PORTRAITS OF AMERICAN WOMEN

PORTRAITS OF AMERICAN WOMEN

From Settlement to the Present

Edited by

G.J. Barker-Benfield
and
Catherine Clinton

Oxford University Press
New York Oxford

Oxford University Press

Oxford New York
Athens Auckland Bangkok Bogotá Bombay
Buenos Aires Calcutta Cape Town Dar es Salaam Delhi
Florence Hong Kong Istanbul Karachi
Kuala Lumpur Madras Madrid Melbourne
Mexico City Nairobi Paris Singapore
Taipei Tokyo Toronto Warsaw

and associated companies in

Berlin Ibadan

First published by St. Martin's Press, 1991

Published by Oxford University Press, Inc.
198 Madison Avenue, New York, New York 10016

Library of Congress Cataloging-in-Publication Data
Portraits of American women: from settlement to the present /
edited by G.J. Barker-Benfield, Catherine Clinton.
p. cm.
Includes bibliographic refrences.
ISBN-13 978-0-19-512048-6

1. Women—United States—Biography. I. Barker-Benfield, G.J.
II. Clinton, Catherine
CT3260.P67 1998
920.72—dc21 97-40361

To our students in women's history,
past, present, and future.

Contents

Preface to the Second Edition

Women's history is here to stay. It shows itself everywhere, on miles of shelves in commercial bookstores, in magazines and newspapers, in films and on television, on the Internet and the World Wide Web. Its most vital impact continues in classrooms from kindergarten through graduate seminars. Popular culture is being rewritten as women's history is absorbed and, one hopes, is breaking free of the perpetuation of the sexual mythology illustrated by our first essay in *Portraits,* on Pocahontas.

Because of the boom in women's history, men's history has begun to be rethought, too, and gender studies has blossomed, although not nearly so extensively or rapidly as women's studies. We hope it is just a matter of time before that happens. Just why women have become so prominent a subject in the new social history since the late 1960s is not a mystery. Women's history has been infused with energy by the second great wave of feminism in America, symbolized by the 1963 publication of *The Feminine Mystique,* by Betty Friedan, our final subject in Portraits.

When we first began to think about this project in the early 1980s, we were exuberant about the range and quality of work on the history of women's lives and the new contributions made by biographies of women. We wanted to pack some of this scholarly excitement between two covers. Over a decade later, this commitment has been reinforced by even more impressive and innovative work. We remain in awe of the continuing bounty of excellent work—work which is finally gaining the kind of recognition women's history so richly deserves, signaled by, for example, the Pulitzer Prizes recently awarded to *A Midwife's Tale,* by Laurel Ulrich (for History in 1991), and to *Harriet Beecher Stowe: A Life,* by Joan Hedrick (for Biography in 1995).

Our goals remain simple and steady. We want to provide an affordable volume of quality scholarship on individual women to engage each new generation of students and readers. The format for this book was suggested by our teaching experience. We found that readers get caught up in the lives of individuals in a personal, immediate way. Students seem eager to absorb the particulars of a life that lead them toward the generalities of women's history. In order to outline those larger contexts, we have arranged the individual portraits chronologically and supplied brief introductory essays before each group of portraits. Our introductory essays have been distilled from courses we have taught over the years, courses in which we have depended on the vast and invaluable scholarship of historians whose very number makes it impossible to acknowledge them individually. These introductory essays, however brief, give accurate overviews of each of the eight chronological eras into which our book has been divided.

How did we make our selections? The number of individuals who can be included in a text of this kind is severely limited, even more so as increasing numbers of historical figures are brought out of the shadows. Proposing alternatives to our choices has been a fruitful source of classroom discussion. Still, readers rightly insist on an answer to the question, What guided our choices?

We decided to include mainly those women who made significant contributions in the public realm, more through actions of their own rather than by way of their relationship to men. Of course, relations with men inevitably played significant parts in the lives of all our subjects, precisely because of the near monopoly men have had on public and economic power until comparatively recently. We have found it historically telling to ask of our subjects, what part did fathers, as well as mothers, play in many of their lives; or brothers and sons, as well as sisters and daughters? Conversely, how independent has it been possible for women to be? In what ways has that changed over time? Why, and for which women?

Two exceptions to this primary criterion (public life on their own) are the lives of Mary Todd Lincoln and Varina Howell Davis, wives of the leaders of the opposing sides in the American Civil War. We departed from our standard because the examples of these women help us better define the larger context of women's lives in the American past. It is illustrative to discover the lives of Lincoln and Davis differed only in degree from the lives of many other women included in Portraits, some of whom were married, some of whom were not, some widowed, some with children, some vilified, some living with disappointment, some bumping up against gender conventions that kept strong-willed women circumscribed.

Our second criterion for choosing the women in *Portraits* was the availability of accessible source material on which to base a viable portrait. In a handful of cases, we felt that previously published essays suited our needs, and we adapted them to *Portraits*. But the majority of our essays are commissioned pieces, written by scholars engaged in ongoing research on their subjects. Since our first edition appeared, several of our contributors have completed books on their subjects, important volumes now listed in our updated "About the Authors."

Third and finally, we were guided by our desire to present as diverse a group as possible within each chronological era, despite our requirement that women included represent those whose contributions were within the public arena. We were able to make choices that offer ideal opportunities to promote lively discussion. For example, the eighteenth century group includes both a slave, Phillis Wheatley, and a slave owner, Eliza Lucas Pinckney. Our "Contemporary Lives" section features both a lawmaker, Congresswoman Helen Gahagan Douglas, and a "lawbreaker," civil rights activist Ella Baker, who pioneered campaigns for civil disobedience to promote racial equality.

We tried to cast our net as wide as possible to include interesting and complex figures. Because autonomy depended to a significant extent on economic resources, that is to say, on class, most poorer women had correspondingly less access to public life. And even though our first criterion (having a public life) may work against our third principle (to include as diverse a group as we could), it remains fascinating to discover that women born in slavery, women denied access to education, women who came to this country in steerage were still able to achieve prominence within their own lifetimes and make important contributions to American public life. Yet even if all of the women we have chosen seized and extended the possibilities of their own times and given circumstances, we also wanted to explore in what sense they were confined by cultural stereotypes and legal impediments. This puzzle continues to draw scholars of women into invigorating debate.

The greatest diversity within our book is revealed by the remarkable range of individuals represented. What relationship do all these women bear to one another, as well as to the groups of which it could be said they were members: Puritans, slaves, reformers, educators, intellectuals, politicians, First Ladies, artists, and writers?

The luxury of a second edition allows us to reflect on what we have learned from being able to use *Portraits* in our courses and having others contact us about their experiences. The book has worked well by combining its readings with related course materials. One of us enjoyed having students read a general work on seventeenth-century New England and then comparing that with the piece on Hutchinson; a work on slavery in colonial South Carolina with the essay on Pinckney; a monograph on Progressivism with the portraits of Gilman and Addams. One of us asked students to explore the impact of race and class on individual lives by comparing two women included in Portraits whose dates were roughly the same—for example, comparing the lives of Indian leader Nancy Ward on the southern frontier and Bostonian Mercy Otis Warren, a historian of the American Revolution, or contrasting the life of African American Charlotte Forten, who taught freedpeople during the Civil War, with that of Confederate First Lady Varina Davis. Others have found that this volume has been an excellent companion to survey texts, to supplement and enhance books that provide less than satisfactory coverage of issues relating to women of color and women in general.

Portraits also works well when assigned in conjunction with rich primary material on American women, especially with new editions of available source material, such as the poetry of Phillis Wheatley, *The Yellow Wallpaper* by Charlotte Perkins Gilman, extracts from Margaret Fuller's *Woman in the Nineteenth Century* or Charlotte Forten's journals, selections from the autobiographies of Jane Addams or Margaret Mead, slides of Georgia O'Keeffe's paintings, and, of course, Betty Friedan's *The Feminine Mystique.* In short, *Portraits* has proved an engaging book to use in a range of courses, as well as a volume with continuing appeal for general readers.

We have been especially pleased that the recent revival in reading groups and book clubs has resulted in fan mail from places as widespread as Maine and Texas. We believe that those who responded so well to the first edition will continue to appreciate the compelling and provocative portraits of our twenty-four extraordinary women.

We also hope that future readers will be stimulated to fresh ways of thinking about women's history and the history of gender, ways that go beyond what we have attempted here.

The very talented colleagues who contributed such exemplary and exciting essays for our collection continue to be inspirational for us both. We were able to include all the pieces but one in our second edition, a tribute to the collegiality and generosity of the overwhelming majority of scholars in women's history.

So many friends and colleagues have given us indispensable support on this project. The following gave of their time and skills in specific ways to make this book happen: Anne Braden, Ellen Fitzpatrick, Jacqueline Jones, Debbie Heuls, Tammy Rich, Angie Simeone, and Bennett Singer. We also want to express our particular gratitude to Craig D'Ooge and Stephen Alcorn for assistance in obtaining images. We received significant institutional support from the W.E.B. Du Bois Institute at Harvard University and the Department of History at the State University of New York at Albany.

We are particularly grateful to Ellen Chodosh of Oxford University Press for her many talents. She is a treasure as well as a treasure hunter, a caring and vibrant editor with whom it has been our pleasure and pride to work. We would also like to thank Joe Schorn and Susan McMichaels, whose prompt and meticulous attention has made our project move ahead smoothly.

Although this project was a labor of love from which we both derived great satisfaction, we can't forget the disrupted dinners and interrupted playtimes with our children, and the patience of our spouses, who fielded dozens of messages, who kept things going during our absences and our absent-mindedness. To thank our families, Patricia West and Chloe Barker-Benfield, and Daniel, Drew, and Ned Colbert for their sacrifices and support seems a cliché of book acknowledgments, but there is nothing hackneyed about the way in which our spouses and offspring have rewarded us in ways we cannot hope to repay, although we will continue to try.

G.J. B.-B.
C.C.

PORTRAITS OF AMERICAN WOMEN

PART I

Colonial Beginnings

Cultures from three continents came together in seventeenth-century North America; they were remarkably different from one another. Already present were dozens of nations of indigenous peoples, who possessed at least a thirty-thousand-year history on the continent. These peoples had created complex societies and political systems, between which there had been long traditions of international relations that included trade, diplomacy, and war. The people from across the Atlantic, seen by the native inhabitants as invaders, came from several European countries. They brought an increasing number of Africans to the land they saw as the "New World." The Africans, like the Indians and the Europeans, came from a wide range of nations, each with a long and complex history.

The different native inhabitants may be grouped together by their common languages. For example, along the Atlantic seaboard, the large number of diverse nations can be divided into four distinct language groups: the Muskogean, Algonkian, Iroquoian, and Siouan. All of their economies were based on a mix of farming and hunting. Within most nations women farmed while men hunted, traded, negotiated, and fought. Those nations in which farming predominated tended to be matrilineal, that is, children traced their lineage through their mothers. Nations in which hunting was the chief source of food tended to be patrilineal; lineage was traced through fathers. The religions of these people shared certain characteristics, among them the belief in spirits, a divine creator, the presence on earth of both the natural and supernatural, and the power of prayer and ritual.

In some matrilineal nations, women may have exercised significant political and social influence. However, it is important not to romanticize the"precontact" authority of Indian women. The political power of Iroquois women was real but indirect. Their greater autonomy within their economic domain may have been derived from their physical separation from their menfolk, who were frequently absent hunting. And if in some nations the women were beneficiaries of greater sexual freedom (notably, divorce was exceedingly simple), they were also subordinated and feared by men because of their reproductive capacities. Childbirth and menstruation were hedged around with powerful taboos; men used the term "woman" as an insult, and in some tribes mutilated women for sexual transgressions.

As ethnohistorians have shown us, the relationship between Europeans and Indians was a two-way street. Europeans introduced guns, alcohol and other kinds of trade goods into the Indian economy. The native peoples taught the Europeans how to understand the new environment, even while fighting them and resisting their encroachments.

By early in the seventeenth century, the English, the Dutch, the French, and the Swedes had all established permanent colonies on the North American mainland. All of these had been preceded by the Spaniards in "New Spain," who had fanned out from Central America and explored vast areas from Florida to California during the previous century. The Spanish conquistadors had taken over the indigenous empires of the Aztecs and the Incas, ransacking them for gold and capitalizing on forced native labor. As other European powers attempted to emulate these exploits, they were frequently in deadly competition with each other as well as with the indigenous nations. The English eventually triumphed over rival Europeans on North America's eastern seaboard. Their settlements grew within two chief regions, along the Chesapeake in the south and on Massachusetts Bay in the north.

The first English settlers on the Chesapeake, organized as the Virginia Company, were an uneasy assortment of male adventurers with fantasies of getting rich quick. After starvation, disease, and deadly warfare led to the near disintegration of the Jamestown, Virginia settlement they found they could flourish only by the exhausting manual labor of tobacco cultivation.

The six Algonkian groups inhabiting that part of the Chesapeake region were confederated under the leadership of Powhatan. Although characterized by raids and skirmishes, relations between the English and Powhatan Confederacy at first served the purposes of both groups. The English were enabled to survive largely because of the food they received from the native peoples in exchange for steel knives and guns, which were adapted by the Indians to their own cultural purposes, including use as weapons in disputes with their neighbors. Pacts of mutual interest between the English and the Powhatans were formalized by a treaty in 1614, of which the marriage between Powhatan's daughter Pocahontas and the English settler John Rolfe was a symbol.

The profitability of tobacco led more and more settlers to encroach onto Powhatan land. On Good Friday in 1622, Opechancough, Powhatan's successor attacked the English and killed about a quarter of the settlement's population. The rest escaped only because of forewarning by two Christianized Indians. With the help of reinforcements from England, the settlers eventually defeated Opechancough; however, the severity of this raid led the English king to take over the Virginia Company. The settlement became a royal colony, to be ruled directly by the king's representative, a development that demonstrates the crucial influence of native peoples' resistance on shaping European settlement as a whole.

Though Opechancough's attack killed 347 English, that figure was only a fraction of the staggering number of deaths incurred by the early settlers. Between 1607 and 1624, over 80 percent of the 8,500 whites who came to Virginia had died. Maintaining the population in the face of disease and a difficult climate meant that the Chesapeake colonies of Virginia and Maryland (chartered in 1632) required a continual flow of immigrants, the majority of whom were men.

The colony failed to "self-reproduce" until the turn of the century. English women had come to Virginia as early as 1608, although in much smaller numbers than men. Most women were indentured servants, but they were also intended as wives. The disproportionate number of men was seen as contributing to the colony's anarchic tendencies. In 1619 the colony's promoters dispatched the list of several boatloads of "maids" to Virginia. Their rationale was the one generally given for encouraging the shipment of women: "the plantation can never flourish till families be planted and the respect of wives and children fix the people on the soil." Women continued to come as indentured servants. They tended to be in their teens and early twenties, looking to get married after their term of servitude expired. Because of the greater proportion of men and the relative freedom from family control, former servants found it easier to get married than in England. They were also able to carve out a more prosperous life than they would have had in England: if women survived to marry and then to outlive their husbands, they would, as widows, gain greater independence than would be the case once the population of the colony began to stabilize demographically.

Regardless of these opportunities during the early years of settlement, women led a hardscrabble life. Many servants worked in the tobacco fields when their masters found it necessary. They encountered the hardship of seasoning (the physical and psychological adjustment to the climate) and diseases such as malaria, and they faced higher rates of death in childbirth and infant mortality. Families were broken continually by early death. But many women survived where the men of their families did not. The premature death of a father and sons made patriarchal authority and lineage more difficult to enforce.

By 1700, the plantation patriarchy, or plantocracy, emerged out of the terrible struggles of early settlement. This caste dominated the social ideals and organization of society from courthouse to household. By then, because it was clear they could depend upon the forced agricultural labor of slaves imported from Africa, Chesapeake plantation owners identified themselves still more closely with Old Testament patriarchs. Furthermore, the hierarchical restraints on women were reinforced by the region's interracial character. As white men attempted to preserve an unmixed white lineage within their own class, they prohibited white women from intercourse with black men. The sexual double standard allowed male slave owners to increase their slave stock by their own intercourse with slave women, and furthermore, African-American women had no legal recourse in cases of rape.

The circumstances of immigrants to Virginia and Maryland differed significantly from those migrating to Massachusetts and other northern colonies. The English women settling in New England came as parts of whole families within communally organized social experiments. They were inspired and led by two kinds of Puritans. In England some Protestant reformers were called Puritans because they believed that the English or "Anglican" Church, while separated from Rome since 1529, had not been "purified" enough from its entanglement with what they saw as worldly corruptions, and the presumption that the individual could buy or work his or her way into heaven. As dissenters, they believed the power of salvation resided with God, not with worldly institutions. Among themselves they differed over the extent to which Puritans should work within the Anglican Church or separate themselves from it. A small group of those who believed they should separate entirely, the Separatists, landed in 1620 at a place they called Plymouth. A much larger group of "non-separating" Congregationalists settled at Massachusetts Bay, beginning in 1628. These later immigrants dispersed very quickly, settling in townships in what would later become the colonies of Connecticut and New Hampshire and the state of Maine. All of the early settlements required exhausting work, but in the northern climate and with communal efforts, the physical strains were dramatically less than those faced by Chesapeake residents.

With a more balanced ratio of men and women, and possessing a more cohesive set of social values, the population and culture of New England reproduced itself virtually from the beginning. This meant a rapid duplication of the traditional gender hierarchy; indeed, with their strict interpretation of scripture, these Puritans attempted to establish a state on an even more patriarchal basis than the one that existed in England. The male heads of household believed that they directly embodied the authority of their Calvinist God. In 1630, a Massachusetts minister publicly praised his wife for her "incomparable meekness of spirit, toward myself, especially." The female members of a clergyman's family, above all, his wife, held exemplary positions in the community as his agents, and they were expected to instill virtue in their household servants and take notes during a husband's sermons. But they were also subordinate to men. They faced a rigid male hierarchy bent on implementing the will of a patriarchal "masculine" God.

Puritanism, therefore, had ambiguous meanings for women. That some were charged with taking notes on sermons indicated that women were literate and were assumed to be intelligent. Women could attain salvation, the most important value of the culture, just as men could. Nevertheless, they were excluded from the operations of the formal, hierarchical institutions of Puritan belief, which in effect defined the terms on which salvation could be reached. The ministry was entirely male. At the same time the ideal in Protestantism of a direct relation between the believer and God promised some self-expression for women which was unmediated by men. The Protestant emphasis on exposure to the word of God in the printed and vernacular Bible could lead to considerable literacy, one of the greatest resources for modern individualism. Two of the most famous women of early Massachusetts history, Anne Hutchinson and Anne Bradstreet, owed their educations to the Protestant beliefs of their fathers. Both fathers were wealthy enough to provide their daughters with access to libraries, all of which were private at the time. But Hutchinson and Bradstreet's literacy led them in different directions. On the one hand, Anne Hutchinson's story illustrates the terrible obstacles that were faced even by a skilled theologian. On the other, the poet Anne Bradstreet was able to turn the possibilities of Protestantism to her own advantage. Born in 1612, Bradstreet survived migration from England to Massachusetts, frequent illness, the birth of ten children, and the demands of women's work in the new colony. While doing so she probed Puritan ideology, just as Hutchinson had done. Bradstreet came down on the side of gender orthodoxy, as her epitaph to her mother illustrates: "A worthy Matron of unspotted life/A loving Mother and obedient wife." Whereas the outspoken Anne Hutchinson was banished and killed, Anne Bradstreet became the greatest artist of seventeenth-century colonial America. Bradstreet's verses show she was "a learned lady," a Renaissance humanist of enormous philosophical sophistication.

Both of these women were exceptional because they were well-known in their own age and were able to leave documentary traces. Bradstreet was a member of the ruling elite and received support from male kin. In England she had been educated in a nobleman's household, where her father held the important office of steward. Spending her adult life in a small distant colony, she was in a position to write "The Dialogue between Old England and New." Hutchinson and Bradstreet had found intellectual and moral inspiration in Protestantism, despite its domination by men. Protestantism would continue to provide women such resources and may be seen as one root of nineteenth-century feminism.

In 1681 the English king granted his friend, the Quaker William Penn, the huge territory that became known as Pennsylvania. The Quaker commitment to toleration, even of Indians, at first made Pennsylvania a haven for many groups of European dissenters, including Swiss Mennonites, French Huguenots, and German Protestants. Philadelphia, along with New York (as "New Amsterdam" had been renamed in 1664 when the English conquered it from the Dutch), became the chief ports of entry for the immigration which poured in during the next century. The New England colonies meanwhile remained far less receptive to non-English or non-Puritan immigrants. One of Anne Hutchinson's supporters, Mary Dyer, had been converted to Quakerism by George Fox, founder of the sect, during a sojourn to England in the 1650s. She returned to Boston to preach her faith but was hanged by the Puritans in 1660, twenty-two years after Anne Hutchinson met her fate.

Seventeenth-century America was a frontier of red, white, and black. Enslaved Africans were brought first to the Caribbean sugar colonies (far and away the most profitable part of the European New World empire through the eighteenth century) and then to the later-established mainland colonies. They mostly came from the agricultural and trading kingdoms between the Senegal and Niger rivers and the Gulf of Benin, and from the Kingdom of Angola. Various in economies and cultures, Africans' long, complex histories rivalled those of European nations. In certain respects their religions resembled the religions of indigenous peoples of America: Africans did not separate the sacred and secular as dramatically as did Protestants, and they invested natural phenomena with spiritual forces. Africans held that their dead ancestors entered a pantheon of gods existing under a supreme being; ancestors could mediate with gods on behalf of their earthly descendants, as could certain living priests.

African gender arrangements varied from nation to nation. In many regions of Africa from which slaves were bought or stolen, women tilled the soil and cultivated crops. (Rice cultivation, unknown in Europe, was probably introduced to the Carolinas by African technology.) Among the Ibo, the sexes worked together throughout the whole agricultural cycle, while among the Yoruba, the men did most of the agricultural labor and women helped only with harvest. In addition to farmwork, African women had the tasks of childcare, spinning, and weaving.

Though traumatized by enslavement and the horrors of the "middle passage" (the transatlantic crossing), the Africans, no less than the Europeans, brought cultural baggage with them to the New World. However, because they arrived in comparatively small numbers throughout the seventeenth century, were drawn from several regions and disparate language groups, and were scattered among aliens and exposed to the full force of European power, Africans had far less opportunity to recreate their Old World than did the English. Their age at their time of capture and the circumstances of their lives in slavery would dictate the terms on which they would attempt to rebuild their culture. By far the largest proportion of Africans was shipped into southern colonies for clearing the land and for harsh field labor. The greater demand for males led to an unbalanced sex ratio. Together with the damaging physical conditions under which Africans were forced to work, this severely reduced African-American prospects for a more stable family life, a condition which lasted until the eighteenth century.

Ætatis suæ 21. A°. 1616.
Matoaks als Rebecka daughter to the mighty Prince
converted and baptized in the Christian faith, and

Pocahontas

(1596?–1617)

Philip Young

From the little verifiable evidence that exists, a remarkable legend about the life of Pocahontas has been passed down through the years. Disputes over her actual role in early America continue to the present day. We do know she was the daughter of a Virginia tidewater chieftain, Powhatan. But even her name creates controversy: although she is referred to as Pocahontas—which means "playful one"—her birth name might have been Matoaka.

At the heart of the legend is the story that she "saved" Captain John Smith from execution by her father's hand. She was held captive in Jamestown, and later converted to Christianity and was baptized Rebecca. In 1614 she married an English widower, John Rolfe; their marriage was meant to symbolize peace efforts between natives and European settlers. In 1616 Rolfe took his wife and their son Thomas to London on a diplomatic mission with the colonial governor, where Pocahontas was sought after in English society and presented at court. In March 1617 she died before she could return to her home and people.

> . . . having feasted him after their best barbarous manner they could, a long consultation was held, but the conclusion was, two great stones were brought before *Powhatan:* then as many as could layd hands on him, dragged him to them, and thereon laid his head, and being ready with their clubs, to beate out his braines, *Pocahontas* the Kings dearest daughter, when no intreaty could prevail, got his head in her armes, and laid her owne upon his to save him from death: whereat the Emperour was contented he should live to make him hatchets, and her bells, beads, and copper. . . .

Of course it may never have happened at all and even if it did we think we may be a little tired of it. Yet three and a half centuries have elapsed, and this interminable sentence about an incident from the travels of Captain John Smith still lives. Americans, their literature swarming with its offspring, still without revulsion can summon up the old image: Smith pinned down by savages, his head on a rock, all those clubs about to smash it; and the lovely Indian princess, curiously moved out from the crowd and across all the allegiances of her family, home and land, her religion and her race, lowering her head to his. Why can this commonplace, even banal, picture absorb us yet?

Shopworn by sentimentality, Pocahontas endures and stands with the most appealing of our saints. She has passed subtly into our folklore, where she lives as a popular fable—a parable taught children who carry some vague memory of her through their lives. She is an American legend, a woman whose actual story has blended with imaginary elements in time become traditional. Finally, she is one of our few, true native myths, for with our poets she has successfully attained the status of goddess, has been beatified, made holy, and offered as a magical and moving explanation of our national origins. What has happened to her story, why did it happen—and in fact what really was her story? It may be that our very familiarity with Pocahontas has kept us from looking at her closely enough to see what is there.

I

Even in the sketchiest of outlines, the story from which all the folklore and legends take off is a good one. As every schoolchild knows, the English arrived in Jamestown in 1607. During December of that year, while exploring the Chickahominy River, Smith—who had worked his way up from prisoner to leader of the expedition—was captured by men of chief Powhatan, and two of his companions were killed. It was at this time that he reputedly was rescued from death by the chief's favorite child, a young girl—no more than twelve or thirteen—called Pocahontas. Then, after what struck him as some very odd behavior on the part of the Indians, he was allowed to return to Jamestown, a place where—the great majority of its members dying within a year of their arrival—one of the most appalling casualty rates in history was being established. By placating Indians and planting corn, and with the help again of Pocahontas, who is said often to have brought supplies, and once to have come through the forest on a dark night to warn of an attack by her father, Smith is usually credited with having temporarily saved the colony. He gave the credit to her, however, as having done most, "next under God," to preserve the settlers.

The Captain returned to England in 1609, and in that year ships under Sir Thomas Gates brought relief to a group of people so desperate that one man had eaten his wife. The *Sea Venture*, flagship of the fleet, was wrecked in Bermuda, but its survivors somehow built a new vessel, and with it made Jamestown. One of its passengers was an Englishman named John Rolfe. Some time elapsed before he saw Pocahontas, because for a while she had no connection with the vicissitudes of the colonists. But in 1613, while visting the chief of the Potomacs, she was tricked into captivity by an Indian bribed with a copper kettle, and taken as security for English men and equipment held by Powhatan. Now she met Rolfe, whose first wife had died in Virginia, and soon they expressed a desire to marry. Powhatan gave his approval but Rolfe had to get permission from his own superiors, and wrote Sir Thomas Dale a passionate, tedious letter protesting that he wished to marry Pocahontas despite, as he put it, her "rude education, manners barbarous and cursed generation," for the good of the plantation, the honor of England, the glory of God, and his own salvation—not "to gorge myself with incontinency" but, according to God's wish, to convert the girl. Even Smith had said that conversion was the first duty of the settlers; permission was granted. Dale gave the girl a good deal of religious instruction, christened her Rebecca—it was the first such conversion by the colonists—and in April of 1614 she and Rolfe were married.

Rolfe, it is generally believed, was primarily responsible for the production of the tobacco—detested by both King James and Smith—which made the colony permanent, and in 1616 he and his wife and their son Thomas were taken abroad by Dale to publicize the success of Jamestown. Thus it was that Pocahontas, less than six weeks after the death of William Shakespeare, arrived in England. In the party too was an Indian named Tomocomo, whom a thoughtful Powhatan had sent as a scout. He had a sheaf of sticks in which he was to place a notch for each white person he encountered, and some equally troublesome instruction to see this "God" about whom the English talked so much.

Pocahontas fared better, for a time. She was honored by the church and feted by the King and Queen, to whom Smith in glowing terms had commended her as his savior. James Stuart demanded to know if her commoner husband had not committed a treasonable act in marrying a princess. The Lady Rebecca became the toast of London, where alert pubs changed their names to "La Belle Sauvage." But not everything went well. She saw Smith again and was mysteriously displeased. Then while preparing for her return to Jamestown she was taken sick, very likely with smallpox, and died. She made a godly end, according to Smith, at the age of perhaps twenty-two, and was buried on the 21st of March, 1617, at Gravesend, on the banks of the Thames.

Her father survived her by only a year. Her husband returned to Virginia alone, married once again, and was killed four years later by Indians. Her son Thomas grew up in England, and then came back to this country to start the line of proud Virginians—of Jeffersons and Lees, of Randolphs, Marshalls, and an estimated two million other people—who to this day trace their ancestry back to the Indian girl. Smith transferred his affections to New England, which he named, but was never able to get the colonial job he wanted and died in bed in 1631. As for Pocahontas, the exact place of her burial is unknown, and the only tangible remains of her are a pair of earrings and a portrait, done in 1616, showing a dark and handsome if uncomfortable young lady, incongruously overdressed in English clothes.

There are other details of a more or less factual nature that have been added to this story by people who knew Pocahontas, or who wrote of her during her lifetime. Smith himself supplies some of them. It is he who describes that day in England when he somehow so upset her, and she "turned about, obscured her face," on seeing him—an event which, since Smith either could not explain it or did not wish to, has tantalized generations of romantics.

There is also the testimony of Samuel Purchas, who was present when Pocahontas was received by the Lord-Bishop of London with even more pomp than was accorded other great ladies of the time, and who records in *Hakluytus Posthumus* or *Purchas his Pilgrimes* (1625) the impressive dignity with which the young lady received her honors. And in his *True Discourse of the Present Estate of Virginia* (1615) Ralph Hamor put down the pious details of her conversion and marriage.

But not all these additions conform to the somewhat stuffy reputation that has been built for her. Smith, for instance, coldly comments that he might have married the girl himself—or "done what he listed" with her. He also supplies a colorful but usually neglected incident relating how she and "her women" came one day "naked out of the woods, onely covered behind and before with a few green leaves . . . singing and dauncing with most excellent ill varietie, oft falling into their infernall passions"; and also tells how, later, "all these Nymphes more tormented him than ever, with crowding, pressing and hanging about him, most tediously crying, Love you not me?"

In addition, William Strachey, in his *Historie of Travaile into Virginia Britannia,* written about 1615, supplies information which does not appear in Sunday School versions of the story. The first secretary of America's oldest colony and the friend of great poets, including Donne, Jonson, and probably Shakespeare, Strachey disturbs the tenderhearted by noting that Rolfe's future bride is already married, to a "private captaine, called Kocoum." Even worse is his description of Pocahontas in earlier days as a "well-featured but wanton yong girle" who used to come to the fort and "get the boyes forth with her into the markett place, and make them wheele, falling on their hands, turning their heels upwards, whome she would followe and wheele so herselfe, naked as she was, all the fort over."

These are all the important sources of the Pocahontas story. Strachey's intelligence was not published until some 234 years after he wrote. Smith's swashbuckling accounts of his own adventures were taken as gospel for even longer, though for quite a while the story of Pocahontas had very little circulation, and was seldom repeated outside a couple of books on Virginia. But when about the start of the nineteenth century Americans began to search intensely for their history the romance was resurrected, and Pocahontas began to loom large as the guardian angel of our oldest colony. Exaggerating even Smith's accounts of her, historians entered into a quaint struggle to outdo each other with praise, concentrating of course on the rescue story. Considering the flimsiness of the evidence, it is odd that for a long time no one seems to have entertained the slightest doubt of its authenticity. On all sides, instead, sprung up the most assiduous and vigilant defense of the lady. Here the case of the Honorable Waddy Thompson is instructive. Poor Thompson, who had been our minister to Mexico, published in 1846 his "Recollections" of that place, and in his desire to praise a girl named Marina, "the *chère amie* and interpreter of Cortez," he let slip a remark he must have regretted the rest of his days. He said that Pocahontas was "thrown into the shade" by her.

The response to these imprudent words was dreadful; an anonymous Kentuckian rushed into print a whole pamphlet Vindicating her Memory. He appealed to all Virginians, to all Americans, and finally "to the admirers of virtue, humanity, and nobleness of soul, wherever to be found," against this Erroneous Judgment. Pocahontas had every gift Marina possessed, and—no *chère amie*—she had also, he added, her "good name." Indeed, it is not possible to improve on her, and to demonstrate either this or his scholarship the gentleman from Kentucky appended long accounts of her from the work of twenty-six historians, including French, German, and Italian representatives. Her character is "not surpassed by any in the whole range of history" is one estimate.

The author of this pamphlet also spoke of "proof" that Pocahontas rescued Smith, which he called "one of the most incontestable facts in history": "The proof is, the account of it given by Captain Smith, a man incapable of falsehood or exaggeration . . . hundreds of eyewitnesses . . . and to this may be added tradition." Here the gentleman defends, somewhat ineptly, what no one is known to have attacked, despite the fact that there have always been excellent reasons for contesting the rescue. For one thing, the Captain had a real inclination toward this sort of tale. His *Generall Historie* of 1624, which tells the full story for the first time, reveals a peculiar talent for being "offered rescue and protection in my greatest dangers" by various "honorable and vertuous Ladies." Most striking of these is the Lady Tragabigzanda, who fell in love with him when he was in bondage, not this time to her father but to her husband, the powerful Bashaw Bogall of Constantinople. She delivered him from this slavery, and sent him to her brother, "till time made her Master of her selfe"—before which, however, Smith made a fantastic escape.

Then, much worse and apparent from the beginning, there is the well-known fact that Smith's *True Relation* of 1608, which tells of his capture by Powhatan, and speaks also of the chief's kindness and assurances of early release, contains no mention at all of any rescue. He had plenty of other opportunities to tell the story, too, but neither he nor anyone else who wrote on Jamestown is known to have referred to the event until 1622, when he remarked in his *New England Trials*, which includes his third version of his capture: "God made Pocahontas the King's daughter the means to deliver me." Then in 1624 when his *Generall Historie* was published he told the story as we know it, and also printed for the first time his letter of eight years before to Queen Anne.

The obvious inference here is that if the rescue was actually performed Smith would have said so in the first place or, if he had not, would have told the story to others who would have repeated it. His *Historie* is boastful; it is hard to know how much of it he may have made up or borrowed from other travelers of the period. And there was a historical precedent for the Pocahontas tale: the story of a soldier, Juan Ortiz, who was lost on an expedition to Florida in 1528 and was found there by De Soto about twelve years later. Ortiz said he had been captured by Indians, and saved at the last second from burning at the stake by the chief's daughter, who later came at night in peril of her life to warn him of her father's plot to kill him. This story had appeared in London, in an English translation by Richard Hakluyt, in 1609, the year of Smith's return to that city.

Despite all grounds for suspicion, however, Smith's tale went unchallenged for well over two centuries—until about 1860, that is, when two historians, Edward D. Neill (who became known as the scavenger of Virginia history) and Charles Deane, began to make what now seem the obvious objections. These men were quickly joined by others, and in order to publicize Deane's case there entered the cause no less an intellect than that of Henry Adams. Writing anonymously in the *North American Review* in 1867, Adams lowered his biggest guns and patiently blasted what he called "the most romantic episode" in our history into what must have seemed to him and his crushed readers total oblivion. Henry Cabot Lodge concurred that the rescue belongs to fiction. Many other great men expressed themselves on the question, and quickly it became the custom to speak of the Pocahontas "legend."

Other historians, however, rushed to the defense. Chief among these were John Fiske, the philosopher and historian, and William Wirt Henry. Fiske in 1879 flatly dismissed the dismissals, and went on to champion the story. Why is it not in the *True Relation* of 1608? Because the editor of that work had obeyed an injunction against printing anything that might discourage potential colonists, and in a preface had explained that Smith had written "somewhat more" than was being published. Certainly the Captain was not allowed simply to go free, after having killed two Indians. The rescue by Pocahontas was quite in accordance with Indian custom. Any member of a tribe had a right to claim a prisoner as son or lover—but how could Smith have known enough about this to invent the tale? That scene in which he describes the weird behavior of his captors following his rescue was clearly a ceremony of adoption into the tribe, the natural consequence of Pocahontas' act. Why didn't Smith tell the story to his compatriots? Because he feared that if they knew the favor of an Indian woman was possible they would desert.

And so the battle, which continues to the present day, was on. There is a rebuttal. Why for example censor from Smith's first book a charming rescue story (which might cause desertions) and include as the editor did an excessively discouraging description of one of Smith's companions, "John Robbinson slaine, with 20 or 30 arrowes" in him? There is no easy answer to that. But, after the short period of the story's disrepute (conveniently passed in time for the Jamestown Tercentenary of 1907), wide acceptance ruled again—especially with proudly celebrating Virginians, who appeared to have forgotten that by their rules the girl was colored. Credence in the story, however, is of course not limited to the South. Indeed by 1957, when the 350th anniversary of the founding was elaborately solemnized, most Americans, including a majority of the published authorities, seemed to subscribe to the tale as fact. For the celebrations Paul Green wrote a "Symphonic Outdoor Drama" called *The Founders,* in which the key events of the young lady's life took on the force of ritual observance in performances at Williamsburg. Since the evidence is not decisive, perhaps everybody has a right to believe as he wishes.

II

Exactly what happened would not seem to make any enormous difference anyway. What counts more is the truly extraordinary way in which the story—despite the profound awkwardness of a climax that comes in the very opening scene—pervades our culture. Pocahontas is represented in countless paintings and monuments; she gives her name to ships, motels, coal mines, towns, counties, and pseudonymous writers, to secret orders and business firms. There are histories of her and Smith by everyone from poet (John Gould Fletcher) to politician ("Alfalfa Bill" Murray, a descendant). But all other signs of her fade before the plays, poems, novels, and children's books which for the last 150 years have flooded our literature. Dramatizing the story from the alleged facts, and filling gaps or inadequacies with invented material usually presented as fact, there are so many different treatments, ranging from the serious to the absurd, that they begin to look numberless.

But they fall into patterns. The first person to make literary use of Pocahontas was no less a writer than the rare Ben Jonson, who included an obscure reference to her in his *Staple of News* of 1625. Then, much later, she was treated at length in a little novel called *The Female American* (1767). Here the story as we know it is, however, simply a rehearsal for far greater events, and the really memorable thing about the book is that its author was an English lady known as Unca Eliza Winkfield, who changed Pocahontas' name to Unca, and Smith's to Winkfield, and gave her a daughter called, once more, Unca.

The writer who really started things, by first romanticizing the story in a proper way, was still another Englishman—an adventuresome fellow named John Davis, a sailor who came to this country in

1798 and spent nearly five years traveling about on foot. Very young and romantic, hyperthyroid, chronically tumescent and rather charming, Davis wrote a book about his journey called *Travels of Four Years and a Half in the United States of America.* As a part of this work he "delivered to the world" the history of Pocahontas which, he announced, was reserved for his pen. Possessed of a lively and libidinous imagination, which he seemed unable to distinguish from his written sources, Davis tore into the story with hearty masculine appetite.

He begins with Smith in the hands of Powhatan, who keeps offering his prisoner a woman. The squaws fight fiercely for the honor, but to Pocahontas' "unspeakable joy" Smith is stern and turns them all down. After she has rescued him she comes to Jamestown, weeping "in all the tumultuous extasy of love." In order to cure her Smith slips off to England, instructing his compatriots to tell the girl he has died. She prostrates herself on his empty grave, beats her bosom, and utters piercing cries. One night while she is strewing flowers about his resting place she is come upon by Rolfe, secretly in love with her and of late much given to taking moonlight walks while composing love poems. ("Of these effusions I have three in my possession," says Davis, and he prints them.) Surprised by Rolfe's appearance, Pocahontas inadvertently falls in his arms, whereupon he seizes his opportunity and drinks from her lips "the poison of delight." A woman is "never more susceptible of a new passion than when agitated by the remains of a former one," is Davis' dark but profitable explanation, and thus it is that hours later, come dawn, Rolfe "still rioted in the draught of intoxication from her lips." Eventually they marry ("nor did satiety necessarily follow from fruition," the author adds anxiously). They go to England, and Pocahontas dies there.

Davis made it clear that he wrote as a historian: "I have adhered inviolably to facts; rejecting every circumstance that had not evidence to support it," he insisted, speaking of "recourse to records and original papers." The man was too modest, for of course these were, like Rolfe's poems, original enough but with him. And he should be given credit too for having seen the possibilities of uniting richly embroidered history with a mammary fixation (habitually the bosoms of his Indian women are either "throbbing" or "in convulsive throes"). That he did see the promise of this combination, and in advance of his time, is indicated by the fact that he himself soon wrote what he called a "historical novel" on "Pokahontas." The book is formally titled *First Settlers of Virginia* (1806), but it simply pads the previous account of the girl's adventures to novel length. Dropping Rolfe's claim to the poetry, Davis managed to add a couple of mildly pornographic native scenes, to use Smith's story of the enamored Indian girls ("Love you not me?") twice, and to present

Pocahontas as "unrobed" in her first scene with Rolfe. He also prefaced a second edition with a letter from Thomas Jefferson to the effect that the President of the United States "subscribed with pleasure" to this Indian Tale.

After Davis, the deluge. This began with a vast number of plays now mostly lost, but including four prominent and commercially successful ones which are preserved. To James Nelson Barker, ex-mayor of Philadelphia and future first controller of the Treasury in Van Buren's cabinet, goes a series of firsts: his *Indian Princess* of 1808 (although anticipated in 1784 by the little-known German *Pocahontas* of Johann Wilhelm Rose) was the first important Pocahontas play and the first to be produced of the Indian plays which soon threatened to take over our stage completely; it is generally cited also as the first American play to appear in London after opening in this country. Hugely popular, and rather deservedly so, Barker's success was followed by that of George Washington Parke Curtis, step-grandson of our first president, with his *Pocahontas* of 1830, and by Robert Dale Owen. The latter, son of the more famous Robert Owen, founder of the radical Owenite communities, and himself a very early advocate of birth control, the free discussion of sex, and the rights of women, made his Pocahontas (1837) an anachronistic feminist. His play, though over-long, is not incompetent and reads very well beside *The Forest Princess* (1844) of Charlotte Barnes Conner. Mrs. Conner, an actress, stuck close to the worst nineteenth-century concepts of theatre and produced a series of unlikely postures which are epitomized in her final scene, where a pious Rebecca dying in England, hand stretched heavenward, speaks her last iambics:

> I hear my father—Husband, fare thee well.
> We part—but we shall meet—above!

after which the hand drops with the curtain.

John Brougham's *Pocahontas* (1855) was honorably designed to stop this sort of thing, and his travesty did stop the production of "serious" Pocahontas plays for quite a time, greatly diminishing the popularity of the Indian drama to boot. But today his play is, to speak politely, "dated," for the humor depends mainly on puns ("What *iron* fortune *led* you to our shores?" "To now ill-use us would be base *illusion!*") (italics his), line after line for two long acts.

Brougham's burlesque was extremely well-received, however, and it performed a service for our drama that nothing has adequately performed for our poetry. Pocahontas poems, produced in the nineteenth century by the carload, are almost uniformly dull, tasteless, and interminable. The efforts of Lydia Huntly Sigourney and William Makepeace Thackeray stand out only a little from the average.

Most nineteenth-century Pocahontas poems seem to begin either with some silly sylvan scene or with "Descend O Muse, and this poor pen . . ." Smith always arrives as expected, but the Muse invariably has other things to do.

Equally forbidding are the Pocahontas poems written in the manner of Henry Wadsworth Longfellow. Longfellow neglected to produce any Pocahontas items himself, but there are a great many poems, and several plays in verse, which have sought to rectify his oversight. These pieces are all distinguished by lines of unrimed trochaic tetrameter ("By the shore of Gitche Gumee / By the shining Big-Sea-Water") which produce a stultifying effect the poets seem to equate with an Indian atmosphere; they suffer from what might properly be known as the Curse of Hiawatha. Of course Longfellow got his famous Hiawatha line from a German translation of a national epic of the Finns, but this is not known to have stopped anyone, and on they go:

> Then the maiden Pocahontas
> Rushes forward, none can stop her,
> Throws her arms about the captive,
> Cries,—"oh spare him! Spare the Paleface!"

What burlesque and abuse cannot destroy will just have to wear itself out. Although the machinery that mass-produces low-quality Pocahontas literature has long shown signs of collapse, the end is not yet. As recently as 1958 a Pocahontas novel by one Noel B. Gerson, with nothing to recommend it but the story, was smiled on by a very large book club. And so still they come with the story, juggling the climax or devising a new one, and trying to make up somehow for the fact that Smith never married the girl. Both problems can of course be solved at once by ending with the scene from Smith in which he and Pocahontas meet in London. Here Rebecca is overcome at the sight of her lost Captain and dies in his arms, usually of a broken heart; indeed it has become a convention to do it that way. But that has not helped, and it is the plays, particularly, which indicate that an industry really is exhausted. The best written and most interesting parts of their scripts are those that deal with such matters as the construction of campfires with electric fans, logs, and strips of red cloth.

One last sign of the popular Pocahontas drama's waning was the appearance (once Brougham was well-forgotten) of an Everything but the Kitchen Sink School. There exists, for instance, an operetta in which Smith has a "regulation negro" servant, comically named Mahogany, who plays a banjo. A better sample is the *Pocahontas* (1906) of Edwin O. Ropp. Mr. Ropp named three of his Indians Hiawatha, Minnehaha, and Geronimo; and there is a rough spot in the action when a man named simply Roger (Williams?), insisting on the freedom of religious thought, disappears for good in the Virginia forest. As for Pocahontas, she is taken through her marriage with Rolfe, to England and back again to Virginia, where she lives out her days in the wilderness with her husband, two children, and their Christian grandpapa, Powhatan, singing the praises of home sweet home, as the play ends with lines lifted from the poem of that name. Mr. Ropp dedicated his play, it should be recorded, to a Moral Purpose, to the Jamestown Exposition of 1907, and to Those Who Construct the Panama Canal. The world was ready for another burlesque when, in 1918, Philip Moeller published his *Beautiful Legend of the Amorous Indian.* In this play only one character, the senile mother of Powhatan, speaks Hiawathan, and there is a heart-warming moment in the dialogue when Powhatan's wife says of her aging mother-in-law: "When she talks in that old manner it nearly drives me crazy."

III

It is not hard to find reasons for the low quality of a large part of our Pocahontas literature: the writers had no talent, for instance. A less obvious difficulty has been that most of the poets and playwrights have prided themselves that their works were founded firmly on "historical sources." This impeded the imaginations of most of them, who tried to romanticize history instead of letting the facts act as a stimulus to fiction. As a result of sentimentality and inaccuracy, there is little or no historical value in their products. And because the works are based so solidly on "history," often footnoted, they seldom have any value as fiction, for invariably events are related not because they are dramatic but because they happened—which is aesthetically irrelevant. If the story is to satisfy a modern audience, it must be treated imaginatively.

Properly told it could be a truly epic story. This is indicated by the fact that elements in the relationships of the characters are so like those in other epics of other countries—the *Aeneid,* for instance. Aeneas, we recall, was an adventurer who also sought a westward land and finally anchored at the mouth of a river. The country there was ruled by a king, Latinus, who had a beautiful daughter, Lavinia. Latinus had dreamed that his daughter's husband would come from a foreign land, and that from this union would spring a race destined to rule the world, so he received Aeneas and feasted him. Later tradition goes on to record the marriage, the birth of a son, and the founding of the city in which Romulus and Remus were born. Other parallels—with the stories of Odysseus and Nausicaa, and of Jason and Medea—likewise suggest the epic possibilities of the American tale.

To be sure, a few writers, usually in a far more modest fashion, have tried to make something of Pocahontas. Fewer still have succeeded, but even some of the failures are interesting. Working from the probability that a letter by Strachey, who was on the wrecked *Sea Venture* with Rolfe, provided Shakespeare with material for *The Tempest*, John Esten Cooke wrote a polite novel called *My Lady Pocahontas* (1885) in which he made Shakespeare dependent on the lady and Smith for his characters Miranda and Ferdinand. At the climax, Pocahontas recognizes herself on the stage of the Globe.

Much of this invention has been blithely repeated as history, but such an attempt at legend fails anyway for being too literary. Other attempts have failed for not being literary enough. Mary Virginia Wall in 1908 wrote a book on Pocahontas as *The Daughter of Virginia Dare*—the child, that is, of this first native-born "American," who mysteriously disappeared, and Powhatan. Thus it is the spirit of Virginia Dare which accounts for the Indian girl's compassion. Now this could be a fruitful merger, uniting two of our best stories and giving Americans a kind of spiritual genealogy. The fact that to have been Pocahontas' mother Virginia would have had to bear a child at eight does not really matter much. But such scenes as the one in which the daughter comes to her end matter a good deal. On her deathbed, a place that has proved scarcely less fatal for authors than for their heroine, Pocahontas stoutly carols "Hark the Herald Angel Sings" (the Amen "begun on earth and ending in heaven"), and what started with some small promise has backed all the way out of it.

Another, but much better, novel which tries to do something with the story is the *Pocahontas* (1933) of David Garnett. This is a good historical novel with a thesis. In scenes of hideous but authentic brutality, Garnett shows the Indian women torturing their naked prisoners to death in orgies of obscene cruelty. These lead directly to orgies of sexual passion which act as a purge. To this sequence he contrasts the cruelty of the whites, which they sanction with self-righteousness and piety and follow with guilt. Garnett's book is a romantic and primitivistic performance after the manner of D. H. Lawrence which uses Pocahontas, more tender than her compatriots, as a vehicle for a lesson on the superiority of uncivilized peoples. Doctrinaire, and intellectually a little sentimental, this is still probably the best Pocahontas novel.[1]

Equally good, or maybe better, are two twentieth-century plays, Margaret Ullman's *Pocahontas* (1912) and Virgil Geddes' *Pocahontas and the Elders* (1933). More interesting than the plays themselves, however, are prefatory remarks their authors made about their material. In an introductory quotation Miss Ullman speaks of her heroine as a "Sweet-smelling sacrifice to the good of Western Planting." Geddes writes that his play is a "folkpiece" and his characters "part of the soul's inheritance." Both writers, in other words, were pointing to some pregnant quality of the story which goes beyond its facts. This was a direction which an informal group of modern poets was taking too. The result was the elevation of Pocahontas to myth.

It is Vachel Lindsay who was primarily responsible for this development. In his "Cool Tombs" Carl Sandburg had asked a question:

> Pocahontas' body, lovely as a poplar, sweet
> as a red haw in November or a pawpaw in May—
> did she wonder? does she remember—in the
> dust—in the cool tombs?

About 1918 Lindsay quoted this passage, answered yes, she remembers, and went on to explain in a poem which transforms the savior of Jamestown into a symbol of the American spirit. He supplies a magical genealogy whereby the girl becomes, as in his title, "Our Mother Pocahontas." Powhatan is the son of lightning and an oak; his daughter is the lover and bride of the forest. Thus

> John Rolfe is not our ancestor.
> We rise from out the soul of her
> Held in native wonderland,
> While the sun's rays kissed her hand,
> In the springtime,
> In Virginia,
> Our mother, Pocahontas.

Though she died in England, Lindsay acknowledges, she returned to Virginia and walked the continent, "Waking, / Thrilling, / The midnight land," and blending with it. We in turn are born not of Europe but of her, like a crop, and we are sustained by our inheritance.

One statement does not make a myth, but this concept was passed to other poets, notably to Hart Crane. First, though, came William Carlos Williams. A part of his prose study of the national past, called *In the American Grain* (1925), was devoted to an excoriation of the Puritans, after the fashion of the '20s, and to praise for the sensual joy of the Indians, who are again taken over as an element of our spiritual ancestry. Williams gave only brief notice to Pocahontas, but he quoted Strachey's description of a naked, wheeling Indian girl.

These are the materials from which Crane, in *The Bridge* (1930), raised Pocahontas to full mythic stature. In some notes he made for the poem, Crane saw her as "the natural body of American fertility," the land that lay before Columbus "like a woman, ripe, waiting to be taken." He followed his notes, and the part of his long poem called "Powhatan's Daughter" develops them. Starting with the quotation from Strachey (which he took from a *transition* review of Williams by Kay Boyle) the poet in a waking dream at the harbor dawn finds someone with him ("Your cool arms murmurously about me lay . . . *a forest shudders in your hair!*"). She disappears, then, from his semiconsciousness to reappear later as the American continent, most familiar to hoboes who "know a body under the wide rain," as the poet himself is familiar with trains that "Wail into distances I knew were hers." The land blooms with her, she becomes a bride (but "virgin to the last of men"), passes herself then to a pioneer mother, a living symbol of the fertility of the land, and makes her last appearance as the earth again—"our native clay . . . red, eternal flesh of Pocahontas. . . ."

Like these four poets, Archibald MacLeish in his *Frescoes for Mr. Rockefeller's City* (1933) was discovering his own land and his faith in its future. Dedicating his book to Sandburg, and deriving a symbol from Crane, MacLeish describes a "Landscape as a Nude"—the American continent as a beautiful naked Indian girl, inviting lovers. With this repetition the concept has taken hold. Thus we have a sort of American Ceres, or Demeter, or Gaea, developed from Pocahontas—a fertility-goddess, the mother of us all. We, by our descent from her, become a new race, innocent of both European and all human origins—a race from the earth, as in ancient mythologies of other lands, but an earth that is made of her. We take on a brave, free, mythical past as our alternative to the more prosaic, sordid explanation of history. And the thing is alive, as an image of the beautiful Indian girl is set in perpetual motion, and comes cartwheeling through our veins and down our generations.

IV

For all our concern with Pocahontas, one of the most interesting facts about her seems to have escaped everyone: the story John Smith told, which we have embraced so long, is one of the oldest stories known to man—not just roughly speaking, as in the Odysseus and Aeneas myths, but precisely in all essential parts. The tale of an adventurer, that is, who becomes the captive of the king of another country and another faith, and is rescued by his beautiful daughter, a princess who then gives up her land and her religion for his, is a story known to the popular literatures of many peoples for many centuries. The theme was so common in the Middle Ages that medieval scholars have a name for it: "The Enamoured Moslem Princess." This figure is a woman who characteristically offers herself to a captive Christian knight, the prisoner of her father, rescues him, is converted to Christianity, and goes to his native land—these events usually being followed by combat between his compatriots and hers.[2] . . . Latin anecdotes from the *Gesta Romanorum*, which contains the germs of plots used by Chaucer and Shakespeare, were widely read in translation in late sixteenth-century England (hence Smith may have known them). Tale V, called "Of Fidelity," is about a youth wasting away as a prisoner of pirates. Their chief has a lovely and virtuous daughter who frees the young man and, being promised marriage, goes to his country. The origins of this version may be in Seneca the Elder, who at the beginning of the Christian era formulated precisely the same situation in his *Controversia* as an imaginary legal case for debate. It is possible that he in turn got the story from the Greek Sophists, who had a lively interest in literature and disputation. . . . It has always been an uncomfortable fact of the Pocahontas story, and an apparently formidable obstacle to its survival, that after appearing to offer herself to Smith the heroine never married the hero. It is a startling fact, and bewildering, that this curiosity has been an element of the story from the beginning. . . . [I]t is extremely curious that there appear to be no accounts in which we are told specifically that what we might expect invariably to happen actually happens.[3]

The presence of a disturbing element in a popular story is hard to explain. The notion that melodies unheard are sweetest and cannot fade, that the lover who has not his bliss then can love forever and she be fair does not seem to account for this peculiarity; it was never that way at all. Yet there must be something obscurely "right" about an apparently unsatisfactory ending, or over the many centuries we should have succeeded in changing it. And the durable popularity of the story also urges the presence of some appeal that is not on the surface, some force that has given an advantage in the struggle for survival which we should make out if we can. The notion that the story is symbolic of something is not new. The monks who used it for religious instruction hundreds of years ago sensed this and had their own reading: the young man, they said, represents the human race. Led irresistably by the force of original sin into the prison of the devil, he is redeemed by Christ, in the form of the girl. But this interpretation incongruously makes Jesus the daughter of Satan, and seems also a little arbitrary. It is too utilitarian—but in that it offers one clue to the story's longevity.

Nothing survives indefinitely without filling some function, and the usefulness of this story is clear: the tale approves and propagates the beliefs of anyone who cares to tell it. An informal survey of the children's sections of two small Midwestern libraries disclosed twenty-six different books on Pocahontas—and no wonder. Quite apart from the opportunity she presents to give children some notion of self-sacrifice, she is, in addition to all her other appeals, perfectly ideal propaganda for both church and state. The story has long been, among other things, a tale of religious conversion, and in its American form is so eloquent a tribute to accepted institutions that there is no need to deflate its power by so much as even mentioning the obvious lesson it teaches. Of course the thing is a little chauvinistic. It is always either indifferent to the attitudes of the betrayed or unconscious of them. Indeed it is a tribute to the high regard we have for ourselves that Pocahontas has never once been cast as a villainess, for she would make an excellent one. From the point of view of her own people her crimes—repeated acts of treason, and cultural and religious apostasy—were serious. But one does not resent a betrayal to his own side, and we can always bear reassurance: love exists, love matters, and we are very eligible, Pocahontas tells us.

The story will work for any culture, informing us, whoever we are, that we are chosen, or preferred. Our own ways, race, religion must be better—so much better that even an Indian (Magian, Moor, Turk), albeit an unusually fine one (witness her recognition of our superiority), perceived our rectitude. But it nicely eases the guilt we have felt, since the start of its popularity, over the way we had already begun, by 1608, to treat the Indians. Pocahontas is a female Quanto, a "good" Indian, and by taking her to our national bosom we experience a partial absolution. In the lowering of her head we feel a benediction. We are so wonderful she loved us anyway.

And yet the story has an appeal which easily transcends such crude and frequently imperialistic functions—especially in the rescue scene, which implies all the new allegiances that follow from it. There is a picture there, at least in the American rendering, which has compelled us for so long that it must certainly contain meanings that go beyond the illustrations of it in the children's books. It is characteristic of all hallowed images that they cannot adequately be put into words, and no single rendering would articulate all that might be stated anyway. But these are feeble excuses for total silence, and it does not take any great sensitivity to perceive that Pocahontas' gesture—accomplished not by any subterfuge, but by the frank placing of her own body between Smith's and death—is fairly ringing with overtones. This is because we see her act as a rite, a ceremonial sign which bestows life. A surface part of that symbolism has always been clear. The Indians understood it as we do, and immediately Smith was alive and free. But what we have not been conscious of, though the modern poets sensed something like it, is that her candor was that of a bride. That is one thing, buried beneath awareness, that has dimly stirred us. Unable to put it into words, we have let the girl keep her secret, but the ritual that we feel in her action is itself an unorthodox and dramatic ceremony of marriage, and we are touched. We see Pocahontas at the moment of womanhood, coming voluntarily from the assembly to the altar, where she pledges the sacrifice of her own integrity for the giving of life. This is an offering up of innocence to experience, a thing that is always—in our recognition of its necessity—oddly moving. It is an act which bespeaks total renunciation, the giving up of home, land, faith, self, and perhaps even life, that life may go on.

Perhaps this helps to explain why it is that what, in its flattery of him, is at first glance so much a man's story should also be greatly promoted by women. Apparently it is a very pleasant vicarious experience for us all. Yet in the depths of our response to the heart of the story, the rescue, there is something more profoundly wishful than a simple identification with persons in a touching adventure. All myths have an element of wish somewhere in them. But there is something about this one that is also wistful, as though it expressed a wish that did not really expect to be gratified. It is as though something in us says "if only it were true. . . ."

We surely ought to know what it is we wish for. In our fondness for Pocahontas can we make out a longing that is buried somewhere below even the affection we bear for our fair selves and white causes? This yearning might be for another kind of love entirely, a love that has forever been hidden under the differences that set countries, creeds, and colors against each other. From the freedom and noble impracticality of childhood, we as a people have taken this Indian girl to heart. Could we be hinting at a wish for a love that would really cross the barriers of race? When the beautiful brown head comes down, does a whole nation dream this dream?

But it is still only a dream. And that fact helps to explain why it is that from the very beginning the story has had what looks like the wrong ending, why the wedding of the protagonists remains a symbol that was never realized. To be sure the girl eventually married, and the groom was usually the hero's compatriot, but by then the event has lost its joy and its force—seems a substitute for the real thing, and not at all satisfactory. But the story might have died centuries before us, and we would have made much less of Pocahontas, if the substitution were not in some way fit and right. We sense that the adventure has to end the way it does partly because we know the difference between what we dream and what we get. We are not particularly happy with the denouement, but we feel its correctness, and with it we acknowledge that this is all just make-believe.

To understand the rest of our dim and reluctant perception of the propriety of the story's outcome, Americans must see the Indian girl in one last way: as progenitress of all the "Dark Ladies" of our culture—all the erotic and joyous temptresses, the sensual, brunette heroines, whom our civilization (particularly our literature: Hawthorne, Cooper, Melville, and many others) has summoned up only to repress. John Smith is the first man on this continent known to have made this rejection; his refusal to embrace "the wild spirit" embodied in the girl was epic, and a precedent for centuries of denial. Prototypes too, and just as important, were the arrogantly hypocritical Rolfe and the rest of the colonists, who baptized, christened, commercialized, and ruined the young lady. With censorship and piety as tools, American writers—a few poets, far too late, aside—completed the job, until Pocahontas was domesticated for the whole of our society, where from the very start any healthy, dark happiness in the flesh is supposed to be hidden, or disapproved. Pocahontas is the archetypal sacrifice to respectability in America—a victim of what has been from the beginning our overwhelming anxiety to housebreak all things in nature, until wilderness and wildness be reduced to a few state parks and a few wild oats. Our affection for Pocahontas is the sign of our temptation, and our feeling that her misfortunes in love have a final, awkward fitness comes from our knowing that all that madness is not for us.

Notes

[1]It is not nearly so good as John Barth's *The Sot-Weed Factor* (1960), but this unprecedented novel is only incidentally about Pocahontas. Included in it, however, are John Smith's *Secret Historie,* parallel—but far superior—to John Davis' discovery of John Rolfe's poems, and the *Privie Journall* of a rival character. In the course of these extended tours-de-force a tribal custom is revealed that requires a prospective suitor to take the maidenhead of his bride before marrying her. In the case of Pocahontas no man has been successful in fracturing this membrane (indeed "most had done them selves hurt withal, in there efforts"). But with the aid of a fantastically invigorating vegetable device Smith publicly accomplishes the feat. In its review of the book, entitled "Novelist Libels Pocahontas Story," the *Richmond News-Leader* demanded to know if, in view of the respectability of the lady's descendants, all this was not "actionable."

[2]See, for instance, F. M. Warren, "The Enamoured Moslem Princess in Orderic Vital and the French Epic," *PMLA,* XXIX (1914), 341–58. It is a mistake, however, to speak of this theme as if it were wholly a matter of the distant past. For instance, the Enamoured Moslem Princess figures prominently in the Fourth Canto (1821) of Byron's *Don Juan.* Here she is Haidée, whose mother was a Moor; her father is Lambro, a pirate leader who holds the Christian Juan captive. The chieftain is about to kill his prisoner "When Haidée threw herself her body before; /. . . 'On me,' she cried, 'let death descend. . . .' " Juan is saved, but is taken off, and Haidée withers away and dies.

[3]The widely known and excellent ballad called "Young Beichan" seems an exception, but only because a new element, the motif of promised marriage, has been grafted on. Beichan is London-born, and longs strange lands for to see, but is taken by a savage Moor whose daughter, Susan Pye, steals her father's keys and releases him from a prison, after which he goes back to England, having promised to marry the girl in seven years. Later she abandons her country for England, is converted to Christianity, and gets a new name. She arrives in England to discover that Young Beichan has just married. But the ceremony is not yet consummated ("of her body I am free") and Susie Pye, now Lady Jane, is able to marry him after all. F. J. Child prints fourteen versions of this ballad in his *English and Scottish Popular Ballads,* while mentioning many related items in Norse, Spanish, Italian, and German. In its various forms it may have been affected by a fairly well-known legend on more or less the same theme, originating in the thirteenth century and concerning Gilbert Beket, father of St. Thomas à Becket. This also has the happy ending.

Anne Hutchinson

(1591–1643)

M. J. Lewis

Born Anne Marbury in 1591, in Alford, England, Anne Hutchinson was educated at home, where she had the benefit of her clergyman father's library. At twenty-one she married William Hutchinson, a successful Alford merchant. They had fifteen children together. In 1634, the Hutchinsons emigrated with a group of fellow Puritans, following their minister, Rev. John Cotton, to Massachusetts Bay Colony in New England. In the aftermath of a fierce political and religious struggle that erupted soon after they arrived, Anne Hutchinson was accused of supporting a church opposed by John Winthrop, the first governor of the colony. In three trials, one by the Bay's General Court and two by the Boston Church. Hutchinson was excommunicated from the church and banished from the colony. The charges against her are virtually all that are known of her life. The falsified official trial records in Winthrop's political pamphlets, published after her death, contribute to a myth surrounding Hutchinson that prevails today. The following essay focuses on the theological and political issues at stake in Hutchinson's public ordeal.

Early in this century one of America's very few statues of a woman was erected in Boston on the State House grounds. It was a memorial to Anne Hutchinson, one of the settlers in the first great English migration to this continent in the 1630s and the first woman to be martyred for her beliefs. The statue's design and its reception, however, are as charged with ambiguity as the historical record of her life. Nearly three hundred and fifty years after her death, she remains a shadowy legend. The plaque at the base of the large bronze memorial recognizes her as a "courageous exponent of religious toleration," but the statue itself conveys a very different message. The figure is passively pious: her throat bared submissively, her eyes weakly appealing to heaven.

Moreover, the memorial was grudgingly received. The federated Women's Clubs of Massachusetts presented the statue to the Commonwealth in 1920, just two months before the Nineteenth Amendment granted women suffrage. The legislature, however, did not formally accept it for three years and has never, apparently, officially dedicated it. Reluctance to do so centered on Anne Hutchinson's reputation. In 1922 a reporter asked a legislator to explain the hesitation to accept the gift. His reply, that the statue represented her "as an idealist while many think she was aggressive," mirrors attitudes about her as strong today as they were in the twenties. The biographical dictionary *Notable American Women* portrays her as "impulsive . . . confused . . . anarchistically subjective; [she] broods morbidly . . . [is] menopausal . . . no champion of religious freedom . . . irrational," yet "a remarkably intelligent and courageous woman."[1]

This reputation and these contradictory attitudes derive entirely from documents fabricated in the seventeenth century by her opponents. Although these documents are obvious political propaganda, they have since been accepted by historians as factual and read literally. Even today, Hutchinson is celebrated as a midwife and an Antinomian* when she was neither.[2] Every effort was made to create a fiction, an official story. John Winthrop, who led one of the two groups in the conflict associated with her and was judge and prosecutor in her civil trials, is responsible for the condition of the records we have. He wrote most of the story, destroyed contrary evidence, and saw to it that most public records were altered or rewritten to be consistent with his version of the events; for example, the General Court records for the three-year period at the height of the conflict are not original, having been mysteriously recopied; the entire Boston Church record was recopied and the entries for eighteen months were removed.

*Antinomian: one who believes that faith alone, not adherence to biblical law, is necessary for salvation.

Winthrop directed the Massachusetts Bay Company's 1630 expedition to New England. Apart from two brief periods, he was governor of the colony until his death in 1649. His writings, in particular the journal he intended to transform into a history of the new country, are the primary sources for subsequent study of the conflict as well as for the first twenty years of New England history.[3] So skillfully does he write and so objective and judicious does he seem, that countless scholars have since accepted his work at face value. In fact, no modern historian has suspected the extent of his efforts to conceal his regime's illegal acts. Yet in spite of his efforts, the conflict was so profound, affected so many people, and had such momentous consequences, that it could not be completely hidden. Enough documents survived to prove beyond reasonable doubt that Winthrop's account was fraudulent. He fabricated a myth to serve his own political ends.

By comparing these documents with Winthrop's writings, we can for the first time begin to distinguish fact from fiction, a believable woman from a caricature. The woman Anne Hutchinson had dignity, self-command, and unusual intellectual and moral courage. She was thoughtful and articulate, and enjoyed the devotion of her husband and family and the respect of her peers. Winthrop casts her in the role of woman as adversary. She is Eve, a seductress luring man into disobedience to his God; the "Whore of Babylon," a metaphor for a harlot church competing with the state for political supremacy. From this role come the derogatory epithets and insinuations—"Mistress Anne," "Jezebel," "prophetess" witch, midwife, woman preacher—characterizing her in the historical legend.

We know relatively little about the woman. Nothing she wrote, no pictorial likeness, little neutral contemporaneous writing about her have been found. Of her life before she emigrated to New England, we know that she was the daughter of Bridget Dryden and Francis Marbury, a silenced Church of England minister, who was tried, imprisoned twice and silenced by church courts for his attacks on incompetent clergy. She was born in Alford, Lincolnshire, and baptized July 20, 1591. When she was fourteen, she moved with her family to London. On August 9, 1612, at twenty-one, she married William Hutchinson, an affluent merchant and native of Alford. They returned to Alford, where they lived for the next twenty years. During this time she bore fourteen children, only two of whom died in childhood—a survival rate that testifies to her great vigor and remarkably competent childrearing. In 1634, when she was forty-three, the family joined a large contingent of emigrants from Lincolnshire to New England. We know little of the first two years of her life in Boston, except that she bore a fifteenth child, baptized in Boston Church in 1636.[4]

The Lincolnshire settlers were followers of the dissident minister John Cotton, who had accepted the pulpit of Boston Church the year before. Rich merchants and minor gentry, their number and quality made them prominent in Bay society. Most joined Boston Church, among them Anne and William Hutchinson. The men assumed leading positions in state and church; William became a Boston town commissioner, inferior court judge, deputy to the Bay's chief governing body, and was ordained a deacon in Boston Church.

The heart of the conflict that eventually drove most of the Lincolnshire settlers into exile seems to have been control of the pulpit. From its beginning, the Bay Company exercised authority over the church: hired ministers, paid passage for them and their families to New England and guaranteed return, provided housing and handsome stipends, determined the number of churches, and limited the franchise to church members. These and other practices transformed a private company into an independent and illegal state government, with the church as a subordinate arm.

John Winthrop later claimed that John Cotton's first sermon in Boston argued against a state-salaried ministry and for the congregation's obligation to pay its own minister. Implicit in Cotton's argument was the power to elect the minister, or lay control of the pulpit—a power exercised in England by hiring lecturers, ministers who preached, but did not dispense the sacraments. Cotton submitted to state support, but the debate over congregational control continued in private meetings. Many, if not most, of those in the influx of new settlers were part of groups led by ministers expecting to form their own congregations. Fearing loss of its authority over the pulpit, Winthrop's government denied these groups permission to congregate separately. Rather than join the established churches, many of them met privately. When increasing numbers chose such meetings, which were, in effect, competing churches, they became a threat to political stability. The meetings deprived the legal churches of members and implicitly repudiated their state-salaried ministers. More importantly, they were powerful vehicles for dissent and resistance to state control. Thus they had to be suppressed. (Roger Williams, for example, was forced into exile for holding such meetings.)

After offering some resistance, many groups gave up and moved out of the Bay jurisdiction. But one minister and his followers, part of the group from Lincolnshire, challenged state control of the pulpit when they were denied the right to form a church. The minister, John Wheelwright, who was Anne Hutchinson's brother-in-law, had arrived in June 1636 with his family, including William Hutchinson's mother. According to John Winthrop's deeply-biased account, a dispute with Wheelwright and his allies began in late October 1636, when most of Boston Church tried to hire him as a lecturer. When their efforts were thwarted by John Winthrop, the group proposed a church at Mount Wollaston, nine miles away, where many of them had large farms. By this time, the group enjoyed considerable power. Among its leaders was Henry Vane, a brilliant young nobleman who came to New England in the fall of 1635 representing enormously wealthy and powerful English investors and political interests. Within months of his arrival, Vane attracted so wide a following that in May 1636 he was elected governor, forcing Winthrop to serve as deputy-governor under a man half his age who had far greater political and economic resources.

Perhaps their strength led Wheelwright's supporters to underestimate the resistance to the proposed church, which was led by the formidable John Winthrop. In the succeeding months, painful strife erupted among the members of Boston Church and bitter controversy among the Bay clergy.[5] To intimidate Wheelwright and his supporters, Winthrop brought charges of sedition against Wheelwright for a sermon he preached by invitation in Boston Church. Unable to control a court over which Vane presided, Winthrop could not silence Wheelwright, who had begun to preach at Mount Wollaston and in Boston, presumably at the Hutchinson farm at the Mount and house in Boston. Faced with such defiance, Winthrop called for a church synod to condemn the doctrines supporting what had become by this time a profound dispute over church-state relations and in May seized the government from Vane by coup d'état. After engaging in written dispute with Winthrop concerning the respective jurisdictions of church and state,[6] Vane returned to England in August, shortly before the September church synod condemned doctrines supporting the dissenters' position. Within two months after the synod, Winthrop had broken the dissident party. When a duly-elected General Court, the colony's governing body, met in October and refused for the fourth time to punish Wheelwright, Winthrop dissolved it and called for a new—and illegal—election. With nearly two-thirds of its members replaced with Winthrop allies, the new Court was considerably more tractable. It dismissed members of the Court who belonged to the dissenting group and disfranchised and banished its leaders, including Wheelwright. Then, after months of fierce quarreling in which Anne Hutchinson played no public part, the Court called her to appear to answer charges of being in alliance with the condemned party and maintaining a meeting in her house.

These charges argue that her Boston house was a center for the dissenters and a pulpit for Wheelwright. Her house was also the scene of women's meetings. Well before she arrived, women had begun the practice of gathering to discuss scripture during the public lecture or week-day sermon they were not permitted to attend. Although she later testified that she did not at first approve of such meetings, she had bowed to public pressure—accusations of pride—and begun to attend. She had, apparently, soon acquired a reputation for learning, for skill in scriptural exegesis. Such meetings were, of course, opportunities to proselytize. By now a strong leader among her sex, she was a threat to containing dissent. To weaken her influence and deprive the group of its meeting place, Winthrop summoned her before the Court. When he asked her to denounce the condemned leaders and agree to hold no more meetings, he must have expected her to submit quietly, to discontinue conduct "not fitting for your sex," as he put it. (Later in her trial he admitted that he "had not meant to deal with those of your sex.") But he underestimated her intellect and her powers of resistance. What seems to have begun as a mopping up of holdouts ended with Winthrop being forced to display the lengths he was willing to go to keep himself in power.

Although Winthrop managed to control the public record of the proceedings against the dissidents, a few documents survived. Among them is a transcript of Anne Hutchinson's civil trial. The text is long, thirty-six printed pages, and appears authentic.[7] Winthrop's opening charge, carefully planned to be extremely threatening, accused her of four grave crimes: sedition, blasphemy, heresy, contempt of court. He then asked her the question he had asked the leaders previously condemned, "whether you do not justify Mr. Wheelwright's sermon and the petition."[8] Unless she denounced the sermon (Wheelwright's doctrines)—and repudiated a petition to the Court protesting his punishment, compiled by her allies—she would receive heavy punishment.

Ignoring the question, she asked to be accused: "I am called here to answer before you but I hear no things laid to my charge." Her reply was dazzling; it proved that she was well-aware that the Court had no case against her, that she was prepared to challenge it to make a case it could prove or to prosecute her illegally. As she had not signed the petition, she could not be convicted on the same evidence as those who had. Furthermore, the Court had passed no order prohibiting private meetings. Forced to be specific, Winthrop countered that she had broken a law by "harboring" the petitioners. Her reply, "that's matter of conscience, Sir," proves that she was also prepared to defend her behavior and the beliefs informing it as matters of conscience. She was making a distinction between secular and sacred authority, defending an independent spiritual order.

Denying any distinction, Winthrop flatly asserted the Court's right to compel her conscience, "Your conscience you must keep or it must be kept for you."

Knowing that English law permitted peaceful petitions, she asked what law the petitioners had broken. Winthrop, extending the fifth commandment to honor parents to rulers of the state, replied: "The law of God and of the state," which requires you to "honour thy father and thy mother." Her answer, "Ay Sir in the Lord," accepted the Court's authority but added the condition that a Christian was bound in duty to obey only just laws.[9] This exchange, perhaps more than any other in what proved to be a long trial, goes to the heart of the matter. For Winthrop, state and church were inextricably fused; for the dissenters, they were separate realms. The political implications of the dispute, the proper relation between state and church, were and are profound. Having suffered under an oppressive church in England, Winthrop was determined to maintain state dominance in the new commonwealth.

Well instructed in the law and in biblical texts, Anne Hutchinson defeated every attempt to convict her. During two days of intense debate, six ministers witnessed against her. In her defense, three witnesses, one of whom was John Cotton, refuted their testimony, arguing that they had distorted her words, added things she did not say, and omitted crucial qualifications. In spite of these witnesses and her claim of a right to speak "what in my conscience I know to be truth," Winthrop relentlessly pursued a conviction. When his intent was clear, she submitted to the Court's authority but quoted a scriptural warning that their acts of persecution would bring a curse upon them and their posterity. When she further claimed that she would be delivered from this adversity, Winthrop seized the opportunity to ensnare her. Twisting her words to pretend that she was speaking prophecy, he asked: "Daniel was delivered by miracle do you think to be deliver'd so too?" Recognizing Winthrop's theological trap—Puritans denied miraculous intervention; God did not act through miracles, only through a predestined providential plan—she answered: "I do here speak it before the court. I look that the Lord should deliver me by his providence."[10] Unable to break her repeated insistence that she meant providential delivery—an appeal members of the Court frequently made—or to enlist Cotton's help to condemn her, Winthrop simply ignored her witnesses' testimonies and pretended that she had claimed a miraculous delivery. Announcing that she must be cut off, he stampeded the Court, declaring her the "ground of all these tumults and troubles."

Cotton recognized the great threat to her these new charges of blasphemy implied and tried to restrain him. Winthrop ignored his efforts. William Coddington, a member of the Court, a lawyer, and now leader of what had become a true political opposition party, also intervened in the face of this added danger. Coddington called attention to the many irregularities in the proceedings—no clear witnesses, her judges were her accusers, she had broken no law of God or man—and appealed to Winthrop: "I beseech you do not speak so to force things along." Winthrop was as undeterred by these pleas—from a man who had long been a personal friend, had been part of the original venture of settling New England, enjoyed nearly as much power and prestige as he, and with whom he was united in a church covenant of brotherhood—as he had been by Cotton's. Denouncing her as "unfit for our society," Winthrop ruled "that she shall be banished out of our liberties and imprisoned till she be sent away." After he imposed these extreme punishments, Anne Hutchinson defended her innocence and called attention to the Court's illegal proceedings by asking: "I desire to know wherefore I am banished?" Winthrop's blatantly arbitrary reply was, "Say no more, the court knows wherefore and is satisfied."

So unexpected and powerful had been her defense, so harsh her punishment that Winthrop feared retaliation—or pretended to. He ordered sympathizers to denounce the leaders or have their guns confiscated, imprisoned Anne Hutchinson in the neighboring town of Roxbury where his support was strong, and had the state's munitions moved from Boston to Roxbury. We have no evidence of anything but peaceful compliance. Yet called to account by Boston Church for the trial and these acts, Winthrop defended them as necessary for the preservation of the country.

In a final attempt to heal a breach that had torn Boston apart or anticipating Winthrop's next move, the leaders of the group petitioned Winthrop in January 1638. Although he promised no further punishment and virtually begged them to capitulate, he demanded surrender. In what appears to be the ultimate step to break their strength, he enlisted the help of ministers hostile to Cotton to force Boston Church to condemn Anne Hutchinson and through her the competing beliefs. After months of inquisition, the ministers contrived enough evidence of alleged heresy to pressure the Church into a public trial. Her allies, her husband among them, admitted defeat. Choosing to leave rather than resist further, they secured permission (careful as they had always been to respect the law) to depart the colony. In early March, as soon as the winter's unusually heavy snow permitted travel, they left Boston to seek a place to form a new settlement. Taking advantage of their absence to insure the unanimity necessary to condemn her, Boston Church peremptorily brought her to trial in mid-March.

Again, fortunately, a record of what became two church trials was preserved. Its text was written and edited by two ministers active in the prosecution, and "proved by four witnesses," none of whom was named.[11] By this time she was showing the debilitating effects of the civil trial, of four months' incarceration, of being without her husband and allies and knowing that their absence made excommunication likely, and of serious illness. A neoplastic growth, with symptoms indistinguishable from those of pregnancy, brought her near death soon after her exile.[12] At the opening of the first trial, the presiding elder apologized for her appearing late and explained that he was "to acquaint all this congregation, that whereas our Sister Hutchinson was not here at the beginning of this exercise, it was not out of any contempt or neglect to the ordinance, but because she hath been long [under] durance. She is so weak that she conceives herself not fit nor able to have been here so long together."[13]

Conducted and recorded in the same manner as the civil trial, the church proceedings were made up of elaborate and unsupported charges, increasingly antagonistic questioning, a shift from particular accusation to inference in the face of her refutation and strong denial, and the use of verbal tricks to justify imposing the heaviest penalties. After many hours of inquisition, she was condemned to be admonished, the church's most serious discipline short of excommunication. Her words interrupting the admonition show her to be greatly weakened but impressively self-possessed: "I desire to speak one word before you proceed: I would forbear but by reason of my weakness. I fear I shall not remember it when you have done."

During the week intervening before her second church trial, her situation was much as it had been at her civil trial: a choice between submission or heavy punishment, renunciation of her beliefs or excommunication. She brought to the second trial a written answer to specific charges of heresy. In the statement paraphrased by Cotton—apparently to make it audible to spectators—she made no mention of doctrinal error, but humbly expressed sorrow for offenses stemming from pride. She heartily regretted her behavior, but not, it must be assumed, her belief. Unappeased, aggravated, her clerical opponents denounced her submission and demanded further satisfaction. But in spite of repeated provocation and distortion of her words and meaning, they were unable to elicit evidence of heresy. By the end of a day of bitter theological dispute, the effects of their harassing and her weakened condition were apparent; she was visibly confused. At a crucial moment when she was being provoked to confess to lying, her son-in-law pleaded: "things is with her in distraction, and she cannot recollect her thoughts."[14] Physically but not spiritually broken, she refused to confess to a lie she had not told. She remained to the end, during harsh excommunication, self-controlled and dignified—at least no evidence of any other kind of behavior was recorded by her opponents.

After her banishment, Anne Hutchinson joined her husband, who, with the large number who chose exile, purchased from the Indians an unpatented tract on the Narragansett Bay, in a region that became Rhode Island, and settled in two towns. Unfortunately, the site they chose had long been coveted by Winthrop for its great intrinsic value and its strategic importance as a base of operations for exterminating intractable Indians and controlling sea trade. With its rich land, temperate weather, access to trade routes linking the Connecticut Valley, the Hudson and Delaware Valleys, Virginia, the Atlantic seaboard, and the West Indies, Narragansett Bay was considered a much more desirable place than Boston.[15]

From the time Winthrop learned of the acquisition, he began to undermine the exiles' efforts to establish a colony. Knowing the land was unpatented, he justified Bay moves to annex the region by denying the legitimacy of rights based on purchase from the Indians only. When the colony sought to protect itself by securing a patent from England, he tried to assume jurisdiction by sending, in the guise of "a brotherly mission of inquiry" from Boston Church, an armed expedition led by three military officers to "require some satisfactory answer about such things as we hear be offensive amongst them."[16] Frightened by the expedition and the assertion of jurisdiction implied in the mission's demand, the settlers established a government similar to that in the Bay. Soon thereafter, when Anne Hutchinson's young son Francis wrote Boston Church asking to be dismissed to join his own church, Boston Church refused, replying that it would dismiss only to a church it accredited; that is, one that became part of the established Bay church. Unable to accept this answer, Francis Hutchinson and his brother-in-law William Collins, a young minister ordained by the English Church, neither of whom had been involved in the earlier part of the conflict, went to Boston to question the refusal. The young men barely escaped with their lives: they were arrested without charge, fined outrageously, imprisoned for months, released under penalty of death if they returned to the Bay.

In an act that had much to do with Anne Hutchinson's ultimate fate, the same Court that dealt so threateningly with the young men admonished the leaders of groups in the Bay who had begun to plan a colony on Long Island under Dutch jurisdiction "not to go to the Dutch because of scandal and offense."[17] At this time New England was extremely vulnerable, its very existence threatened. Affluent, stable settlers were essential to attract and keep investment capital. The Bay's harsh practices deterred immigration from England and provoked large numbers of its own inhabitants to leave. In part because of the exodus, Lord Say, New England's richest English investor, had just written Winthrop that he was shifting his millions from investment in New England to the West Indies—an act that must have had much to do with Winthrop's vindictiveness toward those who left.

Anne Hutchinson and her family were so intimidated by the young men's experience and by the Bay's inexorable moves to annex the Narragansett region, that they and many of its other inhabitants sought the civil and religious freedoms offered by the Dutch. But a third exile did not spare them further hostility.[18] Strong circumstantial evidence suggests that their settlement near New Amsterdam was too opportune a target to miss: Anne Hutchinson and her associates could not be brought back into the fold; their wealth, stability, and reputation strengthened the Dutch and would attract followers; a violent death at the hands of "savages" would be a powerful deterrent to others and would promote the ruin of the Dutch plantation. Depicted as divine justice by the pulpit and in letters to England, such a death could help repair the Bay's reputation among English supporters and investors.

The massacre took place sometime in the early fall of 1643.[19] When news of it reached Samuel Gorton, Anne Hutchinson's Narragansett neighbor and friend, he wrote in outrage to Winthrop that her blood was "so savagely and causelessly spilt." Implying Bay complicity in the murders, his letter continued: "we have heard them [the dissenting exiles] affirm that she would never heave up a hand, no nor move a tongue against any that persecuted or troubled them, but only endeavor to save themselves by flight, not perceiving the nature and end of persecution. . . ."[20]

One contemporary description of the massacre survives in a propaganda tract published in England a decade later by Edward Johnson, a Bay military leader. Johnson's work was intended to counter criticism of New England's "too strict government." Writing his defense in the form of annals, Johnson linked divine retribution with her behavior by including her death in his 1638 description of the conflict. This tactic permitted him to obscure the years between the two events and impede recovery of the truth. (If such was his intent, he was successful; modern scholars still limit the conflict to less than two years.) "The grand Mistress of them all," he wrote,

> who ordinarily prated every Sabbath day, . . . withdrew her self, her husband, and her family also, to a more remote place; . . . The Indians in those parts forewarned them of making their abode there; yet this could be no warning to them, but still they continued, being amongst a multitude of Indians, boasted they were become all one Indian: and indeed, this woman, who had the chief rule of all the roost, being very bold in her strange revelations and misapplications, tells them, though all nations and people were cut off round about them, yet should not they; till on a day certain Indians coming to her house, discoursing with them, they wished to tie up her dogs, for they much bit[.] [T]he man, not mistrusting the Indians' guile, did so; the which no sooner done, but they cruelly murthered her, taking one of their daughters away with them, and another of them seeking to escape is caught, as she was getting over a hedge, and they drew her back again by the hair of the head to the stump of a tree, and there cut off her head with a hatchet; the other that dwelt by them betook them to boat, and fled, to tell the sad news.[21]

The impression Johnson created and the details he chose are consistent with the most probable facts and inconsistent with the claim that Anne Hutchinson and her family were the victims of a random Indian raid.

A likely reconstruction is that Johnson was a participant, for his narrative is filled with revealing details. The Bay government, not the Indians, warned against going to the Dutch. Raiding Indians do not walk up to "discourse" with their victims, nor do victims mindlessly tie their guard dogs. The settlers must have had good reason for trust; either they knew the Indians or the English who must have been with them. How else could Johnson know such particulars as a woman's trying to escape over a hedge being pulled back by her hair to a stump and decapitated with a hatchet. If no English were with the Indians, Johnson's story had to come from "the other" who "took them to boat" to tell the "sad news." But Winthrop claimed in his *Journal* that none survived, that sixteen were killed, including two men in a boat who came to help. John Underhill, who had been a member of the dissenting party in Boston and had a settlement nearby, wrote that only nine, all in the families of Hutchinson and Collins, were massacred. The child taken hostage, Anne Hutchinson's eight-year-old daughter, cannot have been the source because she had forgotten how to speak English when she was returned years later. (Winthrop neglected to mention in his *Journal* account that his October 1643 Court recorded but did not act on a request by Bay relatives and friends of the murdered families, to ransom the child—a request that strongly suggests Winthrop knew which Indians had her.) The inconsistency between Johnson and Winthrop leads us to suspect an attempt to bury the details in obscurity and conceal Johnson's presence.[22]

The present historical record reveals only these facts about the life of Anne Hutchinson. The fiction accepted as fact was created by John Winthrop and his London agents to exonerate his government in the face of heavy condemnation of its practices by investors and allies in England. Winthrop's version was first published anonymously, presumably without his awareness or consent, in a political pamphlet in mid-January 1644, seven years after the trials, at the height of what has been called a "wild and confused period, the very maelstrom of the revolution," the English Civil War. A large embassy sent to promote New England interests arrived in London shortly thereafter to discover the pamphlet and recognize from what immediately became a pamphlet war over its subject the damage it had done. By early February another edition, incorporating the first and prefaced with a long, virulent attack on Anne Hutchinson was rushed into print. Purely an instrument of propaganda, the second work has been accepted by modern scholars as a factual account of the conflict.[22]

But it was written to hide the truth and to defend the New England church and its government's oppression of dissent. Winthrop had to posit a powerful adversary, one for whom no sympathy was possible. Thus he created a demonic Anne Hutchinson, a divine John Winthrop. His narrative portrayed her as the cause of the entire conflict. Describing her behavior and treatment, his language became heavily charged and metaphoric: "All these (except Mr. Wheelwright) were but young branches, sprung out of an old root, the Court had now to do with the head of all this faction . . . a woman who had been the breeder and nourisher of all these distempers, one Mistress Hutchinson. She was "a woman of a haughty and fierce carriage, of a nimble wit and active spirit, and a very voluble tongue, more bold than a man, though in understanding and judgment, inferior to many women."[23] Among the qualities with which he endows her, "voluble tongue" deserves comment. The organ most feared and resented in a woman was her tongue; use of the tongue, the conduit of salvation, was a prerogative exclusive to the male ministry. Women were not permitted to even speak in the church, much less preach. That she did not have a "voluble tongue" Winthrop himself offered the strongest proof. In the record he cautioned the court: "It is well discerned to the court that Mrs. Hutchinson can tell when to speak and when to hold her tongue. Upon the answering of a question which we desire her to tell her thoughts of she desires to be pardoned." Nothing in the trial record resembles the impatient, fierce, boasting spirit who cannot "endure a stop in her way" he depicted in the phamplet.[24]

Winthrop further claimed that she brought her heretical opinions from England and infected others in the infant church. To explain why such a woman was accepted by the Bay church, he wrote: "This woman had learned her skill in England, and had discovered some of her opinions in the ship, as she came over, which had caused some jealousy of her, which gave occasion of some delay of her admission, when she first desired fellowship with the Church of Boston, but she cunningly dissembled and colored her opinions, as she soon got over that block, and was admitted into the Church, then she began to go to work, and being a woman very helpful in the times of childbirth, and other occasions of bodily infirmities, and well furnished with means for those purposes, she easily insinuated herself into the affections of many."[25] Associating Anne Hutchinson with childbirth has led to the false assumption that she was a midwife. As midwives were a favorite target of witch hunters, Winthrop meant to tar her with the brush of witchcraft.[26]

Winthrop further tampered with the trial record to distort her behavior and the court's acts. He twisted the civility, respect, and careful deference she showed the court into insolence and defiance by removing the Sir with which she prefaced most of her replies to his questions and by adding arrogant claims to her testimony. He changed a single, private meeting into multiple public meetings. He struck out her emphatic denial that she had taught men and put in a claim that she had asserted the right to teach men and had taught them publicly.[27] Of far greater importance in the light of her punishment, however, were Winthrop's pretenses that she presumed to be beyond the law and to have prophetic or miraculous powers. The first pretense, to be exempt from the law, was a way to associate her with the Antinomians, a sect much feared in 1644 by orthodox English clergy. She recognized in the court transcript the court's authority over her body, but not over her soul, her conscience. Winthrop has her deny the court's authority over her body. Although she repeatedly denied miraculous intervention, Winthrop not only removed her denials but contrived elaborate evidence that she claimed prophetic powers and spoke prophecy, permitting him to justify her severe punishment.[28] Winthrop even admitted that the court had insufficient proof to proceed against her, then tried to prove that she was self-condemned, that she had fully and freely convicted herself of everything suspected of her. Thus, he concluded with feigned regret, the Court had no choice but to find her guilty and sentence her accordingly.[29]

As a further pretense to authenticity, Winthrop wrote a summary description of her church trial. Needless to say, it bears no relation to her actual behavior and treatment.[30] In it he doubles her alleged heretical opinions, literally creating new offenses. He makes her behave repulsively, hypocritically, rashly, proudly, and obstinately. Winthrop also had to counter criticisms that she was put "to durance," illegally coerced, or treated harshly. Well-trained in the law, he wrote that she "pretended bodily infirmity" but had "only a favourable confinement, so as all of her family and divers others, resorted to her at their pleasure."

By the time the pamphlet was published, Anne Hutchinson and her immediate family were dead. She had no opportunity to defend herself. Winthrop had access to the press, controlled public records, and wrote the first history of New England. His authority has remained unchallenged for over three centuries. Yet his version of the conflict is that of the prosecution only. Having heard no defense, how can we judge? History never stops questioning its own assumptions, its own perspectives. We need to analyze the documents with appropriate rigor, separate fact from fiction, truth from myth. Change one assumption, and another world appears. If, for example, we see the missing dates in the Boston Church Records as an eighteen-month gap rather than a closed record, we ask who made it and why. A long overdue fair hearing would make the words at the base of her memorial, "courageous exponent of civil liberty," intelligible for the first time.

Notes

[1]Emery Battis wrote the entry; his *Saints and Sectaries* (Chapel Hill: University of North Carolina Press, 1962) has been the definitive text on the so-called Antinomian controversy for nearly thirty years.

[2]See G. J. Barker-Benfield, "Anne Hutchinson and the Puritan Attitude toward Women," *Feminist Studies* I, no. 2 (Fall, 1972) and Lyle Koehler, "The Case of the American Jezebels," *William and Mary Quarterly,* 3rd ser. 31 (1974).

[3]James Kendall Hosmer, ed., *Winthrop's Journal: "History of New England, 1630–1649,"* 2 vols. (New York, 1908).

[4]John Denison Champlin, "Hutchinson Ancestry and Descendants of William and Anne Hutchinson," *New York Geneological and Biographical Record,* v. 45 (1914), pp. 164–169.

[5]Scholars have confined their analyses of the conflict to the theological or doctrinal dispute, not recognizing that doctrinal quarrels stemmed from the

political implications of the state-established congregational polity; that is, the seemingly endless quibbling can be reduced to qualifications for church membership and for the ministry. Winthrop and his clerical allies tried to save their concept of church-state relations by making a distinction between discipline—organization, rules, admission practices—and doctrine-theological premises. But doctrine informs discipline; they are inseparable—as the clergy found when it presumed to confirm or deny church membership tied to political franchise rather than spiritual condition.

[6]To oversimplify a very complex issue, Vane's group maintained on the basis of Christ's imperative to render unto Caesar the things that are Caesar's and unto Christ the things that are Christ's that church and state were separate realms.

[7]"The Examination of Mrs. Anne Hutchinson at the Court at Newtown," in David Hall, *The Antinomian Controversy, 1636–1638: A Documentary History* (Middletown, CT: Wesleyan University Press, 1968). Hall reprinted the three documents—a pamphlet and two trial records—in the first selection of primary documents, Charles Francis Adams' *Antinomianism in the Colony of Massachusetts Bay, 1636–1638* (Boston: Publications of the Prince Society, 1894)—and added nine: two letters, five treatises and draft notes of a sixth, and Wheelwright's sermon. Breaks in continuity and defaced lines suggest corruption, but much discreditable detail is left intact.

[8]Hall, p. 312.

[9]Hall, pp. 312, 313.

[10]Hall, p. 338.

[11]Hall reprints the trial report from an eighteenth-century copy of the original that has disappeared. The punctuation "is so erratic as to make the manuscript almost unintelligible" (350).

[12]William Hutchinson wrote John Cotton of her grave illness. Hearing of it, John Winthrop wrote her physician, John Clarke, demanding a full description. Clarke's reply, part of which Winthrop paraphrased in his *Journal*, describes what was probably an hydatidi-form mole. A standard modern medical text calls the condition a "pathological pregnancy," a neoplastic lesion, usually spontaneously aborted by the third month, rarely beyond the sixth. In early stages it is indistinguishable from a normal pregnancy, except that hyperemesis, "morning sickness," is more frequent and apt to be more severe and protracted. The outstanding symptom is uterine bleeding (Nicholson J. Eastman, *Williams Obstetrics* [New York, 1982], pp. 528–532). Clarke wrote that he despaired of her life. Winthrop widely publicized in New and Old England what he called Anne Hutchinson's "monstrous birth."

[13]Hall, p. 351.

[14]Hall, pp. 372, 386.

[15]Cotton Mather called Rhode Island the paradise of New England, "the best garden of all the colonies." *Magnalia Christi Americana*, Hartford, 1853, p. 521.

[16]Richard D. Pierce, ed., *Records of the First Church in Boston 1630–1868*, Colonial Society of Massachusetts, *Publications*, vol. 39. (Boston, 1961), p. 27.

[17]Nathaniel B. Shurtleff, ed., *Records of the Governor and Company of the Massachusetts Bay in New England*, 5 vols. in 6 (Boston, 1853; reprint, New York: AMS Press, 1968), vol. I, p. 337.

[18]Forming a confederation with Connecticut, Plymouth, and New Haven, New England tried to contain the expansion of competing colonies, the Dutch in particular, and punish any who resisted. Winthrop refused to accept the Narragansett government into the confederation. He also used Indian agents to keep those driven from the Bay under close surveillance.

[19]Winthrop wrote of the murders in a letter dated October 10. His *Journal* account of the deaths is a brief, vague undated entry ostensibly made in July. He includes the telling detail that the same Indians went from Anne Hutchinson's settlement to attack Lady Deborah Moody's but found it too strongly defended with palisades and armed men. Lady Moody, Henry Vane's cousin, had found the Salem Church intolerable and had left the Bay to found a colony on Long Island.

[20]Samuel Gorton, *Simplicities Defence against Seven-Headed Policy* (London, 1646), p. 36. Even as he wrote, Gorton was defending his own settlement against annexation. Within days, it was under attack by a Bay military expedition that burned the houses, force-marched the men in shackles to Boston, and appropriated their livestock as booty. Winthrop greeted them with praise and drinks on the house. After keeping Gorton in chains and at hard labor until spring, Winthrop tried unsuccessfully to secure the death penalty on charges very similar to those brought against Anne Hutchinson.

[21]J. Franklin Jameson, ed., *Johnson's Wonder-Working Providence* (New York: Scribner's, 1910), p. 138.

[22]*A Short Story of the Rise, reign, and ruine of Antinomians, Familists, & Libertines....* Page numbers refer to Hall, pp. 199–310. Spelling is modernized.

[23]Hall, p. 262.

[24]Hall, p. 275.

[25]Hall, p. 265.

[26]His intended Puritan English audience was particularly sensitive to this issue. Prosecutions and executions of witches in English history were concentrated in the second half of the sixteenth century and the first half of the seventeenth. Winthrop's 1644 smear of Anne Hutchinson coincided precisely with activities of the most sucessful witch-hunter in English history, Matthew Hopkins. (For Hopkins, see Keith Thomas, *Religion and the Decline of Magic* (New York: Scribner's, 1971), p. 454.

[27]Hall, pp. 267, 314.

[28]Hall, pp. 338, 273.

[29]Hall, p. 265.

[30]This portrayal, indeed the entire pamphlet, should not be read as an attack on the person Anne Hutchinson. It was written to serve quite other political purposes. Winthrop used her figure to represent a recalcitrant church, one which resisted subordination to its divinely-appointed "godly" rulers, the magistrates.

PART II

Many Revolutions

By 1720 the majority of the white population—north and south—had been born in the New World. Population growth was phenomenal throughout the eighteenth century, and competition for land continued to govern the history of European relations with the Indian nations. Decimated by European disease, then by genocidal practices, American Indians saw themselves forced off their ancient lands by European settlers who were relentlessly moving westward. In response, Indian nations formed more permanent confederacies, using all the arts of war and diplomacy to maintain their cultures.

The Cherokee, the largest Indian nation bordering the English, Spanish and French colonies in the South, had used their pivotal geographic position and large number to maintain their autonomy in the seventeenth and eighteenth centuries. They allied themselves with the English Carolinians, although they played off each European group, one against the other. However, after they joined the English for an expedition against the Spanish fort of St. Augustine in 1740–41, the Cherokees were decimated by smallpox. International warfare eventually took its toll as well, as the English proved that they could also play the game of "divide and conquer," by setting one Indian nation against another.

The eagerness of the Indians for European goods ultimately transformed their societies. The fur trade fundamentally altered Indians' relationships with the resources of their environment; some scholars believed this led indigenous peoples to destroy their own ecosystems. Men were drawn away from villages to hunt for prolonged periods of time, and the preparation of furs and skins for market were added to women's agricultural labor. Men's roles in hunting, trading, and diplomacy were aggrandized and the economic basis for women's matrilineal power was diminished. All of this may be interpreted as a form of successful resistance to European encroachment, because it strengthened Indians' economic and military power and their ability to deploy it. But the ability of Indian nations to play one imperial power against another was removed once the English pushed the French out of North America in 1763.

Increasingly, there was a general tendency among Indian nations to develop gender arrangements more like those of the Europeans with whom they intermarried as well as traded. While

Nancy Ward's life perhaps illustrates the resistance of native cultures to such a trend, it was one many American Indian women had to follow. Thomas Jefferson's presidential words in 1802 to Handsome Lake, a Seneca leader, symbolized the official expectations of the white man. "Go on, then, brother, in the great reformation you have undertaken. Persuade our red men to be sober and to cultivate their lands; and their women to spin and weave for their families." This was a message reinforced by missionaries, and Handsome Lake did in fact restructure Seneca life along more patriarchal lines.

By the early eighteenth century, the social order in both the northern and southern colonies had become more uniform in its patriarchal laws and customs. The pressure that the increasing population had on land increased paternal power as the resources that men controlled grew scarcer. Agricultural produce and land speculation were factors in a system of international trade and finance. Colonial economies required men to engage themselves in the market and the law. However, farm women were more isolated from travel and markets than their menfolk. While they seem largely to have accepted their subordination to "the small circle of domestic concerns," women frequently complained about tedium and drudgery. Moreover, a significant number were not so entirely immersed in household production from dawn to dusk as previously thought. The fact that many households did not have the equipment to manufacture clothing, candles, cheese, and butter—even as the production of such items was increasing—suggests that trade networks had come into existence among women.

The advantages of prosperity to women were most evident in colonial cities such as Boston, New York, Philadelphia, Baltimore, and Charleston. The number and misery of poor women in cities was striking, and class divisions were generally sharpened over the course of the century; however, women congregated in cities in part in hopes of the job opportunities (for example, as nurses and seamstresses) not available in the countryside. Other women in towns ran shops and inns, conducting businesses during men's temporary and long-term absences and often inheriting an enterprise to run as their own upon the male owner's death. The law tried to keep women off the charity rolls by according them "feme sole" status as traders—expanding their legal independence if they were adult and unmarried or widowed. Women used such concessions for their own advantage. Some became accomplished in matters of commerce, including Elizabeth Murray, a Scots immigrant. She became a successful merchant, making a fortune in retailing, real estate, and international trade. She profited from the mistakes of her first marriage by using prenuptial agreements to carve out a measure of economic autonomy in her two subsequent marriages. In her own words, she learned to cherish "a spirit of independence."

To be able to acquire education and broaden their interests, women need to be elevated above subsistence. Hence the most literate women throughout much of the eighteenth century came from the upper crust. Large aristocratic plantations emerged in the South after the early years. Plantation mistresses could escape much of the drudgery associated with running a large household by assigning that work to female slaves. Such relief allowed some women to diversify their talents, as exemplified by Eliza Lucas Pinckney. In addition to acquiring the upper-class accomplishments of decorative needlework, music, and French, Pinckney was versed in contemporary philosophy. She taught herself what she called "the rudiments of the law," before engaging in agricultural experiments. Still, with the ownership of slaves came responsibility for their supervision. A plantation mistress usually had far less time for leisure and intellectual interests than the privileged women in the burgeoning cities. There, a pool of female domestic labor provided wealthier women a significantly greater degree of freedom from domestic work. This was especially the case for younger, unmarried women. Some girls attended "dame schools," where an unmarried or widowed woman taught reading and writing. Later in the century, cities saw the growth of small private schools, many run by women trying to escape economic destitution. Such enterprises taught music, dancing, painting, and needlework, as well as academic subjects—accomplishments which enhanced a young woman's attractiveness on the marriage market for which she was destined.

So it is not surprising that we find most evidence of intellectual life among upper-class, urban women in the eighteenth century, especially women in the households of well-educated men. Ben Franklin's famous "Junto" club and his subscription library in Philadelphia are emblems of a growing appetite for education among men, but his daughter, Sarah Franklin Bache, also insisted on an education. In similar fashion, Jane Colden, educated and encouraged by her father, Dr. Cadwallader Colden, became a first-rate botanist—although she may well have given up her vocation when she married in 1759.

Advice books addressed to eighteenth-century female readers aimed to educate them primarily to serve men. Nonetheless, the published debates in England over the purposes of women's education, a daughter's choice in selecting a husband, and female subordination in marriage were echoed transatlantically. One of the most popular vehicles for the dissemination of these issues was the novel. The eighteenth century saw the rise of the first popular, middle-class literate culture among women, expressed in the writing and reading of novels. Their subjects were, above all, those human relationships which were necessarily of the most importance to women.

Many novels were "sentimental," celebrating the qualities of intuitive and instantaneous sympathy between like-minded people with the same "tastefulness" in aesthetic values. Sentimentalism identified human feeling with natural phenomena and celebrated compassion for the poor and exploited. Novelists believed that women could convert men from a hard, immoral approach to life and one contemptuous of women, to a softer, more selfless and Christian view, more respectful of women and more focused on the private delights of family life. The material context of these fictional themes was the changing domestic reality of home. For many it became more comfortable and entertaining over the century. It was the site for the gradual accumulation of domestic items. Chinaware that was easier to wash, manufactured knives and forks, and imported cloth signified a softening of manners and some easing of domestic labor. Among other domestic pleasures was the novel itself.

The popularization of the sentimental novel coincided with a growing religious fervor during the middle decades of the eighteenth century. During the 1730s, Jonathan Edwards, the first preacher identified with what became called the "Great Awakening," convinced thousands of inhabitants in the Connecticut Valley that they were in dire need of spiritual rebirth. In 1740 and 1741, he gathered flocks across New England, paving the way for crusades by fellow evangelicals George Whitefield, Gilbert Tennant, and Samuel Davies, among others, in the middle-Atlantic and southern colonies. Evangelism emphasized the power and value of instantaneous sympathy. It extolled expressive emotionalism—above all, of tears. Colonial congregations had become predominantly female in composition from the turn of the previous century. In the eighteenth-century's own view, religion was being "feminized." Now, in camp meetings, converts of both sexes gave free range to emotional outbursts; they fell down and wept before a God who was represented as a correspondingly more emotional and eventually more sympathetic figure. In this context, several female religious leaders emerged, including Sarah Hagger Osborn of Rhode Island, who made her home a center of religious revivalism in the 1760s.

Newly evangelized males, many from lower-class backgrounds, were (along with women and slaves) up against a formal patriarchy in established state churches. In Virginia, for example Baptists and Methodists challenged the traditional hierarchy of head and heart, of rote liturgy, of expensive church architecture, of a vestimentary code whereby rich clothing signified rank, and, indeed, whole layers of deference. Everywhere in the colonies, fervent converts split churches into opponents and supporters of the Awakening, "Old Light" and "New Light." Their challenges helped lay the groundwork for the American Revolution (1776–1783).

Literacy and religious evangelicalism encouraged individual self-assertion. From mid-century on some young people were more assertive in the private sphere, choosing their spouses for themselves and even restricting or planning pregnancies. Such relative freedoms were intensified by the experience of the American Revolution, the rhetoric for which sometimes drew upon the imagery of conflict between parents and children. The colonists depicted themselves as grown-up offspring, while the English government was portrayed as a decrepit and corrupt old parent. A number of women also extended the political notion of "tyranny" to the relationship of husbands to wives, most famously in the case of Abigail Adams telling her husband, "Remember, all men would be Tyrants if they could," as she implored him to "remember the ladies" during the making of the Constitution.

The Revolution was begun by a kind of economic warfare: the colonists' boycotts of British consumer goods, notably of tea and cloth, required women's cooperation. The majority of women were "patriotic," and enlisted in the rebel cause. Many organized themselves as "Daughters of Liberty," but some women sided with the "Loyalists" or "Tories," as they were derided by the revolutionaries. While men were off fighting, women ran farms, plantations, and businesses, gaining knowledge and self-confidence. As a consequence of such experience and because of the heightened interest in "liberty," the debate over women's education was decisively renewed in the 1780s and '90s. These decades also witnessed considerable debate over the future of American slavery.

The massive importation of Africans as slaves began late in the seventeenth century. This dramatic rise in the number of slaves in the colonies had several long-term consequences. It led to the codification into law of repressive practices which branded black people permanently with slavery. Slave status was automatically inherited by offspring through their mothers, thereby facilitating the economic and sexual purposes of white owners (children of white masters and female slaves were themselves slaves). African-Americans were forced to experience the terrible ambiguity of bearing and rearing children whom slave masters saw as livestock. A second distinctive feature of the lives of African-American women was being forced to labor in the fields along with men, when white women were by and large drawn away from such work. Women slaves worked both in commercialized agricultural gang labor and in households as skilled and drudge labor. Menial household work was the purpose for which Phillis Wheatley was bought.

Despite these circumstances, African-American family life was very significantly stabilized. This was partly one effect of the increased importation of Africans that resulted in a more balanced sex ratio by the 1740s. African-Americans established themselves with family characteristics and customs distinct from those of whites (for example, slaves observed a taboo against marriage between cousins). Even though family members were constantly subject to sexual exploitation and sale, the family was one important base for the creation and transmission of an African-American culture. The second base was religion. The Great Awakening converted slaves to evangelical Protestantism by the thousands. But the enslaved population, conscious of its origins in Africa and wishing to resist slavery, adapted European-American Protestantism and the King James version of the English Bible to its own needs. For example, because the story symbolized their own condition and hopes, African-Americans celebrated the survival, flight and triumph of the Israelites who had been enslaved by Egyptians. African influences permeated the Christian ceremonies of slaves. African-Americans celebrated their religious faith with their own familiar rituals and musical celebrations, in short their own religious culture.

Thus, the social history of African-Americans in the eighteenth century prepared them to meet the decisive changes through which slavery would pass in consequence of the Revolution. The disruptions of the war resulted in a numerically significant free black population in the cities, the staging ground for black abolitionism. Secondly, the Revolution and its rhetoric about freedom and independence added fuel to the religious impulses of a dawning anti-slavery movement. One by one, northern states ended slavery after the Revolution. However, several factors contributed to a counter-trend. The Revolution effectively removed all British roadblocks to restrict colonial expansion. This, along with the invention of the cotton gin in 1793 encouraged the spreading of slave culture into the fertile new lands. Slavery was therefore still more securely entrenched in the South, although cotton production for domestic manufacture and, above all, for exports, was vital to the growth of the nation's economy as a whole. While the Constitution of 1789 compromised U.S. sectional differences over slavery—writing slavery permanently into the new national laws but providing for the abolition of the slave trade in 1808—the stage was set for a potentially explosive division. Nonetheless, the outcome of the Revolution for whites was the achievement of a national identity. It also supplied a rhetorical legacy of revolution on which all Americans eventually could draw. From now on, women claimed a share in the nation's republicanism.

Eliza Lucas Pinckney

(1722–1793)

Constance B. Schulz

Born in the West Indies in 1722 and educated in England, Eliza Lucas was a privileged child of an upper-class planter who moved his family to Wappoo plantation in South Carolina when Eliza was fifteen. When her father was called back to Antigua in 1739, he left Eliza in charge of his three plantations. The young woman proved a talented manager, and successfully introduced the cultivation of indigo (a dye for textiles), a crop she imported from the West Indies in 1740. This agricultural breakthrough was a boon to the young colony, and became the source of fortune for many South Carolinian planters. In 1744 she married widower Charles Pinckney, a wealthy planter, and settled into the traditional role held by many wealthy southern women: plantation mistress and mother.

In 1753 Charles Pinckney's political career transplanted the family to England, where Eliza reestablished her childhood friendships and allegiances, but in 1758 business interests forced the Pinckneys to return to Carolina. The couple left their two sons in English schools and sailed home with their daughter. Within six weeks of their arrival home, Charles Pinckney died, and Eliza Lucas Pinckney was once again left to manage a large plantation on her own.

With the outbreak of the revolutionary war, Pinckney devoted herself to furthering the careers of her two sons, who had returned from England to participate in the colonial rebellion. In doing so, Pinckney rejected her former allegiances to an England she was fond of, and went so far as to lend a large sum of money to the new state of South Carolina in 1779. At war's end, her son Thomas served as governor of South Carolina, and her eldest son Charles Cotesworth became a delegate to the Constitutional Convention. At her death in 1793, George Washington requested to serve as one of her pallbearers, in tribute to her devotion to the revolutionary cause.

Some say that the South Carolina low country is at its most beautiful in the fall. The great watery meadows of sea grass wave in the constant sea breezes behind the sheltering barriers of the outer islands, their tall seeded fronds bending with the tides. Thickets of live oak trees heavy with acorns dress in drifting curtains of Spanish moss, "where a variety of Airry Chorristers pour forth their melody." The newly fallen fresh-scented needles of the longleaf pine carpet the woods of the higher lands, while the great cedar groves reflect what Eliza Lucas Pinckney once called "an Autumnal gloom and solemnity."[1]

Approaching this bountiful land from the water, one can still see today much of what first greeted fifteen-year-old Eliza Lucas in the fall of 1738. Born in the West Indies in 1722, sent by her father to school in England, Eliza had traveled with her parents and younger sister Polly from their home in Antigua to take up residence on inherited Carolina lands that George Lucas hoped would be more healthful for his invalid wife. Eliza's grandfather, John Lucas, owned three properties in Carolina: a plantation of 1,500 acres on the Combahee River, another of 2,950 acres on the Waccamaw, and a third of 600 acres on a bluff overlooking Wappoo Creek, where it flowed into the Stono River not far from the canal constructed to connect the Stono to the Ashley River. This last plantation was the Lucas family's destination.

One can picture the excitement of an observant young woman who loved trees and gardens and the outdoor world around her as the West Indian ship skirted the sandy barriers of Folly, Morris, and James Islands south of the Cooper River, sailing majestically past the southern tip of Sullivan's Island (where slave ships were required to land their cargo for a ten-day period of quarantine lest they bring dreaded diseases like smallpox and malaria into port) and into sight of the bustling harbor city of Charles Town (renamed Charleston after the Revolution), secure on its peninsula between the Ashley and Cooper Rivers. By 1739, eight wharves, or "bridges," jutted into the Cooper, each having on its wooden deck warehouses, shops, and equipment for loading, unloading, and provisioning the numerous vessels docked at its sides. A 1739 painting by Bishop Roberts shows us a handsome urban waterfront, the foreground crowded with vessels of every size and shape: ships, schooners, brigantines, sloops in full sail, with canoes and plantation flats clustered around them.

Although we can see today the sights Eliza Lucas saw—the bustling waterfront of Charles Town, the quiet beauty of the salt marshes, the elegant homes along the city waterfront, and the comfortable plantation houses up the tidal rivers—we have no pictorial image of Eliza herself. That is odd, for by the mid-eighteenth century, Charles Town was becoming a center for the arts and boasted the works of resident and itinerant portrait artists. There are two handsome portraits of her husband, innumerable likenesses of her sons, a miniature of her daughter, and views of her imposing Charles Town home both in a waterfront prospect painted by Thomas Leitch in 1774 and in an 1861 photograph. Hampton plantation house, the home of her daughter Harriott Horry, where Eliza Lucas Pinckney lived after the American Revolution, still stands near Santee. Visitors there might imagine Eliza in 1791 with her daughter and granddaughters welcoming to breakfast George Washington, looking much like he does in the Gilbert Stuart painting, but we no more know what Eliza looked like in her graceful old age than how she appeared in girlhood. "No likeness of Mrs. Pinckney is ever known to have been taken," reported her great-granddaughter and earliest biographer.[2]

To create a portrait of this important woman of the colonial south, then, we must describe the world she lived in, the things she did, and the words she wrote, rather than her appearance at any given point in her life. And perhaps that is fitting, for hers was a life of action rather than of appearance, of the business of plantation agriculture and parental concerns rather than of fashion (although as a girl she gratefully accepted from her father "a piece of rich Yellow Lutstring consisting of 19 yards for my self," and as a young wife she knew enough about luxury apparel to send to London for weaving into damask the silk spun from the production of her own plantation, and to fashion from it three elegant dresses that demonstrated the possibilities of silk manufacture in Carolina).

Charles Town had in 1738 embarked on a remarkable period of growth that would span Eliza Lucas's entire lifetime. The capital of the English colony of South Carolina, it was also the most important English port on the Atlantic Coast south of Philadelphia. Founded in 1670, and moved to its more defensible present-day location in 1680, the city had grown from a struggling village in 1685 to a prosperous town of 6,800 in 1742, fourth largest in all the English mainland colonies. More than half of its inhabitants were black slaves; as early as 1708 blacks had equaled and begun to outnumber whites in the colony as a whole. The slave population had grown with the prosperity derived from the colony's rice cultivation. First introduced late in the seventeenth century, by 1730, rice replaced the earlier trade in deerskins from the Indian tribes of the interior as South Carolina's principal trade commodity. In 1750, the greatest concentration of slaves was in the low-lying coastal areas where rice cultivation based on a system of swamps and diked tidal creeks flourished.

Charles Town's crucial location at the center of an inland water system that stretched from the Cape Fear River in North Carolina to the St. John's River in Florida also made it a center for international commerce. Rice, and later indigo and cotton, fitted in particularly well with the English mercantile system, for all were commodities that England needed, but could not produce. Thus their cultivation and exportation were encouraged by favorable trade legislation, and even by the granting of bounties.

The wealth derived from staple crops and trade, and the commercial ties with England and the Continent, made "Charleston in the Age of the Pinckneys"[3] a remarkably cosmopolitan city. Freedom of religion, despite the firm establishment of the Church of England, attracted Methodists, Huguenots, Baptists, Presbyterians, Jews, Catholics, and Quakers; the presence of Germans, French, Scots-Irish, Dutch, and the majority population of African slaves gave a remarkable diversity to the city. Charles Town merchants intermarried with low-country planters, who maintained elegant homes in town to which they could retreat during the hot summers when "country fevers" (malaria and smallpox) plagued low-country plantations. During the "season," Charles Town offered its residents the best of society: music, theater, balls, a weekly newspaper, and (after 1748) a library society. Most of these amenities were in place, ready to welcome the Lucas family upon their arrival. As the eldest daughter of a wealthy planter family, Eliza Lucas was welcomed on visits to Charles Town where she danced at balls, flirted with naval officers, and attended elegant private dinners, feasting on "oyster soop," turtle, venison, boiled rice, and "dutch blumange" (recipes for all of which she later included in her own cookbook). "Charles Town, the principal one in this province, is a polite, agreeable place," she wrote to Mrs. Boddicutt, the woman with whom she had lived while a student in England.

> The people live very Gentile and very much in the English taste. . . . There is two worthy Ladies in Charles Town, Mrs. Pinckney and Mrs. Cleland, who are partial enough to me to be always pleased to have me with them, and insist upon my making their houses my home when in town and press me to relax a little much oftener than 'tis in my honor to accept of their obliging intreaties. But I some times am with one or the other for 3 weeks or a month at a time, and then enjoy all the pleasures Charles Town affords."[4]

Not all of what Charles Town offered was pleasant, of course, and just as Eliza and her family arrived in Carolina the city was plunged into a series of natural and human disasters. The Yamasee War in 1715 and its aftermath had virtually ended the early threat of Indian unrest to the city (though not to the frontier regions of the colony), but fears of slave revolt replaced those of Creek and Cherokee attack. No comment by Eliza survives on the Stono Rebellion in 1739, although it began less than five miles from her Wappoo plantation. On September 9, about twenty slaves broke into a store near the old Stono Bridge, killing two whites, and, under the leadership of a slave named Jemmy armed themselves. As they marched toward Savannah, their number grew to nearly eighty, many of them recently arrived Angolans. Overtaken by militia, the slaves resisted; by the end of the encounter twenty whites and forty blacks had lost their lives. In response, the Commons House of Assembly enacted a harsh Slave Code in 1740 that included heavy import duties levied on slaves brought from abroad, a financial burden which Eliza did write to her father about in the fall of 1741.

Slave rebellions were not the only source of fear and death in the city. A smallpox epidemic in Charles Town in 1738, and a yellow fever epidemic in 1739 decimated the population. No exact figures are given for the yellow fever attack; but by September 1738 the smallpox had infected 1,675 residents, of whom 295 died. Since 1720, the discovery of "variolation," or inoculation with live vaccine, had lessened the impact of smallpox on those who were willingly exposed to the virus while healthy and strong enough to survive a mild case of the disease and gain immunity. Charles Town became the first city in which this preventative measure was tried on a large scale; 437 citizens were inoculated, of whom only 16 died. Eliza Lucas had "taken the smallpox" while a student in England, and later used her own country house as a temporary hospital for the inoculation of her grandchildren and friends.

Scarcely had Charles Town recovered from the yellow fever attack, so severe that Governor Bull sent the Assembly home rather than risk their lives, when a great fire fanned by winds burned for six hours through the wooden buildings of the heart of the commercial district in November 1740, destroying more than 300 structures. Eliza recorded no comment on this disaster, even though her new friend Charles Pinckney, whose wife had so openly welcomed Eliza to their Charles Town home, lost considerable sums of money from it as one of the founders (with his brother William) of the "Friendly Society of Mutual Insuring of Houses against Fires."

The young woman who came to Wappoo in the fall of 1738 seems to have had both a traditional and an unusual education for a young

Englishwoman. Her lively letters show wit and style; she paid pretty compliments to friends of both sexes, quoted readily from scripture, wrote of playing the flute and taking harpsichord lessons with "Mr. Pachelbel,"[5] and of practicing French and needlework—all accomplishments expected of a young Englishwoman of wealth. But when the outbreak of the War of Jenkins Ear between England and Spain in the fall of 1739 recalled her father to Antigua to fulfill his duties as a lieutenant colonel in the British army and later as royal councilor and lieutenant governor of the colony, he had enough confidence in her practical skills to entrust the care of his estates to Eliza rather than to an outside agent or his ailing wife. "I have the business of 3 plantations to transact, which requires more business and fatigue of other sorts than you can imagine," wrote Eliza on May 2, 1740, to her "good friend Mrs. Boddicott."[6] To her father she wrote knowledgeably of local political and military news, reported complicated transactions of money and goods, and discussed the efficient use of the family's eighty-six Carolina slaves (whom she referred to as "servants").

In her stewardship of her father's property, young Eliza Lucas took on the roles of both plantation master and plantation mistress. In addition to managing the business of the plantation, she was busy concocting medicines for servants and friends, overseeing the activities of house servants, practicing her music, visiting neighboring women, and doing needlework projects—even though she admitted that "my father has an aversion to my employing my time in that poreing work."[7] One of her self-appointed duties was that of schoolteacher to her younger sister Polly, insisting that she should not be sent away to school: "I will undertake to teach her French," she assured her father.[8] But Eliza did more. Despite the 1740 Slave Code prohibition against teaching slaves to read, Eliza included two black girls in her schoolroom; she wrote to her young friend Mary Bartlett, the visiting English niece of Mrs. Pinckney, "if I have my papas's approbation (my Mamas I have got) I intend [them] for school mistres's for the rest of the Negroe children."[9] It is instructive, both in the energy that it reveals, and in the mixture of plantation and household tasks it catalogs, to read the remainder of her lighthearted account to Mary Bartlett of her weekly activities:

> In general then I rise at five o'Clock in the morning, read till Seven, then take a walk in the garden or field, see that the Servants are at their respective business, then to breakfast. The first hour after breakfast is spent at my musick, the next is constantly employed in recolecting something I have learned least for want of practise it should be quite lost, such as French and short hand. After that I devote the rest of the time till I dress for dinner (dinner was served in

mid-afternoon] to our little Polly and two black girls who I teach to read. . . . [T]he first hour after dinner as the first after breakfast is at musick, the rest of the afternoon in Needle work till candle light, and from that time to bed time read or write. . . . I have particular matters for particular days, which is an interruption to mine. Mondays my musick Master is here. Tuesdays my friend Mrs. Chardon (about 3 miles distant) and I are constantly engaged to each other, she at our house one Tuesday—I at hers the next and this is one of the happiest days I spend at Wappoe. Thursday the whole day except what the necessary affairs of the family take up, is spent in writing, either on the business of the plantations, or letters to my friends. Every other Fryday, if no company, we go vizeting so that I go abroad once a week and no oftener. . . . O! I had like to forgot the last thing I have done a great while. I have planted a large figg orchard with design to dry and export them. I have reckoned my expence and the prophets [profits] to arise from these figgs, but was I to tell you how great an Estate I am to make this way, and how 'tis to be laid out you would think me far gone in romance.[10]

The "figg" experiment was no whim, for the Lucas estates and slaves were heavily mortgaged, and Eliza was determined to discover a profitable crop to increase their income. With her father's blessing and seed shipments, and under the tutelage of male neighbors and friends, including Charles Pinckney, she had tried a number of alternatives before the planting recounted in this spring 1742 letter to Bartlett. The first summer after her father's departure, she wrote to describe "the pains I had taken to bring the Indigo, Ginger, Cotton and Lucerne and Casadall[11] to perfection, and had greater hopes from the Indigo (if I could have the seed earlier next year from the West India's) than any of the rest of the things I had tryd."[12] Thus began the experiment that brought her lasting fame—the introduction of successful cultivation of South Carolina's second highly profitable staple crop, *Indigofera*, much prized as a source of the deep blue dye that was an important element in the rapidly expanding European and English textile industry.

Eliza Lucas was by no means the first to grow indigo in the English colonies. Indigo cultivation had been tried by the English in Virginia in the early seventeenth century, and further attempts at cultivating it were carried on in the first years of the Carolina settlement. A perennial native variety, *Indigofera caroliniana* grew wild in the province, but the manufacture of the prized dye either from the indigenous plant or from two imported strains that had to be planted each year from seed, "Guatamala" or "Bahama" (*I. suffruticosa*) and "French" or "Hispaniola" (*I. tinctoria*) eluded Americans until the mid-eighteenth century. It was a combination of her own persistence and luck of ideal timing that helped Eliza Lucas succeed in this enterprise where others had failed. The outbreak of the war with Spain created serious difficulties for planters shipping the bulky rice crop that was Carolina's principal export. A number of European ports were cut off to them altogether, and insurance costs for shipping elsewhere sharply reduced profits. Moreover, the war cut England's textile industry off from its usual supply of French West Indian indigo. Indigo proved to be a natural complement to rice: like rice, it was highly labor-intensive in its cultivation and harvest, but required that labor in the summer growing months, when rice needed less attention, thus promising efficient use of the plantation's slave labor force. Although indigo fared best in the rich loamy soils farther inland, where it was later extensively cultivated at the end of the eighteenth century, indigo was first grown at the coast on the high ground between the flooded rice fields.

The imported West Indian seeds Eliza received from her father grew reasonably well, although she wrote to him of her 1740 crop in June 1741 that "the frost took it before it [the seed] was dry." The difficulty with indigo was in the tedious manufacturing of small cubes of blue dye from the plant. Nothing in the plant itself is actually blue, although the leaves have a bluish tinge. The dye was produced by harvesting leaves and stems before the stem became woody, then immediately steeping them in water to ferment during the hot summer months. Next, at just the right moment, the foul-smelling fermented brew was drained into a second vat, where it was beaten with paddles to assist in the oxidation process that transformed the yellow liquid into the blue sediment. Lime was added at this stage to expedite oxidation. The dyemaker's skill determined when the beating should cease, allowing the dye particles to settle to the bottom of the vat while slaves drained off the excess liquid into a third vat. The sediment left in the second vat was shoveled into sacks and allowed to drip until nearly dry, then spread out to dry more completely until it could be cut into small cubes, which were packed into barrels for shipment. The sheds sheltering the three vats and pumps necessary for draining the liquid were built right in the indigo fields. Although West Indian planters could make up to eight cuttings, in South Carolina, the plants were cut twice (in a mild year, three times) before the plants were allowed to go to seed. Productivity in South Carolina varied with plant species and soil condition (indigo rapidly exhausted the soil in which it grew). An acre of the crop produced an average of thirty-five to forty pounds of commercial indigo; its cultivation and manufacture required the labor of one slave for every two to four acres planted.

Mastering this complicated procedure was the task that Eliza Lucas set herself, with the help and advice of her French Huguenot neighbor, Andrew Deveaux. Her father sent an experienced dyemaker, Nicholas Cromwell, to her in 1741, but she shortly afterward dismissed him on the discovery that he deliberately "threw in so large a quantity of Lime water as to spoil the color" to prevent Carolina indigo manufacture from succeeding and competing with that of his native Montserrat. Nicholas's brother Patrick proved a more loyal expert, and the Wappoo plantation produced "17 pounds of very good Indigo" in 1744, in addition to producing sufficient seed to distribute to her neighbors—a move that proved foresighted as well as generous, for within a year the French had forbidden the exportation of seed.[13] After five years of experimentation, the Lucas investment in indigo realized a return of £225 on dye sent to the London market in 1745 (although by then the plantation had passed out of the Lucas family control). Once the plant was domesticated in South Carolina, indigo cultivation spread rapidly: the colony exported 138,300 pounds of dye in 1747. A bounty of a shilling per pound of indigo voted by the English Parliament in 1748 (reduced to four pence in 1770) encouraged production even further, until South Carolina exports peaked at over one million pounds in 1775. Great fortunes were made in Carolina from indigo, particularly in the Winyah Bay area of Georgetown.

Although she must have rejoiced in the success of her efforts, by the time indigo was well established at Wappoo and the rest of the Carolina coast, Eliza's attentions and energies had shifted to quite a different role. Even before her 1744 crop had been harvested, on May 27, 1744, she married Charles Pinckney, Esq., a recent widower, former speaker of the Commons House of Assembly, member of the governor's Royal Council, extensive landholder—and at forty-four, nearly twice her age. His first wife, also named Elizabeth, was the kindly Mrs. Pinckney who had befriended Eliza on her arrival in Charles Town. She had borne no children, and perhaps regarded the engaging young Eliza almost as a daughter. For six years, the friendship between Eliza Lucas and Charles Pinckney had grown and deepened. In her father's absence, Charles Pinckney advised her on matters of business and law. She wrote to him in great amusement of her adventure in drawing up a will for a poor neighbor. He had loaned her books—Virgil, Plutarch, Malebranche—and taught her shorthand. Her letters to him, and messages to him in the letters she wrote to his wife's niece, suggest that he teased her for the seriousness he himself encouraged in her, and shared with her private jokes. The Pinckneys took Eliza with them when they traveled, and visited her at Wappoo.

Perhaps her father foresaw even in the first days of the Pinckneys' interest in her some danger for his daughter, for in the first letter she received from him after his 1739 departure for Antigua he apparently probed delicately whether she cherished some secret inclination, warned her against "an indiscreet passion for any one"—and offered her the choice of two gentlemen as potential husbands. Her response, carefully couched in the most obedient daughterly terms, had affectionately but firmly rejected both suitors:

> [A]s I know tis my happiness you consult [I] must beg the favour of you to pay my thanks to the old Gentleman for his Generosity and favourable sentiments of me and let him know my thoughts on the affair in such civil terms as you know much better than any I can dictate; and beg leave to say to you that the riches of Peru and Chili if he had them put together could not purchase a sufficient Esteem for him to make him my husband.

For the rest, she assured him:

> I hope heaven will always direct me that I may never disappoint you; and what indeed could induce me to make a secret of my Inclination to my best friend, as I am well aware you would not disaprove it to make me a Sacrifice to Wealth, and I am as certain I would indulge no passion that had not your approbation.

Whether in the spring of 1740 she had already an "Inclination" toward Charles Pinckney is impossible to say.[14]

When Elizabeth Pinckney died in January 1744 after a prolonged illness, the easy camaraderie so evident in the earlier correspondence between Charles Pinckney and Eliza Lucas had hastened to something more by the threat of her immediate removal to Antigua; financial difficulties and a lull in the hostilities led George Lucas to send for his family. The Pinckney "Family Legend" reports that the first Mrs. Pinckney had been "so averse to her [Eliza's] return to Antigua, that she had more than once declared that rather than have her lost to Carolina, she would herself 'be willing to step down and let her take her place.' "[15] Charles Pinckney also had strong affection for Eliza. Her mother and sister delayed their departure, first for George Lucas's permission for the marriage, and then for the wedding. Eliza's dowry was to have been the Wappoo plantation, and the first indigo crop a gift to the groom. Instead, the plantation was claimed by George Lucas's creditors. Ironically, Charles Pinckney distributed the indigo seed to neighbors, publicized widely the news of its successful cultivation, and pressed for the adoption of bounties both in the South Carolina Commons House of Assembly and in London.

The marriage was a happy one, and Eliza Lucas Pinckney threw herself with all her energies into her new life. She had often been a guest at the Pinckney country home, Belmont, on the Cooper River on the Charles Town neck. On her husband's plantation she continued her agricultural experimentation, growing flax and hemp and reviving earlier Carolina attempts at silk cultivation, while he was kept busy in Charles Town supervising the building of a handsome brick townhouse on East Bay Street, overlooking the harbor just up from Market Street. It was there, on February 14, 1746 (February 25, 1746 by today's calendar) that Eliza gave birth to their first son, Charles Cotesworth Pinckney. Motherhood delighted her: "I can discover all his Papa's virtues already dawning in him," she wrote to her friend Mary Bartlett when Charles Cotesworth was still only three months old; to Mary Bartlett's mother (the first Elizabeth Pinckney's sister) she wrote at the same time requesting her "to buy him the new toy . . . to teach him according to Mr. Lock's method (w[hi]ch I have carefully studied) to play himself into learning. Mr. Pinckney himself has been contriving a sett of toys to teach him his letters by the time he can speak, you perceive we begin by times for he is not yet four months old." The plan must have worked, for the proud mother later reported to her sister Polly, then in school in England, that twenty-two-month old Charles Cotesworth "can tell all his letters in any book without hesitation."[16]

The period of Eliza's second pregnancy was not so happy; her father had been taken prisoner by the French while en route to England, and died in captivity in January 1747. Charles Pinckney attempted to keep this news from her, for she loved her father dearly, and had often written of her agitation and concern for him during his military campaigns. Her discovery of the hidden letter so shocked her that she went into premature labor, and the infant, baptized George Lucas in honor of his grandfather, died on June 24, five days after his birth. Within a few months Eliza was pregnant again, and gave birth to a daughter, Harriott, on August 7, 1748. The young family was completed with the birth of Thomas on October 23, 1750. Eliza Lucas Pinckney's childbearing ended abruptly at the age of 28. Remarkably in an age of high infant and child mortality, all three of these children survived to adulthood, and outlived their mother.

Eliza now turned all the energy and dedication that had previously been directed into her plantation and gardening to her children. She did not nurse them as infants; we know this because in a visit with the English royal family several years later, the Princess Augusta asked Mrs. Pinckney directly if she had suckled her children, and Eliza responded "I had attempted it but my constitution would not bear it."[17] Their education, both temporal and spiritual, became one of her chief concerns. In an undated series of resolutions found in the family papers, the young mother resolved:

> to be a good Mother to my children, to pray for them, to set them good examples, to give them good advice, to be careful both of their souls and bodys, to watch over their tender minds, to carefully root out the first appearing and budings of vice, and to instill piety, Virtue and true religion into them; to spair no paines or trouble to do them good; to correct their Errors whatever uneasiness it may give myself; and never omit to encourage every Virtue I may see dawning in them.[18]

The happiness of these years must have been somewhat marred by concerns over Charles Pinckney's political fortunes. Joy at his appointment as chief justice for the colony in 1752 ended abruptly with the news that the king had disallowed the appointment in order to create a "place" for an English officeseeker. Charles accepted instead a position as "special" agent for South Carolina to the merchants in London, and in the spring of 1753 the entire family sailed for England. Eliza was pleased to return to the land where she had both fond memories of her girlhood and many friends. After hiring a house in Richmond (where Eliza supervised the inoculation of her children against smallpox) and traveling outside of London, the Pinckneys finally purchased a house near Ripley, in Surrey, enrolled the boys in school, and prepared to remain residents of England until their children's education was completed.

This plan came to an abrupt end on July 12, 1758. In the spring of that year, Charles Pinckney decided to return to Charles Town to look after his plantation and business interests. Leaving the boys at school, Eliza and Harriott returned with him on what was to have been only a brief visit. But weakened by a long voyage, unused after five years in England to the heat of the Carolina climate, Charles was infected with malaria, and within six weeks was dead. Eliza was almost inconsolable at his loss; too distraught to return to her own home in Charles Town for months, she filled her days and her letterbook writing long letters to their acquaintances in England and Antigua of her loss: "The greatest of human Evils has befallen me," she wrote again and again to friends, "My dear, dear Mr. Pinckney is no more! In him I have lost one of the best and worthiest of men, the tenderest and most affectionate of all husbands, and best of Fathers to my children. . . . I was for more than 14 years the happiest of mortals."[19]

Most difficult for her was breaking such overwhelming news to her young sons in England:

> We have, my dear children, mett with the greatest of human Evils, but we must drink of the cup it has pleased God to Give us, a bitter Cup indeed! but aloted us by Infinite Wisdom, and let us ever remember, terrible and grievous as the stroke is, we have still reason to thank the hand from whence it comes for all his mercys to him, through life and through death, and to us for having given us this inestimable blessing, for having spared him so long to us, for all the Graces and Virtues he endowed him with, for the goodness of his understanding, and the soundness of his judgments.[20]

With her letter, she sent a barrel of rice, with instructions to the headmaster of their school about how to prepare it to their liking. Charles Cotesworth was then twelve, Thomas only eight. Although she missed them, she wished them to continue the education their father had planned for them. She would not see Charles Cotesworth again until May 1769, or Thomas until September 1771. She carried out her earlier resolves to them through a series of letters exhorting them to cultivate industry, piety, good manners, and above all—to write to her at every opportunity.

At the age of thirty-six, Eliza Lucas Pinckney, now a widow, returned to many of the same responsibilities of running a plantation and household that she had shouldered as a young woman. Named by her husband as executor in his will (to be assisted by a competent overseer), she returned to Belmont nearly a year after his death to discover that the estates had suffered greatly from neglect. She observed, "It has gone back to woods again."[21] The plantation needed to be returned to sound management, first to support the expenses of her boys in school, and then to be passed on to them as an inheritance. Once again, her letterbook is full of references to bills of exchange, of crops gathered, of purchases requested. But there is a profound difference from the letters of her youth: the personal letters are of affectionate instructions to her sons, or sent in thanks to those who befriended them in England, not to her beloved Mr. Pinckney; the letters of business are to Mr. Morley, her man of business, not to an indulgent father. As she returned to her tasks, she wrote to Morley:

> I find it requires great care, attention and activity to attend properly to a Carolina Estate, tho' but a moderate one, to do ones duty and make it turn to account, that I find I have as much business as I can go through of one sort or another. Perhaps 'tis better for me, and I believe it is. Had there not been a necessity for it, I might have sunk to the grave by this time in that Lethargy of stupidity which had seized me. . . . A variety of imployment gives my thoughts a relief from melloncholy subjects, tho' 'tis but a temporary one, and gives

> me air and exercise, which I believe I should not have had resolution enough to take if I had not been roused to it by motives of duty and parental affection."[22]

The creativity and inventiveness of her earlier agricultural experiments were not repeated, though her love for her gardening continued. A long illness in 1760–61 sapped her energy. Although we do not know the name of the gentleman, she apparently received an offer of marriage, which she immediately rejected, "as entering into a second marriage never once entered my head"—although gossip about it reached her friends in England. For the next thirty years she remained faithful to the memory of her "dear, dear Mr. Pinckney."[23]

Her life might thus have passed uneventfully to its end in enjoyment of her children and grandchildren. Her daughter Harriott, who learned the skills of plantation management by observing and perhaps by assisting her mother, made an excellent marriage in 1768 to Daniel Horry, a widower with two children. She was then nineteen; a year later Eliza celebrated the birth of her first grandson, whose infant ways delighted her nearly as much as had those of her own first son. Charles Cotesworth Pinckney had by then returned to Carolina a mature and grave young man, trained in the law, ready to take the responsible role in the province urged upon him in his father's will; within months he had been elected to the Assembly, and in 1773 married Sarah Middleton, the daughter of planter and royal councilor Henry Middleton. Thomas too returned to Carolina: briefly in the fall of 1771, and permanently in 1774 after having been admitted to the bar in London. Eliza's pride in her children and their accomplishments seemed assured.

But public events now enlisted Eliza for yet another role. If she considered herself "on the whole a very loyal subject," with her "share of joy in ye agreable account of my Sovereign and his Consort,"[24] her sons had grown to adulthood in England loyal to their native America. The Stamp Act aroused in them such patriotic feelings that Charles Cotesworth Pinckney was painted in 1765 by the artist Zoffany proclaiming against the act, and Thomas Pinckney in his enthusiasm became known to his friends as "The Little Rebel."[25] Within a few years of their return to Charles Town, both young men were heavily involved in the revolutionary movement, receiving captain's commissions in the First Regiment of South Carolina troops. For Eliza the rush of events must have been disheartening; her childhood and many of her friends had been English, and some of the happy years of her marriage had been spent with the very English ruling class her sons and neighbors were now denouncing. But the loyalties of her sons became hers, and Eliza Lucas Pinckney earned through their military and political efforts and honors yet another honor of her own: "mother of patriots."

The revolutionary war years were not easy for South Carolina. By 1779, the British offensive campaign had shifted to the South. Responding to desperate appeals by the Assembly for funds to prepare the province's defenses, Eliza loaned £ 4,000 currency to the State of South Carolina at 10 percent interest in September 1779. In May 1780, Sir Henry Clinton's forces defeated General Benjamin Lincoln and captured Charles Town for the British. Charles Cotesworth Pinckney was captured in the fall of Charles Town; Thomas Pinckney escaped to rejoin Betsey Motte, whom he had married on July 22, 1779, but in August he too was captured, with his leg shattered by a bullet in the battle at Camden, South Carolina. The British confiscated the Pinckney properties in September 1780. To her English friend Mrs. Revance, Eliza wrote of her losses: "I have been rob[b]ed and deserted by my Slaves; my property pulled to pieces, burnt and destroyed; my money of no value, my Children sick and prisoners. . . . Such is the deplorable state of our Country from two armies being in it for nearly two years."[26]

Nor did the end of the war end Eliza's losses. Charles Cotesworth's wife Sarah died of tuberculosis in the spring of 1784, and within a short time, Harriott's husband Daniel Horry was dead of a "bilious fever." Charles Cotesworth brought his three young daughters to Harriott's Hampton plantation, which now became Eliza's permanent home. Like her mother, Harriott proved adept at running a plantation and directing the education of the assembled children.

In the early days of the new republic, Eliza's sons continued to distinguish themselves. Charles Cotesworth remarried, and shortly after, left for Philadelphia as a delegate to the Constitutional Convention of 1787; Thomas was elected governor of South Carolina in the same year, and presided over the state during the ratification debates. When newly elected President George Washington toured South Carolina in 1791 as part of his efforts to unite the country, he honored the two brothers by breakfasting at Hampton plantation with their mother and sister. The ladies greeted him "arrayed in sashes and bandeaux painted with the general's portrait and mottoes of welcome." He admired Harriott's rice fields, and knowing of Eliza's earlier agricultural contributions, spoke favorably of the indigo fields he had visited. Eliza's life had indeed come full circle.

Not long after, Eliza developed breast cancer. Told of Eliza's condition, Thomas, on a diplomatic mission in London, sent leeches home to be used as a cure, and in April 1793 Charles Cotesworth persuaded her to go to Philadelphia for additional treatment by Dr. William Shippen, a pioneer in the study of anatomy and midwifery, and James Tate. These doctors could do little for her, although while Eliza was there, Martha Washington and the wives of the cabinet officers honored her with visits. At her death, on May 26, George Washington at his own request served as one of her pallbearers. She was buried in Philadelphia's St. Peter's churchyard, far from her beloved Carolina.

Eliza Lucas Pinckney is not an unsung heroine; she has been honored by her country in many of its histories, beginning with David Ramsay's *History of South Carolina from Its First Settlement in 1670 to the Year 1808* (Charleston, 1809). Her contributions as described in these histories sometimes seem to suggest a paradox: Was she the independent young lady who ran a plantation by herself at the age of eighteen and singlehandedly introduced the crop that insured Carolina's wealth? Or was she the archetype of the faithful "republican mother," who sacrificed herself in raising two sons to become such splendid patriots? She is remarkable precisely because she did not herself see any contradiction in those two roles. Her own belief that it was natural and right for a southern woman to be prepared to run all aspects of a plantation can be seen in her willingness to give her daughter much the same training and opportunity that she herself had, and to the same good effect. Perhaps she was fortunate: the men who were closest to her respected her abilities, and encouraged her to use them. Her father provided her with a good education, and then trusted her with the management of his considerable properties. Her husband encouraged her serious reading, and paid her the ultimate compliment of leaving his estates in her competent care. Her sons brought their wives and children to her home when they themselves could not protect them. Eliza Lucas Pinckney was not an early feminist; she was not in open rebellion against the lot of women of her day. But she was a woman who took the considerable advantages with which she was gifted, and used her intelligence, her interest in the world around her, and her sense of duty to herself, her family, and her community to make important contributions, the benefits of which survive two centuries after her death.

Notes

[1]Elise Pinckney, *The Letterbook of Eliza Lucas Pinckney, 1739–1762* (Chapel Hill: University of North Carolina Press, 1972), pp. 61, 36.

[2]Harriet Horry Ravenel, *Eliza Pinckney* (Spartanburg, SC: The Reprint Company, 1967; reprint of Scribner's 1896 edition), p. 199.

[3]See *Charleston in the Age of the Pinckneys*, an excellent book by George C. Rogers, Jr., describing the evolution of Charleston from 1730 to 1830 (Columbia: University of South Carolina Press, 1969).

[4]Pinckney, *Letterbook*, pp. 7–8.

[5]This son of the composer Augustus Pachelbel served as organist in St. Philip's Church, and became one of the great early musicians of Charles Town; ibid., p. 25.

[6]Ibid., pp. 6–7.

[7]Ibid., p. 35.

[8]March 1740, ibid., p. 5.

[9]Ibid., p. 34.

[10]April 1742, ibid., pp. 34–35.

[11]Probably *cassava*, a root product that was a staple food of the tropics.

[12]July 1740, ibid., p. 8.

[13]Ravenel, *Eliza Pinckney*, pp. 104–05.

[14]Pinckney, *Letterbook*, p. 6.

[15]Ravenel, *Eliza Pinckney*, p. 68.

[16]Ibid., pp. 109–114.

[17]The conversation continued on the differences between "putting children" out to nurse in England, and the Carolina practice of using "Nurses in our houses." "Princess Augusta was surprized at the suckling blacks; the Princess stroakd Harriott's cheek, said it made no alteration in the complexion." Ravenel, pp. 151–152.

[18]Ibid., p. 117.

[19]To Mrs. Pocklington, 1759, Pinckney, *Letterbook*, p. 114.

[20]Ibid., pp. 94–95.

[21]Ravenel, *Eliza Pinckney*, p. 189.

[22]March 14th, 1760, Pinckney, *Letterbook*, p. 144.

[23]Ibid., p. 176.

[24]Ravenel, *Eliza Pinckney*, p. 217.

[25]Ibid., p. 247.

[26]Pinckney, *Letterbook*, p. xxiii.

Nancy Ward

(1738?–1822)

Theda Perdue

Although little is known of Nancy Ward's life in general and especially her early years, we suspect that she was born in a Cherokee settlement along the Little Tennessee River near Monroe County, Tennessee. She was the daughter of a Cherokee mother of the Wolf clan and a Delaware father. After her traditional Cherokee upbringing, Nanye'hi (her Cherokee name) married a Cherokee named Kingfisher, with whom she bore two children, Fivekiller and Catherine. Taking her husband's place after he fell in battle against the Creeks, the young Cherokee woman earned the title and privileges of "War Woman." She later married Bryant Ward, a white trader, took the name of Nancy Ward, and gave birth to a daughter, Elizabeth. Her husband eventually returned to South Carolina. She is reputed to have saved a white settlement in 1776 by warning of an impending Cherokee attack. She also used her prerogative as War Woman to save a white woman from being burned at the stake. Ward went on to assume many leadership roles, addressing treaty conferences between the United States and the Cherokee nation in 1781 and in 1785 and advising Cherokee leaders during negotiations in 1817. Political and economic changes in the Cherokee nation diminished the role of War Woman, but Nancy Ward adapted with the changes. She died an innkeeper in 1822 on the Ocoee River in a part of the Cherokee nation that today is eastern Tennessee.

In 1785, representatives of the Cherokee Indians met United States commissioners at Hopewell, South Carolina, to negotiate a peace treaty and land cession. Among the speakers at the conference was Nancy Ward, the War Woman of Chota, who addressed the assembly:

> ... I look on you and the red people as my children. Your having determined on peace is most pleasing to me, for I have seen much trouble during the late war. I am old [about 47], but I hope yet to bear children, who will grow up and people our nation, as we are now to be under the protection of Congress and shall have no more disturbance. The talk I have given is from the young warriors I have raised in my town, as well as myself. They rejoice that we have peace, and we hope the chain of friendship will never more be broken.[1]

By addressing the treaty conference, Nancy Ward violated the Anglo-American convention that barred women from speaking publicly on political matters. As a Cherokee, however, her action embodied another tradition, one in which women enjoyed political status, acknowledged economic power, and a high degree of personal autonomy.

So alien was this tradition to Anglo-Americans, on whose written accounts we must rely for most information about preliterate native peoples, that few references to the political rights and roles of native American women exist in the traditional historical record. One reason for the paucity of information is that most Anglo-Americans who had contact with native peoples and left records were men. Because native men and women led very separate lives, these observers saw little of how Cherokee women lived, and what role they played in Cherokee society. These observers would have been excluded from women's councils, rituals, and ceremonies, as well as more mundane activities. Furthermore, Anglo-Americans had little interest in native women, except occasionally to buy corn from them or to take them as wives. The observers' ethnocentrism, the inability to interpret events from any perspective other than one's own culture, also poses problems for researchers using Anglo-American sources about native women. For example, many observers commented that Indian men were lazy and that women were virtual slaves who performed all the manual labor.[2] Europeans arrived at this conclusion because native women farmed while men hunted and fished, activities the Europeans considered to be sport instead of important contributions to subsistence. Yet we do have a few references, particularly to Nancy Ward, and through them, we can infer not only how Cherokee women lived in the late eighteenth and early nineteenth centuries but also how many of them obtained the privileges and extraordinary status of "War Women."

The Cherokees were a powerful people who lived in the southern Appalachians. Linguistically, they were related to the Iroquoian peoples of the north, but culturally, the Cherokees were part of the southeastern cultural complex. They shared many practices and beliefs with the Creeks, Choctaws, and Chickasaws; in particular, their economy was based on agriculture, a condition that was reflected in their ceremonial life. The Cherokees first came into contact with Europeans in the late seventeenth century. For much of the eighteenth century the Cherokees had access to the British along the Atlantic seaboard, the French in Canada and Louisiana, and the Spanish in Florida. Throughout this period they retained a degree of independence from any one group of Europeans, although their sentiments early in the century generally rested with the British. The eighteenth century was a period of recurring wars with European powers and with other native peoples. Cherokee warriors often participated in European military expeditions, and their chiefs traveled to colonial capitals and across the Atlantic on diplomatic missions. In the Seven Years' (French and Indian) War, most Cherokees supported the French—whose colonists were more interested in furs than land. The American Revolution found the Cherokee Nation divided, although the majority of Cherokees, motivated by the king's proclamation limiting expansion of colonial settlement, sympathized with the British.

Shifting diplomatic alliances were not the only changes the Cherokees experienced. By the early eighteenth century European traders had established trading posts among them. In response to the European demand for deerskins and their own desire for European goods, hunting came to dominate Cherokee economy. Warfare with European and native enemies disrupted village and family life, while defeat in the Seven Years' War and the American Revolution led to land cessions. Disease and famine took a heavy toll, calling into question the efficacy of certain religious rituals designed to ward off such hardships. By the time the Cherokees met with the representatives of the United States at Hopewell, their culture had begun a major transformation, best characterized as an attempt to preserve what they deemed truly valuable in their own way of life while adopting aspects of colonial culture in order to survive in the changing environment.

Nancy Ward's life spans these cultural changes. She was born about 1738 in Chota, the preeminent town of the Overhill Cherokees who lived in what is today eastern Tennessee.[3] It is thought that her Cherokee name was Nanye'hi, and that she was a member of the Wolf clan and a niece of Attakullakulla, or "The Little Carpenter." The Cherokees had no ruling clan, but many prominent eighteenth-century leaders came from the Wolf clan. One of the most distinguished was Attakullakulla, who visited England with a group of Cherokee chiefs in 1730 and returned to become a leading spokesperson for peace and friendship with Anglo-Americans. Attakullakulla was the brother of Nanye'hi's mother; in the Cherokees' matrilineal kinship system, this meant that he was the primary male figure in Nanye'hi's life.[4] According to the principle of matrilineal descent, a children's only kin were those on their mother's side—their mother's mother, sisters, other children (even those by different fathers), sisters' children, and brothers. Attakullakulla, as Nanye'hi's maternal uncle, assumed the role that Europeans ascribed to fathers.

In the early 1750s Nanye'hi married Kingfisher, a member of the Deer clan. The Wolf and Deer clans were two of seven clans to which Cherokees belonged. Members of a clan believed that they shared a common ancestor, even if they did not know precisely who the ancestor was or how they were related. Clans were essential to Cherokee life because one's clan offered protection. The Cherokees had no formal laws or courts: any wrongdoing was punished by the victim's clan. For example, in the case of murder, the clan of the slain Cherokee would kill the murderer or one of the murderer's relatives. Within this system of justice, a person without a clan was often a target of violence because there would be no threat of retribution to act as a deterrent.

In the eighteenth century, Cherokee towns reached from upcountry South Carolina into the mountain valleys of western North Carolina, eastern Tennessee, and northern Georgia. Most towns had households of each of the seven clans. Because of kinship customs, a Cherokee could expect a warm welcome in any household of his or her clan even if he or she had never met these people before. Because all members of a given clan were blood relatives, marriages were always between members of different clans. Cherokees usually married outside their father's clan. They considered a marriage to a member of the grandfather's clan to be the most desirable arrangement. Within these rules, Cherokees married whomever they chose; no one dictated spouses. Marriage did not alter clan affiliation; thus, Nanye'hi remained a Wolf and Kingfisher remained a Deer. Their two children, Fivekiller and Catherine belonged, because of the matrilineal system, to the Wolf clan.

Kingfisher and the children probably lived in Nanye'hi's household because the Cherokees were matrilocal as well as matrilineal. That is, a man lived with his wife and children in a house which belonged to her, or perhaps more accurately, to her family. Unmarried men lived with their mothers or their sisters, but they usually slept in the communal council house because they really had no house of their own. As the principal farmers, women also "owned" storage buildings, fields, crops, and agricultural produce—corn, beans, squash, sunflowers, and pumpkins. While the Cherokees technically held land in common and anyone could use unoccupied land, improved fields belonged to specific matrilineal households. In one sense then, Cherokees vested title to improved land in women.[5] Farming was essential to the Cherokees' way of life, and they highly regarded the economic role of women, which they commemorated in their most important religious festival, the Green Corn Ceremony. The central events of the Green Corn Ceremony were the rekindling of the sacred fire by the medicine man and the presentation of the new corn crop by the women.[6]

In 1755 Nanye'hi joined her husband on a military expedition against the Creeks, the Cherokees' ancient enemies to the south. Women sometimes accompanied war parties to draw water, gather firewood, and cook. In the Cherokees' rather rigid division of labor by gender, these activities were distinctly female. For a man to do them, particularly a warrior, jeopardized his manhood. That Nanye'hi went on an expedition at an early age may indicate a high status for her family or her husband, and it certainly suggests that she was regarded as knowledgeable of restrictions and scrupulous in observing them. For example, relations between men and women were strictly dictated. Men on the warpath, for example, did not engage in sexual intercourse because semen, coming from inside the body, possessed spiritual power. Other taboos prevented menstruating women from accompanying warriors; in fact, they sequestered themselves in special huts in the village during their menses. Even contact with meat from which blood had been spilled was considered potentially dangerous to a military expedition. Therefore, warriors (and, interestingly, menstruating women) ate only a little corn and never meat.[7] War parties that failed to follow these rules courted disaster.

At Taliwa in north Georgia, the Cherokees engaged the Creeks. As Nanye'hi lay behind a log, a Creek bullet found its mark, and Kingfisher dropped dead beside her. She seized his gun and took his place in the fray until the Creeks were driven off. By doing so, she became part of a tradition of women warriors among the Cherokees. Usually these women, like Nanye'hi, became warriors by circumstance, but according to John Howard Payne, who collected information about Cherokee customs in the 1830s, "women have in certain cases dressed in men's clothes and went [*sic*] to battle." In the American Revolution, one of the casualities of the Cherokee defeat by General Griffith Rutherford at Waya Gap in North Carolina was a woman "painted and stripped like a warrior and armed with bows and arrows." In the early nineteenth century, the Moravian missionary John Gambold had an opportunity to converse with one of these women warriors whose age he estimated to be 100: "The aged woman, named Chicouhla, claimed that she had gone to war against hostile Indians and suffered several severe wounds." The Cherokee Joseph Vann's wives verified this and said that she was "very highly respected and loved by browns and whites alike." One of anthropologist James Mooney's informants in the 1880s had known an old woman whose Cherokee name meant "Sharp Warrior." The Wahnenauhi manuscript that Mooney obtained from a Cherokee medicine man contained another account of a Cherokee woman who rallied the warriors when her husband died defending their village against enemy attack. This woman, Cuhtahlutah (Gatun'lati or "Wild Hemp"), saw her husband fall, grabbed his tomahawk, shouted "Kill! Kill!" and led the Cherokees to victory.[8]

Women who distinguished themselves in battle, like Nanye'hi, went on to occupy an exalted place in Cherokee political and ceremonial life. The eighteenth-century naturalist William Bartram translated the Cherokee title, which is no longer certain, as "War Woman," and he noted that a stream in north Georgia bore the name War Woman's Creek. A trader told him that the name of the stream came "from a decisive battle which the Cherokees had gained over their enemies on the banks of this creek, through the battle and strategem of an Indian woman who was present. She was afterwards raised to the dignity and honor of a Queen or Chief of the nation, as a reward for her superior virtues and abilities, and presided in the State during her life."[9] Anglo-Americans also translated the title as "Beloved Woman" and used the two interchangeably. Cherokees may, however, have reserved the term meaning "Beloved Woman" for postmenopausal women who had acquired unusual spiritual power by surviving both menstruation and warfare.

The Cherokees probably honored women who excelled in battle because these women challenged the usual categorization of the sexes. As we have seen, the Cherokee culture assigned specific roles to each sex. Neither sex was considered superior and neither set of roles was more important than the other. Both were essential to the Cherokee way of life, to their social well-being, and to cosmic order. For there to be harmony in the world, however, each sex had to fulfill its own role. Women were not supposed to engage directly in warfare; only men who had carefully prepared themselves for war through fasting and purification could expect to meet with success. How then could the Cherokees explain a woman who behaved like a man without bringing disaster, a woman who killed enemy warriors and led Cherokee men to victory? Such a woman was obviously an anomaly, and like certain other anomalies, had exceptional power.[10] She was no longer merely a woman nor, however, was she a warrior. She was a "War Woman," and the Cherokees permitted her to manifest her apparent spiritual power in a number of temporal ways.

Only War Women could perform martial dances along with the men. Mooney heard about a woman who had killed her husband's slayer in battle during the American Revolution: "For this deed she was treated with so much consideration that she was permitted to join the warriors in the war dance, carrying her gun and tomahawk." War Women also participated in the Eagle Dance, which commemorated previous victories. Athletic young men performed the actual dance, but in one part, old warriors and War Women related their exploits. These women sat apart from other women and children on ceremonial occasions and partook of food and drink not normally given to women.[11]

Lieutenant Henry Timberlake, who was stationed at Fort Loudoun near Nanye'hi's town of Chota in the 1750s, pointed out that while War Woman was the only title awarded to women, "it abundantly recompenses them, by the power they acquire by it, which is so great, that they can, by the wave of a swan's wing, deliver a wretch condemned by the council, and already tied to the stake." Nanye'hi, who by then was known as Nancy Ward because of her marriage to Bryant Ward, a white trader, exercised this power in 1776 when she rescued a white woman named Mrs. William Bean. Mrs. Bean lived in one of the illegal settlements along the Holston River in what is today northeastern Tennessee. The Cherokees captured her, took her to the town of Toquo, and bound her to the stake. They were about to ignite the tinder at her feet when Nancy Ward appeared and ordered her release. Nancy Ward took Mrs. Bean to her house and, according to an oral tradition, learned from her how to make butter. Ultimately Mrs. Bean was restored to her family. In 1781 Nancy Ward once again rescued prisoners—but this time she acted clandestinely. The Cherokees at Scitigi (Sitico) had imprisoned five white traders and intended to execute two of them before embarking on a raid against white frontier settlements. Instead of publicly demanding the freedom of the traders, Nancy Ward and several other women helped them escape and reach safety.[12]

Mercy was not the only factor that motivated War Women to spare condemned captives. Often they wanted to adopt the captives into their clans to replace members who had been killed in the incessant warfare of the eighteenth century. An adopted captive enjoyed all the rights and privileges of a person born into a clan, and the important decision of whether to accept a captive rested with the women of the clan. David Menzies, an English physician captured during the

Cherokee War of 1760, recounted the experience of being offered to and rejected by a clan:

> In proceeding to the town I understood that these Cherokees had in this expedition lost one of their head warriors, in a skirmish with some of our rangers; and that I was destined to be presented to that chief's mother and family in his room: At which I was overjoyed, as knowing that I thereby stood a chance of not only being secured from death and exempted from torture, but even of good usage and carresses. I perceived that I had overrated much my matter of consolation. . . . The mother fixt first her haggard bloodshot eyes upon me, then riveting them to the ground, gargled out my rejection and destruction.[13]

The warriors clearly favored Menzies' adoption; the chief's mother, however, prevailed. Menzies was subjected to torture but survived, and eventually secured his release.

War Women had an additional incentive to spare prisoners. European captives could be ransomed for a handsome sum, while native captives could be sold to white traders for use as slaves on plantations in the South and in the West Indies. Indeed, the Indian slave trade was a major enterprise throughout much of the eighteenth century involving, according to historian J. Leitch Wright, "tens of thousands" of war captives. As a result of the market for captives, competition for them developed in some towns. John Gerar William De Brahm, a British surveyor, observed the tactics used by some War Women:

> All prisoners must be delivered alive (without any Punishment) as her Slave, if she requires it, which is a Privilege no man can enjoy, not even their Emperor, Kings, or Warriors; there are but a few towns in which [there] is a War Woman; and if she can come near enough to the Prisoner as to put her hand upon him, and say, this is my Slave, the Warriors (tho' with the greatest Reluctancy) must deliver him up to Her, which to prevent they in a great hurry drive a Hatchet in the Prisoner's Head, before the War Woman can reach him; therefore the War Women use that Strategem to disguise themselves as Traders, and come in Company with them, as if out of Curiosity to see the Spectacle of the cruel War-dance.

Occasionally, an Indian woman did appear in Charleston with a prisoner to ransom or sell.[14]

Generally, however, War Women did not exercise their prerogative, but acquiesced to the people's desire for vengeance and condemned captives to torture. While there is no evidence that Nancy Ward actively engaged in torture, she did not rescue a boy who was about to be tortured along with Mrs. Bean, the white woman she had saved in 1776. Instead, she left the boy tied to the stake, where he was burned to death. Mooney recorded an oral tradition in which two women with snakes tattooed on their lips directed the other women to burn the feet of a captive Seneca war chief until they blistered. Then they put corn kernels under the burned skin, chased him with clubs, and ultimately beat him to death. A similar fate at the hands of the women awaited most captives. Usually they thrashed the prisoners, tied them to stakes, "larded their Skins with bits of Lightwood," and seared them with flaming torches. If victims collapsed from the pain, their tormentors threw water on them and gave them time to revive. Sometimes torture lasted for over twenty hours. Adair observed: "Not a soul, of whatever age or sex, manifests the least pity during the prisoner's tortures: the women sing with religious joy, all the while they are torturing the devoted victim, and peals of laughter resound through the crowded theatre—especially if he fears to die." Many victims, particularly Indian warriors, manifested no fear but bragged about martial deeds. When the women concluded that vengeance had been sufficiently exacted or the victim died, they took the scalp and dismembered the body.[15]

As appalling as such behavior is to us today, we must consider torture in its cultural context. Cherokees went to war for vengeance alone. They believed that relatives killed by an enemy could not go to the Darkening Land where spirits resided until their "crying blood" had been avenged. Indeed, kinfolk had a moral and sacred obligation to avenge "crying blood." Under normal conditions, only men had the opportunity to fulfill this obligation—on the warpath. Yet women grieved for their fallen kin as well and longed to participate in the freeing of their spirits. Consequently, the torture of captives brought back by warriors for this purpose was the only way in which women could satisfy their sacred duty.[16]

Occasionally women, including Nancy Ward, provided intelligence to people whom many Cherokee warriors considered enemies. Such activities, which we would consider treasonous, were possible because the Cherokees lacked a coercive centralized government and accorded individuals considerable autonomy. The British garrison at Fort Loudoun often relied on female spies, many of whom were married to soldiers. The commander, Raymond Demere, wrote Governor Henry Lyttleton of South Carolina that "intelligence from women amongst the Indians are always best." In 1756 the native woman employed to procure food for the garrison told Demere that the "Old War Woman" at Chota had confided in her about an Indian and French conspiracy against the English. After Cherokee warriors began a siege of the English fort, women continued to visit the garrison with both information and provisions. According to Timberlake, the women laughed at the threats of the war chief who tried to stop them, and told him "that if he killed them, their relations would make his death atone for theirs."[17]

During the American Revolution, Nancy Ward supported the cause of the new United States, a minority position among the Cherokees who resented colonial encroachments on their land. In 1776 she warned the trader Isaac Thomas of a Cherokee plan to attack settlements along the Holston River; he conveyed the message to the settlers in time for them to prepare for the attack. Four years later, she once again warned white settlers of imminent Cherokee attack. For this reason, perhaps, United States officials received Nancy Ward as a Cherokee emissary and diplomat. In 1781, when Arthur Campbell led the Virginia militia into Cherokee territory, burning several towns and capturing Chota, Nancy Ward called on him. Campbell reported to Governor Thomas Jefferson of her visit:

> In the time the famous Indian woman Nancy Ward came to camp, she gave us various intelligence, and made an overture in behalf of some of the chiefs for peace; to which I then evaded giving an explicit answer, as I wished first to visit the vindictive part of the nation, mostly settled at Hiwassee and Chistowee: and to distress the whole as much as possible, by destroying their habitations and provisions.

Despite Nancy Ward's visit, Campbell burned Chota and moved on to destroy other Cherokee villages. Yet she herself apparently was accorded kinder treatment. Jefferson replied to Campbell's report: "Nancy Ward seems rather to have taken refuge with you. In this case her inclination ought to be followed as to what is done with her."[18]

Nancy Ward was not alone in the role of female ambassador. In 1725 the Creeks trusted a Cherokee woman who had been taken prisoner to represent them in treaty negotiations. She had been present during Creek council deliberations that centered on the mistaken belief that the Cherokees, rather than the "French Indians," had killed a number of Creek people and on the rumor that a joint attack of the English and Cherokees was imminent. Fully apprised of the Creek view, "Slave Woman" accompanied a Creek man, perhaps as a translator, to a Cherokee town to petition for peace. The man fled in fear, but he left Slave Woman behind and "particularly gave her in charge to talk about a peace."[19] Cherokee women also represented their own people in negotiations with foreign powers. In the 1750s a Cherokee woman traveled to Fort Toulouse, in what is today Alabama, with French John, a captive whom the English suspected of espionage, to discuss the building of a French fort among the Overhill towns. And the wife of the Mankiller of Tellico, who had conspired with the French against the English, joined her husband in complaining to Demere at Fort Loudon about English treatment of the Indians.[20]

In negotiations, women may have met with women's councils among other native peoples. Women were almost always present at treaty conferences, but white male commissioners who were keeping records paid little attention to them except to complain about the additional expense of feeding them. Consequently, only indirect references to women's roles in diplomacy exist. In 1768, for example, Cherokee warriors negotiating with Iroquoian peoples at Johnson Hall in New York presented a wampum belt, used to symbolize and record agreements, that had been sent by Cherokee women to Iroquois women. Oconostota, a Cherokee war chief who was urging peace, relayed the women's message: "We know that they will hear us for it is they who undergo the pains of Childbirth and produce Men. Surely therefore they must feel Mothers pains for those killed in War, and be desirous to prevent it."[21]

Nancy Ward used similar language when she appeared in July 1781 at a treaty conference with United States commissioners held on the Long Island of the Holston in northeastern Tennessee. Because most Cherokees had allied with Britain in the American Revolution, the United States sought to exercise sovereignty over the trans-Appalachian region by forcing land cessions from its native inhabitants. In speaking at the conference, Nancy Ward reminded the commissioners that not all Cherokees had supported the British. She spoke eloquently for peace:

> You know that women are always looked upon as nothing; but we are your mothers; you are our sons. Our cry is all for peace; let it continue. This peace must last forever. Let your women's sons be ours; our sons be yours. Let your women hear our words.[22]

Her words had the desired effect, and the Cherokees ceded no land to the United States at the Long Island of the Holston. Her speech at Hopewell in 1785 echoed the same theme, but this time the Cherokees paid dearly for their alliance with the British during the American Revolution by losing thousands of acres of their national domain.

When Nancy Ward told the commissioners at the Long Island of the Holston that "women are always looked upon as nothing" she demonstrated considerable knowledge of Anglo-American attitudes toward her sex. She may have acquired this knowledge while she was married to the white trader Bryant Ward. Ward had taken up residence at Chota in the late 1750s, married the War Woman, and fathered one daughter, Elizabeth. At this time Nanye'hi anglicized her name, and subsequently was known as Nancy Ward. By the end of the decade, however, Bryant Ward had returned to his other family in South Carolina. Elizabeth remained with her mother, and Bryant Ward's desertion probably did not radically alter their lives.

Nancy Ward was only one of many Cherokee women who married white traders in the eighteenth century.[23] Traders sought native wives not only for companionship but also for the entree matrimony gave them into Cherokee society. Their wives acted as translators as well as tutors of the difficult Cherokee language. Furthermore, in dealing with a society dominated by kin networks, a wife belonging to a Cherokee clan was highly desirable. Marriage did not extend clan membership to a trader, of course, but his children inherited that affiliation from their mother. Since kinship—not race—determined who was a Cherokee, these children were truly a part of Cherokee society.

Unlike Bryant Ward, many traders remained with their native families throughout their lives and bequeathed to their children prosperous businesses, familiarity with Anglo-American ways, and fluency in English. By so doing, they wreaked social havoc on the Cherokees. Traditionally, Cherokees buried personal property with the deceased, but that, of course, was impractical with the entire inventory of a frontier trading post. Furthermore, children usually had acquired their fathers' materialistic values and had no intention of seeing their inheritance interred. By adopting their fathers' names and values, these children also began a reordering of kinship patterns, and paternity came to take precedence. In 1808 a council of Cherokee headmen (there is no evidence of women participating) formalized these trends by establishing a national police force to safeguard a person's possessions during life and "to give protection to children as heirs to their father's property, and to the widow's share."[24]

The importance of matrilineal clans waned. In 1810 a council representing the seven clans, but once again apparently including no women, abolished the practice of blood vengeance and surrendered to the Cherokee national government the responsibility to punish crime.[25] A class system began to replace the clans in ordering social relations as wealthy Anglo-Cherokees tended to marry whites or each other. Nancy Ward's daughter Elizabeth, for example, married Joseph Martin, the North Carolina agent to the Cherokees; their daughter Nannie married Michael Hildebrand, the son of a white miller and a Cherokee woman.[26]

The superior wealth of Anglo-Cherokees inspired envy in some of the native Cherokees, who began to imitate the descendants of traders by anglicizing their names, turning to trade and commercial agriculture, and bequeathing to their children the earthly rewards they managed to reap. Other Cherokees, less willing to alter traditional lifestyles, nevertheless treated highly acculturated Cherokees and Anglo-Cherokees with respect and deference. The ability of these people to interact easily with Anglo-Americans increasingly led the Cherokees to delegate political power to them. By 1830, a disproportionate number of Cherokee leaders descended from traders and/or possessed great wealth.[27]

Just as individual Cherokees began to adopt the values and lifestyles of Anglo-Americans, so the Cherokee Nation began to pattern itself after the United States. The near anarchy that had permitted Nancy Ward to warn colonists of Cherokee attacks in the American Revolution made the Nation vulnerable to the white people's insatiable hunger for land. Without a formal political structure and coercive power, a few individuals susceptible to threats and bribes could, and did, sell off much of the Cherokee homeland. Yet the political system that emerged had little room in it for Nancy Ward, the War Woman of Chota, and other women. The people who began to centralize political power in the Cherokee Nation were the male warriors, who could enforce national decisions, and the descendants of traders, who could deal more effectively with whites. With the defeat and pacification of a small band of Cherokees who had continued to wage war with the United States into the 1790s, the warriors' role declined—as did that of War Women—and the genetic and ideological heirs of traders gained ascendancy. For these people, women did not belong in the political arena. In 1818, Charles Hicks, who would become principal chief in the 1820s, described the most prominent men in the Nation as "those who have kept their women and children at home and in comfortable circumstances."[28]

These changes had the approval and encouragement of missionaries and United States agents who hoped to "civilize" the Cherokees. "Civilization" meant adopting the cultural norms of Anglo-American society—literacy in English, commercial agriculture, Christianity, republican government, and a patriarchal family structure. The "civilized" Cherokee John Ridge described what this meant for women: "They sew, they weave, they spin, they cook our meals and act well the duties assigned them by Nature as mothers." They clearly, in Ridge's view, did not go to war, speak in council, or negotiate treaties. Nancy Ward had become an anachronism.[29]

The final official pronouncement by the War Woman of Chota regarded a proposed sale of Cherokee land. In 1817, the United States sought a large land cession that would result in the removal of the Cherokees to land west of the Mississippi River.[30] Because of her advanced age, Nancy Ward was unable to attend the treaty conference, but she and twelve other women sent a message to the Cherokee National Council:

> The Cherokee ladys now being present at the meeting of the Chiefs and warriors in council have thought it their duties as mothers to address their beloved Chiefs and warriors now assembled.
>
> Our beloved children and head men of the Cherokee nation we address you warriors in council[. W]e have raised all of you on the land which we now have, which God gave us to inhabit and raise provisions[. W]e know that our country has once been extensive but by repeated sales has become circumscribed to a small tract and never have thought it our duty to interfere in the disposition of it till now, if a father or mother was to sell all their lands which they had to depend on[,] which their children had to raise their living on[,] which would be bad indeed and to be removed to another country[. W]e do not wish to go to an unknown country which we have understood some of our children wish to go over the Mississippi but this act of our children would be like destroying your mothers. Your mother and sisters ask and beg of you not to part with any more of our lands. . . .
>
> Nancy Ward to her children Warriors to take pity and listen to the talks of your sisters, although I am very old yet cannot but pity the situation in which you will hear of their minds. I have great many grand children which I wish them to do well on our land.[31]

Nancy Ward probably did not appear the next year when Cherokee women pleaded with the Council, "our beloved children," to reject the United States' proposal for allotment of land to individuals and "to hold our country in common as hitherto."[32] She may very well, however, have advised them on the subject.

The effect of these women's petitions is difficult to ascertain. In 1817 the Cherokees ceded tracts of land in Georgia, Alabama, and Tennessee, and in 1819, they made a larger cession that included Nancy Ward's town of Chota. Nevertheless, they rejected individual allotments, retained common ownership of land, and strengthened restrictions on the sale of improvements individuals had made to the commonly held land. Furthermore, the Cherokee Nation gave notice that it would negotiate no additional cessions—a resolution so strongly supported that the United States ultimately had to turn to a small unauthorized faction in order to obtain the removal treaty from a minority group of Cherokee in 1835.

With the cession of her town, Nancy Ward moved south to the Ocoee River valley, where she operated an inn along the federal road that ran from Georgia to Nashville, Tennessee, through the Cherokee Nation. In 1822 the War Woman of Chota died, leaving behind a Nation in which the status of women was suffering a precipitous decline. Only five years after her death, the Cherokees enacted a new constitution that restricted the franchise to "free male citizens" and specified that only "a free Cherokee male" could sit in the General Council.[33]

Nancy Ward's life spanned the time in which the Cherokees abandoned a government in which women had a voice, an economy in which women's work was recognized as essential, not peripheral, and a definition of gender roles that did not subordinate one sex to the other. The society after which they patterned their new institutions relegated women to a secondary role, one which Nancy Ward probably found incomprehensible. Her life reminds us that such a subordinate position is not the natural order, that it is merely cultural, and that other cultures regard women in a different light than Western "civilization." And that is reason enough to remember the War Woman of Chota.

Notes

[1]*American State Papers,* Class 2: *Indian Affairs* (Washington, DC, 1832), 1: 41.

[2]Bernard Romans, *A Concise Natural History of East and West Florida* (New York, 1775), pp. 40–43; James Adair, *Adair's History of the American Indian,* ed. Samuel Cole Williams (Johnson City, TN, 1930), pp. 434–41.

[3]Biographies of Nancy Ward include Robert G. Adams, *Nancy Ward, Beautiful Woman of Two Worlds* (Chattanooga, TN, 1979); Pat Alderman, *Nancy Ward: Cherokee Chieftainess* (Johnson City, TN, 1978); J. P. Brown, "Nancy Ward, Little Owl's Cousin," *Flower and Feather* 13 (1957): 57–59; Annie Walker Burns, *Military and Genealogical Records of the Famous Indian Woman, Nancy Ward* (Washington, DC, 1957); Katherine Elizabeth Crane, "Nancy Ward" in *Dictionary of American Biography* (Washington, DC, 1936) 19: 433; Harold W. Felton, *Nancy Ward, Cherokee* (New York, 1975); Carolyn Thomas Foreman, *Indian Women Chiefs* (Muskogee, OK, 1954), pp. 72–86; Ben Harris McClary, "Nancy Ward: Last Beloved Woman of the Cherokees," *Tennessee Historical Quarterly* 21 (1962): 336–52, Norma Tucker, "Nancy Ward, Ghighau of the Cherokees," *Georgia Historical Quarterly* 53 (1969): 192–200. These range in quality from McClary's scholarly study to E. Sterling King's highly fictionalized *The Wild Rose of the Cherokee . . . or, Nancy Ward, The Pocahontas of the West* (Nashville, TN, 1895).

[4]The best study of the Cherokees' kinship system is John P. Reid, *A Law of Blood: Primitive Law of the Cherokee Nation* (New York, 1970).

[5]William Bartram, "Observations on the Creek and Cherokee Indians, 1789," *Transactions of the American Ethnological Society* 3 (1854): 66.

[6]Adair, *History*, pp. 105–15; Henry Timberlake, *Lieut. Henry Timberlake's Memoirs, 1756–1765*, ed. by Samuel Cole Williams (Johnson City, TN, 1927), pp. 64, 88.

[7]For a theoretical discussion of attitudes toward body fluids, see Mary Douglas, *Purity and Danger* (London, 1966).

[8]John Howard Payne Papers (Newberry Library, Chicago, Ill.), 3: 124, 4: 170; Diary of the Moravian Mission at Spring Place, 5 July 1807, trans. Carl C. Mauleshagen (typescript, Georgia Historical Commission, Department of Natural Resources, Atlanta, Ga.); James Mooney, "Myths of the Cherokee," *Nineteenth Annual Report of the American Bureau of Ethnology* (Washington, DC, 1900), p. 395.

[9]Bartram, "Observations," p. 32.

[10]Charles Hudson, *The Southeastern Indians* (Knoxville, TN, 1976), pp. 139–47.

[11]Mooney, "Myths," p. 395; Payne Papers, 6: 220; Alexander Longe, "A Small Postscript on the Ways and Manners of the Indians Called Cherokees," ed. David H. Corkran, *Southern Indian Studies* 21 (1969): 14, 16, 20, 22, 24.

[12]Timberlake, *Memoirs*, p. 94; John Haywood, *The Natural and Aboriginal History of Tennessee up to the First Settlements Therein by the White People in the Year 1768* (Jackson, TN, 1959, orig. ed. 1823), 278; William P. Palmer, ed., *Calendar of Virginia State Papers and Other Manuscripts, 1652–1781* (Richmond, 1875), 1: 446–47.

[13]David Menzies, "A True Relation of the Unheard-of Sufferings of David Menzies, Surgeon, among the Cherokees, and of His Surprising Deliverance," *Royal Magazine* (July 1761), p. 27.

[14]J. Leitch Wright, Jr., *The Only Land They Knew: The Tragic Story of the American Indians in the Old South* (New York, 1981), p. 148; John Gerar William De Brahm, *Report of the General Survey in the Southern District of North America*, ed. Louis De Vorsey (Columbia, SC, 1971), p. 109.

[15]Mooney, "Observations," pp. 360, 363; De Brahm, *General Survey*, p. 108; Adair, *History*, pp. 418–19.

[16]Adair, *History*, p. 155; Timberlake, *Memoirs*, p. 82.

[17]Timberlake, Memoirs, pp. 89–90.

[18]Samuel Cole Williams, *Tennessee during the Revolutionary War* (Rpt. Knoxville, 1974, orig. ed. 1944), pp. 36, 184; Palmer, 1: 435, Julian P. Boyd, ed., *The Papers of Thomas Jefferson* (Princeton, NJ, 1951), 4: 361.

[19]Newton D. Mereness, ed., *Travels in the American Colonies* (New York, 1916), pp. 120–21, 134–35.

[20]William L. McDowell, ed., *Documents Relating to Indian Affairs, 1754–1765* (Columbia, SC, 1970), pp. 201, 268.

[21]E. B. O'Callaghan and B. Fernow, eds., *Documents Relative to the Colonial History of the State of New York* (Albany, NY, 1849–51), 8: 43.

[22]Nathaniel Green Papers (Library of Congress, Washington, D.C.) quoted in Williams, p. 201.

[23]For the role of trade and traders in Cherokee society, see Verner W. Crane, *The Southern Frontier, 1670–1732* (Durham, NC, 1928); John P. Reid, *A Better Kind of Hatchet: Law, Trade and Diplomacy in the Cherokee Nation during the Early Years of European Contact* (University Park, PA, 1976); J. Leitch Wright, *The Only Land They Knew: The Tragic Story of American Indians in the Old South* (New York, 1981).

[24]*Laws of the Cherokee Nation: Adopted by the Council at Various Times, Printed for the Benefit of the Nation* (Tahlequah, Cherokee Nation, 1852), p. 3.

[25]Ibid., p. 4.

[26]Penelope Johnson Allen, "Leaves from the Family Tree," *Chattanooga Times* 12 August 1934.

[27]For the changes experienced by the Cherokees, see Henry T. Malone, *Cherokees of the Old South: A People in Transition* (Athens, GA, 1956); Willam G. McLoughlin, *Cherokee Renascence in the New Republic* (Princeton, NJ, 1986); McLoughlin, *Cherokees and Missionaries, 1789–1839* (New Haven, CT, 1984); Theda Perdue, *Slavery and the Evolution of Cherokee Society, 1540–1866* (Knoxville, TN, 1979).

[28]Ard Hoyt, Moody Hall, William Chamberlain, and D.S. Butrick to Samuel Worcester, 25 July 1818 (Papers of the American Board of Commissioners for Foreign Missions, Houghton Library, Harvard University, Cambridge, MA). For the effect of cultural changes on Cherokee women, see Mary E. Young, "Women, Civilization, and the Indian Question" in Mabel E. Deutrich and Virginia C. Purdy, eds., *Clio Was a Woman: Studies in the History of American Women* (Washington, DC, 1980); Perdue, "Southern Indians and the Cult of True Womanhood" in Walter J. Fraser, et al., eds., *The Web of Southern Social Relations: Women, Family, & Education* (Athens, GA, 1985).

[29]John Ridge to Albert Gallatin, 27 February 1826, Payne Papers.

[30]The removal policy is dealt with in Francis Paul Prucha, *American Indian Policy in the Formative Years: The Indian Trade and Intercourse Acts, 1790–1834* (Cambridge, MA, 1962); Ronald N. Satz, *American Indian Policy in the Jacksonian Era* (Lincoln, NE, 1975).

[31]Presidential Papers Microfilm: Andrew Jackson (Washington, DC, 1961), Series 1, Reel 22.

[32]Brainerd Journal, 30 June 1818 (American Board Papers).

[33]*Laws*, pp. 120–21.

PHILLIS WHEATLEY, NEGRO SERVANT to MR. JOHN WHEATLEY, of BOSTON.

Phillis Wheatley

(1753?–1784)

Charles Scruggs

Born in West Africa, the person to be named Phillis Wheatley was enslaved as a child and sold in Boston in 1761. Her purchaser, John Wheatley, intended her to be a domestic servant to help his wife Susanna. However, because Phillis showed great intellectual precocity, Susanna Wheatley educated her and fostered her talent. With the rest of the family, she became a member of Boston's Old South Church. Having demonstrated her poetic abilities, Phillis Wheatley was sent by her owners to England in 1773 to further her literary career. There, the most prominent evangelical woman in England, the Countess of Huntingdon (who was a friend of Susanna and Phillis through George Whitefield, one of the first and most popular evangelical Methodist preachers) sponsored the publication of Wheatley's poems. In 1773 she was manumitted in accordance with Susanna Wheatley's dying wish and then lived in the Wheatley household until John Wheatley died in 1778. Shortly thereafter, Wheatley married a free black man. She died a poor domestic servant in 1784.

Phillis Wheatley was born about 1753, in Senegal, West Africa. She was enslaved perhaps shortly before 1761. In that year a slave ship brought the Fulani child (whose African name is now lost) to Boston. White merchants in northern seaports had dramatically increased their importation of slaves during the first half of the eighteenth century. By the 1720s about one-fifth of Boston's families held slaves, and by 1742 about 8.5 percent of the population were slaves. African men frequently worked in the shipyards and on board ships while African women worked as domestic slaves.[1]

The young Fulani was purchased directly off the ship in Boston harbor by a prosperous merchant tailor named John Wheatley, to be the personal servant of his wife, Susanna. She was renamed and taught English in the Wheatley household and, as Phillis Wheatley, she would come to look on Susanna Wheatley as her adoptive and spiritual parent. After Susanna Wheatley's death when Phillis was twenty-one, Phillis said she felt "like one forsaken by her parent in a desolate wilderness," for Susanna Wheatley had given her both "uncommon tenderness for thirteen years" and above all "unwearied diligence to instruct me in the principles of the true Religion."[2]

As a child, Phillis soon demonstrated her extraordinary intellectual abilities. According to John Wheatley, "by only what she was taught in the family," which included the Wheatley's twin children, Mary and Nathaniel, "in Sixteen Months Time from her Arrival, [Phillis] attained the English Language, to such a Degree, as to read any [of] the most difficult Parts of the Sacred Writings, to the greatest Astonishment of all who heard her."[3] Like other well-educated persons of that era, she mastered Latin as well as English. By age thirteen she was writing poetry, publishing her first poem nine years after arriving from Africa.[4] English was now her private and public language, the cultural vehicle for her genius.

Phillis Wheatley became known in Boston as,

> a very Extraordinary female Slave, who had made some verses on our mutually dear deceased Friend [George Whitefield]: I visited her mistress, and found by conversing with the African she was no Imposter. . . .[5]

She was "extraordinary" not because of the quality of her verse but because, as a slave, an African, and a female, she made verses at all.

The writer of that "Extraordinary female Slave" letter was Thomas Wooldridge, well known to Susanna Wheatley because both were members of a transatlantic network of evangelicals inspired by the Great Awakening. Wooldridge's addressee was the Earl of Dartmouth, after whom Dartmouth College was named: its ostensible purpose was the evangelization of American Indians. We see from the letter that both Wooldridge and Dartmouth were close to the Rev. George Whitefield, perhaps the greatest preacher of the Great Awakening, the man who had originally converted Susanna Wheatley. We can assume that she, in turn, converted Phillis. These connections and Susanna's "principles of the true Religion" were reflected in the publication in 1770 of the Phillis Wheatley poem to which Wooldridge's letter refers, "An Elegaic Poem on the Death of the Celebrated Divine . . . George Whitefield." Whitefield and those inspired by him and his fellow itinerant preachers reached hundreds of thousands of the poor and enslaved, most in huge, outdoor camp meetings. When Wooldridge met "the African" she was already in correspondence with evangelicals on both sides of the Atlantic. Among them were Lady Huntingdon, as head of her "Connexion" a leading aristocratic sponsor of English evangelism and a good friend of Susanna Wheatley; and John Thornton, a rich English merchant at whose house in London would form the "Clapham sect," at the heart of the white component of English abolitionism.[6]

Phillis Wheatley visited England in 1773, where Susanna Wheatley believed that a volume of her poetry would stand a better chance of being published. Phillis had already published three poems in London and four in Boston, but had had proposals for a book of poems rejected in Boston. Susanna Wheatley then cultivated the support in London of the Countess of Huntingdon, who not only agreed that Phillis Wheatley might dedicate a volume of poems to her, but arranged to have a likeness of the author engraved for a frontispiece.

When Phillis Wheatley arrived in London, she was received there with more fanfare than she would ever receive in her lifetime in America. With the Lady Huntingdon as her patron, this humble young woman found herself courted and lionized by the city's literati. The former Lord Mayor of London presented her with a copy of John Milton's *Paradise Lost*, regarded as one of the greatest poems in the English language. And *Poems on Various Subjects* was actually published in England—primarily owing to Lady Huntingdon's efforts.[7]

Phillis Wheatley's public life was to reach a climax upon her presentation at the English royal court. But it was prevented by news from Wheatley's Boston home. Hearing of Susanna Wheatley's serious illness, Phillis left for America after only five weeks in England. Back in Boston, however, she was granted her freedom in December 1773—in her own words, "three months before the death of my dear mistress and at her desire, as well as [John Wheatley's] own humanity. . . ." It seems that the dying Susanna Wheatley was ensuring that Phillis would, indeed, be freed before she died. In the letter grieving her "parent's" death, Phillis noted the change in "the behavior of those who seem'd to respect me while under my mistresses [*sic*] patronage; . . . some of those have already put on a reserve. . . ."[8] She faced continuing racism. Her correspondent in this case, the evangelical John Thornton, advised Wheatley to return to Africa as a missionary, more specifically, by marrying one of two Rhode Island evangelized blacks named Bristol Yamma and John Quamine, neither of whom she had ever met.[9] It is crucial to recognize the historical meaning of Phillis Wheatley's reply to Thornton: "Upon my arrival [in Africa] how like a Barbarian shou'd I look to the natives; I can promise that my tongue shall be quiet, for a strong reason indeed, being an utter stranger to the Language of Anamaboe."[10] She had become "British and American." Returning to Africa would silence her.

She continued to live in the Wheatley household in Boston, a city dominated by the Revolution during the remainder of Phillis Wheatley's life. Responding to her "To His Excellency George Washington," published in Tom Paine's *Pennsylvania Magazine* (1776) when Washington was appointed commander in chief of the revolutionary armies, Washington invited Phillis Wheatley to his Cambridge headquarters. In March 1778, John Wheatley died, finally dissolving the secure circumstances under which Phillis Wheatley had lived since her arrival in America. The following month she married a free black shopkeeper, John Peters. They had three children (all of whom died young) before he left her life and the historical record. One of her last poems, "Liberty and Peace" (1784) celebrating the end of the American Revolution, was published under her married name. Phillis Wheatley was working as a servant in a cheap boardinghouse when she and her last remaining child died, on December 5, 1784. Her poetry was kept alive in the early nineteenth century by abolitionist publishers.[11]

Although we have learned a good deal in recent years about Phillis Wheatley's life and literary career, we have rarely attempted to discuss her poetry as poetry. A starting point is her reception in London. What was the reason for such lavish attention given to a lowly slave poet? The answer lies in England's fascination for poets who illustrated the principle of "natural genius." This principle can best be explained by the Latin aphorism, *poeta nascitur, non fit* ("a poet is born, and not made").[12] Although the idea of "natural genius" is ancient, it was given a new interpretation by the middle of the eighteenth century. This interpretation not only helps us to understand the English response to Phillis Wheatley, but it also enables us to see how she could use the idea of "natural genius" to her own poetical advantage.

The essayist Joseph Addison popularized the concept of "natural genius" in the eighteenth century. In 1711, in his very influential magazine, *The Spectator,* Addison had distinguished between two kinds of poetic genius. The first kind is those artists "who by the mere strength of natural parts, and without any assistance of art or learning, have produced works that were the delight of their own times and the wonder of posterity." The second kind is artists who "have formed themselves by rules and submitted the greatness of their natural talents to the corrections and restraints of art." Addison claims to make no disparaging comparison between the two types of genius, but he does admit that there is something "nobly wild, and extravagant in . . . natural geniuses that is infinitely more beautiful than all the turn and polishing of what the French call a *bel esprit,* by which they would express a genius refined by conversation, reflection, and the reading of the most polite authors."[13] As Addison defined the term, "natural genius" implied an elitist view of the poet—some are born with this divine talent, others are not—for he never imagined that the idea of "natural genius" could be applied to a working-class poet.

Nevertheless, at mid-century this concept was given a distinctly democratic twist. Some members of the English aristocracy became convinced that among the poor were to be found "mute, inglorious Miltons," who if only given the chance would burst forth in glorious song.[14] Thus poets were seized upon because they were "unlettered," and in the thirty-five or so years before Phillis Wheatley began to write in the late 1760s, we find numerous examples of bards from the lower classes who were patronized by people of position. For example, Joseph Spence sponsored Stephen Duck, the "Thresher-Poet"; Lord Lyttelton encouraged James Woodhouse, the "Shoemaker-Poet"; Lord Chesterfield helped Henry Jones, the "Bricklayer-Poet"; and in little more than a decade after Phillis Wheatley's death, Hannah More sponsored Ann Yearsley, the poet known as Lactilla, the "Milkmaid-Poet."[15]

Given this atmosphere, it is understandable that Lady Huntingdon became excited over the poetry of a young slave woman.[16] To Lady Huntingdon, Phillis Wheatley was another example of "natural genius" among the impoverished classes. Furthermore, Lady Huntingdon knew that others would respond to this new manifestation of the "Unlettered Muse" and that a picture of the author as the frontispiece of *Poems on Various Subjects* would call attention to the author's humble station.

The advertisement for Phillis Wheatley's book also emphasized the author's "natural genius." This notice appeared in the *London Chronicle* (September 9–11, 11–14) and in the *Morning Post and Advertiser* (September 13 and 18), and it included a testimonial from people "distinguished for their learning" who "unanimously expressed their approbation of her genius, and their amazement at the gifts with which infinite Wisdom has furnished her." The language of the advertisement implies that Phillis Wheatley and Africa were inseparably linked in the minds of the eighteenth-century English readers:

> The Book here proposed for publication displays perhaps one of the greatest instances of pure, unassisted genius, that the world ever produced. The Author is a native of Africa, and left not that dark part of the habitable system, till she was eight years old. She is now no more than nineteen, and many of the poems were penned before she arrived at near that age.
>
> They were wrote upon a variety of interesting subjects, and in a stile rather to be expected from those who . . . have had the happiness of a liberal education, than from one born in the wilds of Africa.[17]

Phillis Wheatley is not praised because she expressed her naked, unadorned self; she is praised because, deprived of a "liberal education," she intuitively knows the adornments of art.

The tradition of "natural genius" continues well into the nineteenth century and is the basis of Margaretta Odell's short biography of the African poet. A strange mixture of fact and fancy, Odell's *Memoir* (1834) is our major source of information about Phillis Wheatley's life, and the myth which Odell expounds has its roots in eighteenth-century England. We learn, for instance, that as a young girl, Phillis Wheatley took to poetry as naturally as ducks take to water. Although people encouraged her to read and write, "nothing was forced upon her, nothing was suggested, or placed before her as a lure; her literary efforts were altogether the natural workings of her own mind." Also, she never had "any grammatical instructor, or knowledge of the structure or idiom of the English language, except which she imbibed from a perusal of the best English writers, and from mingling in polite circles. . . ." Furthermore, she was visited by visions in the night which awakened her and which she wrote down as poems. The next morning, she could not remember these dreams which had inspired her to write poetry.[18]

The extent to which Phillis Wheatley believed she was a "natural genius" is difficult to determine, but she did skillfully employ this public image of herself in her poetry. The appearance of the idea of "natural genius" in her poems presented a familiar paradox, as her age would have instantly recognized. In a poetical correspondence with Lieutenant Rochfort of His Majesty's Navy, Phillis Wheatley modestly disclaims the use of artifice, at the same time that she artfully defines the kind of poet she is and hopes to be.

Phillis Wheatley had written a poem, addressed to Rochfort, in which she had praised the sailor's martial valor, and Rochfort responded by sending her a poem of his own. In "The Answer," Rochfort eulogizes Phillis Wheatley by glorifying the country of her birth. Africa is depicted as a "happy land" where "shady forests . . . scarce know a bound." Here there are

The artless grottos, and the soft retreats;
"At once the lover and the muse's seats."
Where nature taught, (tho strange it is to tell,)
Her flowing pencil Europe to excell. (84)

In these lines, Rochfort romanticizes Africa. Primitivistic and picturesque, this Africa is as unreal as the "dark continent" of the advertisement to *Poems on Various Subjects.* Rochfort sees Africa as the cause of Phillis Wheatley's power as a poet; the simple "artless" land has given birth to an "artless" poet. In later lines, he celebrates "Wheatley's song" as having "seraphic fire" and an "art, which art could ne'er acquire."

When Phillis Wheatley wrote a poetic reply to this poem, she employed the same motifs which Rochfort had used. She refers to Africa as a luxuriant "Eden." Then she humbly says of Rochfort's flattery:

The generous plaudit 'tis not mine to claim,
A muse untutor'd, and unknown to fame. (86)

She laments further that her "pen . . . Can never rival, never equal thine," but she will nevertheless continue to study the best authors to improve her talent. She illustrates this thought by soaring into poetic flight:

Then fix the humble Afric muse's seat
At British Homer's and Sir Isaac's feet*
Those bards whose fame in deathless strains arise
Creation's boast, and fav'rites of the skies. (86)

It is easy to see that Rochfort and Phillis Wheatley are playing an elaborate game in these poems, with the assumptions on both sides well understood. Rochfort tells her that she is an "artless" poet, and she modestly agrees, only to prove his thesis that her "untutored" muse has the capacity for true "seraphic fire." She is the "artless" poet as wise *ingénue.* It is worth noting that in the above passage,

*The "British Homer" is the poet Alexander Pope, who translated Homer; "Sir Isaac" is the scientist and astronomer Sir Isaac Newton.

Phillis Wheatley says that she will worship at the shrines of Pope and Newton, two of the greatest "bards" of the age.

What Phillis Wheatley learned from Alexander Pope, her favorite author, was an ability to transform her real self into an imagined self, a *persona,* that functioned as a means to a precise end, rhetorical persuasion. Instead of being a liability, this imagined self became a poetic asset. Often it was used as the cornerstone of an argument which she was building in a poem, and since the imagined self was based upon assumptions about race and "natural genius" that she and her age understood, the poem was convincing to the people who read it. Whatever her real feelings, it was her imagined self that she showed to the world. Whatever the disadvantages, her imagined self made her eloquent in places where she might have been simply maudlin.

Let us look more closely at a poem in which Phillis Wheatley uses her imagined self for rhetorical purposes. In "To The Right Honourable William, Earl of Dartmouth, His Majesty's Principal Secretary of State for North America," she congratulates Dartmouth on his new political post and pleads with him to protect and preserve the rights of Americans, vis-à-vis England, in the New World. To reinforce her point, she makes an analogy between America's situation and her own:

> I, young in life, by seeming cruel fate
> Was snatch'd from *Afric's* fancy'd happy seat:
> What pangs excruciating must molest,
> What sorrows labour in my parent's breast?
> Steel'd was that soul and by no misery mov'd
> That from a father seiz'd his babe belov'd:
> Such, such my case. And can I then but pray
> Others may never feel tyrannic sway? (34)

These lines have been alternately praised and blamed for their sincerity or lack of sincerity. As we know from Dr. Johnson's dictionary (1775), although the word "fancy" can be a synonym for "delusion", it can also be a synonym for the "imagination" which, in Johnson's words, "forms to itself representations of things, persons, or scenes of being." In this definition, "fancy" is that part of the mind that makes images, ones that in turn have their origin in sense experience. Phillis Wheatley's "Afric's fancy'd happy seat" might be "the happy seat" which other poets have pictured Africa to be—either from seeing it themselves or from seeing it in their imaginations. We know that Phillis Wheatley was aware of the primitivistic tradition in eighteenth-century England that often conceived of Africa as a fruitful paradise.[19] Not only did she use this idea in her poem to Rochfort, but we also know that in her poem "To Imagination" she used "fancy" and "imagination" interchangeably and that both words were placed in the context of the mind's ability to perceive a truth beyond one's own immediate experience.

Thus, the entire passage above might be read as follows:

> I, Phillis Wheatley, now a Christian slave, was once taken from my native land, Africa, which others besides myself have recognized as a Golden World. Not only did it cause my father much grief but also it has given me an understanding of the word "freedom." Fortunately for me, everything worked out for the best, for now I am a Christian (the "fate" is only "seeming cruel"), but others like myself, the Americans of these colonies, are being threatened by political tyranny.

In this poem, Phillis Wheatley has artfully used the pathos of her own past to persuade Dartmouth to assuage the wrongs done to the Americans by the British. This is neither the poetry of self-expression nor the poetry of cold elegance; rather it is the poetry of argument and rhetorical persuasion. As such, this poem is reminiscent—not in excellence but in intention—of some of the great poems of the Restoration and eighteenth century: John Dryden's "Absalom and Achitophel," and Alexander Pope's "An Essay on Man," and "An Epistle to Dr. Arbuthnot."

"To the University of Cambridge, in New England" also illustrates Phillis Wheatley's ability to manipulate an imagined self for the sake of rhetorical persuasion. This poem is addressed to the students at Harvard who are urged by this young African slave to mend their profligate ways. To underscore her didactic theme, Phillis Wheatley describes the world from which she came:

> 'Twas not long since I left my native shore
> The land of errors, and *Egyptian* gloom:
> Father of mercy, 'twas thy gracious hand
> Brought me in safety from those dark abodes. (5)

This is a different picture of Africa from the one of happy primitives; it is an Africa without Christianity and without civilization. Although this portrait is not flattering to her native land, it is rhetorically useful; it creates an ironic contrast between her lot and that of the Harvard students. The latter are Christians by birth, and because they have the privileges of class, they are offered a knowledge of the highest civilization that human beings have attained. Yet they are abusing this god-given gift, one that has been denied to members of Phillis Wheatley's race. A lowly African must remind them that they too, like all people, may be destroyed by sin:

Ye blooming plants of human race devine
An *Ethiop* tells you 'tis your greatest foe;
Its transient sweetness turns to endless pain,
And in immense perdition sinks the soul. (6)

As an "Ethiop," that is, an African, Phillis Wheatley is exploiting a situation here that is quite familiar to her audience. In this instance, the simple savage *knows* more than the sophisticated Harvard students.

In another well-known poem, "On Being Brought from Africa to America," we see a similar rhetorical strategy. Phillis Wheatley begins by celebrating God's mercy in bringing her from her "Pagan land" to the New World: "Once I redemption neither sought nor knew." Nevertheless, she is aware that some Christians in America "view our sable race with scornful eye." These Americans see the "Negro's" color as "diabolic," and thus Phillis Wheatley reminds them in the last two lines of the poem:

Remember, *Christians, Negroes,* black as *Cain,*
May be refin'd, and join th' angelic train. (7)

As Phillis Wheatley said in one of her letters, God "was no respecter of Persons."[20] Although the Negro appears to be Cain to white Americans,[21] he is not Cain in Christ's eyes. The italicized words not only emphasize the falsehood of the analogy but they also serve as a reminder that all human beings—including whites—need to be "refined" before they "join th' angelic train."

The quiet irony of these last two lines seems to echo Pope's "lo, the poor Indian" passage in "An Essay on Man." In Pope's poem, civilized man thinks himself superior to the simple savage; yet it is the savage's simplicity that serves as a satiric comment upon the actual behavior of those people who call themselves "Christians." For the "poor Indian," heaven is a place where "No fiends torment, no Christians thirst for Gold." By placing her imagined self in ironic juxtaposition to the "Christians" who would view her as "diabolic," Phillis Wheatley is making the same satiric point.

Pope was not the only one to teach her how to use a *persona* to rhetorical advantage. One poem recently discovered in manuscript indicates that Phillis Wheatley was probably aware of John Dryden's poetry. "To Deism" is similar to Dryden's "Religio Laici" in both theme and technique; both authors use the *persona* of the "layperson" to attack the web-spinning sophistry of Deism. In the eighteenth century, Deism was called "natural religion" because it assumed that human reason was sufficient to discover the intricate workings of God's universe. The world, in other words, was like a clock, and one need only understand the mechanism to understand the clockmaker. Thus, Christianity is not mysterious and there is no need for revelation to make God known to humankind.

Phillis Wheatley appears in "To Deism" as an unlettered African who nevertheless knows the fundamental truths of Christianity. Her antagonist, a Deist, is out to disprove the doctrines of revelation and the trinity, and like John Dryden, Phillis Wheatley cannot hide her indignation at such folly:

> Must Ethiopians be imploy'd for you
> [I] greatly rejoice if any good I do
> I ask O unbeliever satan's child
> Has not thy savior been to[o] meek [&] mild. . . .[22]

Phillis Wheatley weighs God's mercy against the Deist's reason and finds the latter light indeed; the Deist rejects the very attribute of God, His infinite mercy, that for his sake he ought to hope exists. For if the Savior had not been "meek [&] mild," He would have already damned the Deist to endless perdition for his impudence. Again like John Dryden, Phillis Wheatley suggests that only the direct, simple truth will cut through the tissue of the complicated reasoning that has so entrapped the Deist.

Phillis Wheatley's mastery of poetic technique, such as her ability to shape a *persona* for rhetorical purposes, shows her to be a more artful poet than we have previously recognized. At times she eloquently wrote in the "sublime" mode which so fascinated her age. As a religious poet, she found the "sublime" a perfect vehicle for expressing transcendent emotions. As an artist, she responded to the secular theories of the "sublime," a kind of poetry which tried to be grandiloquent rather than clear, astonishing in its effects rather than logical. In this verse, whether sacred or profane, Milton and the Old Testament were influences upon her—but so was Alexander Pope.

We are told by Margaretta Odell that Phillis Wheatley specifically admired "Pope's Homer."[23] This fact is significant, for Pope's preface to *The Iliad* and translation of it helped to create the critical opinion in the eighteenth century that Homer was the master of "sublimity."[24] The "sublime" reached the zenith of its popularity around the same time that Phillis Wheatley began writing poetry.[25] In "To Maecenas," Wheatley describes herself as a humble poet who wishes to soar in exalted flight. Homer, she says, is her model, but she laments that she cannot "paint" with his power. Homer makes lightning "blaze across the vaulted skies," and causes the thunder to shake "the heavenly plains," and as she reads his lines: "A deep-felt horror thrills through my veins." She too would fly like both Homer and Virgil but complains:

. . . here I sit, and mourn a grov'ling mind,
That fain would mount, and ride upon the wind. (3)

Not only is there an oblique reference to the Old Testament in the last line, but she is also remembering two lines from Pope's "An Essay on Man":

Nor God alone in the still Calm we find;
He mounts the Storm, and *walks upon the wind.*[26]

Phillis Wheatley identifies herself with Pope because as the translator of Homer and as the author of "An Essay on Man," Pope is a poet who has already excelled in the "sublime" mode; in these two works, he has, as it were, mounted "the storm" and walked "upon the wind." To the pious young slave poet, for instance, "An Essay on Man" would be an example of the highest kind of "sublimity," for Pope's poems contain passages which grandly describe the vast, mysterious, awe-inspiring universe of God's creation.[27]

The "sublime" takes various forms in Phillis Wheatley's poetry. One of the instruments enabling one to reach the sublime was "terror." In "Goliath of Gath," she is consciously creating an epic character who terrifies us through our inability to imagine him as finite. In "On Imagination," she celebrates the imagination's capacity to seize upon what our senses cannot hold, the vast immensity of the universe. In "Ode to Neptune" and "To a Lady on Her Remarkable Preservation in an Hurricane in North Carolina," she is concerned with the "natural sublime," the fact that some objects in nature such as storms and hurricanes fill us with terror because of their uncontrollable power. In "Niobe in Distress for Her Children Slain by Apollo," Phillis Wheatley is domesticating a mythological figure by treating Niobe as a distressed mother. Not only is the poet's portrait contemporary in that Niobe is a favorite figure in the "Age of Sensibility," but Phillis Wheatley is also illustrating an aesthetic commonplace of the period: pathos is a branch of the "sublime."

If we examine two of her "sublime" poems, we shall see just how thoroughly Phillis Wheatley knew the taste of her age. In "Goliath of Gath," for instance, she illustrates aesthetician Edmund Burke's famous dictum in *The Sublime and the Beautiful* (1757) that "to make anything very terrible, obscurity seems in general to be necessary."[28] Burke's point is that if a character is going to affect our imaginations with ideas of terror and power, the artist must not draw him or her too precisely. Hence, Phillis Wheatley describes Goliath as a "monster" stalking "the terror of the field" as he comes forth to meet the Hebrews. She mentions his "fierce deportment" and "gigantic frame," but never descends to particulars when she refers to his physical characteristics. Rather, she obliquely depicts Goliath by focusing upon his armor and weapons:

> A brazen helmet on his head was plac'd,
> A coat of mail his form terrific grac'd,
> The greaves his legs, the targe his shoulders prest:
> Dreadful in arms high-tow'ring o'er the rest
> A spear he proudly wav'd, whose iron head,
> Strange to relate, six hundred shekels weigh'd;
> He strode along, and shook the ample field,
> While *Phoebus* blaz'd refulgent on his shield:
> Through *Jacob's* race a chilling horror ran. . . . (14)

Like Achilles in Book 22 of Homer's *The Iliad* and Sat in Book 1 of Milton's *Paradise Lost,* Goliath is terrifying because our sensory perceptions fail to contain him. If she had not read Edmund Burke, she at least knew about his psychological theory of the "sublime."

Goliath is meant to frighten us (like storms and hurricanes in nature), but the imagination in "To Imagination" is meant to bring us to an emotional state of religious awe. Following poet Mark Akenside's lead ("The Pleasures of the Imagination" [1744]), Phillis Wheatley sees the infinite soul of a human being as a microcosm of God's infinite universe; only the imagination can capture a sense of that infinity:

> *Imagination*! who can sing thy force?
> Or who describe the swiftness of thy course?
> Soaring through air to find the bright abode,
> Th' empyreal palace of the thund'ring God,
> We on thy pinions can surpass the wind,
> And leave the rolling universe behind:
> From star to star the mental optics rove,
> Measure the skies, and range the realms above.
> There in one view we grasp the mighty whole,
> Or with new worlds amaze th' unbounded soul. (30)

The imagination is a kind of mental eyesight ("optics") which allows us to penetrate the finite world and discover, to use Marjorie Nicolson's phrase, "the aesthetics of the infinite."[29] In this context, it is no wonder that Phillis Wheatley referred to Sir Isaac Newton as one of the greatest "bards" of the age, for Newton's theories about the universe expanded God's world at the same time that they explained it.

Although eighteenth-century England saw Phillis Wheatley as a "natural genius," she had larger plans for herself. She aspired to be an artist in the manner of Homer, Milton, and Pope. If we still complain that she failed as a poet because she did not express, with sufficient vehemence, her suffering black self, then we might do well to listen to Ralph Ellison, a contemporary black writer, who has argued against "unrelieved suffering" as the only basis of Afro-American art:

> . . . there is also an American Negro tradition which teaches one . . . to master and contain pain. It is a tradition which abhors as obscene any trading on one's own anguish for gain and sympathy; which springs not from a desire to deny the harshness of existence but from a will to deal with it as men at their best have always done. It takes fortitude to be a man and no less to be an artist. Perhaps it takes even more if the black man would be an artist.[30]

Phillis Wheatley could be called the founding mother of this tradition which Ellison describes, for the eighteenth century provided her with the tools to transmute her pain into art. She saw herself as a *poeta,* a maker of poems, and not as a suffering black slave who happened to be a poet.

Notes

[1]Gary Nash, *The Urban Crucible: Social Change, Political Consciousness, and the Origins of the American Revolution* (Cambridge, MA: Harvard University Press, 1979), 445.

[2]Phillis Wheatley to John Thornton, 30, Oct. 1774, quoted in James A. Rawley, "The World of Phillis Wheatley," *New England Quarterly* 50 (1977), 666–77; 669.

[3]Quoted in Terence Collins, "Phillis Wheatley: The Dark Side of the Poetry," *Phylon* 36 (1975), 78–88; 78.

[4]In 1966, Julian Mason published a modern critical edition of Phillis Wheatley's poetry, including a biographical sketch and critical introduction. Since then several new letters and poems have been found. Two essays in particular have provided us with biographical information that Mason seemed to have missed: James R. Rawley, "World of Phillis Wheatley," *New England Quarterly,* 50 (1977), 666–77; and William H. Robinson, "Phillis Wheatley in London," *College Language Association Journal,* 21 (1977), 187–201. Rawley's article also includes a list of recent discoveries in the Phillis Wheatley canon, and *PMLA* bibliographies from 1970 to the present show that our interest in her has not diminished. Specific references to Phillis Wheatley's poetry are to Mason's edition, *The Poems of Phillis Wheatley* (Chapel Hill: North Carolina Press, 1966), and will appear in the text.

[5]Thomas Wooldridge to the Earl of Dartmouth, 24, Nov. 1772, quoted in Rawley, "World of Phillis Wheatley, p. 670.

[6]Rawley's "World of Phillis Wheatley," describes these connections.

[7]We know that Phillis Wheatley first tried to get her book published in Boston in 1772. See Muktar Ali Isani, "The First Proposed Edition of *Poems on Various Subjects* and the Phillis Wheatley Canon," *American Literature,* 49 (1977), p. 98. The project mysteriously failed. An American edition of her poems was not published until 1789, five years after her death (Rawley, p. 677).

[8]Phillis Wheatley to John Thornton, 29, Mar. 1774, quoted in Rawley, "World of Phillis Wheatley," p. 673.

[9]Rawley, "World of Phillis Wheatley," p. 674.

[10]30, Oct. 1774, in Rawley "World of Phillis Wheatley," p. 674.

[11]Saunders Redding, "Phillis Wheatley," *Notable American Women, 1607–1950,* 3 vols. (Cambridge, MA: Belknap Press, 1971), 3: 573–74; 574.

[12]See Jefferson Carter, "The Unlettered Muse: The Uneducated Poets and the Concept of Natural Genius in Eighteenth-Century England" (Diss. University of Arizona 1972), pp. 6, 7. Although Carter does not discuss Phillis Wheatley, I am using his ideas when describing the eighteenth century's interest in "natural genius" and the "unlettered" poets.

[13]Scott Elledge, *Eighteenth-Century Critical Essays* (Ithaca: Cornell University Press, 1961), I, 27–29.

[14]Carter, "Unlettered Muse" p. 103.

[15]Ibid., pp. 69–238.

[16]According to Susanna Wheatley, when Phillis Wheatley's poems were first read to the Countess of Huntingdon, the latter would interrupt by saying, "Is not this, or that very fine? Do read another." See Kenneth Silverman, "Four New Letters by Phillis Wheatley," *Early American Literature,* 8 (1973–74), p. 269.

[17]As quoted in Robinson's "Phillis Wheatley in London," p. 97.

[18]*Memoir and Poems of Phillis Wheatley, A Native African and A Slave* (1838; facs. rpt. Miami: Mnemosyne, 1969), pp. 18, 20. The *Memoir* was published anonymously in 1834.

[19]See Wylie Sypher, *Guinea's Captive Kings: British Anti-Slavery Literature of the XVIIIth Century* (1942; rpt. New York: Farrar, Straus, 1969), pp. 103–55. Sypher notes that the African as "Noble Savage" had strong roots in eighteenth-century English culture; whereas Winthrop Jordan points out that this tradition fell on barren soil in America, *White over Black: American Attitudes toward the Negro, 1550–1812* (1968; rpt. Baltimore: Penguin, 1969), p. 27.

[20]See Silverman, "Four New Letters," p. 265. Also, see Acts 10:34.

[21]That the Negro's black skin is the mark worn by Cain seems to be a predominantly American idea. See Jordan, *White over Black,* pp. 42, 416.

[22]Phil Lapsansky, "Deism: An Unpublished Poem by Phillis Wheatley," *New England Quarterly,* 50 (1977), 519. Lapsansky does not mention the rather obvious connection to Dryden's poem.

[23]*Memoir,* p. 20.

[24]See Pope's "Preface to the Translation of *The Iliad*" and his "Postscript to the Translation of *The Odyssey*" in *Eighteenth-Century Critical Essays,* I, 257–78, 291–300. Pope especially emphasized the "sublimity" and daring "invention" of *The Iliad.*

[25]Samuel H. Monk, *The Sublime: A Study of Critical Theories in Eighteenth-Century England* (1935; rpt. Ann Arbor: University of Michigan Press, 1960), pp. 101–33.

[26]"An Essay on Man," II, 11. 109–10. Also, see Psalms 104:3.

[27]For example, "An Essay on Man," I, 11. 22–32; I, 11. 247–58.

[28]Edmund Burke, *A Philosophical Inquiry into . . . the Sublime and Beautiful,* in *Eighteenth-Century Poetry and Prose* (1939; rpt. New York: Ronald Press, 1956), p. 1166.

[29]Marjorie Nicolson, *Mountain Gloom and Mountain Glory: The Development of the Aesthetics of the Infinite* (Ithaca: Cornell University Press, 1959). In *Newton Demands the Muse: Newton's "Optics" and the Eighteenth-Century Poets* (Princeton: Princeton University Press, 1946), Nicolson makes a connection between Newton's *Optics* and the poetry of the imagination which became popular in the 1740s. Phillis Wheatley's reference to "mental optics" may be another illustration of the impact of Newton's treatise on the poetry of the eighteenth century.

[30]Ralph Ellison, *Shadow and Act* (1953; rpt. New York, Random House, 1966), p. 119. Also, see Henry-Louis Gates, "Dis and Dat: Dialect and the Descent," in *Afro-American Literature: The Reconstruction of Instruction* (New York: MLA, 1979), pp. 88–119. Gates's fascinating essay focuses upon the relationship of the African "mask" to Afro-American poetry. He does not discuss Phillis Wheatley's poetry, but some of the implications of his essay have relevance to her art. Perhaps Phillis Wheatley's poetical *persona* has its roots in African culture as well as in the artistic practices of eighteenth-century England.

Mercy Otis Warren

(1728–1814)

Marianne B. Geiger

Born in Barnstable, Massachusetts, on September 14, 1728, Mercy Otis Warren was not formally schooled, despite the middle-class trappings of her family. She learned from her brother James's tutors and was relatively well educated by the time of her marriage in November 1754 to James Warren, who became a leader within Massachusetts Revolutionary circles. The couple had five sons.

Warren's roles as wife and mother did not satisfy her during an age of explosive ideas and radical transformations, and she became one of a generation of prolific American political writers, publishing three satiric plays, although like many of her male contemporaries she published under a pen name. Despite their pseudonymous publication, her works became known as a product of her prolific wit. Warren also, at age seventy-six, distinguished herself as a historian when she published, under her own name, a three-volume history of the American Revolution. Her history was one of the first accounts written by an American, and is widely recognized as a classic eighteenth-century interpretation of the era. Warren died in Plymouth in 1814.

Mercy Otis Warren was born into a politically active family, married into a politically active family, and raised sons who in their maturity held appointive federal office. Although she was interested in politics all her life, her participation in politics was circumscribed, for women in the eighteenth century were not permitted to participate directly in public life. Nevertheless, Warren made her voice heard in public political discourse, decade after decade, through her writing, by her cultivation of a "salon," and through an extensive correspondence with men active in political life. Warren also cultivated a wide circle of female correspondents, including women like herself with close ties to political leaders. Through their correspondence, these women shared and shaped each others' political understanding and implicitly that of their husbands and sons, and perhaps even their daughters.

As Linda Kerber has observed, "the newly created republic made little room for [women] as political beings." Republicanism, in the Anglo-American meaning of the word, was the advocacy of representative self-government by a "people," which meant in effect, men. Men who qualified for participation in such government possessed land or held it in nondependent tenure, which also entitled them to bear arms. Republican government was intended to allow the expression of personal virtue through "civic" and public participation. Republican men excluded women from political rights and required them to be "submissive to men . . . as loving wives, prudent mothers, and mistress of families, faithful friends and good Christians."[1]

Mercy Otis Warren departed from this limited definition by becoming a woman who was clearly and publicly a political being. However, she also served as an exemplar for the ideal of the "republican mother," a woman who served her country politically by educating her sons to lead lives of lofty republican virtue, putting the good of the state ahead of their own personal good.

Warren's life followed conventional lines, as she played the roles of daughter, wife, and mother, until she was in her mid-forties. Her brother, James Otis, had led the resistance to the British Parliament's new program for dealing with the colonies, thundering, "Taxation without representation is tyranny." Mercy Otis Warren had shared all his early education as a child, and ardently shared his political views as an adult. Her letters reveal a literary talent comparable to his, and when James Otis fell ill, a victim of a disease akin to manic depression, Mercy Otis Warren, encouraged by her husband James Warren and his friends, particularly John Adams, used her talents to promote the patriotic cause in his place. Her views were well regarded because she clearly articulated a political philosophy that her friends, men on the brink of revolution, believed in. In addition, her flair for vivid expression compelled assent and, at times, delight.

Warren could not act in the political realm for herself, but she could, and did, speak both for herself, for her family, and for the thousands who shared their political convictions. Warren's political credo, exemplified by her brother James Otis's opposition to British authority in the 1760s, was labeled the "Real Whig," or "Country," ideology. It held that republicanism was the best form of government, that those who were ruled must participate in the choice of those who were to rule. Rulers must frequently rotate out of their offices in order to participate anew in the life of ordinary people. The tendency to undue ambition and avarice in officials must be controlled through the practice of civic virtue, the placing of the good of the whole people before one's individual good. These Real Whigs, or republicans, were characteristically suspicious of the motives of those in power and always concerned about the independence both of electors and of members of representative assemblies.[2]

Mercy Otis was born in Barnstable in Cape Cod, Massachusetts, in 1728, the first daughter and third child of thirteen. The Otises were descendants of farmers from Glastonbury, England, who had come to New England in the 1630s. Mercy's father, James Otis, Sr., was a third son and sixth child of a branch of the family that had settled on the Great Salt Marshes at Barnstable. Fiercely ambitious, but without the Harvard education given his two elder brothers, James Otis, Sr., combined farming, storekeeping, merchant-trading, and the practice of provincial law to make himelf a leading citizen of Massachusetts. He was always known as "Colonel Otis" because of his office in the Barnstable County militia.

The Otis children received their early education from their uncle Jonathan Russell, minister of the Barnstable church, who enjoyed young James and Mercy's quick intelligence, and fostered in them his love for the works of William Shakespeare and Alexander Pope. The cadences of Pope and of Shakespeare reverberate in all the published work of both James and Mercy.

After graduation from Harvard in 1743, James did postgraduate work in literature for two years, spending a great deal of time at home in Barnstable while writing a manual of Latin prosody. His sister Mercy's obvious skill in using formal techniques of versification and classical drama reflect familiarity with the works her brother James was studying at this time.

James Otis was one of the few revolutionaries to express dissatisfaction with the political status of women in his time. In his 1764 pamphlet, *The Rights of the British Colonies Asserted and Proved,* speculating on the origins of government, James Otis said, "May there not be as many original compacts as there are men and women born or to be born? Are not women born as free as men? Would it not be infamous to assert the ladies are all slaves by nature?"[3] The man whose education had begun at the side of Mercy Otis Warren could never acquiesce to his age's denigration of women's intellectual capacities. His sister was to justify his faith in women's abilities when she carried on his political work after he no longer could.

James Otis studied for the Massachusetts Bar under one of its leading members, Jeremiah Gridley. Once admitted, James became his father's envoy in seeking colony-wide office. The elder Otis hoped to be named to the next vacant seat on the Superior Court. But when there was a vacancy, a new royal governor, Francis Bernard, gave the Court's chief justiceship to Thomas Hutchinson (a descendant of Anne Hutchinson), a man who already had more than his share of colonial offices. The elder Otis's bitterness grew, flowering into a great resentment of Hutchinson and of all his extensive family. The Colonel imbued his children with his resentment: James's most vivid speeches and Mercy's most vivid writings referred to the Hutchinsons, always in searing negatives.[4]

Mercy Otis married James Warren of Plymouth, a gentleman farmer and merchant, in November 1754. In the impressive Warren house at North and Main Streets in Plymouth, Mercy gave birth to five sons between 1757 and 1766. James Warren succeeded his father as sheriff of Plymouth County and, in 1766, was elected to the General Court, serving often as Speaker.

John Adams, a longtime admirer of James Otis's political oratory, became a close friend and political ally of James Warren; he and his wife Abigail also developed strong bonds with Mercy Otis Warren. The families exchanged visits, and many letters. Abigail and Mercy in their letters mixed politics, literature, and musings about the dilemmas of bringing up children in the comfortable manner of people whose minds are in deep sympathy. The Adamses encouraged Warren's literary and political interests. Abigail Adams warmly admired the literary gifts of the woman fifteen years her senior, assuring her, "I love characters drawn by your pen."[5]

Abigail Adams thought Warren had a particular wisdom in divining political motivations, praising her as one "who have so thoroughly looked thro the Deeds of Men, and Develloped the Dark designs of a Rapatio [Thomas Hutchinson] soul."[6]

In the early 1770s, encouraged by both John and Abigail Adams and, as time went on, by popular approval, Warren anonymously published a series of three satirical plays in pamphlet form, denouncing a thinly disguised Thomas Hutchinson. Since anonymous satirical publications were a common vehicle for eighteenth-century political expression, Warren could manuever within customary boundaries to gain a political voice without revealing her identity as a woman.

The first of Warren's plays, *The Adulateur,* was published in the *Boston Gazette* in the spring of 1773. It centers around the villain Rapatio, obviously Thomas Hutchinson, planning revenge for the wreck of his house during the 1765 Stamp Act riots. *The Defeat,* which appeared a few months later, satirizes Hutchinson's perceived sacrifice of virtue for political advancement.[7] The third play, *The Group,* mocks the men who accepted places on the new, gubernatorially appointed, council established by the hated 1774 Massachusetts Government Act.

The plays make no attempt at plot or character development. Warren's villains are consciously evil. They proudly face the audience and recite their ignoble motives, the acquisition of power and money. The good men are virtuous beyond compare; the people's good is their only motive. There are no women in the trilogy: these plays deal with the public arena, from which women were excluded.

It is touching to see how Warren continually has James Otis, usually called "Brutus" and described as "The First Patriot," act in the plays the noble part he was unable to take in real life because of his increasing mental deterioration. His speeches in the play resound with the most high-flown patriotic rhetoric:

> I spring from men, who fought, who bled
> for freedom:
> From men, who in the conflict laugh'd at danger:
> Struggl'd like patriots, and through seas of
> blood,
> Waded to conquests.—I'll not disgrace them.[8]

Mercy Otis Warren was not alone as a woman interested in writing as a political person. Her brother James, and other American patriots, had during the late 1760s and early 1770s corresponded with Catharine Macaulay, a British historian whose work, critical of the seventeenth-century Stuart monarchy, was more widely popular in America than in Britain. Macaulay also wrote political pamphlets deploring the actions of the current British government and expressing sympathy for the American cause. At the suggestion of John Adams, Mercy Otis Warren began to correspond with Macaulay. Warren and Macaulay exchanged letters on political topics for the next two decades, until Macaulay's death in 1791.[9]

During the 1770s, James Warren became ever more active in the revolutionary cause. His service gave Warren access to the information she was to use in the great work of her life, the *History of the Rise, Progress, and Termination of the American Revolution.* A leader in the Massachusetts General Court since 1766, James Warren served as president of the Massachusetts Provincial Congress in 1775. After George Washington was appointed commander in chief of the Continental army, Warren assumed the post of paymaster.

Mercy Warren frequently visited her husband at army headquarters at Watertown, and there she began to write what she thought of as her "Memoir," a description of the exciting revolutionary activity that swirled around her. She sent personality descriptions, which she called "characters," to John Adams in Philadelphia. Warren was later to use these for some of the most appreciated pages of her *History* of the American Revolution.

James Warren continued to serve as John Adam's eyes and ears in Massachusetts while Adams spent years in Philadelphia at the Continental Congress. Through their extensive correspondence with Adams, the Warrens became familiar with all the ramifications of political and military developments in the rest of the states. The correspondence continued during the years Adams served in diplomatic posts in Europe.

The years after the American victory at Yorktown were difficult for Mercy and James Warren. Despite his consistent preference for asserting himself in state rather than national politics, James Warren was not politically successful in Massachusetts during these years. Elections were most often won by John Hancock and men allied with him. The Warrens and the Adamses regarded Hancock as an intellectual lightweight and a political opportunist who lacked the stern virtues proper to one who aspired to govern in a republican state. They thought he flattered people too much and spent too much of his own fortune on lavish entertainments designed to build political support, behavior anathema to committed republicans.

James Warren recognized that Plymouth was too isolated a location on which to build a firm political base, and decided to become more a part of the ongoing political life of the state by moving closer to Boston. In an exquisite irony, in 1780 the Warrens purchased Milton Hill, the former home of their archenemy, the now deceased Thomas Hutchinson. Ten miles south of Boston, the beautiful estate was meant to be the headquarters for the Warrens and their political dynasty.

Catharine Macaulay came to the United States in 1784, staying in the Boston vicinity for the winter. She spent several days with the Warrens at Milton Hill, and Mercy Warren wrote a series of letters to introduce Macaulay to political leaders in New York and Philadelphia, as Macaulay and her young second husband William Graham undertook a tour of the new United States. After Macaulay spent ten days with George and Martha Washington at Mount Vernon, she decided that she would not, after all, write a history of the American Revolution. On the eve of embarking for Europe in 1785, she wrote to Warren to tell her so, leaving the field clear for her American friend.

None of the five Warren sons showed the flair for politics their Otis forebears had demonstrated. The eldest, James Warren, Jr., who had lost a leg as a result of service on the *Alliance* during a revolutionary war naval battle, spent most of the decade following the war coming to terms with his disability. He revealed a tendency to melancholy similar to that of his uncle James Otis. James Otis himself died in 1783, dramatically, when struck by a bolt of lightning. The Warrens' second son, Charles, stricken with that scourge of the age, tuberculosis, spent part of the decade searching for health, dying in Lisbon in 1785. Their third son, the mercurial Winslow, hoped to become a successful merchant, but succeeded only in amassing large debts both in the United States and Europe. After being imprisoned for debt, he joined the army, only to be killed in an Indian attack in the Ohio country in 1791, while serving under the ever-luckless General Arthur St. Clair. The fifth son, George, became a landowner and merchant in the Maine region; he died in 1801, at age thirty-five. Henry, the fourth son, settled on the Plymouth farm, the one son to marry and have children.

Finding neither the political nor economic rewards they had anticipated, deeply saddened by their sons' lack of worldly success, the Warrens put Milton Hill up for sale and returned to their Plymouth house in 1786. Mercy Warren's brothers Joseph and Samuel Alleyne Otis underwent bankruptcy in this decade, because of their misreading of the turbulent trade patterns that followed resumption of trade with Great Britain after the Treaty of Paris in 1783. Regretting the Otis and Warren misfortunes, John Adams declared, "I dont believe there is one Family upon Earth to which the United States are so indebted for their Preservation from Thraldom," adding, "There was scarcely any family in New England had such Prospects of Opulence and Power . . . they have sacrificed them all."[10]

The economic hardships endured by the Otis brothers reflected patterns throughout Massachusetts. A group of people led by Daniel Shays attempted to force the courts in the western part of the state to remain closed, so that no more bankruptcies could be declared. This lawlessness lent urgency to the interstate meeting called for Philadelphia in 1787 to consider ways to strengthen the Articles of Confederation that bound the states together. Although young Henry Warren was among those who marched to suppress the Shaysites, James and Mercy Warren were not convinced that a new instrument of central government was needed. Because of this

Antifederalist opposition to the resulting Constitution that created a stronger central government, James Warren was not elected to represent Plymouth at the state ratifying convention. However, Mercy Otis Warren wrote antiratification speeches for some who were elected, making her words heard even though her husband's voice was silenced.

When the Constitution was narrowly approved in Massachusetts, Warren wrote a nineteen-page pamphlet, again anonymously, to dissuade New York delegates from approving the Constitution in their convention. She began by imagining the "slavery" that would occur under the Constitution, "when the inhabitants of the Eastern States are dragging out a miserable existence, *only* on the gleanings of their fields; . . . languishing in hopeless poverty" because they had had to send "the flower of their crop, and the rich produce of their farms" to "the *Federal City*."[11]

Warren pointed out that there was no provision for freedom of conscience or of the press; there were "no well defined limits of the Judiciary Powers, they seem to be left as a boundless ocean."[12] She objected to the lack of provision for rotation in office, saying, "By this neglect we lose the advantage of that check to the overbearing insolence of office, which . . . keeps the mind of man in equilibrio, and teaches him the feelings of the governed."[13] Warren knew that after approval by Massachusetts, ratification by the required nine states was likely. "But if after all," she concludes, "on a dispassionate and fair discussion, the people generally give their voice for a voluntary dereliction of their privileges, let every individual who chooses the active scenes of life, strive to support the peace and unanimity of his country."[14]

In 1790, Mercy Warren for the first time published under her own name, dedicating her volume, *Poems, Dramatic and Miscellaneous*, to President George Washington. Warren, who had suffered the deaths of three of the sons for whom she had hoped so much, did not publish anything else for the next fifteen years. She did, however, work on her "Memoir" about the Revolution, writing to Washington, General Benjamin Lincoln, the commander of the revolutionary forces in the South, and John Adams to gather documents.

However, James and Mercy Warren felt themselves increasingly separate from political developments in the nation's capital. They saw in Alexander Hamilton's financial program the beginnings of the victory of the money power and the fostering of political and financial corruption that had triumphed in 1760s Britain, forcing the American Revolution. Further, the Warrens disapproved of Jay's Treaty with Great Britain, which was designed to resolve commerce and navigation issues as well as violations of the Treaty of Paris. They viewed it as an unseemly capitulation of the new United States to its former enemy. The Warrens considered themselves the true republicans, and dismissed their Federalist opponents as "monarchists."

Ardent Republicans, believers in the Democratic-Republican principles of Thomas Jefferson and James Madison, the Warrens in the 1790s found themselves increasingly out of sympathy with the man in the presidency, first with George Washington and then with their old friend John Adams.

But after an easy victory at the polls (sometimes referred to as the "Revolution of 1800") placed Thomas Jefferson in office, Mercy Otis Warren thought the country was ready at last to read a truthful, unbiased republican account of the American Revolution. She worked feverishly, with her son James serving as her scribe, compiling, arranging, and rewriting the materials gathered over three decades. Late in 1805, she published a three-volume account of the *History of the Rise, Progress, and Termination of the American Revolution. Interspersed with Biographical, Political and Moral Observations.* Mercy Warren was seventy-six years old; this book was the first overtly political publication she had ever signed with her own name.

Warren admitted in the introduction that "There are certain appropriate duties assigned to each sex."[15] Men not only fight the battles, they also write the battle accounts, attempting "in the nervous style of manly eloquence, to describe the blood-stained field, and relate the story of slaughtered armies." Yet she defended her historical work by pointing out that everyone feels "a concern for the welfare of society." Women, the hearthkeepers, suffer if deprived of liberty, since "every domestic enjoyment depends on the unimpaired possession of civil and religious liberty."[16]

Warren outlined her qualifications for writing: a brother and a husband deeply involved in the early days of the conflict, continuing relationships with such political leaders as John Adams and such military leaders as General Benjamin Lincoln. She maintained, "Connected by nature, friendship, and every social tie, with many of the first patriots and most influential characters on the continent . . . I had the best information."[17]

Warren made clear at the outset that she would carefully present the character of the people responsible for events, since the writer and the reader of history must have "a just knowledge of character, to investigate the sources of action."[18] Warren here expressed her strong belief, typical of the majority of eighteenth-century historians, that people make history, that what happens in the world happens because people plan, even plot, for it to happen. By the time Warren published, sophisticated historical explanation had abandoned this interpretive stance, taking greater account of the role of the contingent in human affairs. But at the time Warren wrote, this more skeptical viewpoint was not yet influential in America.

People are the key to events, Warren said, and ambition is the key to an understanding of people's character. Ambition, "the love of distinction," is "a noble principle," she maintained, "when kept under the control of reason."[19]

Warren paired ambition with avarice, saying that these are the "primary sources of corruption" from which "have arisen all the rapine and confusion, the depredation and ruin, that have spread distress over the face of the earth from the days of Nimrod to Cesar [*sic*] and from Cesar to an arbitrary prince of the house of Brunswick."[20]

Thinking morally, wanting to bring her readers to a sense of possible doom if the ideals of the Revolution were compromised, Warren used the language of the New England jeremiad, language that had reverberated in her ears and in her heart from earliest memory. She rejected the notion of inevitable progress. It would be all too easy for the fragile new republic to slip under the yoke of some foreign power, to decline into slavery. Warren sought, through the *History,* to avert this by presenting a stirring and truthful story of the sufferings that had brought Americans to their present happy republic.

Considering her own family's political eclipse, Warren observed that "virtue and talents do not always hold their rank in the public esteem. Malice, intrigue, envy . . . frequently cast a shade over the most meritorious characters." She was convinced that "Fortune [good luck] . . . established the reputation of her favorites," leaving posterity to regard them with an admiration "which perhaps they never earned."[21]

Calling her brother James "the celebrated Mr. Otis," and "the first martyr to American freedom," she said "truth will enrol his name among the distinguished who have expired on the 'blood-stained theatre of human action.' " Warren described her brother as almost an angel of light, possessed of "independent principles, comprehensive genius, strong mind, retentive memory and great penetration" with "extensive professional knowledge."[22]

In the first, most vivid volume of the *History,* James Otis is the hero, Thomas Hutchinson the villain. Warren had first treated this conflict in her 1770s satires: the dramatic struggle between the forces of light (the Otises and their allies) and of darkness (Hutchinson and his clan) shaped her presentation in the *History.* The malevolent, almost satanic figure of Thomas Hutchinson stalks through all Warren's political work, both the pamphlet-plays and the *History.* Accusingly, she said: "Few ages have produced a more fit instrument for the purposes of a corrupt court. He was dark, intriguing, insinuating, haughty and ambitious, while the extreme of avarice marked each feature of his character."[23]

Warren set up a tension between Hutchinson and James Otis, one the personification of evil, the other the impassioned advocate of the right and the true. She blamed Hutchinson for "instigating . . . the innovating spirit of the British ministry." This "prostituter of power, nurtured in the lap of America, and bound by every tie of honor and gratitude," had "for some time" encouraged the British minister to "interrupt. . . the tranquility of the province."[24]

Warren's second and third volumes are a more conventional chronological narrative account of the course of the Revolution and its aftermath. Because of her and her husband's extensive correspondence with John Adams, her accounts of revolutionary diplomacy are particularly detailed and authoritative. Warren's descriptions of battles are well organized and dramatic; the playwright's flair for scene-setting and for choosing the right incident are abundantly in evidence.

Reading Warren's account of the Constitutional Convention, one would never know how vehement had been her objections to its work. True to her stated purpose, Warren in the *History* did all she could to foster loyalty and love for the new American republic for which she and her family had longed. Mercy Otis Warren wanted to teach the new country's citizens how to live as the kind of free people her brother James Otis had idealized; criticisms of the instrument of government could have no place in her lesson.

Warren had praise in her history for everyone except Thomas Hutchinson. Even her old enemy John Hancock was let off lightly. She deleted a reference to him under her old nickname for him of "the state baby" (so called because his gout necessitated assistance in walking) and buried her unflattering assessment of his capacities and actions in an endnote.[25]

It was then with some shock that Warren in the summer of 1807 received a letter from a furious John Adams protesting her treatment of his career. About Adams's presidency, Warren had merely said she would treat "summarily" the administration of George Washington's "immediate successor." She did point out that "the heart of the annalist may sometimes be hurt by political deviations which the pen of the historian is obliged to record."[26] She conceded that "Mr. Adams was undoubtedly a statesman of penetration and ability; but his prejudices and his passions were sometimes too strong for his sagacity and judgment."[27]

Enraged and deeply hurt, Adams in a series of fourteen tempestuous letters proceeded to demonstrate the truth of Warren's judgment. He accused her of writing to the taste of the nineteenth century, meaning to the taste of Jeffersonian Republicans. Not intimidated by the eminence her old friend had achieved, Warren replied with asperity, reminding him that her work had been mainly written before he had become president. Further, she taunted him that he himself had often urged her to write the history of the Revolution. In exasperation, Warren criticized Adams for "feelings so deficient in the benign and heavenly spirit of friendship," saying his concluding lines "cap the climax of rancor, indecency, and vulgarism."[28] No answer came from Adams.

Mercy Otis Warren retired from the political lists at age seventy-eight. Her eyesight had long been failing; with the death of James Warren in 1808 much of the zest for partisan battle left her. With her pen she had fought for the principles her brother James trumpeted to the world. She had lived to see those principles triumph. There seemed no battle that needed to be, or could be, fought by a woman of her age, in isolated Plymouth.

In 1812, after a five-year estrangement because of their differences over the *History*, Warren was reconciled with John and Abigail Adams, through the good offices of Elbridge Gerry, a prominent figure throughout the Revolution, and at this time governor of Massachusetts. The old revolutionaries exchanged visits, choosing to remember what united rather than what had divided them. It is not recorded, but surely present at the Adamses' visit to Plymouth was young Marcia Warren, Mercy's eldest granddaughter, named in honor of the "republican" pseudonym her grandmother had used in writing to the Adamses when they and the Warrens and the American Revolution were young.[29]

Mercy Warren lived on into the second administration of James Madison, enduring another war with Great Britain, the War of 1812. Her son Henry was deeply embroiled in conflicts with the Plymouth townspeople during the war, since, as Collector of the Port of Plymouth he was a Madison appointee, and "Mr. Madison's War" was ruining the town's commerce. However, it does not appear Mercy Warren kept any papers to help write a history of that war.

Warren died on October 19, 1814, a month after her eighty-sixth birthday, in the Plymouth house at the corner of North and Main Streets. As an articulate, impassioned member of a political family, she had had her say on wars, revolutions, and republics long before, and what she said had made a difference. Through her pen, Warren achieved something unique: her political satires of the 1770s, her extensive correspondence with American and British political figures, her publishing a *History* written from the unique point of view of a woman and a Jeffersonian Republican were the means Mercy Otis Warren used to move the politics of her time and place.

Notes

[1]Linda Kerber, *Women of the Republic: Intellect and Ideology in Revolutionary America* (Chapel Hill: University of North Carolina Press for the Institute of Early American History and Culture at Williamsburg, 1980), 11, 27–32.

Some of Warren's letters are transcribed in the manuscript Mercy Warren Letter Book held at the Massachusetts Historical Society. But since these transcriptions were done in the nineteenth century, in various hands, none of which is Warren's, they must be used cautiously when drawing conclusions about Warren's intellectual development. The original letter-copies used to make the transcriptions appear to have been lost.

[2]For an examination of the context and significance of these ideas in the period of the American Revolution, see Bernard Bailyn, *The Ideological Origins of the American Revolution* (Cambridge, MA: Belknap Press of Harvard University Press, 1967), and Gordon Wood, *The Creation of the American Republic* (New York: W. W. Norton, 1972). The content of the ideas is provocatively examined in Edmund S. Morgan, *Inventing the People: The Rise of Popular Sovereignty in England and America* (New York: W. W. Norton, 1988).

[3]James Otis, *The Rights of the British Colonies Asserted and Proved*, Boston, 1764. Reprinted in Bernard Bailyn, ed., *Pamphlets of the American Revolution, 1750–1776* (Cambridge, MA: Belknap Press of Harvard University Press, 1965), 1: 420.

[4]Thomas Hutchinson to Israel Williams, 21 Jan. 1761, Mass. His. Soc., Williams MSS, II, 155. Cited in Douglass Adair and John A. Schutz, eds., *Peter Oliver's Origin and Progress of the American Rebellion* (Stanford, CA: Stanford University Press, 1967), p. 28, n. 3.

[5]Abigail Adams to Mercy Warren, 13 Apr. 1776, in Lyman Butterfield, ed., *Adams Family Correspondence* (Cambridge, MA: Belknap Press of Harvard University Press, 1963), 1: 378.

[6]Abigail Adams to Mercy Otis Warren, 5 Dec. 1773, in *Warren-Adams Letters: Being Chiefly a Correspondence among John Adams, Samuel Adams, and James Warren.* Massachusetts Historical Society *Collections*, 72 (1917). Reprint ed. New York: AMS Press, 1972, vol. 1: 18–19.

[7]An identification key to the characters is in a fragment of *The Defeat* in the Mercy Warren Papers at the Massachusetts Historical Society. Rapatio is Thomas Hutchinson; Limpet is Andrew Oliver; Rusticus is James Warren; Hortensius is John Adams; Brutus is James Otis.

[8][Mercy Otis Warren], *The Adulateur*, act I, sc. i. Benjamin Franklin V, ed., *The Plays and Poems of Mercy Otis Warren: Facsimile Reproductions.* (Delmar, NY: Scholars' Facsimiles & Reprints, 1980), p. 6.

[9]This series of letters is placed first in the compilation known as the Mercy Warren Letter Book, suggesting that Warren, or whoever compiled it, considered this correspondence the most important of Warren's life.

Warren wrote an introduction for the 1791 American edition of Macaulay's pamphlet attacking Edmund Burke's *Reflections on the Revolution in France.*

[10]John Adams to Thomas Jefferson, 13 Dec. 1785, in Lester J. Cappon, ed., *The Adams-Jefferson Letters* (Chapel Hill: University of North Carolina Press for the Institute of Early American History and Culture at Williamsburg, 1959), p. 107.

[11][Mercy Otis Warren] *Observations on the New Constitution, and on the Federal and State Conventions, By a Columbian Patriot.* (Chicago: Quadrangle Books, 1962. Reprint of New York 1788 ed. Bound with [Richard Henry Lee?] *An Additional Number of Letters From the Federal Farmer to the Republican . . .),* 1.

[12][Warren], *Observations,* p. 7.

[13][Warren], *Observations,* p. 9.

[14][Warren], *Observations,* p. 19.

[15]Mercy Otis Warren, *History of the Rise, Progress, and Termination of the American Revolution. Interspersed with Biographical, Political and Moral Observations.* 3 vols. (Boston, 1805. Reprint: New York: AMS, 1970) 1: iv. Hereafter, MOW *History.*

[16]MOW *History* 1: iii.

[17]MOW *History* 1: i.

[18]MOW *History* 1: 1.

[19]MOW *History* 1: 1.

[20]MOW *History* 1: 2.

[21]MOW *History* 2: 247.

[22]MOW *History* 1: 85.

[23]MOW *History* 1: 79.

[24]MOW *History* 2: 37.

[25]See MOW *History* 1: 430, note 13.

[26]MOW *History* 3: 391.

[27]MOW *History* 3: 393.

[28]Mercy Otis Warren to John Adams, 27 Aug. 1807, in Charles F. Adams, ed., *Correspondence between John Adams and Mercy Warren, Collections of the Massachusetts Historical Society,* Vol. 4, 5th series, Boston, 1878. [Reprint ed.: New York: Arno Pres, 1972], p. 490.

[29]Warren left her copy of Catharine Macaulay's *Letters on Education* to this granddaughter, whom she hoped would see in her lifetime the implementation of the new kind of women's education Macaulay advocated.

PART III

The Flowering of Antebellum Culture

The year 1800 marked not only the opening of a new century but also the beginning of major transformations in women's lives. In the wake of the American Revolution, political leaders celebrated the crucial role mothers might play in the growth of the new nation. The importance of women's roles in the new nation was stressed by statesmen who wanted the "production of children" recognized as vital to national prosperity. Within the new regime, "republican mothers" were encouraged to rear "liberty-loving sons."

As a result, the initial impetus for the reform and improvement of women's education stemmed directly from women's roles as educators of their own children. Colonial parents welcomed the replacement of dame schools, which taught ornamental arts such as dancing and embroidery, with more rigorous academies to provide young women with "classic English educations." These new curriculums included geography, history, and other more intellectually demanding subjects. Though these changes were not intended specifically to enhance the opportunities available for women to improve their status, they did enrich the intellectual climate for daughters of the upper and middle classes. Many young women, afforded improved training, became educators themselves; they founded and taught in academies up and down the eastern seaboard.

A transition during this era that had an even more widespread and immediate effect upon women was the development of centralized manufacturing or the "Waltham system." This shift in the production of an enormous range of goods from the individual household to the factory dramatically sharpened the division of women's and men's spheres. Women were now identified more exclusively with the home or private domain, where their duties included maintenance of family stability, protection of traditional values, and advancement of children's welfare. The public or male sphere included all other realms outside the household, including politics, law and business. Within this new framework of separate spheres, "work" was assigned a new meaning. With the expansion of manufacturing outside the home, household production, the core of the agrarian colonial economy, declined in economic influence. As domestic labor in the household became "women's work," its status declined relative to wage-paying work in the public realm. Thus while in early nineteenth-century America, society accorded women an enhanced social status as the moral leaders and protectors of their families, their economic roles were accorded less value. This exchange was not satisfying to those women unfulfilled by their images as republican mothers. In the ferment of reform during the 1830s, '40s and '50s, many women forged new movements to reshape their image as moral leaders to their own advantage.

Though the factory system made firmer the ideology of republican motherhood and the division of men and women into separate spheres, economic necessity did draw a small but significant number of women out of the private domain and into the public world. As the West attracted legions of men, many of the young women left behind flocked to factories to supply the workforce for the textile industry. Yankee fathers welcomed their daughters' opportunities to earn wages, as most sent a portion of their income back to their families. Thousands of young women in New England and the middle-Atlantic states abandoned family farms and became "mill girls."

Women's lives in these factory towns were still governed by extreme paternalism. Factory owners required that women live in company-sponsored boarding houses, attend church regularly, and maintain a curfew. Moreover, both their fathers and their bosses expected that women would be wage earners for only a short time, until they married. This was the pattern during the first part of the century; however, by the 1830s, many women who saw their work in the factory as more than temporary began to organize to protect their interests. As late as 1850, despite the increase in immigrant workers and the fact that less than ten percent of American women earned wages outside the home, women were the majority of textile operators. Work as labor organizers gave women such as Harriet Hanson Robinson of the Lowell Cotton Mills their first experiences as reformers. Robinson and others raised public consciousness about women's roles and encouraged active participation in the women's rights movements and other reform campaigns.

The expansion of industrial markets may have drawn only a minority of women into production, but it had a dramatic effect on all women as consumers, and affected patterns of domesticity for all classes. Literacy and consumerism stimulated an explosion of magazines, advertising enterprises and, eventually, the invention of "domestic science." Although many of these enterprises would develop later in the century, the seeds for this revolution were sown during the pre-Civil War era.

Because of the popularity of academies, New England women like Maria Weston Chapman and her sisters, Anne, Deborah and Caroline, received the kind of intellectual foundation which allowed them to cultivate literary and reform pursuits. Many sought careers as teachers—Catharine Beecher promoted reform and women's education throughout her lifetime, and Chapman taught before marriage and her antislavery career. Education allowed women of all classes to expand their horizons.

In order to maintain the integrity and stability of their families, many women felt compelled to extend their concerns to the evils of the world outside the household, including drunkenness, licentiousness, and impiety. Through religious and reform institutions, women attacked those elements in the public sphere that provided a threat to the security of the family. Though such attempts might have undermined male authority, they were, as a logical consequence of female preoccupation with moral reform, an extension of concerns of the private sphere into the public domain. Evangelical Christianity and reform movements spurred many women into action—actions based on religious and moral principles, which could and often did lead women out of the home and into the wider world.

One of the most powerful movements of the era, antislavery, attracted thousands of women. Prominent in the abolitionist movement were the Grimké sisters, Sarah and Angelina, who abandoned their home in South Carolina to practice their faith as Quakers in a more receptive New England climate. The Grimkés joined a thriving network of women abolitionists, including Lucretia Mott, Abigail Kelley, and Lydia Maria Child. African-American members of the network such as Maria Stewart and Sarah Parker Remond formed separate societies for black women, as well as working within the larger movement.

Slavery took its toll on both men and women. However, the exploitation of female slaves was extraordinary. With the abolition of the external slave trade in 1807, the only way plantation owners could increase their slave labor force was by reproduction among the current slave population. The fertility rate for slave women exceeded that of white women, North and South which contributed to the phenomenal growth of the slave population. (This was at a time when the slave infant mortality rate has been calculated as high as 25 percent.) Many masters treated slaves as valuable stock to be bred and, perhaps, even sold for profit. Despite their reproductive values, female slaves were integrated into almost all aspects of agricultural production on the plantation. Pregnancy and nursing did not exempt women from work in the fields during hoeing and harvest. Then, after a hard day in the fields, women returned to slave cabins where they were expected to fulfill their domestic labors as wives and mothers.

It is testimony to the strength of these African-American women that crucial elements of their culture and values were preserved. Slave mothers instilled a sense of family pride and cultural tradition into children. Many preserved and passed on aspects of African culture (language, medicinal practices, rituals) despite the massive campaign of white slaveowners to indoctrinate slaves against their own cultural heritage. Not only did slave women resist their masters' intellectual coercion, many resisted the sexual harrassment, sexual coercion and rape exploitative masters practiced from the colonial period onward. Slave mothers could rarely gain protection or legal freedom for their children, but they struggled to impart to them a sense of self and heritage that might help sons and daughters escape the rigid confines slavery and racism attempted to impose. The efforts of slave mothers struck a chord with women abolitionists. Again and again, white abolitionist women posed their appeals on the common ground of motherhood and sisterhood, but bonds of common decency emerged.

Antislavery was but one of a whole range of charitable endeavors and reforms. Others included the improvement of living conditions of immigrants and the urban poor, fighting alcoholism (the Daughters of Temperance), opposing prostitution (Mary Magdalene societies), and ameliorating the conditions of convicts and the inmates of lunatic asylums. Margaret Fuller worked on behalf of female convicts at Rikers Island, New York. Dorothea Dix, the most famous reformer of conditions in asylums, began her career as a teacher in Boston. In 1841 she began ministering to the insane when she was asked to conduct Sunday school in a local prison and discovered felons and disturbed persons mixed together irrespective of age, sex, and mental capabilities. Through her campaign efforts, over thirty mental hospitals were established in over 15 different states. Despite her repeated bouts of bad health which included tuberculosis, she was a vigorous champion of the rights of those unable to fight for better conditions.

All of these reform activities could be made to square with women's "primary function" as a maternal nurturer, guardian of those who needed special care. At the same time, such involvements allowed women the opportunity for a more public life, for the explorations of new capacities (from politicking within organizations to fundraising) and, above all perhaps, for a new sense of group awareness.

Women armed with education and intellectual curiosity could and did launch other pioneering efforts for reform. Sarah Josepha Hale edited *Godey's Lady Book*, one of a score of successful magazines aimed at a burgeoning female readership. Designed to inform and entertain ladies, the antebellum literary magazine addressed a range of issues designed to inform and entertain ladies, including domestic and moral reform, hygiene, leisure and recreation, health, religion and most subjects except electoral politics. They linked a wide female readership to the efforts of a small vanguard of reformers. Another female entrepreneur, Lydia Pinkham, mass-marketed home remedies, notably her "Vegetable compound." She saw her work as contributing to health reform and addressed herself specifically to "female complaints" in a way that the new male medical specialists could not. The segregation of women into this "domestic sphere" resulted ironically in female captains of newly-created industries.

As women began to establish their own literary and critical voice, male critics began to carp at "scribbling women," as Nathaniel Hawthorne called the prolific female writers who were his contemporaries. Catharine Maria Sedgwick, Caroline Gilman, Lydia Maria Child, Caroline Hentz, Lydia Sigourney, and the most popular of them all, Emma D.E.N. Southworth (whose novels were issued in forty-two volumes in 1877), found fame by appealing to female audiences through a range of literary forms, most notably the novel. (Ironically, the most brilliant and talented woman writer of this generation did not even have an audience, as poet Emily Dickinson was a recluse who did not publish any of her verse during her lifetime—1830–1886.)

Most women writers imbued their work with themes of female sacrifice, maternal stoicism, and the three "p"s: purity, propriety and piety. Some pushed beyond the limits of the sentimental novel and incorporated powerful messages about domestic politics that celebrated women's capacities for sustaining family relationships. Tyrannical fathers and husbands were favorite targets for these novelists. Indeed, the "male sphere" was ridiculed in many novels as being a world bankrupt of enduring worth and abundant in greed and selfishness. Most familiar of all such books was *Uncle Tom's Cabin,* published in 1852 by Harriet Beecher Stowe, Catharine Beecher's sister. A work of abolitionist propaganda, the novel illuminated the hypocrisy of politicians and the evils of human bondage, especially in its heartwrenching descriptions of slavecatching. Stowe's novel branded slavery as a product of the ruthless greed honored in the male-dominated public sphere. Her audience and influence reached far beyond American women. The novel was widely read in Europe and heavily criticized by slaveowners in the South. Abraham Lincoln, referring to the Civil War and acknowledging the power and popularity of Stowe's attack on slavery addressed her during their meeting in 1863 as "the little lady who made this big war."

As early as the 1830s, many women transferred their influence beyond social and moral reforms to the growing movement in women's rights. Scottish immigrant Frances Wright, founder of a Utopian community in 1825 in Nashoba, Tennessee, moved to New York to co-edit *The Free Enquirer* with social reformer Robert Dale Owen in 1828. They advocated, among other changes, property rights for married women and the practice of birth control. They also contributed to the formation of the New York Workingmen's Party in 1829. Wright boldly involved herself in the world of male politics which women like Stowe addressed only indirectly. She was part of the early group of activists and writers of her day committed to women's rights. Women of the New York Female Reform Society established a respected forum for their views, *The Advocate,* in the 1830s. The journal attracted over 16,000 subscribers and continued well into the 1850s. Sarah Grimké published *The Equality of the Sexes* in 1838, one of the most important early works to call for women's legal rights. Margaret Fuller's *Woman in the Nineteenth Century* (1845) was another ground-breaking feminist work. These developments signalled the stimulation of a feminist sensibility which initiated a series of political conventions at mid-century, beginning at Seneca Falls, New York in 1848.

Many outstanding women during the first half of the nineteenth century battled for the cause of those less fortunate and in doing so articulated their own individuality. Many sought to increase their authority and independence beyond the confines of "woman's sphere" and the household, while others eventually challenged altogether the notion of separate spheres and pursued leadership positions in reform movements. Maria Weston Chapman and abolitionist women crusaded on behalf of slaves, especially women subjected to sexual exploitation and mothers deprived of their children. Catharine Beecher and her disciples sought to transform the lot of the isolated farmers' daughters scattered across the countryside. Margaret Fuller fought for autonomy on behalf of her sex. The energies of these pioneers contributed to enormous changes within American society as a whole and women's role within this dynamic era.

Maria Weston Chapman

(1806–1885)

Catherine Clinton

Born into an affluent Massachusetts family, Maria Weston Chapman was educated in local ladies' academies and in England before she became a school principal. After her marriage to Henry Grafton Chapman, a Boston merchant, she left her position to fulfill the role of wife and mother. Adopting the Chapman family's antislavery stance as her own, Maria Weston Chapman became an influential abolitionist in addition to rearing six children and serving as wife—and nurse—to her invalid husband until his death.

Allying herself with William Lloyd Garrison and his followers, Chapman organized the Boston Female Anti-Slavery Society in 1832 to complement Garrison's all-male New England Anti-Slavery Society. Although she was a forceful personality, she never developed a platform speaking style and was content to wield influence from behind the scenes or with her pen. Chapman spent over thirty years as organizer, fundraiser, and valued executive for several antislavery groups, and as writer and editor of various abolitionist journals. She was especially active during the split in the movement in 1839 that involved dissent concerning women's roles, among other issues, but her advocacy for women's equal participation was never extended beyond the antislavery movement to political feminism. With the end of slavery following the Civil War, Chapman retired from public life, devoting herself to her children and their business interests. She also focused her energies on writing, and produced a biography of Harriet Martineau, the famed English reformer and chronicler of American society, as well as her own autobiographical writing. Chapman died in Weymouth in 1885.

A wealth of letters and papers from Maria Weston Chapman to noted abolitionist William Lloyd Garrison and his followers attest to Chapman's invaluable contributions to the crusade against slavery. The abolitionists, like many other social and political reformers, had leaders who functioned exclusively within the organizational fold. Although this left them prey to historical neglect, their political impact was not diminished.[1] The platform personalities played a major role in antislavery leadership, but were by no means the sole parties determining abolitionist policy and productivity. Maria Weston Chapman was a member of the less visible but not less influential leadership who, as she herself put it, spent their time "in the trenches, filling up on the way for others to mount the break."[2]

Maria Weston Chapman was born July 25, 1806, in Weymouth, Massachusetts, the eldest of Warren and Anne Bates Weston's six children. She grew up on her parents' farm and attended local schools until her teens, when she was sent to England to live with a maternal uncle, Joshua Bates. Her years abroad acquainted Maria Weston with a highly cultivated circle of people concerned with political as well as cultural affairs. From them, she acquired a cosmopolitan polish and a taste for reform that shaped her future—she later credited this experience with starting her on her activist career. Upon her return to America, she maintained similar ties with political thinkers. When she returned to Massachusetts in 1828, she served as the first "lady principal" of Ebenezer Bailey's Young Ladies' High School in Boston, wanting more to her life than the traditional roles of wife and mother expected of her.

Within a year of her return to Boston, Maria Weston fell in love with Henry Grafton Chapman, a wealthy Brahmin merchant. Although little is known of their romance and courtship—no letters have survived from this early period—the two probably met through their common affiliation with William Ellery Channing's Unitarian Church. They were married on October 6, 1830. Maria Weston Chapman discontinued her work as principal to embark on what she believed at the time was an even more challenging career, abolition.

The Chapman family were abolitionist sympathizers; Henry himself was an ardent Garrisonian. By marrying into the Chapman family, Maria Weston became firmly ensconced within the Boston antislavery circle. She chose to become a follower of the outspoken Garrison instead of a disciple of Channing, whose Unitarian church advocated a conservative approach to abolition, because, as she wrote: "I have never been cured by a busy, battling controversial laborious lifetime of the very great imperfection of inability to wait patiently, even for greater satisfaction."[3] Her political zeal was further nurtured by her rebellious personal style: "It is we who are against the world. But then, . . . it is the only comfort of our lives—this being in the opposition."[4] Chapman saw her antislavery work as a "mission," believing herself neither saint not martyr, merely an instrument of God.

Chapman devoted herself to the antislavery cause with a religious fervor. Believing in the absolute existence of a right and wrong path, she felt antislavery was her only choice. She often described her mission in highly emotive terms ("our views are larger and our souls steadier than those of man"), yet her rhetoric of self-glorification was restrained for its day. When she was praised by a friend as a martyr to the cause, Chapman replied, "I can't say I have made any sacrifices. I have had my choice."[5] In another piece of correspondence Chapman answered the accusation that abolitionists were not the saints they pretended to be: "We deeply feel that the reformer ought to be perfect, but when would reform begin if it were to wait till there were perfect reformers?"[6]

Chapman was acutely aware of many of her imperfections as well as her contradictions. She was firm in her opposition to slavery and able to defend herself in public, but in private she suffered extreme anxiety about her shortcomings. Her doubts about her career plagued her throughout her life. In a letter to a friend, she listed her sins: "How heretical, harsh, fanatical, moon-struck, unsexed I am. I hate much."[7] The terms in which she expressed her doubts are as intriguing as her sense of guilt about her faults. The controversy that her career provoked in Chapman was reflected in her internal conflict. This dilemma proved an unending struggle for Chapman. The personal and political riddles of her role as a female activist mystified Chapman herself and continue to puzzle the social historian.

The issue of slavery divided the upper-classes north of the Mason-Dixon line during the antebellum era. In response, the abolitionists developed their own society and hierarchy within that society.[8] Chapman sensed no loss of status through her association with antislavery: "We were possessors of great social influence before we were abolitionists. Now let us use it—for we have never lost it."[9] Content to form their own social spheres, many aristocratic abolitionists considered any social ostracism a minor element in the scheme of their lives; this was certainly the case with Chapman.

Her abolitionist accomplishments were achieved in the context of a more traditional domestic life than most of her female colleagues. She was married, unlike Sallie Holley. She was a mother, unlike Lydia Maria Child. She did not limit her antislavery activity with the birth of her children, unlike Angelina Grimké Weld (who also drafted her sister Sarah as domestic companion during her confinement). Maria Weston Chapman's participation in the movement far outweighed her husband's abolitionist contribution, unlike Abby Kelley Foster's compared to her husband Stephen's. Managing a household, bearing four children and raising three (one daughter died in infancy) while nursing her consumptive husband (Henry contracted tuberculosis in 1834), Maria Weston Chapman created for herself one of the most productive careers of the movement.

On October 14, 1832, Chapman joined with several other women to form the Boston Female Anti-Slavery Society, an organization inspired by the formation of the all-male New England Anti-Slavery Society earlier in the year. Both groups rejected gradual emancipation and African colonization, measures endorsed by more conservative antislavery organizations, arguing for more immediate action through moral persuasion that slavery is wrong. The Boston women held weekly meetings, conducted prayer vigils, circulated antislavery petitions, and distributed Garrison's popular weekly journal, the *Liberator.* Their work expanded the antislavery realm incalculably.

In 1834 Chapman organized the first of what was to become an annual event, the antislavery fair. The first fair netted $1,000 through the sale of gift items and handcrafted goods contributed by sympathizers. Through the years "antislavery friends" throughout the country and abroad (principally England and France) shipped tons of material to Boston for the fairs. Maria Chapman tirelessly solicited monetary or material contributions for these antislavery fairs which became well attended and effective both as fundraisers and as propaganda. By the 1850s the annual profit averaged $4,000, providing funds desperately needed by the near-bankrupt antislavery operation. Thus, this activity cannot be dismissed as "mere" charity work; Chapman's ingenuity often saved the Garrisonians from financial ruin.

In 1835 Chapman assumed the first of what was to become a series of concurrently held antislavery leadership positions. She became corresponding secretary of the Boston Female Anti-Slavery Society, and in 1836 began writing its annual reports. During the twenty-seven years of her executive career (1835–1862), she displayed enviable stamina, serving fourteen terms on the business committee of the Massachusetts Anti-Slavery Society, thirteen years as a member of the American Anti-Slavery Society Executive Board, and throughout the 1830s and 1840s on the Central Committee of the Boston Female Anti-Slavery Society. In addition, Chapman continued to organize the annual bazaars.

In 1839 Chapman initiated a new antislavery fundraiser, the *Liberty Bell,* a collection of abolitionist writings. Her pet project, this gift book with a golden bell on the cover was conceived and edited by Chapman to raise desperately needed money. Chapman solicited contributions from antislavery sympathizers throughout the world: political writers Harriet Martineau (who was a close personal friend of Chapman's) and Alexis de Tocqueville, feminists Fredrika Bremer and Margaret Fuller, and poets Elizabeth Barrett Browning, Henry Wadsworth Longfellow, and James Russell Lowell. The collection of poetry and prose by "Friends of Freedom" was in great demand and continued in popularity until its final issue in 1858. The annual subscription revenue greatly augmented the abolitionist treasury. Chapman hardly wrote a letter to a literary personage without requesting some short article as a donation. Although it was but one of her many activities, she reminded a friend: "Don't forget the Bell, it is a trifle, but it does much good."[10] Not only did this volume net profit, but it promoted the message of abolitionism in a sugar-coated format.

Chapman, unlike most influential abolitionists, was unwilling to take to the public platform. In 1835 when a mob threatened violence during an interracial abolitionist meeting in Boston and the mayor ordered immediate dispersal, Chapman replied: "If this is the last bulwark of freedom, we may as well die here as anywhere." (At length, the group adjourned to the Chapman home.) This oft-quoted phrase is the only public remark with which Chapman has been associated. Although many of her female contemporaries—Angelina Grimké, Abby Kelley Foster, and Lucretia Mott, to name but a few—were known for their stirring abolitionist lectures, Chapman was not comfortable with public speaking. In private or on paper she was articulate and persuasive. She did not shy away from oration for reasons of propriety; in fact, Chapman openly attacked criticisms of "promiscuous audiences" and women lecturers. She simply suffered from a form of stage fright.

She did deliver one public speech, at the Women's Anti-Slavery Convention in Philadelphia in 1838. Her performance was widely acclaimed, and she was lauded as a dynamic speaker. Unfortunately for her speaking career, she suffered a complete breakdown on the train returning to Boston. Her husband's illness and the strains of an overactive schedule contributed to her collapse, but the breakdown apparently was triggered by the unnerving experience of speaking at the convention.[11] She was removed from the train and placed in a convalescent home in Stonington, Connecticut. During her hospitalization, friends and family alike feared she would never recover, so severe had been her mental collapse. Yet after a few months rest, Chapman emerged to resume her former activities with an increased commitment. She refused to reduce her work load after her return, nor would she elaborate on the causes of the breakdown or the reasons for recovery. She tried to erase this episode from her record through a regimen of strenuous antislavery activity. However, Chapman never again took the podium after her Philadelphia experience, instead confining herself to her primary talents as fundraiser, editor, and essayist.

Following her recovery from her breakdown, Chapman began to produce reform literature at a phenomenal rate. After launching the *Liberty Bell,* yet while continuing her executive and secretarial posts as well as managing the annual fairs, Chapman organized a pacifist group, the New England Non-Resistance Society with Garrison. (Non-resistance was tantamount to withdrawal from all institutions deemed to operate by way of force.) She became its corresponding secretary and assistant editor of its periodical, the *Non-Resistant,* from 1839 to 1842. Chapman next collected manuscripts and published an antislavery songbook in 1839 titled *Songs of the Free.* In 1840 she initiated and financed a new abolitionist paper in New York as an attempt to strengthen the American Anti-Slavery Society, which had undergone severe damage during an organizational split.

The new journal, the *National Anti-Slavery Standard,* had a shaky start with Nathanial P. Rogers as temporary editor and Chapman advising by post. Chapman had gained a working knowledge of journalism through her association with the *Liberator* and the *Non-Resistant.* When Garrison had been away on tour or during one of his frequent illnesses, Chapman had been drafted to compose editorials, solicit articles, rewrite copy, and even do layouts for the *Liberator.* In 1841 Lydia Maria Child became editor of the *Standard,* proceeding to fashion the weekly into a "family paper." This doubled the circulation of the *Standard,* but the Garrisonians were not pleased with Child's political moderation, as the *Standard* under her direction did not feature controversial abolitionist news and avoided inflammatory issues. The Boston radical clique withdrew their support. In 1843 David Child succeeded his wife as editor, but he, too, failed to reflect the political sensibilities of the sponsoring organizers, and in 1844 was replaced by an editorial board consisting of Edmund Quincy, Sydney Howard Gay, and Maria Weston Chapman.[12]

Chapman's involvement with the paper became all-consuming, for at this point in her career, her work was especially important to her. In 1841 she had accompanied her invalid husband to Haiti, a trip undertaken to benefit his waning health. While in the Caribbean she had not only continued her efforts for the Boston fair, but had worked for the Philanthropic Society of Porto Plate, a West Indian auxiliary of the American Anti-Slavery Society.[13] Upon his return to the United States, Henry Chapman's health failed rapidly and he died in 1842. Caroline Weston, Maria's sister, reported Henry's deathbed words to his wife: "I leave you to the Cause."[14] Rather than retire into a prolonged mourning, Maria Chapman took her husband's words to heart. She allowed only the responsibilities of rearing her children to temper her abandoning herself to abolitionism.

From 1844 to 1848 Chapman contributed a ceaseless stream of articles and advice to the *Standard's* New York headquarters. Her letters to Gay are full of suggestions for layout, subscription drives, and editorial policy. She wrote to a female abolitionist: "I am hard at work. What I do makes no show, and only I tell you that you may not feel deserted and alone .... I average five columns a week for the *Standard,* so the rest of the days to do writing to stir up people's minds about the fair."[15]

Under the direction of Gay, Chapman, and Quincy, the *Standard* declined in popularity, but Chapman reveled in the unpopularity, confiding to Gay:

> E. M. Davis pays us the highest possible compliment—quite takes away Garrison's crown—says the *Standard* is the most despised of any of the papers. If we had not passed the age of caring for honours it is enough to make us vain.[16]

At a low point, when Gay feared the *Standard* was failing to accomplish its propagandistic purpose because of declining subscriptions, Chapman counseled: "The existence of the *Standard* is a proof to the eyes of the nation that the highest morality does yet *live* in this nation. I do know that fact is torment enough for the satisfied."[17] She saw the abolitionist journals as essential to the cause.[18] The antislavery press was Chapman's foremost effort among her many concerns.

Even at a peak of her editorial reign, Chapman did not lessen her organizational efforts. She was a prime mover in the 1839 power coup within the Boston Female Anti-Slavery Society, during which Garrisonian forces ousted more moderate leadership. Throughout abolitionist infighting Chapman was a ferocious warrior, always involved in one debate or another. Most of her arguments, however, were published as anonymous editorials and she refrained from personalizations. Thus when asked to publish a rebuttal to an article by Harriet Beecher Stowe that Chapman composed for personal correspondence, Chapman refused:

> I would have nothing controversial rise between her and me at this juncture. You know how good I think controversy is at the right time that like somebody, I forget who, in Bunyan, I can "fight till the swordhilt cleaves to my hand as if they were one piece." I have no abstract dislike of controversy—quite the contrary.[19]

Chapman felt that personal exchanges should not be aired in public, urging abolitionists to present a united front. Of proslavery critics, she commented, "It is their policy to represent the abolitionists as broken up into parties. This is not the case. There are in our ranks diversities of opinion, but there are not divisions of hearts."[20]

Yet in her correspondence she lashed out at "diversities of opinion" that took their toll during the 1840s and 1850s. For instance, she bemoaned the actions of Gerrit Smith, "who has formally merged the Liberty Party in free soilism which is the natural form of imperfect devotedness and waning convictions."[21] Of James Buffam's defection, she is only a little more sympathetic: "*Who* leads the procession and *where* is it going—and what have they got in their pockets? Dear good Buffam! I pity him, I do. What is an honest man in the hands of knaves?"[22] Over the years she grew bitter about those who broke from the ranks, and about her own embattled position. In 1852 she lashed out indignantly:

> When you see a quarrel, it is not about words, but about base personal betrayal and treason to the cause and abandonment of its principles—all trying to conceal themselves under the cloak of love of the cause. Think how hard it must be to stand upright in such a current of iniquity as this and not swim with it.[23]

While she witnessed others drifting away from the "one true path," Chapman stood steadfast, pledging her unwavering support of Garrison: "It is my freedom to keep my faith unbroken."[24] Her unfailing assistance was a source of comfort to the much maligned *Liberator* editor. Garrison expressed his gratitude in a letter dated 1848: "We have a few suggestive creative, executive minds and such is yours in an eminent degree. . . . How immensely indebted I am to you for counsel, encouragement, commendation and support."[25]

Chapman, however, did not blindly follow Garrison through the years. She trusted him implicitly on matters of principle and philosophy, although she often found his methods "soft-hearted." In turn, Garrison never questioned Chapman's actions, recognizing that her motives were as he considered his own, above reproach. During the long years of their association Garrison constantly consulted Chapman on a variety of issues. (Due to their proximity, they rarely communicated by letter; thus, only a minimum of documentary evidence concerning their relationship exists.) One antislavery crusader held that Garrison was entirely ruled by Chapman.[26] Although an obvious overstatement, Chapman's influence should not be underestimated. Perhaps Garrison himself best summed up their relationship in a letter to her:

> How could the *Liberator* have been sustained . . . without your powerful cooperation? Where would have been the Boston Female Anti-Slavery Society? How could the Massachusetts and American Anti-Slavery Society have put forth such exertions, independently of your own! The National Bazaar—what does it not owe you! Your position and influence have been preeminently valuable.[27]

There was one instance in their long years of friendship when Chapman, impatient with what she felt to be Garrison's incompetence, took matters into her own hands. When Frederick Douglass was on a lecture tour of England, Chapman became convinced of his treachery to the cause. She confided to Harriet Beecher Stowe:

> We shall be obliged, I think (we the American Anti-Slavery Society, I mean) to withdraw our recommendation of Frederick Douglass in Great Britain as promptly as we gave it—since by means of it he is enabled to use money to tell falsehoods to raise more money to tell more falsehoods, all under the false pretense of serving a cause he has not the slightest interest in but as it serves his selfish purposes. He changes his politics and his tactics exactly like a base white man. And we have been, I fear, weak on account of his color.[28]

This tirade was brought about by Douglass's purchase of his freedom, against the express wishes—for tactical purposes—of the Boston antislavery clique.[29] Chapman drummed up opposition to Douglass among her colleagues. Her harassment of Douglass prompted him to warn Chapman in 1846: "If you wish to drive me from the Anti-Slavery Society, put me under overseership and the work is done. Set someone to watch me—for evil—and let them be so simple-minded as to inform me of the office and the last blow is struck."[30]

Although an "overseer" never materialized, Chapman launched a series of attacks upon Douglass in her private correspondence. Douglass's campaign to sell his autobiography and his neglect of his family for the sake of more "refined" companionship elicited severe criticism. Chapman wrote a confidante: "As for F. Douglass, he is like Harry Wind 'fighting for his own hand'—and he will always take the course that most promotes his own interest."[31]

The controversy centered on Douglass's independence from the Boston power base and was aggravated by his association with the "refined" Julia Griffiths, his white female assistant who returned with him to the United States following his British tour. In 1847 Douglass initiated and edited the *North Star,* an abolitionist paper based in Rochester, New York. While Garrison was content merely to scold Douglass for his "impulsiveness," the rest of the abolitionist community was livid. Chapman expressed herself in public with restraint, wishing Douglass well on his new endeavor for the cause, but in private she was enraged:

> The measure of his crimes is full. It is high time we took away his character. He *never had any* but what we gave him, we were all [unintelligible] into thinking he was capable of having one by his cunning artfulness. Our committee say—"what can one expect better of a slave" true—but it does not absolve us from the duty of exposing him—to my judgement.[32]

The Douglass episode demonstrates some of Chapman's "contradictions": self-righteousness, stubbornness, the power of her influence, and racist attitudes.[33] She felt it was *her* duty to expose Douglass (within the realm of the organization) for what she felt him to be and to drive him from the movement, even against Garrison's expressed wishes to the contrary. She accomplished this task with little regret.

In the midst of her career and at the height of her influence, Chapman chose to leave America. She believed her life had been transformed by her education abroad, and she was determined that her children should profit from a similar advantage. Colleagues were shocked at her apparent "abandonment of the cause" just at the time the Mexican War was fanning the flames of the debate over slavery. Chapman was convinced her trip to Europe would not eliminate but merely reduce her antislavery activity. With her three children and her sister Caroline, Chapman sailed in the summer of 1848. During her seven years abroad she tirelessly continued her campaign, raising enormous sums of money in London and Paris. Although Chapman left the annual bazaar in the able hands of her sisters Anne and Deborah, she fired off a continuous stream of postal directives to supervise their activities. The *Liberty Bell* continued under her editorship, and Chapman wrote articles for the antislavery press as a foreign correspondent.

Upon her return in 1855, she resumed her old executive duties, regaining her former power. As an example of renewed strength, in 1858 she singlehandedly forced discontinuance of the fairs. In Europe she had witnessed the success of antislavery salons—some of which she herself organized—galas staged for cultural edification rather than commercial sales. Patrons invited to attend the galas pledged donations to the cause. Chapman thought the bazaar had become an outmoded event, and wanted to replace it with an annual salon. The antislavery women of Boston who had worked for years with Chapman and her sisters were enraged, not only because of her cancellation of the fairs, but because of Chapman's callous dismissal of their objections. With minimal assistance, Chapman organized her "Subscription Anniversary" in an atmosphere of thinly veiled hostility. In spite of antagonism, the benefit netted a profit of $5,700—$1,200 more than the most lucrative of fairs. Chapman's critics were silenced. When there was money to be had for antislavery, Chapman exerted her iron will to gain it.

Her domineering manner provoked severe criticism from other sources as well. Fellow abolitionist John Greenleaf Whittier called her Garrison's "evil genius."[34] Branded the "Lady Macbeth" of the movement, Chapman's inflexible personality kept her from compromise on many matters. She argued it was a "necessity for walking right over a good many things and persons that have not sense of good feeling to do their best for good order."[35] Her willfulness was certainly a response to the requirements of leadership. It is significant to note that most of her enemies within the movement were men—her sex as much as her methods sparked many attacks upon her.

Her coolness gave her an aura of detachment that many abolitionists believed was a reflection of "aristocratic disdain." She was labeled a blueblood and a snob by some of her critics. Yet Chapman never expressed any of these characteristics in her correspondence; to the contrary, she believed that antislavery affiliation was a great and positive leveler.[36] Raised as an aristocrat and married into a Brahmin family, Chapman struggled to repress her inherent snobbery for the good of the cause. Her success in doing so was praised by colleague Abby Kelley Foster:

> So far as I have been able to learn the minds of the abolitionists, M. W. Chapman is the person to bear up our banner, boldly and gallantly, and at the same time with all due hum'ty to *all* persons whatever may have been their different degrees of progress, if they are sound at heart.[37]

In spite of Chapman's public endorsement of antislavery solidarity, a stance she believed was the most tactically advantageous to the cause, she privately advocated individualism. She wrote to a coworker: "I can never make myself responsible for any man's language, nor do I wish any man to be responsible for mine."[38] Her sense of independence often undermined the representative nature of the abolitionist movement. Her individualism was in direct conflict with her collectivist politics, a contradiction she failed to resolve throughout her career.

Chapman was an ardent critic of the government. The murder of abolitionist editor Elijah Lovejoy at the hands of a mob proved a catalytic experience for her and many other abolitionists, and after his death she declared: "There is no law for us."[39] Her political sensibilities hardened. In 1837, she wrote:

> I fear when I see the strength of slavery *here* [Boston] and how the institutions of the South are interwoven with our own free ones—not openly indeed, but like the roots of a giant tree, *beneath the soil*—I fear that abolition will be resisted by the South to her own destruction and by the North until the last possible day of grace.[40]

And in 1861, Chapman concluded: "Civil war . . . is not so bad as slavery."[41] Early in her political career she had rejected the Constitution as "a compact by which the South bound herself to the North on the condition that the North should guarantee the existence of slavery in perpetuity,"[42] in favor of the Declaration of Independence which she saw as "an expression of the abstract opinions of the framers of the Constitution."[43] To Chapman the political aims of the abolitionist movement were a "renovation" of the Constitution and a restoration of democratic principles. Although opposed to war on principle, she saw the conflict as irrepressible.[44] When the Civil War broke out, Chapman was hopeful for "the Cause."

By the surrender of the Confederacy five years later, Chapman was jubilant, confiding to Garrison: "I believe we are of the number (smaller than I had hoped) who can really rejoice with the slaves at the downfall of the system."[45] At the close of the war she retired from the abolitionist ranks, rationalizing:

> There is no need for me now—I mean in any strenuous absorbing sense—for I draw with the millions the stones of reconstruction though we were alone in the duty of demolition. . . . Quiet hard work now is better than anything else. I cannot be too glad that I had an experience of life, anterior to our anti-slavery life so that I did not get so bent to battle in the days when battle was *sina qua non*, that I am unable to fulfill the duties of victory.[46]

Chapman radically misjudged the power of the law and the South's commitment to Reconstruction. She mistakenly believed the emancipated slaves would be guaranteed equality through political necessity.[47]

By war's end, Chapman was weary of her activist career. Although her work had been freely chosen as a rewarding vocation, her letters amply document the strenuous aspects of a quarter century of abolitionism. She described her working conditions to a friend: "Any excuse, the haste in which I *always* write, surrounded by children getting their lessons, Board meeting in full sail, of laughing girls in full sail—young men singing and snapping their fingers at the universe and a stream of people passing through all the while."[48] Her schedule was no less hectic:

> I have been all summer driven hither and thither with matters pertaining to death and shall probably be all winter driven still more furiously by affairs of life. So that it seems to matter of life and death with me all the time. . . . [T]he Fair gets every instant of my life with the mortifying reflection that if I were only on a level with a cat and had nine lives, I could carry on the work with geometrically proportional results.[49]

Chapman having but one life, and although well spent on a worthy cause, was to reflect regretfully in 1866:

> My public work in life did not come to me as I should have planned for it to come. I should have given my earlier life to my children wholly, I suppose, if I had been laying a plan at the outset and have wrought for public good in later life. But it was not to be so.[50]

Like many mothers who worked outside the home, she would suffer guilt and anguish over the tension between family commitment and the demands of a career.

Following the war, Chapman spent several years in the New York home of her son, Henry, occupying herself with his business concerns before retiring permanently to Boston. In 1877 she edited a memorial edition of Harriet Martineau's autobiography. Chapman died in Weymouth in 1885 at age seventy-nine.

Maria Weston Chapman's abolitionism stemmed from her complex view of self and society. Her strong religious beliefs dictated for her a rigid path to "right" behavior. She believed her individual freedom was to do the greatest good for society and she pegged slavery as the ultimate evil. Just as her convictions led her to divide the world into good and evil, private and public, temporal and spiritual, so her sense of duality dictated masculine and feminine spheres. She believed men and women were identical in a spiritual realm—rendering their souls and intellects equal, yet Chapman maintained that the sexes were, by necessity, separate and distinct in a temporal realm.

Because she believed antislavery to be a matter of conscience, Chapman championed the equal participation of women in the movement:

> Women, whose efforts for the cause could not be hindered by men were more valuable auxiliaries than the men whose dignity forbade them to be fellow laborers with women.[51]

She even welcomed the opportunity for women to demonstrate their "God-given" talents, claiming "in situations of peril and difficulty, they [men] have looked for aid to women superior to themselves in ability."[52] Yet she never channeled her energies into any women's rights activity. She greeted Margaret Fuller's *Women in the Nineteenth Century* with tepid approval, praising the author's "general feeling that a woman's duties like a man's are to her country, her race and her religion: as well as to her personal ties and to her home."[53] Her conservative response to any feminist doctrine continued throughout her career. It is especially ironic that on the opening day of the first women's rights convention in Seneca Falls, New York, while one of her poems was being read to the delegates, Chapman sailed for Europe with her family. Despite her singlemindedness, her involvement with non-resistance demonstrated an interest in reform outside the antislavery umbrella. Her lack of enthusiasm for women's rights must be judged a disapproval of feminist organization rather than indifference to it.

Maria Weston Chapman, like many women of her generation and those of her milieu who followed, was not attracted to feminism. Feminists sought political equality, and Chapman would have none of it. Women who did not ally themselves with the women's rights movement have been properly termed "nonfeminist." But to leave the matter at that is to rob ourselves of clearer understanding of both the era and those women challenging established social roles.

Barbara Welter's work illuminates the popular alternative to political feminism in the antebellum era with the cult of domesticity.[54] Ann Douglas's sophisticated and provocative treatment of Victorian America sheds light on a concurrent if not overlapping phenomenon, the cult of sentimentality.[55] Another less prominent but nonetheless significant group of women developed what might be called a "cult of influence."[56]

This particular group drew its ideological tenets from a variety of texts ranging from Mary Astell's *Serious Proposal to the Ladies for Advancement of Their True and Greatest Interest* (1694) to Daniel Defoe's *Essay on Projects* (1698) and most significantly from the works of the "high priestess" of influence, Hannah More: *Essays on Various Subjects* (1777), *Sacred Dramas* (1782), *Estimate of the Religion and the Practical World* (1790), *Structures on the Modern System of Female Education* (1799).

Just as the intellectual origins of political feminism stemmed from European political thought, American domestic feminism also drew from British sources. The split between domestic and political feminism was as wide a gulf in the United States as it was in England. Kathryn Kish Sklar illustrates this dichotomy by contrasting the leadership styles of Angelina Grimké and Catharine Beecher in her biography of Beecher. An even more striking counterpoint is found by comparing Catharine Beecher and Margaret Fuller. These two women were essentially American counterparts of a pair of influential British activists, Hannah More and Mary Wollstonecraft. Whereas More and Beecher were both conservative theorists who spent their lives unmarried and committed to educating women and writing texts of domestic feminism, both Wollstonecraft and Fuller committed themselves to radical political causes, experimented with marriage and childbearing, and wrote major influential works of political feminism.

Much has been written about the colorful figures of Fuller and Wollstonecraft, who both suffered premature and tragic deaths. Beecher and More led less melodramatic lives, but had no less an impact on the culture. While the works of Fuller and Wollstonecraft enjoy notoriety and popularity during the twentieth century and Beecher and More suffer relative obscurity, the opposite was true in antebellum Anglo-America. Beecher, More, and other promoters of women's moral superiority and domestic priority triumphed during the middle of the ninteenth century. Their ideology of influence challenged and in a very real sense crippled political feminism. The cult of influence, built on a blue-stocking model, created an intellectual alternative to political feminism for the female elite.

These particular nonfeminists believed that although women were intellectually equal, if not morally superior to men, the world was divided into two spheres (the public and the private) as well as into two sexes. The female sex, being restricted to the private sphere, was in no way inferior to the male sex who occupied the public arena. The believers in the cult of influence wished to enlarge the female domain by redefining the domestic sphere.[57] Their employment of enlightenment theory and in many cases republican ideology[58] bolstered their arguments for a program of social redistribution of responsibility—without tampering with traditional authority. Yet their philosophy in no way endangered either sex segregation of social spheres or by extension, male domination in political and economic realms. Feminists, by contrast, presented a triple threat: they demanded equal political rights, an end to male domination in economic matters, and a fundamental restructuring of society.[59]

The concept of "influence," much like "virtue," has undergone considerable change since the eighteenth century. Influence was perhaps as crucial to social change in antebellum America as "media" is to cultural transformation in the present day. Women sought influence through education, through religion, and lastly, through reform. Their struggle for influence was essentially a bid for power, yet their challenge was for themselves as an elite minority, not for women as a whole. And these women failed to take into consideration that their gains of influence might result in influence's immediate social and political devaluation.

Maria Weston Chapman spent the most productive part of her adult life fighting for freedom, against slavery. Her struggle for influence generated a very real impact in her lifetime. Although she expressed explicitly feminist ideas with her support of female orators and her contempt for men who objected to women's participation in the antislavery movement, Chapman also endorsed separate (but equal) abolitionist societies for women and refused to join with female colleagues in their political organization for women's rights. She resisted the intellectual shift from fighting white's enslavement of blacks to battling men's domination over women. Her career as an activist was fraught with conflict. Whereas she was often attacked in antifeminist terms, as an "aggressive" and "domineering" woman, Chapman was unable to embrace feminism and deflect male criticism. She took derision personally, and to heart; her self-doubts created waves of emotional unrest. While she could function smoothly and effectively within the private realm of the antislavery circles, the instant she took a more public abolitionist role, such as orator, Chapman collapsed. She was not loathe to make her antislavery views public, as her politics were well known in print, but Chapman's conflict concerning woman's roles in society was perhaps the crucial factor in her breakdown. Although she recovered to resume an even more dynamic role in abolitionist activities, Chapman never again ventured into the public arena. Her experimental attempt at "mounting the break," rather than "filling in the trenches," was disastrous. She firmly settled on the principle of separate spheres for men and women, in both her personal and political philosophy.

Conflict, so much a part of the abolitionist struggle within and without, plagued Chapman's personal life as well as her career. She was committed to antislavery, indeed it was her husband's dying wish that she continue her abolitionist crusade. Yet motherhood proved an emotional and ideological stumbling block. In 1848 Chapman left the United States to further her children's education, in spite of her colleagues' scorn that she was "abandoning the Cause." Chapman countered that motherhood was necessarily her primary concern. In later years she expressed guilt over time not spent with her children during her antislavery career, and her "lament of the working mother" was quite moving. Indeed Chapman endorsed a woman's duty to her conscience, and the moral necessity of antislavery activity, yet when this abolitionism interfered with domestic and maternal roles, as it was bound to do on a long range if not daily basis, problems were inevitable. The conflict between nonfeminist principles and social activism produced a constant and critical dilemma for Maria Weston Chapman, a dilemma which remained unsolved throughout her lifetime, even though she managed to fulfill both her domestic and activist roles.

Maria Weston Chapman alone does not demand a more complex rendering of the feminist context. Many women of her generation—Catharine Beecher, Catharine Sedgwick, and Fanny Kemble to name but a few—constituted a discernible opposition to the women's rights movement yet maintained an important alternative to the anti-intellectualism of the majority of nonfeminists. These women merit more careful attention as they have too long been condemned to the lower historical depths of "minor figures." Chapman and many other women of her day made significant contributions within their context of femininity, outside the bounds of feminism, carving out for themselves creative and above all influential careers.

Notes

[1]There is no biography of Maria Weston Chapman. A majority of antislavery literature deals little if at all with the remarkable accomplishments of her career. The work of Alma Lutz (*Crusade for Freedom*) and William and Jane Pease (*Bound with Them in Chains*), and Blanche Hersch (*Slavery of Sex*) treat Chapman.

[2]Letter of Maria Weston Chapman (MWC), n.d., n.a., Gay Collection, Columbia University Library.

[3]MWC, March 1853, Weston Collection, Boston Public Library.

[4]MWC to Estlin, March 1852, Estlin Collection, Boston Public Library.

[5]MWC, n.d., 1855, Weston Collections, Boston Public Library.

[6]MWC, n.d., 1852, Boston Public Library.

[7]MWC, March, 1853, Weston Collection, Boston Public Library.

[8]MWC, 8 March, 1873, Jay Collection, Columbia University Library.

[9]MWC, n.d., 1855, Weston Collection, Boston Public Library.

[10]MWC, n.d., n.a., Weston Collection, Boston Public Library.

[11]The trauma of the burning of Independence Hall during the convention had an effect on Chapman's mental state, in addition to her public speaking ordeal.

[12]Much of what is known about Chapman's political views is to be found in the remains of her correspondence with coeditor Gay. Chapman had the utmost respect for her colleague, not only for his journalistic abilities, but

also for his abolitionist commitment. Gay went on to edit the *New York Tribune* during the Civil War years, where his antislavery sympathies made him an effective propagandist for the abolitionist crusade. Gay, like Chapman, suffers from historical neglect despite the significance of his contributions and the availability of manuscripts.

[13]In a January 1841 letter to Garrison, Chapman requested 1,000 extra copies of the *Liberator* for distribution.

[14]Caroline Weston, 23 Feburary, n.a., Harriet Beecher Stowe Collection, Schlesinger Library, Radcliffe College.

[15]MWC quoted in Alma Lutz, *Crusade for Freedom: Women of the Anti-Slavery Movement*, 1968, p. 201.

[16]MWC, 8 Septemeber 1845, Gay Collection, Columbia University Library.

[17]MWC, n.d., n.a., Gay Collection, Columbia University Library.

[18]MWC to Estlin, n.d., n.a., Estlin Collection, Boston Public Library.

[19]MWC, March 1853, Weston Collection, Boston Public Library.

[20]MWC, n.d., n.a., Weston Collection, Boston Public Library.

[21]MWC, September 1852, Weston Collection, Boston Public Library.

[22]MWC to William Lloyd Garrison, 4 August 1843, William Lloyd Garrison Collection, Boston Public Library.

[23]MWC to Estlin, n.d., 1852, Estlin Collection, Boston Public Library.

[24]MWC to WLG, 4 August 1843, William Lloyd Garrison Collection, Boston Collection, Boston Public Library.

[25]WLG to MWC, quoted in W. P. and F. J. Garrison, *William Lloyd Garrison*, New York, 1885–1889, 3, p. 229.

[26]Deborah Weston to Anne Weston, 16 April, n.a., Weston Collection, Boston Public Library.

[27]WLG to MWC quoted in W. P. and F. J. Garrison, *op. cit.*, p. 229.

[28]MWC to Harriet Beecher Stowe, 1845, Stowe Collection, Schlesinger Library, Radcliffe College.

[29]Chapman's reaction is particularly insensitive. In spite of his "interference" with the tactics of the Boston abolitionist clique, it is reprehensible for Chapman to accuse Douglass of not having the "slightest interest" in antislavery.

[30]Frederick Douglass to MWC, 29 March 1846, Weston Collection, Boston Public Library.

[31]MWC, n.d., n.a., Weston Collection, Boston Public Library.

[32]MWC, n.d., 1855, Weston Collection, Boston Public Library.

[33]Although much of her criticism of Douglass is tinged with racism, it is notable that Chapman consistently endorsed the campaign to allow racial intermarriage in Massachusetts and she gave her unfailing support to black abolitionist Charles Redmond.

[34]Whittier quoted in Alma Lutz, *Crusade for Freedom*, 1968, p. 191.

[35]MWC, 13 September, n.a., Weston Collection, Boston Public Library.

[36]MWC, n.d., 1852, Weston Collection, Boston Public Library.

[37]Foster quoted in William and Jane Pease, *Bound with Them in Chains: A Biographical History of the Anti-Slavery Movement*, 1972, p. 56.

[38]MWC, n.d., 1852, Weston Collection, Boston Public Library.

[39]MWC, n.d., 1837, Weston Collection, Boston Public Library.

[40]*Ibid.*

[41]MWC, n.d., 1861, Weston Collection, Boston Public Library.

[42]MWC, 10 December 1853, Weston Collection, Boston Public Library.

[43]MWC, n.d., n.a., Weston Collection, Boston Public Library.

[44]MWC to WLG, n.d., n.a., William Lloyd Garrison Collection, Boston Public Library.

[45]MWC to WLG, n.d., 1861, William Lloyd Garrison Collection, Boston Public Library.

[46]MWC to WLG, n.d., 1863, William Lloyd Garrison Collection, Boston Public Library.

[47]MWC, n.d., n.a., Weston Collection, Boston Public Library.

[48]MWC, 13 September n.a., Weston Collection, Boston Public Library.

[49]MWC to Sydney Howard Gay, 7 November 1847, Gay Collection, Columbia University Library.

[50]MWC, February 1866, Weston Collection, Boston Public Library.

[51]MWC, *Right and Wrong*, 1838, 1, p. 12.

[52]15 April 1848, *Liberator.*

[53]20 March 1845, *National Anti-Slavery Standard.*

[54]See Barbara Welter, *Dimity Convictions: The American Woman in the Ninteeenth Century*, 1976.

[55]See Ann Douglas, *The Feminization of American Culture*, 1977.

[56]These upper-class women sought access to intellectual circles, armed with classical educations and democratic ideologies. They were the American equivalent of the blue-stockings in England. Their challenge to male domination was cosmetic rather than fundamental, but nonetheless significant. These women proposed tokenism not unlike W. E. B. Dubois' "talented tenth" strategy to undermine white male establishment a century later.

[57]See Marlene Stein Wortman, "Domesticating the Nineteenth Century City," *Prospects: An Annual of American Cultural Studies*, Vol. 3, Fall 1977, pp. 531–72.

[58]Linda Kerber, "The Republican Mother: Women and the Enlightenment, An American Perspective," *American Quarterly*, Vol. 27, Summer, 1976.

[59]Not all feminists during the nineteenth century embodied the "triple threat." But those men and women who joined together under the banner of women's rights are my primary concern. Although each and every individual might not have supported radical reform and a movement by its organizational nature restricts itself to a limited program of demands, the actual binding together for feminism is a defining principle. Collective action both reflects and initiates consciousness while undermining domination.

Catharine Beecher

(1800–1878)

Kathryn Kish Sklar

Catharine Esther Beecher was born September 6, 1800, in East Hampton, Long Island, New York, the eldest of the eight children of Lyman and Roxanna Foote Beecher. Her father, a Congregational preacher, was a leader of the Second Great Awakening, the resurgence of religious revivals in the nineteenth century. Briefly attending Sarah Pierce's school in Litchfield, Connecticut, Beecher began teaching in New London in 1821. She challenged the harsher doctrines of her father's Calvinism in two publications: Letters on the Difficulties of Religion *(1836) and* Common Sense Applied to Religion *(1857). With her sister, Mary, Beecher founded the Hartford Female Seminary in 1823. In 1837 Beecher published* An Essay on Slavery and Abolition, with Reference to the Duty of American Females, *chastising noted abolitionist Angelina Grimké for leaving what Beecher called "her appropriate sphere" in order to speak publicly against slavery. Beecher believed women should only exert themselves within their domestic spheres. However, as the following portrait demonstrates, Beecher advocated a kind of "domestic feminism" within the home. Beecher believed that within the separate sphere of the household, middle-class women could assert their domestic authority by making responsible decisions, thus gaining control over immediate circumstances. Moreover, she claimed that women at home had vital social importance. On that basis, she worked for improvement in women's education. After 1837 Beecher traveled incessantly, lobbying, fundraising, and organizing for the training of women as teachers, especially in the West. She wrote many books devoted to the practical education of women, supplementing her extraordinarily influential* A Treatise on Domestic Economy for the Use of Young Ladies at Home and School *(1841). An ex-*

panded version of her Treatise, American Woman's Home *(1869) was written in collaboration with her sister, author Harriet Beecher Stowe. Catharine Beecher died in Elmira, New York, in 1878.*

Catharine Beecher was primarily known in her own time for *A Treatise on Domestic Economy,* first published in 1841. Considered historically significant today, the *Treatise* is also a document of importance in the history of nineteenth-century feminism. Printed at the dawn of a new era in American publishing, Catharine's *Treatise* was among the first books to be distributed by the modern methods established between 1830 and 1860.[1] Reprinted annually from 1841 to 1856,[2] the *Treatise* enjoyed its hegemony in American domestic affairs during the same years in which book marketing became more responsive to popular demand and feminism flowered into a political movement.

Initially printed by a small Boston firm that distributed most of its publications locally over its own counter, the *Treatise* was purchased immediately by Harper and Brothers, who distributed it through the new system whereby publishers abandoned their own retail efforts and specialized in supplying a network of booksellers with volumes on consignment. Bookstores sprang up whenever urban populations were forming during this period. They served the regional hinterland as well as their own communities. During the 1840s and 1850s, Catharine's *Treatise* was carried by trains and boats to established provincial centers such as Hartford and Albany, as well as to newer cities like Rochester and Buffalo, and through the Ohio Valley to Cincinnati, Louisville, and St. Louis, and across the northern Great Lakes route to Cleveland, Detroit, and Milwaukee.[3]

This new system printed larger editions, distributed them more widely, and made possible the development of specialized reading constituencies, the largest of which was middle class and female. Although no exact measurement has been taken of the proportion of books and magazines aimed at female readers during the mid-nineteenth century, these readers and the women authors who addressed them were a well established feature of the American literary landscape by 1840. More than one-third of the American novels published before 1820 were written by women and it is well known that women dominated the literary marketplace by mid-century.[4] The times were therefore propitious for female authorship, and Catharine was one of hundreds of women who found domestic writing a profitable enterprise.

The biographical context in which the *Treatise* was written was not, however, nearly so promising as the literary one. If one were to graph the contours of Catharine Beecher's career from the time she founded the Hartford Female Seminary in 1823 until her quasi-retirement in the late 1850s, . . . he would note that the *Treatise* was written during the career nadir that followed her emigration with her father, Lyman, to Cincinnati in 1832 and the career low that preceded her national prominence in women's education during the 1850s. The West was more an arena of struggle than achievement for the Beecher family in the 1830s, and Catharine's experience was no exception.[5] Determined to increase her sphere of influence from the local parameters she had known at Hartford, she founded the Western Female Institute in Cincinnati in 1833, but she saved her own energies for prospective work in the larger national arena and refused to direct the school herself. Yet with the exception of her 1835 speech to the American Lyceum in New York on *The Education of Female Teachers,* her efforts to reach a national audience proved futile. By the time her local school failed for lack of enrollment in 1837, Catharine's career was foundering without an economic base or a support constituency.

In the spring of 1838, therefore, it was not surprising that she turned to the female literary constituency that her sister, Harriet, had already begun to tap as a lucrative source of self-support. Writing her friend, Lydia Sigourney, Catharine asked advice as to what magazines she should write for. Her purpose, she said, was "to make myself known, and as popular as I can with all classes of readers. I need not tell you that this may be aimed at without any craving for fame or notoriety, but as one means of increasing the sphere of usefulness."[6]

Yet Catharine Beecher's forays into the literary arena and away from her field of education were less successful than Harriet's example had led her to hope, and during that year she earned only one-tenth what Harriet did—far from enough to relieve her financial dependence on Lyman and worlds away from the substantial income that had allowed her to rent her own house at Hartford a decade earlier.

In a mood of personal pessimism and professional disarray, Catharine consoled herself during 1839 with technical religious writings and with the belief that "good must be done for its own sake and not for any gain or profit that may come from it."[7] In that year and the next, during which she wrote *A Treatise on Domestic Economy,* Catharine came close to the role occupied by her aunt, Esther Beecher—that is, an unmarried female dependent who contributed her labor to the household in exchange for room and board. It was from this dead end in her career that Catharine produced the work establishing her national reputation and her historical significance.

Catharine's relative failure to support herself during these years must have made her admire all the more Harriet's ability to earn autonomous space for herself within her own household. This achievement was accomplished even though Harriet bore three children during her first two years of marriage. Harriet bore twins nine months after she married Calvin Stowe, and she was pregnant again a few months afterwards. Catharine described Harriet's plight to their sister, Mary Beecher Perkins, in 1837.

> Harriet has one baby put out for the winter, the other at home, and number three will be here the middle of January. Poor thing, she bears up wonderfully well, and I hope will live through this first tug of matrimonial warfare, and then she says she shall not have any more *children, she knows for certain* for one while. Though how she found this out I cannot say, but she seems quite confident about it.[8]

Harriet's "matrimonial warfare" was, it seems, only part of her effort to control the circumstances of her life as a married woman rather than be controlled by them. In a letter to Mary Dutton in 1838 Harriet described her new domestic regime.

> I have about three hours per day in writing, and if you see my name coming out everywhere you may be sure of one thing, that I *do it for the pay.* I have determined not to be a mere domestic slave without even the leisure to excel in my duties. I mean to have money enough to have my house kept in the best manner and yet to have time for reflection and that preparation for the education of my children which every mother needs. I have every prospect of succeeding in this plan.[9]

Harriet's determination "not to be a mere domestic slave" and her successful implementation of a systematic plan to avoid sinking to such a condition makes her the unsung heroine of Catharine's *Treatise.* For Catharine's book was written for women with Harriet's double view of the potential of the nineteenth-century domestic arena: that it could increase as well as decrease the autonomy women experienced within it.

Catharine's *Treatise* was a response to the circumstances in which mid-nineteenth-century middle class American women found themselves. The transfer of economic production from family-sized units to units of larger scale profoundly disrupted traditional patterns of domestic life. Children, whose labor had once been necessary to sustain the family economy, now served no such direct economic purpose. Native white fertility rates fell throughout the nineteenth century, reflecting the demographic transition from high birth and death rates to low birth and death rates that every industrializing European nation was experiencing during this time. Even as motherhood was praised as life's most desirable state, more women were experiencing fewer births than ever before, and the number of spinsters tripled.[10] With this long term decline in fertility came a more rapid decline in household-made goods. By 1860 the ease with which a woman could contribute to her family's support while raising children at the same time was considerably reduced compared to 1800 when much of the gross national product was produced in family units.[11] The dispersion of the traditional work of the household outward into specialized work arenas—whether in Lowell mills or in common schools—created new work for single women outside the home, but this shift cast the work status of married women within the home into doubt. Housewives were left with a collection of preindustrial tasks and skills seemingly disassociated from the modern world around them.

Catharine's response to this historical situation was to emphasize the modernity of women's domestic responsibilities. She treated motherhood and childbearing as the production of the new democracy's most valued commodity—the good citizen. She described the entirety of women's work within the household in industrial terms. She emphasized the need for women as individuals to exercise responsible decision-making power over the circumstances of their lives. Concerned throughout the *Treatise* with enhancing both the theoretical and practical value of women's work, Catharine's goal was to link the female work sphere in a positive way with the currents transforming it. As such, her book was an ideological as well as a practical achievement. The function of ideology, Clifford Geertz has written, is to "make an autonomous politics possible by providing the authoritative concepts that render it meaningful, the suasive images by means of which it can be sensibly grasped."[12]

Catharine Beecher's *Treatise* created an autonomous politics through the use of concepts and images related to democracy and to modern work forms. It will be seen that this politics, though based in the home and founded on motherhood, was both behaviorally and conceptually congenial to nineteenth-century feminism because it promoted autonomous or self-motivated behavior. Catharine analyzed the domestic arena so as to make clear its internal constraints and its social resources, creating a vocabulary and a methodology by which nineteeth-century women could assess their needs and assert their interests.

No concept was more central to the *Treatise* than that of democracy. The first chapter, entitled "The Peculiar Responsibilities of American Women," was a paean to the potential of democratic individualism—with a warning that only women could make it work.

> The success of democratic institutions, as is conceded by all, depends upon the intellectual and moral character of the mass of the people. If they are intelligent and virtuous, democracy is a blessing; but if they are ignorant and wicked, it is only a curse. . . . It is equally conceded, that the formation of the moral and intellectual character of the young is committed mainly to the female hand.[13]

Describing traditional female responsibilities as political or social responsibilities, Catharine depicted women as an elite[14] who had special access to moral resources because they themselves were engaged in the production of a valuable resource—namely, the "character of the mass of the people."

Her book was an effort to give women a sense of their social mission and to describe appropriate means for carrying it out. Women needed a proper sense of mission, Catharine believed, in order to perform their work successfully.

> The mind is so made, as to be elevated and cheered by a sense of far-reaching influence and usefulness. A woman, who feels that she is a cipher, and that it makes little difference how she performs her duties, has far less to sustain and invigorate her, than one, who truly estimates the importance of her station.[15]

The dramatic tension of Catharine's *Treatise* arose from the contrast she drew between the importance of work "committed mainly to the female hand" and the lack of resources available to most women for the successful performance of their work. The value and effectiveness of women's lives were seriously undermined, Catharine said, because, unlike men, women received no specialized training for their work. Such training was needed, she implied, because the modern world confronted women with experience incongruent with traditional patterns of behavior and belief. What once seemed inevitable now was problematic. As Catharine wrote: "Many a reflecting young woman is looking to her future prospects, with very different feelings and hopes from those which Providence designed."[16] She dramatized the distance modern society had placed between biological design and actual experience with vivid personal testimony.

> The writer has repeatedly heard mothers say, that they had wept tears of bitterness over their infant daughters, at the thought of the sufferings which they were destined to undergo; while they cherished the decided wish, that these daughters should never marry.[17]

Catharine's answer to these grave circumstances was to advise women to approach the female life cycle as a work cycle and prepare for it as a man would prepare for a vocation. She urged her readers to "systematize" as much of domestic life as possible and gain control of their lives by gaining control of their work. To begin a system, she suggested that her readers compose a list of all their "religious, intellectual, social, and domestic" duties[18] and use time as the basic standard by which they measured their priorities.

> Let a calculation be made, whether there be time enough, in the day or the week, for all these duties. If there be not, let the least important be sticken from the list, as not being duties, and which must be omitted.[19]

This assessment of female responsibilities was a long way from traditional prescriptions. It was pragmatic rather than dogmatic, time-oriented rather than task-oriented. Above all, it was individuated and designed to enhance autonomous female decision-making in the domestic arena. For Catharine Beecher the most important fact in a woman's life was not whether she was moral or pious but whether she controlled her life circumstances or they controlled her. This distinction was basic to her *Treatise*.

> Without attempting any such systematic employment of time, and carrying it out, so far as they can control circumstances, most women are rather driven along, by the daily occurrences of life, so that, instead of being the intelligent regulators of their own time, they are the mere sport of circumstances. There is nothing, which so distinctly marks the difference between weak and strong minds, as the fact, whether they control circumstances, or circumstances control them.[20]

Not passive submission to their biological identity, nor fetching dependency on their husbands, but active control of their immediate life circumstances was the model Catharine held out to her readers.

Catharine collected the data for her *Treatise* from the extensive travels that replaced her steady employment during the 1830s. Traveling for her health, for pleasure, and for the cause of education, she routinely inquired about local household practices. The breadth of her inquiry and her sharp eye for detail were recorded by Edward King when she visited his family in Chillicothe in 1835. "She asked more questions than one could answer in a day," King wrote to his daughter.

> Why the fields were so square! Why there were not better houses! Why the current ran where it did! Whose property was this and that! She asked innumerable questions about the house, how long it had

> been built, why the walls were so thick, when everybody slept, why Lizzy slept in that room, whether mother managed her farm, whether she gave orders to the men, whether labor was difficult to procure, what was the price of help, why this fence was built and that.[21]

Catharine incorporated the conclusions drawn from such inquiries into thirty-seven chapters of about eleven pages each. Each chapter was laced with examples of real life experience, making her book more intimate and immediate than it would otherwise have been and providing behavioral evidence to show that her ideas were workable. Four of her chapters were devoted to theoretical considerations of women's work. Seven major chapters were devoted to health, five to interpersonal topics such as "On Preservation of a Good Temper in a Housekeeper," and four to explicitly economic considerations such as that "On Habits of System and Order." Only three were devoted to the care of the dependent young and the ill. Nearly half the book, seventeen chapters, was devoted to house construction, furnishing, and grounds, together with specific receipts and designs. Whatever the topic, "systematization" was the answer and wherever true system was employed, autonomous female responsibility was expanded.

In her chapter "On Economy of Time and Expenses," for example, after establishing the general principle that "care be taken to know the amount of income and of current expenses, so that the proper relative proportion be preserved,"[22] Catharine acknowledged that many women could not balance income with expenditures because their husbands were "business-men" who had trouble predicting their incomes, or because the expenses of the family were "more under the control of the man than of the woman."[23] Asserting, nevertheless, that "every woman is bound to do as much as is in her power, to accomplish a systematic mode of expenditure, and the regulation of it by Christian principles,"[24] Catharine related several anecdotes drawn from real life showing how women could effectively control their household finances.

> [One woman] whose husband is engaged in a business, which he thinks makes it impossible for him to know what his yearly income will be, took this method. She kept an account of all her disbursements, for one year. This she submitted to her husband, and obtained his consent, that the same sum should be under her control, the coming year, for similar purposes, with the understanding, that she might modify future apportionments, in any way her judgement and conscience might approve.[25]

In this case, as in others throughout the *Treatise*, Catharine used real life experience to show that true systematization and the assertion of female control went hand in hand.

In keeping with her view of domestic life as an arena of work and responsibility for women, Catharine persistently discredited unproductive leisure. Women should "subtract from [their] domestic employments, all the time, given to pursuits which are of no use, except as they gratify a taste for ornament,"[26] she wrote. Intellectual improvement, benevolent activity, and religious reflection all had a place within Catharine's work system, but unproductive leisured activities such as "dressing, visiting, evening parties, and stimulating amusements"[27] came in for severe criticism as unhealthy, selfish, and ultimately degrading. When women of the wealthier classes "are called to the responsibilities and trials of domestic life, their constitution fails, and their whole existence is rendered a burden,"[28] Catharine wrote. She attributed this widespread malaise to insufficient familiarity with manual labor. Modern attitudes no longer held labor to be "the badge of a lower class,"[29] Catharine said, and she recommended that mothers of all classes "make it their first aim to secure a strong and healthful constitution for their daughters, by active domestic employments."[30]

Discrediting the unproductive use of the leisure that middle class women increasingly found at their disposal, Catharine also discouraged its traditional corollary: the employment of domestic servants. "Awkward," "ignorant," and "careless" were her typical characterizations of hired domestic labor, although she encouraged her readers to pay their servants a living wage and to sympathize with their life circumstances.[31]

Treating the domestic sphere as a specialized segment of modern society, Catharine rejected the notion that women were naturally equipped to perform their complex duties. Skills and training were as necessary for them as for men. To meet this need she advocated the creation of endowed institutions of learning for women, and she urged her readers to support this cause.

> Are not the most responsible of all duties committed to the charge of woman? Is it not her profession to take care of mind, body, and soul? and that, too, at the most critical of all periods of existence? And is it not as much a matter of public concern, that she should be properly qualified for her duties, as that ministers, lawyers, and physicians, should be prepared for theirs? And is it not as important, to endow institutions which shall make a superior education accessible to all classes,—for females, as for the other sex?[32]

Called by their society to serve others, Catharine concluded that women were first required to serve themselves through education—specifically through an education in the basics of independent decision-making. Since their duties as mothers and housekeepers required them to exercise "quickness of perception, steadiness of purpose, regularity of system, and perseverence in action," Catharine urged that women be trained in "the formation of habits of investigation, of correct reasoning, of persevering attention, of regular system, of accurate analysis, and of vigorous mental action."[33] Catharine's call for a superior education for females of all classes was the keystone to her domestic politics. Because women's work was equal in value to men's, women had a right to equal access to the educational resources of their society. Catharine's fullest statement of her domestic politics came thirty years after her *Treatise*, but it deserves full quotation here as an extension of the ideas contained in the *Treatise*.

> We agree . . . that women's happiness and usefulness are equal in value to those of man's, and, consequently, that, she has a right to equal advantages for securing them. We agree also that woman, even in our own age and country, has never been allowed such equal advantages, and that multiplied wrongs and suffering have resulted from this injustice. Finally, we agree that it is the right and the duty of every woman to employ the power of organization and agitation, in order to gain those advantages which are given to the one sex, and unjustly withheld from the other.[34]

Although based on motherhood and located in the home, Catharine's domestic politics was designed to consolidate rather than erode the links between women and their society.

Catharine's politics did more than idealize the value of women's domestic responsibilities—it identified them as socially-derived, hence meriting commensurate social reward. The popularity of her *Treatise* has long been thought to lie in the fact that in it her readers found a formula for understanding their social context as well as their personal responsibilities, but the modern cast she gave to female responsibilities has not been fully appreciated for the modern potential it gave to female social participation. The importance of the close link Catharine established between female responsibilities and adequate means of carrying out these responsibilities can be seen in an anthropological essay written by William Graham Sumner in 1909.

> In all societies usages which were devised to cherish and pet women become restraints on their liberty and independence, for when they

are treated as unequal to the risks and tasks of life by men who take care of them, the next stage is that men treat them as inferior and contemptible and will not grant them dignity and respect. When they escape responsibility they lose liberty.[35]

For Catharine Beecher the definition of women's responsibilities led directly to an assertion of their "right to equal advantages." For her women were not passive bystanders, imprisoned in their biology, but social actors capable of independently assessing their own responsibilities and asserting their own rights.

What overall sense can be made of the domestic politics of Catharine's *Treatise* both with the development of her own thought and the development of nineteenth-century feminism? Within her own thought the *Treatise* constituted a dramatic break with the evangelical tradition that had informed her earlier writings on women. In *An Essay on Slavery and Abolitionism* (1837) she had argued against Angelina and Sarah Grimké's example of female activism by invoking divine law and its immutable deference to male authority.

> It is the grand feature of the Divine economy, that there should be different stations of superiority and subordination, and it is impossible to annihilate this beneficent and immutable law . . . Heaven has appointed to one sex the superior, and to the other the subordinate station.[36]

Yet in her own life Catharine had found this "Divine economy" more restraining than liberating, and in her next breath she added an important loophole to it.

> While woman holds a subordinate relation in society to the other sex, it is not because it was designed that her duties or her influence should be any the less important, or all-pervading.[37]

Sometime between 1837 and 1841, Catharine read Alexis de Tocqueville's *Democracy in America* and found there the principle that could extricate her from the confusion of a divinely decreed sexual hierarchy. In Tocqueville she found an alternative and more functional explanation for gender distinctions. She quoted him in her *Treatise.*

> Americans have applied to the sexes the great principle of political economy, which governs the manufactories of our age, by carefully dividing the duties of man from those of woman, in order that the great work of society may be the better carried on.[38]

In his study, *The Division of Labor in Society,* Emile Durkheim said that the modern era had one categorical imperative: "*Make yourself usefully fulfill a determinate function.*"[39] Obeying this modern imperative in her *Treatise*, Catharine escaped the strictures of perennial female inferiority and thereby moved from the margin to the mainstream of nineteenth-century feminism.

She published other volumes on domestic life, including her *Letters to the People on Health and Happiness* (1855) and her *American Woman's Home* (1869), essentially an expansion of the *Treatise* but with Harriet as co-author. Neither of these books was reprinted for more than two years, whereas the *Treatise* was reissued annually for a decade and a half. The proceeds from its sale supported the second phase of Catharine's career during which she founded and directed the American Woman's Educational Association and nurtured the growth of educational institutions for women throughout the East and West. She traveled widely during the 1840s and 1850s, and from Boston to Burlington, Iowa, she was welcomed, in the words of the *Iowa State Gazette* in 1848, as one "whose name has long since become a household divinity."[40]

Catharine's reputation as a domestic commentator smoothed her path as an educator, but the last year that the *Treatise* was reprinted was also her last year of active work in behalf of women's education. In 1857 she returned once again to religious writings, seeking to clarify further her place in the Beecher theological pantheon.

It makes a certain amount of sense that American women in the antebellum period should have taken their domestic directives from a woman not herself embroiled in the day-to-day reality of family life. Her view from the sidelines gave her greater perspective on the historical forces transforming the family and, thus, on the effect of those transformations on women. Catharine's contribution to these transformations was to idealize not the ascriptive qualities of submission, delicacy, and weakness that had been attributed to women by those, who in Sumner's words, wished "to cherish and pet" them but to idealize the achieved qualities of "correct reasoning," "accurate analysis," and "vigorous mental action"—exactly those qualities she herself exercised as a single woman seeking to support herself.

A considerable amount of excellent scholarship has recently been devoted to nineteenth-century feminism, and its findings uphold Aileen Kraditor's 1968 definition of feminism as essentially the assertion of female autonomy.

> What the feminists have wanted has added up to something more fundamental than any specific set of rights or the sum total of all the rights men have had. This fundamental something can perhaps be designated by the term "autonomy." Whether a feminist's demand has been for all the rights men have had, or for some but not all the rights men have had, or for some men have *not* had, the grievance

> behind the demand has always seemed to be that women have been regarded not as people but as female relatives of people.[41]

The basic message of Catharine Beecher's *Treatise* is that women should regard themselves as people as well as "female relatives of people"—as people who try to assert autonomous control over their immediate life circumstances and act as self-motivating individuals.

A hypothesis about nineteenth-century feminism may account for the autonomous politics seen in Catharine Beecher's *Treatise.* This hypothesis proposes that nineteenth-century feminism continues along a spectrum called the assertion of female autonomy. This spectrum begins with the assertion of female sexual autonomy and ends with the assertion of female civil autonomy. In between there is room for a wide variety of feminist expressions, one of which might be called the assertion of female domestic autonomy. Harriet Beecher Stowe, Catharine Beecher, and Isabella Beecher Hooker[42] seem to exemplify three variations of feminist expression. The hypothesis further proposes that these three merge into and grow out of one another, that they constitute a continuum rather than divergent paths.

To test this hypothesis one must return to the letter that Catharine wrote to Mary about Harriet in 1838. There Harriet vowed "not [to] have any more *children, . . . for certain* for one while." How general was such a vow among Harriet's contemporaries and, thus, among the readers of Catharine's *Treatise*? How was such a vow implemented? It is by pursuing these questions that one can see even more clearly why Catharine's *Treatise* deserves a place in the history of nineteenth-century feminism.

Although Catharine expressed surprise at Harriet's vow and pretended ignorance as to the means Harriet might use in implementing it, recent studies, particularly Daniel Scott Smith's 1972 article, "Family Limitation, Sexual Control, and Domestic Feminism in Victorian America," have shown that nineteenth-century sexual ideas facilitated the female control of family planning that Harriet's remarks implied.[43] Caught in the grips of the demographic transition from high birth and death rates to low birth and death rates, Victorian society valued the control and limitations of sexuality and, seeing women as the best representatives of such a policy, gave them considerable social and ideological support for asserting control over their own bodies and limiting their husband's traditional right of sexual access. Elizabeth Cady Stanton and other suffragists attacked the legal base of this traditional right, but most women, like Harriet Beecher Stowe, fought this battle in the domestic rather than the public arena. The sexual ideas that accompanied the nineteenth-century fertility decline meant that the biological imperatives of the past were broken in a climate that encouraged the exercise of female sexual autonomy. Thus behavior and ideology conspired to promote an arena of female autonomy that did not previously exist. From 1830 and 1880 the number of children under five years of age per one thousand women of childbearing age declined by a third.[44] Adopting Smith's hypothesis that "the wife significantly controlled family planning in the 19th century,"[45] one can conclude that Harriet's vow of 1838 was typical of a large number of her contemporaries.

The way Harriet implemented this vow was also typical. Quantitative studies have shown that the American fertility decline, like fertility decline elsewhere, was achieved by two means: first, by longer intervals between births during the early and middle childbearing years; and second, by a dramatic reduction of births in the late childbearing years.[46] Harriet's experience followed this pattern. While she bore three children during the first two years of her marriage, she bore only two during the next five years and then maintained a six-year interval between the birth of her fifth and sixth children. Roxana Beecher, in contrast to her daughter, did not exhibit such fertility control and bore children regularly every other year until her death in 1816 at the age of forty-one. Thus Harriet, like most nineteeth-century women did effectively limit her fertility, and with increasing maturity, she became increasingly successful at it.

Such a resolve did not inevitably lead Harriet or her contemporaries into gradually greater personal autonomy but, frequently, to its contrary—invalidism. Since the only reliable contraceptive techniques—coitus interruptus and abstinence—involved direct intervention with sexual behavior and, thus, the overt exercise of personal choice, such methods overtly violated the traditional and still strongly held belief that family limitation was ungodly and unnatural. By adopting invalidism rather than autonomy as a strategy for managing the dilemmas posed by the nineteenth-century female life cycle, women could justify their desire for sexual abstinence without seeming to have made a personal choice in the matter. Harriet adopted this strategy when she spent months at a time away from her husband, Calvin, at the Brattleboro Water Cure in the mid-1840s.

In her *Treatise* Catharine addressed the strategy of invalidism as though it were her primary behavioral and ideological opponent. Her volume was filled with the personal testimony of those whose constitutions failed when they were "called to the responsibilities and trials of domestic life," and whose whole lives were subsequently rendered a burden to themselves and their families. She acknowledged invalidism as a characteristic shared to some extent by almost all middle class women.

> A perfectly healthy woman, especially a perfectly healthy mother is so unfrequent in some of the wealthier classes, that those who are so may be regarded as the exceptions, and not as the general rule.[47]

Although she did not hint at the conscious or self-motivated origin of this general ill health, demographic evidence does show that native born women were growing more healthy rather than less healthy during the nineteenth century. The percentage of women who had children but died before the age of fifty-five decreased from twelve percent in 1830 to eight percent in 1880.[48] Although this topic has not been studied systematically, it does seem as though this slight decrease in female mortality during and after the childbearing years of the life cycle was the result of the sharp decrease in contemporary fertility rates, which fell by a third from 1830 to 1880. For many nineteenth-century women, therefore, invalidism may paradoxically have been a means by which they lived longer lives and enjoyed good health. An unwell woman was a sexually abstemious woman.

Catharine addressed women who pursued this strategy sympathetically but firmly. Not challenging the traditional premise on which invalidism was based—that the female constitution was by nature weak and flawed—she, nevertheless, urged her readers to see their health as susceptible to the same kind of control they could exercise over other aspects of their domestic life. Complete with anatomical drawings, the *Treatise* presented a full discussion of most of the body's physiological processes.

> There is no really efficacious mode of preparing a woman to take a *rational* care of the health of a family, except by communicating that knowledge, in regard to the construction of the body, and the laws of health, which is the basis of the medical profession.[49]

Her many chapters on health urged women to discard fashionable practices that contributed to their enfeeblement—tightly laced corsets and the lack of physical exercise. She urged women to choose health, to choose to exercise personal choice in their lives, and to move from forms of dependency to forms of self-assertion as a life strategy. For women posed with the choice between continued dependency through invalidism or overt assertion of their decision-making power over their own lives, the *Treatise* offered a total strategy for autonomous growth, a behavioral blueprint and ideological support for their self-determination in the domestic arena. This is the importance of her *Treatise,* and this is the reason it belongs on the scale of nineteenth-century feminism somewhere in between the assertion of sexual autonomy and the assertion of civil autonomy.

Harriet Beecher Stowe, Catharine Beecher, and Isabella Beecher Hooker all sought in various ways to enlarge the arena in which they acted as self-determining agents. Each of these daughters of Lyman Beecher also explored themes in her own writing relating to domestic life and female influence. Anne Farnam has shown how Isabella moved from the assertion of domestic autonomy to the assertion of civil autonomy.[50] Catharine Beecher aided nineteenth-century women toward autonomous personal growth. Her version of domesticity can be seen as congruent with, not in opposition to, the basic thrust of nineteenth-century feminism.

Notes

[1]W. S. Tryon, "Book Distribution in Mid-Nineteenth Century America," *Papers of the Bibliographic Society of America*, Vol. 41 (3rd Quarter, 1947), pp. 210–230.

[2]For a full discussion of the printing history of *A Treatise on Domestic Economy* see Kathryn Kish Sklar, *Catharine Beecher: A Study in American Domesticity* (New Haven: Yale University Press, 1973), p. 305.

[3]"Book Distribution," p. 219.

[4]For the best discussion of the domestic novel and female authors see Herbert Ross Brown, *The Sentimental Novel in America, 1789–1860* (Durham: Duke University Press, 1940), pp. 281–322. See also Carl Bode, *The Anatomy of American Popular Culture, 1840–1861* (Berkeley: University of California Press, 1959), pp. 169–188.

[5]For a discussion of Catharine Beecher's experience in Cincinnati in the 1830s see *Catharine Beecher*, pp. 107–150.

[6]Letter, Catharine Beecher to Lydia Huntley Sigourney, 1838 April 24, The Connecticut Historical Society, Hartford.

[7]Letter, Catharine Beecher to Mary Dutton, 1839 February 13, Mary Dutton—Beecher Letters, Yale University, New Haven.

[8]Letter, Catharine Beecher to Mary Beecher Perkins, 1837 Fall, Beecher—Stowe Collection, Radcliffe College, Cambridge.

[9]Letter, Harriet Beecher Stowe to Mary Dutton, 1838 December 13, Mary Dutton–Beecher Letters, Yale University, New Haven.

[10]Wilson H. Grabill, Clyde V. Kiser, and Pascal K. Whelpton, "A Long View," *The American Family in Social-Historical Perspective*, ed. Michael Gordon (New York: St. Martin's Press, 1937), pp. 374–396, especially p. 387.

[11]Rolla M. Tryon, *Household Manufacturers in the United States, 1640–1860: A Study in Industrial History* (Chicago: University of Chicago Press, 1917), pp. 242–303.

[12]Clifford Geertz, "Ideology as a Cultural System," *Ideology and Its Discontents*, ed. David Apter (New York: Free Press of Glencoe, 1964), p. 63. For a discussion of autonomous politics see pp. 47–75.

[13]Catharine Beecher, *A Treatise on Domestic Economy*, rev. ed. (Boston: Thomas H. Webb & Co., 1842), pp. 36–37.

[14]For a discussion of strategic elites see Suzanne Keller, *Beyond the Ruling Class: Strategic Elites in Modern Society* (New York: Random House, 1963), pp. 30–38, 134–145.

[15]*Treatise*, pp. 150–151.

[16]*Treatise*, p. 43.

[17]*Treatise*, pp. 42–43.

[18]*Treatise*, pp. 157–158.

[19]*Treatise*, p. 166.

[20]*Treatise*, p. 160.

[21]Letter, Edward King to Sarah King, 1834 December 24, King Family Papers, Cincinnati Historical Society, Cincinnati.

[22]*Treatise*, p. 186.

[23]*Treatise*, p. 186.

[24]*Treatise*, p. 186.

[25]*Treatise*, p. 187.

[26]*Treatise*, p. 161.

[27]*Treatise*, p. 45.

[28]*Treatise*, p. 42.

[29]*Treatise*, p. 147.

[30]*Treatise*, p. 50.

[31]*Treatise*, pp. 204–208.

[32]*Treatise*, p. 52.

[33]*Treatise*, p. 56.

[34]Catharine Beecher, *Woman's Profession as Mother and Educator, with Views in Opposition to Woman Suffrage* (Philadelphia: Geo. Maclean, 1872), p. 4.

[35]William Graham Sumner, "The Status of Women," *War and Other Essays*, ed. Albert Keller (New York: AMS Press, 1970), p. 71. Reprint of 1911 original.

[36]Catharine Beecher, *An Essay on Slavery and Abolitionism, with Reference to the Duty of American Females* (Philadelphia: Henry Perkins, 1837), pp. 98–99.

[37]*An Essay on Slavery*, pp. 99–100.

[38]*Treatise*, p. 28.

[39]Emile Durkheim, *The Division of Labor in Society* (New York: The Macmillan Co., 1933), p. 43.

[40]*Iowa State Gazette*, March 29, 1848.

[41]Aileen Kraditor, ed., *Up from the Pedestal: Selected Writings in the History of American Feminism* (New York: Quadrangle Books, 1968), p. 8.

[42]See Anne Farnam, "Woman Suffrage as an Alternative to the Beecher Ministry," *Portraits of a Nineteenth-Century Family*, eds. Earl A. French and Diana Royce (Hartford: The Stowe-Day Foundation, 1976).

[43]Daniel Scott Smith, "Family Limitation, Sexual Control, and Domestic Feminism in Victorian America," *Feminist Studies*, Vol. I, Nos. 3–4 (Winter–Spring, 1973), p. 48.

[44]"A Long View," p. 384.

[45]"Family Limitation," p. 48.

[46]For a study of this pattern in one New England community from its origins to the mid-eighteenth century see Daniel Scott Smith, "Change in American Family Structure before the Demographic Transition: The Case of Hingham, Massachusetts" (Unpublished paper presented to the American Society for Ethnohistory, October, 1972), p. 3.

[47]*Treatise*, p. 48.

[48]Peter Uhlenberg, "A Study of Cohort Life Cycles: Cohorts of Native Born Massachusetts Women, 1830–1920," *Population Studies*, Vol. 23 (1969), pp. 407–420.

[49]*Treatise*, p. 69.

[50]See "Woman Suffrage as an Alternative to the Beecher Ministry."

Margaret Fuller

(1810–1850)

Bell Gale Chevigny

Margaret Fuller was born on May 23rd, 1810, in Cambridgeport, Massachusetts, to Mary Crane Fuller and Timothy Fuller. Fuller attended Miss Prescott's school in Groton and then Mr. Perkins's school in Cambridge. In 1839 she translated Johann P. Eckermann's Conversation with Goethe. *By that time Fuller had left home, supporting herself by teaching. Between 1840 and 1842 Fuller edited the radically innovative magazine the* Dial, *with Ralph Waldo Emerson. She continued to write criticism for the* New York Tribune, *moving to New York for that purpose in 1844. Fuller published* Summer on the Lakes *that year, recording a visit she had made to the West in 1843. In 1845 she published* Woman in the Nineteenth Century. *Fuller had long been immersed in reform, involved in the Brook Farm communal experiment and, while in New York, visiting and writing about Sing Sing and Blackwell's Island prisons. Fuller's last book was* Papers on Literature and Art *(1846). That year the* Tribune *sent Fuller to Europe as its foreign correspondent. In Rome, Fuller became the lover of Giovanni Angelo, Marchese d'Ossoli, and in September, 1848, had a son by him. They may have been married the following year. Fuller was, with Ossoli, an active participant in the Italian revolution. They became refugees when Rome fell in 1849. In Florence she worked on her history of the brief Roman republic. Fuller, Ossoli, and their child were drowned July 19, 1850, in a storm off Fire Island, New York, as she returned to publish her book in America.*

After Margaret Fuller's death, the poet Elizabeth Barrett Browning wrote of her friend, "If I wished anyone to do her justice, I should say 'Never read what she has written.' " And although Ralph Waldo Emerson, a great admirer, judged her conversation "the most entertaining in America," he also said, "her pen was a non-conductor." Countless others testify that Fuller's writing never matched the vividness of her presence and, above all, her life story.*

Certainly the barest recitation of the facts of her remarkable life command attention. Reared in the intellectually stimulating climate of Massachusetts at the turn of the nineteenth century, Fuller received a remarkable upbringing. From the age of six, she was tutored so rigorously by her father that, by her teen years, she could match wits with the brightest men at Harvard. She is supposed to have said, "I now know all the people worth knowing in America, and I find no intellect comparable to my own." She was no beauty, but her conversation was so clever and eloquent that her plainness was forgotten. A plan to go to Europe at age twenty-five was deferred for eleven years by family demands placed upon her by her father's death. Fuller was an intimate of the transcendentalists, the community of utopian literary figures including Ralph Waldo Emerson, Henry David Thoreau, and William Henry Channing, in New England. She edited their journal, the *Dial,* and taught at an experimental academy run by fellow transcendentalist Bronson Alcott, a member of the literary family from Concord, Massachusetts.

Each winter from 1839 to 1844 Fuller offered "conversations" for the leading women of Boston, a series of meetings in which the group explored intellectual issues within a broad range of topics. In 1845 she published *Woman in the Nineteenth Century,* one of the first American texts to examine the condition of women's lives. A book of her travels in the West, *Summer on the Lakes in 1843* (1844), won her a position as the first female journalist for a major newspaper—Horace Greeley's *New York Tribune.* She produced articles on social questions and a body of literary criticism that in her time was rivaled only by that of Edgar Allen Poe. A collection of these articles, *Papers on Literature and Art,* was issued in 1846. She went on assignment to Europe and became involved in literary and radical political circles, earning fame as a war correspondent when the revolutions of 1848 broke out. In Rome, she secretly became the lover of an Italian revolutionary, Giovanni Angelo Ossoli, with whom she bore a child. She remained in Rome for the brief days of the Roman republic and directed a hospital when the French held the city in siege. After the fall of Rome, she claimed that she was married to Ossoli, but offered no details or documentation. She removed to Florence with her family and prepared a book on the Italian revolution.

Her political radicalism made Elizabeth Barrett Browning, her confidante in Florence, call her "an out and out Red" and warn that her book was drenched in "the blood colours of Socialistic views, which would have drawn the wolves on her . . . both in England and America." In 1850, when she returned to America to promote her book, "the wolves" were cheated by the shipwreck that took her life—and that of Ossoli and their child—within sight of the American shore. Her great friend Henry David Thoreau spent days on Fire Island off the coast of New York's Long Island searching for her body and her manuscript—but neither were recovered. The cutting short of such a dramatic and enigmatic life has helped to keep her legend alive—tantalizing, infuriating, and elusive.

From our twentieth-century perspective, it is tempting to see Fuller as a woman of the nineteenth century nurturing a modern woman within. Such an approach helps us to analyze her problematic writing. This modern woman, wary of being trapped by the conventional language of her day, only intermittently sought expression in Fuller's life and writings. Fuller's writing strained toward a future, a transformed society, a culture that would mirror and validate her reality as nineteenth-century America could not do. Her failures were marked by romantic rhetoric, or an outlandish jargon of her own. Sometimes she saw lucidly that the language of modern feeling had to be invented and that the deep cultural change must accompany such speech. Increasingly, as she encountered such change in her last years, she found words—and her writing became easy, eloquent, and forceful.

More useful to us than Elizabeth Barrett Browning's warning is Poe's observation: "Her acts are bookish and her books are less thoughts than acts." It is interesting to read her life and work as if they formed a single text. Although Fuller's literary criticism was her most praised work within her lifetime, we now profit most from the critical light her life and work cast on the situation of American women and on the underlying social assumptions of her time.

Alexis de Tocqueville saw better than any American the unique position of women within this new democratic nation. Visiting the United States in the 1830s, Tocqueville noted that, as a "puritanical people and a commercial nation," Americans had a double motive for binding women in conventional marriages: ensuring the purity of their morals and securing order and prosperity in the home. But as a democratic people, placing high value on individual independence, Americans preferred not to repress woman's passions but rather to trust her to restrain herself, by placing "more reliance . . . on the free vigor of her will," by arming her with reason as well as with virtue.

So reared, nineteenth-century unmarried American women revealed a freedom of mind and action unmatched in Europe. But as wives, they were more submissive, dependent, dutiful, and conformist than their European counterparts. What wrought this change? Tocqueville believed it was the young American women themselves, who, in the culminating exercise of their virtue, reason, and free will, chose marriage. Tocqueville further noted that American women "attach a sort of pride to the voluntary surrender of their own will, and make it their boast to bend themselves to the yoke, not to shake it off."

Fuller, however, was one of many American women who sought to continue this youthful freedom of mind in their adult lives. As Tocqueville showed, the religious and economic objectives which defined the nation defined the American woman as a creature destined for marriage and fulfilled and useful only in the family circle. To conceive of women differently was tantamount to challenging the assumptions on which the nation was built. Ultimately, Fuller did this while living in Italy, implicitly challenging Puritanical assumptions by her sexual behavior, and explicitly questioning the economic assumptions and especially their social, and political corollaries through her writing.

Fuller's path to the understanding of herself and fulfillment of her vocation that she gained while living abroad was paved by her willingness to be considered a freak in America. According to Poe, humanity is divided into three classes: men, women, and Margaret Fuller. As others did, she saw herself as a hybrid, a union of two usually exclusive tendencies: more often than not, these tendencies were labeled "masculine" and "feminine."

By their natures, Fuller's parents reinforced American sexual stereotypes, and by their method of rearing her, they contributed to her sense of being hopelessly divided between these stereotypes. Her mother, Margaret Crane Fuller, seems to have followed without effort the model of the "true woman" esteemed at the time. As a teenaged schoolteacher she could keep rough boys in line, but as a mature woman she submitted serenely to her husband's domination, and patiently endured illness and the bearing of nine children, two of whom died in infancy.

The earliest American Fullers had arrived in Massachusetts in 1629. Individuality, and strong and even controversial, behavior seem to be the paternal legacy. Her father, Timothy Fuller, served two terms in Congress before becoming Speaker of the Massachusetts House. Something of a renegade, he opposed the expatriation of the Seminoles and the Missouri Compromise, remaining a staunch supporter of John Quincy Adams despite Adams's declining popularity. Fuller's political discouragement drove him back into the country to pursue farming as his father before him had done.

At the age of thirty, Margaret Fuller wrote an autobiographical romance, in which she gave an ideal account of her parents that connects her mother with physical nature, emotionalism, spirituality, and idealism, and her father with the social world, intellectual discipline, and practicality. The usual practice of the daughter following her mother's role was distorted in Fuller's case by her father's enormous influence on her and her mother's unusually retiring role in her life. Spurred on by his daughter's precocity, Timothy Fuller initiated an unusual and rigorous program of classical education when she was six. Quizzing her in Latin and English grammar until long past her bedtime, he rejected apology, hesitation, or qualification in her performance, effectively cutting her off from prevailing styles of female discourse. Eventually realizing the cost of his one-sided approach, Fuller urged his daughter to be less bold in speech, less bookish, and more concerned with manners. It was too late: by age twelve, his daughter had resolved to be "bright and ugly."

Fuller later wrote that her father's odd and exacting education whetted her appetite for heroic action and for meeting the challenges of the world with a disciplined will—values she associated with the ancient Romans. "I kept their statues as belonging to the hall of my ancestors, and loved to conquer obstacles, and fed my youth and strength for their sake," she wrote, as if a New England girl might simply grow into a Roman hero. On the negative side, she felt her father's nocturnal drills contributed to her nightmares as a child and later to her "continual headache, weakness and nervous afflictions, of all kinds." In addition, some deeper distortion stemmed from the imposition of the values of will and intellect at the expense of imagination and passion. "The child fed with meat instead of milk becomes too soon mature," Fuller confessed. "With me, much of life was devoured in the bud."

The effect of this rigid perfectionism of the Romans and Timothy Fuller was in some way counterbalanced by Fuller's appreciation of the Greeks, and of Molière, Cervantes, and especially Shakespeare. She wrote of the Greeks that she "loved to creep from amid the Roman pikes to lie beneath this great vine, and see the smiling serene shapes go by. . . . I loved to get away from the hum of the forum and the mailed clang of Roman speech, to these shifting shows of nature, these Gods and Nymphs born of the sunbeam, the wave, the shadows on the hill." Fuller's imagery bisects the classical world by gender: male Rome (vertical pikes, "mail," the forum) and female Greece (horizontal vines, nymphs, nature). Her earliest refuge from her father's books was the garden, significantly her mother's cherished workplace. Thus Fuller felt herself divided into separate selves. As the side nurtured by her father came into public view, that associated with her mother became private, and even invisible:

> His influence on me was great, and opposed to the natural unfolding of my character, which was fervent, of strong grasp and disposed to infatuation, and self-forgetfulness. He made the common prose world so present to me, that my . . . own world sank deep within. . . . But my true life was only the dearer that it was secluded and veiled over by a thick curtain of available intellect, and that coarse but wearable stuff worn by the ages—Common Sense.

Fuller's finding her vocation depended upon her breaking down the divisions that plagued her during childhood. She would have to learn to reject the notions of masculine and feminine that were locked into the culture, for as long as she described her problem in these terms, she conspired in delaying her progress to selfhood and freedom.

By 1824, Timothy Fuller was anxious enough about his daughter to send her, against her will, to Miss Prescott's School for Young Ladies in Groton, Massachusetts, where he hoped she would acquire "female propriety." Fuller's affection for the headmistress, Susan Prescott, had the desired effect of making her wish for womanly "tact and polish" to complement the genius she took for granted. Back at home in Cambridge in 1825, she found her studies had filled her with a "gladiatorial disposition" that prevented her enjoyment of casual society. Social ease came late to this lonely adolescent.

Cambridge in the late 1820s was full of brilliant talkers, intellectuals dedicated to the romantic cult of friendship. Margaret Fuller's arrival was a spectacular event, her style startling. Many were initially repelled by this long-necked, robust figure with eyes alternately squinting and dilating, by her dominating use of erudition and scathing wit. Unitarian minister and author William Henry Channing confessed that he initially avoided one "so armed from head to foot in saucy sprightliness," and Emerson underscored the martial image: "the men thought she carried too many guns." For an extraordinary number of men and women, however, closer acquaintance with Fuller broke down initial resistance. One woman confessed, "Though she spoke rudely searching words, and told you startling truths, though she broke down your little shams and defenses, you felt exhilarated by the compliment of being found out."

Now in her late teens, Fuller enjoyed a rich life of letters with a small circle of Cambridge friends, several from Harvard's class of 1829. Together they read the English romantics, Charles Lamb, William Wordsworth, Samuel Taylor Coleridge, and Thomas Carlyle. Then when her father, disillusioned with political life, retired to the country in 1833 and took the family to Groton, Fuller's pace changed dramatically. She found herself tutoring her siblings five to eight hours daily, and taking on an onerous share of domestic work because her grandmother, mother, and brothers were often ill. One infant sibling died in Fuller's arms. During what spare time she found, Fuller read up on architecture and astronomy, devoured European and American history, and kept up her translations of German and French romantics.

While in Groton she conceived the bold idea of writing a life of the great German writer Johann Goethe, one of her intellectual heroes, who was relatively unread and underappreciated in America. Fuller was sure she would have to go to Europe to collect data on him because none of the American scholars who knew Goethe were willing to share the details of his life with a woman. Moreover, there was no American woman who could provide a model for Fuller as a writer.

Her female forerunners were in Europe, where the institution of the salon had long given women of intelligence and wit an influential role with men of letters and politics, a role rare in America. At fifteen, Fuller had been attracted by the example of French writer Madame de Staël; her reputedly brilliant conversation, intense friendships, and influential writing had been said to have compensated amply for her plain appearance. Fuller's contemporaries later compared her with de Staël. In the late 1830s Fuller was drawn to another unconventional French writer, George Sand, despite what she called Sand's "womanish" failings: "She has genius and a manly heart! Will there never be a being to combine a man's mind and woman's heart, and who yet finds life too rich to weep over?" The "common sense" instilled in her by her father caused Fuller to disparage in women artists the emotionality she cherished in her companions.

Her father's sudden death from cholera in 1835 forced Fuller to abandon her writing projects and trip to Europe and take on the role of head of the household. She began by attempting to disentangle his financial affairs. Her next challenge was to seize control of the rearing and education of her siblings over the protestations of a domineering uncle. Most difficult of all for Fuller was being emotionally orphaned; for the next few years she searched for a father figure as well as a mentor.

When Fuller met Ralph Waldo Emerson in 1836, she felt she had found a spiritual guide. Seven years her senior, Emerson, who had had to define his own vocation, offered what her father had not: encouragement for Fuller to define her own path. When he read his essay "Nature" aloud to her, she might have drawn strength from its closing: "Build therefore your own world." Emerson's vision sanctioned a world built around individualism. Fuller thus could fashion her own world in which she could simultaneously cultivate a circle of high-minded intimates and expand her sense of private self. She praised Emerson: "From him I first learned what is meant by the inward life."

The interest each took in the other was powerful. While Emerson inducted Fuller into the worlds of solitude and natural harmony, she offered him the best of society. Sometimes Emerson was exuberantly grateful for Fuller's company and her young friends. But as Fuller eventually felt constrained by Emerson's "inwardness," so Emerson clung to his inveterate reserve. A tension grew between the two, which each expressed in similar terms. Emerson's adoption of Montaigne's phrase "Oh, *my friends,* there are no friends," was, to Fuller, "a paralyzing conviction." After one of Fuller's visits, Emerson confided to his journal, "Life too near paralyzes art." Given the ascetic basis of Emerson's craft and Fuller's craving for dynamic relationships, the friendship dwindled within a few years. In her last visit with Emerson in 1844, Fuller teased him about how Concord lacked "the animating influences of Discord."

Before Fuller discovered her own path, she drew heavily on the stimulating and steadying influence of Concord and the transcendentalists. Fuller's intellectual exchange with Emerson helped fill gaps in her knowledge of English literature while she broadened Emerson's appreciation of Continental literature. Emerson also encouraged Fuller's acquaintance with Bronson Alcott, who offered Fuller her first job at his Temple School. Although teaching was the most conventional of female occupations during this era, Alcott's teaching philosophy was anything but conventional. He believed that children are nearer their "celestial origins" than adults, and directed their education inward. His principles were branded as heretical, blasphemous, and even obscene. Fuller preferred Alcott's methods to her father's forced march, although she was a critic of some of Alcott's methods. When she switched to a more lucrative and less radical school in Providence, she found herself restless after her stimulating tenure at Alcott's school.

Early in 1840, Fuller embarked on the most demanding of her transcendentalist enterprises, the editing of the *Dial.* Members of this elite literary circle, the so-called Transcendental Club, decided to produce a journal of their own. Their first editorial proposed "not to multiply books, but to report life." Despite initial enthusiasm, Fuller had to beg for contributions, and for one issue of 136 pages, had hastily provided 85 pages from her own notebooks. She was sharply criticized despite her heroic efforts. Emerson complained, "I hope our *Dial* will get to be a little *bad*," while theologian and fellow transcendentalist Theodore Parker even more pointedly suggested that the publication "needed a beard." These calls for greater boldness drove Fuller into an uncharacteristically "feminine" neutrality, resulting in work of poorer quality than most of her later efforts.

Fuller's poems and art and music criticism are too subjective for evaluation now, but her literary criticism provides us with a systematic record of critical practice in America. Fuller argued that criticism should go beyond the impressionism that chiefly characterized the critic; it should combine empathetic elucidation of literary works on their own terms with objective standards outside them.

During her twenty months in New York in 1844–46 writing for Horace Greeley's *New York Tribune*, Fuller wrote two literary pieces a week, outstripping any in her New England circle in practical criticism such as book reviews. Fuller was happy to "aid in the great work of popular education." She was uniquely able to mediate between the ordinary reader and the likes of Goethe, Byron, and Sand. Explaining the themes of these difficult writers by placing them in the contexts of their ages and options, Fuller made them accessible, even enlightening. This perspective brought her to favor American literature that was individual but not provincial. She criticized James Russell Lowell and the lionized Henry Wadsworth Longfellow, but praised Frederick Douglass, Edgar Allen Poe, Nathaniel Hawthorne, and the as yet unknown Herman Melville. She tried to rescue from literary oblivion the novelist Charles Brockden Brown (a feminist, as she read him). In private and in public, she was satirized by many, including Lowell and Poe (who thought her praise did not match his talents), although in the *Brooklyn Daily Eagle* the young Walt Whitman welcomed "right heartily" her collected criticism, *Papers on Literature and Art*.

Fuller's ideological break with Emerson was initiated in what was ironically one of her most transcendentalist works. In her *Dial* essay, "The Great Lawsuit," Fuller applied transcendentalist tenets to women, particularly the universal sacred right and duty to develop fully one's nature. Her need to prove woman's humanity shows that however warmly Fuller had been received by transcendentalist men, she was still made to feel "other."

Probably the earliest source of Fuller's feminism was her feeling for her mother. She wrote that after her father's nocturnal drills she often had nightmares of following her mother's corpse to the grave, as she had followed her infant sister. In her biography of Fuller, Katharine Anthony made this dream the keystone of her Oedipal reading of

Fuller. But a fragmentary manuscript, in which Fuller fictionalizes her parents' marriage, suggests other readings. In this fragment, Fuller takes two stunning liberties in fact. She disguises herself, the narrator, as a *son*, and tells how the mother—weakened by her husband's neglect of her inner life and destroyed by grief over her second child's death—*dies*. The narrator speculates, "had she lived there was enough in me corresponding with her unconscious wants to have aroused her intellect and occupied her affections. Perhaps her son might have made up to her for want of that full development of feeling which youth demands from love." Fuller's fictional tale incorporates her real recurrent nightmare of her mother's death, her mother's real relative absence from Fuller's rearing and inability to provide her daughter with a model, and the death of the internalized female in the child when both parents fail to value and nurture feminine characteristics. The son's fantasized rescue of the mother can be read perhaps as Fuller's attempt to *create* a mothering self that could provide the acceptance she was unable to find elsewhere.

Fuller's friendships with other women were marked by these needs to be loved and accepted *and* her desire to transform the "other." The fervent language of her friendship owes something to the cult of romanticism. In addition, the culture's rigorous separation of human qualities by gender might have encouraged women to believe only they could understand one another. But the intensity of Fuller's love of women also came from a need to heal a wound sustained in childhood, and to enlarge women's mutual understanding, and hence their capacities. "It is so true that a woman may be in love with a woman and a man with a man," she wrote of a friend in youth whom she had loved "with as much passion as I was then strong enough to feel."

Understanding women was not the same as endorsing them or their "separate sphere." As Fuller wrote sharply, "Plain sewing is decidedly immoral." Her sense that she was an exception was a habitual defense as a young woman. As she grew older, though, her desire to work for other women replaced it: Her "conversations" for women, likely inspired by her sessions with the transcendentalists, nourished a sense of herself and of possible vocations.

In 1839 Fuller proposed to assemble a circle of "well-educated and thinking women" to help them "systematize thought and give a precision and clearness in which our sex are so deficient, chiefly, I think because they have so few inducements." Her first series of conversations was on Greek mythology, but over five winters she covered fine arts, ethics, education, and women's influence of the family, school, church, society, and literature. Paying a small fee, from twenty-five to forty women gathered once a week in fellow transcendentalist and educator Elizabeth Peabody's bookstore. The aims might have been modest, but the effort had profound effects.

Fuller's very premise that women should nurture their serious responses to each other as well as their obligations to family was trailblazing. Women's rights pioneer Elizabeth Cady Stanton later found the "vindication of woman's right to think" in the conversations subtly subversive. Fuller's notion that for women the precincts of love stretched beyond the hearth and that morality is based on free choice and personal responsibility was nothing short of revolutionary. Fuller's channeling of her talents toward women's issues led her to personal wholeness and the free exercise of her power.

The conversations also helped Fuller to develop her writing style. When she published her *Dial* essay on women, "The Great Lawsuit," Thoreau praised it as "rich extempore writing, talking with pen in hand." Fuller expanded this essay into *Woman in the Nineteenth Century* while living in Fishkill, New York, before she settled in Manhattan. She was about to start work for Horace Greeley, who had offered her a job after reading her *Summer on the Lakes in 1843*. The trip to the Great Lakes and Wisconsin that inspired this book, weaned her from New England thought; *Woman* reflects her quickened sense of independence and her new interest in the claims of society and politics.

Her psychological confidence reveals itself in her treatment of female nature. Although she concurs with the cultural conviction that woman's nature is distinct, she insists that this female essence never appears unmixed: "two sides of the great radical dualism," male and female "are perpetually passing into one another," and "there is no wholly masculine man, no purely feminine woman." Another measure of transformation comes with her portrait of her "friend" Miranda—really an idealized self-portrait—who seeks to dispose of these classifications: "Let it not be said, wherever there is energy or creative genius, 'She had a masculine mind.' " Moreover, in Miranda's story, Fuller reevaluates her father's training, and the contrast is sharp. In her 1840 autobiographical romance, Fuller condemned her father's methods as his "great mistake," but here she says it stemmed from "a firm belief in the equality of the sexes." Where previously she argued that she was cheated of her female nature, now she appreciates that he addressed her as "a living mind," and not a plaything. Where the effect earlier was a life "devoured in the bud," now it is "a dignified sense of self-dependence." Both versions are polemical exaggerations, but the experience of the conversations must help explain the shift from despair to pride.

The independence that Fuller stresses for women is a combination of the transcendentalist virtue of self-reliance and the activist one of "self-impulse." She believed that until a woman represented herself she was "only an overgrown child."

In analyzing society's effects on women and the role women should take in society *Woman* is curiously hybrid. In it, Fuller's calls for various social reforms and even for militant action sound through the old music of pure transcendentalist individualism. Her homely democratic faith in the Declaration of Independence is grafted onto the philosophy of romantic self-culture. The former leads her to praise the abolitionist movement she had ignored during her conversations and admire its activists, Angelina Grimké and Abby Kelley Foster. She also calls upon women to respond as a united group to the threatened annexation of Texas and heralds public speaking and petition campaigns by women, both widely censored as immodest and offensive. She writes with remarkable candor for the time about the double standard in marriage and on women's need to understand sexuality and prostitution.

Fuller shows acid scorn for those who felt women should be sheltered within a domestic circle: "Those who think the physical circumstances of Woman would make a part in the affairs of national government unsuitable, are by no means those who think it impossible for negresses to endure field-work, even during pregnancy, or for sempstresses to go through their killing labors." At such moments, and with the calls to action, Fuller moves for the first time toward radicalism, though she appears not yet aware of its cost.

Active feminism clarified for Fuller the ways in which pure transcendentalism was inadequate for her and initiated her career of activist journalism. It also led her into wider engagement with the world. Her feminist perspective triggered her involvement with political activism and carried her beyond the struggle for women alone. In New York, Fuller celebrated the refuge of immigrants of all classes: standing in the city, she felt "the life blood rushing from an entire continent to swell her heart." She preferred New York to New England, writing, "I don't dislike wickedness and wretchedness more than pettiness and coldness."

Horace Greeley, her editor, became a teacher of sorts for Fuller. In her weekly column on social issues—the Irish, antislavery, opposition to the Mexican War—she often supported his causes. Fuller produced controversial columns stemming from her own convictions as well: She attacked capital punishment, welcomed persecuted Jews from Europe, and sought better education and broader work opportunities for the poor and for women. No longer restricted to acquaintance within her class, Fuller's concern for women in trouble flourished and her feminism grew along with her social awareness. She visited women in Sing Sing prison and helped plan the first halfway house for female convicts. As revolutionary as these ventures into worlds formerly closed to women of her class were for Fuller, they were still rather genteel muckraking.

With the beginning of America's aggressive foreign policy, particularly after the annexation of Texas and the threat of expansion into Mexico, Fuller became disillusioned with the myth of America's special destiny. She took an interest in many varieties of socialism and even translated from a German immigrant newspaper one of the earliest discussions of Marx and Engels in this country. But as no ideology could replace the myth of special destiny, it is likely that if she had not left the country to write for the *Tribune* about Europe, her perspective would simply have soured.

In August 1846, Greeley sent Fuller to England as one of the first American overseas correspondents of either sex. Although at a younger age she might have soaked up the culture and "genius" of Great Britain, during this visit she explored social conditions and intensified her commitment to reform after being shocked by the omnipresence of poverty in England. Throughout Europe, Fuller was appalled by the horrors of industrial slums—the underside of Europe's "costly tapestry"—especially the female victims "too dull to carouse" and their children fed on opium. Although we know she had toured the slums of Five Points in New York, Fuller nevertheless wrote, "Poverty in England has terrors of which I never dreamed at home." What her unconscious adherence to the democratic rhetoric of America made her miss at home, the tradition in Europe of critical political rhetoric laid bare. In addition, she was visiting France on the eve of the 1848 revolution. The life of the streets and the salons was crackling with rival socialist theories, heightening her sense of the need for political action.

An illuminating series of private events kept pace with Fuller's public tour. As Europe heated up for the revolution, experiences and encounters prepared Fuller for fundamental and irrevocable change in her personal life. In New York, a troubling romance with an opportunistic businessman of German-Jewish descent, James Nathan, had made her long, for the only time in her life, for the traditional subordinate role of woman. Apparently the relationship became too demanding or convoluted and Nathan retreated to Europe. If Fuller had come to Europe still hoping for a reconciliation, that hope was effectively dashed when she received a letter in Edinburgh announcing Nathan's engagement to a German woman.

But at the same time, Fuller found her work warmly received in Europe and intellectual discourse more comfortable for her abroad than at home. She wrote to Emerson, "I find myself in my element in European society. It does not, indeed, come up to my ideal, but so many of the encumbrances are cleared away that used to weary me in America, that I can enjoy a freer play of faculty and feel, if not like a bird in the air, at least as easy as a fish in the water." Europe offered her two crucial sensations America had denied: the shock of class consciousness and the warm bath of personal acceptance. She was more than ready for the liberating political and literary influences she encountered in London and Paris that helped her discover how to move against the social and religious pressures that bound American women in "their place."

While in England, Fuller met Giuseppe Mazzini, an Italian revolutionary in exile who was hoping to overthrow Austrian imperialists and unite the eight separate Italian states into a democratic republic. Mazzini knew the struggle would take more than idealism, and would include mobilizing the masses and taking concrete, violent action. Fuller did not succumb to hero-worship, but she did support his cause and accept Mazzini's list of his secret agents on the Continent.

While in France, Fuller met George Sand, whose work Fuller had defended in America, although always with an added regret for her lapses in private virtue. However, after meeting Sand in the freer atmosphere of France, Fuller confessed, "I never liked a woman better. She needs no defence, but only to be understood, for she has bravely acted out her nature, and always with good intentions." It was a moment of prophetic self-recognition, for Fuller would later adapt this phrase to explain her liaison with Ossoli. In Rome, historical events would combine with Fuller's capacity for change to alter transcendentalism's influence on her and to offer her an opportunity for self-realization and her most satisfying work.

When Fuller arrived in Rome during the spring of 1847 a state of optimistic excitement prevailed. The liberal Pope Pius IX, elected a year earlier, had proclaimed a universal amnesty for political prisoners, admitted laypersons into the council of state, and authorized a civic guard. These measures undermined the Pope's temporal powers and stimulated pressure for reform in Italy's seven other states.

Most of Fuller's twenty-one dispatches from Italy have more concentrated force and style than almost anything else she wrote. The effect is panoramic, a combination of quick sketches of conditions in Germany, Austria, and France with colorful and shrewd predictions of sociopolitical evolutions; denser drawings of mounting struggles throughout Italy; and a close, evolving portrait of the Pope and the people of Rome. Fuller chronicled the Pope's gradual decline and the Italian people's growing consciousness and awakening to their own civic responsibilities. Fuller's values are so focused that they make her partisan accounts of hope, restlessness, political suspense, and battle riveting reading. Something of the bite and flash said to have characterized her conversation at last dominates her prose.

Fuller sought out radicals in Genoa, Milan, Florence, and Rome. One of these, met by chance, was Giovanni Angelo Ossoli, a Roman nobleman of meager means who was expected to follow his father and three older brothers into the Pope's service. Late in 1847 the twenty-seven-year-old Ossoli defied his family and rejected his livelihood by turning his back on the Pope and joining the radicals' civic guard. During this same period he became Fuller's lover.

The couple served one another's emotional needs. Ossoli, the youngest of six children, still grieving over the death of his mother when he was six, found in Fuller, ten years his senior, an authoritative woman. Fuller cherished in Ossoli his gentleness and the way he defeated "masculine" stereotyping. An American acquaintance who knew Ossoli commented, "She [Fuller] probably married him as a representative of an imagined possibility in the Italian character which I have not yet been able to believe in." Fuller had been committed to "imagined possibilities" all her life, but she took her greatest risk in her liaison with Ossoli. She wrote to her sister later, "I acted upon a strong impulse. I neither rejoice nor grieve, for bad or good, I acted out my character."

At the same time that she committed herself to Ossoli, Fuller became more deeply involved with the Italian people in the cause of a free Italy. While most American visitors in Italy at this time saw the Italian people as becoming a frightening rabble, Fuller saw in them a heroic struggle. She now saw no Americans more worthy of honor than the abolitionists (to whom she apologized in print for earlier assessments), for with the exception of antislavery, Fuller felt that the "spirit of America flares no more" but had leaped the ocean to blaze in Italy. So, until 1850, she refused the entreaties of Emerson and her family to return home, believing she had more to say to Americans from Italy.

Her refusal to repatriate demonstrates Fuller's repudiation of Emerson's perspective. Fuller denied the mythic specialness of American destiny and offered herself to the struggles of a foreign people as a guide to completing the American Revolution and entering "brotherhood of nations." So Fuller remained in Italy, anchored by political as well as personal ties.

In January 1848, when uprisings flared across Europe like a string of firecrackers, Fuller, nearly thirty-eight and chronically ill, discovered that she was pregnant. She may well have feared survival scarcely less than death in childbirth, for without much more money, Ossoli's marriage to a foreign Protestant radical would probably be impossible. Moreover, Fuller had strong reservations about marriage. Unwell and unsure of her personal circumstances, Fuller turned with relief to the public crisis—devouring news of the February revolution in Paris, the March uprising in Vienna, and especially the "Five Glorious Days" in Milan when the Autstrian garrison was expelled. "It is a time such as I always dreamed of," Fuller wrote, and she contemplated becoming its historian. Seeking seclusion ostensibly to write her history, Fuller withdrew to the Abruzzi mountains. That summer she awaited with equal anxiety the birth of her child and news of friends in reoccupied Milan. Angelo Eugenio Filippo Ossoli was born September 4, 1848, in the village of Rieti. Fuller was overwhelmed with joy at being a mother, yet she felt obliged to leave the child in November with a wet nurse in the hills and to rejoin Ossoli in Rome. She sent enthusiastic reports to the *Tribune* of the murder of the Pope's minister, the Pope's flight to Naples, and the dignity of Romans in their first attempt at self-government.

On the eve of the declaration of the Roman republic in February 1849, Fuller begged the United States (in the pages of the *Tribune*) to send a sensitive and statesmanlike ambassador to the new nation, adding, "Another century and I might ask to be made Ambassador myself." But even with the triumphal return of Mazzini to preside in the new republic, America was only willing to send a lowly chargé d'affaires. Then France, in the full sway of reaction, sent its army to defeat isolated Rome. During the long siege of June, with news of her child cut off from her, Fuller stayed behind with Ossoli in Rome while other Americans fled the city. Fuller worked long hours as director of a hospital while Ossoli remained at his battery command, but the city's bombardment and the wounded made her "forget the great ideas" and confess she was not of the heroic "mould." After Rome fell, Fuller, Ossoli, and their child moved in the autumn of 1849 into exile in Florence, where she reexamined the events of the past few months and began a broader social critique.

There is no minimizing her sense of loss. "Private hopes of mine are fallen with the hopes of Italy. I have played for a new stake and lost it," she wrote. Had the republic triumphed, work for Fuller and Ossoli might have emerged and continued to give form to their lives. But even defeated and living in Florence, which was again under despotic rule, facing a future empty of earlier promise, Fuller and Ossoli tasted great happiness. Fuller wrote of the "power and sweetness" of Ossoli's presence and rejoiced in the love of their child. Ossoli's love for her seemed to deepen during this period as well; Fuller wrote that he "loves me from simple affinity." More illuminatingly, Fuller compares the tenderness of Ossoli's love for her with that of her mother and expresses confidence that they, in particular, will love each other when they meet.

Yet Fuller's announcement of her marriage and motherhood in the summer of 1849 was not without problems. There was gossip about a "Socialist marriage, without the external ceremony." No document or reliable account survives. Fuller was either lying and avoiding embroidery as much as possible, or telling the truth in such a way as to signal the unorthodox view she had of legal unions. She had advanced ideas about her liaison: "Our relation covers only a part of my life," but "I do not feel constrained or limited." Further, she believed that Ossoli, being younger, might one day love another, in which case she pledged, "I shall do all that this false state of society permits to give him what freedom he may need."

The family was dogged by the fear of police surveillance and poverty, and Fuller, the breadwinner, felt she could no longer rely on presents and loans to support them. Work for the *Tribune* had stopped inexplicably. Believing that her book was the most important project she had undertaken, she decided to sell it in person in America. Yet she knew that at home she would face "the social inquisition of the United States." Both she and Ossoli were superstitious about sea-travel. Moreover, on the eve of her May departure, some good friends, in consultation with Emerson, urged her to remain in Italy for the time being.

This warning was clear: the person she had become could not return to America. The long trajectory of her short life was not circular. To learn to respect herself as an intellectual woman, Fuller had first had to use what was at hand in America, the idealism of the transcendentalists. When this had made her strong enough, she left New England and began in New York to apply her energies more directly to herself, to society, and to the world, but her repressed sexuality and her simplistic faith in divinely ordained national destiny reveal she was still subject to the limits of American attitudes. Only her European experiences, especially those in Italy, could illuminate for her the meaning of her most intimate prayer, "Give me truth, cheat me by no illusion."

Despite fears and warnings, Fuller, Ossoli, and their child set sail on what became an ill-fated journey. The details of Fuller's death remain uncertain. We know that within sight of American shores, her ship struck rocks off Fire Island. During the twelve hours between the time the ship began to sink and when it finally went under, Fuller was on deck watching some swim to safety and others drown. She repeatedly refused to leave the boat. She saw the lifeboat brought to the beach by persons unwilling to risk a rescue. We know she told the ship's cook, "I see nothing but death before me." We do not know whether or not she tried to swim ashore, clinging to a board. Her body and those of Ossoli and her child were never recovered. After her drowning, Emerson confided to his journal, "I have lost in her my audience." As for Fuller's audience, it remained to be created.

Note

* The longer version of this essay may be found in Leonard Unger and A. Walton Litz, *American Writers: A Collection of Literary Biographies* (New York: Scribner's 1981).

PART IV

Divided Loyalties

The dramatic challenges faced by American women during the first half of the nineteenth century were overshadowed by events taking place at mid-century. By 1860, the ferment of reform and the explosive impact of sectional politics on national policy led America into civil war. All women felt the impact of this national calamity, except perhaps those on the far western frontier. The Civil War (1861–1865), an attempt to preserve the Union against the forces of secession, eventually would determine the fate of slavery. Because of women's disproportionate role in the antislavery movement, they can be said to have contributed decisively to the momentum toward war.

After the election of Abraham Lincoln in November 1860, the southern states—led by South Carolina—began a slow but steady departure from the federal Union to form their own Confederacy. The mobilization for war tore families apart as many women watched helplessly as their kin divided over choosing sides. Lincoln's own wife, Mary Todd, saw members of her family fight and die with the Confederacy. Further, women's feelings about the war effort changed over time. At the outset women might have gaily waved their men off to war; however, as the casualties mounted, they watched reluctantly as men donned uniforms to join in prolonged and bloody military campaigns. The issue of war pulled women's emotions and energies in different directions. Both as individuals and as a group, women faced a crisis when the nation erupted into a full-scale armed conflict.

In the wake of the Mexican War in 1846, many women abolitionists launched a pacifist crusade, forming the New England Non-Resistance Society. Yet the firing on Fort Sumter in April 1861 galvanized most antislavery women into enthusiastic support of the Union. The talents and skills which they had brought to bear in the fight to end slavery were put to invaluable use by Federal authorities. Following the Fort Sumter battle, three thousand New Yorkers attended a benefit at Cooper Union Hall. The New York Central Association of Relief tapped this patriotic outpouring for donations and volunteers. This group was one of over seven thousand local organizations that collected and distributed supplies, trained nurses, and aided widows and orphans. Out of this effort, the U.S. Sanitary Commission established itself as an ambitious and effective conduit for civilian resources. The administration of this quasi-official organization was primarily male, but women quickly established competence as fundraisers, supply collectors, and recruiters of medical staff. In their zeal to promote the cause, female agents of the Sanitary Commission, especially in the Midwest, frequently exceeded their authority, issuing orders independently without consulting supervisors in times of urgent need. However, the circumstances of war made the freely donated labor of women more valuable than the maintenance of feminine submissiveness. Hundreds of women gained valuable experience and enormous confidence through their wartime service in the Commission.

Women also joined the war effort by volunteering in hospitals, rolling bandages and performing other menial but essential labor. Another important group (including Louisa May Alcott, better known as the author of *Little Women*) joined the effort by serving as skilled nurses. Young women from a wide range of class and ethnic backgrounds supported the Union—and themselves. Social reformer Dorothea Dix became Superintendent of Nurses for the Union Army in 1861. Some nurses served not only in hospital wards, but on the battlefield as well; women such as Mary Ann ("Mother") Bickerdyke were a welcome sight for the wounded at battle sites. Self-taught in "botanic" medicine, the early widowed Bickerdyke simply went to work on her own in the filthy hospital tents near her home in Illinois. She eventually joined Grant's army along the Tennessee River and was present at some of the bloodiest contests of the war—at Fort Donelson, Lookout Mountain, Missionary Ridge, and the sieges of Vicksburg and Atlanta.

Southern "ladies" set propriety aside to participate in activities usually reserved for servants or slaves. Sally Tompkins of Richmond borrowed the home of a friend to set up a clinic for the Confederate wounded. The female members of the upper class staffed her hospital, performing menial and taxing labors. By war's end, Tompkins had been commissioned as a captain by Confederate President Jefferson Davis, and well over 1,000 men had been successfully treated at her facility.

African-American women also made significant contributions during the war as illustrated by the career of Charlotte Forten, a schoolteacher who went south to help freedpeople at Port Royal,

South Carolina. The most famous of black nurses during the war, former slave Suzy King Taylor, began work in the camps as a laundress before serving as a nurse in the Union Army. During Reconstruction she launched her career as an educator.

Women on both sides of the conflict entered government service, working alongside men for the first time as clerks. With men away at war, female labor was crucial to both the efforts in Washington and Richmond, the Confederate capital. Increasingly, widows and mothers sought employment as well as pensions and charity. Even with jobs, single mothers and widows faced mounting difficulties. Though Confederate women were especially hard hit by wartime inflation which made minimum wages nearly worthless, families North and South were confronted with the harsh realities of war. Mary Todd Lincoln and Varina Davis witnessed enormous suffering from their respective White Houses; the numbers of homeless and hungry increased rapidly during wartime.

While almost all women felt a sense of dislocation and loss, one group viewed the war as a means to gain that most precious commodity: freedom. African-American women in the North and South identified the Confederacy as their enemy and saw the war as a necessary evil. Those slave women who watched beloved men march off to battle knew that their sacrifices might bring peace and improved conditions for future generations. Blacks were enlisted on both sides, but predictably the Confederacy was more reluctant to use slave labor and was willing to contemplate using African-Americans as soldiers only in sheer desperation during the war's final weeks.

The North did drag its heels when it came to utilizing willing and able African-American soldiers—including free blacks from the North and the "contraband" slaves who deserted masters for the protection of the Union Army in droves. However, following the Emancipation Proclamation in January 1863, black soldiers took a more decisive role in the war against the Rebels. The arming of African-Americans changed the nature of the battle for white soldiers who fought alongside blacks, as well as for the white soldiers at the end of black gunsights. Certainly the presence of African-American soldiers in the occupied Confederacy broke the famed southern spirit during the prolonged period which preceded surrender. But even more importantly, African-

American soldiers were empowered by their fight on their own behalf, for a freedom so long denied.

When Lee surrendered at Appomattox in April 1865, more than half a million soldiers had perished: the North lost over 360,000 and the South 260,000. Four long years of conflict wiped part of a generation of young men off the face of the earth. The human toll was even larger, as many more were maimed and towns were filled with scores of one-legged or one-armed men. Those wounded by war also included the widowed and orphaned, the displaced and devastated women left homeless after surrender.

In the years immediately following the war, hundreds of men and women traveled south in hopes that education would provide a boost to the recently emancipated African-Americans. Yankee "schoolmarms," whom W. E. B. DuBois deemed crusaders, planted schools in a barren and hostile environment. Not only was black illiteracy a problem, but white illiteracy in the South was the highest in the nation. Some northern women ventured south during wartime, such as black educator Charlotte Forten who settled at Port Royal, South Carolina, and Laura Towne, a white reformer from Philadelphia, who set up her Penn School on St. Helena Island off the coast of South Carolina in September 1862. By the war's end, these crusaders had grown in number to over four thousand Yankee women laboring in Freedmen's Bureau schools throughout the South. With the withdrawal of federal troops from the South in 1877, which signalled an end to Reconstruction, most women abandoned their posts—although Penn School founder Laura Towne, and others similarly dedicated, remained south.

Northern women in the Reconstruction South found themselves drawn not just into educational issues, but into all aspects of reform. Women began to petition against the abuses of the apprentice system which was used virtually to re-enslave many African-American children. They petitioned, too, for land reform and other economic and civil measures to stem exploitation of freedpeople as well as white sharecroppers. But women, white and black, confronted the immovable force of southern racism and many felt defeated.

Women's rights advocates who believed that the end of war would signal rewards for their loyalty to the Union cause were equally disappointed. When Elizabeth Cady Stanton, wife of abolitionist Henry Stanton, along with Lucretia Mott, a Philadelphia Quaker abolitionist leader, and other organizers launched their campaign for women's rights at Seneca Falls in 1848, they had linked the battle for female status with an end to chattel slavery. Throughout the 1850s, at conventions in New York and Ohio, Susan B. Anthony and Sojourner Truth preached the gospel of abolitionism along with women's rights.

Reform efforts resulted in the Married Women's Property Acts. These guaranteed married women control over the property that they brought into marriage with them as well as any they might inherit. Other statutes liberalized divorce. Wealthy legislators were not opposed to amending *feme covert* principles. Under English common law and in American statutes, a woman who was adult and single had *feme sole* status, or "legal personality." However, when a woman married she relinquished this status and became *feme covert.* Her legal personality was subsumed by her husband's rights over her person and property. Some husbands were interested in protecting their property from creditors by passing on assets to their wives. They also wanted their own property controlled by deserving daughters rather than by sons-in-law exclusively. In 1839 the Mississippi legislature approved such a measure. However, in other states, such as New York, reform proceeded much more slowly. A similar law, first introduced by women's rights advocates in Albany in 1836, was not finally approved until 1848; and then only the real and personal property of women was protected. It took another twenty years before wives could retain control over their own wages, and mothers might be given equal consideration in child custody.

Many feminists hoped that the cataclysm of war would accelerate their gains—pushing up the timetable for legislative reforms—and even lead to a rapid acceptance of women's suffrage, the goal of radical activists during the antebellum era. To many female activists, northern victory symbolized a triumph of reform; advocates of woman's suffrage believed they should be rewarded with the franchise, as ex-slaves had been by Constitutional amendment. Too many male reformers failed to agree. Frederick Douglass, the most famous African-American of his day, had championed woman's suffrage from Seneca Falls onward. Women reformers stood firmly behind the 13th Amendment which abolished slavery but, when controversy flared in

1867 during debates over the 15th Amendment, even Douglass declared that it was "the negro's hour."

Outraged by the exclusion, Susan B. Anthony, Elizabeth Cady Stanton, and many feminist supporters abandoned the Republican party and aligned with the Democrats in 1867 in exchange for the party's support of woman's suffrage. When this strategy failed miserably during a referendum campaign in Kansas and local elections in New York, Stanton and Anthony abandoned party politics altogether and formed an independent political organization in 1869: the National Woman Suffrage Association (NWSA). Additionally, in 1875, feminists tackled the courts with the *Minor v. Happersett* case, proposing that suffrage was a right conferred on all national citizens. The Supreme Court, however, ruled that the vote was a privilege granted by individual states and not guaranteed through federal protection.

Victoria Woodhull had been an early proponent of the strategy to sue for the vote, based on rights protected by the Constitution. An unusually flamboyant personality, Woodhull's early life was marked by upheaval: she and her sister Tennessee Claflin travelled with their parents' medicine and fortune-telling show. Married at fifteen, she divorced her husband in 1864 after bearing two children. Four years later she captured the interest of Cornelius Vanderbilt, a widowed millionaire, who set up Woodhull and her sister in a successful stock brokerage business. In 1870, the sisters established a women's rights paper, *Woodhull and Claflin's Weekly* which advocated dress reform, free love, legalized prostitution, and other radical reforms. In 1872, she organized an "Equal Rights" party and accepted their nomination as President. Her designated running mate, Frederick Douglass, chose not to participate as a candidate; nonetheless, the protest campaign brought Woodhull and feminist issues attention in the national press.

Relatively few women were even exposed to the kinds of feminism espoused by Woodhull, Anthony, and Stanton. While radicals like Stanton and Anthony formed the NWSA, a separate organization, the American Woman Suffrage Association (AWSA), was established by Lucy Stone, Henry Blackwell and Henry Ward Beecher (Catharine and Harriet's brother). This rival group provided a more moderate framework for reform, which appealed to those unwilling to join beneath the banner of NWSA's journal, the *Revolution*. The reunification of the movement would await a later generation of women.

It was not surprising that race tore apart the suffrage movement. The whole of white American society was preoccupied with racial issues in the nineteenth century: at first over the issue of slavery, and once slavery was ended, over the issue of extending rights and recognizing African-Americans as part of free society. The 1860s witnessed the rise of several white supremacist organizations in the South, most significantly the Ku Klux Klan. Many northern whites, even some who had dedicated their lives to abolitionism, exhibited racist attitudes when it came to granting blacks full and equal membership within society.

Nativist movements (groups of white "native born" people) gained support both North and South. Groups such as the American Protective Association (APA) founded in 1887, hoped to limit immigration and to enforce stricter naturalization laws. Xenophobia and religious intolerance flourished in the postwar years.

The *real* native Americans, Indians, found their already reduced land holdings being sacrificed to the wave of white pioneer farmers and ranchers moving westward. From the Gold Rush of 1849 onward, white settlers began a steady march to fill up the Great Plains and the Pacific seaboard. Congress enacted the Homestead Act in 1862, which allowed any twenty-one-year-old or head of household to stake a claim of 160 acres for $14, a provision which benefited women as well as men. White settlers demanded Indian land, pushing the government to break treaties in order to guarantee the fulfillment of the nation's "manifest destiny." Thus in 1887 Congress passed the Dawes Act, which provided for individual land holdings, voiding the Indian custom of collective ownership. This led to the further economic and political disintegration of native peoples.

The scope of these human developments in nineteenth-century America was matched by another major transformation in the wake of the war—the expansion of heavy industry and a revolution in transportation. Mining, manufacturing, shipping and railroads all boomed in the postwar era. The gleaming gold of the closing spike that joined the two tracks of the first transcontinental railroad in 1869 symbolized not only the unification of the continent but the seemingly "golden" opportunity for expanding markets and continuing economic growth. By 1890 there were six transcontinental lines, with settlements and businesses flourishing from coast to coast. These transformations propelled women as well as men into the modern industrial era.

Elizabeth Cady Stanton

(1815–1902)

Bruce Miroff

Elizabeth Cady was born in Johnstown, New York, in 1815. Educated at Johnstown Academy and at the Troy Female Seminary (now the Emma Willard School) in Troy, New York, she married abolitionist Henry Stanton in 1840. When in that year she and Quaker lecturer Lucretia Mott were outraged by the exclusion of female delegates from the floor of the World Anti-Slavery Convention in London, they decided to call for a women's rights convention. Although the plan was not immediately carried out, a meeting of Stanton, Mott, and three other women in 1848 resulted in the first women's rights convention, which began a few days later in Seneca Falls, New York. At this convention, Stanton drafted the Declaration of Sentiments, which called for economic and social equality and suffrage for women. In 1851, she began a lifelong collaboration toward this goal with Susan B. Anthony. Busy rearing her seven children, born between 1842 and 1859, Stanton nonetheless worked continuously in the women's movement and successfully advocated married women's legal rights in New York state. During the Civil War she and Anthony organized the National Woman's Loyal League to support Abraham Lincoln's party and to petition Congress for the immediate abolition of slavery by constitutional amendment. Stanton was president of the National Woman Suffrage Association, which she founded with Anthony in 1869, for twenty-one years, and of the National American Woman Suffrage Association from 1890 to 1892. She wrote and lectured all her life, and with Anthony, edited the radical periodical, the Revolution *(1868–1870). Together they published three volumes of the documentary* History of Woman Suffrage *(1881–1886). Stanton also published* The Woman's Bible *(1895–1898) and her autobiography,* Eighty Years and More *(1898).*

At the first women's rights convention in America, held in her home town of Seneca Falls, New York, in 1848, Elizabeth Cady Stanton discovered the vocation that would shape the remainder of her life. She would become a public voice for women's grievances and a prophet of genuine equality between the sexes. Battling for this vocation against the ridicule of men, the fears of women, and the continuing claims of her own family upon her, she emerged after the Civil War as the most vocal agitator and the most penetrating thinker in the ranks of nineteenth-century American feminists. Stanton's subsequent public career was not without disturbing episodes. The pain of women's exclusion from the rights of citizenship led her, on occasion, to outbursts of nativist and racist sentiments. Yet her career was always animated by a profound insight into women's subjugation and a passionate commitment to the freedom of all women.

Prior to the convention at Seneca Falls, Elizabeth Cady Stanton had struggled unsuccessfully against the dominant social convention of "separate spheres," which reserved the fields of politics and business for men, while restricting women to the "sphere" of domesticity. She was born in 1815 in Johnstown, New York. Her mother was a strong woman, but it was Elizabeth's father, a wealthy landowner and judge, who exercised the decisive influence on her childhood. When her father became distraught over the death of his only son, Elizabeth, then aged ten, resolved to take her brother's place and fulfill her father's shattered ambitions. She learned to ride on horseback, studied Greek, and became a star student at the local academy.[1]

But as much as her father loved her and took pride in her accomplishments, he set strict limits as to how far Elizabeth could breach the proprieties of a "woman's sphere." When the male classmates that she had bested in school competitions went off to college, he forbade her to go. Many years later, in one of her most popular lectures, "Our Young Girls," Elizabeth Cady Stanton would tell a story of a "proud girl" who, rejecting "these invidious distinctions" between the sexes and feeling herself to be "the peer of any boy she knows," would find everything conspiring to defeat her aspirations. Perhaps remembering her own defeat, she would conclude the tale by asking: "But what can one brave girl do against the world?"[2]

Although Elizabeth's father insisted that her life follow a conventional path of marriage and domesticity, he could not prevent her from following that path into unconventional circles. Making frequent visits to the Peterboro, New York, home of her older cousin, Gerrit Smith, a prominent antislavery leader, she came into contact with numerous abolitionists and other reformers who congregated under the hospitable Smith's roof. Among these was Henry Stanton, a romantic young abolitionist agitator, whom she married in 1840. Elizabeth was now drawn into the most radical network in antebellum America. Like a number of other women in this network, she responded passionately to its language of equality, finding in the arguments directed toward emancipating the slave a potent vocabulary for women's needs as well. Still, her husband was the public actor, and she was his domestic counterpart. Elizabeth's only public identity was as Henry Stanton's wife.

The Stantons settled in Boston, the capital of political and intellectual reform, in 1844. For Elizabeth, domestic life in Boston, balanced as it was by intellectual and social stimulation, was pleasurable. She threw her enormous energies and talents into housekeeping and motherhood (she had two small children at the time), and imagined the home as an arena for female power. But when the family moved a few years later to the town of Seneca Falls in the Finger Lakes region of New York, domesticity lost its savor. Cut off from the wider world in the isolated environs of Seneca Falls, Elizabeth was exhausted and sometimes depressed by the demands of a growing household. To her cousin, Elizabeth Smith Miller, she wrote: "I am desperate sick of working and attending to the fleshly needs."[3]

With her rebellious temperament and her grounding in reform movements, Elizabeth Cady Stanton was not likely to succumb to isolation and depression, or to accept domesticity as defeat. Instead, she began to view her own confinement in the home as representative, her own hunger for a larger life as a metaphor for women's hunger for political and social equality. The slogan of the modern women's movement—"the personal is political"—would have come as no surprise to Stanton. From her personal discontent with women's restricted "sphere," she derived a fundamental insight into an oppression that needed to be combatted through political action. Stanton had ample amounts of the frustration, passion, and vision necessary for the founding of a feminist politics in America. All that she lacked was a catalyst.

That catalyst was Lucretia Mott. Stanton had become friendly with Mott, a pioneer abolitionist and feminist, at an international antislavery gathering in London in 1840. The two had been outraged by the overwhelming majority vote at this convention to exclude women as delegates, and had talked of convening a meeting to discuss women's rights as soon as they returned to America. Although this plan was not carried out, Stanton remained in touch with Mott, whom she came to look upon as her mentor and role model. In the summer of 1848, Mott came on a visit to Waterloo, a town near Seneca Falls. Meeting there with her and three other women on July

13, 1848, Stanton knew that at last she had a sympathetic audience for her rebellious thoughts. As she recalled in her autobiography, *Eighty Years and More,* "I poured out, that day, the torrent of my long-accumulating discontent, with such vehemence and indignation that I stirred myself, as well as the rest of the party, to do and dare anything. . . . We decided, then and there, to call a 'Woman's Rights Convention'. . . ."[4]

Lacking a model of feminist political discourse, the five women seized upon the Declaration of Independence as a framework for their Declaration of Sentiments. It was a fortunate choice. As Stanton reworked the language of the Declaration of Independence, it became a potent vehicle for women's declaration of independence. In her adaptation, men as a class stood accused of practices as onerous as those the American colonists had ascribed to George III: "The history of mankind is a history of repeated injuries and usurpations on the part of man toward woman, having in direct object the establishment of an absolute tyranny over her."[5] The Declaration of Sentiments listed eighteen grievances, the same number as the colonists had advanced, in a revolutionary indictment of men's oppression of women.

The Declaration of Sentiments was Stanton's first venture into political theory and rhetoric, but it already contained the marks of her distinctive feminist style. Stanton took a classic American idiom and infused it with a radical message not contemplated by its authors. She took the most democratic and egalitarian American values and turned them against a dominant culture that claimed to uphold them. The Declaration of Independence was genuinely sacred to Stanton, who remained throughout her life a passionate believer in the republican ideals of liberty, equality, and virtuous citizenship. At Seneca Falls, she discovered the feminist possibilities in those ideals.

On July 19, 1848, only six days after Stanton had poured out her personal discontents, the first women's rights convention began. The hastily organized convention was well attended. Several hundred women and several dozen men came from a radius of fifty miles to the small Wesleyan chapel at Seneca Falls to hear Stanton and her colleagues proclaim a new struggle for female equality. The response of the audience was favorable; at the conclusion of the convention, sixty-eight women and thirty-two men signed the resolutions that Stanton had prepared.

Stanton's speech at the convention refuted every ground—physical, intellectual, moral—for men's self-proclaimed superiority over women. This speech was more, however, than a brief for women's equality; it was also a personal declaration of vocation.

Propelling herself from domesticity to public activity in a single leap, Stanton made herself into a political voice for her sex. In the opening lines of her speech, she announced her life's work:

> I should feel exceedingly diffident to appear before you at this time, having never before spoken in public, were I not nerved by a sense of right and duty, did I not feel the time had fully come for the question of woman's wrongs to be laid before the public, did I not believe that woman herself must do this work; for woman alone can understand the height, the depth, the length, and the breadth of her own degradation. Man cannot speak for her. . . .[6]

That women must speak for themselves, that they must find their own public voice, was, for Stanton, the key to their struggle. Men had monopolized public speech up to now, and had used their monopoly to define women into subservience. The Declaration of Sentiments spelled out the consequences of man's power over public discourse: "He has usurped the prerogative of Jehovah himself, claiming it as his right to assign for her a sphere of action, when that belongs to her conscience and to her God. He has endeavored, in every way that he could, to destroy her confidence in her own powers, to lessen her self-respect, and to make her willing to lead a dependent and abject life."[7]

Stanton insisted that the voice of a woman also be the voice of a citizen. It was through her efforts that suffrage for women became a demand of the Seneca Falls convention. Lucretia Mott did not want to include enfranchisement of women among the proposed resolutions, fearing that it would make the convention appear foolish. Henry Stanton warned his wife in much the same terms. But Elizabeth Cady Stanton swept aside these cautions. With the support of black abolitionist Frederick Douglass, she carried her suffrage resolution—the only one not to receive unanimous approval—by a small majority.

Because Stanton and other pioneer feminists entertained inflated hopes for women's suffrage as an instrument of political reform, it has been common for later observers to criticize their focus on voting rights as misguided and naive. Ellen Dubois has countered this criticism by pointing to the radical meaning of women's suffrage in the context of a culture divided into sexual spheres: "By demanding a permanent, public role for all women, suffragists began to demolish the absolute, sexually defined barrier marking the public world of men off from the private world of women."[8] Stanton did exaggerate the benefits that would flow from the enfranchisement of women. But she was correct to stress that the suffrage was an indispensable prerequisite to women's freedom and dignity.

With the Seneca Falls convention of 1848, Elizabeth Cady Stanton began a public career that would span more than half a century. But before she could fully come into her own as a feminist leader, she would have to surmount a series of formidable obstacles. The first of these obstacles was the ridicule of men. In her speech at the convention, Stanton had predicted that the women's protest would raise a storm. But she and her colleagues were unprepared for the sarcastic contempt with which their handiwork was greeted. Newspapers throughout the nation vied in lampooning the Seneca Falls declaration and resolutions. And they sharply reproached Stanton and her colleagues for forgetting their proper "sphere." In the words of a Philadelphia paper: "A woman is a nobody. A wife is everything. A pretty girl is equal to ten thousand men, and a mother is, next to God, all powerful. . . ."[9]

Stanton soon learned to counter or ignore male ridicule. A more disturbing obstacle than the sarcasm of men was the silence of women. The great majority of American women did not immediately flock to the banners that had been unfurled at Seneca Falls. Some agreed with the new feminist arguments, but held back from public support out of a fear of male disapproval. A larger number clung to the dominant conventions of "separate spheres." The imperviousness of the latter group to a discourse of equality sometimes stung Stanton into vehement exclamations of frustration. In 1857, when Susan B. Anthony reported her failure to stir a meeting of female teachers to demand equal pay with male teachers, Stanton wrote back:

> What an infernal set of fools these schoolmarms must be!! Well, if in order to please men they wish to live on air, let them. The sooner the present generation of women die out the better. We have jackasses enough in the world now without such women propagating any more.[10]

The obstacles to Stanton's feminist leadership were also closer to home. She was a founding mother of the women's rights movement in a literal as well as a figurative sense; by 1859, she had seven children to bind her to the domestic sphere. Her husband, frequently absent on legal and political business, expected her to stay at home and place maternal and household cares above feminist endeavors. Her father, the person whose approval she wanted most desperately, warned her that she would pay an emotional and financial price for her public voice, threatening to disinherit her if she became a feminist lecturer. (He carried through with the threat, but later relented.) Loving her children intensely, glorying in her experiences as a mother, Stanton still repeatedly lamented the restricted public role that seemed to be the concomitant of her motherhood. Writing to

Susan B. Anthony in 1852, she cried out: "I am at the boiling point! If I do not find some day the use of my tongue on this question, I shall die of an intellectual repression, a woman's rights convulsion!"[11]

Throughout these years of domestic confinement, however, Stanton was honing her feminist consciousness. Anthony came often to visit, bringing Stanton news of the suffrage movement, and temporarily relieving her of household duties so that she could write the speeches and tracts that made her the leading theoretician of the women's cause. The laments about how domestic cares hobbled the public career for which she yearned were balanced by a realization that those cares strengthened her identification with other women and deepened her perception of what a women's movement would have to overcome. Stanton recognized that she would have to bide her time, waiting for a period when the demands of domesticity would recede and her rebellious feminist spirit could have full play. In 1857, she laid out her future in a prescient prediction to Anthony: "You and I have a prospect of a good long life. We shall not be in our prime before fifty, and after that we shall be good for twenty years at least."[12]

Shortly before she turned fifty, Stanton shed the remaining constraints of domesticity—there were no more babies to bind her to home—and took up a full-time public career amid the heated political atmosphere of the Civil War and Reconstruction. Once the dominant political forces of the Reconstruction era began to promote the rights of black men, while ignoring the rights of the women who had labored for their emancipation, she threw herself into what was to be the most painful episode in her entire public life. In the name of a passionate and outraged defense of women's rights, Stanton broke with her former abolitionist and radical Republican allies, and opposed passage of the Fourteenth and Fifteenth Amendments because they excluded women. She went beyond principled opposition to black manhood suffrage to articulate a racist and nativist position that violated her own egalitarian convictions. Fighting for women's cause with every weapon at her command, she helped to shape a more autonomous women's movement—but at a heavy cost to her own democratic vision.

The abolitionists and radical Republicans with whom Stanton and Susan B. Anthony had long associated themselves emerged as an influential bloc in the postwar politics of Reconstruction. But as the abolitionists began to press for black legal equality and then for black manhood suffrage, they also made it plain that any similar advances for women would have to wait. In their view, to couple suffrage for women with suffrage for the freedmen would ensure the defeat of both. Feminists were thus advised that this was "the negro's hour," not theirs. For some Republican politicians, the question was one of expedience; their concern in pushing black manhood suffrage was to guarantee Republican political dominance in the South. For lifelong champions of the slave, though, the sense of urgency in obtaining black rights and black manhood suffrage was sincere. Without a federal guarantee of black rights, the former slaves would have no chance to make economic progress. Without a federal guarantee of black voting power, the former slaves would be at the mercy of white violence and terror.

If there was a strong case to be made for the priority of the rights of black men, there was also a strong one to be made by Elizabeth Cady Stanton for placing women on a par with black men. Stanton insisted that Reconstruction must be "the woman's hour also. . . ."[13] Once the most progressive political forces appeared to be in the driver's seat, they should seize the moment to fulfill the equal rights promise of the Civil War struggle. The time for reform was brief; if the cause of women's rights was deferred for a few years to give precedence to black rights, it would be lost for a generation. Stanton charged her former male allies not only with political timidity, but with political hypocrisy as well. Champions of republican equality, they were proposing a universal manhood suffrage that made all men a superior and all women an inferior caste. Former patrons of the suffering slaves, they were transferring half of the emancipated population—black women—from bondage to the slavemaster to bondage to the black male. Stanton eloquently deployed the rhetoric of universal rights that the abolitionists and radical Republicans had largely abandoned, turning that rhetoric against its former practitioners: "We demand in the reconstruction, suffrage for all the citizens of the Republic. I would not talk of negroes or women, but of citizens."[14]

The initial impulse of Stanton and Anthony in the Reconstruction era was to win back erstwhile male allies to the standpoint of universal rights. But as the majority of abolitionists and Republicans opposed or evaded their arguments, they began to search elsewhere for support for the women's cause. They turned first to the Democrats—a party that included the Copperhead (pro-slavery) elements they had excoriated during the Civil War. Elizabeth Cady Stanton's and Susan B. Anthony's abolitionist friends were appalled by their association with George Francis Train, a strong supporter of women's rights but also a self-promoting crank whose Copperhead past was reflected in flagrant racist rhetoric. Train's patronage furthered—yet did not initiate—Stanton's and Anthony's own turn to the rhetoric of racism.

Although many of Stanton's arguments against giving priority to black men over women were principled and cogent, her use of racism showed her at her worst. Stanton began to devalue blacks and immigrants as a way of boosting the claims of women. One of her frequent rhetorical devices during the Reconstruction period was to project middle-class white women as the only possible saviors of the American republic from the dangerous hordes empowered by universal manhood suffrage: "In view of the fact that the Freedmen of the South and the millions of foreigners now crowding our shores, most of whom represent neither property, education, nor civilization, are all in the progress of events to be enfranchised, the best interests of the nation demand that we outweigh this incoming pauperism, ignorance, and degradation, with the wealth, education, and refinement of the women of the republic."[15] Her language of class superiority sometimes became overtly racist: "If woman finds it hard to bear the oppressive laws of a few Saxon fathers, of the best orders of manhood, what may she not be called to endure when all the lower orders, natives and foreigners, Dutch, Irish, Chinese, and African, legislate for her and her daughters?"[16]

In the search for new friends to back the cause of women's rights, Stanton and Anthony soon discovered the limits of the Democratic party and its racist elements. Rebuffed by the Democrats in 1868, Stanton and Anthony associated the women's movement with the National Labor Union, and Anthony took the lead in organizing working-class women. During the brief period when militant unionism provided a framework for Stanton's thought, the language of racism was supplanted in her speeches and articles by a language of collaboration between women and blacks. She became inspired by a vision of fundamental political and economic change in which all of the oppressed would work together: "The producers—the workingmen, the women, the negroes—are destined to form a triple power that shall speedily wrest the sceptre of government from the non-producers—the land monopolists, the bondholders, the politicians."[17] The coalition that Stanton envisioned was, however, to be short-lived, doomed both by sexist traditions among male unionists and middle-class biases on the part of the feminists. And with its unraveling, coupled with the fresh outrage to women of their exclusion from the Fifteenth Amendment, Stanton returned to the rhetoric of racism.

Elizabeth Cady Stanton could hardly have been comfortable in employing racist and nativist rhetoric. Her republican faith, expressed with great fervor during the Civil War, made her a passionate advocate of equality and a sworn enemy of caste and class distinctions. Racial prejudice was not a part of her makeup; after the Reconstruction struggles were past, Stanton would again become a defender of the rights and the dignity of blacks. Why, then, did she choose during the Reconstruction era to adopt a rhetoric so at odds with her own values?

Stanton's turn to racism was, in part, an expression of frustrated hopes for justice. To Stanton, the proclamation of a "negro's hour" that excluded women was more than another extended postponement of equality for women, more even than a betrayal by revered male allies. It was an outrageous demonstration of the gendered nature of justice in America. Asked to keep silent and to wait, women were in reality being told, as always, to subordinate their own needs and aspirations to the requirements of a group of men. They were being told that they should sacrifice their interests to those of black men, reproducing in public life the ethic of domestic self-sacrifice dictated to women by the doctrine of "separate spheres."

But Stanton's racist rhetoric also reflected her class bias. Coming from a background of privilege, and living the life of a bourgeois matron as well as a feminist agitator, Stanton's vision was obstructed by the blinders of her class. Believing that the emancipation of the freedmen placed them on a par with middle-class white women—both groups lacking only the ballot to attain full equality—she failed to grasp the beleaguered economic position of southern blacks in the new industrial-capitalist order. Stanton's Reconstruction rhetoric was, finally, a descent into political expedience. She employed racist language deliberately in an attempt to persuade middle-class white males that they needed their female counterparts as allies if they hoped to control the rising political power of immigrants and blacks. In so doing, she pitted the political aspirations of one excluded group against those of another, rather than seeking common ground among the oppressed.

Neither Stanton's principled arguments nor her racist ones made much headway. The Reconstruction era advanced black rights but left women just as excluded from public freedoms as before. For Stanton, the pain of this failure was only exacerbated by the anguish of her break with old friends. She emerged from Reconstruction shaken but undaunted. If women's immediate political prospects were bleak, the commitment of Elizabeth Cady Stanton and Susan B. Anthony to continue the fight for equal rights was underscored by their formation of the National Woman Suffrage Association in 1869. The Reconstruction era had produced a more autonomous women's movement, interested in alliances with other progressive forces but insistent on avoiding the subordination of women's cause to any other. The fashioning of this movement has been hailed by Ellen Dubois as "the greatest achievement of feminists in the postwar period. . . ."[18]

The three decades remaining to Stanton after Reconstruction, up to her death in 1902, were filled with the vigorous public activities of a feminist agitator. In the 1870s, her principal role was as a traveling lecturer, spreading her feminist views across the nation. In the 1880s, she joined with Susan B. Anthony and Matilda Joslyn Gage to compile the multivolume *History of Woman Suffrage,* preserving the words and deeds of early feminists for later generations. During the final years of her life, she became convinced that religious teachings about the inferiority of women stood in the way of equality between the sexes, and produced *The Woman's Bible* as a critical commentary on the biblical depiction of women. This work was repudiated by an increasingly conservative and Christian women's movement, leaving the elderly Stanton isolated but proudly defiant in her prophetic feminist militancy.

If we turn to examine Stanton in her roles as an agitator and theorist, we find a figure of rich feminist complexity. As an agitator, Stanton had a striking public personality. The feminist vision she voiced was explosively radical for her time. Stanton went beyond the demand for equality for women in every sphere of life, and insisted upon profound transformations of both the public and the private spheres. She was a critic of marriage and a proponent of sexual radicalism. Yet this voice that threatened the political and social proprieties of nineteenth-century America came from a woman whose appearances in public were unthreatening, indeed reassuring. On the public platform, Stanton was matronly, charming, genial. She dressed in respectable black silk, with white lace collars and cuffs.

How can this peculiar combination of militant feminist and middle-class matron be explained? According to biographer Elisabeth Griffith, Stanton's radical message was her real public personality; the feminine garb and style were her mask. As Griffith puts it: "At the same time that she was moving out of her domestic sphere, Stanton began to use her maternal role to legitimize her public activities. She shrewdly chose to appear matronly, respectable, charming, and genial."[19]

There is some evidence that Stanton did self-consciously attempt to make her radical message more palatable. But the femininity and maternity she displayed on the public platform were not masks, but essential facets of her character. Stanton was not only the mother of seven children, but a woman who prided herself on her knowledge and skills at mothering; she was genuinely eager to present herself as a sort of supermother. She loved beautiful clothes and graceful appearances. While she knew moments of private rage against male oppression, she was generally a genial and humorous person in private as well as public. Stanton was just what she appeared to be: a militant feminist *and* a middle-class matron.

If Stanton's public personality seems contradictory, especially to a modern observer, such contradiction may have made her more effective as a feminist agitator. Her public personality embodied the experiences of the majority of women, making it easier for her audiences to identify with her. That personality spoke to the ambivalence that many women, torn between prevailing codes of femininity and feminist visions of changed womanhood, seemed to be feeling in nineteenth-century America. What appears in one light as contradiction can even be seen, in a different light, as an essential attribute of Stanton's feminism. Through her public personality, as much as through her public arguments, Stanton was asserting that women did not have to give up valued experiences *as* women—such as motherhood or the expression of a special moral sensitivity—in order to stake their claims to share all the domains that men had previously monopolized. What she wrote in 1885—"surely maternity is an added power and development of some of the most tender sentiments of the human heart and not a limitation" upon women in politics—she lived out on the public stage.[20]

Stanton drew power as an agitator from her contradictory public personality, but she did not want her particular fusion of feminism and femininity to be obligatory for other female activists. She often praised the unstinting efforts that unmarried women, such as Susan B. Anthony, were able to provide to the feminist movement. She defended these women against charges that they were "masculine," arguing that men hurled this epithet at the bravest and most independent women. If Stanton remained attached to beautiful clothing and gloried in the signs of her motherhood, she was not without knowledge of the price women paid for these feminine pleasures. She knew that woman "is a slave to her rags."[21] And she knew the ambiguous joy of feminist motherhood. Upon her return home from a brief political trip in 1855, she wrote to her cousin, Elizabeth Smith Miller: "The joy a mother feels on seeing her baby after a short absence is a bliss that no man's soul can ever know. There we have something that they have not! But we have purchased the ecstasy in deep sorrow and suffering."[22]

Possessing a compelling personality and an eloquent tongue, Stanton enjoyed her role as an agitator. First initiated into politics through the abolitionist movement, she had powerful role models in William Lloyd Garrison and Wendell Phillips. Although Stanton was more willing than Garrison or Phillips to work within the framework of political parties, she shared their disdain for the politician and their pride in the stance of the agitator.

An agitator, in Stanton's self-conception, was to be guided by the truth of a principle rather than by the numbers who adhered to it. Agitators should anticipate an initial hostility and scorn from the majority rather than understanding and applause: "The history of the world shows that the vast majority in every generation passively accept the conditions into which they are born, while those who demand larger liberties are ever a small, ostracised minority whose claims are ridiculed and ignored."[23] The task of the agitator was both to defy and to transform public opinion. Confronting a majority steeped in outmoded customs and unjust values, the agitator sought to open their eyes to political rights and moral responsibilities. Stanton held to a simple, even naive, faith that true principles, if effectively agitated, would ultimately be accepted by the majority. In 1888, writing in her diary, she observed: "If I were to draw up a set of rules for the guidance of reformers, . . . I should put at the head of the list: 'Do all you can, *no matter what,* to get people to think on your reform, and then, if the reform is good, it will come about in due season.' "[24]

Stanton's pleasure in agitation was matched by her dislike for organizational politics. She viewed organizational responsibilities as cribbing her independent and militant voice. Her avoidance of organizational duties might have weakened her influence on the women's rights movement, had she not been fortunate to enjoy a close partnership with Susan B. Anthony. Where Stanton was delighted when she could obtain her freedom from organizational constraints, Anthony was most happy and most effective in the organizational milieu that suited her special talents. While Anthony organized the growing ranks of women's suffrage supporters, Stanton developed a political vision that spoke to women's most profound aspirations for changes in their lives.

Stanton's feminist vision was as complex—and often seemed as contradictory—as her public personality. Conflicting strains and impulses pulled her thought in different directions. She emphasized that women were no different than men in their mental qualities and capacities—but also argued that they were fundamentally different through their special proclivity for morality and mercy. She demanded equal access for women to all the spheres of life that men currently monopolized—but also demanded a revolution in male-female relations. She reshaped the liberal ideal of self-reliance into a doctrine of female individualism—but also bound women together through a vision of sisterhood.

On one level, these strains and conflicts in Stanton's thoughts reflect inconsistency. On another level, they are signs of a legitimate tension at the heart of her feminist vision. Recognizing the sharp dichotomies in prevailing codes of male domination and female subordination, Stanton constantly struggled to transcend them. She wanted to deny that women had to choose between their identity as women and their complete freedom and equality. She wanted to affirm that women could value their distinctive experiences, ethics, and solidarity, while still overcoming any limits placed upon them by men.

In Stanton's comparisons of women with men, arguments from women's sameness and arguments from women's difference from men were sometimes mixed together in the same speech or letter. Writing to an Ohio women's rights convention in 1850, she complained that "it is impossible for us to convince man that we think and feel exactly as he does; that we have the same sense of right and justice, the same love of freedom and independence." In the very next paragraph, however, she made it plain that women did not "think and feel exactly" like men: "Had the women of this country had a voice in the Government, think you our national escutcheon would have been stained with the guilt of aggressive warfare upon such weak, defenseless nations as the Seminoles and Mexicans?"[25]

Whether Stanton emphasized sameness or difference was, as she once candidly admitted, in large part a matter of tactics, of what made the most compelling case for women's rights. Philosophically, she wanted to push beyond the existing dichotomy between male and female. At her most visionary, she proclaimed that "in the education and elevation of woman we are yet to learn the true manhood and womanhood, the true masculine and feminine elements."[26] Stanton recognized that male oppression and female subordination had distorted the qualities of both genders. What women and men would truly be like was a question that only the future could answer. Yet that future was not predestined; it was the task of the feminist movement to create it.

Stanton always demanded equality for women—but the equality she sought had multiple meanings. One of these meanings was equal rights for women, principally in the area of the suffrage, but also in such fields as ownership of property and access to trades and professions. The disfranchisement of women was, in her view, a basic disability that lay at the core of women's grievances. Deprived of political power, women could not gain equal opportunity in any sphere of life. Deprived of citizen responsibilities, they could not gain equal respect either. Throughout her long public career, Stanton condemned what she called "the degradation of disfranchisement."[27]

If much of Stanton's case for women's equality stressed equal opportunity within existing structures, her conception of equality could not be satisfied merely by inclusion of women into the political and economic status quo. Increasingly, she came to regard the home, even more than the state, as the locus of women's oppression. In the home, she wrote, "the woman is uniformly sacrificed to the wife and mother."[28] Law reinforced custom in making the marital bond into "the man marriage," in which "the woman is regarded and spoken of simply as the toy of man . . . ."[29] Feminists must not, Stanton argued, ignore inequality in the home in their campaign for equality in the state.

Tracking down inequality in the home, Stanton courageously ventured into the domain of sexuality. She came to argue that men's power over women was anchored in an autocratic assertion of sexual prerogative. To be genuinely equal with men, women would have to fight for their sexual self-determination: "Man in his lust has regulated long enough this whole question of sexual intercourse."[30] Stanton wanted women not only to be able to say no to their husbands, but to have the personal and economic freedom to dispense with marriage if they found it oppressive. She thus championed liberalized divorce laws, and advocated greater freedom of sexual choice. Bringing the political back to the personal, Stanton fought for a radical transformation of relations between the sexes.

Just as Stanton was pulled toward the opposing poles of sameness and difference, of equal opportunity and radical transformation of gender relationships, so was she tugged toward the opposing poles of individualism and sisterhood. The language of individual freedom and self-development was one of the enduring themes in her rhetoric after 1848. Stanton's individualism only reached its apogee, however, with her 1892 speech, "The Solitude of Self." In this speech (which she considered her best), she declared that women's campaign for equality had its ultimate justification in the solitariness of each human life.

> The strongest reason why we ask for woman a voice in the government under which she lives; in the religion she is asked to believe; equality in social life, where she is the chief factor; a place in the trades and professions, where she may earn her bread, is because of her birthright to self-sovereignty; because as an individual, she must rely on herself. No matter how much women prefer to lean, to be protected and supported, no matter how much men desire to have them do so, they must make the voyage of life alone. . . .

At times in the speech, Stanton spoke a language of individual development reminiscent of Ralph Waldo Emerson, whom she admired. At the end of the speech, however, she underscored with bleak images the distances separating each individual from all others: "There is a solitude which each and every one of us has always carried with him, more inaccessible than the ice-cold mountains, more profound than the midnight sea: the solitude of self."[31]

As a sermon on the need for women to take responsibility for their own lives, "The Solitude of Self" was powerful and moving. But when Stanton posited freedom as the condition of a solitary self—even making reference to "an imaginary Robinson Crusoe, with her woman, Friday, on a solitary island"—she neglected the bonds of sisterhood that sustained women in their struggles to overcome oppression.[32] It was precisely those bonds that pulled Stanton away from her own "solitude of self."

Stanton's broad sympathies for women of all kinds were especially evident during the same period in which she produced "The Solitude of Self." In the final decades of the nineteenth century, the women's movement grew increasingly narrow. Shedding more radical demands and concentrating only on suffrage, the movement was now dominated by white, middle-class, Christian women who sought respectability in the eyes of the powerful. Elizabeth Cady Stanton found herself at odds with such a movement—and with her closest friend, Susan B. Anthony, who accommodated herself to the new conservatism—because it no longer spoke for all of women's needs or for all classes of women. Against the new tendency to work only for suffrage, Stanton insisted on a struggle in every arena in which women were oppressed. Against the new tendency to push only the claims of the most respectable women, she called upon feminists to regain an enlarged vision of sisterhood. Speaking before the founding convention of the National American Woman Suffrage Association (formed by the merger of the National Woman Suffrage Association and the American Woman Suffrage Association) in 1890, Stanton swam against the conservative tide:

> Wherever and whatever any class of women suffer whether in the home, the church, the courts, in the world of work, in the statute books, a voice in their behalf should be heard in our conventions. We must manifest a broad catholic spirit for all shades of opinion in which we may differ and recognize the equal right of all parties, sects and races, tribes and colors. Colored women, Indian women, Mormon women and women from every quarter of the globe have been heard in these Washington conventions and I trust they always will be.[33]

Elizabeth Cady Stanton could be self-righteous in her feminist individualism. Her proud self-assertion sometimes conveyed an air of superiority. But the principal force in her public life was always a sense of outrage at the degradation of women and an empathy for all women confronting that degradation. The individualist who plumbed her own "solitude of self" never forgot her bond to the multitudes of women whose redemption she once described as her "whole-souled, all-absorbing, agonizing interest."[34]

Notes

[1]For biographical details on Stanton, see Elisabeth Griffith, *In Her Own Right: The Life of Elizabeth Cady Stanton* (New York: Oxford University Press, 1984) and Alma Lutz, *Created Equal: A Biography of Elizabeth Cady Stanton* (New York: The John Day Company, 1940).

[2]Elizabeth Cady Stanton Papers, Vassar College Library.

[3]Ibid.

[4]Elizabeth Cady Stanton, *Eighty Years and More: Reminiscences, 1815–1897* (New York: Schocken Books, 1971), p. 148.

[5]Elizabeth Cady Stanton et al., *History of Woman Suffrage*, vol. 1 (Rochester: Susan B. Anthony, 1881), p. 70.

[6]Ellen Carol Dubois, ed., *Elizabeth Cady Stanton/Susan B. Anthony: Correspondence, Writings, Speeches* (New York: Schocken Books, 1981), p. 28.

[7]Stanton et al., *History of Woman Suffrage*, vol. 1, p. 71.

[8]Ellen Carol Dubois, "The Radicalism of the Woman Suffrage Movement: Notes toward the Reconstruction of Nineteenth-Century Feminism," in Anne Phillips, ed., *Feminism and Equality* (New York: New York University Press, 1987), p. 130.

[9]Stanton et al., *History of Woman Suffrage*, vol. 1, p. 804.

[10]Stanton Papers, Vassar College Library.

[11]Theodore Stanton and Harriott Stanton Blatch, eds., *Elizabeth Cady Stanton as Revealed in Her Letters, Diary and Reminiscences*, vol. 2 (New York: Harper & Brothers Publishers, 1922), p. 41.

[12]Ibid., p. 71.

[13]Elizabeth Cady Stanton et al., *History of Woman Suffrage*, vol. 2 (Rochester: Susan B. Anthony, 1881), p. 319.

[14]Stanton and Blatch, eds., *Elizabeth Cady Stanton as Revealed*, p. 120.

[15]Stanton et al., *History of Woman Suffrage*, vol. 2, p. 181.

[16]*The Revolution*, 24 Dec. 1868.

[17]Ibid., 1 Oct. 1868.

[18]Ellen Carol Dubois, *Feminism and Suffrage: The Emergence of an Independent Women's Movement in America: 1848–1869* (Ithaca: Cornell University Press, 1978), p. 164.

[19]Griffith, *In Her Own Right*, p. 143.

[20]Susan B. Anthony and Ida Husted Harper, *History of Woman Suffrage*, vol. 4 (Rochester: Susan B. Anthony, 1902), p. 58.

[21]Stanton and Blatch, eds., *Elizabeth Cady Stanton as Revealed*, p. 45.

[22]Ibid., p. 61.

[23]Elizabeth Cady Stanton et al., *History of Woman Suffrage*, vol. 3 (Rochester: Susan B. Anthony, 1886), p. 56.

[24]Stanton and Blatch, eds., *Elizabeth Cady Stanton as Revealed*, p. 252.

[25]Stanton et al., *History of Woman Suffrage*, vol. 1, p. 811.

[26]Stanton et al., *History of Woman Suffrage*, vol. 2, pp. 189–90.

[27]Anthony and Harper, *History of Woman Suffrage*, vol. 4, p. 176.

[28]Stanton et al., *History of Woman Suffrage*, vol. 1, p. 22.

[29]Ibid., p. 722.

[30]Stanton and Blatch, eds., *Elizabeth Cady Stanton as Revealed*, p. 49.

[31]Dubois, ed., *Elizabeth Cady Stanton/Susan B. Anthony*, pp. 247–54.

[32]Ibid., p. 247.

[33]Ibid., p. 226.

[34]Stanton and Blatch, eds., *Elizabeth Cady Stanton as Revealed*, p. 81.

Mary Todd Lincoln

(1818–1882)

Jean Baker

Born into the household of a wealthy Kentucky slaveholder in 1818, Mary Todd received an unusually good education for a woman of her day. In 1839 she went to live with her sister in Springfield, Illinois. There, Mary Todd entered the social circle that included the brightest young men in Illinois politics, and attracted the attention of one of them, Abraham Lincoln, a local lawyer. Despite her family's objections and a troubled courtship, in November 1842 the couple were married. Abraham Lincoln's legal career flourished, and he was elected to the state legislature and then to Congress. The Lincolns had four sons and a marriage that appears to have been a happy one. When her husband was elected president in 1860, and with the outbreak of the Civil War, Mary Todd Lincoln came under attack as a Southern woman married to the Union president, and because of her expensive tastes in creating a lavish White House. Tormented by the criticism and by the death of one of her sons (another child had died earlier), Mary Todd Lincoln became increasingly prone to melancholy and distress. With her husband's assassination in 1865, she was left homeless and with little money. During her later years she was confined to a sanitarium by her only living son on claims of her "insanity," but she was eventually able to secure her freedom. She died in Springfield, Illinois, in 1882.

Mary Todd Lincoln's prominence depended upon her connection to her husband. Her life suggests much about the relation of women to successful husbands and to the public world of nineteenth-century politics. Although the privilege she gained through marriage allowed her a voice in the public arena, it made her a target for the hostile prejudices to which outspoken women were subject.

At the end of her life, Mary Todd Lincoln referred to herself as "poor me" and exhorted "the ruler of us all to soften the pathway I have been called upon to tread." Her advice to anyone who would listen—and few did—was to have a good time, "for trouble comes soon enough." Surely this was the lesson she had learned from a life of exaggerated misery; others—from male contemporaries to later biographers of Lincoln—would try to make Mary Lincoln's story a cautionary tale of what respectable women should *not* be. Yet, earlier, it had seemed that hers would be the easy, pampered existence of the Lexington gentry—a life framed by the affections and the money of the Kentucky Parkers and Todds and the conventions of female behavior in the early nineteenth century. In these circumstances, like too many women, she would have disappeared from history's view, but Mary Todd Lincoln ensured her historical remembrance by her marriage to an American hero, her interpretation of the role of First Lady, and the tragedies that she sustained during her life.[1]

Like most American women of her time, it was marriage that defined Mary Todd Lincoln's adult status. Yet, before his election to the presidency in 1860, Abraham Lincoln was neither a hero nor even a suitable choice for a young woman of Mary Todd's social and economic background. Born a poor farmer's son in a Kentucky setting that shared little besides geographic proximity to Mary Todd's Lexington, Abraham Lincoln, like so many young men of his generation, had moved to town, first to New Salem and then to nearby Springfield, Illinois. A self-taught lawyer who had less than a year of formal schooling, he nonetheless impressed some of the Springfield community with his intelligence and common sense. Still, even after four terms in the state legislature in the 1830s and 1840s, Lincoln was twice defeated for the United States Senate, and his selection as the Republican nominee and his subsequent victory in the 1860 presidential election were explained by his surprised contemporaries as the result of a split in the Democratic party, which ran two candidates in the election. Nor was Lincoln a heroic figure during the war. His election in 1864 over the Democrat and former commanding general of the Union forces George B. McClellan was only assured by the votes of soldiers in the field.

Only after his assassination did Lincoln emerge as the symbol of the American Union. For blacks and antislavery whites, the sixteenth president became the "Great Emancipator" who had freed from bondage nearly four million slaves. After his death, Lincoln was seen to have dedicated his life to the restoration of the American Republic, and the leader who was assassinated the very week that Robert E. Lee's Confederate army surrendered seemed to symbolize the 600,000 young Americans who had died in military service. The wartime gibes about "Old Abe—The Black Gorilla" were forgotten, as even the South after Lincoln's death came to locate in him more benign approaches to the problem of reconstructing the Union. And as the myths around Lincoln grew and moved farther and farther away from the historical reality of his life, his wife's reputation deteriorated. Like a see-saw, the greatness of the husband provided a contrast to the myths that clustered, unfairly, around the wife. But in the beginning of their relationship, it was Mary, not Abraham, who was the more socially respectable.

Mary Todd was born in Lexington, Kentucky, in 1818, the daughter of Eliza Parker Todd and Eliza's distant cousin Robert Smith Todd; she died in 1882 at her sister's home in Springfield, Illinois. Christened Mary Ann after her father's sister, she began life as a member of an expanding household of siblings and slaves in a town that had been organized by her grandfathers and great-uncles. The Todd brothers—Levi, John, and Robert—had named Lexington after the famous battle fought in 1775 in faraway Massachusetts. With an energy and spirit that the Todds would pass along to many of their descendants, including Mary, the founders expected to transform a grassy meadow surrounded by woods into a center of culture and commerce. In these frontier times, their wives, daughters, and sisters wove textiles; bore, raised, and fed their families; took care of the livestock; and worked in the hemp and corn fields as well as the small gardens that provided this generation with its herbs and vegetables.

By Mary Ann Todd's day Lexington had become a sophisticated city of over six thousand residents with good schools, a college (Kentuckians boasted that Transylvania was the best institution in the country), stores that catered to the rich planter families of Fayette county, and an economy that depended on the transportation of agricultural products and slaves to the markets in New Orleans. But when steamboats began making the journey upstream from New Orleans to rival Louisville on the Ohio River in only three weeks, the Todds' great expectations for Lexington to become "the Athens of the West" floundered.

So too did young Mary Todd's attachment to the place. In 1826 her mother died of puerperal fever, an infection that often followed childbirth and that made childbearing a life-threatening event in every woman's life. Like most Kentucky women, Eliza Todd had a child every two or three years, a spacing dictated not by any conscious control over the process of reproduction, but rather by the natural form of contraception afforded by lactation. At a critical age to lose a mother, Mary promptly lost some of her father's affection to her mother's replacement, just as earlier she had lost part of her name to a younger sister Ann. For all her virtues, Robert Smith Todd's new wife proved to be an uncongenial stepmother.

Surrounded by a growing household that would eventually number fourteen children and ten slaves along with her parents, Mary stood out because, unlike her three sisters and five half-sisters, her behavior crossed some of the barriers of gender that separated young boys and girls in Lexington, and indeed throughout the United States. First she went to school too long; by the time Mary finished both John Ward's day school and Madame Mentelle's French School for Young Ladies she had completed twelve years of schooling, and though Lexington was well known for its educated women, only a handful of women in the United States had that much education. By the 1840s, Catharine Beecher, Mary Lyons, and Almira Phelps would make the case for girls' schooling not so much for their husbands' and children's benefit, but so that women could become schoolteachers. Still, girls were not supposed to compete as intellectual equals with boys, and Mary violated this taboo when she argued with the tutor brought from New England to advance the learning of the Todd sons. And no doubt she also set herself apart from the other girls at the Lexington parties through her book-learning. "[L]iterary topics," advised one southern woman, "make [the boys] run from you as if you had the plague."[2]

So, too, did political topics. Women who talked about public affairs, except perhaps those who consoled male relatives who had lost an election, risked gossip. Evidently Mary did not care. She may have hoped to catch a busy father's attention, for Robert Smith Todd was an important member of the Whig party, a major political party of the time, by the 1830s. She may have been influenced by a home where politicians came to grumble about President Andrew Jackson's veto of a Bank Bill and, worse, his veto of the Maysville bill that would have allocated federal funds to a road connecting northern Kentucky counties to the Ohio River. She may have been influenced by the great Whig senator, Henry Clay, who lived across the pike from her boarding school. In any case, Mary proclaimed herself a Whig, and in an early display of what became an enduring characteristic, she took an active interest in politics. This was in a time when well-born women, especially those in the South, shunned any interest in the public world, instead making their contributions to the private realm of home, family, and church. Those few who did not, like Angelina and Sarah Grimké, the daughters of a South Carolina slaveholder, found it necessary to leave the South.[3]

Mary Todd took her interest in public affairs to Springfield, Illinois, where, by 1839, she lived with her older married sister as an exile from her stepmother's house. For a time, like many young women of her class and time, she went to parties, read, sewed, and formed a close, affectionate relationship with another woman. The modern historian Caroll Smith-Rosenberg calls this "the female world of love and ritual" and means by it a female culture shared by those excluded from the male life of politics, work outside the home, and special meeting places such as taverns, coffee shops, and clubs. Women prohibited from public places made the home and the church their special preserve, while at the same time creating strong bonds with other women. Certainly, Mary participated in this female world in her friendship with Mercy Levering, and their intimacy is apparent in the letters that they wrote when separated by what Mary once called "so many long and weary miles." Wrote Mary in 1840 to Mercy: "You know the deep interest I feel for you. . . . [T]he brightest associations of the past years are connected to thee." Both of these women expected to marry; it was their obligatory status and one that would determine their future in a consuming way that would not be the same for their spouses. During this time of idleness both Mary and Mercy courted; Mary's dance cards were always full and she had an eye for men of politics. But after the parties she and Mercy shared an affection which was not necessarily sexual or erotic but which was a common response to the separated spheres of men and women.[4]

In time, Mary made her choice, and it was Abraham Lincoln, the Whig legislator and lawyer whom she married at a small ceremony held at her sister's house in November 1842. Some thought him the ugliest man in Springfield, and Mary's sister and brother-in-law had opposed the marriage on the grounds that Abraham would not go far. But behind his country manners and clothing, Mary appreciated his potential, and she also sensed his tolerance for women and his desire for the partnership that she believed marriage must be. Traditionally, the husband had been the head of the family, and the comparison of the family to a little kingdom with the wife and children as subjects was a familiar one during the colonial period. But in the nineteenth century a newer style of domestic feminism enabled wives to make crucial decisions about childrearing, the allocation of family resources, and childbearing, even if they did not control the household pursestrings. And as all Springfield soon knew, Abraham Lincoln, according to his friend, and biographer, William Herndon, "exercised no government at home."[5]

It is through an appreciation of Mary's domesticity, and her conventional years as a mother, wife, and homemaker in the western town of Springfield, that we gain an understanding of the experiences shared by many if not most American women of her era. For eighteen years, from 1842 until 1861, when the Lincolns left for the

White House, Mary Lincoln ran the household at Eighth and Jackson. She organized the menus, relying on *Miss Leslie's Cookery and Miss Leslie's House Book* for the recipes that she had never learned in Lexington, where household slaves had done the cooking. She took care of her husband in the nurturing manner that was expected of self-sacrificing middle-class women of this generation who were to smother their own individuality and autonomy with the needs of others. For according to one of the popular prescription manuals of the day:

> Best pleased to be admired at home
> And hear reflected from her husband's praise
> That her house was ordered well,
> Her children taught the way of life.[6]

Certainly it was Mary Lincoln who molded the character and values of her four sons. While Abraham Lincoln was an example of the more companionate father of the future, he was usually absent from Springfield for over a third of the year. Both business and politics took him to the dusty courtrooms of the Eighth Judicial Circuit, leaving Mary Lincoln at home with the boys for long stretches of time. In the permissive mothering style of the future, she organized games and gave large birthday parties. At a time in which most mothers were not so child-directed, she nursed her babies longer than most women, and she erupted in anger if anyone criticized her boys. She also provided most of the medical care for her children, for this was a time and Springfield was a place where the only treatments for the bacterial infections that threatened the young were ineffective drugs such as calomel, a purgative, along with the bloodletting that remained a respectable method of dealing with many diseases. Like most women, Mary Lincoln lost a child to disease; young Eddie Lincoln—"My Angel Boy," as she called him—died at age four of tuberculosis, the most common of the infectious diseases in children under five.[7]

Besides cooking and childraising, Mary was also responsible for keeping the house and the clothes clean. Washing in an age without any electrical devices was a dreaded three-day chore, and Mary paid servants to heat the water, lather the clothes, rinse them in cast-iron tubs, beat them dry, and finally iron them with the awkward stove-heated contrivances of the mid-nineteenth century. She was also responsible for clothing the family, though increasingly—and especially for the boys and her husband—she could buy ready-made clothes in the shops along the courthouse square where Abraham Lincoln kept a second-story office. Unlike her grandmothers, she did not work outside the home, for town living in the mid-nineteenth century provided no possibilities for gardening. Still, the expanding definitions of middle-class domesticity provided a ceaseless round of activities. No doubt it was Mary who organized and paid for the renovation and continuing improvements of the Lincoln cottage, which by the mid-1850s had become what Americans who wanted to summon up an image of the ideal setting for their families called "The House Beautiful."[8] Increasingly, the Lincoln house required more time and energy to maintain the bric-a-brac and the Belgian carpets purchased (for Springfield had no such luxurious goods) in St. Louis. Despite the hard, repetitive labor devoted to uninteresting tasks, Mary would look back on her years as a homemaker as among her happiest. After all, she wrote her daughter-in-law later, all women should hold as their ideal what she once had enjoyed—"a nice home, a loving husband and precious child."[9]

She was busy in Springfield but never too busy to talk politics or to encourage her husband's participation in a career that had stalled after four terms in the state legislature followed by one term in Congress. He wanted to be a United States Senator, but lost twice, once in 1854 and then again after the debates with Democrat Stephen Douglas in 1858. Throughout, Mary Lincoln played more than a supporting role: she wrote patronage letters, she calculated the partisan choices of the legislature that would vote for the senator, she tried to encourage in her husband the conviction that he could become president, and she entertained those who might help what she considered their mutual campaign. To a prominent state politician in 1858, she extended an invitation when Abraham Lincoln was out of town: "I would be pleased to have you wander up our way. . . . I should like to see you." The hospitality she offered was strawberries and cream and conversation, but the subject of her meeting with the Illinois secretary of state was the future of what she came to think of as "our Lincoln party." One lawyer in Springfield admitted that she "did a great deal to educate Lincoln up to action," but in so doing she trespassed onto territory reserved for men in the nineteenth century. When the Republican National Committee traveled to Springfield to notify her husband of his nomination for president, they met an accomplished hostess—the most genteel of ladies—who had set a fashionable table of cakes, sandwiches, and under the table so as not to upset the temperance vote, a bottle of champagne.[10]

Other women, especially in the Northeast, had begun to campaign for public roles for women—the right to address public meetings without being harassed, the right to sign contracts and control property as married women, and even, at the Seneca Falls convention in July 1848, the right to vote. Mary Lincoln thought such activities unladylike, yet she revealed her opposition to a system that denied women their natural rights through her bold involvement in her husband's political life. Like most Americans in this time when "all the world was politics" and three of four voters turned out to vote in elections, she was fascinated with the great game of partisanship. But she chose to challenge the system in a different way from most other politically aware women of her time.

March 1861 marked the beginning of Mary Todd Lincoln's notorious years in the White House, and like so much of her life, the experience was simultaneously grandiose and tragic, unusual and conventional. From the moment of her arrival in Washington, Mary Lincoln continued to trespass into the public world reserved for men. First she intended to improve what she considered the shabby interior of the thirty-one-room White House. While each president was granted $20,000 for repairs and maintenance, the allocation had never supported redecorating. For Mary Lincoln the appearance of the president's house represented more than just a frivolous effort to show off her good taste. Rather, in her redecoration of the Green and Red Rooms, she sought to provide a symbolic statement of the power of the Union during a Civil War when the impressions of foreign diplomats posted in Washington might determine the recognition of the Confederacy by their governments. Soon after the Confederate guns of Charleston fired on the Union batteries at Fort Sumter in April 1861 and her husband began his long toil of winning a war, Mary embarked on her campaign to redo the White House.

To New York and Philadelphia the "President's Lady" went to buy the best wallpaper and furnishings along with expensive dresses; she was soon christened the "First Lady" by a perceptive English correspondent.[11] In the past, presidents' wives had retired to the second-floor family quarters, their names forgotten, as the Commissioner of Public Buildings supervised the maintenance of a house that Europeans dismissed as no grander than "the country house of a merchant."[12] Mrs. President Lincoln (as she became officially known), however, took charge as the lady of the house and served as the interior decorator as well as the director of the social occasions that served as informal opportunities not only to meet the president, but also to discuss military affairs and politics.

Although in so doing she had only transplanted her domestic feminism from one setting to another, she was soon the butt of Washington gossip. In fact, the criticism had begun before she had even gotten to Washington and as such it represented—for Washington was a Southern city—an attack on her Republican husband who was bringing a "vulgar Western wife from the prairies" to the capital's high-toned society. After Mary Lincoln overspent the congressional appropriation and was rumored to have spent $6,800 for French wallpaper and $3,195 for a magnificent set of state china with an entwined gold border signifying the union of North and South, the newspapers forgot their earlier commentary on her supposed uncouthness and instead printed stories of her extravagance. In addition, some Republicans suspected Mary Lincoln of disloyalty, in part because of her ineradicable Southern drawl, and in part because her three stepbrothers were fighting in the Confederate army. Meanwhile, Abraham Lincoln, who was accustomed to turning over the management of the home to his wife, bristled at the expenses, which Mary with some success tried to persuade others to pay. The publicity that enveloped what some were calling the "Presidentess" infuriated many members of the government; at the same time, Mary Lincoln became a symbol of elegance and success for others.

But for the subject of this gossip, her status as a celebrity provided alternating cycles of elation and humiliation. She could never forego reading about herself as a fashion-queen, dressed, according to one description in the *Washington Chronicle,* in a "rich-watered silk deeply bordered, with camellias in her hair and pearl ornaments," but such praise was offset by harsh accounts of the Illinois "queen" who was aping Louis Napoleon's empress, the red-haired beauty Eugenie. To harassed officials trying to find funds to buy blankets and muskets for the hard-pressed Union army, there was an inappropriateness and bad timing to Mary Lincoln's efforts. In time Mary complained that she had become the "scapegoat for both North and South," although she was also the victim of the prevailing attitude toward women that bound them to the private sphere of family, home, and selflessness.[13] Despising what she called the unfeminine women who took up causes, Mary Lincoln suffered because nowhere could she find a precedent for her role as President Lincoln's active partner.

Some of the complaints against Mary Lincoln focused on her incursions into politics. In Springfield she had known Abraham Lincoln's colleagues personally and believed that her special intuitiveness as a woman provided a scanning device to be used for her husband's benefit. But in Washington her husband presided over a vast war-inflated patronage. Mary Lincoln was not deterred by this, for she continued to claim appointments for her friends and relatives, and at the same time to offer advice to her husband and to his cabinet officers. But the cabinet members were often offended by what they considered her impertinent demands, for their own wives did not interfere in public affairs.

Early in her years as First Lady, Mary Lincoln organized a party that revealed the style of her life in the White House. She intended, during the dull winter of 1862, to give a lavish affair that would display the economic power of a government that had been hammered on the battlefield by the Confederate troops at Bull Run and by Nathan Forrest's Confederate cavalry raids in the West. The First Lady invited the most important members of official Washington—Union officers, the diplomatic corps, and leading Republicans. Certainly, as Mary Lincoln reasoned, their acquaintance might be useful in the future, and in the refurbished public rooms of the White House she would advance her husband's career, and through him, her own ambitions as hostess, First Lady, and promoter of what she described as "our Lincoln party." The painters had only just repainted the Gold Room walls scarred by the damage of federal troops billeted there to protect the Lincoln family from a rumored Confederate raid; all was in readiness. But like so much in her ill-starred life, as the guests streamed into the state dining room for the magnificent buffet produced by a New York caterer, young Willie Lincoln lay dying of typhoid fever. This favorite son died two weeks after the party.

Then three years later, in another of those family abandonments that had begun with her mother's death, Mary Lincoln lost her husband as they sat holding hands, enjoying the popular farce *An American Cousin* at Ford's Theater. For most of the Union it was a time of celebration. Robert E. Lee had surrendered his Confederate army only five days before, and on April 6 Mary had toured Richmond, the defeated capital of the Confederacy. But Mary Lincoln's life was always counterpoint. At a time when she looked forward to peacetime Washington and an end to the violence of the Civil War (of which her eldest son Robert was now a part as a member of Grant's army), her husband was murdered. "Alas," she wrote a friend, "all is over with me," and in the poignant expression of her grief she echoed the agonies of thousands of American widows.

The Civil War with its 620,000 dead, along with another 50,000 civilian casualties, had widowed many women, North and South. Widowhood was an especially cruel fate for those who had been trained to see themselves as dependent adjuncts to their husbands. With a characteristic sense of her specialness, Mary claimed that "No *such sorrow* was ever visited upon a people or family, as when we were bereaved of my darling husband, everyday, causes me to feel more crushed and brokenhearted. . . . Time, does not soften [my grief] nor can I ever be reconciled to my loss until the grave closes over the remembrance and I am reunited with him."[14]

For the next sixteen years, from April 1865 until her death in July 1882, Mary Lincoln dressed in the traditional mourning clothes required by her time. Most women gave up the widow's weeds (garments) after the prescribed two years, but Mary Lincoln continued to mourn, and was never able to absorb the memories of her husband into a new life. No matter where she was—for now she had no home as well as no husband—she remembered her losses, of brothers and sisters, of two elder sons and in 1871 of her youngest son Tad, and always of her husband—whom she called "my All."

She also suffered another problem common to widows—a lack of money and of experience in financial affairs. For three years she had no idea what the size of her husband's estate would be. Innocent of interest rates and money matters, she was neglected by both her son Robert and the administrator of her husband's estate, the Supreme Court Justice David Davis, who believed her a spendthrift. As was the case with most women, the bars of the male experience had separated her from the business world, and so she struggled to provide for herself. She had no profession, and other than hiring herself out as a schoolteacher or governess, there was—given the restrictions of her class—little she could do. The possibility of boarders disappeared when she could not afford the taxes and maintenance on the house she purchased in Chicago in 1866 with the $22,000 congressional donation of her husband's residual salary for 1865.

But in 1868 Mary Lincoln decided on a bold plan. She would sell her clothes, the only asset she like most other widows possessed, and though she at first tried to do so anonymously, soon everyone in America knew of Mary Lincoln's Second-Hand Clothing Sale. "Was there ever such cruel newspaper abuse lavished upon an unoffending woman as has been showered on my head?," she wondered, and there were those, including her son Robert, who believed that the most charitable construction that could be put on the behavior of what one newspaper called "this mercenary prostitute" was that she was insane.[15]

Deeply humiliated, Mary Lincoln took her son Tad and left for Germany. Before she went, with suspicious suddenness (for the probate process had languished under Judge Davis's authority until the Second-Hand Clothing Sale), her husband's estate was distributed, and along with Tad and Robert she received $36,000. She was by any standard a rich woman, though her own sense of herself as "poor me" made it impossible for her to be comfortable. Certainly the size of Lincoln's estate testified to her frugality, for the success of her efforts to get others to pay her bills had permitted the president to invest his money in Civil War bonds.

Now began Mary Lincoln's restless years. She had no home and so traveled with her son Tad until his death in 1871, and then by herself. Increasingly, Mary Lincoln turned to spiritualism for the solace that her Presbyterian faith did not provide. While the conviction that the dead could return to visit the living was not restricted to women, it was nonetheless a preeminently female approach to dealing with death. It was also a dangerous one. In Illinois a Presbyterian minister, Reverend Packard, had recently declared his wife Elizabeth a lunatic on the grounds of her spiritualism; in effect, Elizabeth Packard had been institutionalized for two years in a state asylum solely because her belief in the spirits of the other world challenged her husband's ideas. But because of the laws of the time, Reverend Packard needed no other testimony than his own to convince the superintendent of the asylum that his wife was mentally ill.

After the Civil War a growing number of institutions clamored to cure the neurasthenic, the maniacal, and the hysterical, and for the first time in American history women outnumbered men in institutions, although both, according to the U.S. Census, were at equal risk for lunacy. Among the more common diagnoses was that of *mania*, a catchall term used by doctors to include spiritualism.

But for a lonely woman, female mediums provided companionship and the opportunity to talk to a dead husband—through what the believers in the spirit world knew as "hovering," the presence of the dead in the nearby atmosphere. Since Willie Lincoln's death, spiritualism had become an essential part of her life. As Mary Lincoln had told her half-sister Emilie, sometimes Willie returned by himself or with his dead brother Eddie, and once he came with her Todd half-brothers who had fought and died in the Confederate army. With no one left of her family but her eldest son Robert, Mary listened carefully to the medium's appraisals of her eldest son's health.

In 1875 he was, according to her voices from the spirit world, about to die. Terrified, she hastened back to Chicago, where a healthy Robert, a rising star in Chicago's legal circles, met her at the station. Soon Mary Lincoln was living in a Chicago hotel and filling her days with what Robert considered unnecessary shopping. It was easy enough for Robert to persuade his medical friends that his mother was mentally ill. And in this shabby episode of family business, in May 1875 Mary Lincoln was brought before an Illinois jury, charged with being *non compos mentis* (not mentally competent). Convicted in a humiliating public trial, she was sentenced to an asylum for an indefinite period.

In this episode Mary Lincoln suffered the results of a gender system that removed women from the economic and legal sources of power and gave them the insufficient substitute of a male protector. During her trial her lawyer had been chosen by her son, not herself, and the doctors who testified against her had been paid by a son anxious in his paternalistic understanding to do "the best thing" for his mother. During the trial, Mary Lincoln was not called to testify, though had she been, she would have explained the reasons for her undeniably "different" behavior that was the legacy not of lunacy, but rather of the emptiness created by her family losses.[16]

Once in the private asylum outside Chicago, Mary Lincoln began a campaign for freedom that demonstrated her rationality and feminism. She needed an ally to effect her emancipation. For different reasons, both her son and the superintendent of the institution would extend her confinement indefinitely. But given the censorship of all outgoing mail it was difficult to find a supporter to challenge the lawfulness of her continuing confinement. In the end it was a sympathetic woman—one engaged in public activities that Mary Lincoln used to disparage as unfeminine—who accomplished her release. Without Myra Bradwell's intervention it is doubtful that Mary Lincoln would ever have left the mental institution that she likened to prison.

Myra Bradwell was a lawyer who, having successfully completed law school, had subsequently sought to be the first woman practicing attorney in the United States. Debarred from her profession by the state courts of Illinois, she appealed to the Supreme Court, which based its ruling on the ancient doctrine that a married woman was not an independent autonomous being, but instead was "one with the husband and he the one." The court's ruling followed the prejudice with which Mary Lincoln had earlier agreed—that "the paramount destiny and mission of women are to fulfill the noble and benign offices of wife and mother." Given this social understanding, a married woman could not sign contracts or represent clients, for she was not, as common law had long held, an autonomous individual.[17]

But Bradwell was more successful in Mary Lincoln's case than her own. First she found a home for Mary at Mary's sister's and then, familiar with the legal world of writs, grand juries, and appeals, she negotiated Mary's release with the grudging approval of Robert and the superintendent of the asylum.[18] No doubt Mary's notoriety helped, for hers was a case for the reporters who since her husband's assassination had chased her everywhere. Other women were not so lucky, and there is no way of knowing how many women of this generation became the permanent victims of a system that was organized to their disadvantage.

After her release Mary again fled to Europe, this time to France, an exile from the United States and the son whom she never forgave. But even before she left, the reality of her life had disappeared into two myths that determined her historical reputation. Both mirrored the attitudes of American society towards women and their proper status.

Even before her death, Mary Todd Lincoln was viewed as a shrew, a termagant, a virago, and these gendered terms—for there are no equivalents for men—were used about her on the floor of the United States Senate during the debate over her pension. She was, according to one aggrieved senator, "[a]n unrepublican, unAmerican, unfeminine" creature.[19] In such thinking the humanity of a great assassinated leader was expanded through the supposition that his selfish, ill-tempered wife had created for her husband "a domestic hell. . . . For the last twenty-three years of his life, Mr. Lincoln had no joy," wrote William Herndon, the biographer who helped to shape American opinion on Lincoln. Thus Lincoln was thought to have learned the tolerance he displayed with generals, freed slaves, and Republican politicians from navigating his allegedly tortured relations with his wife.[20]

The second myth of Mary Lincoln's historical reputation made her responsible for the trials she endured. Such feelings were a residual effect of the American reliance on Providence, for the idea that nothing happened save through God's will suggested a Job-like punishment for those who sinned. In the way that victims are often blamed for the evil that befalls them, Mary was judged guilty of neglecting her children for the glory that she sought not for her husband but for herself. This prevailing view emerged mainly from the necessity of a male-ordered society to maintain its system of male supremacy during a time of changing roles for women. It was easy enough to convict this prominent, disorderly woman of being an unruly female who violated the separated spheres of the sexes. From such a perspective, it was not surprising that history remembers her as ending her days (for her quick release was often forgotten) in a mental institution.

Today we do better to remember Mary Todd Lincoln as a conventional Victorian woman whose endurance amid the disasters of her life displays the strength that was characteristic of thousands of other American woman.

Notes

[1]Justin and Linda Turner, *Mary Lincoln—Her Life and Letters* (Knopf, 1972), p. 633; Insanity File, Letter Fragment, Lincoln National Life Library, Fort Wayne, Indiana.

[2]Katherine Helm, *The True Story of Mary, Wife of Lincoln* (Harpers', 1928), p. 52; Bertram Wyatt-Brown, *Southern Honor: Ethics and Behavior in the Old South* (Oxford, 1982), p. 201

[3]For development of this point, see Jean Friedman, *The Enclosed Garden: Women and the Community in the Evangelical South, 1830–1900,* (University of North Carolina Press, 1985). Also Gerda Lerner, *The Grimké Sisters,* (Schocken Books, 1971).

[4]Caroll Smith-Rosenberg, "The Female World of Love and Ritual: Relationships between Women in Nineteenth Century America," *Signs,* 1 (Autumn 1975), pp. 1–29.

[5]William Herndon and Jesse Weik, *Herndon's Life of Lincoln* (Cleveland Publishing Company, 1930), pp. 344–45.

[6]*The Mother's Assistant,* vol. 6(January, 1845), pref.

[7]United States Census, Seventh Census, Mortality Schedule, Springfield, Illinois, "Causes of Death," 1850.

[8]David Handlin, *The American Home: Architecture and Society, 1815–1915,* (Little,Brown, 1979), p. 232.

[9]Jean H. Baker, *Mary Todd Lincoln: A Biography,* (W. W. Norton, 1987), p. xiv.

[10]Turner, *Mary Lincoln,* p. 60; Herndon and Weik, *Herndon's Lincoln,* p. 201; Gustave Koerner, *Memoirs of Gustave Koerner,* vol. 2 (Torch Press, 1909), pp. 93–95.

[11]William Howard Russell, *My Diary North and South* (Breadbury, 1863), pp., 132,269; Edna Colman, *Seventy-Five Years of White House Gossip* (Doubleday, 1926).

[12]W. O. Stoddard, *Inside the White House in War Times,* (Webster, 1890).

[13]*Washington Daily Chronicle,* 4 Mar. 1863, 10, 23 May 1863, 17 Nov. 1863, 15 Dec. 1863; *Independent,* 10 August 1882; Helm, *The True Story,* p. 225.

[14]Turner, *Mary Lincoln,* pp. 260, 268.

[15]*Columbus (Ga.) Advertiser,* 4 October 1867.

[16]Baker, *Mary Todd Lincoln,* pp. 318–330

[17]*Bradwell vs. Illinois,* U.S., 30 (1873).

[18]Robert Spector, "Woman against the Law: Myra Bradwell's Struggle for Admission to the Illinois Bar," *Journal of the Illinois State Historical Society* 68 (June 1975), pp. 228–42.

[19]*Congressional Globe,* 41st. Cong., 2nd sess., pp. 5559–60.

[20]Herndon and Weik, *Herndon's Lincoln,* pp. 180–181, 348–350, 105–113.

Varina Howell Davis

(1826–1906)

Joan Cashin

Born into the wealthy planter class in Mississippi, Varina Howell enjoyed the trappings of privilege that were conspicuous in the antebellum South. Her upbringing had many Northern influences, however, for her father, William Burr Howell, was from New Jersey. He sent his young daughter to an academy in Philadelphia, and on her return home engaged for her a tutor from Massachusetts. Varina Howell met the widower Jefferson Davis, a member of a Mississippi planter family, when she was sixteen. Two years later, in 1845, they married. Varina Howell Davis's strong personality sometimes countered the behavior expected of her as a Southern "lady," and caused conflicts between Varina and her husband's family, and often between her and Jefferson. After early years marred by these conflicts and by separation, Varina Davis joined her husband in Washington and settled into the busy social life of a senator's wife. In Washington, Varina Davis bore four children, to whom she was devoted, and gathered a circle of prominent figures as friends. With the secession of the Southern states and Jefferson Davis's selection as the president of the Confederacy in 1861, Varina Davis took on the role of First Lady of the Confederacy. She maintained the Confederate White House in Richmond and bore two more children, at the same time becoming a visible First Lady, a role that brought her much criticism. As the fortunes of the South fell, so too did those of the Davises, as one of their children died in an accident, and Jefferson Davis was imprisoned for treason at the end of the war. After Jefferson Davis's release the family faced illness, financial worries, homelessness, and the loss of two other children. Varina Davis also faced another estrangement, as her husband took up residence on the plantation of a wealthy widow. Reconciled later, the Davises lived together until Jeffer-

son Davis died in 1889. Despite the trouble that had sometimes characterized their marriage, Varina Davis was devastated by her husband's death, and set out to write a memoir of him in which she defends him. In 1892 she moved to New York, where she lived until her death in 1906.

Like Mary Todd Lincoln, Varina Howell Davis did not choose the public spotlight, but became prominent because of her marriage to a leading political figure of the time. The similarity of their lives, despite being identified with opposite sides of the Civil War, suggests the centrality of marriage in shaping women's lives in the nineteenth century—how much women were invested in marriage for their self-esteem, social status, and even perhaps, their reason for living.

Varina Howell Davis was probably the most famous Southern woman of the nineteenth century. The wife of Jefferson Davis, president of the Confederacy, she was a fascinating person in her own right, an intelligent, dynamic, and sensitive woman. One of the most important themes of her life concerns her deep ambivalence about her identity as a Southern woman. Varina Howell Davis was born into the slave-owning elite and accepted many of the conservative values of her region, race, and class, but she could never abide completely by the rules of behavior appropriate to a Southern "lady." Her ambivalence had its origins in the particular circumstances of her personal background, but it was compounded by the oppressive conditions that she and every planter woman faced as a member of the slave-owning class.[1]

Her story begins in Mississippi, where her father, William Burr Howell of New Jersey, settled after his service in the War of 1812. Howell was the scion of a distinguished family; his father Richard was a major in the Revolutionary War and in the 1790s was governor of New Jersey. A talented but irresponsible man, William Howell dabbled in several occupations until he married Margaret Kempe, the daughter of a wealthy slave-owner, in 1823. Margaret Kempe's father gave the young couple a plantation in Warren County, Mississippi, near the banks of the Mississippi River, as a wedding gift, so Howell began a career as a Southern planter. Over the next several decades, the Howells reared their six surviving children. Varina, the second child and oldest daughter, was born on May 7, 1826.

In the 1830s, when Varina Howell was a girl, the role of the Southern "lady" coalesced, part of the South's response to the abolitionist attack on slavery. When Northerners criticized bondage as cruel, immoral, and unchristian, Southerners responded with a battery of arguments defending slavery, among them the notion that the wife of a slave-owner, the plantation mistress, humanized and softened the institution by her kind treatment of slaves. The ideal had larger implications for a woman's role in all of her relationships. She was supposed to defer in all things to her husband, who gave her security, protection, and guidance in return. She should be literate and know something about the arts, but she should not become so well educated that she forgot that her most important duty was to care for her family. Languid, gentle, and retiring, she lived entirely in the private world of the family. The image took deep root in Southern culture and remained the standard by which the behavior of women of the planter class was measured throughout the generation before the Civil War.

In reality, planter-class women had great responsibilities and few freedoms in this conservative, patriarchal society. They typically received poor educations, married at young ages, bore many children, and lived on isolated plantations where they performed a great deal of work—well documented by historians—in rearing children and managing slaves. But these responsibilities did not translate into decision-making power within the family. Men made the key decisions, such as where the family would live, as well as the smaller decisions, such as when women would be allowed to visit their relatives on distant plantations. If a man violated his marriage vows, mistreated his wife or children, or abrogated his responsibilities to provide for his family, his wife had few alternatives. Divorce was illegal in many Southern states, and it was extremely difficult to obtain even in states that did permit it; the stigma was so terrible that most women would rather endure an unhappy marriage than get a divorce.

It is true that elite Southern women had privileges that poor white women did not enjoy; they were literate, lived in physical comfort, and had the assistance of slave house servants in running their households. But they were also denied the freedoms enjoyed by Northern white women of the upper classes or even the middle classes, such as sound educations, the opportunity to work outside the home, and the stimulation of town and city life, and through it all they had to live up to the demanding ideal of the lady. Varina Howell Davis escaped some of these strictures, partly because of her family's Northern roots and partly because she married a man who became a national figure, but she too had to struggle all of her life to behave as a lady, and she was often confronted with her powerlessness in the family.

Her difficulties began, ironically, with her education, which was almost completely Northern in orientation. She attended an elite girls' academy in Philadelphia and then studied at home with a private tutor, George Winchester of Massachusetts, a stern Yankee who recognized that his pupil had a keen, lively mind. He gave her a rigorous education in the classics, history, literature, and languages, and he nurtured her love of reading, something that stayed with her for the rest of her life. Winchester also imparted his political views to her—he was a confirmed Whig but no abolitionist—and encouraged her to take an interest in current events. Perhaps most important of all, he taught her to think for herself and value her own intelligence. Varina Howell did not attend college, but she was better educated than most Southern women (and most men) of her generation. Throughout her life, she showed a hearty interest in cultural and political matters, an interest that was considered bold and unfeminine.

As Varina Howell grew up, it became clear that her personality would not conform to the ideal of the lady. She was an energetic, affectionate, and brave girl, who felt things vividly and tended to say exactly what she thought. She took on family responsibilities at an early age, helping to run the household at the family's plantation, the Briers. As the oldest daughter, she helped her mother care for the other children, and she once saved her siblings from a housefire. Margaret Howell, reared in Louisiana, was much like a typical lady, completely submerged in family life, not very well educated, and deferential toward her husband. She was also a loving woman and understood her daughter's temperament. Varina in turn was devoted to her mother, but she could not play the ideal female role as her mother did.

Varina Howell's relationship with her father was more complex and much more strained. Although William Howell gave her a far better education than most young women received, he expected her to behave like a typical lady, and he never encouraged her to aspire to any occupation other than wife and mother. Furthermore, there was an emotional barrier between them. When she was in her thirties, she remarked that her father did not like children, and some of his missives to her have a callous, indifferent tone. One letter he wrote after the birth of one of her children, when Varina nearly died from puerperal fever, a common post-childbirth infection, was so cold that she burst into tears. Nor was he a good provider for his family: he squandered his wife's dowry and lost the plantation in 1850, when he moved to New Orleans to work as a customs official. Margaret Howell suffered quietly as her husband went deeper into debt, but Varina resented his irresponsibility. She stepped into the vacuum and guided the education and upbringing of her younger siblings; after she married, several of them lived with her, rather than with their parents, for long periods of time. At an early age, Varina began learning a hard lesson: men did not always behave consistently or provide the security that was their duty to provide as fathers and husbands.

Yet the young Varina Howell was not completely at odds with the Southern world in which she grew up. She enjoyed the status, privileges, and physical comforts that went with being a lady. All of her life she loved beautiful clothes, good food, and elegant homes, and she wanted to be around powerful, accomplished people. In fact, she was always an elitist, feeling distaste and pity for whites who were not members of the slave-owning class. Her racial views were also representative of the planter class: she saw blacks as inferior, childlike, and untrustworthy, and she accepted slavery as a God-given institution. By the time Howell was in her teens, she had been socialized as a member of the planter class, but she was not completely at one with its values. Her education and her family background prevented her from becoming a lady in the traditional mold.

When sixteen-year-old Varina Howell met Jefferson Davis at a Christmas party in 1843, she was a tall young woman with pale skin, dark hair, and great dark eyes, and she already had a reputation as a wit. In an observant letter to her mother, she described their meeting: "He impresses me as a remarkable kind of man but of uncertain temper, and has a way of taking for granted that everybody agrees with him when he expresses an opinion, which offends me." She added, "He is the kind of person I should expect to rescue one from a mad dog at any risk, but to insist upon a stoical indifference to the fright afterward." Yet he could also be "most agreeable" with "a winning manner of asserting himself," and he was a gentleman, handsome, "refined," and "cultivated," even though he was a Democrat. Jefferson Davis left no account of their meeting, but he told his brother soon afterwards that she was beautiful and had a fine mind. The couple fell in love, but they had a rocky courtship, and Margaret Howell initially opposed Jefferson's suit because he was a widower and considerably older than Varina. She finally gave them her blessing, and the couple was married at the Briers on February 26, 1845.[2]

Seventeen years older than Varina, Jefferson Davis was the son of Mississippi planter Samuel Davis, who died in 1824 when Jefferson was sixteen years old. The oldest son, strong-willed Joseph, completed Jefferson's upbringing, sending him to Transylvania College and then to West Point Military Academy, from which he graduated in 1828. He served in the army in the Midwest, where he fell in love with Sarah Knox Taylor (called "Knox"), the daughter of Colonel Zachary Taylor. His brother Joseph gave him slaves and a plantation called Brierfield near his own plantation in the Mississippi River Delta so that Jefferson might begin a new career as a planter. Jefferson married Knox Taylor in 1835, and the couple proceeded on a honeymoon trip to the South where the bride was to meet the Davis family.

Little is known about Knox Taylor Davis, but she seems to have been much like the ideal lady—sweet, pliable, and even-tempered. Her new in-laws adored her. But the marriage ended tragically when the newlyweds both contracted malaria while visiting relatives in Louisiana. Knox Davis died only three months after the wedding. Jefferson Davis plunged into a profound grief, retreating to Brierfield, where he saw few people other than his own relatives. For eight years, he lived virtually alone, spending his time reading and talking to his brother Joseph when he was not working on his plantation. The brevity of the marriage allowed Jefferson and everyone else to idealize Knox, and he mourned for her for years.

The death of Knox Davis probably accentuated the austere, rigid aspects of Jefferson Davis's personality. Even as a boy, he was dignified and self-controlled, and as an adult many people found him aloof, as Varina Howell did when they first met. He suffered from bad health for most of his life, enduring a variety of neurological disorders, eye problems, and recurring bouts of malaria, so that his nerves were easily frayed. Yet Jefferson Davis worked hard at whatever task he chose, driving himself whether he was a soldier, planter, or politician. There was a warmer, more humane side to his makeup. With intimates he could be funny and engaging, and some of his letters to his family members were surprisingly sweet. He was idealistic and devoted to principles as he understood them, but he could easily become self-righteous. It would soon become clear that he had very conventional attitudes about women's roles. These unappealing qualities appeared early on in his marriage to Varina Howell.

The match was shadowed from the beginning, and not only by the ghost of Knox Taylor Davis. For several years, both Davises believed (falsely, as it turned out) that they could not have children, and for reasons that are not clear, they both thought the problem lay with Varina. When the couple settled in 1845 on Jefferson's plantation, domestic peace was disrupted by heated conflicts between Joseph Davis and his new sister-in-law. The elder Davis first suggested that the couple share living quarters with one of Jefferson's widowed relatives, but Varina objected. Then she found that Joseph Davis had drawn up a will that prevented her from inheriting Jefferson's plantation; since Joseph had never given his brother title to the property, he still had control over its disposition. Joseph had initially approved of his brother's second marriage, but he had then taken a deep dislike to Varina, probably because of her strong personality and the fact that she was much better educated than the other women in the Davis family. Joseph, Jefferson, and Varina exchanged harsh words over all of these issues.

Jefferson Davis was offended by the conduct of both his brother and his wife, but he seems to have blamed Varina for much of the conflict and, more generally, for the incompatibilities that surfaced in the marriage. Jefferson and Varina Davis had very different personalities, and Jefferson was in the habit of commanding others, whether in the military or on the plantation. Varina tried hard to please him and behave as a submissive wife, but she resented the punishing behavior of her brother-in-law and her husband. During the first year of their marriage, the couple became estranged. In the midst of this turmoil, Jefferson Davis was elected to the House of Representatives, serving briefly in Washington, D.C., before he left to join the American army in the Mexican War. Varina Davis remained in Mississippi with in-laws who were increasingly uncharitable to the teenaged bride and subtly reminded her that she was not Jefferson's first love. The Davises ostracized her much of the time, so that she even ate her meals alone, telling her mother that "my one plate looks very lonely, and I tear my food in silence." She moved from one household to another, living alternately with her brothers- and sisters-in-law until her husband returned from Mexico in 1847.[3]

Their reunion was not a happy one, aggravated by Jefferson Davis's ill health and continuing rancor over Joseph Davis's will. Jefferson Davis had become a war hero after the battle of Buena Vista, and he was appointed to serve in the United States Senate. He left his wife in Mississippi and went alone to Washington, where he wrote her a series of blistering letters. In one letter, he lambasted Varina for "suspicions and threats . . . equally unjust and unnecessary" and told her to act in a way "demanded by your duties as a wife," when in fact Joseph Davis was clearly trying to stop Varina from obtaining property that should have been hers as the wife of Jefferson Davis. Varina's response to this letter is not recorded, but no doubt she was angry that her interests were being shunted aside; when her in-laws discussed these property disputes, she raged that "it has not been thought proper to inform me" about the outcome. Few letters survive from this fateful year in their marriage, possibly because Varina or Jefferson later destroyed them, but by mid-1848, the couple reconciled on his terms. Joseph Davis's will remained unchanged, but Varina joined her husband in Washington, where she lived for most of the next twelve years. She somehow forgave her spouse, whom she still loved, but she never forgave Joseph Davis, and her relationships with most of the Davis family were cool and formal.[4]

Thus in the early years of her marriage Varina Davis was confronted with the power, and the inconsistency, of two of the most important men in her life. Her brother-in-law, a prototypical Southern patriarch, deprived her of property that should have been hers, and her husband did not take her side or protect her interests. Her spouse also had the power to decide when, or if, she could live with him in Washington. Her response was one of initial rebellion followed by eventual acquiescence, which became a recurring pattern in the Davis marriage. Jefferson Davis loved his wife and respected her intelligence, but he expected her to submit to his will; he simply accepted the sex roles of his era and never understood or sympathized with her frustrations, which he tended to dismiss as the outbursts of an emotional woman. He had the decision-making power in the relationship in matters large and small. Varina once told her mother that she had been "begging" her husband to allow her to visit her family, but added, "He does not say yea or nay."[5]

The marriage nonetheless had its compensations and satisfactions. The couple seemed to be sexually compatible, according to the few oblique comments they made in their letters. Jefferson once told his wife that he longed to "clasp my own Winnie [his nickname for her] in my arms." And when the couple finally had children, both parents delighted in them. Varina bore four children in the 1850s, Samuel, Margaret, Jefferson Jr., and Joseph. Varina Davis worked as her husband's secretary, helping him read and write letters when his vision troubled him, and they often discussed books and politics together. Davis's political career flourished, as he served as secretary of war under President Franklin Pierce and for a second time in the United States Senate in 1857. Varina gave up her Whig sympathies for his Democratic views, and she was proud of her husband's success. But even his triumphs had a bitter edge: she regretted his long absences from home, and as an old woman she wrote that long before the Civil War she realized that the lot of a politician's wife was a lonely one.[6]

Varina Davis was a hard-working mother as well as a wife. She occasionally had the help of female slaves who worked as house servants, but she longed for the assistance of her mother at home, whom she missed very much. She raised her children, a "precocious" bunch with "unbroken wills," with little help from her busy husband. Varina nursed her offspring herself, and her letters are filled with anxious accounts of their many illnesses. Medical knowledge was primitive in the mid-nineteenth century, and every childhood ailment was a potentially serious one. Her firstborn, Samuel, died in 1854, probably from the measles, and his death traumatized

Varina. Yet the Davises were able to comfort each other and devote themselves to their other children.[7]

In the 1850s, Varina Davis developed her distinctive views on the subject of women's roles, reflecting her experiences and those of her friends. She had a number of close female friends in Washington, and she remarked after the birth of her son Joseph in 1859 that they "did everything in the world for me." A friend later commented that "clever women" tended to gravitate toward Varina Davis, and in this decade she forged friendships with such vital women as Mary Boykin Chesnut, the wife of Senator James Chesnut of South Carolina. Davis believed that there were deep differences between the sexes and that intimacy between men and women was difficult, if not impossible; she could share her most private thoughts, her inner self, only with other women. She also believed that the many demands made on women in their capacities as wives and mothers were unfair, an opinion she expressed throughout her life. In 1858, at age thirty-two, she told her mother that young wives had to take on the responsibilities of adulthood at too early an age. She lamented that "Cares do wear out one's youth," but added, "I think they refine, and purify at the same time." Here Davis's innate conservatism was evident: she objected to the heavy burdens of being a woman in a man's world, and she probably regretted her early marriage, but she strove to find something redeeming in her sacrifices. These views she expressed privately in her correspondence, never in public, and she showed no interest in the burgeoning woman's rights movement of the mid-nineteenth century.[8]

Varina Davis did find time to take part in the social life of the capital. As the wife of a cabinet member and senator, she attended dinners, teas, and other social events with the most powerful people in the nation. She became known for her wit, which was sometimes cutting, but her warmth and spirit won her a wide circle of friends, including President Franklin Pierce, his wife Jane Pierce, President James Buchanan, and Judah P. Benjamin, the senator from Louisiana. Davis was a shrewd observer of human nature, and her writings contained some wise judgments and funny comments about political figures of the day. She once went to a masquerade ball dressed as Madame de Staël, delivering "caustic repartee" in French and English. She relished the social and intellectual stimulation of the capital that life on a Southern plantation could not provide.[9]

Varina Davis was very much alarmed by the secession crisis of 1860–61. Although she believed that slavery had to be protected and that the Southern states had the right to secede from the Union, she prayed for peace and wished that she had lived in an another age. She was anything but optimistic when her husband was chosen president of the new Confederacy in February 1861. Davis allegedly told a friend in 1860 that if the South seceded "the whole thing is bound to be a failure," and she confided to her mother in 1861 that the North had a great advantage in manufacturing power. She described her husband as "depressed" about the Confederacy's prospects, but he accepted the office as his duty. Varina Davis did her duty and followed him to Montgomery, Alabama, and then to Richmond, Virginia, when it was selected as the Confederate capital.[10]

As First Lady of the Confederacy, Varina Davis was once again part of a brilliant social circle. She resumed her friendship with Judah Benjamin, the canny Louisianian who held several posts in the Davis government, and she became the confidante of the equally gifted Mary Chesnut, whose husband was an aide to President Davis. She was a highly visible First Lady, sparkling at parties and dinners, so much so that her sister-in-law, Eliza Davis, the wife of Joseph Davis, left a disapproving account of Varina's behavior in the summer of 1861. She received callers every evening, so that the parlors of the Confederate White House were "filled with strange gentlemen" and "[A] few ladies." (Eliza Davis, by contrast, kept to her room.) What made Varina Davis's behavior even more unsuitable was the fact that she was pregnant with her fifth child. In and of itself, this was a serious transgression of proper behavior for a Southern lady, and it helps explain why Varina became such a controversial individual.[11]

Varina Davis repeatedly violated other standards of genteel feminine behavior, and now that her husband was president she came in for criticism from many sides, not just from her sister-in-law. Jefferson Davis's political enemies criticized his wife as imperious, and some said that she dominated her husband. The blue-blooded ladies of Virginia shunned her, and one of them derided her as a "coarse western woman." Men and women said that her forthright, spirited manner was unrefined. Davis did have an exuberant sense of humor with an especially acute sense of the ridiculous, which got her into trouble. She once attended a dinner during which a general's wife said that the underdrawers for an entire regiment had mistakenly been made with two right legs. Davis burst out laughing, much to the horror of the other guests. The First Lady was just as controversial in the eyes of the Confederate public, and for much the same reasons. A plantation mistress in North Carolina remarked that Varina Davis was not "Ladylike" in her dress or her conduct and that she was not a "truehearted Southern woman."[12]

Jefferson Davis did not publicly rebuke his wife for her behavior, although we will never know what he said to her in private. He was too traditional a man to be dominated by Varina, but it is clear from letters written when they were occasionally separated during the war that their relationship was much like it had been in Washington. He discussed military developments with his wife and gave her his frank views about the capabilities of Confederate generals and politicians. She played a supportive role in their correspondence, agreeing with his opinions and passing on rumors and information she heard from various sources. These letters also demonstrated the love that Varina still felt for her husband. In 1862, when she and the children had to evacuate Richmond because a Union invasion seemed imminent, she felt "every months [*sic*] absence an irreparable loss."[13]

The Davis family continued to grow in the 1860s, as two more children were born, William in 1861 and Varina Anne in 1864, but for Varina motherhood continued to bring worry and sorrow. Much of her time was taken up with rearing and caring for her children, just as it had been before the war. Doctors, nurses, and female slaves attended them, but Davis herself tended to her children through their many illnesses. She lost another child in a freak accident in 1864, when five-year-old Joseph died after falling from the second story of the Confederate White House. Davis was distraught, and her husband walked the floor at night, consumed with grief.

As the war went on, both Davises continued to take a pessimistic but stoical view of the conflict. In the spring of 1865, Varina and the children fled Richmond once again, heading south. Her husband followed after the city fell to the Union army, and the family reunited, planning to go to Texas, where Jefferson Davis hoped to continue the fight. After a nightmarish flight, they were captured in southern Georgia near the town of Irwinville by a contingent of Northern troops. When the soldiers closed in on Jefferson Davis, Varina apparently threw a shawl over his head to disguise him, giving rise to the rumor that he had tried to escape in the dress of a woman. Both the Davises denied the rumor for years afterwards because it called Jefferson's courage into question, but the incident is just as interesting for what it reveals about Varina, who once again refused to play the helpless lady.

Soon after his capture, Jefferson Davis went to prison for treason in Fort Monroe, Virginia, and the children left for Canada in the company of their grandmother Margaret Howell. Varina lived near the prison with her infant daughter, feeling "very desolate" about the fate of her husband and scattered family. The couple wrote regularly to each other and were allowed to visit occasionally; in 1866 she confided to a friend that her husband had changed a great deal since he had gone to prison, growing weaker as the months and years went by, and she later wrote that during all of the postwar years she never once heard her husband laugh, suggesting that something vital had gone out of him forever. Meanwhile, Varina handled their financial problems, borrowing money from friends to support her mother, her children, and herself. It was a harbinger of days to come, because Jefferson Davis was never able to provide for his family after he was released from prison in the spring of 1867.[14]

Now began a period of homelessness, poverty, and illness for Varina Davis and her family. The Davises traveled to Canada and rejoiced to see their children, but Varina lost her beloved mother a few months later when Margaret Howell died of typhoid fever. The family set sail for England in 1868 in hopes that a change of scene would improve Jefferson's health. The family spent two years abroad, living in a succession of hotels, while Varina cared for her sick and restless husband. "I watch over him unceasingly," she told a friend, and lived "in terror" that he would collapse and die. She also struggled to care for her brood of children and was determined that they should get the best education the family's limited means could permit. She sent her sons and daughters to several noted schools, such as an academy in Karlsruhe, Germany, where she placed young Varina Anne.[15]

The Davises were still public figures, and they were sometimes cheered on the streets of England and France by sympathetic strangers. They received social invitations from the European elite, including members of the British aristocracy and the emperor of France, who were curious about the ex-president. Varina was grateful for the kindnesses she received, especially when her children fell ill, but she longed for quiet and privacy. They occasionally met other Confederate exiles, such as Judah Benjamin, who had begun practicing law in England and eventually built up a lucrative practice. Jefferson Davis lacked Benjamin's resilience, however, and found it very difficult to adapt to the postwar world.

In 1870, the family returned to the United States, where Varina faced a new round of struggles. Her husband accepted a job as head of the Carolina Life Insurance Company in Memphis, Tennessee, but he had no experience in business, and the company foundered. The Davises lost yet another of their children, William, who died of diphtheria in 1872 at age eleven. Another family dispute marred these difficult years, when Jefferson Davis sued to break the will of his brother Joseph, who died in 1870 without leaving Jefferson the title of the plantation, Brierfield, which he had given him in the 1830s. Jefferson Davis won the case in 1878, but the plantation brought in little revenue, so he moved to Beauvoir, a plantation owned by Sarah Dorsey on the Gulf coast of Mississippi, and decided to begin writing a history of the Confederacy. Varina Davis, who had developed heart trouble, was in England being cared for by a physician. She was furious when she discovered where her husband had relocated.

Jefferson Davis's decision to live on the estate of Sarah Dorsey, a widow whom the Davises had known for many years, seems surprising even today. Sarah Dorsey idolized Davis and may have been in love with him; in any event, she quickly usurped his wife's role, acting as his secretary and helping him with his book. He rented a separate cottage on the estate, but he had nonetheless abandoned his wife while she was ill and gone to live with a woman who was not his wife. Davis's behavior may have been part of a more general deterioration in his judgment and personality that seems to have begun while he was in prison. Varina Davis was wounded and mortified by his settlement at Beauvoir, which soon became a subject of gossip. When she returned from England, she lived in Memphis with her daughter Margaret for almost a year.

This episode illustrates not only the issues in the Davis marriage, but also suggests the outlines of sex roles for women in the postwar South. Historians still know little about how the upheavals of the Civil War and Reconstruction era changed the lives of women from the old slaveholding class, but these events resulted in more burdens on Varina Davis and only exacerbated the inequities in her marriage. Despite Varina's growing responsibilities and her husband's inability to provide for his family, he nonetheless retained the power to do as he wished, to forsake the role that he as a Southern man, husband, and father should have played. This was Joseph Davis and William Howell all over again, and Varina acquiesced once again, as a proper lady and loyal wife had to do. If she ever considered divorcing her husband, she never mentioned it in writing. She finally went to Beauvoir in 1878 on the most humiliating terms, living with her husband in the main house with Sarah Dorsey.

The wretchedness of this era in Varina's life had not yet come to an end. Her last surviving son, Jefferson Davis, Jr., died of yellow fever at age twenty-one in Memphis, and his death sent both of his parents into a still, silent grief. Once again Varina was robbed of a home when Sarah Dorsey, who died in 1879, willed Beauvoir to Jefferson Davis and his daughter Varina Anne, also called "Winnie," excluding Varina from ownership altogether. The Davises continued to live in the house because they could not afford to go elsewhere. When in 1881 Jefferson Davis published his history of the Confederacy—a dry account that justified the right of secession—it sold poorly and brought in little revenue.

The last years of Varina Davis's married life were somewhat more contented. The household brightened when her daughter Winnie returned from abroad to live with her parents. A delicate, thoughtful woman, Winnie wrote poetry and fiction, and like her parents, she was an avid reader. She soon became her father's constant companion. The family received many visits from old friends and inquisitive strangers, such as Oscar Wilde, who came to Beauvoir in 1882 to meet the ex-president and his wife. Jefferson himself became ever more frail and suffered from insomnia. Winnie and Varina both cared for him, writing letters, helping him with articles and speeches, and reading to him into the night when he could not sleep. Davis tended to relive the war years, fighting battles again and discussing them endlessly with his wife, daughter, and friends. Varina became the mainstay of the household, its greatest source of vitality and strength.

She showed little interest when Southerners began celebrating the war and the "Lost Cause" in the late nineteenth century, even though she was a natural candidate, as the wife of the ex-president, for some role in these activities. Varina seems to have valued her privacy too much to give it up, and she may have thought that she had already sacrificed enough for the Confederacy. Her daughter Winnie did play a ceremonial role and became something of a public figure in the 1880s. Born in 1864, she had been nicknamed "The Daughter of the Confederacy." She had spent most of her youth abroad and knew little of the South when she came home, but when she appeared at a meeting of Confederate soldiers in Atlanta in 1885, the crowd gave her a thunderous ovation. Soon Winnie was appearing at other reunions and public gatherings. She apparently played this role out of love for her parents, especially her father, rather than her personal commitment to the "Lost Cause." In the 1880s, she fell in love with a Northerner, Alfred Wilkinson, Jr., who was the grandson of a noted abolitionist. Jefferson Davis opposed the match on these grounds, but later reluctantly consented when he realized how deeply she loved Wilkinson; Varina did not relent, however, and objected even more strongly when she discovered that Wilkinson was not as affluent as he pretended to be. Winnie finally broke the engagement, and she never married.

Varina Davis had long suspected that she would outlive her husband, and his death finally came in December 1889. Jefferson contracted acute bronchitis on a trip through New Orleans, brought on because he characteristically insisted on traveling on a cold rainy day. She rushed to New Orleans to care for him, and she was holding his hand at his bedside, sobbing and calling his name, when he died. The funeral was an enormous public event, but the widow behaved with dignity and maintained her composure. She collapsed afterward, however, and went into a period of deep mourning, at one point telling a friend that she felt that her life was over. Varina had indeed devoted most of her life to her husband's needs, like so many nineteenth-century Southern women, and she never publicly criticized her husband or voiced what must have been her considerable anger at his behavior with Sarah Dorsey. The death of her spouse, despite the many problems in the marriage, was a great loss to Varina.

She then threw herself into the task of writing a book about her husband. Published in 1890, the memoir is a monumental work, a total of 1,638 pages in two volumes. Like many nineteenth-century biographies, it includes excerpts from Jefferson Davis's speeches and correspondence interspersed with Varina's own account of events. Written in clear, strong prose, the book has some poetic touches, such as her description of the wildflowers at Brierfield which shone like "banks of gold." The memoir is a valuable source of information about Varina Davis herself, especially her early life, and it wonderfully evokes the lush tropical beauty of the Southern countryside and the rhythm of plantation life.[16]

It is somewhat disappointing, however, as a commentary on her forty-four-year relationship with Jefferson Davis, since her chief purpose seems to have been to vindicate her husband, and in doing so, to justify the many sacrifices she made throughout their life together. She depicted her late husband in reverential terms as a noble, principled man, and she did not mention most of the conflicts and tensions that plagued the marriage, such as her long-standing feud with Joseph Davis. She did discuss her husband's sojourn with Sarah Dorsey, which may indicate how much she was hurt by it. Obviously attempting to dispel the rumors surrounding the incident, she emphasized that Sarah Dorsey acted as her husband's secretary "at stated hours during the day." The only critical remark she made about her husband was that he should have been a general during the Civil War because he "did not know the arts of the politician, and would not practise them" if he did know them. Varina may have thought that his entire career as a politician was a mistake; she knew that he lacked the flexibility necessary for successful political leadership, a judgment later reached by many historians of the Confederacy.[17]

Her ambivalence about the South was also evident in certain passages of the memoir. She continued to believe that the states had the right to secede, and she praised the courage of Confederate soldiers, but she still bristled at the restrictions of the role of the Southern lady. Varina Davis commented on the role indirectly in her description of the Virginians who had snubbed her during the war. They were cold, merely "practical," and not very cosmopolitan—a sharp retort from a woman who had received an invitation from the emperor of France. She ridiculed attempts to prevent women from reading widely and freely in the 1840s and 1850s, when authors such as

Charles Dickens were considered too dangerous for the female mind—something that still galled Davis over forty years later. Yet nowhere in the book did she directly challenge traditional sex roles, despite her manifest unhappiness with the role proscribed for her.[18]

In 1892 Davis decided to leave Beauvoir and live elsewhere. For the first time in her life, she was able to decide for herself where she wanted to live, and she moved to New York City. Her choice stunned many Southerners, who felt betrayed when the former Confederate First Lady settled in the North. Davis had several practical reasons for the move: New York was full of ex-Confederates, some of them prosperous, who were willing to befriend the family. She hoped that Winnie's literary abilities might be recognized in the metropolis, and she wanted to escape the hot climate of the Deep South, which had begun to bother her as she aged. These reasons were all plausible enough, but at the heart of her decision there was nonetheless an unmistakable rejection of the South itself. After all, cities in the Upper South such as Richmond or Baltimore offered similar attractions. Davis wanted the cosmopolitan atmosphere that only a great Northern city like New York could provide.

So mother and daughter settled in the Marlborough Hotel, the first of many hotels Varina was to inhabit for the rest of her life. They worried constantly over money, writing articles for pay and receiving financial help from friends and family members. It was a precarious existence, but an interesting one. Members of the city's social and cultural elite flocked to her door, drawn by her fame, charm, and conversational powers. Her life was filled with improbable encounters: she became a good friend of John W. Burgess, a prominent intellectual and political scientist, and in 1893 she met Julia Dent Grant, the widow of Ulysses S. Grant, with whom she had an extended, friendly conversation.

Varina Davis lost yet another child, however, when Winnie died of some gastro-intestinal disorder in 1898 at age thirty-three. Varina felt very much alone, deprived of her daughter's "precious companionship and sympathy." She was also wracked with guilt, not only because she had insisted that Winnie take the trip Varina thought had precipitated the illness, but because she had been primarily responsible for Winnie's broken engagement. She had put tremendous energy into her role as a mother, raising six children, but only one of her offspring lived long enough to marry and have children, and this daughter had settled far from her mother. Margaret Davis had wed Addison Hayes, a bank officer, in Memphis in 1876, and the couple moved to Colorado Springs in the 1880s for Addison's health.[19]

The remaining years of Varina Davis's life she lived on her own terms. She supported herself by writing articles on the Civil War and other subjects for such publications as the *New York World*. She continued to draw friends, relatives, and acquaintances to her sitting room, and she took part in the city's cultural life, attending the opera, the theater, and concerts. Freed of her demanding duties as a wife and mother, she was able to control the use of her time and indulge her taste for accomplished people, good books, and good conversation. She remained a fundamentally conservative woman, however, and to the end of her life she was a tireless defender of her husband. Yet there was a breach in her conservatism, as always; she maintained her views that women were treated unfairly. In her old age, she opposed woman's suffrage, but on the grounds that women already had enough responsibilities. Varina Davis felt that "my duties have always been more numerous and arduous than I could satisfactorily perform." It was a sad comment, a confession of failure after a lifetime of trying to conform to the ideal of the Southern lady.[20]

Varina Howell Davis died of pneumonia in New York on October 16, 1906, and was buried beside her husband in Richmond. Raised in the South, she absorbed many, but not all, of its values, and she could never be wholeheartedly loyal to it. The First Lady of the Confederacy was always ambivalent about her identity as a Southern lady, and her feelings were evident throughout her long, turbulent life.

Notes

[1]I am writing a full-scale biography of Varina Howell Davis, the first professional historian to do so. Students seeking information on her life have to go to a variety of sources: Davis's memoir of her husband, Varina Davis, *Jefferson Davis, Ex-President of the Confederate States of America: A Memoir*, 2 vols. (New York: Belford Company, 1890); Haskell M. Monroe, Jr., James T. McIntosh, Lynda L. Crist, and Mary S. Dix, eds., *The Papers of Jefferson Davis*, 5 vols. (Baton Rouge: Louisiana State University Press, 1971–1985); Eli N. Evans, *Judah P. Benjamin, The Jewish Confederate* (New York: The Free Press, 1988); C. Vann Woodward, ed., *Mary Chesnut's Civil War* (New Haven: Yale University Press, 1981); Bell Irvin Wiley, *Confederate Women*, Contributions in American History, no. 38 (Westport, CT: Greenwood Press, 1975). Ishbel Ross, a journalist, wrote the most recent biography, *First Lady of the South: The Life of Mrs. Jefferson Davis* (New York: Harper & Brothers Publishers, 1958). I thank the National Endowment for the Humanities for a Travel to Collections Grant that enabled me to conduct some of the research for this article.

[2]Varina Banks Howell to Margaret K. Howell, 19 December 1843, *The Papers of Jefferson Davis*, vol. 2, *June 1841–July 1846*, ed. James T. McIntosh (Baton Rouge: Louisiana State University Press, 1974), pp. 52–57.

[3]Varina Davis to Margaret Kempe Howell, 4 January 1847, Jefferson Davis Papers, University of Alabama.

[4]Jefferson Davis to Varina Davis, 3 January 1848, *The American Scene: A Panorama of Autographs 1504–1980*, Paul C. Richards (n. p., n. d.), p. 66; *The Papers of Jefferson Davis*, vol. 3, *July 1846–December 1848*, eds. James T. McIntosh, Lynda L. Crist, and Mary S. Dix (Baton Rouge: Louisiana State University Press, 1981), pp. 301–304; Varina Davis to Margaret Kempe Howell, n. d. [January 1848], Jefferson Davis Papers, University of Alabama.

[5]Varina Davis to Margaret Howell, 15 September 1858, Jefferson Davis Papers, University of Alabama.

[6]Jefferson Davis to Varina Davis, 5 November 1850, original owned by Joel Webb.

[7]Woodward, ed., *Mary Chesnut's Civil War*, p. 595.

[8]Varina Davis to William B. Howell, 1 September 1859, Jefferson Davis Papers, University of Alabama; Woodward, ed., *Mary Chesnut's Civil War*, p. 80; Varina Davis to Margaret Howell, 21 November 1858, Jefferson Davis Papers, University of Alabama.

[9]Virginia Clay-Clopton, *A Belle of the Fifties: Memoirs of Mrs. Clay, of Alabama, covering Social and Political Life in Washington and the South, 1853–66, Put into narrative form by Ada Sterling* (New York: Doubleday, Page & Company, 1905), p. 134.

[10]Woodward, ed., *Mary Chesnut's Civil War*, p. 800; [Varina Davis] to [Margaret Howell], n. d. [June] 1861, Mrs. Jefferson Davis Letters, Iowa Department of History and Archives, Copy at Jefferson Davis Papers, Rice University.

[11]"Aunty" [Eliza Davis] to "Dear Mattie" [Martha Harrison?], 10 August 1861, Lise Mitchell Papers, Tulane University.

[12]Woodward, ed., *Mary Chesnut's Civil War,* p. 136; Catherine Anne Devereux Edmonston, 20 May 1862, *"The Journal of a Secesh Lady": The Diary of Catherine Ann Devereux Edmonston, 1860–1866,* eds. Beth G. Crabtree and James W. Patton (Raleigh: Division of Archives and History, Department of Cultural Resources, 1979), p. 180.

[13]Varina Davis to Jefferson Davis, 28 June 1862, original owned by Jefferson Hayes-Davis.

[14]Varina Davis to William Preston Johnston, 2 November 1865, Johnston Family Papers, The Filson Club. William Howell died in 1863.

[15]Varina Davis to Mrs. Howell Cobb, 22 October 1868, *The Correspondence of Robert Toombs, Alexander H. Stephens, and Howell Cobb,* ed. Ulrich Bonnell Phillips, 2 vols. (Washington, D. C.: Ninth Report of the Historical Manuscripts Commission, 1913), 2: 704.

[16]Varina Davis, *Jefferson Davis,* 1: 475.

[17]Davis, *Jefferson Davis,* 2: 828, 12.

[18]Davis, *Jefferson Davis,* 2: 202.

[19]Varina Davis to Charles Dudley Warner, 2 October 1898, Charles Dudley Warner Papers, Watkinson Library, Trinity College.

[20]"Should Women Vote," in unknown newspaper, n. d., Kate Cumming Collection, Alabama Department of Archives and History.

Charlotte Forten

(1837–1914)

Brenda Stevenson

Born in 1837 into a prominent free black family in Philadelphia, Charlotte Forten lost her mother when she was three. After her father's remarriage, Forten spent much of her childhood under the guidance of relatives living in the Forten household, who encouraged the young girl in her studies, and influenced her with the abolitionist and other reform ideals. In 1853 she was sent to Salem, Massachusetts, where she received an excellent education and was again exposed to prominent African-American activists. Despite her shyness, Forten carved out a career for herself as a teacher, became self-supporting, and continued to live in Salem. In 1858 she was forced by illness to resign her position and returned to Philadelphia to the home and care of maternal aunts. While recuperating, she published essays and poems in antislavery journals and taught her young cousins. The great challenge of her career came during the Civil War, when Forten moved in 1862 to the Sea Islands of South Carolina to work as a teacher among "contraband" slaves (those who had escaped and were under the protection of the Union army). Forten was one of the first black teachers to join this educational effort and was the first and only one at her outpost on St. Helena Island. Her journals of this period provide scholars with an invaluable record of this dramatic historical experiment and epoch. A two-part article chronicling her experience, "Life on the Sea Islands," appeared in The Atlantic Monthly *in May 1864. At this same time, faced with another bout of illness and the impact of her father's death, she returned to the North, traveling and living for short periods in both Pennsylvania and Massachusetts. She returned to the South in 1871, to teach a year in Charleston, South Carolina, after which she moved to Washington, D.C., to teach at a black preparatory school. During these years in Washington,*

Forten met her future husband, Francis Grimké. Married in 1878, the couple had one child, who died in infancy. The couple spent most of their lives in Washington, with Francis Grimké pursuing his career as a minister and Charlotte Forten retiring from teaching to continue her interest in writing and reform. Forten died in Washington in 1914.

Charlotte Forten was born on August 17, 1837 in Philadelphia, Pennsylvania. She was the only child of Robert Bridges Forten (1813–1864) and his first wife, Mary Virginia Woods Forten (1816–1840), who died when Charlotte was only three. The Forten family was among the most prestigious and wealthy of the Philadelphia free black community. Moreover, they used their financial and social standing to support local and regional reform movements, most particularly the efforts to abolish slavery and to establish legal equality for free blacks. Charlotte's earliest paternal ancestor in this country had been an African slave, but that was five generations before her birth. She represented the fourth generation of Fortens who were born free, a generation that would live long enough to realize some of the political goals that her family of activists advocated.

James Forten, Sr., Charlotte's paternal grandfather, initially articulated these ideals that so profoundly influenced the lives of his children and his granddaughter in particular.[1] In 1800, Forten was among other prominent Philadelphia free blacks who, led by the Reverend Absalom Jones, petitioned the U.S. Congress to end the African slave trade, establish guidelines for the gradual abolition of slavery, and provide legislation to weaken the Fugitive Slave Act of 1793.[2] Congress voted 85 to 1 not to consider the petition.[3]

Forten and his peers, however, were not discouraged in their determination to gain legal and economic equality for blacks. In 1813, Charlotte's grandfather published a pamphlet of five letters rebutting statements supportive of legislation that would ban the entrance of free blacks into the state of Pennsylvania. Moreover, he was an adamant critic of the American Colonization Society. The members of the society, which was formed in December 1816, proposed the voluntary removal of free blacks from the United States to some location in Africa or elsewhere. Most members did not support abolition, but offered a ready remedy for the social and economic problems that they believed free blacks imposed on American society. Colonizationists, as they were called, couched their appeal to blacks in "benevolent" terms, asserting that prejudiced whites in the United States would never accept blacks as full citizens. Outside the country, however, blacks could live more peaceably and "freely." Forten and other free black activists, on the other hand, believed that blacks and whites had equal intellectual and physical capabilities, and that blacks had contributed much to the creation and development of the United States as a nation, and thus should have equal access to the country's resources and equal protection under its laws. Free blacks should not be forced to move elsewhere, Forten maintained, but should receive the appropriate training to enable them to live productive lives in American society. He supported protest meetings against the colonizationist movement in both 1817 and 1819.

In 1830, Forten was one of the driving forces behind a National Negro Convention held in Philadelphia. Participants of this convention not only condemned colonizationist efforts, but also discussed strategies to expand the rights of free blacks and abolish slavery. Black reformers held several similar meetings during the 1830s, and Forten figured prominently in all of them.[4] This was an important decade for all blacks within the nation, for it was during these years that disparate antislavery efforts became united in powerful organizations, locally and regionally. James Forten and most of the adult members of his household were at the forefront of these efforts. Thus, the Forten home of the 1830s was a hub of radical thought and activity, and certainly none of its members could have escaped the influence of such dedication and activity.[5] Into this household Charlotte Forten was born in 1837.

James Forten and his wife, Charlotte, Sr. (1784–1884), taught their children to take responsibility both for their lives and for the fate of their race. Scholarship, morality, achievement, selfless dedication to the improvement of the political and economic conditions of blacks—these were the important elements of the socialization process that took place at 92 Lombard Street during Charlotte's childhood as well as during her father's. James and his wife had eight children, four sons and four daughters. Among them, Margaretta, Sarah, Harriet, and Robert Forten were the most politically active.[6]

Forten's daughters, his wife, and his future daughter-in-law (Mary Virginia Woods)[7] were all founding members of the Philadelphia Female Anti-Slavery Society in 1833, an organization that figured prominently in their activities. Margaretta (1808–1875), teacher and administrator of a school for black children in Philadelphia, had a special interest in education and served on the society's educational committee for several years. Moreover, she was one of the few remaining founding members who still supported the organization when it dispersed in 1870. Sarah, her younger sister, also served on the Female Anti-Slavery Society's Board of Managers, representing the organization at the Anti-Slavery Convention of American Women in 1837. Harriet Forten herself was a delegate to this conference in 1837 and 1838.[8]

Sarah Forten and her sister Harriet also were active supporters of women's rights and representative of a growing number of antebellum women who believed in the equality of the sexes. They especially understood the great social and political changes women could help to effect and believed women had a contribution to make to society. Their husbands, the brothers Robert and Joseph Purvis, held similar views. Harriet's spouse, Robert, was a particularly influential abolitionist as well as an advocate of temperance and women's rights. Young Charlotte Forten was very impressed with her Uncle Robert's activism and enlightened perspective, and she drew personal comfort and intellectual delight when in the company of her Aunt Harriet's family. In their home and in her grandparents' Charlotte met and heard some of the most important members of the abolitionist movement, locally and nationally.

Her father, Robert Bridges Forten dedicated himself to efforts to improve the status of blacks in America. It was a commitment that his father demanded of him and that he expected of his daughter. Born in 1813 and educated privately, Charlotte's father was considered by family, friends, and acquaintances as the most talented of his clan. As a young man, he was known locally as a mathematician, poet, and orator. It was during his youth that he constructed a nine-foot telescope that was exhibited at Philadelphia's Franklin Institute. And it was at an early age that he began to participate in various antislavery organizations and activities. Forten was a member of the Young Men's Anti-Slavery Society of Philadelphia and served on its Board of Managers from 1835 to 1836. He also was a member of the Philadelphia Vigilance Committee and the New England Anti-Slavery Society.[9]

Robert Forten's activities document his dedication to antislavery and civil rights, and yet the years of frustration and anger he sustained while growing up as a talented black man in a racist society took its toll. He found it impossible to live a productive and happy life in the United States and moved abroad, first to Canada in 1855 and then to England in 1858.

In 1862 Robert Forten returned to the United States to enlist in the Union forces then at war with the Confederacy. Although his family counseled him not to expose himself to the harshness of military life, he was determined to join the U.S. Army and did so at Camp William Penn on March 2, 1864. His initial rank was that of a private in Company A of the 43rd U.S. Colored Infantry. A month later, he was promoted to sergeant-major and transferred to Maryland, where he was to help recruit black soldiers. Forten became ill almost immediately after reaching Maryland and, on April 18, 1864, requested sick leave to return to his family home in Philadelphia. Robert Forten died of typhoid fever on April 25, 1864. He was the first black to receive a military funeral in Philadelphia.[10]

Charlotte's father and other politically active family members must have had a tremendous impact on her. She grew up in a home where abolition and equal rights for blacks were key issues to discuss and act upon. Daily she was in the presence of important designers and participants in the abolitionist and civil rights movements. William Lloyd Garrison, John Greenleaf Whittier, Harriet Martineau, William Nell, and Charles Remond were but a few of the prominent abolitionists who visited the Forten and Purvis homes. Moreover, there were present in her family and their groups of friends several impressive female activists who served as important role models for Charlotte. Her mother, grandmother, and aunts were all well-educated, hardworking, morally upright, socially astute women who quite willingly gave much of their energy, financial resources, and time to abolition, civil rights, and the general improvement of conditions within the free black community. Charlotte's mother, Mary Virginia Woods Forten, who was described by her contemporaries as a "beautiful mulatto," was herself a member of a prominent abolitionist family of Philadelphia. Undoubtedly, the young mother believed that her little girl too would grow up to participate in such worthy activities. Unfortunately, Mary Virginia Forten died when Charlotte was quite young and thus was unable to influence her child directly.[11] Yet Charlotte's relatives provided recollections of her mother that served as an inspiration to her as she grew older.

After Mary Virginia Forten's death, Charlotte's paternal grandmother, Charlotte Forten, Sr., and her aunts—particularly Margaretta, who was unmarried—took over the maternal role in her life. Because her aunts and their families lived so near each other, Charlotte benefited from an extended family network that was particularly close-knit. She spent many of her childhood days at the Forten family home at 92 Lombard Street, but also would often visit her aunts Sarah and Harriet Purvis who had moved to nearby Bucks County. She adored her cousins and the beauty of the land surrounding their homes, spending many summer days riding, reading, playing games, acting out plays, discussing important issues, picking flowers and berries, and generally enjoying herself. And it seems she never was as relaxed or happy as when surrounded by family. After she moved to Salem in late 1853, Charlotte often thought of the happy times she had spent with her large family and wished once again to be in their presence. Yet she was not one for leisurely vacations at home. She left Philadelphia to complete her education. Her personal needs, even family affection, she maintained, were unimportant in comparison.[12]

On May 24, 1854, Charlotte Forten began to keep a daily journal. At the time, she was sixteen years old and had moved to Salem, Massachusetts, from her native Pennsylvania just six months before. At home, Charlotte had received years of private instruction from tutors since Robert Forten refused to send her to the poorly equipped and racially segregated schools designated for black children in Philadelphia. When an opportunity came for her to receive an excellent public school education outside of Philadelphia, Charlotte was sent. Forten discovered from friends that Salem had integrated schools of sound reputation. It was also the location of a fine normal school which her father wanted her eventually to attend so that she could prepare for a teaching career. This profession, he believed, would give Charlotte some practical skill with which to aid her race, for there were few well-trained teachers available to the black community. Moreover, he surmised, such a profession would allow Charlotte some secure means of financial support.

It is not clear whether Charlotte ever really wanted to become a teacher. It seems as though she preferred the life of a scholar or writer. The young Charlotte Forten was, however, eager to please her father and to contribute to the uplift of her race and, therefore, she was determined to complete her studies successfully. "I will spare no effort to become what he desires that I should be; . . . to prepare myself well for the responsible duties of a teacher, and to live for the good that I can do my oppressed and suffering fellow-creatures."[13]

Robert Forten arranged that his precocious, but shy, daughter reside in the Salem home of old friends, the prominent abolitionist Charles Lenox Remond and his wife, Amy Matilda. Charles Remond was active as an orator and supporter of the abolitionist cause and was still in the forefront of the movement during Charlotte's stay in his home. In fact, it was while she resided with the Remonds that she met William Lloyd Garrison, Wendell Phillips, John Whittier, Abigail and Stephen Foster, Lydia Maria Child, Maria Chapman, William C. Nell, William Wells Brown, and other noted abolitionists. Many of these persons were close friends of Charlotte's family and the Remonds, and wholeheartedly welcomed her into their fold. Her host's sister, Sarah Parker Remond, did not live with her brother, but was a frequent visitor. A lecturer for the American Anti-Slavery Society, Sarah Remond inspired Charlotte with stories of her lecturing tours at home and abroad.

As time passed, Charlotte came to know and love Salem. Its climate, political activism, and particularly its intellectual offerings suited her tastes. She was well aware of the racism of some of its residents and various instances of institutionalized discrimination, but in comparison with Philadelphia, she found Salem much less oppressive. On those occasions when she had to leave New England for Pennsylvania, Charlotte was routinely apprehensive of the treatment she would receive in her racially hostile home state.

During the first year and a half of her stay in Salem, Charlotte was a student at the Higginson Grammar School. Intellectually, Charlotte thrived at the school from which she graduated with "decided éclat" in March 1855. Charlotte's poem "A Parting Hymn" was chosen as the best submitted by her class, and she gained a modest local reputation as a young poet of some merit. In fact, she had begun to submit her poetry for publication a year before. In March 1855, a poem that she wrote in praise of William Lloyd Garrison was published in the *Liberator* magazine.[14] Charlotte entered the Salem Normal School after her final examinations at Higginson and graduated in July 1856.

Charlotte lamented the end of her school days, but she pursued knowledge even more avidly in the following years. She most often spent her free time studying French, German, Latin, European and classical history, and reading the works of both her contemporaries and of the great authors of the past. Charlotte was particularly fond of good literature and searched for companions with similar tastes. Fortunately, she found such persons in her "society" of housemates and their local relations. Still, she deemed her studies her "closest friends" and approached them with a vitality and passion rarely expressed in other facets of her life. A typical week of self-imposed study was rigorous. On January 5, 1857 she noted: "Still alone, and should be lonesome were not my time so constantly occupied,—teaching all day and reading and studying all the evening. Translated several passages from the 'Commentaries,' and finished the 'Conquest of Mexico.' "[15] The following evening she read and criticized Tennyson.[16] The afternoon of the seventh she spent studying Latin.[17] The next evening she dedicated herself to translating Caesar, a task of which she wrote: "Find it rather difficult, but am determined to persevere. Excelsior! shall be my motto, now and forever."[18] On the ninth, she relaxed and attended a concert by the pianist Thalberg, but followed this with a thorough reading of the *Liberator* when she returned home.[19]

Such was the scholar's life that young Charlotte Forten chose for herself. To pursue her studies in this uninhibited manner she considered a wonderful blessing. Deeply religious, Charlotte believed that

God had indeed chosen her for a particular mission—to use her natural talents to inspire and improve her race. Denial of this calling, Charlotte believed, could jeopardize her own Christian salvation.

Charlotte's insistence on selfless dedication to her race—which in her mind denied her the right of such basic human needs as love, pride, and concern for "self-culture"—was at best a burdensome ideal that caused her immeasurable frustration during her youth. It was a goal that, in time, Charlotte came to know as unattainable. As a young adult, however, she could not accept this rationally and failed to appreciate the valuable contributions she could and did make. Thus a pervasive sense of unworthiness and insecurity characterized Charlotte's adolescence and young adulthood. Yet her unhappiness and frustration during this period not only was derived from a growing sense of failure with regard to her mission but also from the deteriorating relationship with her father.

Charlotte came to Salem in 1853 hoping her father and stepfamily would soon relocate to Massachusetts, where together they could establish a home.[20] She was crushed when Robert Forten decided in 1855 to move his family to Canada. Once he left the country, Charlotte received little communication from him, which prompted her to believe that his interest in and affection for his only daughter had somehow diminished. She felt a profound sense of parental abandonment during this important period of her development.

Charlotte's estrangement from her father posed practical problems, too, for she was left with no financial support except that which she earned herself. When her father's aid ceased, she was a full-time student at the Salem Normal School and suddenly was unable to pay some of her school expenses as well as her room and board to the Remonds. Her growing indebtedness was another source of frustration and depression. As Charlotte's relationship with her father disintegrated, she seemed to think more of her deceased mother and of the loving relationship they would have had if she had lived. Charlotte's fantasies of her mother depicted a beautiful, warm, loving woman to whom an unhappy and often ill daughter could always turn for comfort.[21] Although for days and weeks at a time Charlotte thought much about her mother, her fantasies did not bring her long-lasting comfort.

Charlotte's unhappiness and negative self-perception undoubtedly also stemmed from the racism and rejection of whites with whom she came in contact. During her adolescence and early adulthood, she keenly felt the racism of classmates and, later, of teachers in Salem. A shy, sensitive, sometimes angry and defensive adolescent, Charlotte absolutely refused to compromise her standards with regard to friends. Thus, from her experience, Charlotte grew suspicious of the racial attitudes of whites and usually withheld her judgment of a person until she found out if that person held the "correct" views on racial issues. She was, however, able to establish a few meaningful relationships with some of her schoolroom associates, most particularly a deep friendship with Mary Shepard, Charlotte's principal at the Higginson Grammar School.

Despite her criticism of many of her associates, Charlotte judged her own character and actions more harshly than she did those of her friends and family. She was particularly generous in her assessment of those whites whom she believed had overcome their racism and were involved actively in the abolitionist movement. She also praised those who, like Shepard, offered her genuine acceptance and friendship. And while Charlotte was familiar with the overt racial hostility of most whites in mid-nineteenth-century America, she continued to be angered and hurt when faced with discrimination or outright rejection.

Yet as a young adult, Charlotte Forten never realized the enormous impact that she had on those whites with whom she came in contact. Her insecurity and extreme modesty blinded her to their appreciation of her demeanor, intelligence, and accomplishments. These persons—primarily abolitionists, intellectuals, and literary artists—viewed her as exceptional in character and talent. Her close friend, John Greenleaf Whittier, for example, described Charlotte to Theodore Dwight Weld as "a young lady of exquisite refinement, quiet culture and ladylike and engaging manners, and personal appearance." "I look upon her as one of the most gifted representatives of her class," he concluded.[22] A writer for the *Salem Register* wrote of Charlotte in 1856: "She presented in her own mental endowments and propriety of demeanor an honorable vindication of the claims of her race to the rights of mental culture and privileges of humanity."[23] Forten never allowed herself to take such compliments seriously.

Perhaps Charlotte's negative self-esteem resulted from her subconscious inculcation of popular views of black inferiority. Publicly she never wavered in her belief in the natural equality of the races and, indeed, dedicated her life to asserting through personal example the legitimacy of that doctrine. Yet privately she struggled not so much with the basic premise of natural equality, but with the question of whether members of her race were willing to work diligently to achieve the reality of equality, given their limited access to it. Her criticism of blacks, as of herself, was often severe, and it was difficult for her to accept their moral nobility, much more so than it was for her to recognize the nobility of whites. She described a good friend from Salem, Henry Cassey, for example, as a young black man with a "noble nature, and high aspirations, both moral and mental." She went on, however, to sharply contrast his nobility with those of other black males, noting that these characteristics of Henry made "him a different being from the generality of colored young men that one sees;—though I know that the unhappy circumstances in which these are placed, are often more to blame than they themselves."[24]

Charlotte certainly adopted white standards for beauty that caused her to think of herself as unattractive when by all accounts she was a pretty woman. While she was visiting John Whittier's home in 1862, for example, the poet's sister, Elizabeth, presented her with a portrait of an Italian woman that everyone present thought resembled Charlotte. She noted of the incident, however: "I utterly failed to see it: *I* thought the Italian girl very pretty, and I know myself to be the very opposite."[25] On another occasion Charlotte described a Caucasian acquaintance as quite attractive, with "just such long, light hair, and beautiful blue eyes. . . . She is a little poetess—a sweet, gentle creature. I have fallen quite in love with her."[26] When describing the face of a wounded black soldier in the 54th Massachusetts, she again indicated her standards for beauty. "He has such a good honest face. It is pleasant to look at it—although it is black."[27] Thus Charlotte herself internalized racist attitudes that undoubtedly would have a negative effect on her self-image.

While issues of race continued to figure largely in Charlotte's life, her health problems became a major source of frustration as early as 1856. Like so many of her friends and family, she suffered from respiratory ailments that frequently imposed an immense physical and emotional burden on her. Charlotte first began to suffer from severe headaches and respiratory illnesses in November 1856, not long after she accepted a teaching position at the Epes Grammar School. She was intermittently ill for the next six months and, in May 1857, she was forced to return to Philadelphia to rest and regain her health. Charlotte returned to Salem in July 1857 to resume her teaching position at Epes, but was forced to resign in early March 1858 due to illness.

Following her resignation, Charlotte returned to Pennsylvania where she rested, taught the younger children of Harriet Purvis, and wrote poems and essays for publication. Although her health had interrupted her teaching career, the less hectic pace of the Purvis household allowed her to focus on professional writing. She received her first payment for writing, a modest sum of one dollar, from Bishop Daniel Payne of the *Christian Recorder* magazine, on May 20, 1858, for a poem entitled "Flowers."[28] The next month, her essay "Glimpses of New England" appeared in the *National Anti-Slavery Standard*.[29] In 1859, two poems—"The Two Voices" and "The Wind

Among the Poplars"—appeared in print.[30] And in January 1860, Charlotte's poem "The Slave Girl's Prayer" was published in the *National Anti-Slavery Standard.*[31]

Charlotte remained with her family until September 1859, when she again returned to Salem to teach in the Higginson Grammar School. By the spring, however, she became ill with "lung fever" and resigned her post. Charlotte then traveled to Bridgewater and later to Worcester to seek physical therapy at the water cure establishment of Dr. Seth Rogers.[32] By the fall of 1860, she had recuperated enough to resume work, but again became seriously ill in late October 1860 and had to return to Philadelphia. There she rested but remained active in the abolitionist cause while she taught in a school for black children. Charlotte returned to Salem during the summer of 1862 to teach summer classes, and on August 9, 1862, she visited John Whittier at his home in Amesbury. It was during this visit that Whittier suggested to Charlotte that she could render a great service to her people if she went to teach among the contraband slaves who had run away to Union camps in the Confederate South.[33]

On October 22, 1862, Charlotte Forten sailed from New York for Port Royal, South Carolina, where she remained for about eighteen months. Under the auspices of the Port Royal Relief Association, Charlotte secured the position of teacher among the contraband slaves of the South Carolina Sea Islands. She was among hundreds of teachers from the Northeast who had come South for various reasons, but primarily to prepare the recently released slaves for their new role as free citizens of the United States.

Charlotte Forten was among the first black teachers in the South and, at the time she arrived, the first and only one stationed on St. Helena Island. Proportionately, there continued to be a very small number of blacks who were trained as teachers. Moreover, some agencies were less than cooperative in their efforts to place qualified black teachers in these positions. Charlotte Forten, for example, initially tried to reach South Carolina under the auspices of the Boston Educational Commission, later renamed the New England Freedman's Aid Society. After several unsuccessful attempts to gain their sponsorship in August 1862, she returned to Philadelphia where she retained the support of the Port Royal Relief Association of that city.[34]

Charlotte Forten believed that working among the contraband slaves of South Carolina would afford her an excellent opportunity to help her race. Frustrated by the restrictions of poor health, she welcomed the opportunity to travel South where she hoped the mild climate would allow her to remain tolerably healthy while she performed the "noble" task of preparing illiterate blacks for their roles as free Americans.

From the very beginning of her stay on St. Helena Island, Charlotte thought fondly of the contraband slaves with whom she came in contact. Sensitive to their plight of trying to adjust to the status of free persons, she was quick to explain that their cultural expression and lifestyles, which seemed peculiar and sometimes crude to Northerners, were largely a result of their past as slaves.[35] Yet like the other teachers and missionaries who came to instruct the contraband, Charlotte sometimes was both amused and repulsed by the social, linguistic and religious practices of the Sea Island blacks. Overall, however, she appreciated their friendly and deferential manner, their determination to gain freedom and educate their children, and particularly their affectionate treatment of loved ones and friends. Her general fondness for the adults as well as her students caused her to be solicitous of their individual and group needs, especially their health and material welfare.[36]

Forten's primary task was to teach the contraband children the rudiments of a formal education. Placed in a one-room schoolhouse with children of all ages, Charlotte taught reading, writing, spelling, history, and math. She also instructed older blacks on proper moral and social behavior. Freedman aid societies, such as the one that sponsored Charlotte's work, strongly advocated this kind of informal but instructive contact between contraband slaves and their Northern workers. Charlotte, who was an avid assimilationist, was no different in this respect from her white peers and adamantly believed that blacks would never be accepted as equals if they remained culturally distinct. Certainly she enjoyed the culture of the Sea Island blacks, especially their unique singing style, but she was greatly relieved that the contraband were conforming to Northern mores, such as solemnizing their relationships through legal marriage.[37]

Most of her time on St. Helena was happy. It was undoubtedly the most challenging period of her life, a time of immense personal growth. As the first black teacher among the contraband who resided there, Charlotte faced the mixed feelings of both teachers and military personnel. Although she reported that most of the Union whites she interacted with were pleasant, she did note that initially she felt no "congeniality" among those with whom she lived.[38] This feeling, however, changed when old abolitionist friends and acquaintances began to arrive.

Colonel Thomas Wentworth Higginson was one of the several close friends that Charlotte acquired while residing on St. Helena Island. A native of Massachusetts, Higginson had been a dedicated abolitionist who gained widespread notoriety in 1854 when he tried unsuccessfully to aid in the escape of the fugitive slave Anthony Burns, who was then on trial in Boston. Higginson was by profession a Unitarian minister and lived in Worcester, Massachusetts. When Charlotte saw him in South Carolina in the fall of 1862, she recalled that she had seen him the summer before drilling soldiers of the all-white 51st Massachusetts before they left for duty in the South, and she remembered his enthusiasm in commanding the troops. Such a man, "so full of life and energy" and so obviously dedicated to the black race, was "the one best fitted to command a regiment of colored soldiers," she thought.[39] So did General Rufus Saxton, commander of the Union forces in the Port Royal region, who decided to place Higginson in command of the First South Carolina Volunteers, a regiment of Sea Island blacks.[40] Charlotte followed closely the recruitment and training of this historic regiment. Both blacks and white abolitionists hoped that they would soon impress America with their bravery and determination.

Charlotte also befriended other military personnel, as well as teachers and plantation superintendents. She met, for example, and was very impressed with Colonel Robert Gould Shaw, son of the noted abolitionist Francis Shaw of New York and commander of the all-black 54th Massachusetts regiment. She was moved by Colonel Shaw's gentlemanly qualities, intellect, and his great appreciation for his position as commander of the first regiment of free blacks from the North to be engaged in the Civil War.[41] She was stunned by the death of Colonel Shaw at the bloody battle of Fort Wagner on Morris Island, South Carolina, on July 18, 1863.

But, by far the most important relationship that Charlotte established on St. Helena Island was her deep romantic attachment to a white surgeon in Higginson's First South Carolina Volunteers, Dr. Seth Rogers. Forten first met Dr. Rogers during the spring of 1860, when she frequented his water cure establishment in Worcester. He arrived at Camp Saxton, South Carolina, during the latter part of December 1862. When Charlotte traveled to the camp on New Year's Day 1863 to celebrate the Emancipation Proclamation, she was elated to see her friend and physician again, and their friendship flourished. Entry after entry in Charlotte's diary describe the times they spent together—taking walks and riding horseback, having dinner, traveling together to nearby plantations, playing chess, reading to one another, and just talking about themselves, their work, and literature.[42] It is not certain how profoundly Dr. Rogers felt about Charlotte, for the journal only depicts her feelings. It does tell us, however, that Rogers certainly devoted a great deal of time and energy to her while they were in South Carolina. Moreover, it was his suggestion that they write to one another when they could not visit often. He also sent her gifts, read to her when she was ill, and was generally very attentive.[43] Although his gestures appear to have been romantic in intent, Charlotte explained in a diary entry on February 2, 1863 that Dr. Rogers wanted her to think of him "as a brother." "And I will glady do so," she responded.[44]

Charlotte did not forget that Rogers was married and white. He in turn, seeming to anticipate the possibility of a more intimate relationship with her, tried to quell it by insisting that Charlotte regard him as a brother and by reminding her of his wife. Charlotte viewed these as "noble" gestures and was apt to respond to them by feeling closer to him. Charlotte's journal indicates that she and Seth Rogers continued to have a close relationship throughout most of 1863, until he resigned from his post in the Union Army in December 1863, and went back to Worcester.

Overall, Charlotte's experiences on St. Helena Island were fruitful. She wrote of her time among the contraband in two letters addressed to William Lloyd Garrison, which subsequently were published in the *Liberator* in 1862. A two-part article, which Charlotte called "Life on the Sea Islands," appeared in *The Atlantic Monthly* in 1864.[45] It was a rewarding and exciting period of her life not only because opportunities existed for it to be so, but also because she had acquired the emotional maturity necessary to realistically perceive and act on these opportunities. After a troubled and prolonged adolescence, she was long overdue for the happiness and sense of fulfillment that she obtained while working among the ex-slaves. Unfortunately, her health began to fail again. That circumstance, and undoubtedly her father's untimely death on April 25, 1864, precipitated her decision to return to the North for good where she hoped to recover her health and draw comfort from her family.[46]

Charlotte did not remain very long in Philadelphia once she left the South. Her health was poor, and she wrote to her friend John Whittier from Detroit during the summer of 1865 to solicit his aid in securing her a place in the sanatorium of Dioclesian Lewis at Lexington, Massachusetts. For reasons that are unclear, Charlotte never went to Lexington. Instead, in October 1865, she accepted a position as Secretary of the Teachers Committee of the New England Branch of the Freedman's Union Commission for a salary of ten dollars a week.[47] Located in Boston, Charlotte socialized with her many New England friends and continued with her personal studies. Her determination to master the French language culminated in her translation of Emile Erckmann and Alexandre Chatrain's novel *Madame Thérèse; or, The Volunteers of '92,* which Scribner's published in 1869.[48] As Secretary of the Teachers Committee, Charlotte acted as liaison between the teachers in the South who tutored the ex-slaves and those in the North who supplied them with financial and material support through the auspices of the Commission. She held this position until October 1871[49], then resigned to teach for a year at the (Robert Gould) Shaw Memorial School in Charleston, South Carolina.[50] She then moved to Washington, D.C., where from 1872 until 1873 she was a teacher in a black preparatory high school (later named Dunbar High) under the direction of Alexander Crummell. Charlotte left this position to accept a job as first-class clerk in the Fourth Auditor's Office of the U.S. Treasury Department.[51]

Charlotte stayed in Washington for almost the remainder of her life. Her first few years in the capital were no doubt spent working, meeting new friends, renewing old acquaintances, writing, and studying. She also enjoyed the stimulating company of her cousin, Charles Burleigh Purvis, who was at that time a surgeon in the Freedmen's Hospital at Howard University.[52] Charlotte continued to suffer from poor health, and kind but chauvinistic friends, such as John Whittier, wished that "the poor girl could be better situated—the wife of some good, true man who could appreciate her as she deserves."[53] Several years later, Whittier's wish for "the poor girl" came true. During her late thirties, Charlotte met and fell in love with a young, black graduate student of divinity who was twelve years her junior—Francis Grimké, the mulatto nephew of Angelina Grimké Weld. Charlotte and Francis married in December 19, 1878.[54]

Intelligent, sensitive, morally upright, and fiercely dedicated to his profession and race, the Princeton-trained minister was certainly the husband Charlotte and her friends hoped that she would have some day. The two set up house in Washington, and Charlotte retired from public work. They had one child, Theodora Cornelia, who died as an infant in 1880. Given Charlotte's age and persistent bad health, it was inconceivable that she could bear another child, though she dearly loved children.

Charlotte now viewed her mission as intimately intertwined with that of her husband's. Francis Grimké used his pulpit as a religious forum to attack discrimination. He and Charlotte wrote and published many essays that were critical of racial oppression. They obviously worked well together, combining fierce intellectual acumen with a passionate commitment to alleviating the racial hostility prevalent in late nineteenth- and early twentieth-century America.[55]

In 1885, Charlotte and her husband left Washington to reside in Jacksonville, Florida, where Francis Grimké had accepted the pastorate at the Laura Street Presbyterian Church. They remained there for four years but then returned to Washington and the Fifteenth Street Presbyterian Church. Although they were both busy with missionary work and the many commitments that Francis Grimké's growing political influence mandated, Charlotte and her husband continued to pursue an active intellectual life. They both regularly attended two weekly reading groups, one on Friday and the other on Sunday, where they discussed art, literature, history, politics, religion, and any other topic of interest to the members of the societies.[56]

After her marriage, Charlotte continued her interest in writing poetry and essays. Her poems from that period include "A June Song" (1885), "Charlotte Corday" (1885), "At Newport" (1888), "The Gathering of the Grand Army" (1890), and "In Florida" (1893). Only a handful of essays that she wrote during the 1880s and 1890s survive: "On Mr. Savage's Sermon: 'The Problem of the Hour' " (1885), a lengthy letter addressed to the editor of the *Boston Commonwealth*; "One Phase of the Race Question" (1885), another letter written to the *Commonwealth* editor; "Colored People in New England" (1889), which was sent to the editor of *The Evangelist*; and "Personal Recollections of Whittier" (1893), which appeared in the *New England Magazine*. Four other essays, probably written during the 1890s, were not assigned a specific date of completion: "The Umbrian and Roman School of Art"; "The Flower Fairies' Reception"; "At the Home of Frederick Douglass"; and "Midsummer Days in the Capitol: 'The Corcoran Art Gallery.' "[57]

The last decade of the nineteenth century was a busy one for Charlotte, not only because of her intellectual pursuits, writing, and missionary work, but also because of her special relationship with her niece, Angelina Weld Grimké. Angelina Grimké was the only child of Francis Grimké's brother, Archibald. While he served as consul to Santo Domingo from 1894 to 1898 Charlotte and her husband acted as Angelina's legal guardians. Charlotte always had a deep affection for her niece, who was born just two years after her own infant daughter died. When Archibald and his wife, Sarah Stanley, separated, Charlotte became an important maternal figure in Angelina's life. Moreover, after 1905, Archibald and Angelina Grimké moved into Charlotte's home, where they remained until well after her death in 1914. Their permanent inclusion in Charlotte's house enlivened it socially and intellectually—further cementing the bond between aunt and niece. As always, Charlotte was surrounded by well-educated political activists. And she must have drawn immense pleasure from the fact that this time it was her own home that was the hub of activity. Although continually ill, she undoubtedly was happy to be among her loved ones, to be cared for by a "noble" and loving husband whose mission was so compatible with her own, and to be able to pursue her intellectual growth and development.[58] Charlotte Forten Grimké died quietly in her Washington home, on July 22, 1914, at the age of seventy-six.

Notes

Charlotte Forten Grimké (1837–1914) completed five journals. The dates and locations of each journal are as follows: Journal One, 1854–1856, Salem, Massachusetts; Journal Two, 1857–1858, Salem and Philadelphia, Pennsylvania; Journal Three, 1858–1863, Salem, Philadelphia, Boston, Massachusetts, and St. Helena Island, South Carolina; Journal Four, 1863–1864, St. Helena Island, Philadelphia, and Salem; Journal Five, 1885–1892, Jacksonville, Florida, Washington, D.C., Philadelphia, and Ler, Massachusetts. The manuscript copies of Grimké's journals are located in the Moorland-Springarn Research Center, Howard University, Washington, D.C.

[1]Gloria C. Oden, "*The Journal of Charlotte L. Forten:* The Salem-Philadelphia Years (1851–1862) Reexamined," *Essex Institute Historical Collections* 119 (1983): 121; Rayford W. Logan and Michael R. Winston, eds., *Dictionary of American Negro Biography* (New York, 1982), 233–234 (cited hereafter as *DANB*).

[2]The Fugitive Slave Law of 1793 allowed slave owners to seize their runaway slaves in any location in the United States, slave or free, and upon documentation of ownership to a federal or state magistrate, could return the fugitive to his former residence and status. Moreover, this law stipulated that it was a criminal act for anyone to knowingly harbor fugitive slaves or to aid their evasion of arrest. John Hope Franklin, *From Slavery to Freedom: A History of Negro Americans*, 3rd ed. (New York, 1967), 151–152; Peter M. Bergman and Mort N. Bergman, *The Chronological History of the Negro in America* (New York, 1969), 73.

[3]Bergman and Bergman, *Chronological History of the Negro*, 83.

[4]Howard Holman Bell, *A Survey of the Negro Convention Movement, 1830–1861* (New York, 1969), 10–37; Nell, *Colored Patriots*, 177–178; *DANB*, 235; Franklin, *From Slavery to Freedom*, 237–241.

[5]Bell, *Negro Convention Movement*, 43–53; Nell, *Colored Patriots*, 178–179; *DANB*, 235.

[6]Oden, "*Journal of Charlotte L. Forten* . . . Reexamined," 122.

[7]Mary Virginia Woods, Charlotte's mother, was not married to Robert Bridges Forten in 1833, the year of the formation of the Philadelphia Female Anti-Slavery Society. They were married in 1836. For an informative account of the lives of Charlotte Forten's parents, see Janice Sumler Lewis, "The Fortens of Philadelphia: An Afro-American Family and Nineteenth Century Reform," Ph.D. Dissertation, Georgetown University (1979), 14–128, passim; Sterling, *We Are Your Sisters*, 119–120.

[8]Lewis, "Fortens of Philadelphia," 43–44, 61; Sterling, *We Are Your Sisters*, 114, 120–121.

[9]Lewis, "Fortens of Philadelphia," 24–128, passim.

[10]Lewis, "Fortens of Philadelphia," 14–128, passim.

[11]Oden, "*Journal of Charlotte L. Forten* . . . Reexamined," 121.

[12]Journal One, September 3, 1854; Journal Two, February 14, 1857, April 12, 1857.

[13]Journal One, October 23, 1854.

[14]*Liberator*, March 16, 1855.

[15]Journal Two, January 5, 1857.

[16]Journal Two, January 6, 1857.

[17]Journal Two, January 7, 1857.

[18]Journal Two, January 8, 1857.

[19]Journal Two, January 9, 1857.

[20]Journal One, September 3, 1854.

[21]Journal Two, April 12, 1857, July 16, 1857; Journal Three, June 18, 1858.

[22]John B. Pickard, ed., *The Letters of John Greenleaf Whittier, Vol. 3, 1861–1892* (Cambridge, 1975), 97.

[23]*Salem Register*, July 24, 1856.

[24]Journal Three, June 22, 1862.

[25]Journal Three, August 9, 1862.

[26]Journal Three, April 11, 1858.

[27]Journal Four, July 23, 1863.

[28]Journal Three, May 20, 1858.

[29]*National Anti-Slavery Standard*, June 18, 1858.

[30]*Liberator*, May 27, 1859; *National Anti-Slavery Standard*, January 15, 1859.

[31]*National Anti-Slavery Standard*, January 14, 1860.

[32]Journal Three, June 22, 1862.

[33]Journal Three, August 9, 1862.

[34]Journal Three, August 13, 1862 to October 22, 1862.

[35]Journal Three, November 30, 1862; and "Life on the Sea Islands," draft in the Francis Grimké Papers, Moorland-Springarn Research Center, Howard University.

[36]Journal Three, November 7, 1862, November 18, 1862.

[37]Journal Three, October 29, 1862, November 7, 1862, November 23, 1862.

[38]Journal Three, November 23, 1862.

[39]Journal Three, November 27, 1862.

[40]Thomas Wentworth Higginson, *Army Life in a Black Regiment* (Boston, 1870), 1–3.

[41]Willie Lee Rose, *Rehearsal for Reconstruction: The Port Royal Experiment* (1964; New York, 1967), 248–250.

[42]Journal Three, January 1, 1863, January 7, 1863, January 26, 1863, February 8, 1863, February 9, 1863, Journal Four, February 19, 1863, February 22, 1863, March 2, 1863, April 11, 1863, July 25, 1863.

[43]Journal Three, January 7, 1863, January 26, 1863; Journal Four, February 19, 1863, March 2, 1863, April 3, 1863.

[44]Journal Three, February 8, 1863.

[45]*Liberator*, December 12, 1862; *Liberator*, December 19, 1862; *The Atlantic Monthly*, May 1864; *Atlantic Monthly*, June 1864.

[46]Lewis, "Fortens of Philadelphia," 126–128.

[47]Pickard, *Letters of John Greenleaf Whittier, Vol. 3*, 97, 98, nn. 1, 4. Whittier wrote to Theodore Dwight Weld concerning Charlotte Forten's desire to seek a place at Lewis's establishment, asking Weld if he could arrange a "reduced" price for her. Pickard quotes a letter of Whittier's dated September 13, 1865, in which Whittier mentions Forten's request and notes that she did not go to the sanatorium because all concerned thought it unwise. He did not give a reason for this decision, but only wrote, "To take her at all would I fear be hazardous to his enterprise, and I am sure Charlotte would not wish to run the risk of that"; Sterling, *We Are Your Sisters*, 284.

[48]Emile Erckmann and Alexandre Chatrain, *Madame Thérèse; or, The Volunteers of '92*, Charlotte Forten, trans. (Boston, 1869).

[49]Sterling, *We Are Your Sisters*, 284–285.

[50]Sterling, *We Are Your Sisters*, 283.

[51]*New National Ear*, July 3, 1873.

[52]*DANB*, 507.

[53]Pickard, *Letters of John Greenleaf Whittier, Vol. 3*, 278.

[54]Sterling, *We Are Your Sisters*, 285–286.

[55]*DANB*, 274–275.

[56]Anna Julia Cooper, "Reminiscences," Francis Grimké Papers, Moorland-Spingarn Research Center, Howard University.

[57]Copies of Charlotte Forten Grimké's writings from this period are all part of the Francis Grimké Papers , Moorland-Springarn Research Center, Howard University.

[58]*DANB*, 272–273; correspondence of Charlotte Forten Grimké, to Angelina Weld Grimké dated September 23, 1899, January 23, 1903, May 7, 1911, June 4, 1911, July 18, 1911, August 4, 1911, August 25, 1911, Francis Grimké Papers, Moorland-Spingarn Research Center, Howard University.

PART V

The Reform Era

The range, variety, and success of women's efforts in caring for the sick and wounded of America's explodingly expansive cities and industries allow us to describe the period from 1877 to 1914 as "the reform era." These efforts remained consistent with the nineteenth-century social idea of "separate spheres"—the private sphere of home and motherhood for women and the larger public sphere of everything else, with which men identified themselves. Because women had specialized in morality in the family and housekeeping, most claimed to enter the public sphere in order to clean up its "sins." Before the Civil War, they had started with prostitution, drunkenness, and slavery.

After the Civil War, the public world to which women brought such traditional values changed with dramatic intensity. Changes included the growth of mechanized farming, the massive expansion of industry and the growth of cities, and of the immigration that industry stimulated. By 1900, the oil, iron, steel, railroad, milling, mining, manufacturing, and merchandizing industries had been transformed into interlocking monopolies, creating a single, standardized national economy. The direction taken by women reformers cannot be understood without taking note of these major changes in American society.

The mechanization of farming allowed farmers to produce vast quantities of cotton and cereals for a world market, as well as for the burgeoning American cities. The transportation, marketing, and financing of these crops were in the hands of corporate businessmen. When supplies of farm products outstripped demand, there was a steady and disastrous fall in prices that resulted in foreclosures, indebtedness, and an increase in the number of landless tenant farmers. Starting in the 1860s, farmers banded together as the "Grange," an economic self-help organization, in which farm women played a significant role. Managing separate "female" concerns, women also had full voting rights in the organization. Not so in the Grange's successor organizations, the Farmers' Alliances, which created the populist movement, one of the largest democratic mass movements in American history. While populist women lectured, organized locally, and helped educate masses of rural people in the innovative, cooperative economics proposed by the alliances, they were denied organizational voting rights and any voice at the national level. In response, in 1891 Fannie Mc-

Cormick and Emma Pack started the National Women's Alliance. Supporting the economic reforms demanded by their male counterparts, they also endorsed women's suffrage and temperance, as had Grange women before them. Both issues were refused support by male Populists.

White Farmers' Alliances did cooperate with the Colored Farmers' Alliances, which counted a million members in the South, but the relationship was a vulnerable one, succumbing to the racist attacks launched by the enemies of Populism. And the farmers' groups never managed to form the largest alliance at which they had aimed: one with urban workers.

Between the Civil War and 1900 there was a huge increase in the number of wage-earners employed in heavy industry and transportation. The number of female wage-earners went from 2.5 million in 1880 to 8.5 million in 1900. Moreover, the proportion of women employed as domestic servants, laundresses, and cooks dropped as their employment in the public service sector of the economy increased, for example, as clerical and retail workers. Women comprised 4 percent of the clerical work force in 1880; by 1920 they comprised nearly 50 percent. While women earned far less than their male contemporaries, their income was essential to the family income because living costs kept ahead of wages, even though wages increased over this entire period. A large number of children were drawn into paid labor for the same reason. Much wage-earning was seasonal, and all of it subject to the tidal waves of economic depression, notably in 1873–78, 1884–85, and 1893–97.

The rich got richer and America produced more and more millionaires. Employers kept wages as low and hours as long as they could. They had a free hand to dictate working conditions because the prevailing economic ethos among society's leaders was laissez-faire. While this policy claimed to be minimum action by government in the marketplace, in fact the U.S. government has always given lavish assistance and protection to business. In accordance with the same ideology of laissez-faire, "individualism" was preached from the top to the bottom of society. The "self-made" man was exemplified by the male heroes of Horatio Alger's novels. Such a male ideal existed in sharp contrast to the domestic ideology of harmonious and moral relations with which women were supposed to identify themselves, and which were preached in such novels as *Little Women.* One result of laissez-faire capitalism was the failure to consider even the most basic safety of workers; industrial accidents killed and maimed hundreds of thousands of workers each year. In 1913, 1 million workers were injured and 25,000 were killed, even after employees began to respond to the reform campaigns which women led and joined. Protective legislation was one result of their efforts.

In facing terrible living as well as working conditions, female and male industrial workers, the majority of whom were immigrants, were sustained by the traditions of their various ethnic heritages, ranging from age-old religious beliefs to equally strong secular political beliefs. People banded together in churches and clubs, keeping their old ways alive in their marriage patterns, religious festivals, and ethnic newspapers. These traditions were diversified even more with the changing proportions of immigrants—less arrived from the northern and western countries of Europe, while huge numbers poured in from the eastern and southern countries (the shift from the so-called Old Immigrants to the New Immigrants). It would take several generations before immigrant groups achieved social mobility by way of property ownership, education, or both.

The flood of European immigrants had been drawn to America by industrialization's demand for labor. For years, workers, union organizers, and other reformers decried the living and working conditions of industry's employees, which were appalling by any standard. At the same time, urban political machines played an important role in fostering city services, brokering different interests, and disbursing a wide range of charity where no one else would. These political machines were rooted in ethnic constituencies and were self-interested in the good as well as the bad they did. Such self-interest laid the machines open to middle-class reformers' charges that the machines were corrupt. In attacking political machines, reformers claimed that they were applying neutral, social-scientific standards to bring about progress. There was another dimension to the reformers' attack, one that linked it to the campaign for female suffrage. Political machines and clubhouse politics were imbued with traditional masculine values. Symbolically, voting took place in bars and taverns. What room was there in such machine politics for women? Jane Addams's early conflicts with Chicago's bosses were symbolic of the conflict.

In opening her campaign in the city, Jane Addams undertook a formidable task. Chicago, like many American cities, was growing rapidly. The nationwide urban population increased five-and-a-half times between 1870 and 1920, by which time 54 million Americans (a clear majority of the total population) lived in cities. The living conditions of the urban working class were, as Addams observed, "horrid." The influx of people exceeded housing supplies; people were crammed into filthy tenements. In many cases tenements were workplaces, too, especially for women in the needles trades, desperately combining family care with work, trying to scrape together some income. Reformers like Jacob Riis publicized the terrible overcrowding and unsanitary living conditions experienced by the working class.

Cities were transformed in shape as well as size because mass transit systems facilitated the sprawling of cities into suburbs. There the single-family, suburban home would be made into the all-American ideal. Among their other achievements, reformers Addams and Charlotte Perkins Gilman were pioneers of alternative living arrangements. Addams's settlement house—a community of reformers established in working-class neighborhoods—and Gilman's kitchenless apartment house symbolize the alternative ways of organizing which were being explored within the larger and traumatically transformed urban spaces of late nineteenth- and early twentieth-century America.

Women rose to the challenge posed by the careless individualism of self-made men with an outpouring of "expanded domestic housekeeping" and "social mothering." They qualified themselves for such a challenge by their successful inroads on the male bastions of higher learning. The Morrill Act of 1862 had sponsored the founding of coeducational state universities. Although many of these universities maintained a gender differentiated curriculum, by 1879, nearly half of all American colleges were coeducational. Stanford and the University of Chicago, both founded in 1890, were open to women. Women went on to demand entry into the professions for which their education now qualified them; they became natural scientists, social scientists, academics, and lawyers, despite meeting obstacles at every turn. Female doctors were the most successful of professional women before 1900, but this was because they concentrated their careers in obstetrics and gynecology and many based their claim on women's "natural" proclivity for nurturance. They were trained largely in separate colleges and hospitals. Many women patients preferred women doctors. In short, women's modest success in entering the medical profession must be explained by its congruence with Victorian, separate-sex culture.

Some men supported women's educational advance, but many found it deeply threatening. One form of resistance to equal education for women was an updating of the traditional argument that women were physically incapable of being educated. This was the context within which one must place Addams's struggle to go to medical school. The attitude that she and women with ambition like hers challenged was represented by Dr. Edward Clarke, a trustee of Harvard's medical school (which at the time faced women's insistence on being admitted). In 1873 Clarke published *Sex in Education*, an attack on women's having any college or high-school education. Clarke said that young women could not compete intellectually with men and develop their ovaries at the same time. Clarke's additional suggestion that female factory workers' reproductive capacity was damaged by similar "unnatural" demands on their system was developed by Dr. Azel Ames in *Sex in Industry* (1875). Ames had been instrumental in making these views the rationale for a 1874 Massachusetts law attempting to limit women's factory-work hours to ten a day. While exceptional and unenforced, this law was an early effort at "protective legislation," aimed at "protecting" women in the paid workplace. In addition to shorter hours (to protect women's reproductive and mothering capacities), later "protective" laws aimed to establish minimum-wage requirements (better wages meant shorter hours and therefore more time for mothering); restrictions on nightwork (again, to leave more time for mothering); the provision of places and seats to rest (to protect women's health); and separate toilets. In short, while it was based on apparently medical and therefore "scientific" evidence, "protective legislation" in fact expressed middle-class Victorian gender values.

Throughout the century, courts and legislatures continued to upold the sanctity of laissez-faire capitalism against the effort of reformers. Lawyers and labor organizations tried and failed to limit the hours of industrial workers but were defeated by the courts. Government, said the courts, could not intervene in the freely entered contract between employer and employee. Finally, the reformers decided to use the tactic of appealing to the gender ideal embodied in protective legislation. In their successful 1908 brief, *Muller* vs. *Oregon*, lawyer Louis Brandeis and his sister-in-law Jacqueline Goldmark cited that 1874 law rationalized by the Clarke-Ames argument. (Oregon had passed a law limiting a woman's daily work hours to ten, which a commercial laundry operator named Muller,[12] had ignored.) Brandeis and Goldmark amassed apparent proof that extended hours of work damaged menarche and healthy menstruation. Those processes represented *potential* motherhood—menstruation was common to all women—therefore, the argument was a way of classifying women by way of reproduction, whether they became mothers or not. By upholding the Oregon law, the Supreme Court placed motherhood above laissez-faire.

The case also symbolized the acceptance of medical and social-scientific authority as the arbiter of social policy. After the Civil War, the study of society, claiming to have the authority and prestige of hard science, began to flourish in the new and growing research universities. Social science provided careers and a rationale for reformers. Eventually entering higher education in significant numbers, women had come to combine their moral claim to reform, which was based on a highly idealized motherhood, with the language, authority, and institutions of social science. This fusion made late nineteenth-century reform significantly different from women's reform activities earlier in the century. Women shed their more genteel outlook in order to increase their influence on public affairs. They began forming female clubs and associations. In 1890, they organized themselves into the General Federation of Women's Clubs; by 1910, 800,000 women had joined this national network. Members collected data for the solution and protection of large-scale social problems. Their efforts and those of many others, including settlement-house workers, helped to desentimentalize motherhood and to make it more "scientific." One illustration was the supposedly biological rationale for protective legislation.

While concerned with the circumstances faced by workers of both sexes, women reformers were particularly focused on the plight of women. For example, the Woman's Christian Temperance Union (WCTU), founded in 1874, addressed the terrible damage that men's alcoholism did to their families, that is, to most women's primary concern at the time. The WCTU was the largest women's organization of the nineteenth century. It had roots among women in country and city. Its combination of middle-class, "female," Protestant, and social science values was typical of its era. Its greatest leader, Frances Willard, recognized the only effective way to bring power to bear on national social problems was politics. Temperance reformers, like settlement-house workers, embraced suffragism.

Fostering education, establishing settlement houses, and forming pressure groups, educated women became central to Progressivism, the loosely defined movement that culminated in the "reform" presidencies of Theodore Roosevelt (1901–1909), William Howard Taft (1909–1913), and Woodrow Wilson (1913–1921). Following in the wake of populist reformers, Progressives aimed to check the excesses of corporate power, from the abusive railroad rates charged farmers to the monopoly of city power companies. Feminist Progressives exposed the terrible conditions of women factory workers and attempted to reform them through labor legislation. These efforts were consistent with Progressive journalism's "muckraking" of the meat-packing and oil industries and the passage of laws to check those abuses, and its cleansing and opening of politics by way of the secret ballot, the initiative, referendum, and recall. Women's demand for suffrage can be seen as part of this whole progressive thrust.

Female reformers' identification with motherhood was sometimes at odds with other impulses in reformers themselves and in popular culture at large. Americanization and greater material prosperity can be correlated with declining family size, an increasing number of women choosing not to marry, and an increasing rate of divorce. While celebrating marriage and motherhood for women generally, Jane Addams never married; Charlotte Perkins Gilman eventually sent her child to her husband to raise; and late in life, the great suffragist Elizabeth Cady Stanton was to identify herself with "The Solitude of the Self" even in the experience of motherhood. "Alone" she wrote, woman "goes to the gates of death to give her life to every man that is born into the world; no one can share her fears, no one can mitigate her pangs." Perhaps the most dramatic expression of this appetite for individual identity is Kate Chopin's 1899 novel, *The Awakening.* Its heroine "awakens" to sensuality and individual consciousness—

in short, to freedom—which she chooses over conventional marriage and motherhood. But such clarity was rare; far more characteristic of women's intellectual lives was the conflict between, on the one hand, subordination of self to larger entities (family, society, or "womanhood") and, on the other, the assertion of individual freedom.

African-American female reformers shared certain characteristics of late nineteenth-century white female reformers. Educated, middle-class in comparison to most African-Americans, and struggling with some success to enter the professions, black reformers also established settlement houses and a national network of women's clubs. Ida Wells-Barnett's extraordinary work against lynching may be seen as both muckraking and as the social-scientific gathering of data. But as her targeting of lynching illustrates, black women's intellectual orientation was fundamentally different from white women's. Pervasive and continuous racism affected African-American women and men in every dimension of their lives, whatever the success of their attempts to resist it and maintain their cultural identity.

As white, urban-dwelling women left paid domestic service for the tertiary sector, African-American women took their places because they were excluded from other kinds of work. In the southern states, they were allowed into the booming tobacco industry only in the hardest, dirtiest, and worst-paid jobs. The vast majority of African-American women worked as sharecroppers and farmers. In many places they were visible as convict labor on the roads as well as in the fields. Nonetheless, a few African-American women fought their way into middle-class jobs, most notably into teaching. Lucy Craft Chaney established the Haines Institute in Augusta, Georgia, in 1886, which trained African-American women for teaching and nursing. Middle-class black women formed clubs to foster the same goals (child care, health care, relief for the impoverished, moral and educational reform) that were fostered by white women's clubs. When the white General Federation of Women's Clubs rejected black women's clubs, black women formed their own national organizations. They also founded suffrage associations, which similarly faced rejection by white suffrage associations, most notably in 1919 at the hands of Carrie Chapman Catt, the head of the National American Woman Suffrage Association. While some African-American women then rejected the suffrage movement altogether because of this racism, others continued to fight for the vote in local, regional, and national associations.

This era was in large part one of reform because of the large-scale emergence of educated women into public life. Overcoming resistance to their desire for higher education, arming themselves with social expertise, and banding together in overlapping networks of associations, middle-class women took on a daunting array of social problems that were largely the effects of unchecked capitalism. Ironically, perhaps, America's economic success provided its female reformers with the resources, of time and education, on which they depended. Jane Addams's inheritance from her "capitalist" father paid her way for the rest of her life. On the other hand, capitalism itself benefitted inestimably from the cheap labor of women, who provided at least one-fifth of the factory labor force throughout this period. It also encouraged and relied upon all classes of women to purchase consumer goods and services.

Charlotte Perkins Gilman

(1860–1935)

Carol Ruth Berkin

Charlotte Perkins Gilman was born July 3, 1860, in Hartford, Connecticut, to parents who separated soon after she was born. Following her own divorce from her first husband in 1894, Gilman moved to California where she began to establish her career of social reform by publishing in several literary forms and by lecturing to women's clubs and to socialist and working men's associations. In 1898 Gilman published Women and Economics: The Economic Factor between Men and Women as a Factor in Social Evolution, *a work that made her internationally famous and has remained the best known of her many writings. Gilman's goal was to end women's subjection to degrading and unpaid housework; child care, cooking, and cleaning, she argued, should be separated from other aspects of women's lives and assigned to paid professional specialists. Gilman's architectural plans for kitchenless living quarters were designed to facilitate this purpose. They stemmed from a long-standing tradition of socialist and feminist thought. With Jane Addams and other women, Gilman was a founder of the Women's Peace Party during World War I.*

Charlotte Perkins Gilman married her cousin, Houghton Gilman, in 1900. The couple lived together in New York and in Connecticut. Diagnosed as having terminal cancer, she committed suicide in 1935 in California, where she had moved to be with her daughter soon after Houghton Gilman's death in 1934.

Once upon a time, 10-year-old Charlotte Perkins wrote in 1870, the good King Ezephon and his besieged kingdom were saved by the heroic battlefield performance of Princess Araphenia, only daughter of the king. Araphenia had not vanquished the wicked enemy alone, however; she had magical help from the fabulous Elmondine, a beautiful visitor from a distant planet. Bejeweled and bewitching, Elmondine had come to a lonely Araphenia in the palace garden and had offered advice and assistance. To save the king and his kingdom, Elmondine created, out of thin air, an army of a thousand men. And to the young earthly princess, this fairy princess gave a magic sword with which to fight and an invincible horse on which to ride while disguised as a warrior-prince. When victory came, the brave girl threw off her disguise, and her astonished father embraced her.

Tales like this one appear in different versions throughout Charlotte Perkins's diaries.[1] The central characters remain the same in each story: a young woman who can, through some magic, overstep the prescribed boundaries of her life and enter into active participation in the great struggles between good and evil in her society; an older woman, resplendently female yet wise and independent and powerful, who guides the novice's path; and always a grateful father whose respect had been won.

Charlotte Perkins was a young girl with an active fantasy life and a lonely reality when she spun these tales. But as a mature woman of 50, she continued to write stories of wise, older women, strong and independent doctors or philanthropists, who appeared out of nowhere to guide some struggling girl to maturity. The setting was no longer fabulous, but the characters were unchanged.[2]

No Elmondine ever appeared in the life of Charlotte Perkins Stetson Gilman. But for many younger women—in her lifetime and today—she has seemed to play that fabled role herself. Writer, philosopher, socialist, and feminist, Gilman has come to stand for the potentialities of American womanhood. She appears very much the self-made woman, overcoming sexual stereotype and social pressures to emerge as a woman of depth and dimension.

Valuable as this Elmondine may seem to those searching for a model, Gilman did not come from a distant planet, free of the conflicts that a woman might have faced at the turn of the century or faces today. Nor was she magically transformed by any fabulous figure into a secure, stable, integrated personality without the marks of a difficult childhood. Her life bears witness to the difficulties of feminism, not as an ideology or a political commitment, but as a personal experience. Charlotte Perkins Gilman struggled for intellectual and emotional liberation, hampered through much of her life by an internalization of the very split vision of masculine and feminine spheres and destinies that, in her work, she would expose as artificial. She struggled later in her life to achieve a balance between independence and an interdependence with others. This essay seeks to chart her personal confrontation with feminism, because it is in that experience that she may serve as a model for American women.

Charlotte Perkins was born on July 3, 1860.[3] Her parents' family trees, rooted in New England soil, were already intertwined, with cousins marrying cousins in discreet confirmation of their pride in association. Her father was a Beecher, grandson of Lyman Beecher, and nephew, as Charlotte put it, of twelve "world servers," a young man nearly smothered in the mantle of reform. Frederick Beecher Perkins's mother had been a rebel of sorts, the odd sister who had never taken any interest in public affairs.

Frederick Beecher Perkins struck a compromise between family tradition and maternal heresy; He dedicated himself to the pursuit of knowledge, thus satisfying his own personal desires in the interest of society. It was his world service to know everything, in case anyone might ask. He was quick-tempered, sensitive, with a well-mannered hostility to authority. He was never much of a financial success and never seemed to care. In 1858 Perkins married his 31-year-old cousin, Mary Fitch Wescott of Providence, Rhode Island. As a girl, Wescott had been "the darling of an elderly father and a juvenile mother," a naive, lovely, flirtatious girl who broke hearts and prompted numerous proposals at first sight. Her own branch of the family was known for its strong attachment to one another and its indifference to the outside world.

If Mary Fitch Wescott had been naive and frivolous as a maiden, her marriage cured her of both failings with cruel abruptness. Within less than three years she bore three children. The eldest died. Thomas Perkins and his younger sister, Charlotte Perkins, survived. When the exhausted mother was told that another pregnancy would kill her, her husband abandoned her.

The dissolution of the Perkins family worked upon the consciousness and character of each member differently. Despite the poverty, the humiliating dependence on family charity that kept her moving from home to home and city to city, Mary Perkins never voiced a word of criticism at her abandonment. Thus, her children were left to struggle with its mystery. Their father's motives could only be imagined and their mother's continuing attachment to him only accepted as a reality.

Mary Wescott Perkins kept her silence, but she drew from this marital experience a lesson that surely helped shape her daughter's life. She learned, she said, that affection was a fatal vulnerability.

What was true physiologically became for her psychologically true as well: Love could kill. She strove, therefore, with devotion and steely determination, to arm her own children against emotional disappointment. She resolved to nurture stoics, immune to rejection because no appetite for love had been developed. This denial of affection to her children was, of necessity, also self-denial; out of love for her children she kept her distance from them. "I used to put away your little hand from my cheek when you were a nursing baby," she once remarked with pride and regret to her adult daughter. But her stoicism was acquired rather than natural, and there were lapses; in secret moments, when she thought her daughter Charlotte safely asleep, she held and caressed and kissed her.

It was Charlotte Perkins—precocious, intensely lonely, isolated from other children by her family's nomadic life, and alienated from her brother by his teasing style and his "bad" behavior—who bore most heavily the burden of her mother's contradictions. From Mary Wescott Perkins she learned the unintended but crucial lesson that there was a public, rational, independent self and a secret, emotional, vulnerable self. The young girl took the public self to be estimable and held the private self suspect. By the age of 10 she had constructed this dichotomy.

Her childhood diaries reveal a self-consciously stoical Charlotte, a character ruthlessly creating itself, always disciplining and reprimanding, always self-critical, trusting in rigorous programs for self-improvement to overcome unacceptable character traits. This was, for her, the real Charlotte Perkins. Yet she indulged a secret self. At night she immersed herself in a rich fantasy life, allowing her imagination to transport her to beautiful and exotic paradises where (as she later remembered) "the stern restrictions, drab routines, unbending discipline that hemmed me in became of no consequence." But allowing free rein to her imagination provided more than an escape from drab situational realities. Her fantasy worlds were never so randomly constructed as she might have believed. Repeatedly she peopled them with open and affectionate maternal figures who provided her with the secrets to winning a father's affection and esteem.

As sustaining as she knew her fantasy worlds to be, Charlotte Perkins felt the need to prove that she kept her imagination under control. Unwilling to relinquish it, she struck a bargain with herself that would preserve it: "Every night," she wrote, she would think of pleasant things that could really occur; once a week, of "lovelier, stranger things"; once a month, "of wonders"; and once a year, of "anything."

This bargain held until her adolescence. When she was 13, as Gilman recalled in her autobiography, her mother discovered the evening fantasies and ordered her daughter to end them. To this, Gilman wrote, an obedient child instantly acceded. Perhaps, however, Charlotte Perkins demanded of herself that the fantasies be abandoned, or transformed into something less disturbing to her conscious self. Such a transformation did occur, for even as she dissolved the kingdom of Ezephon she began to nurture an absorbing enthusiasm for the "things that could really occur" in the world of science and sociology. Social "wonders," existing and potential, began to preoccupy her; physics, with the power of its absolute laws, made magic pale; and the plausible utopias the social reformer could design were "lovelier stranger things," than the fairy kingdoms had ever been.

The bridge between the old fantasy world and the new scientific one was her own role in them. In either setting, Charlotte Perkins's part was heroic. In the new and less-disturbing secret life that took shape, she dreamed of becoming a renowned world server, a major figure in the reorganization of her society. The shift in focus to the real world offered her a better chance to release her productive and constructive energies. But lost in this transformation was the expression of a desire for intimacy and the frank recognition that loneliness was a negative condition.

Her imaginary worlds had helped her confront her feelings. They were populated by individuals who came to cherish her and to love her and, thus, to end her emotional isolation. But in the new world of social realities, Charlotte Perkins saw herself befriended by no one in particular and a friend to no one but impersonal humanity. In such a self-image, loneliness was elevated to a necessity; it was transformed into the price one paid for the heroic self. Through the prism of her new ambitions, the years of stoical training at last revealed their clear purpose. Her mother had intended to prepare her for survival only; now Charlotte Perkins saw that self-denial and discipline prepared one not simply to endure life, but to perform great deeds in it.

As this perception of her life hardened into an ideology, Charlotte Perkins lost the power to discern genuine interests from defensive commitments. The attraction of social reform became a shield against the appeals and the dangers of personal intimacy. The two modes of living were forced into contradiction. Armed with a rationale for dismissing her feelings, she often refused to probe their meaning. Some emotions she could incorporate into or redefine within her heroic image. Responses and impulses she could not thus account for, she simply denied. Her conscious certainty masked her deep ambivalence.

Her new self-image and its ambitions drew Charlotte Perkins to a closer identification with her father. He loomed in her mind—as figures often do who are not familiar realities—as the embodiment of his ideals rather than his performance. His reputation as a humanitarian was as well known to her as he was unknown. His apparent dedication to public service contrasted, in her mind, with her mother's slavish commitment to her children and the narrow circle of domestic life. Certain that her mother led a "thwarted life," she became equally certain that her father did not.

Thus, attraction to Frederick Perkins increased, even as the key to gaining his attention seemed to be found. Charlotte Perkins had sought that attention before, appealing to him to write to her because she was lonely. Appeals for support and approval now gave way to requests for reading lists in history, anthropology, and science. To these came speedy and lengthy replies. In this manner she reached out to him, speaking of her intellectual isolation, not a personal loneliness but an absence of tutelage and collegiality. No one at home, she wrote, could understand as he could her ambitions to relate to social issues. It was in this shared breadth of vision that she pressed their kinship. But for all her efforts to rise above "personal pain or pleasure," her disappointment at his frequent coolness and distance slipped into the letters. "Should I continue to write," she asked after a long period without response from Frederick Perkins, "for I am anything but desirous to intrude."

Her mother conveyed a sense of danger in the admission of personal needs, and her father seemed simply to dismiss them as trivial. Thus, both parents denied the validity of feelings to their daughter. But without knowing it, mother and father conspired in a second way. The young Charlotte Perkins came to believe that the compensations for self-control and self-negation were real in the public sphere and were only a mean mockery in the circle of the home; that the avenue to satisfaction and the path to despair were as inevitably separated as this man and woman. She must choose between them. And she must be allowed to choose between them. The choice was a demand upon her own resources; the possibility of choice was a demand upon the society in which she lived. The Victorian society she encountered seemed more hostile than receptive to her pursuit of a public life, and this would direct her reformist energies to the place of women in American society.

The new self-image that took shape in the early 1870s may have cushioned Charlotte Perkins while family relationships and economic circumstances disintegrated further. In 1871, after a decade of separation, Mary Wescott Perkins began a suit for divorce. Her motives are unknown, but the decision brought a dramatic alteration in her public image. When the divorce came in 1873, Mary Perkins was no longer a loyal and suffering wife; she had become a scandalous divorcée. Once-sympathetic Beechers and Perkinses closed their doors to her, and she and her children were left entirely on their own.

In 1873 the three moved to Providence, Rhode Island. They spent a brief time experimenting in cooperative living. When this failed, the Perkinses settled into independent poverty. While her mother struggled to support the family, Charlotte struggled for autonomy. At 15 she openly challenged her mother's rule of complete obedience, with ironic success. Free of parental control at last, she promptly disciplined herself: She swore to give total obedience to her mother until she reached age 21.

Superficially the results of rebellion and of defeat were one and the same; in more ways than she yet understood, Charlotte Perkins remained a dutiful daughter. Her real rebellion was not in character but in the uses to which she intended to put the stern self-discipline and the dire vision of a woman's lot in the world that were her inheritance. Mary Wescott Perkins intended to protect her daughter from disappointment, and to prepare her for life. But that protection was situational: It was in marriage, as wife and mother, that Charlotte Perkins was expected to face her tests. Charlotte Perkins intended, however, to escape marriage, to avoid the despair and defeat it guaranteed, and to meet her test in a world her mother could not know or imagine.

The reality of her adolescent years offered few opportunities to test the meaning of her commitment to spinsterhood. Her mother's excessive restrictions on Charlotte Perkins's social life limited her access to men and even to women. Without any real attachments and always desperately lonely, she fell back upon her imagination for relief. She formed a wild and absorbing crush on an actor she had seen perform but had never met. She nursed an adoration of an older woman who had been only casually kind. In her diaries she regularly denounced love and marriage, yet she filled its pages with speculation: "Who will you marry?" "What will be his age?" "What will you wear on your wedding day?"

At the age of 18 Charlotte Perkins described herself in her diary: "18 years old. 5′6½″ high. Weigh some 120 lbs or thereabout. Looks, not bad. At times handsome. At others, decidedly homely. Health, perfect. Strength—amazing. Character—ah! . . . I am not in love with anybody; I don't think I ever shall be." This was written in January 1879. In February a short diary entry reasserted her lack of attachments. "No Valentines! No Regrets!" Perhaps there were no regrets. But in March of that year, her mother allowed Charlotte to accompany her on a visit to relatives in Cambridge and Boston. Here, suddenly, the 18-year-old found herself the belle her mother had so often been in her own youth. She was surrounded by young college men, courted by Arthurs, Edwards, and Charles Walter Stetson, a "Nice boy . . . but young." She frankly enjoyed the flirtation, and when she returned home in July, her mood grew gloomy.

That fall she returned to Cambridge and then went to Connecticut, and again was faced with a happy embarrassment of beaux. Back home in November, she kept herself busy writing letters to her new male friends, among them a younger cousin from Connecticut, George Houghton Gilman. For several months letters passed between "Dear Ho!" and "Dear Chopkins," and it was to Houghton Gilman that she most openly wrote of the boredom and the tension of living under the heavy hand of her mother. On March 6, 1878, she had chastised herself in her diary: "I must really abolish all desire for comfort or any sort of happiness if I expect to have any peace." But back in Cambridge for New Year's Day 1880, she recorded with pleasure a day of excitement and expectation, the "best day of my life."

Charlotte Perkins was nearly 20 when this brief flurry of social life broke the monotony of her Providence existence. When the excitement ended, she settled once more into biding her time until, at 21, she could embark upon her own life. Even in her impatience, however, she knew that things at home had greatly improved. She had studied art, and recently had enjoyed some independent income through the sale of miniatures and other decorative pieces. She found release for her physical energies—and an opportunity for sorority—at a local woman's gymnasium.

And despite her mother's continuing interference with her life—reading her mail, intercepting and rejecting social invitations—Charlotte Perkins had established her first genuine friendships with other women. One of these women was Grace Channing, daughter of a noted New England clerical family, a girl with a background similar to Charlotte's. Together, Grace Channing and Charlotte Perkins wrote plays and poems to entertain themselves and their families. But most intimate and most important was the friendship formed with Martha Luther, a young girl who for almost four years held Charlotte Perkins's unguarded confidence.

These friendships were hard-earned. Charlotte Perkins was as deeply wary of them as she was eager for them, thinking affection to be a trap and a drain on one's energies, but feeling it as a voluntary vulnerability. To protect herself, she compelled Martha Luther to make a pact, pledging that their affection would be "permanent and safe." Even with such a guarantee, Charlotte worried that she would jeopardize the relationship either by excessive demands for affection or, conversely, by sudden withdrawals of affection. "I was always in a fervor," she later recalled, "that for a time I should want to see her continually, and that there would be spaces when affection seemed to wane."

Sometime before the end of 1881 Martha Luther married and moved from Providence. Perkins felt the separation keenly, experiencing the old isolation and loneliness more intensely after the years of sharing with Luther. She was, by her own account, in a vulnerable state when, in January 1882, Charles Walter Stetson re-entered her life. Like Perkins, Stetson had trained as an artist. Art was an immediate bond between them, though perhaps it involved more competitive tension than either thought to admit. Even deeper was the bond of circumstance. "He was," Gilman later recalled, "a great man—but lonely, isolated, poor, misunderstood." Stetson's state of mind and worldly condition seemed to mirror her own perfectly. The two quickly fell in love and, within a short time, Walter Stetson proposed.

The effect of Stetson's proposal upon Charlotte Perkins was deep and disturbing. It came in her twenty-first year, and thus it set her cruelly at odds with herself. She was, by the terms of her bargain with herself, free at last of parental control. She felt an urgency to give her past meaning by pursuing its heroic dreams. Her self-esteem depended upon an energetic dedication to her social goals. To abandon the pursuit of a life of world service before it had begun, and to embrace instead love and marriage, would be to shatter a self-image that had, despite its problems, been sustaining.

Just when she needed most to understand what she truly desired and what she might realistically work to have, Charlotte Perkins was most completely at a loss. She could not separate her genuine commitment to social reform from the power she had invested in it to justify her emotional isolation; and because she had invested her commitment with that power in order to defend against emotional rejection and disappointment, she could not risk disarming it in the face of a proposal of marriage, with its confusing threats and promises of intimacy. She loved Walter Stetson and wanted to be with him. But she could neither overcome the powerful image of her mother's thwarted life nor separate that image from the institution of marriage itself; the two concepts were merged.

In order to avoid confronting her confusion, Charlotte recast her dilemma. She posed the choice as one between two mutually exclusive duties rather than two strongly felt desires. She faced, she told herself and Charles Walter Stetson, a decision to be made between a duty to life and a duty to love. Thus she distorted her feelings and the issues entirely; she sacrificed any awareness of her positive yearnings for both choices in order to avoid the reasons for rejecting either. In her diaries and her letters to Stetson, she hid behind a rhetoric of obligation and self-sacrifice that not even she could resist in the end. She made no effort to accommodate both duties. She was protected from this approach not simply by her psychic patterns, but also by her sociological perceptions. For women, life and love were not overlapping spheres. Men could have marriage and careers; women, responsible for home and children, could not. A sense of injustice that she could not entirely hide sprang from the fact that it was exactly this social division of labor and duties that she intended to reform.

For months, Charlotte Perkins pleaded with Walter Stetson for delay. This she won in large part simply by her indecision. Although he suffered, she felt she suffered more, because she was torn this way and that, and had, she told him, no peace. "How often one duty contradicts another," she exclaimed when, in the midst of reading in order to acquire a "general notion of how the world worked," she stopped to write him a letter. "And what a world of careful practice it needs to distinguish the highest!" It was the skill required to distinguish the highest duty that she felt sorely lacking. And this, she argued, accounted for her delay.

"I am not a tenderhearted child," she assured him, and herself, "neither am I an impulsive girl: But a clearheaded woman who is weighing a life time in her hands." How could she know what she would lose or gain if she had no experience of either life? On marriage and motherhood there were, she knew, all-too-many voices of authority to guide her. "This is noble, natural and right," said "all the ages." Her own body, she admitted, urged her to yield. Against her independence ran "all the ages" as well, for "no woman yet has ever attempted to stand alone as I intended." The grandiosity of this statement was entirely innocent, although it did not reflect social reality.

In the 1880s American women of her race and region were experimenting with independence. The existing social currents for change had, in fact, suggested to her the role of public woman and reformer; her ambitions confirmed that the struggle had already begun. Of course, the general contours of her society reinforced both her notion of women's segregated sphere and the heretical quality of her career aspirations. But when Charlotte Perkins spoke of standing alone, it was the expectation of emotional isolation rather than the concrete problems of economic support or practical opportunities that gave force to her personal drama.

What did she want to do? She had taken care to bury the answers and could not now plumb her own depths. She tried to clarify her thoughts in letters to Walter Stetson, in soliloquy rather than conversation. But she could not explain—or understand—herself. Why, she wrote, do I hesitate? Life with him promised paradise, she said, but love seemed to ask "more than I can give." Repeatedly, and with an unwitting callousness for his feelings, she pressed for a relationship that was limited, a friendship, like the one agreed upon with Martha Luther, that would free her from the necessity of choice. Companionship and friendship would satisfy her; why must there be love and marriage? "I ought not to complain of being offered the crown of womanhood," she confessed, voicing her own and her mother's tenacious romanticism about all that they feared; but she did not fully wish to accept it.

Slowly the choice crystallized into one of duty to submit and endure, or duty to rebel. Posed in these terms, love lost all its positive potential, and independence had its romance restored. But at the last moment, with frustrating perversity, she denied even her own freedom and responsibility to choose. Instead she bowed to the moral imperative of finding one's "right duty." The "right duty" was surely the more difficult one. As she weighed each choice, her pride—and the hint of pleasure—in her insistence "that my life is mine in spite of a myriad lost sisters before me" made her crucially uneasy with the choice of independence: thus, she chose marriage. On December 31, 1882, she wrote in her diary: "With no pride, with little hope, with uncertain occasional happiness, with no glad energy and living power; with no faith or nearly none, but still, thank God! with firm belief in what is right and wrong; I begin the new year."

A deep nostalgia and a sense of loss showed in her diary for 1883 as she made plans for marriage. Self-pity, wholly shrouded from her own consciousness, marked every page. Dread—equally of unhappiness and of happiness—pervaded this secret record of events.

On May 2, 1884, Charlotte Perkins and Walter Stetson were married. Despite all her mother's care and preparation, despite her own, Charlotte Stetson entered marriage as an innocent and a romantic: "My Wedding Day . . . HOME. . . ."

> I install Walter in the parlor and dining room while I retire to the bed chamber and finish its decoration. The bed looks like a fairy bower with lace, white silk, and flowers. Make my self a crown of white roses. Wash again, and put on a thin shift of white mull fastened with a rose bud and velvet and pearl civeture. My little white velvet slippers and a white snood. Go in to my husband. He meets me

> joyfully; we promise to be true to each other; and he puts on the ring and the crown. Then he lifts the crown, loosens the snood, unfastens the girdle, and then— and then. O my God! I thank thee for this heavenly happiness! O make me one with thy great life that I may best fulfill my duties to my love! to my Husband!

May was filled with diary reports of great personal happiness and a total commitment of energy and ego to cooking, baking breads, visiting, and house care. She aimed for perfection and was furious at any domestic failures. Culinary errors made her "disgusted with myself." By mid-June efforts to prove herself a perfect wife were interrupted by an illness that left her weak and bedridden. By June 25 she was miserable, not because of domestic failures, but now because her "old woe"—"conviction of being too outwardly expressive of affection"—had begun to fill her with fears of driving Walter Stetson away. Assurances by her husband could only temporarily ease her mind. In early August she learned she was pregnant.

Through most of her pregnancy, Charlotte Stetson was both sick and depressed. The physical incapacity and loss of the body tone she had acquired through hours in the woman's gymnasium disturbed her, and they no doubt contributed to her sense of unnatural lethargy and of a passivity she held in contempt. Holding herself in ever lower esteem as the months went by, she feared Walter Stetson must share her disgust with herself. But her husband—almost stubbornly—proved sympathetic and supportive. "He has worked for me and for us both, waited on me in every tenderest way. . . . God be thanked for my husband!"

The pregnancy brought her little pleasure. Still, as the months passed, Charlotte Stetson began to adjust to her child-to-be in the terms she best understood: in the language of duty. Her hopes, she wrote, were that the child she carried would be a "world helper" and that she herself could serve the world by a devotion to the child. "Brief ecstasy, long pain. Then years of joy again," she wrote on the morning of March 23, 1885, when Katherine (Kate) Beecher Stetson was born.

But pain and joy seemed to wage a confusing struggle that left her helpless. Despite desperate efforts to be a perfect mother, Charlotte Stetson had given over the care of her daughter to her own mother by August 1885. Depressed, ill, bedridden, she had few days without "every morning the same hopeless waking." She could not explain her deepening depression. Her child was lovely, her husband was loving; she berated herself for not regaining control over her emotions and carefully shied away from locating in her illness any hostility or anger. She was suffering, she was certain, from a new disease called "nervous prostration," and she came to fear that she had contracted an infection of the brain.

Walter Stetson, however, surmised that marriage and motherhood were his wife's problems. Although he did not understand why this was the case, he accepted it. That fall he offered her a separation. But with desperate insistence Charlotte Stetson refused this relief. "He cannot see how irrevocably bound I am, for life, for life. No, unless he dies and the baby die, or he change or I change there is no way out." The dilemma was once again, if not of her own making, at least one she would not allow to be too easily resolved. She could not permit herself to be relieved or consoled; she was invested in this painful punishment. And, with the unintentional blindness of the determined sufferer, she forced husband, daughter, and mother to participate in her nightmare.

Then, in the summer of 1886, Charlotte Stetson bowed to family urgings and left, alone, for California. She looked forward to a host of reunions, visiting her brother Thomas in Utah, her father in San Francisco, and her good friend Grace Channing in Pasadena. The trip restored her health and spirits almost magically. The lush, rich floral splendor of Pasadena satisfied her childhood dreams of beauty; to her, the city was Edenic.

But her return home brought immediate relapse into illness and despair. That winter her husband took her to the famous woman's doctor, S. Weir Mitchell, for treatment at his clinic. Here, her worst fears that either love or "her driving force" must be relinquished were given confirmation by a representative of that impartial science she had always trusted. Mitchell, famous for his belief that anatomy was a woman's destiny, argued that the passivity of the womb must be echoed in the woman's daily life in order for true health to be hers. He prescribed for Charlotte Stetson a totally domestic life, the constant companionship of her child, and an absolute end to any writing or serious reading. Determined to obey this dictum of absolute domesticity, Charlotte Stetson reached the dangerous edge of insanity.

This total collapse, with its admission of failure and its punishment, seemed to release Charlotte Stetson from her commitment to her marriage. Every effort had been made. Thus, in early 1887 she agreed to a separation from her husband. She had, in significant if shrouded ways, recapitulated her parents' marital history. Her mother's physical danger from childbearing found its counterpart in her own near-insanity. But the Stetsons' separation, unlike that of Frederick and Mary Wescott Perkins, had no taint of a husband's abandonment.

Walter Stetson remained nearby, visiting whenever his wife allowed, some weeks coming to see her every day. He brought her gifts, cared for Kate when his wife or child was sick, and, as Charlotte Stetson frequently recorded in her diary with gratitude, did not press any demands upon her. Yet when she looked at the examples of marriage and motherhood around her, she identified with the despair of vulnerable and abused women. "Talked with Mrs. Smythe," she wrote on February 20, 1887. "She is another victim! Young, girlish, unexperienced, sickly, with a sickly child, and no servant . . . ignorant both, and he using his 'marital rights' at her vital expense."

By the end of the year, Charlotte Stetson had begun to think again of California and its healing effect on both body and mind. In 1888, with her daughter and her mother, she set out once again for Pasadena. She had done her duty to love; now she meant to fulfill her desire "to have my utmost capabilities called out in some necessary work."

In this manner, the Charlotte Perkins Gilman known to us through her books, lectures, novels, magazine articles, and poetry began her career. If this were a fairy tale, the woman who left New England "ashamed, degraded and despairing" to become an independent woman and a leading intellectual and social critic of her day would have soon experienced the personal satisfaction and self-esteem her achievements should have brought her. But this woman was who and what she was, and like us all she carried her past into her present.

With her mother (soon to develop cancer) and Kate, Charlotte Perkins Stetson lived a precarious existence, economically and emotionally, in California. She was formally uneducated, and unskilled except in commercial art. This occupation she did not pursue. Her goal was a public life and her career the preaching of a gospel of reform. She tried to support her family by giving public lectures on reform topics, but the proceeds from a passed hat were small. Extra income came from taking in boarders. Debts piled up; soon the triad was moving from house to house in a nomadic pattern reminiscent of her own childhood. If her experience as the head of a husbandless household echoed her mother's years of struggle, Stetson's love life became an odd parody of her marriage.

In 1890 she formed a relationship with another woman writer. The affair was not necessarily sexual; the intensity of emotion did not demand, though it may have included, physical expression. Perhaps Stetson was only seeking a friendship similar to the sustaining one with Martha Luther, but with "Dora" she accepted the subservient and self-negating role she had always associated with "wife." The aspects that had driven her from marriage she now experienced with, even seemed to invite from, Dora. Dora was generous with money, and Charlotte, who would take no financial aid from her estranged husband, accepted assistance from Dora—with every string attached. In return for the money and the companionship, Charlotte provided Dora with her domestic services, "making a home for her," and with intellectual support, cheating her own career by "furnishing material for [Dora's] work."

But the companionship was not so gentle and constant as that she had received from "her dear boy," Walter. Dora was an openly abusive partner. She was "malevolent. She lied . . . she drank . . . she swore freely, at me as well as others. She lifted her hand to strike me in one of her tempers." This affair, begun with the decade, ended when Dora left Charlotte in 1893. From this demeaning experience, Charlotte Stetson refused to learn anything except disappointment. She did not examine her choice of loves or raise any questions about what the affair reflected of her needs and her insecurities. She would only chastise herself in her diary: "Out of it all I ought surely to learn final detachment from all personal concerns."

These private turmoils did not prevent, but coincided with, Charlotte Stetson's growing recognition as a public figure. Her skills at extemporaneous speaking had earned her little money in her early years in California, but they had brought her a reputation, just as her first essays and published articles had brought national notice. Her radical views on the rights of labor and of women, on child care, and other social reforms earned her influential friends in California, as well as the expected enemies. In an essentially conservative state, there were nevertheless several active women's organizations and a few lively communities of intellectuals and writers. These groups welcomed Charlotte Stetson without hesitation, helped her find speaking engagements, and encouraged her to develop and expand her ideas.

Through her work with women's organizations like the Pacific Coast Women's Press Association, she made contact with the national leaders of the women's rights movement—Stanton, Stone, and the settlement house organizer, Jane Addams. To these friends and associates Charlotte Stetson appeared as an energetic, creative, remarkably productive, and admirable woman. But this image contrasted sharply with her own critical sense of herself. In her public life, as in her private life, she seemed determined to demean herself. She was not to be applauded for her raw energy or its constructive channeling, she felt. In reality, she was no better than a cripple; illness, fatigue, and the accompanying mental lethargy that she insisted were the legacy of her married life had permanently damaged her intellectual abilities. She was certain never to realize her potential, and thus she was a disappointment to herself, as she should be to others.

In her first year in California, amid the confusion of establishing a new life, with financial worries and a young child to care for, she had written 33 articles and 23 poems. But this was not enough to bring a sense of satisfaction. In every possible way she seemed to flee the self-esteem her work could and, by her own declared philosophy, should provide. She was hampered by an inability to take her work (rather than herself) seriously. Her speaking and her writing she dismissed as "natural" for her and therefore not to be confused with true work. Work she defined as everything she could not do easily, well, or at all, and she could not hope to do such work because her nervous condition prevented it. Thus, she felt her marriage remained with her; she had not escaped.

It was not the marriage itself that Charlotte Stetson remained wedded to, but rather her concept of her feminine identity. This identity was rooted in disappointment and the thwarted life. As she moved into what she viewed as a masculine sphere, the world of the mind and of action, she would not abandon its opposite. Ironically, though perhaps not surprisingly, the very things she defined as legitimate, enviable intellectual work—"reading, going into a library, learning languages"—were her father's skills, joys, and professional duties as a librarian. And these were, she insisted (and thus it was so), the achievements her past made impossible.

But Gilman's abilities were extraordinary. Quick, creative, able to grasp immediately the essentials of an argument and to generalize from seemingly disparate particulars, she had trained and tutored herself well during her lonely youth. Her true genius lay in her ability to transform her personal contradictions into valuable and legitimate insights on social problems and on the institutions and ideologies that created and sustained the problems.

In her ability to bridge the gap from personal experience to social understanding, she liberated her intellect from the immobility she protested she suffered. What fueled the process was her conviction that social solutions could be found that would some day obviate psychological dilemmas like her own. In this there was potential irony, for she had committed her energies to the elimination of a source of her creativity.

The intellectual framework of her insight was that of the evolutionary and progressive social analysts of her era. Like Lester Ward, Edward Bellamy, and other social critics of the late nineteenth century, she believed that the always shifting patterns of social organization could be understood, predicted, and to some extent manipulated if the evolutionary laws Charles Darwin had discovered were properly applied to human society. By understanding the laws of sociology, human participation in the shaping of human destiny was possible—and, for the concerned citizen, imperative.

Charlotte Perkins Stetson Gilman, like her peers, wrote and lectured to suggest the appropriate actions. For committed evolutionist reformers like herself, change was synonymous with progress. No matter how dark or regressive they might seem, the past and the present always served as a useful and ultimately justifiable base for a better future. Thus, there was equanimity in her perspective, despite the tone of urgency or impatience in pressing reform or the polemical style of her argument. She was dedicated to prodding for changes she was convinced would eventually come. It was only a matter of when and how smoothly the changes would arrive.

Gilman's own work was devoted to the analysis of the relationship of women to their society.[4] Her ideas were not formally or systematically presented until *Women and Economics* was published in 1898, but they had been formulated many years before and were already introduced in the work of her California days. As a historical social anthropologist, she traced the rise and institutionalization of patriarchy as a necessary step in human growth and progress. Until the development of modern industrial society, this patriarchal structure with its rigid segregation of women into sex-related functions had been essential for race preservation. But modern society no longer required such a segregation, nor its aggrandizement to the male of privilege and power through the monopoly of the social sphere. The laws and customs sustaining male monopoly on socially productive activity were now clearly without legitimacy. This kind of social division of labor was neither permanent nor fixed by nature; permanent sexual differences did not, as social conservatives argued, mean permanent differences in capacity for social productivity.

Women's potential for contribution in the social—or, as Gilman called it, the human—sphere must now be released and realized. This would mean a radical restructuring of the society, which would be resisted by men jealous of their privileges and by women ignorant of their deprivation. But, she wrote in 1912: "Social evolution has never waited for the complete enlightenment of mankind."

Gilman's vision of the future did not eliminate the genuine sex-related functions. Reproduction remained woman's specific natural specialization, essential to the preservation of the race. But she wholly renounced the traditional social institutions and duties that surrounded this sexual function. In books like *The Home* or in her *Forerunner* essays, she entirely dismantled the imprisoning female sphere of home-making and child care.

Astute and direct, Gilman located the institutionalization of women's oppression in the home and the family, and in the conditioned mentality that channeled all love and all sense of responsibility and potential for self-esteem into limited personal relationships rather than social activities and humanitarianism. Women were not merely trapped in the home, but also psychologically crippled so that they must only hope to remain there. Not only was their world too narrow, but they could not hope to master it. The sphere itself, with its multiple and dissimilar duties, its undifferentiated requirements, its mystique that forbade systematic training for what was "natural"—this chaotic agglomeration called home and child care could not be successfully managed by the average woman.

The fault lay with the role, not with the woman, Gilman insisted. Only a total disassembling and rationalization of "women's sphere" would be acceptable, with each component of women's traditional roles transformed into a modern, scientific, and professional activity. Once this process had begun, women could abandon their old tasks with confidence that none suffered as a result. They could release their energies in the larger world. Professional "baby gardens" or nurseries, professional food services, and house-cleaning services—on these Gilman's hopes rested. Woman's role would thus disappear, and she would not be accused of deserting it.

Femininity itself would be redefined and attainable: "As women grow, losing nothing that is essential to womanhood, but adding steadily the later qualities of humanness, they will win and hold a far larger, deeper reverence than that hitherto vouchsafed them. As they so rise and broaden, filling their full place in the world as members of society, as well as their partial places as mothers of it, they will gradually rear a new race of men, men with minds large enough to see in human beings something besides males and females."[5] Gilman's woman of the evolutionary future would be Elmondine, female and independent, at ease with her sex and her work.

Yet, ironically, Gilman's new woman carried with her the crucial social and psychic trappings of the old. Gilman, like many of her contemporary feminists, could not ultimately envision woman liberated from the task of nurturance itself, could not imagine woman pursuing work for her own personal satisfaction or solely for its challenge to her mind and ambitions. Although she was genuinely radical in the surgery she wanted to see performed on society and all its sacred institutions in order to free women from a sex-defined sphere of domesticity, her goal was to expand the area in which women might serve, not be served. Admittedly she placed the same standard of morality upon men; a desire to cooperate with and to contribute to the welfare of the greater society was, if anything could be said to be, the defining impulse of true humanity.

Here was the reform vision of her century, perhaps, but those who struggled to meet its demands with an obliteration of self were too often women like Charlotte Perkins Gilman. Too many of her own psychic struggles were over defining *self,* its boundaries never stable, the distinction between self-fulfillment and selfishness never clear. She had married, driven to a great extent by a repulsion at her *pride* in defining herself as a woman different from others and independent. Her self-esteem was stifled once she achieved that independence because, to take pride in her own creativity and talents, to cherish them for their own sake, could only be understood as selfish. Surprisingly, she would have more success in her private life resolving this dilemma of self and selfishness than her intellectual work incorporated or revealed.

Gilman's feminist ideas were shared by other women of her generation. Although her radical programs, such as dismantling the home, were resisted by feminists and nonfeminists, her central analysis of women and society was embraced. In her thinking and writing, in the realm of ideas, she was not isolated from others, but had found companionship.

In 1895 Charlotte Stetson left California. Within those eight years she had established herself as a writer, admired in literary as well as intellectual circles and praised by social reformers across the country. She had lectured for socialist and women's organizations. She had edited a financially unsuccessful but intellectually exciting radical newspaper. She had helped organize and had participated in women's conferences that earned her a place among the leading ranks of international feminists. She had organized a unique employment office, through which "day work" domestics could find temporary jobs. She had written about evolutionary socialism, anthropology, history, and feminism. But at the age of 35, when she left for the East, she judged herself a failure.

Charlotte Stetson returned East alone. Her mother had died in 1894. That same year Walter Stetson had remarried, choosing his ex-wife's friend Grace Channing as his bride. To many people's surprise—and disgust—Charlotte Stetson appeared delighted with this match. Soon after their marriage, she sent Katherine to live with them.

The decision to relinquish Katherine had been characteristically a blend of rational considerations and deep emotional ambivalence. Her relationship with Katherine was so complicated by fears of failing to be a good mother, by self-conscious and rigid pursuit of a program of "good mothering," and by doubts about its success, that her daughter made her both anxious and guilty. Like her own mother before her, she found it difficult to express directly the love and sympathy she felt for Katherine, often because she feared it would burden the child in some way.

She chose, again as her own mother had, to be useful to her daughter, to protect her by building in her a "right character." She substituted the doctrines of "understanding and self-control" for Mary Wescott Perkin's "obedience and discipline," and she produced a perfectly behaved, sober, responsible, emotionally distant young girl. When in 1894 Charlotte Stetson decided to send her daughter to the more stable home of the Stetsons and thus to the care of Grace Channing, she refused to let Katherine see that the separation would hurt her. In this way, she said, she protected Katherine from any uneasiness at deserting her mother. The cost of this denial Charlotte Stetson thought only she had to absorb.

Nothing she ever did raised such hostility or brought her such notoriety as this act of voluntary separation from her child. She was labeled an unnatural mother, accused not of failing as a mother but of renouncing her duty to be one. Duty and self-indulgence seemed to reverse themselves in the public eye, like a reflection in the mirror: She thought she was helping Katherine by giving her up; the newspapers said she was freeing herself. Her critics' insight was only semantic: The freedom they spoke of, a self-conscious self-interest, was not yet within her reach.

The year 1895 was spent in Chicago, with Stetson working for Jane Addams in the Chicago settlement-house projects. In January 1896 she attended a suffrage convention in Washington, D.C., where she met and befriended the famous pioneer in American sociology, Lester Ward. Between January and July of that year she took to the road, lecturing and giving guest sermons at 57 different churches or meeting halls in the Corn Belt.

In the midst of a hectic schedule she found time in April to visit New York City where her father, now remarried, had settled. Stetson liked her new stepmother and her grown daughters. Her father seemed content, their meeting was warm, and she allowed herself the sweet contemplation of a home at last—with her father. But by November 1896, when she returned to New York, Frederick Perkins had been moved to a sanatorium. He was helpless, growing rapidly senile as the arteries in his brain hardened. Her own intellectual powers were on the rise; his had ebbed. He would not be there to welcome or commend her to the larger world he had so long symbolized.

The next two years were important ones in Stetson's life. Free entirely of personal ties, she devoted herself to her work. She kept up an extraordinary pace, traveling for months at a time, lecturing, attending feminist meetings and conventions, and in her uncommitted hours, reading and writing. Everywhere she went she was confronted by the tangible evidence of her success. Men and women greeted her in each town, receptive to her ideas and eager to be near the energy she radiated. Younger women confessed that she was their model of independent womanhood. Her litany of self-doubt and self-criticism was weakened by this daily routine confirmation that she was indeed what she had wished and worked to be.

Reality thus seemed to catch up with Stetson during these years, and the passage of time seemed to make her more comfortable in her chosen role as spokeswoman for reform. Yet surely this maturation process pointed to a new receptivity to self-esteem. Perhaps the loss of both her parents freed her from the need to view her life in the old pattern of dichotomous loyalties and aversions, a duality that allowed her no victory without its companion, defeat.

One thing is clear: The acceptance of her success changed her understanding of her personal loneliness. Loneliness lost its heroic quality and she came to feel it not as a necessity or a punishment or the price of success, but simply as an emptiness. This changed perception influenced the course of her renewed friendship with Houghton Gilman.

On March 8, 1897, Charlotte Perkins Stetson visited Houghton Gilman's New York office for advice on a legal matter. It had been almost 20 years since "Ho" and "Chopkins" had exchanged letters, yet Houghton recognized her at once. "This," she later wrote, "was the beginning of a delightful renewal of an earlier friendship."

George Houghton Gilman was seven years his cousin's junior, a handsome, courtly, intelligent man. He was gentle, steady, generally likable. He had for most of his life been burdened with responsibility that had tied him down, emotionally and financially, for his mother was an invalid, his brother Francis a dwarf. These family obligations, heavy enough to oppress others, seemed not to embitter Houghton Gilman or to produce in him any debilitating sense of lost opportunities. He may have lived a circumscribed life, but he nevertheless found enjoyable moments and interesting pastimes. He was modestly ambitious and honorable; he liked his work as an attorney. He was not politically active or much attuned to the issues that so engrossed Charlotte Stetson. But he very much enjoyed her company.

Charlotte Stetson was obviously pleased with the new friendship and could not stay off the subject of Houghton Gilman, even in a letter to her daughter. "Last week I made a delightful discovery!

Found a cousin! . . . This cousin is Houghton Gilman . . . he is now a grown man nearly thirty, but when I remember him he was just your age." Then, only a few sentences later, she found herself writing: "To return to my newly discovered cousin; he is in the 7th regiment, and is going to take me to see them perform next Tuesday."

By March 18 the cousins were corresponding again, as they had decades ago. Charlotte, full of things to say and feelings to show, chose to write them to "Ho" even though they were both in New York City. "In some ways," she explained, "paper is freer than speech." The paper served her well, for the letters are frank and intense. "What a good time I did have the other night!" she wrote on March 18. "You now float and hover in my brain in a changing cloud of delectable surroundings."

Enjoying Houghton Gilman's company and his confidence seemed to reinforce Charlotte Stetson's awareness of how carefully she had repressed her feelings over the last several years and had escaped dealing with them by a frenzy of activity. "These years, when I stop doing things and my mind settles and things come up into view, most of these are of so painful a nature that I have to rush around and cram them back into their various (right here I have to stop and write a poem on 'Closet Doors' . . .)." But Gilman had created a mental space for her. "Now when I am quiet," she wrote, "there's a pleasantest sort of feeling—warm and cosy and safe."

Although her friendship with Gilman had allowed her room to test her capacity for affection once more, and helped her come to terms with its long absence, she was still wary and insecure. She often insisted that the relationship was platonic, familial, with herself the idiosyncratic but interesting older cousin and him the elegant and courtly young boy who found her educational and amusing in a maiden-aunt fashion. "I am looking ahead and wishing most earnestly and tenderly that you may have such a house as you deserve and one of the very charmingest of wives," Charlotte Stetson typically included in a long and effusive letter, using her pose as "Aunt Charlotte" like a talisman against disappointment.

As the odd courtship continued, these letters became—as those to Walter Stetson had once appeared to be—an open battleground for her conflicting emotions. But Charlotte Perkins Stetson had grown. There may have been defensive cul-de-sacs and charades, but there was nevertheless a true effort to discover her feelings, to know her desires, and to act as she wanted to act rather than as she ought. She knew that Houghton Gilman made her feel good about herself, good enough for her to admit how very low her self-esteem had always been. "Truly Houghton, for all the invulnerable self-belief and self-reliance which I have to have to live at all, you have no idea how small potatoes I think of myself at heart, how slow I am to believe that anyone's kindness to me is other than benevolence."

Houghton Gilman could not help but know. She had revealed her insecurity in every letter, in a transparent flippancy that was too earnest to be coy. "It won't surprise me in the least when you get over liking me as they all do," she had written, and in a hundred different forms she repeated the same fears over the next years. It was an appeal for reassurance woven into the letters with others. "Do [my letters] annoy you? I couldn't write for a week 'cause this fear depressed me," she wrote while in Kansas; "*Say* you like me if you do—often!" she added to a letter that summer.

For four years Charlotte Stetson confided her present and her past to Houghton Gilman, in a dialogue largely with herself. And, although much of the content was self-denigrating and self-pitying, there were moments of a new comfortable feeling about herself. She began to treat herself well, to buy clothing, and to indulge in gratuitous touches of luxury. She had begun to celebrate herself. Although this delight in self would previously have repelled her, now she began to accept personal pleasures that harmed no one by their fulfillment. Most important, she re-examined the very basis of affection.

Duty, she discovered, could not always promote or sustain love. "I have loved many people, in various ways, mostly because they needed it," she wrote Houghton, "but . . . the way you make me feel is different. It is not merely in the nature of wanting you—in the sense of a demanding personal affection, or even of—well, any kind of hungriness. And it is not at all in the sense of wishing to serve . . . the uppermost feeling is of pure personal gratification because you are so!"

What surprised Charlotte Stetson most was that the frank commitment to love did not destroy the sense of commitment to her life's work. Self-denial and self-satisfaction were not after all mutually exclusive rulers of character and destiny; there was room in her to accommodate both states. Her work improved, she told Houghton, her energies increased, her desire to write was not diminished but intensified. She had moments of genuine optimism. "The new charmed being now accepted by Madam Conscience, who has been struggling violently to choke it up for some time past, works admirably and I begin to see my way to let out more love towards Kate, too."

In truth, Charlotte Stetson was at the peak of her career when she wrote these letters to Houghton Gilman. *Women and Economics* was published in 1898 and won instant international acclaim. Even before it was published she was at work on a second book. In the summer of 1899 she returned to England, a star among equals at the international women's conference. Her lecture tours at last showed a profit, with Houghton Gilman acting as her agent and adviser. Her personal philosophy, equating living with growing, had once located growth in the soil of pain, denial, and disappointment. Now she conceded a growing that was expansive and inclusive. What could be a clearer sign of the changes in Charlotte Perkins Stetson than that she had at least developed a sense of humor. The heroic figure could now laugh a little at herself.

In June 1900 Houghton Gilman traveled to the Midwest to meet Charlotte Stetson. She was in the midst of a speaking tour; he had taken the summer away from his law practice. They had not seen each other for almost a year. On June 11 they were married. Of this wedding day, Charlotte Perkins Gilman, now 40, wrote:

> Monday . . . Our Day . . . the end of waiting, not to let the happiness blind and mislead me—dull my sensitiveness, check my sympathy, stop my work. It will not, I know; it has not so far and it will not. On the contrary I shall do more work and better. . . . I suppose I shall get used to love and peace and comfort and forget to be grateful everyday! But I doubt it. The other life has been too long. . . . I have liked as well as loved you from the first. . . . So strong and quiet and kind . . . to your pure and noble Manhood I come humbly, gladly full, bringing all that I have and am—willing to be taken as I am. . . . I am coming to be your happy Wife.

Gilman's new confidence in the harmony possible between her public and private lives proved well founded. For 34 years her personal happiness neither hampered her work nor eroded her feminist perspective. When, on August 17, 1935, she ended her own life to avoid debilitation by cancer, she was no longer an influential figure in the world of ideas or politics. The war and the decade that followed had destroyed the world she knew. The era of optimistic reform had passed; and the search in the 1920s by young women for self-gratification and satisfaction without any commitment to public service had made her militant but nurturant feminism obsolete. Despite her eclipse, Charlotte Perkins Gilman continued to write and to advocate the restructuring of society. Her last book, however, was not social anthropology but autobiography, charting an inner odyssey to both independence and interdependence. It was a conscious effort to mark the path for other, younger women.

In the end, Charlotte Gilman's philosophy and her psychic needs seemed, after all, to be one. She sought a social and psychological androgyny: a full humanity, to be experienced by each individual, that would create harmony among them through shared experience rather than the isolation and dualism of the sexually segregated world into which she had been born. She sought the pride in contribution and participation that ensured self-esteem, and the condition of independence that ensured equality. She sought the integrated self, and even at those moments when she felt it impossible for herself in her own lifetime, she was determined to secure it for future generations of women and men.

Notes

[1]In this essay, all materials from Gilman's diaries and personal correspondence with family and friends are drawn from the Charlotte Perkins Gilman Papers, Schlesinger Library, Radcliffe College, Cambridge, Massachusetts.

[2]See, for example, the novelettes serialized in *The Forerunner* (1911–1916), reprinted by Greenwood Press, New York, 1968.

[3]Gilman's own account of her family history and her life, from which much of the information in this essay is drawn, can be found in her autobiography, *The Living of Charlotte Perkins Gilman*, D. Appleton-Century, New York and London, 1935.

[4]Gilman's books, published between 1898 and 1935, are: *Women and Economics*, Small, Maynard, Boston, 1898; *In This Our World*, Small, Maynard, Boston, 1898; *Concerning Children*, Small, Maynard, Boston, 1900; *The Home: Its Work and Influence*, McClure, Phillips, New York, 1903; *Human Work*, McClure, Phillips, New York, 1904; *What Diantha Did*, Charlton, New York, 1910; *The Man-Made World*, Charlton, New York, 1911; *His Religion and Hers: The Faith of Our Fathers and the Work of Our Mothers*, D. Appleton-Century, New York, 1923; *The Living of Charlotte Perkins Gilman*.

[5]Charlotte Perkins Gilman, "Are Women Human Beings? A Consideration of the Major Error in the Discussion of Woman Suffrage," *Harper's Weekly* (May 25, 1912).

Jane Addams

(1860–1935)

G. J. Barker-Benfield

Jane Addams, born in 1860, was the founder of Hull House in 1889. This was one of the earliest of American "settlements," community houses established in poor urban neighborhoods to stimulate social reform. Addams publicized the goals and achievements of settlements in hundreds of lectures around the country, which she used as the basis of a dozen books published between 1902 and 1930. In 1895 she collaborated with her fellow workers on Hull House Maps and Papers, *one of the first sociological studies of tenements and sweatshops. She published* Twenty Years at Hull House *in 1910. Addams's reform impulses led her to suffrage, to political progressivism, and to help establish an international peace movement during World War I (1914–1918). The latter activity subjected Addams to jingoistic vilification. She was expelled from the Daughters of the American Revolution, but elected the first president of the International League of Peace and Freedom in 1919. Further resisting conformist pressures, Addams was a founder of the American Civil Liberties Union in 1920 and worked for it for most of the rest of her life. She also continued to work for peace and remained a controversial figure throughout the 1920s. Addams maintained her relationship with Hull House and in 1930, she published* The Second Twenty Years at Hull House. *In 1931, Addams shared the Nobel Peace Prize with Nicholas Murray Butler, the noted educator, and was frequently named the "Greatest American Woman" by public opinion polls. Her political heritage and her work with Herbert Hoover's relief agency in Europe during and after World War I led Addams to support Hoover for presidency in 1928 and 1932. Addams died of cancer in 1935.*

The following essay examines the decisive phases of Ad-

dams's life in order to cast light on how middle-class women overcame opposition to their entering public life. The essay challenges the reader to do two things: to follow Addams's own detective work in diagnosing her illness; and to watch carefully for the connections between this intimate story and the larger social changes of which it was part.

Jane Addams came from a family with deep roots in Pennsylvania and Quaker history. She was born in 1860, in Cedarville, Stephenson County, northern Illinois, to John and Sarah Addams, who had moved there from Pennsylvania right after their marriage in 1844, nine years after the first white settlers had arrived. Staked by his own father, John Huy Addams (1822–1881) had bought a saw and grist mill which, in the primarily lumbering and agricultural region that he helped link to Chicago by rail, provided the basis for his economic success. He moved into banking, investment, and politics, where he was an associate of Abraham Lincoln.

Jane was the youngest of the five children who survived infancy: Mary, born in 1846; Martha, 1850 (she would die at 16); James Weber, 1853; and Alice, in 1854. Their mother, Sarah Weber Addams (1817–1863), who had attended "boarding school" in Philadelphia, was "accomplished in music and drawing," and was pregnant nine times, her last pregnancy terminating with her death.[1] The bereaved family was augmented in 1868 by John Addams's marriage to the widowed Anna Haldeman; she brought two sons into the household from her former marriage. Harry,* then aged 18, and George, at 7, close to Jane Addams's age. From 1868 until they went to college in 1877, Jane and George were "inseparable companions."[2] Like her siblings, Addams had attended the one-room school house in Cedarville, her education there supplemented by private lessons in music and drawing. While George went to Beloit College, Jane followed her female siblings to Rockford Female Seminary (1877–1881). She then successfully completed the first year of medical studies at the Pennsylvania Woman's Medical College in Philadelphia (1881–1882). But in her autobiography she would include that year in the period of sickness and uncertainty that lasted, she wrote, "from the time I left Rockford in the summer of 1881 until Hull House was opened in the autumn of 1889."[3]

While traveling in Europe in 1888, Addams visited Toynbee Hall

*Harry Haldeman married Alice Addams in 1876 and therefore bore the double relation of stepbrother and brother-in-law to Jane Addams.

in London, an all-male "community of University men who live there, have their recreation and clubs and society all among the poor people, yet live in the same style they would live in their own circle." This visit seems to have crystallized Addams's purpose, which she would share with many others: the establishment of reform centers, or "settlements," to bridge the social gulf that had opened up in American cities as the result of the expansion of industrialism and the immigration which it sucked in. Addams's achievement was to do for women what she often said Lincoln had done for men: open up a "channel through which the moral life of his countrymen might flow," a channel that is, into public life.[4]

By 1900 there were over a hundred settlements in American cities.[5] Addams became the leader of this national movement, and in 1911 was elected the first head of the National Federation of Settlements, a position she held until 1935. Settlements were the tips of an iceberg of reform activities during this period. Drawing on the sociological studies they helped to create at the same time they were creating "social work," settlement house workers devoted themselves to improving the physical and mental health of the working-class population. They attempted to rid city dwellers of unsanitary housing, poisonous sewage, contaminated water, high infant mortality, adulterated food, smoke-laden air, juvenile crime, and overcrowded tenements. They gave classes in many subjects, including the English language and American civics, and they provided the space and means for a host of recreational activities, from debate to dance, athletics to theater. Addams made a point of celebrating immigrant cultures, including women's traditional work. Most obvious in this huge range of issues was an emphasis on the concerns of women and children.[6]

The frustrations of attempts to ameliorate living and working conditions of poor working women and men led Addams and her fellow workers into municipal and then national politics. The settlement house workers were the "spearheads of reform." They wished to establish that government's function included the protection of the public's health and welfare. Facing nitty-gritty machine politics in Chicago, they led the middle-class effort to transform it, to open up those clogged channels to the scientific-mindedness of progressivism. Hull House generated leaders, such as Florence Kelley and Grace Abbott, who would go on to head government agencies of inspection and reform. Addams, therefore was vitally important in connecting the scientized but traditional separate-sphere idea of "social housekeeping" with politics. She was a vice president of the National American Woman Suffrage Association from 1911 to 1914. In 1912 she seconded Theodore Roosevelt's nomination as the presidential candidate of the breakaway Progressive party, which, committed to the same goals as Hull House, would, Addams said, "appeal to women, and seek to draw upon the great reservoir of their moral energy so long undesired and unutilized in practical politics. . . ."[7]

Hull House was a meeting place for intellectuals and leaders of all sorts, a seedbed for social work and sociology, and a place where socialism was seriously debated. In the aftermath of the Haymarket riot of 1887, in which violence broke out at a labor rally, Hull House gained a reputation for radicalism because it sponsored speakers across the whole political spectrum. Addams was influenced by Marxism but in the end drew back because of the ideological rigidity of the Chicago socialists. She was rooted in American political traditions of free speech and a belief in "the slow march of human progress." Her conviction "that social arrangements can be transformed through man's conscious and deliberate effort" ran counter, she said, to a "crude interpretation of class conflict" which, to Chicago socialists, was "the test of the faith."[8] In her view of American democratic possibilities, Addams inherited Lincoln's political beliefs. The second chapter of her autobiography is entitled "The Influence of Lincoln," an influence intertwined in her imagination with the influence of her father. To immigrants she "held up Lincoln for their admiration as the greatest American" in a way that spoke to their heritage and to her own. "I invariably pointed out his marvelous ability to retain and utilize past experiences." In asserting that those experiences were of "the common people," Lincoln cleared the title to "our democracy," which was America's most "valuable contribution" to "the moral life of the world." Addams's terms combined Lincoln's views with what she, like the majority of suffragists and reformers at this time, saw as women's special contribution to public life.[9]

Of course, Lincoln had directed the enormous expansion of the federal government during the Civil War, although it had contracted afterwards. Addams held fast to her belief in the free-enterprise system but she, too, advocated the expansion of the powers of the federal government, in effect to prevent class war.[10] Using the expansion of government to clean up the abuses of capitalism can be seen as the application to the public sphere of domestic values, virtue, harmony, and caring, with which women and the "woman's sphere" had been invested. This is what is meant by "social housekeeping."

Her outspoken leadership of the peace movement in World War I brought Addams up against the clear limits of women's activity in the public sphere. In a notorious speech in 1915, Addams suggested that young soldiers on both sides were mutinying against war; many, she said, had to be doped up to make bayonet charges. Instantly her reputation was reversed. She was called "a silly, vain, impertinent old maid. . . . Her dabbling in politics, her suffrage activity and her ill-advised methods of working for peace have materially lowered her in the esteem of her former admirers." Thereafter Addams carefully identified herself as a "Corn Mother," an archetypal figure of a provider, and simply raised supplies of food for wartime refugees.[11]

Out-of-step in the matter of war, she was also out-of-step in peacetime popular culture. Although she regained her reputation, Addams remained a "Victorian lady" and was no longer a "role model for college women."[12]

Jane Addams never married and never had children. Her family relationships were those she established first with Ellen Gates Stars and then with Mary Rozet Smith. In this she resembled a large proportion of college women of their generation[13] who thought of motherhood and public individuality as mutually exclusive alternatives. This was another facet of the culture's belief in a doctrine of separate spheres, the public, dominated by men, the private, inhabited by women with children, the idolized mothers.

Middle- and upper-class women who moved into public life did so by claiming that they were expanding the domestic sphere rather than leaving it. It was precisely on the grounds that "society" beyond the home—men's world—was in such desperate need of the qualities associated with the home and its most constant inhabitant—mother—that from early in the nineteenth century women claimed public roles as charity workers, reformers, teachers, nurses, and eventually, doctors and social workers. Social housekeeping was squared with "the ideology of mother." The apparently widespread adherence to such an ideology after the industrial revolution, by men as well as by women, can be explained in part perhaps as the psychological effect of the experience of children spending increasing hours and years at home with middle- and upper-class women, themselves increasingly isolated at home, their meaningful work confined to childrearing.

Whatever its origins, maternal ideology came to stand for American feminism's "only abiding culture" in a context of pervasive sexual prejudice, antifeminism, and the deep divisions of religion and immigration, as well as class.[14] Of course, there was a profound limitation built into the doctrine of separate spheres because it was held to rest on "nature." Women's capacities, it was asserted time and again, were determined by their reproductive organs. We shall see how this governed the diagnoses of women's illnesses. The male sphere was never held to be determined by nature in that way. Men could transcend nature; this was the rationale for their claim to command women.

The conflict between motherhood and public life was one of several conflicts caused women by the identification of female with private, and male with public. A second lay in the relations between fathers and daughters. At least that is what Addams's own words suggest. In approaching such a difficult subject, the historian must be as careful with the evidence as in the case of any other subject. So, the following history rests squarely on what Addams herself chose to tell. It is a story of which everyone has a particular and historical version, since everyone has a psychic life dependent on childhood, the challenge of growing up. Women's versions have had to take into account the force of sexual prejudice and the variability of resources available to combat it. Success here, as everywhere, depends on consciousness.

Addams wrote a dozen books. Her niece, Anna Marcet Haldeman-Julius describes the scrupulousness with which she did so. Addams "had a compulsion to find exactly the right word and she needed to write, re-write, and write again. This often involved considerable transposition. The mechanical device by which she accomplished this most efficiently, and which she taught me, was that of cutting paragraphs or sentences out of one page of her manuscript and pinning them as inserts in their shifted sequence on another page. This gave her books that flowing spontaneity which is so often the rich reward of thought and toil."[15] Her most famous book was *Twenty Years at Hull House with Autobiographical Notes* (1910), the major text for the rest of this essay. That Addams made it both autobiographical and nonautobiographical, as well as that she wrote it with so much care should be borne in mind.

A significant portion of *Twenty Years* explaining the motive and rationale for the creation of settlement houses is Addams's diagnosis of the mysterious illness from which she suffered between 1881 and 1889, when she founded Hull House. To her, that illness was enormously important, not the least because she thought it one which millions of women shared. She linked it to her ambivalent relationship with her father and suggested the limitations of daughters' identifying with fathers and doing their parents' will. She described how she came to enjoy a multitude of roles—writer, administrator, fundraiser, and politician. But, she showed how she found the "ideology of mother" to be of particular value. By 1910 Addams was clearly identified as a social mother, a reputation she was usually careful to foster. The *Los Angeles Times* called her "a woman who has ever mothered humanity, though herself unwed."[16]

The early death of Addams's mother, Sarah Weber Addams, left Jane's father as the formative influence on her. "I centered upon him all that careful imitation which a little girl ordinarily gives to her mother's ways and habits. My mother had died when I was a baby and my father's second marriage did not occur until my eighth year."[17] While her primary emphasis here is obviously on imitation of her father, we should note in this passage Addams's recognition of conventional sexual identification (daughters with mothers) and the contrast between "My mother" and the exclusion of her father's second wife, Anna Haldeman, Jane's stepmother. Sarah Weber Addams's obituary suggests a general similarity between her reputation and that of her daughter: "Mrs. Addams will be missed everywhere, at home, in society, in the church, in all places where good is to be done and suffering relieved."[18] Sarah Addams had led the kind of life idealized by those moralists so alarmed by the frivolity and ill-health of later generations of young women. According to Allen Davis, Addams's mother

> supervised the operation of what was virtually a domestic factory; she also did a great portion of the actual work herself. The household produced its own soap, lard, candles, rugs, quilts and stockings; it preserved fruits and vegetables, salted meats, baked bread, and prepared meats for as many as twenty farm and mill hands in addition to the family.[19]

As Jane Addams would find herself acting as a midwife to the poor immigrant peasants of Chicago, so Sarah Addams, forty-nine years old and nine months pregnant, had gone one Friday years earlier, "in the best traditions of the rural village to the aid of another woman in labor. The doctor was out on another call and Sarah took complete charge." She "overexerted" herself, and became deathly sick.[20]

After going blind, having convulsions, being delivered of a dead infant, and falling unconscious for long periods, Sarah Addams died the following Wednesday. Jane Addams's uncle, George Weber, described Jane's reactions to her dying mother. Sarah Addams had lain "unconscious until Sunday about 11 o'clock. The first we noticed of any consciousness was when their little daughter Jenny [Jane Addams] cried with a loud shriek. Sarah raised up in bed, but oh the wild look she had! she soon sunk back again."[21] Seventy years later, Addams recalled this episode from her early childhood for her nephew, James Weber Linn, who was writing her biography, Addams insisted that she remembered one of her mother's responses to her as her mother lay dying:

> She remembered being aware that her mother was in the ground-floor bedroom of the house; pounding on the door with her fist, and hearing her mother say, 'Let her in, she is only a baby herself.' As she [Jane Addams] declared, "No one ever told me this, and it is impossible that I could have invented it."[22]

Addams's own declaration about this scene shows the importance to her of that maternal caring and of her remembering it.

After Sarah Addams's death, Jane's eldest sister Mary, "her mother's replica," managed the Addams household. Jane is believed to have said to Mary's son, James Linn, that Mary was "so far forgetting of herself in others that by them she became unforgettable."[23] It remained the same kind of household as it had been under Sarah Addams and must have been full of memories of her. Jane became especially attached to her old sister Martha, and must have experienced a second maternal deprivation on Martha's death when Jane was six. Naturally Jane then apprehended the loss of her mother's replica: "my horrible dream every night would be Mary's death and no one to love me."[24] Mary provided her with maternal continuity, as it were, until it was disrupted by John Addams's marriage in 1868 to Anna Haldeman, when Jane was eight. At the same time, Mary moved away first to the college at Rockford, then to marry John Linn. The household also changed in character from what it had been under Sarah Addams and her daughters, that is, from a "domestic factory" along traditional lines to as close to a "center of culture and art" as Anna Haldeman Addams could make it.[25]

Jane Addams resisted going to Rockford Female Seminary. In 1877 the seventeen-year-old Addams had visited Smith College (which had opened two years earlier), passed the entrance examination, and had been admitted, but John Addams had insisted she go to Rockford to which he had sent Jane's elder sisters. Addams published an account of this conflict with her father in *Twenty Years:*

> As my three older sisters had already attended the seminary at Rockford, of which my father was trustee, without any question I entered there at seventeen. . . . I was very ambitious to go to Smith College, although I well knew that my father's theory in regard to the education of his daughters implied a school as near at home as possible, to be followed by travel abroad in lieu of the wider advantages which an eastern college is supposed to afford. . . . I was greatly disappointed at the moment of starting to humdrum Rockford.[26]

The passions on each side of this conflict are unmistakable. On one side Jane Addams was "very ambitious" and then "greatly disappointed." On the other side was the immovable, indeed, the unchallengeable will of her father. For years his feelings had been elaborated into a rigid "theory" regarding female education which required daughters to stay as close to parental supervision as possible. Such parental supervision would have been supplemented, in both his eyes and his daughters', by his authority as a Rockford trustee. Obviously,

John Addams lacked institutional authority at the college his daughter preferred: his parental supervision would also have been curtailed had she gone to faraway Smith. Although it was slowly changing, Rockford, like other female seminaries, emphasized "accomplishments" and morality for young ladies being shaped for marriage. Smith, with its contemporaries Vassar, Wells, Elmira, and Wellesley, was founded in part as criticism of the inequalities offered "females" by the seminary. The colleges would offer women an education equal to that offered men.

The trouble was that if John Addams believed that after her seminary education his daughter should follow the traditional role of domestic women, he had also "passed on to her his own driving sense of ambition" and social responsibility.[27] Addams tells us in *Twenty Years* how he had paid her "as a little girl, five cents a 'Life' for each Plutarch hero I could intelligently report to him, and twenty-five cents for every volume of Irving's *Life of Washington.*" He supplied her with masculine models and she had reciprocated by modeling herself after him. John Addams conveyed to her his reverence for Lincoln, his ally and friend in Illinois politics, and she responded by always associating Lincoln "with the tenderest thoughts of my father." Addams's identification with her father included her "consuming ambition" to have hands shaped, like his, by milling: "This sincere tribute of imitation, which affection offers its adored subject, had later, I hope, subtler manifestations, but certainly these first ones were altogether genuine. In this case, too, I doubtless contributed my share to that stream of admiration which our generation so generously poured forth for the self-made man." From the vantage point of 1910, when she wrote this, Addams reaches back to locate her particular experience in a broad social context, that of laissez-faire. But how could a daughter become a self-made man?[28]

At Rockford, Addams became a friend and inspiration to teachers as well as fellow students. The latter looked to her for advice and leadership and her teachers regarded her as at least their equal. This is clear in the letters they continued to write her after she left Rockford. They all expected her to act on the ambition she had expressed, to study medicine and live with the poor, in spite of the physical weakness and pains to which they knew she was vulnerable. They were vulnerable to them too. In *Twenty Years,* Addams tells us that "long before the end of my school days [at Rockford] it was quite settled in my mind that I would study medicine. . . ." Because Rockford did not yet grant degrees, she planned to take a B.A. from Smith before going to medical school. She had never given up the ambition her father had blocked when she was seventeen. But she became sick immediately before leaving Rockford in 1881. She must have anticipated the opposition to her future plans that she knew she would meet at home. Her graduating essay, entitled "Cassandra," embodied the conflict. While it was optimistic about the future of the "contemporary woman," Addams wrote it was her tragic-fate "always to be in the right and always to be disbelieved and rejected."[29]

Addams presents the conflict to her public a second time in *Twenty Years*, but on this occasion it is generalized to the typical female graduate. Nonetheless, its context makes it clear that such a conflict had occurred in her own life and that Addams intended this to be understood. That context is Addams's explanation for her post-college illness and cure, amounting to what Addams calls "The Subjective Necessity for Social Settlements."[30] It was the amplification of the personal diagnosis she had made of her sickness in a previous chapter, "The Snare of Preparation." She says of what she presents as the typically frustrated graduate facing her parents on her return from college: "She is besotted with innocent little ambitions, and does not understand this apparent waste of herself, this elaborate preparation if no work is provided for her." She is prepared by her parents to expect a life devoted to "the good of the whole" and then, she implies, is confined to a cultivation of "the good of the ego."

> Parents are often inconsistent: they deliberately expose their daughters to knowledge of the distress in the world; they send them to hear missionary addresses on famines in India and China; they agitate together over a forgotten region of East London. . . . from babyhood the altruistic tendencies of these daughters are persistently cultivated. They are taught to be self-forgetting and self-sacrificing, to consider the good of the whole before the good of the ego. But when all this information and culture show results, when the daughter comes back from college and begins to recognize her social claim to the "submerged tenth," and to evince a disposition to fulfill it, the family claim is strenously asserted. . . .[31]

Addam's disposition when she left college had been "to study medicine and 'live with the poor.' " It was her father who, in her words, had opened up to her in childhood "the great world of moral enterprise and serious undertaking," a sense of the genuine relationship which may exist between men who share large hopes and like desires, even though they differ in nationality, language, and creed; that those things count for absolutely nothing between groups of men who are trying to abolish slavery in America or to throw off Hapsburg oppression in Italy." It was her father, she is telling her readers in the meticulously constructed *Twenty Years*, who had been "inconsistent."[32]

Addams had published another description of this parent-daughter conflict eight years earlier, as chapter two of *Democracy and Social Ethics* (1902), "Filial Relations." Here she pointed out that modern education had finally recognized woman "apart from family or society claims. . . ." This quality allowed women potentially to identify with the individualism claimed by men, even with the self-making Addams believed her father epitomized. Modern education she said, gave woman "the training which for many years has been deemed successful for highly developing a man's individuality and freeing his powers for independent action." But when she returned home from college she found that her parents assumed "that the daughter is solely an inspiration and refinement to the family itself and its own immediate circle, that her delicacy and polish are but outward symbols of her father's protection and prosperity. . . . She was fitted to grace the fireside and to add lustre to that social circle which her parents selected for her." The educated woman had to struggle against the family's, above all the father's, definition of her as "a family possession." The struggle was between this "family claim" and the "social claim" to "act her part as a citizen of the world." Addams said that most daughters "repress" the social claim in the face of the concrete and strenuous assertion of the family claim. Each one "quietly submits," but not without a continual feeling of having been "wronged." It was in this same chapter, "Filial Relations," that Addams presented most dramatically her insight into a father's attempt to limit a daughter: "It was new to him that his daughter should be moved by a principle obtained outside himself, which even his imagination could not follow; that she had caught the notion of an existence in which her relation as a daughter played but a part."[33]

The family claim was asserted, Addams said, by "parents." While I am suggesting that Jane Addams's veneration of her father was to prove the chief obstacle to her attainment of independence, we should not ignore the woman she faced at her father's side on her return from college. John Addams's second wife is absent from Jane Addams's autobiography. Anna Haldeman Addams's letters to her stepdaughter show her to have been anxious, petty, and demanding in her attempt to fulfill the rich woman's cultured and decorative role and to have Jane Addams fulfill it as well. Jane Addams's using her education to add "lustre" to her father's social circle would have been simply augmenting the role Anna Haldeman Addams played for her husband. Addams's eventual repudiation of the cultured role exemplified by her stepmother would entail the rejection of marriage in general, and marriage to Anna Haldeman Addams's beloved youngest son George in particular. He had hoped to marry Jane as his brother Harry had married Jane's sister, Alice, after she had completed her education at Rockford.[34]

So each member of the Addams family who went on a combined business and pleasure trip to northern Wisconsin in August after Jane's return home from Rockford in 1881 had considerable interest in her future. They were John, Jane, Anna, and George. This common concern and the preceding struggle over Jane's "Smith plan" suggests that the Wisconsin trip could have been in part a reassertion of family purpose, one of those minimally conciliative group ventures whose aim is in fact to reinforce the decision of the strongest members or the largest number. George may well have courted his stepsister—he was to "press his affections" the following spring and summer after the intervening trauma—while John and Anna could have believed that Jane was too weak to go to college and would settle down to adorn her father's home while George was finishing his education, as her sister had done before marrying Harry.[35]

But if she was to appear to defer to her father's wishes during this summer (as she had done already in 1877 by attending Rockford), Addams had decided to enter the Woman's Medical College in Philadelphia for the 1881 winter term. Giving up Smith (as she had done by July) to go directly to medical school was only a telescoping of plans she had described to a friend at Rockford. We do not know whether or not Addams had told her father during the summer that she still planned on going to medical school. In any case, on August 17, 1881, after a strenuous day on the mining property in which he was considering investing, John Addams died in Green Bay, Wisconsin, of "inflammation of the bowels." How now could Jane reconcile herself with her father? How could she betray him by responding to the social claim?[36]

Addams sent letters and telegrams telling friends and relatives the news. Their replies show us how powerful a psychological presence he was in his daughter's life: "I remember how affectionately you used to speak of him—and the time when we came home together, how happy you looked when you saw him waiting outside"; "the poignancy of your grief arises from many causes, principally from the fact that your heart and life were wrapped up in your Pa"; "by a word you spoke at one time I know your father's life transfused itself through yours. . . ." These observations testify to the profound difficulty Addams would have in arriving at some sense of herself independent of the identification with him.[37]

Four months after her father's death, her Rockford teacher and friend, Sarah Blaisdell, wrote to the still deeply grieving Addams, referring to the influence of John Addams's principles on Jane Addams's "own character," and reinforcing this attempt to get Addams to distinguish herself from her father by criticizing him, albeit very subtly. She said that a father can act as "a wall of defence" for a young girl, "but when he is gone she stands out in her own person to meet the responsibilities of life." A wall around someone can be as much a prison as a defense. But when Jane Addams received this prescient letter she had been in medical school for three months, since the term had started on October 6. She had gone in spite of physical weakness and "vertebrae" problems that had persisted through the summer.[38]

Addams went to Philadelphia as part of a family group, this circumstance representing more of a compromise (perhaps literally negotiated by the parties) between "family" and "social" claims than her solo attendance at Smith would have represented. Harry Haldeman attended a third session of the Medical Department of the University of Pennsylvania, while Alice matriculated with Jane at the Woman's Medical College of Pennsylvania. His session began October 17, theirs October 6.[39] Anna Haldeman Addams came with them. Given the vicissitudes in Addams's health, her father's recent death, and the struggle over her future, one can see the family's logic in making this a group venture, whether one construes it as support or pressure. Addams had become sick enough by the middle of December 1881 to be placed under the supervision of a doctor.[40] Her apparent problem was exhaustion, which she was soon to call "nervous." Addams had, in Sarah Blaisdell's December 24 paraphrase of Addams's own description, "lost . . . physical vigor," having "taxed it . . . very severely both in study and in doing for others and at their suggestion." She had depleted her "original stock" of vigor. The "doing for others" must have referred in part to Addams's attempts to comply with her stepmother's demands that she play the lady with and for her accompanying family, as well as with the demands made by her fellow medical students. Nonetheless, Addams had written to a Rockford friend before the end of the year that her "physical strength" was returning; perhaps her medical treatment at that time was working. She passed the first year's examination in March. But then she relapsed.[41]

The condition, which, Addams tells us, forced her into "Mitchell's hospital" in the spring of 1882, was a "development of the spinal difficulty which had shadowed me from childhood." Later she would say that "development" (in 1882) was "a nervous affliction which compelled me to abandon my studies."[42] Her use of the word *nervous* reflected nineteenth-century belief. Although doctors and students of physiology had not yet fully mapped or understood the nervous system, they believed it was only a matter of time before all disorders of function would be explained as diseases of the nervous system. Nerves, they thought, provided the key to understanding the relations between functional and organic disorders, between mind and body. Physical, organic disease could give rise to what the twentieth century calls psychological disorders by way of the nerves; conversely, psychological disease could give rise to physical disorders by way of the nerves. The physical treatment of mysterious functional or psychological problems was thus easily justified.

Addams provides our first lead into the tangled question of the somatic dimensions to her illness in the period between leaving Rockford in 1881 and founding Hull House in 1889. When she tells us in *Twenty Years* that her spinal difficulty originated in childhood, she is referring the reader back to the chapter "Earliest Impressions," which mentions her "crooked back" and her "disability of the curved spine." She later said that her spinal curvature resulted "from an illness at the age of four." While there are several childhood illnesses that can have this result, her biographers are probably correct in ascribing Addams's crooked back to tuberculosis of the spine.[43] Significantly, in *Twenty Years* Addams does not tell us when or how it was believed her disease originated, progressed, or was treated in her childhood. Instead she explains the effects of the disability on her childhood sense of herself, just as she did with the "development of the spinal difficulty" in her twenties.

Addams first refers to her spine in her account of a childhood dream. The contexts she presents to her readers for this account are "the theory that our genuine impulses may be connected with our childish experiences," the belief that all of her impressions of childhood were "connected with my father," and the organizing principle of stringing "these first memories on [the] single cord of the connection" with her father because he "was so distinctly the dominant influence. . . ." It is tempting to point out the connection that the ambiguous word *cord* suggests between Addams's sense of herself as a child and of her father who provided her with a central sense of self, standing back of her moral values as well as becoming so much of an authoritative burden as to crook her back. Yet the dream "exhibits" Addams's own childhood sense of significance to the world, to society. "I dreamed night after night that everyone in the world was dead excepting myself, and that upon me rested the responsibility for making a wagon wheel. . . . no human being was within sight. They had all gone around the edge of the hill to the village cemetery, and I alone remained alive in the deserted world." A page earlier she had described the dread she had of dying while in a state of sin (specifically of having told a lie) and therefore going to hell, which was combined with the fear that her father, "representing the entire adult world which I had basely deceived," should "himself die before I had time to tell him." (We can see that such a circumstance had happened on the fatal 1881 trip to Wisconsin, between the childhood dream and Addams's adult recording of it.) The wagon-wheel dream was, then, in part a realization of this fear; and both fear and dream may well have reflected Addams's apprehension of final abandonment by her father, already having experienced her mother's death. It also registered the sheer power of her father as moral judge and bridge (or wall) to the adult world. It also may well have represented her wish (fulfilled by 1910 when she published this description) to stand alone, free particularly of that dominant/dominating figure. Her account then goes on to juxtapose the figure of herself as a child, weak by way of "delicacy," size, sex, age, and deformity, with the figure of the powerful, skilled, adult, male blacksmith. The juxtaposition foreshadows the contrast for which it serves as introduction or "doorway" to Addams matching herself against the man and workplace she found even more powerful, that is, against her father, his intellectual and political skills and his workplace in public life. That matching in turn served as the doorway for Addams' entry into public life.[44]

Her second reference in *Twenty Years* to her spinal deformity in childhood is part of her invidious comparison of herself—an "ugly, pigeon-toed little girl, whose crooked back obliged her to walk with her head held very much on one side"—to her powerful, physically imposing father, a comparison she invited in a sentence beginning "My great veneration and pride in my father. . . ." The paragraph goes on to conflate the memories of several days "doubtless occurring in two or three different years" when the "Union Sunday School of the village was visited by strangers." Their presence allowed Addams to dramatize the vast difference she felt existed between herself and her father, who taught the large Bible class. She "could not endure the thought that 'strange people' should know that my handsome father owned this homely little girl." She describes this attempt as an example of her "doglike affection." It seems to be self-abasement; conversely, the elevation of the venerated, "fine," "imposing," "dignified," paternal, religious teacher, "rising high above all the others" in the church, is to almost godlike eminence. But she corrects this child's eye view even as she gives it, writing with the hindsight of someone who has successfully overcome too strong an identification with her father. The tone of the whole description is humorous. She calls that "doglike affection" "grotesque." And everybody knows the truth of "the ugly duckling" to which Addams compared herself in the same passage—the duck turns out to have been a cygnet (and can thus disassociate itself from its "parents"), a creature that would grow into a big beautiful swan.[45]

In sum, while it was Addams herself who pointed out to her readers how her illness "shadowed" her from childhood, both of the references to her spinal difficulty present (1) the striking physical contrast between her filial, female self and a powerful adult male, above all, her father; and (2) the certainty that by 1910 when she presents this past contrast, she has outgrown it and overcome the inequality.

She concluded her discussion of her deformity in childhood by describing how her father ridiculed the notion that he shared her feeling about her "personal appearance . . . [that] thrust itself as an incongruity into my father's life." Lifting his "high and shining silk hat" to her on a main street, he had made her "an imposing bow." This parodied both of their statures. Addams is showing her readers that she had let John Addams overshadow her; his figure with its "shining" hat had come between her and the sun, stunting her growth. Part of her "difficulty" had been her contrast of herself to her father and her having internalized his judgment of her.

Of course there were other factors influencing the nature of her sickness, such as the fact that she had suffered from Pott's disease (spinal tuberculosis); the social expectation that the strain of education would lead to sickness in women; and the widespread belief that a major focus for such sickness was the spine. The autobiographical sentence in 1910 leading back to the childhood origin and meaning of her "spinal difficulty" in 1860 also leads into "Mitchell's hospital" in the late spring of 1882. To the famous neurologist and self-proclaimed woman-expert, S. Weir Mitchell, Addams's case must have looked exactly like that of hundreds of cases of nervous exhaustion accompanied by spinal difficulties. Mitchell believed that spinal problems in young women were usually symptoms of a disorder of the entire nervous system and therefore susceptible to Mitchell's special source of wealth and claim to fame, his "rest treatment." He and his contemporaries were primed to address such female patients through hostile and devaluative stereotypes. Instead of the person we know Jane Addams, for one, to have been in 1882, talented, torn, idealistic, frustrated, pained, ambitious, and depressed, this doctor was prepared to see her as, in his words, "a creature" "with a back."[46]

This is not the place to describe or examine Mitchell's "rest treatment," save to mention (for later reference) that it included fattening the patient, in part by a diet of milk. It is fair to characterize the treatment as an attempt to impose Mitchell's conventional, literally paternalistic view of woman's role onto his patients by infantilizing and reeducating them.[47] In the very short run it seems to have been effective in restoring Addams's physical strength and in bringing her up from the "breakdown" so that she could at least move about, write letters, plan travel, and honor social obligations. Sarah Anderson's letters to Addams in April and June 1882 confirm that the therapy was aimed at her gaining strength. They show that Anderson and, in all likelihood Addams, agreed with convention and with Mitchell that such an aim had to be at the expense of study and that study itself had been debilitating to her. Anderson advised Addams to take a restorative trip to the seashore should she not have "made good progress" by the end of June, advice consistent with the frequent practice of Mitchell's patients following the rest treatment. In July Addams did visit Nantucket in her pursuit of "strength" and "color." At the end of August Sarah Blaisdell wrote Addams a letter that illustrated and reinforced the widespread apprehension that a woman's health was vulnerable to education, even though Blaisdell, a college teacher, was committed to education and wanted Addams to go on. As might be expected, ambition and apprehension emerged as a typical syndrome in the college women of this period.[48]

Addams's weakness, nervousness, and spinal problems, including backache, lassitude, melancholy, and "general crookedness" of temper, and all of her therapies—the rest treatment, travel to the seashore, experimental surgery, recumbency on an orthopractic couch to which she was strapped, and her wearing of a mechanical support,—were the common experiences of thousands of women of her class, a fact that would become a major concern of Addams. The symptoms became a major concern because the therapies failed her. They failed her and the large proportion of women with cognate disorders because they were offered from a particular set of social and sexual assumptions that were in fact a fundamental cause of the symptoms. Doctors' diagnoses of women's spinal problems and nervous disorders generally provide evidence of large-scale social change perceived in the lives of middle- and upper-class women, in contrast to the lives led by their grandmothers. Most spinal experts agreed with Dr. Charles Fayette Taylor's proposition that women's spinal difficulties were causes or symptoms of what he called a "lack of power." He also called general muscular weakness "delicacy" in the book describing his therapeutic couch, probably similar to the one to which Addams was strapped. The irony and appropriateness of such diagnoses becomes apparent from a feminist perspective. Women were supposed to lack power, lack energy, in contrast to men.[49]

Addams's account in *Twenty Years* of her own diagnosis and treatment gives short shrift to the kinds of explanations that had dominated her doctors' diagnoses. In *Democracy and Social Ethics* (1902)

Addams had challenged Mitchell directly, opposing active, emancipating work to passive, confining rest. The educated, repressed, and therefore, frustrated young woman

> looks out into the world, longing that some demand be made upon her powers, for they are too untrained to furnish an initiative. When her health gives way under this strain, as it often does, her physician invariably advises a rest. But to be put to bed and fed milk is not what she requires. What she needs is simple health-giving activity, which, involving the use of all her faculties, shall be a response to all the claims which she so keenly feels.

By "claims," of course, she refers to the "social claim" of meaningful work beyond the home, in contrast to the "family claim" that Mitchell, like her father, had attempted to enforce. She now explains the sickness she had experienced to have been the result of conflict. The woman graduate who defers to her parents' wishes "either hides her hurt, and splendid reserves of enthusiasm and capacity go to waste, or her zeal and emotions are turned inward, and the result is an unhappy woman, whose heart is consumed by vain regrets and desires." To it Addams adds an account of the physiological effects of such conflict (not of weak nerves nor of spinal curvature), the effects of which were precisely the ones she had suffered on leaving Rockford:

> the situation is not even so simple as a conflict between her affections and her intellectual convictions, although even that is tumultuous enough, also the emotional nature is divided against itself. The social claim is a demand upon the emotions as well as upon the intellect, and in ignoring it she represses not only her convictions but lowers her springs of vitality. Her life is full of contradictions.[50]

In the same chapter of *Twenty Years,* Addams broadened her diagnosis to include the whole "first generation of college women." While she has shown us it is rooted in her own experience of conflict leading to nervous exhaustion, lack of energy, deep nervous depression, spiritual struggle, a sense of failure, clutching at the heart, despair, resentment, paralysis of will, and disgust with herself, her diagnosis from now on (and she frequently returned to it in books and articles) would always be projected onto a larger social canvas, from the first generation of college women to middle-class women to all women and to young people in general. Addams assumed the symbolic value of her diagnosis and cure, and in doing so followed her characteristic pattern of dealing with her own pain by seeing it as something that connected her with others. In *The Spirit of Youth and the City Streets* (1909), where Addams pointed out the frustration of poor and largely immigrant urban youth—not simply of educated, middle-class women—she wrote, "We allow a great deal of this precious stuff—this Welt-Schmerz of which each generation has need—not only to go unutilized, but to work havoc among the young people themselves."[51]

Addams goes on to summarize the diagnosis and anticipate the therapy she elaborated in "The Subjective Necessity for Social Settlements."

> I gradually reached a conviction that the first generation of college women had taken their learning too quickly, had departed too suddenly from the active emotional life led by their grandmothers and great-grandmothers; that the contemporary education of young women had developed too exclusively the power of acquiring knowledge and of merely receiving impressions; that somewhere in the process of "being educated" they had lost that simple and almost automatic response to the human appeal, that old healthful reaction resulting in activity from the mere presence of suffering or of helplessness; that they are so sheltered and pampered they have no chance even to make "the great refusal."

This generation of woman, she went on to say, was "smothered and sickened with advantages."[52]

This romantic view of the lives of previous generations of women had a great deal in common with those authorities on women's health from whom I am concerned to distinguish Addams. In regard to generations, to sex, and to explanatory models, the view was a cliché of her era. Doctors frequently compared sickly young women with their healthy forebears. The most salient and, from the point of view of the overwhelmingly male analysts, most appalling symptom of what one of them called this "physical decline of American women," was the declining birth rate. Women, they said, were unable or unwilling to bear babies in the numbers they knew their ancestresses had. Unwillingness was as much an expression of sickness as incapacity, since such an attitude had to be the expression of an enfeebled constitution: "healthy women were willing mothers." Most unwilling of all were those rich and leisured enough to attend college; the birth rate of female graduates was especially low. Attendance at college and decrease in fertility were explained as cause and effect. At the crucial stage of sexual development, it was argued, young women's energies were being absorbed by their brains instead of going to the development of their sexual organs. The higher education of women, a key goal of feminists, was contributing to what Theodore Roosevelt would call "race suicide."[53]

This was the context for the half-century-long debate over the effects of the higher education of women on society. It was also the context for the concern of Addams, her classmates, and her teachers over the effects of study on women's health. Addams's founding of Hull House and her description in *Twenty Years* of the process whereby she came to do it must be seen as a contribution to this debate. Addams agreed that the outcome of higher education was to make "girls" sick by cutting them off from a part of themselves she characterized as more fundamental than mere thought. But unlike medical orthodoxy, Addams did not say that women's meaningful connection with life should be submersion in traditional motherhood. In Addams's view, the more fundamental part of women consisted of an emotion (comprising zeal, enthusiasm, capacities) that she called "social sentiment" to be "utilized" in "social" work. Addams's answer to nervous disorders among women, including "nervous exhaustion," was the expression of self in meaningful work rather than the repression of self in the interests of "society." This is how Starr had explained Addams's conception of settlements during the time they were looking for a house in Chicago:

> Jane's idea which she puts very much to the front and on no account will give up is that it is more for the benefit of the people who do it than for the other class. She has worked that out of her own experience and ill health. She discovered that when recovering from her spinal trouble that she could take care of children, actually lift them up and not feel worse but better for being with them. While an effort to see people and be up to things used her up completely. . . . Nervous people do not crave rest but activity of a certain kind.

Drumming up support for Hull House in the spring of 1889, Addams told a Chicago club woman that Hull House would be "a place for invalid girls to go and help the poor."[54]

Addams was not alone in arguing that meaningful work could be a cure for the nervous disorders that her own case illustrated. For example, Ann Preston, an early dean and guiding spirit in the founding of the Pennsylvania Woman's Medical College, was deeply pained that young, educated women led "wasted, suffering, unsatisfied lives." Like Addams, Preston diverged from orthodox therapy by recommending against medication in favor of putting "to ennobling uses the powers of faculties which are the glorious birth-right of humanity." The answer to those women's sickness was work. "You know," she told her students, "that quiet, interesting, imperative work—work for hand and for mind—is essential to [such women's] health."[55] But Addams's version of this discovery was, in my view, of much greater moment than Preston's for three reasons. Addams opened up a myriad of new kinds of healthy, satisfying work for women, all based on Hull House. She established herself as a national symbol of such work for women, whatever the class limitations of her symbolism. And, most important, she showed in *Twenty Years* precisely how she had struggled from sickness to health by way of her own analysis and how others could do it as well.

If Addams saw a correspondence between her own depression and the wretchedness of the poor, she found health in those whom she called "the most vital part of humanity." Addams found that the humanity in them corresponded to the humanity she was eventually able to find in herself. The crucial connection here for my argument is that Addams saw those resources, outside as well as inside herself, as maternal. It was in this diagnosis written so soon after her founding of Hull House (in "The Subjective Necessity for Social Settlements") that Addams characterized the uneducated, unshriveled, live, vital, cooperative, emotional, and healthful resources she had in common with working people as "the great mother breasts of our common humanity."[56]

This maternal metaphor is repeated in different forms throughout Addams's writings. She personified art, religion, and modern industry as mothers, and referred to life as "she." Memory, she wrote in 1916, was "the Mother of the Muses . . . that Protean Mother. . . ." Her explanation for the dynamic of the peace movement was nearly the same.

> There are . . . strenuous forces at work reaching down to impulses and experiences as primitive and profound as are those of struggle itself. That "ancient kindliness which sat beside the cradle of the race," and which is ever ready to assert itself against ambition and greed and the desire for achievement, is manifesting itself now with unusual force, and for the first time presents international aspects.[57]

The same image had existed very powerfully in Addams's imagination in 1879 when her chief concern was religion. (So her reaching back to a primal mother represented three great passions of Addams' life—religion, the settlement movement, and peace.) In 1879 she wrote to Starr:

> As a general rule I regard [the Deity] with indifference, think of the Jewish faith just as I do of Mohammadism or any other system of religion. Lately it seems to me that I am getting back to all of it—superior to it, I almost feel. Back to a great Primal Cause; not Nature exactly, but a fostering mother, a necessity brooding and watching over all things, above every human passion & yet not passive, the mystery of creation. I make a botch trying to describe it & yet the idea has been lots of comfort to me lately . . . you see I am not so unsettled,

> as I resettle so often, but my creed is everyone be sincere and don't fuss. I began with an honest desire to say something in myself which is intangible—'impale a man on the personal pronoun.'—I give you my blessing my dear. . . .[58]

In 1879, she was unable to base her "I" on her father because she was female (impaled, it can be suggested, by having ambitions only men could have). Yet there are clues in this letter, and in the maternal references just quoted, to the "settlement" she would eventually find, that is, to a sense of self not utterly based on her father. Again the idiom of the age, this time conceptualizing selves in terms of "the childhood of the race," held a very personal meaning for its heroine, whose mother had died when she was two years and four months old. Her depiction of her sense of a primal mother is both literally tangible (cradle, breast) and a depiction of feelings (kindliness, comfort, brooding, watching, godlike power, mysteries of creation) that together give the sense of an infant's intimate experience of its mother or rather the experience that Jenny Addams had until her mother's traumatic death. To reach this sense Addams had to move back even more systematically, more consciously, than she did in 1879 ("it seems to me I am getting back to all of it . . . Back . . .") to describe something "in myself which is tangible." Back to before she felt burdened—by that appalling sense of loss represented by the wagon-wheel dream, before perhaps she came to depend on her father so much and to learn from him the burden-bearing of social responsibility, and more to my point here, before her spinal tuberculosis at four, before she had a crooked back at all, back, in short, to health. . . . She was reaching back to her mother. The "subjective necessity which led to the founding of Hull House," that is to Addams's own "motherhood," incorporated, she said in *Twenty Years,* "the impulse beating at the very source of our lives. . . ." Addams's commitment to her kind of maternity and her position as the mother of mothers was rooted in her childhood. She would cure herself by discovering something that she believed had been there all along and which existed in clear contrast to the values she associated with her father.[59]

So it was that Addams criticized competition and advocated cooperation. She shared such views with her fellow progressives, male and female, who emphasized cooperation for the good of the whole social organism, and with those corporate leaders who were tending increasingly toward "rationalization" of the economy and against wasteful competition. But such views coincided with Addams's own very individual experience. She said it was maternity and woman's other roles in family life that held society together, even if she also maintained, quite consistently, that male adherence to Victorian domestic ideals was important. She celebrated women as specialists in cooperation. She held that good "mothers, through their sympathy and adaptability, substitute keen present interests and activity for solemn warnings and restraint, self-expression for repression. Their vigorous family life allies itself by a dozen bonds to the educational, the industrial and the recreational organizations of the modern city. . . ." Parents', especially mothers' "wonderful devotion to the child seems at times in the midst of our stupid social and industrial arrangements, all that keeps society human, the touch of nature which unites it, as it was that same devotion which first lifted it out of the swamp of bestiality."[60] Those most responsible for "stupid social industrial arrangements" were men. She pitted the new, ameliorative, cooperative ethic (rooted in the "great mother breasts of our common humanity") against the male ethic of laissez-faire. Her "settlement" had several connotations, especially in the light of the "Primal Cause" letter to Starr, and stood in opposition to the dominant male ideology.

> A Settlement is above all . . . a spot to which those who have a passion for the equalization of human joys and opportunities are early attracted. It is this type of mind which is in itself so often obnoxious to the man of conquering business faculty, to whom the practical world of affairs seems so supremely rational that he would never vote to change the type of it even if he could.

In *Twenty Years*, Addams described the opposition of large glass companies and other manufacturers to child labor legislation in Illinois. While she acknowledged the attraction to the glass manufacturers of saving money by employing cheap, child labor, Addams devoted more time in her account to the psychological motives of the men involved, believers in "untrammeled energy and 'early start' " as "generators of success." A child labor law ran "counter to the instinct and tradition, almost to the very religion of the manufacturers of the state, who were for the most part self-made men."[61] Again personal history fuses with sexual and political ideology to emphasize the full meaning of Addams's cure of herself. Her characterization of the opposition echoed the opposition of her father to her fulfillment in a broad social role. He had been a "pioneer" in Illinois, a miller, banker, land speculator, investor in railroads, and president of an insurance company. Addams herself had described him as a representative "self-made man" in the same book now criticizing the values of the type he epitomized. These values can be contrasted with "the wonderful devotion" of her dying mother's concern for her baby.

In sum, in reaching out to independence, to a new role, Addams had to traverse the psychic reality that her father was both a bridge and a wall. Her traversal was marked by sickness and cure. While I am describing a contrast in Addams's view between the values represented by her father, and those she associated with her mother, I do not want to suggest she simply jettisoned the former. In her *A New Conscience and an Ancient Evil*, Addams said it "is better to overcome the dangers in this newer and freer life, which modern industry had opened to women, than it is to attempt to retreat into the domestic industry of the past." She wanted to recover "*something* [my emphasis] of the . . . sanctity and meaning" of such women's work.[62] The reaching back was a psychical one, not a literal one, coexisting with, indeed supporting, the host of new roles sponsored by Hull House. Those roles incorporated the skills and values Addams had learned from her father, most obviously the political, Lincolnesque ones. Her history led Addams to explore ways for women to reconcile Lincoln's liberalism with maternal ideology. Soon after *Twenty Years* was published, a Boston newspaper called Addams "that mother Emancipator from Illinois."[63] She had found a way of continuing to share her father's values without crippling herself.

Notes

[1]James Weber Linn, *Jane Addams: A Biography* (New York: Appleton-Century, 1935), p. 6.

[2]Linn, *Addams*, p. 32.

[3]Jane Addams, *Twenty Years at Hull House with Autobiographical Notes* (New York: Signet, 1960 [1910]), p. 59.

[4]Jane Addams to Alice Haldeman, 14 June 1888, Jane Addams Memorial Collection, University of Illinois, Chicago; Anne Firor Scott, "Jane Addams," *Notable American Women*, 3 vols. (Cambridge, MA: Belknap Press, 1971), 1:16–22; 22.

[5]Allen F. Davis, *American Heroine: The Life and Legend of Jane Addams* (New York: Oxford University Press, 1973), p. 92. I am deeply indebted to this splendid biography—as my frequent citations indicate.

[6]The best sources for Hull House's activities are Addams's own writings, especially *Twenty Years*. For a very helpful and brief recent account, see Nancy Woloch, *Women and the American Experience* (New York: Alfred Knopf, 1984), ch. 11.

[7]Davis, *Spearheads for Reform: The Social Settlements and the Progressive Movement, 1890–1914* (New York: Oxford University Press, 1907); Addams, *The Second Twenty Years at Hull House* (New York: Macmillan, 1930), pp. 33–34.

[8]Addams, *Twenty Years*, pp. 137–39.

[9]Addams, *Twenty Years*, pp. 42, 45.

[10]Davis, *American Heroine*, p. 287.

[11]Davis, *American Heroine*, pp. 226–29.

[12]Davis, *American Heroine*, pp. 277–78. See Donald B. Meyer, *Sex and Power: The Rise of Women in America, Russia, Sweden and Italy* (Middletown, CT: Wesleyan University Press, 1988), pp. 354–62.

[13]Davis, *American Heroine*, pp. 85–91.

[14]Donald B. Meyer, "Capitalism and Feminism in Italy, Sweden and the United States 1870–1970," American Historical Association Annual Meeting, San Francisco, 1978. This anticipated Meyer, *Sex and Power*, pp. 311–30.

[15]Anna Marcet Haldeman-Julius, "Jane Addams as I Knew Her," *The Reviewers Library* 7 (1936), 3–30; 30.

[16]Quoted in Davis, *American Heroine*, p. 250.

[17]Addams, *Twenty Years*, p. 25.

[18]Quoted in Linn, *Addams*, pp. 22–23.

[19]Davis, *American Heroine*, p. 5.

[20]Addams, *Twenty Years*, p. 88; Davis, *American Heroine*, p. 5.

[21]George Weber to Elizabeth and Enoch Rieff, 17 Jan. 1863, Jane Addams Correspondence, Swarthmore College Peace Collection (hereafter cited as SCPC). I am very grateful to Ann Gordon for drawing my attention to this letter.

[22]Linn, *Addams*, p. 25. Addams collaborated with Linn in writing this biography to a significant extent; he tells us in the preface that "my aunt read over and annotated the first draft of the first eight chapters of this book, talked over the next three, and agreed upon the proportion of the remainder." It is reasonable to assume that many of the unacknowledged quotations in the book are Addams's own commentary on the past events.

[23]Linn, *Addams*, p. 25.

[24]Addams to Alice Haldeman, 20 Aug. 1890, quoted in Davis, *American Heroine*, p. 6.

[25]Davis, *American Heroine*, p. 6.

[26]Addams, *Twenty Years*, p. 46.

[27]Davis, *American Heroine*, p. 9. Davis has emphasized the contradictory messages John Addams gave his daughter and his account of Addams's sickness and her "Creative Solution" is consistent with mine (*American Heroine*, ch. III). We have both been influenced by Meyer's pathbreaking *The Positive Thinkers* (Garden City, New York: Doubleday, 1965), ch. 3.

[28]Addams, *Twenty Years*, pp. 48–49; 38; 26.

[29]Addams, *Twenty Years*, 57.

[30]Addams, *Twenty Years*, ch. 6. This was a paper she had given in 1892, only three years after the founding of Hull House.

[31]Addams, *Twenty Years*, pp. 93–94.

[32]Addams, *Twenty Years*, pp. 57; 31–2.

[33]Addams, *Democracy and Social Ethics* (New York: Macmillan, 1902), pp. 83; 85; 96. The last reference is to Lear's relation with Cordelia.

[34]Linn, *Addams*, p. 30.

[35]Linn, *Addams*, p. 65; Davis, *American Heroine*, p. 29.

[36]Linn, *Addams*, p. 68; Mary B. Down to Addams, 23 May 1880, SCPC; Davis, *American Heroine*, p. 26.

[37]L. D. Cummings to Addams, 20 August 1881; J. M. Linn to Addams, 26 Aug. 1881; C. A. Potter to Addams, 20 Aug. 1881, SCPC.

[38]Sarah Blaisdell to Addams, 24 Dec. 1881, SCPC; Women's Medical College of Pennsylvania, "Announcement," 1881–82; Sarah Anderson to Addams, 11 Sept. 1881, SCPC.

[39]University of Pennsylvania Archives, 1866–84: Med. Matrics. Book, UPC 2.7 # 17); Women's Medical College of Matriculates, 1881–82, Archives and Special Collections on Women in Medicine, Florence A. Moore Library of Medicine, Medical (WMC) College of Pennsylvania.

[40]Davis, *American Heroine*, p. 27; Sarah Blaisdell to Addams, 24 Dec. 1881, SCPC.

[41]Davis, *American Heroine*, p. 78; Emma Briggs to Addams, 30 Dec. 1881, SCPC.

[42]Addams, *Twenty Years*, p. 60; A. L. Bowen, "The World Is Better That This Woman Lived," *New Age Illustrated* 11 (1927), 84–87; 84.

[43]Addams, *Twenty Years*, pp. 22–23; Bowen, "This Woman," p. 27; John Farrell, *Beloved Lady: A History of Jane Addams' Ideas on Reform and Peace* (Baltimore, MD: Johns Hopkins University Press, 1967), p. 40; Davis, *American Heroine*, p. 6. For a more detailed account of this issue and other aspects of this article, see Barker-Benfield, " 'Mother Emancipator': The Meaning of Jane Addams' Sickness and Cure," *Journal of Family History* 4 (1979), 395–420.

[44]Addams, *Twenty Years*, pp. 19; 21.

[45]Addams, *Twenty Years*, pp. 23–24.

[46]Silas Weir Mitchell, "The Annual Oration," *Transactions Medical and Chirurgical Faculty of Maryland* (1877), 51–68; 63–64.

[47]Barker-Benfield, "S. Weir Mitchell and the 'Woman Question': Gender, Therapy and Social History," *Quarterly Journal of Ideology* 5:3 (1981), 25–37.

[48]Anderson to Addams, 27 Apr. 1881, SCPC; Harrington to Addams, 25 July 1882, SCPC; Blaisdell to Addams, 29 Aug. 1881, SCPC.

[49]Barker-Benfield, " 'Mother Emancipator,' " pp. 26–28.

[50]Addams, *Democracy and Social Ethics*, p. 87.

[51]Addams, *The Spirit of Youth and the City Streets* (New York: Macmillan, 1909), pp. 146–47.

[52]Addams, *Twenty Years*, p. 64.

[53]James Reed, *From Private Vice to Public Virtue: The Birth Control Movement and American Society Since 1930* (New York: Basic Books, 1977), p. 28.

[54]Starr to Mary Blaisdell, 23 Feb. 1889, Smith Collection, Smith College, Northampton, Mass.; Addams quoted in Davis, *American Heroine*, p. 64.

[55]Preston quoted in Guilielma Fell Alsop, *History of the Women's Medical College, Philadelphia, Pennsylvania, 1850–1950* (Philadelphia: J. B. Lippincott, 1950), 76–77.

[56]Addams, *Twenty Years*, p. 93.

[57]Addams, *The Long Road of Woman's Memory* (New York: Macmillan, 1916 [1907]), p. 8.

[58]Addams to Starr, 11 Aug. 1879, in Christopher Lasch, ed., *The Social Thought of Jane Addams* (Indianapolis: Bobbs-Merrill, 1965), pp. 3–4.

[59]Addams, *Twenty Years*, p. 98.

[60]Addams, *Spirit of Youth*, pp. 47, 33.

[61]Addams, *Twenty Years*, p. 153.

[62]Addams, *A New Conscience and an Ancient Evil* (New York: Macmillan, 1912), p. 92; Addams, *Twenty Years*, p. 175.

[63]*Boston American*, 15 Feb. 1911, quoted in Davis, *American Heroine*, p. 164.

PART VI

The Transition to Modernity

By 1900 the great American industrial machine was geared for the mass production of consumer goods. The conditions inviting reform remained, but their context was gradually changing. In 1890, the average work week in manufacturing was 60 hours long; by 1910 it was 51 hours. Although these averages hide wide variations and continuing exploitation, more and more families could participate in consumerism as men's wages improved and were augmented by the wages of women and children. Significantly, too, single working-class women found ways to pursue the pleasures of a growing consumer culture.

The increase of life expectancy by six years between 1900 and 1920 was connected with the decline in deaths from diptheria, typhoid, and influenza. The flush toilet and sewage treatment facilities contributed to this decline. Such factors, along with the limitation of family size, had a significant impact on domestic environments. Traditionally strenuous domestic demands on women's work at home were mitigated by the availability of processed foods and much more ready-made clothing, although these items were being produced by women who were among the most exploited of industrial wage-earners.

A host of similarly mass-produced items and mass-marketed goods permitted new levels of self-expression. For example, although young department-store saleswomen worked for low pay and long hours, they could also be exponents of style. Additionally, more and more young people could read at higher levels, as the enrollments in high schools grew from 203,000 in 1890 to 2.3 million in 1920. The new service-sector jobs, as well as mass advertising and certain forms of mass entertainment, required new levels of literacy. And if on the one hand, the decline in the hours of work was in large part the result of a mechanization that deprived some workers of traditional skills, on the other, it also permitted the enormous expansion of leisure activities. Like fashionable clothing and literacy, these were avenues for self-expression.

Leisure, too, became big business. There were 10 million bicycles in America by 1900. Bicycling was one of a number of activities which encouraged women to wear less cumbersome and constrictive clothing that allowed more physical activity. Furthermore, the anxiety over the effects of concentrated study on young women's brains led to their widespread participation in college athletics such as basketball, rowing, and swimming, with a consequent enhancement of their sense of strength and physical freedom. Whether young women went to college or not, they could attend circuses, vaudeville, musical comedy, and ocean resorts in increasing numbers, again suggesting new ways to imagine selfhood. Commerce responded to working women's demands in these respects. Dance halls became very significant sites for working-class women's "cheap amusements," including the expression of sexual desire although women also ran sexual risks in enjoying themselves there. And after 1900, the movies were established as one of America's greatest dream machines encouraging even married women to extend their pleasures outside the home.

In the 1920s, women surged into business and the professions. They entered coeducational colleges in far greater numbers than ever before. There they would enjoy a very different cultural environment than that of their pre-war predecessors in women's colleges: their circumstances were part of a new "youth culture" that was fostering new ways for young women and men to enjoy themselves in each other's company and drawing on the possibilities for self-conception in clothing, cosmetics, cars, movies, radio, and music. While it included a renewed emphasis on marriage and motherhood, in contrast to the doubts raised by previous generations over the compatibility of marriage and college education, it also fostered greater acceptance of female desire and the ideal of greater sexual equality in marriage. This youth culture extended from the middle to the working class, both groups exposed regularly to the powerful influence of the movies.

The rise of a consumer culture, then, had special meanings for the great mass of American women, in their homes, in that women's work was made easier, but also in opening up a public life based on pleasure, not reform. This dimension of consumerism has often been neglected in favor of the negative aspect—making women mere sex objects—which was also a tendency. In any case, the pursuit of pleasure was sanctioned by the most powerful voices in American society, those of big business. Access to such pleasure was immediately attractive to all classes. By the end of the nineteenth century, isolated farm households had been linked to the consumer culture by the mail-order houses, Montgomery Ward and Sears Roebuck, through their catalogs and the new Rural Free Delivery Service. In the cities, the daughters of the "new immigration" were just as eager as rural women to join a "consumption community." After the trauma of uprooting themselves, immigrant families were reconstituted in some cases to become stronger than had been possible under the disintegrative effects of impoverishment in their land of origin. Family ties played a key role in easing the transition of the millions of immigrants, who flooded into America in their greatest numbers in the years immediately prior to World War I.

Among other things, trade unionist Rose Schneiderman's story symbolizes the fact that different traditions of gender relations have responded to the American tradition of domesticity in different ways. Schneiderman's generation of Eastern European Jews had been preceded by the German Jews of the 1840s who, by the 1890s, had become Americanized enough to become leading contributors to that "new world" of "social feminism," prominent in suffragism and in many aspects of reform. Many immigrant women carried with them deeply conservative attitudes toward gender; others yearned to escape patriarchal traditions by coming to the United States. Immigrant Italian women limited their births, but still focused their lives on their families. Americanization provided women opportunities for literacy and (after 1920) for voting participation, as well as for work and pleasure outside the home. Immigrant wives could look to the laws and customs of the new country for protection from beatings within their families. Settlement houses could be the sites for a sympathetic and respectful acknowledgment of Old World cultures as well as what must be seen as the necessary education into the traditions of the new. At the same time, the middle-class female reformers' temperance crusade, eventually leading to Prohibition, was at odds with the festive traditions of immigrant cultures. This symbolizes the powerful tensions in American life, generated by the contrasts between cultures.

Immigrant families, then, consolidated for the future. Eventually they became more prosperous than would be possible in their countries of origin for decades. But along with the families of native-born, white Americans migrating to the cities in record numbers, immigrant families faced a more rapid shifting of their traditional functions. Formerly, children had learned skills at home. There, too, family members had entertained themselves in a variety of ways. Now children went to school, and as they grew older, to dance halls and movie houses. Young women formed peer groups by way of the paid workforce, as well as in schools and college. Families saw their daughters joining a national consumer culture that generated vastly new role models.

The outbreak of World War I in 1914 temporarily halted the massive influx of immigration. Amidst jingoistic hatreds left by the war, including the "red scare" that Crystal Eastman faced, conservative groups of white Anglo-Saxon Protestants made a last stand. The Emergency Quota Act was passed in 1921, aimed at restricting the new immigration from southern and eastern Europe, in favor of the old immigration from the north and west. The restrictions were made still more effective by the National Origins Act of 1924. Big business had adequate supplies of labor, which it kept cheap by systematic union-busting; thus, it no longer resisted the nativist campaign as it had done in earlier decades, when it had looked to immigration for cheap labor. Immigrant cultures were no longer being invigorated by fresh infusions from the old countries and now they were exposed to the full force of consumer culture. The result was to accelerate Americanization. From a political and reform point of view, the 1920s were intensely conservative, whatever the liberalizing juices unleashed by consumerism's triumphs.

Conservative forces were also provoked by a particular migration within the United States. Poor African-Americans from rural areas met far more enduring and pervasive discrimination when they migrated to northern cities than their contemporary immigrants who came from outside the nation's borders. African-Americans had begun significant migration to the north in the 1880s as whites intensified their economic and political oppression in the rural south. In southern states, African-Americans were systematically purged from any participation in the political system in the wake of the defeat of Populism. Moreover, temporary employment opportunities of World War I greatly increased black migration to northern cities. Detroit's black population, for example, increased 300 percent between 1910 and 1920, and it more than doubled in the next ten years. But if black people moved away from the constant threat and reality of southern lynchings, their mass migration to the north often provoked northern whites to riot against them. In violence following the murder of a black person swimming at a whites-only beach in Chicago on a hot July day in 1919, thirty-eight people, black and white, were killed.

Expanding ghettoes were to be powerful centers for the generating of African-American culture. In the 1920s, jazz emerged as "a major art form" celebrated in mainstream popular culture. Among the creators and performers of jazz were a series of magnificent women singers, including Bessie Smith, and later, Billie Holiday. Jazz was rooted in generations of African-American experience. It fearlessly expressed pain and sexuality, injustice and transcendence. Jazz would be the chief wellspring for that twentieth-century popular American music upon which each generation would draw to define itself. The ability to do so was fostered in the 1920s by radio and recordings.

Harlem, in New York City, was the site of an outpouring of many other forms of African-American self-expression, in addition to music. They ranged from painting to poetry and fiction (shaped by the same cultural traditions as music) and from social science to the separatist politics of Marcus Garvey. This outpouring has become known as the Harlem Renaissance. The poets included Claude McKay, of whom Crystal Eastman was a friend, and Langston Hughes. One of the greatest of the Harlem Renaissance's writers was Zora Neale Hurston. Trained as an anthropologist, Hurston celebrated the uniqueness of African-American culture, insisted on a woman's ability and right to participate fully in it, and demonstrated its integrity in the face of racism.

The creation of a national consumer culture; the massive immigration of new immigrants into the cities; and the intensification of racist politics, south and north, formed the context for suffragism's final push during the second decade of the twentieth century. The Nineteenth Amendment to the Constitution, finally passed in 1920, declared that the "right of citizens of the United States to vote shall not be denied or abridged . . . on account of sex." Originating in the social reforms of the 1820s and 1830s, women's suffrage was the culmination of the first women's movement in which suffragists identified themselves as a distinct, collective interest. It formally connected women to public life in a culture where political participation was fundamental in ideology and in practice. It symbolized sexual equality, although it did not achieve it. The winning of suffrage had taken nearly a "century of struggle." Suffragists only achieved a critical mass of support in the second decade of the twentieth century. The heritage of "separate-sphere" domesticity and of social science converged with the political goals of progressivism. During the two decades after the Civil War, suffragists had split acrimoniously over the granting of the vote to black males. One of the two suffrage associations, the National Woman Suffrage Association, pressed for a national amendment, while the American Woman Suffrage Association continued its state-by-state strategy. But of the 480 state campaigns between 1870 and 1910, only 17 resulted in state referenda and suffragists won in only 2 of those, Wyoming and Colorado. In 1890 the two associations merged as the National American Woman Suffrage Association (NAWSA). It was infused with new life in 1907 when Elizabeth Cady Stanton's daughter, Harriet Stanton Blatch, and a younger generation of suffragists reached out to a broader constituency and initiated more dramatic tactics. Rose Schneiderman's career illustrates that working-class women participated in the suffrage campaign. Alice Paul, schooled in the English suffrage movement, became a suffrage leader in America and led still more militant protests. In 1913 she and her followers broke away to form the Congressional Union, which became the National Woman's Party in 1916. It took a hard line against the Democrats in power under President Woodrow Wilson, which distinguished it from NAWSA, which tried to stand above party politics.

When the United States entered the first World War against Germany and its allies in 1917, more militant suffragists compared Wilson to the German Kaiser. They dramatized the contradiction of President Wilson's war goal, asking how America could be "saving the world for democracy," while half of all Americans were denied the vote. They chained themselves to the White House fence and when they were arrested they went on hunger strikes in prison. The media made them martyrs and this advance guard of radicals made the more numerous and less militant NAWSA seem the lesser of two evils to the male establishment. Both Democrats and Republicans embraced women's suffrage and Wilson reversed his opposition to it.

At another level, less radical suffragists had worked hard since the turn of the century to show it was in either of the two major parties' interests to support women's suffrage. Suffragists shared common ground with progressives generally, including the goal of political "reform." For example, mainstream politics were still deeply racist. To make themselves more acceptable to those men who could grant them the ballot, some white suffragists used racist tactics. They emphasized the "superiority" of educated white women to illiterate African-Americans and non-English-speaking and illiterate immigrant males.

Suffragists also emphasized the conventionality of their beliefs about gender roles. They argued that women would bring the special gender qualities to bear on public life. They presented women as "social housekeepers" for the public sphere. Then, during the war, the majority of suffragists patriotically threw themselves into the war effort, demonstrating their loyalty to the same imperatives as men. Suffragists argued that women's wartime work, in factories and near the battlefields as medical volunteers, in addition to various charitable efforts on behalf of the troops, further demonstrated women's qualifications for the vote.

By contrast, a number of women socialists and pacifists, including Jane Addams and Crystal Eastman were made outcasts by their opposition to the war. Another was Emma Goldman, who had come to the United States from Russia to find freedom from traditional patriarchy in the form of a marriage arranged by her father. Always individualistic, her politics were those of an anarchist. She was a magnificent public speaker. Her topics ranged from the evils of capitalism to advocacy of birth control. Repeatedly imprisoned and finally deported from the United States to Russia in 1919 during the "red scare," Goldman became deeply critical of the emerging totalitarianism there. She died in Canada on a trip to raise money to fight General Francisco Franco, the fascist usurper in Spain. A lifelong feminist, Goldman distinguished herself from most of her contemporary American feminists by her open expression of sexual appetite. Goldman criticized her fellow feminists for their "narrow Puritanical vision" which sought to banish "man, as a disturber and doubtful character, out of their emotional life."

The directions that feminists had taken in order to win the vote had been disquieting to several of their leaders. Those directions included capitalizing on racial and class prejudices. They also included repressing the issue of sex. But tapping Victorian roots, separately nourished in domesticity and deeply suspicious of the association of male power with sexuality, a significant proportion of female college graduates and social feminists found public life and conventional family lives mutually exclusive. Some chose homosocial relationships. Others hoped to establish a single, sexual standard for heterosexual relations. They saw sexual puritanism and even celibacy as necessary strategies in women's historical conflict with men. Hence suffragists succeeded in winning women the vote but left aside the issue of sexual freedom. This powerful element in the dominant, middle-class feminist tradition put it at odds with a freer, more sexual popular culture.

By the 1920s, much of feminism was, in a crucial sense, anachronistic. This is why it languished. Charlotte Perkins Gilman was contemptuous of "the newly freed" women's giving in to a sexuality that Gilman could only see as "masculine," as women mastered "birth control" and acquired "experience." It was in the 1920s that contraception finally became a respectable subject of discussion. While quite effective techniques had been known for at least a century, social beliefs—especially religious ones—had inhibited their dissemination. In 1921 Margaret Sanger set up the American Birth Control League in Brooklyn, New York, through which the new secular authorities on such matters, doctors and social workers, were persuaded to give their expert imprimatur to birth control. But users had their own reasons, too. Gilman, Addams, and others of their generation were deeply conscious of the gulf between themselves and younger women over the issue of sex and style, a gulf that showed itself within feminism, as the story of Crystal Eastman illustrates. She, like many of her generation, attempted to combine career and family. On the other hand, Alice Paul sustained the traditional asceticism of feminism and Rose Schneiderman devoted herself to reform rather than family.

While differing sharply in personal and sexual styles, Paul and Eastman jointly campaigned in the 1920s on behalf of the full equality of the sexes. Paul's party introduced the Equal Rights Amendment in 1923. It opposed "protective legislation" on the grounds that it assumed women needed protection, that is, that women were naturally weaker than men. Their opponents, among them Rose Schneiderman, preferred to maintain reform legislation defending female workers, whatever its rationale. They saw this as especially important because of big business' successful anti-labor campaign of the 1920s. Protective legislation's effects were ambiguous; the laws went largely unenforced and were used frequently to exclude women from certain jobs. This was one of many struggles splitting feminism in the 1920s, a decade which for some symbolized the end of the old feminism and the beginnings of the new.

Rose Schneiderman

(1882–1972)

Annelise Orleck

Rose Schneiderman was born in Saven, Poland, in 1882 to a close-knit Orthodox Jewish family. In 1890 the family came to New York City. Poverty forced Schneiderman to enter the paid work force at thirteen, first as a saleswoman and then as a capmaker. By 1904 she was the first woman to be elected to the general executive board of an American labor union, the United Cloth Hat and Cap Makers Union. Schneiderman then became a vice president of the New York Women's Trade Union League (WTUL) in 1906 and its chief organizer in 1908. She helped organize the great uprising of New York shirtwaist makers in 1909–1910, and between 1914 and 1916 was the general organizer for the International Ladies' Garment Workers Union. In 1911 she helped found the Wage Earner's League for Woman Suffrage and in 1917 she was elected president of the Industrial Section of the New York Woman Suffrage Party, the working-class wing of the party. Schneiderman was elected president of the New York WTUL in 1917 and president of the National WTUL in 1926, retaining both positions until her retirement in 1949. In 1933 President Roosevelt appointed her the only woman on his National Labor Advisory Board. From 1937 until 1945 Schneiderman served as secretary of labor for the state of New York. She retired in 1949, after which she wrote her memoirs, made radio speeches, and appeared at various union functions. She lived alone in New York City until 1969, when declining health forced her to enter a nursing home. She died in 1972 at age ninety.

Rose Schneiderman always liked to remind people that she was "a redhead." In speeches and writings she used her hair color as a symbol of her fiery personality. So did her detractors, who called her, among other things, "the Red Rose of Anarchy." Only four feet nine inches tall, the diminutive immigrant Jew from Poland had an uncanny ability to cut to the heart of an issue. That quality won her both lifelong friends and enemies. For nearly half a century, from 1905 through the early 1950s, Schneiderman stirred crowds with her words. Speaking on street corners, soapboxes, lecture platforms, and, during the 1930s, over the radio, the militant trade unionist and women's rights advocate could move even those who were prepared to dislike her. New York City patrol officer John Kelly was one unlikely convert. During the spring of 1911 he decided to attend a memorial for victims of the Triangle Shirtwaist Company fire, at which Rose Schneiderman was to be the featured speaker. He did not expect to hear anything he liked from ". . . one of them foreigners. But she herself can make you weep," he commented afterward. "She is the finest speaker I ever heard." A year later, when Schneiderman toured Ohio to build support for a statewide woman suffrage referendum, a local suffragist wrote to a friend that she was amazed by Schneiderman's affect on crowds. "We have had splendid speakers here before, but not one who impressed the people as she did. Strong men sat with tears rolling down their faces. Her pathos and earnestness held the audiences spellbound."[1]

From the time she was first introduced to socialism as an eighteen-year-old capmaker at the turn of the twentieth century, to her retirement in 1949, Rose Schneiderman committed herself to improving the conditions of working-class women's lives in the United States. Despite only four years of formal schooling in the United States, Rose Schneiderman moved to the forefront of the American labor and woman suffrage movements. She became a friend and adviser to progressive Democrats including Al Smith, Eleanor and Franklin Roosevelt, and eventually won the presidency of both the New York and National Women's Trade Union Leagues, to a seat as the only woman on Franklin Roosevelt's Labor Advisory Board, and to a seven-year term as secretary of labor for the state of New York. She organized tens of thousands of working women into unions and convinced them of the importance of getting the vote. She promoted the organization of housewives into a nationwide network of neighborhood consumer organizations. She lobbied effectively for maximum hour, minimum wage, maternity, disability, and unemployment insurance legislation that affected millions of women. When she died in 1972, a *New York Times* editorial summed up her life and work this way: "A tiny red haired bundle of social dynamite, Rose Schneiderman did more to upgrade the dignity and living standards of working women than any other American."[2]

Acclaimed as she was, Rose Schneiderman was not without her critics. Her pragmatic focus sometimes made her seem conservative to radical feminists, such as the leaders of the National Woman's Party, who had broken with the National American Woman Suffrage Association to take more direct action in securing the vote. She was a passionate advocate of women's rights; and yet, for decades she fought bitterly against a proposed Equal Rights Amendment to the federal Constitution, which would ban sex discrimination, because she feared that it would nullify hard-won legislation protecting female workers. She was sharply criticized for this stance by activists in the National Woman's Party, who accused her of ignoring the needs of American women. Schneiderman was also chastised by communists, during the twenties and thirties, for her work with upper-class women and her service to the state and federal administrations of Franklin Roosevelt. She did not flinch under either attack. She had a single goal in mind, to aid American working-class women, and she pursued that goal with the combined pragmatism and passion that were the hallmarks of her long career.

But a lifetime of standing her ground had its costs. Fewer than a dozen people attended Rose Schneiderman's funeral. Her oldest friend, Pauline Newman, was shocked. "I thought I'd find a lot of people who knew her and for whom she worked all her life," she recalled sadly. "I could not believe it, you know?" In part the small turnout was due to the fact that Schneiderman had no children and had outlived many of her contemporaries. But it was also a reflection of the fact that her life and work did not always meet with approval from the media, the Democratic party, or even the men with whom she worked in the labor movement. Male colleagues praised her often for her contributions to the cause of labor, but they also resented her for her insistence that the American labor movement address women's needs and make full use of women's talents. They appeared with her at union functions where they cheered the solidarity of men and women in the labor movement, but they were not comfortable with this Jewish woman who never married, who chose to live a public life when women were expected to devote themselves exclusively to home and family.[3]

Schneiderman's own writings and her repeated refusals to reveal any details about her private life to reporters or, after her retirement, to historians, reflect a deep ambivalence about the private costs of her public life. By all accounts her personal life seems to have been a rich one. Still she was torn, as she put it in a letter to Pauline Newman, by a "yearning, yearning for warmth and tenderness."

Like many of her contemporaries, Schneiderman had absorbed the belief that women who chose a public career had to be willing to forgo ". . . the fulfillment of love." She was aware of what she lacked. "I am," she wrote to Newman at age thirty-five, "used to going without the things most wanted." A lifetime of activism brought Schneiderman excitement, fulfillment, and a measure of fame, but it also left her open to criticism. She did not mind battling those who attacked her for her politics. It was harder having to deal with those who would not accept her personal choices. An immigrant, working-class woman challenging the limitations that American society imposed on people of her ethnicity, her class, and her sex risked giving up the comfort of being socially acceptable. Though it did not stop her from fighting, Schneiderman was never able to resolve to her own satisfaction the tension between cherishing difference and demanding equality. She felt the strain of that tension throughout her life.[4]

Rose Schneiderman's early life was in many ways typical of her generation of Eastern European Jewish immigrants. She was born in Saven, Poland, in 1882, a time when the thousand-year-old traditions of Eastern European Jewry were cracking apart. Political repression combined with economic dislocation as the Russian empire industrialized rapidly and suddenly, leaving Jewish craftspeople and artisans unable to compete. Tens of thousands migrated to the cities hoping to find work in one of Russia's new garment factories.

There Jewish young people came into contact for the first time with a wide range of secular ideas. Young men and women who socialized, worked, and studied together in Kiev, Odessa, Vilna, and Warsaw began to see traditional Jewish religious life as old-fashioned, narrow, and provincial. Typical of that provincialism, many Jewish intellectuals argued, was the belief that women did not need to be, indeed should not be, educated. The intellectual, political, and artistic ferment of the cities soon reached small Jewish towns like Saven. As in the cities, study groups sprang up, composed of equal numbers of men and women. Some traditionalist parents still sought to prevent their daughters from receiving any education, religious or secular, but others, like Deborah Schneiderman, perhaps taking a vicarious pleasure in it, encouraged their daughters to learn as much as they could.

"I started going to Hebrew school when I was four," Rose Schneiderman later recalled. "Though it was somewhat unusual for girls to study . . . Mother was determined that I learn Hebrew so I could read and understand the prayers recited at home and in the synagogue." When the family moved from the small town of Saven to the city of Khelm they sent Rose to a public school where she learned to read, write, and speak Russian. Though Schneiderman would later express embarrassment at her limited education, perhaps because so many of the American women she worked with had college degrees, her reading knowledge of Hebrew and Russian made her an educated woman by comparison with her mother's generation of small-town Jewish women.[5]

In 1890, Rose Schneiderman, her mother, and brothers left Poland for New York City, where Rose's father Samuel waited for them, having gone on ahead to find work and living quarters for his family. Part of a mass migration that brought 1.25 million Jews from Russia and Poland to the United States between 1881 and 1914, the Schneidermans settled on the Lower East Side of Manhattan, in a crowded, dirty ghetto that was also a center of trade union and socialist activity. Like thousands of other new Jewish immigrants, Samuel found work there in the burgeoning garment trade.

Less than two years later, Samuel Schneiderman died of the flu, leaving thirty-year-old Deborah with the prospect of providing for three small children and a baby soon to be born. Like many Eastern European Jewish women, Deborah Schneiderman was accustomed to earning money to help support her family. In Poland, she had supplemented the small income Samuel derived from his tailoring business by doing a little bit of everything. She sewed for neighbors, baked ritual breads and cakes for local weddings, treated the sick with homemade herbal medicines, and tended bar in a nearby saloon when the proprietor was too drunk to do it herself. Now in New York she did what the majority of immigrant women of all ethnicities did during the early twentieth century when they needed to enhance the family income: Deborah took in boarders.[6]

For a while after Samuel Schneiderman's sudden death, the family had no income besides the daily basket of food provided by United Hebrew Charities. Deborah Schneiderman was forced to send six-year-old Harry to the Hebrew Orphan Asylum. The arrival of a boarder fresh from Poland temporarily postponed further breakup of the family.

> After father died, we rented out the living room of our apartment to a young man, a tailor who worked at home, and we kept the bedroom and the kitchen. As long as he stayed we were able to pay the rent of $7.00 a month.[7]

For a year, while Deborah Schneiderman worked to supplement the boarder's contribution, Rose stayed home from school to care for the baby. But when her mother lost her outside job, Rose was sent to live for a year in a Jewish orphanage. Deborah Schneiderman found another job lining capes and slowly saved enough money to rent a room in the home of a family on Norfolk Street where she brought her two daughters, Rose and Jane, to live with her.

When the family again was faced with starvation after Deborah Schneiderman lost this new job, thirteen-year-old Rose decided to leave school. Fearful of what would happen to her on the factory floor, Deborah insisted Rose instead take a job in a department store where she might get to know "a higher class of people" who could help her escape the Lower East Side. The United Hebrew Charities, an organization staffed by middle- and upper-class German Jewish women who had helped the young family through many crises, got Rose her first job. For three years she was the sole support of her family, until her mother took a job as superintendent of their Lower East Side tenement.

Schneiderman enjoyed her three years as a shop girl. She particularly appreciated the camaraderie of the saleswomen. However, she could not earn enough at the store to support her family. The family moved to a tenement on Sulfolk Street where her mother got a job as Superintendent. Though her mother's labor cleaning the outhouses, halls, and stairways of their building entitled them to free rental, Rose's salary was all they had to buy food and clothing. When she started she was paid $2.25 for a sixty-four-hour week, out of which she had to subtract the cost of laundering her uniform. During the Christmas season the shopwomen worked an eighty-four-hour week, without any compensation for overtime. After three years on the job, she was only earning $2.75 per week and she found out that one female supervisor, a fourteen-year veteran, was paid just $7.00 per week. "I decided I couldn't possibly wait fourteen years, as Martha had, and so must find another job," Schneiderman later recalled. She decided to look for work in a garment factory.[8]

When a neighbor offered to teach her to line caps, Rose jumped at the chance. In 1898, she was hired by Fox and Lederer, where she began at $6.00 per week. Out of that she had to pay for her own thirty-dollar sewing machine and thread, for lunches and transportation. Still, she felt confident that the move would pay off. She hoped to work her way up to a more skilled position in the trade. Then Rose was introduced to the principles of trade unionism by a young coworker, Bessie Braut.

> Bessie was an unusual person. Her beautiful eyes shone out of a badly pockmarked face and the effect was startling. An outspoken anarchist she made a strong impression on us. She wasted no time in giving us the facts of life—that the men in our trade belonged to a union and were, therefore, able to better their conditions. She added

pointedly that it would be a good thing for the lining-makers to join a union along with the trimmers, who were all women.[9]

Schneiderman agreed to join with Braut, Bessie Mannis, and other lining-makers in requesting a charter from the United Cloth Hat and Cap Makers Union (UCHCU). The young women were told to enroll twenty-five women working in different factories. Schneiderman and her comrades stationed themselves at factory doors and, with membership blanks in hand, approached women workers as they were ending their shifts. Within a few days they had enough signatures to win a charter for Local 23 of the UCHCU, and Schneiderman was elected secretary. In her new position, Schneiderman met with women workers at the end of each shift to hear their problems, then attempted to intervene with management on their behalf. She was elected to the Central Labor Union of New York. By 1904 Schneiderman was involved in a strike against a runaway shop* in New Jersey, during which she addressed a crowd of workers for the first time. Schneiderman found that she enjoyed organizing, but her mother was disturbed by Schneiderman's penchant for public speaking. She warned Rose that if she continued along this path she would never marry: Men did not want a woman with a big mouth.

At the 1904 convention of the United Cloth and Cap Makers Union, Rose Schneiderman was elected to the general executive board, the first woman to achieve an executive position in the American labor movement. During the winter of 1904–1905, the cap-makers were faced with an attempt by owners to open up union shops to nonunion workers. In response, the largely immigrant Cap Makers Union struck. The strike would be a turning point for Schneiderman, for her role in the strike brought her to the attention of the infant Women's Trade Union League (WTUL), an organization of progressive middle-class women founded in 1903 to help working women organize themselves into trade unions. Although Schneiderman had misgivings about the group because she "could not believe that men and women who were not wage earners themselves understood the problems that workers faced," the favorable publicity that the WTUL won for the strikers moved her to become a member. By the end of March 1905 Schneiderman was elected to the executive board of the New York WTUL. It was a position she would hold for the next forty-five years.[10]

Schneiderman's entrance into the New York WTUL was an important turning point not only in her career, but for the fledgling organi-

**Runaway shop* was the name given to manufacturing businesses that relocated outside of major cities to avoid paying union wages.

zation. Despite a genuine commitment on the part of the organization's officers to organizing working women into unions, the WTUL had credibility problems among workers. Although the WTUL was proud that it had representatives from most of New York's major unions on its executive board, union members rarely attended. The league's work and emphasis was dominated by upper-class women who described themselves as "allies" of the working class. Although the league would, as years went on, come to have an increasingly working-class leadership and tone, its primary financial support always came from very wealthy women rather than from the unions.[11] It was a contradiction that Schneiderman was never able to resolve.

Friendships with middle-class and wealthy women in the league deeply influenced young working women, making them aware of the possibility of women's solidarity across class lines. But, while they derived tremendous emotional nourishment from these alliances, Schneiderman, Pauline Newman, and Irish shirtmaker Leonora O'Reilly never lost sight of the ways in which their class background distinguished them from the league's wealthier members. Sisterhood was exhilarating but, outside the WTUL, their lives were starkly different and their political agendas diverged. The progressive reformers who dominated the league were committed to helping working-class women organize but they were also concerned with steering them away from radical influences. Schneiderman, Newman, and O'Reilly, on the other hand, were active members of the Socialist party. Caught between the indifference or outright hostility of men in the labor movement and the well-meaning but often patronizing benevolence of upper-class women, working-class members of the league struggled to insure that their own voices would not be lost.

This political and social tension heightened working women's emotional dependence upon one another. Schneiderman, Newman, O'Reilly and other working-class league organizers formed deep bonds. When heart disease and an invalid mother bound O'Reilly for years to her home in Brooklyn, Newman and Schneiderman visited her every Saturday and, when they weren't in New York, wrote weekly. Letters among the three are filled with political advice, affectionate banter, and perhaps most important, with expressions of gratitude for the friendship of other activist working-class women. In the midst of all the turbulence of union organizers' lives, they needed to know that there were at least a few people with whom they could relax and just be themselves.[12]

With the appointment of Schneiderman as organizer, the New York WTUL initiated a new policy—listening to workers. Previously, league women had approached organizing as social reformers might, focusing on the most exploited workers. The results were discouraging. By the end of 1906, league leaders decided only to respond to requests for aid from workers already trying to organize. The garment trades seemed a fertile field for testing this strategy, but many of the workers were Jewish immigrants and the league had no Yiddish-speaking organizers. Eloquent as she was, Irish garment worker Leonora O'Reilly could only organize English speakers. Schneiderman provided a vital link between the WTUL and the Jewish female workers of the Lower East Side. In 1906, hoping to improve the crediblity of the WTUL within the labor movement, the New York League elected Rose Schneiderman vice president.[13]

Schneiderman organized feverishly for the next three years. Though fear and hunger made it slow going at first, female workers in New York suddenly began to express their anger through strikes, surprising male garment union organizers who had tended to ignore them. "It was not unusual for unorganized workers to walk out without having any direct union affiliation," Schneiderman later wrote about that restless season.[14]

In April 1907 a group of women's underwear makers at the Milgrim shop on Grand Street staged a spontaneous walkout to protest speedups, wage cuts, and the requirement that employees pay for thread. Schneiderman came in to guide the strike, setting up picket lines and arranging for a committee of strike leaders to negotiate with the owner. The strikers won almost all of their demands, including the establishment of a permanent grievance committee to negotiate future problems. Schneiderman believed that the Milgrim strike reflected a growing sense of group consciousness among young women workers on the East Side. She later remembered

> the young Russian woman who was the leader of the group . . . told me how different things had been in her shop before the strike. The women looked upon each other as enemies because one might get a better bundle of work done than the other. But now, since they had organized and had fought together, there was a kinship among them.[15]

Schneiderman sought to build on such successes. Every day she and her fresh converts mounted soapboxes on crowded street corners, calling to other women to join their union. It was an effective strategy that took full advantage of the speaking skills of the East Side organizers. Fearful that manufacturers were attempting to stir up antagonism among Jewish, Italian, and American workers, organizers conducted street meetings in Yiddish, Italian, and English. Their campaign succeeded beyond their expectations.[16]

In November 1909 New York's shirtwaist and dressmakers, the

vast majority of them immigrant women under age twenty-five, walked off their jobs in a general strike. As chief organizer for the New York WTUL, Schneiderman attended countless workers' meetings, spoke to crowds, and walked the picket lines. The tender age and courage of the young strikers during that long winter of 1909–1910 in the face of hunger, cold, police brutality, and attacks by hired company guards won them support from an unexpected source. In December 1909 some of New York's wealthiest women, including suffragists Alva Belmont and Anne Morgan, daughter of financier J. P. Morgan, decided to join the young strikers on the picket lines to prevent further violence. These wealthy women were able to generate positive press coverage for the strikers, and contributions for their strike fund. The active proselytizing of suffragists on the picket lines also brought masses of working women into the woman suffrage movement for the first time, marking a turning point in working-class women's struggle for improved conditions.

During the next decade working-class women would fight on two battlefields: for both political and economic rights. Between 1909 and 1916, women workers struck across the Northeast and Midwest. The 1909 shirtwaist "uprising" in New York was echoed by women's strikes in Philadelphia; Brooklyn; Boston; Chicago; Cleveland; Muscatine, Iowa; Kalamazoo, Michigan; Lawrence, Massachusetts; and Paterson, New Jersey. Schneiderman was involved in a number of those strikes as organizer, speaker, or mediator. But the strike that most deeply involved her was the 1913 general strike of underwear and lingerie makers in Brooklyn and Manhattan. Thirty-five thousand young women, many of them little more than children, poured onto picket lines and captured the attention of such leading progressives as former President Theodore Roosevelt and Wisconsin Senator Robert La Follette. After nearly five years of intensive organizing, Schneiderman had pulled together young women from a wide variety of ethnic backgrounds and proved that they could stick together through a bitter struggle. Once again progressives were moved by the eloquence and determination of the young female workers. The strike, which received national press coverage, heightened pressure for state regulation of the conditions under which women and children worked.

The militance displayed by immigrant female workers exacerbated class and ethnic tensions within the WTUL. Almost as soon as the 1909 shirtwaist strike ended, upper-class members of the league's executive board had begun to argue that too much attention was being paid to immigrant workers, particularly to Jewish women. Schneiderman fought hard to keep the league from withdrawing its support for Jewish workers. She was hurt and angered when league secretary Helen Marot, a socialist and someone Schneiderman had considered a good friend, lashed out at Jewish organizers: "We have . . . realized for several years that the Russian Jew had little sense of administration and we have been used to . . . their depending solely on their emotions and not on constructive work." In response, Schneiderman handed in her resignation, which the league refused to accept because she was in the middle of organizing the white-goods workers. After the strike, she decided to run for president of the New York League. She might have been willing to accept her loss to American organizer Melinda Scott had she not been informed by Newman and O'Reilly that upper-class league members had lobbied secretly for her defeat. The trade union women were all behind her, Newman assured Schneiderman shortly after the election. Schneiderman lost, she wrote, "because [she was] a Socialist, a Jewess and one interested in suffrage."[17]

This time when Schneiderman resigned, the league let her go. From 1914–1916, she worked as general organizer for the International Ladies Garment Workers Union (ILGWU), traveling throughout the Midwest and New England. Frustrated by the union leadership's lack of support for her efforts at organizing women, Schneiderman resigned from her position with the ILGWU after only two years. In a vote that reflected how much they wanted her back, the New York WTUL elected Schneiderman president in 1917. She returned to New York to take over the league and also to replace her ailing friend Leonora O'Reilly as president of the Industrial Section of the New York Woman Suffrage Party (WSP).[18]

Increasingly through the decade that followed the 1909 "uprising," Schneiderman had come to focus on the vote as a key weapon in the struggle to empower working-class women. Drawn to suffrage as early as 1907, when she became the most popular speaker for Harriot Stanton Blatch's Equality League of Self Supporting Women, Schneiderman had in 1911 helped to found the first suffrage organization composed primarily of industrial workers—the Wage Earner's League For Woman Suffrage. The Wage Earner's League reached out not only to working women but to the wives and mothers of workers by pointing out ways women could use the vote to improve conditions in their homes and communities.[19]

In 1912 the Wage Earner's League and the Collegiate Equal Suffrage League called a mass meeting to protest the New York state legislature's failure to pass a resolution endorsing woman suffrage. The working-class suffrage movement showcased the best speakers it had in New York to answer the "sentimentality of New York Senators," with the "common sense of working women." On the night of April 22, 1912, the Great Hall of the People in Cooper Union, where in 1909 the waistmakers had met, was once again filled with cheering women.

Rising to her full height of four foot nine, Schneiderman imitated the New York senator who claimed, "Get women into the arena of politics with its alliances and distressing contests—the delicacy is gone, the charm is gone, and you emasculize women." Schneiderman the pragmatist had no patience for such romanticized nonsense. She immediately won cheers with an open question.

> What does all this talk about becoming mannish signify? I wonder if it will add to my height when I get the vote. I might work for it all the harder if it did. It is just too ridiculous, this talk of becoming less womanly, just as if a woman could be anything else except a woman.

Schneiderman believed that men and women had different talents and values. However, she was deeply offended by a double standard of femininity that required working women to be strong and sexless in the factory, helpless and modest outside it.

> It seems to me that the working woman ought to wake up to the truth of her situation; all this talk about women's charm does not mean working women. Working women are expected to work and produce their kind so that they too may work until they die of some industrial disease.

Whatever benefits upper-class women derive from the men who admire their feminine charms, Schneiderman told her audience bluntly, will never accrue to the working women.

> Senators and legislators are not blind to the horrible conditions around them. . . . It does not speak well for the intelligence of our Senators to come out with statements about women losing their charm and attractiveness. . . . Women in the laundries . . . stand thirteen hours or fourteen hours in terrible steam and heat with their hands in hot starch. Surely these women won't lose any more of their beauty and charm by putting a ballot in a ballot box once a year than they are likely to lose standing in . . . laundries all year round.[20]

Schneiderman continued her suffrage activism through the 1910s, touring Ohio for the National American Woman Suffrage Association, heading up the WTUL Suffrage Committee and finally leading the Industrial Section of the New York WSP. When women won the vote in New York in 1917, Schneiderman made regular trips to the state capital in Albany, to lobby for passage of bills granting a forty-eight-hour week for New York working women, and a minimum wage. The latter, she argued, would benefit working men as well as women in insuring that employers would not replace male workers with lower paid female workers.

Schneiderman wanted to make sure, now that New York women had the vote, that they used it. In 1918 she led a group of working women in a neighborhood campaign to defeat several New York state legislators who had been particularly hostile to wage, hours, and working conditions legislation. Schneiderman, with her powerful voice, spoke from the back of a horsedrawn truck as it moved slowly up and down the streets of each legislator's district. The campaigns were relatively successful. Four antilabor legislators were defeated; two of them replaced by women who strongly supported legislation regulating workplace conditions.[21]

In 1919 Schneiderman was nominated, along with former shoe worker Mary Anderson, to serve as the only women in the trade union delegation to the Paris Peace Conference. While in Paris, Schneiderman commenced a long friendship with British Labour party leader Margaret Bondfield, who would later become England's first female minister of labor. Excited by their own friendship, and their late night conversations, the two women began to plan for an international conference of working women. It was held in Washington, D.C., in November of 1919, the first in a series of such conferences and the beginning of a new era in working women's politics—an era of internationalism, during which the ideas and aims of activist working women in the United States and in Europe would be shaped by regular communication across the Atlantic.

Schneiderman's international experience was an important consideration when, in May 1920, the newly formed New York State Labor party nominated Schneiderman for the U.S. Senate. Although Schneiderman never expected to win, the seriousness with which her campaign was treated by the press reflects the power of labor as a force in New York state politics at the end of the First World War. The *New York Times* reported her nomination on page two. The domestic goals of Schneiderman's campaign for the Senate are also worth noting because they highlight Schneiderman's increasing emphasis on government intervention. Just as the Wage Earner's League for Woman Suffrage had called for legislation protecting the worker both in the workplace and in the home, so in her campaign for the Senate Schneiderman suggested that government must become involved in all aspects of workers' lives. Her broad platform also called for the use of public monies to pay for construction of nonprofit housing for workers, improved neighborhood schools, publicly owned utilities and food markets, and for state-funded health and unemployment insurance for all Americans.[22]

During the 1920s, the labor movement was severely weakened by conservative backlash. Government repression following World War I and the Russian Revolution, and internecine struggles between communists, socialists, and progressives racked the unions. As a result Schneiderman and other female labor leaders began to focus increasingly on women's concerns outside the workplace. Rose Schneiderman believed that one of the most important things she could do for working-class women was combat their sense of inferiority.

In order to enrich the lives of women laborers and to cultivate a younger generation of leaders, Schneiderman and ILGWU colleagues Fania Cohn and Pauline Newman helped design a series of education courses geared specifically to working women. As early as 1915, Schneiderman, Newman, and Cohn had collaborated with a young Barnard professor named Juliet Poyntz to establish an education program for the ILGWU dressmakers who had struck in 1909. The largely young, immigrant women of ILGWU's Local 25 responded enthusiastically to classes in economics, history, labor law, art and music appreciation, and public speaking. That program was so successful that the union established a worker-education department to coordinate courses for workers across the country. In 1920 Schneiderman and Cohn were approached by the president of Bryn Mawr College, M. Carey Thomas, and asked to help design a special summer school there for women workers. The Bryn Mawr Summer School for Women Workers became the model for several others that followed, including the Hudson Shore School which lasted until 1952. In 1923, the New York WTUL also established a school of its own that grew in the range of its offerings and in the size of its classes through the 1940s. These schools for female workers were based on an idea shared by Cohn and Schneiderman that the greatest obstacle working-class women faced was their own lack of confidence.[23]

The second front on which Schneiderman and her colleagues battled working-class women's sense of inferiority, was literally the homefront. In an era when the costs of food, rent, and clothing were quickly climbing higher than many housewives could afford, Schneiderman knew that this sector of the working class was ripe for organization. Immigrant housewives on the Lower East Side had rioted numerous times between 1902 and 1917, boycotting butchers and bakers who would not bring their prices down, smashing store windows and pouring kerosene on the stock of any business owner who would not close to honor their boycotts. During the 1920s and 1930s, Schneiderman sought to organize housewives into permanent organizations that would parallel workers' trade unions and allow them to inject the larger concerns of home and neighborhood into the working-class movement.

In 1922, Schneiderman and Grace Klueg, wife of a Brooklyn Navy Yard worker and president of the Women's Auxiliary of the International Association of Machinists, established the Housewives Industrial League to organize wives of workers from a variety of trades. The two women hoped to build up existing women's union auxiliaries into a broad-based, militant movement. Supplementing their organizing drives by lobbying the government, Schneiderman and the leadership of the WTUL called for federal investigation into the status of non–wage-earning women—their labor conditions in the home, housing conditions, and health. Such an investigation, they believed, would also lay the groundwork for an organization of domestic workers. Domestic workers, then as now, were difficult to organize because they were scattered across every city and nearly impossible to protect legally because of the problem of enforcing labor laws in private homes. Schneiderman wanted the labor movement and the government to recognize the home as a workplace. It was a radical concept then as it is now.[24]

In June 1928, after six years of agitating and educating in communities across the country, Schneiderman and ILGWU Education Secretary Fania Cohn convened the First Women's Auxiliary Conference. Held at the garment workers' cooperatively owned resort, Unity House, it was attended by delegates from women's auxiliaries across the country. Their goal was to set priorities and plan strategies for an organized movement of working-class housewives, regionally based, but national in its scope. In her welcome to the delegates, Schneiderman stressed the need for community-based action. Lose your timidity, she chided. Stop clinging to ideas about women's inferiority. The mother's role in her children's education should not be restricted to the home. Mother's committees should demand a voice in shaping the curricula in public schools. Run for local school boards or make sure that pro-labor people get on them. Women have power as consumers, she told them. Exercise it. Set up cooperative buying arrangements to keep prices down. Set up cooperative child care so that mothers in the communities have the time to become active in community-based organizations. Learn to lobby for legislation that affects working-class women, Schneiderman told them. "It is time," she concluded, "the women's auxiliaries become something more than agencies for sick benefits, relief work and tea parties."[25]

They did. In the decade that followed the Unity House Conference, women's union auxiliaries responded to the challenges issued by Schneiderman, Cohn, and Klueg. The 1930s saw a radicalization of women's union auxiliaries across the United States, particularly in coal, steel, and automobile towns where one major employer's outright ownership or domination of local housing, banks, and food stores meant that women were directly oppressed by management, just as their husbands were. From the coal and steel towns of western Pennsylvania and southern Illinois to the automobile towns of northern Michigan, from New York City to Los Angeles, women's union auxiliaries aided working men and women's strikes, formed and guarded soup kitchens, walked picket lines, and fought with police. Participation in such activities broadened their political horizons; by the end of the decade they were demanding not only a just price for food but also education, child care, and a greater say in the running of their lives and their children's lives.

Following Schneiderman's advice, women's councils and auxiliaries also gathered information about food prices, utility rates, and school curricula in their neighborhoods and used that information both to build grass-roots organizations and to lobby for social legislation. They were so effective in gathering and disseminating information about the quality of life in their respective communities that, in 1941, when Franklin Roosevelt was facing pressure to cut social programs to appropriate money for the war effort, Eleanor Roosevelt called on the housewives' groups to provide information to the president and his advisers.[26] Eleanor Roosevelt was an old friend of the WTUL.

Twenty years earlier Eleanor Roosevelt's interest in women's politics had drawn her into a circle of women deeply committed to social welfare legislation. By 1921, Roosevelt had thrown herself into Women's Trade Union League work with all her characteristic passion. Rose Schneiderman became a regular guest at the scrambled-egg suppers that Roosevelt liked to cook for friends and, through her Roosevelt came into contact for the first time with the world of the immigrant working class. Both her friendship with Schneiderman and Roosevelt's interest in working-class women deepened quickly.[27]

Using her considerable influence with Democratic party leaders, including Governor Al Smith, Roosevelt did much to sensitize the Democratic party in New York State to the needs of women workers. As an important step in her own political career, Roosevelt became a lobbyist for the Joint Legislative Conference (JCL), a consortium of New York women's organizations founded by the WTUL to promote social legislation, including child-labor laws, minimum-wage and maximum-hour laws, unemployment insurance, and old-age pensions. By the mid-1920s Roosevelt had became one of the most effective and indefatigable lobbyists in the Joint Legislative Conference. Another of the JLC's most persuasive lobbyists was Rose Schneiderman. She and Roosevelt taught each other a great deal.

Schneiderman knew, from personal experience, that labor laws were far more than abstract policies defining government's relationship with workers. Women's and children's lives depended on them. Ever since 1911, when hazardous conditions had resulted in a fire at the Triangle Shirtwaist Factory that killed 146 young women, Schneiderman had been a passionate advocate of legislation regulating workplace conditions. Organization was a painfully slow process; legislation was comparatively easy and far more efficient. Over her quarter century as an organizer, Schneiderman was personally involved in organizing strikes that affected, at most, several hundred thousand women workers. The legislation that she lobbied for from 1917 to 1949 ultimately affected millions of female workers and established the model for fair labor legislation that would affect millions of male workers. Schneiderman's success as a lobbyist exhilarated her, and by the late 1920s, the former socialist had become a committed supporter of the Democratic party.

Schneiderman's attraction to the Democratic party had more than a little bit to do with her growing affection for Eleanor and Franklin Roosevelt. Rose Schneiderman's forty-year friendship with Eleanor Roosevelt, and her twenty-five-year friendship with Franklin, had a profound impact on her. It also deeply affected the Roosevelts. Although there was none of the intimacy between Schneiderman and FDR that she shared with Eleanor Roosevelt, FDR spent a good deal of time with Schneiderman, particularly during the 1920s.

Eleanor Roosevelt first invited Schneiderman and her companion Maud Swartz, the outgoing president of the Women's Trade Union League, to Campobello in 1925 and to Hyde Park in 1926. Franklin Roosevelt was so attracted by their forcefulness and clarity that they became frequent guests. The young, aristocratic politician would talk for hours with the two trade unionists. Frances Perkins, Franklin Roosevelt's secretary of labor, later commented that FDR's ideas about government's proper relationship to labor were crystallized and fleshed out during those conversations: "Relying on the knowledge he had gained from these girls," Perkins concluded, "he appeared to have a real understanding of the trade-union movement." The two unionists gave him a theoretical framework for the policies he later developed as governor and then as president.[28]

In 1933, President Roosevelt appointed Rose Schneiderman to the National Recovery Administration's Labor Advisory Board. The task of the board was to establish codes for each industry, setting minimum wages, maximum hours, and price controls for finished goods. Schneiderman was the only woman on the twelve-person board and as a result was expected to supervise all codes affecting female workers. To keep up with her new responsibilities Schneiderman took a leave of absence from the WTUL and temporarily relocated to Washington. There she was drawn into the New Deal women's political network headed by Eleanor Roosevelt and including Frances Perkins (secretary of labor), Mary Anderson (director of the Labor Department Women's Bureau), Molly Dewson (director of the Women's Division of the Democratic National Committee), and many others. It was an exciting time for Schneiderman: as she said, it was "the most exhilarating and inspiring of my life."

These women, many of whom had come to know, respect, and love each other over long years of struggling together in the suffrage movement and the movement for social legislation, now were in position to inject their ideas about government's social responsibilities into the New Deal. To participate in the shaping of a new state structure was a remarkable experience for all of them, but for none so much as for the immigrant whose formal schooling had ended when she was thirteen years old.[29]

In 1937 Rose Schneiderman was appointed secretary of labor for the state of New York. In Albany, as in Washington, Schneiderman's closest colleagues were also her closest friends. Longtime friend Nell Swartz (no relation to Maud) worked with Schneiderman on the state compensation board. Frieda Miller, the companion for many years of Schneiderman's closest friend Pauline Newman, served as director of the New York State Labor Department Women's Bureau and in 1941 became industrial commissioner for New York State. Newman herself represented the ILGWU and the WTUL on a great many of the investigative boards convened by the New York State Labor Department. Outsiders in an almost exclusively male political preserve, these four, along with National WTUL Secretary Elizabeth Christman, formed their own political network. They had regular dinners at Nell Swartz's house, held serious discussions about political strategy, and, when there was nothing more they could do, the five friends played poker.[30]

When American soldiers returned home at the end of the Second World War, Schneiderman resigned her post in the New York State Labor Department and turned her attention to the problem of how to preserve the gains female workers had made while working to support the war effort. As Schneiderman well knew, most women could not afford to leave the work force at the end of the war. Rather than shifting them back into unskilled industrial and low-paid clerical jobs, Schneiderman argued, the government should provide training programs that would allow women to maintain their newly won position as skilled laborers.

She and the WTUL also fought for a comparable-worth bill in New York State which they hoped would establish a model for other states. An equal-pay law was meaningless, she argued on the radio and in front of the New York State Factory Investigating Commission in 1947, because employers could simply continue arguing that the jobs they hired men to do were worth more than the jobs they hired women to do. There must, she insisted, be some objective criteria for establishing the worth of all jobs in a factory. Few American employers were ready for such an idea. Many have still not accepted it.[31]

In April 1949, at sixty-seven, Rose Schneiderman surprised everyone who knew her by announcing her retirement. Eleanor Roosevelt and the Women's Trade Union League hosted a testimonial luncheon attended by many of the leading lights of the American labor movement. Letters and telegrams poured in from around the country expressing a mixture of sadness at her departure from public life and pleasure that she would finally have time to rest. Over the next decade, Schneiderman continued to attend league meetings, appeared from time to time at union functions, made a few radio speeches, protested the activities of the House Committee on Un-American Activities, and worked on her memoirs.

As she faded into old age, so the organization that she had championed for fifty years also faded away. The National Women's Trade Union League closed its doors in 1950 and the New York WTUL voted to dissolve itself in 1955. The women who had run it and funded it since the first decade of the century were now all old, some had died, and few young women workers seemed to care about the league. The leadership of the newly united, predominantly male AFL-CIO had little interest in lending financial support to an organization they had long viewed as a nuisance. Male union leaders had never, Schneiderman noted, "realized how important it was to have an organization like the League to interpret trade unionism to women. . . ." Through the conservative 1950s and early 1960s it seemed as though much of Schneiderman's work might die with her.

But the 1960s saw a resurgence both of militant labor activism and of a nationwide women's movement. In 1969 a group of female trade unionists founded the Coalition of Labor Union Women (CLUW). The CLUW was in many ways the grandchild of the Women's Trade Union League. A generation had been skipped, but once again women in the labor movement were asserting their rights, and they paid homage to those who had come before them—Schneiderman, Newman, and others.

Though, in her old age, Schneiderman liked to portray herself as mild-mannered and nonthreatening, many of her ideas seemed radical even in the late 1980s. Long before the most recent wave of feminist activism began, Schneiderman was attacking sexual segregation in the workplace, trying to unionize not only industrial women but also white-collar and domestic workers, calling for state regulation not only of factory and office working conditions, but also of working conditions in the home. She organized housewives on a community basis to fight for fair rents and food prices, better housing and public education. She argued for comparable-worth laws, government-funded child care, and maternity insurance. And always, she reminded audiences that "the woman worker must have bread but she must have roses too." For more than half a century, Rose Schneiderman organized women to fight not just for economic independence, but also for the right to have meaning and beauty in their lives. She died in 1972, just as a new women's movement was growing in the United States. But many of her ideas and dreams were taken up by that movement and they are still being debated in classrooms, courtrooms, and congressional chambers today. Those ideas and dreams, as much as the government protections that most American workers now take for granted, are the legacy of Rose Schneiderman.

Notes

[1]For a fuller treatment of Rose Schneiderman's life see Annelise Orleck, "Common Sense and a Little Fire: Working Class Women's Activism in the Twentieth Century U.S." (Ph.D. diss., New York University, 1989). During the Red Scare of 1919–1920, New York State Senator Thaddeus Sweet was the first public official to call Schneiderman "Red Rose." The name stuck. In 1940, Schneiderman's lawyer Dorothy Kenyon mounted a libel suit against William Wirt who had called Schneiderman "The Red Rose of Anarchy" in print; see Dorothy Kenyon to RS, 6 March, 1940. The testimony of the police officer is recounted in Margaret Dreier Robins to RS, 14 June, 1943; Schneiderman's suffrage speaking tour in M. Sherwood to Harriet Taylor Upton, 15 July, 1912; Rose Schneiderman Papers, Reel 3082, Tamiment Library, New York City.

[2]*New York Times*, 14 August, 1972.

[3]Pauline Newman interviewed by Barbara Wertheimer, November 1976, Pauline Newman Papers, Schlesinger Library, Cambridge, MA.

[4]Rose Schneiderman to Pauline Newman, 11 August 1917; Pauline Newman Papers, Box 1.

[5]Rose Schneiderman with Lucy Goldthwaite, *All for One* (New York: Paul S. Eriksson, 1967), pp. 10–22.

[6]Schneiderman, *All for One*, pp. 11–15.

[7]Schneiderman, *All for One*, p. 29.

[8]Schneiderman, *All for One*, pp. 35–47.

[9]Schneiderman, *All for One*, p. 48.

[10]Schneiderman, *All for One*, p. 77; Minutes of the New York WTUL Executive Board, 24 February and 24 March, 1905, Reel 3044, Tamiment Library, NYC.

[11]Minutes of the New York WTUL Executive Board, 24 February, 24 March, 5 May, 25 August, 24 September, 26 October 1905; 25 January, February, 29 March, 26 April, 28 June, 1 August, 12 September, 22 November, 20 December, 1906; 28 February, 24 April, 27 June, 25 July, 22 August, 26 September, 26 November, 1907; 28 January, 1908; NYWTUL Papers; Schneiderman, *All for One*, p. 83.

[12]See letters among Schneiderman, Newman, and O'Reilly in the Leonora O'Reilly Papers, Reels 3075–76, Tamiment Library, New York City, and the Rose Schneiderman Papers Reel 3082 and File 18A; and the Pauline M. Newman Papers, Box 1.

[13]Minutes of the Executive Board NYWTUL, 24 February 1905–1 February 1909, NYWTUL Papers.

[14]Schneiderman, *All for One*, p. 84.

[15]Schneiderman, *All for One*, p. 86.

[16]Schneiderman, *All for One*, pp. 84–88; Minutes of the New York WTUL Executive Board, 21 May, 1 June, 25 August, 27 October, 1908; 24 August, 15 September 1909. NYWTUL Papers.

[17]Minutes of the NYWTUL Executive Board, Secretary's Report, 15 February, 27 April 1911. NYWTUL Papers; PMN to RS, n.d., Rose Schneiderman Papers.

[18]Schneiderman, *All for One*, pp. 110–117; RS to Benjamin Schlesinger 6 February 1916; RS to Abe Baroff 1 December 1916, Schneiderman Papers; RS to PMN 6 February 1916; RS to PMN 6 August 1917, Newman Papers.

[19]See Ellen Carol Dubois, "Working Women, Class Relations and Suffrage Militance: Harriot Stanton Blatch and the New York Woman Suffrage Movement, 1894–1909," *Journal Of American History* (June 1987); also "Miss Rose Schneiderman, Gifted Young Lecturer," Leaflet of the American Suffragettes, n.d. Rose Schneiderman Papers; see also Papers of the Wage Earner's League for Woman Suffrage in the Leonora O'Reilly Papers, Reel 3080.

[20]"Senators vs. Working Women," handbill for the April 22 meeting, and *Senators Vs. Working Women*, pamphlet, both by the Wage Earner's League for Woman Suffrage, included in the O'Reilly Papers.

[21]Rose Schneiderman. "WTUL Legislative Efforts," typescript for a radio speech, June 1955, Schneiderman Papers, Reel 3083; see also Nancy Cott, *The Grounding of Modern Feminism* (New Haven: Yale University Press, 1988), p. 105.

[22]*New York Times*, 31 May 1920; RS to Margaret Dreier Robins, 10 March 1919, Schneiderman Papers; Schneiderman, *All for One*, pp. 146–148; Cott, *The Grounding of Modern Feminism*, p. 65.

[23] Annual Reports of the New York Women's Trade Union League, 1922–1955, Papers of the WTUL, Reels 3045–3048, Tamiment Library. See also Alice Kessler-Harris "Problems of Coalition Building: Women and Trade Unions in the 1920's," in Ruth Milkman, ed., *Women, Work and Protest* (London: Routledge, Kegan & Paul, 1985); Schneiderman, *All for One*, pp. 157–163.

[24]Proceedings of the Ninth Biennial NWTUL Conference, held in New York, 1924.

[25]Summary of Speeches, Women's Auxiliary Conference Unity House, Forest Park, PA, 30 June–1 July, 1928, Mary Van Kleeck Papers, Sophia Smith Collection, Northampton, MA.

[26]*New York Times*, 26 October 1941.

[27]See Joseph P. Lash, *Eleanor and Franklin* (New York: Signet, 1971); Schneiderman, *All for One*, pp. 150–153, 156–157, 175–184; *New York Times*, 3 June, 8 June 1929.

[28]Swartz, who worked briefly as a proofreader, was a member of the typographical union, but, although she came from a family of modest means in Ireland, she had some extremely wealthy relatives in the United States. This distinguished her from Schneiderman, who had absolutely no money in her family. See Frances Perkins, *The Roosevelt I Knew* (New York: Vintage Press, 1946), pp. 32–33. See also Lash, *Eleanor and Franklin*, p. 380; Schneiderman, *All for One*, pp. 177–180 (both cite Perkins). After FDR became governor of New York in 1928 he kept up a steady if sketchy correspondence with Schneiderman. He appointed her to represent the state in the International Association of Public Employment Services, and to serve on committees dealing with prison labor and workers' compensation. FDR to RS, 11 January, 17 September 1929; 12 May, 2 August 1930; 12 October, 1932; RS to FDR, 16 March, 18 November, 1932; Schneiderman Papers.

[29]*New York Times* 20 June 1933; Rose Schneiderman Papers, Reel 3083, Part I, Frames 450–661 and Part II, Frames 221–232; Susan Ware, *Beyond Suffrage: Women and the New Deal* (Cambridge, MA: Harvard University Press, 1981).

[30]Interview with Elizabeth Berger, 15 December 1987. (Berger was adopted as an infant by Frieda Miller and raised by Miller and Newman); Schneiderman, *All for One*, pp. 121–130.

[31]New York WTUL Annual Reports 1930–1950, Reels 3046–3048, Tamiment Library, New York City; Radio Speech, "Women's Role in Labor Legislation," 1955, Rose Schneiderman Papers, Reel 3083; *New York Times*, 16 March, 20 September 1936; 4 March, 14 March, 12 April, 13 May, 20 May 1937; 8 January 1939; 28 October 1943; 28 January 1945.

Crystal Eastman

(1881–1928)

Blanche Wiesen Cook

Crystal Eastman was born on June 25, 1881, in Marlborough, Massachusetts. She graduated with a B.A. from Vassar in 1903, an M.A. in sociology from Columbia in 1904, and, in 1907, an LL.B. from New York University Law School. She was appointed member and secretary of the New York State Employer's Liability Commission from 1909 to 1911. In 1910 she published Work Accidents and the Law, *a book that contributed to the passage of worker-safety laws. In 1914 she helped found the Congressional Union, along with Alice Paul and Lucy Burns. She was chairperson of the New York branch of the Woman's Peace Party and on the executive committee of the American Union Against Militarism (AUAM), organizations formed to protest the United States' entrance into World War I. In 1917, Eastman was a founder of the Civil Liberties Bureau, a committee of the AUAM established to defend conscientious objectors to the draft. In March 1918, she began coediting the socialist publication* The Liberator *with her brother Max, a position she held until 1922. Throughout her life she wrote on a wide range of feminist and socialist issues. In 1916 she divorced her first husband and married English pacifist Walter Fuller, with whom Crystal Eastman had two children, Jeffrey and Annis. In England with her husband for most of the years 1921–1927, she wrote regularly for* Time and Tide, *a radical feminist journal. She returned to the United States in 1927 where she died on July 8, 1928.*

For full citations to this essay, readers should consult the introduction to *Crystal Eastman on Women and Revolution* by Blanche Wiesen Cook (New York: Oxford University Press, 1978) from which this essay is adapted.

To lean on and be protected by a man, Crystal Eastman wrote, is not the same as standing on your own two feet. Patriarchal protection of workers is not the same as workers' control. Equal rights for all; work for all; peace and justice and equal opportunity; the end to privilege as well as poverty—those are very radical demands. They were Crystal Eastman's demands, and it is no accident that her work has for so long remained unknown—along with her joy in life and enthusiasm for people. The neglect and disappearance of Crystal Eastman's work is partly explained by the fact that history tends to bury what it seeks to reject. There was little room for the writings of a militant feminist who was also a socialist in the annals of America as it went from Red Scare to Depression to Cold War and back again.

Surely, Crystal Eastman would not have been so lost to history if she had been more conventional. It is perhaps more comfortable to picture a woman of her views tragic in exile, rather than undaunted at the speaker's platform in Rome, Budapest, Paris, London. It would have been simpler if she had not also socialized with Charlie Chaplin, titled nobility, black intellectuals, and government officials; and when she partied with women she dressed entirely for herself and their company with a flamboyance for which she become noted. For women to dress for themselves and each other was really unfathomable. How was history to appraise the militant feminist wing of the international "smart set"? How could history appraise the life of a tough woman lawyer who was not only a feminist, but a mother and socialist?

There was nothing simple about her work, her political vision, or the nature of her personal relationships. Her vision demanded radical, profound, and absolute changes. Crystal Eastman's ideas were heretical and dangerous. Her life by its very example embodied a threat to customary order. "Freedom is a large word," she wrote in 1920. It demanded a large struggle, a long battle. She committed the entire range and intensity of her energy and spirit to that struggle.

Crystal Eastman loved life and was generally surrounded by friends. Protected and fortified by the support of women and men who shared her ideals and battled beside her, she was free and bold. Her close friend Jeannette Lowe said that "you wouldn't believe her freedom—she was entirely free, open, full of joy in life." Her brother Max wrote that "she poured magnetic streams of generous love around her all the time" and boldly plunged into new experiences. Roger Baldwin, who worked closely with her during World War I in the American Union Against Militarism and the Civil Liberties Bureau which they jointly created, remembered Crystal as "a natural leader: outspoken (often tactless), determined, charming, beautiful, courageous. . . ." She spoke in a deep and musical voice and could be entirely captivating as she dashed about the country on behalf of suffrage or peace or to organize against an injustice. Her sincerity was absolute and she frequently grew red with anger. She was impulsive and passionate and once consulted Dr. A. A. Brill, the first Freudian psychoanalyst to practice in America, to bring her intense "libido down."

Crystal Eastman was a woman-identified woman. She neither sought male approval for her activities nor courted male protection. While she delighted in the company of women, she enjoyed male alliances whenever she found them genuine. She worked with and loved easily many women and men who were her friends and comrades. She was also determined. Hazel Hunkins Hallinan, the suffragist organizer who knew Crystal best when she lived in England, recalled that she was "very realistic but not very docile. We used to call her a 'tigress' because she was so vital and aggressive."

Crystal Eastman spent most of her childhood in Glenora, a small town on the shore of Seneca Lake in New York. The daughter of suffragist parents, both of whom were ordained Congregational ministers, she claimed feminism as her birthright. Toward the end of her life Crystal wrote that "the story of my background is the story of my mother." Her mother, Annis Ford Eastman, was "the most noted minister of her time," an inspiring orator who found new ideas from Santayana to Freud "dangerously fascinating." She encouraged Crystal and her two brothers, Max and Anstice, always to be independent in thought and vigorous in action. (A third brother, the oldest son, Morgan, died of scarlet fever in 1884. Crystal had scarlet fever at the same time and it marked her health throughout her life.)

When Crystal was fifteen, her mother organized a summer symposium at which Crystal read a paper called "Woman." She dedicated the rest of her life to the fulfillment of the theme of that paper: Women "must have work of their own . . . because the only way to be happy is to have an absorbing interest in life which is not bound up with any particular person. No woman who allows husband and children to absorb her whole time and interest is safe against disaster."

Although Crystal Eastman hated the traditional institutionalization of marriage and "homemaking," she believed that most women shared "the normal desire to be mothers." An early advocate of birth control, she wrote in 1918: "Feminists are not nuns. That should be established." Although she ultimately married twice, she did not marry until she was almost thirty. Both she and her brother Max remained single until after their mother's death. And all their friends apparently believed that Crystal and Max really loved each other above all. In his autobiography, *Love and Revolution,* Max wrote: "As a boy . . . I used to announce that I would never marry any girl but my sister."

During her junior year at Vassar in 1902 Crystal wrote in her journal that men were typically "clever, powerful, selfish and animal"—except for her brother Max. Should she ever marry a man he would have to have Max's qualities: "I don't believe there is a feeling in the world too refined and imagined for him to appreciate." Crystal thought her brother might not like it, but it was "the highest compliment you can pay a man to say that he has the fineness of feeling and sympathy of a woman. . . . All mothers ought to cultivate it in their boys."

Many of Crystal's later writings reflect her high sense of gender injustice—bolstered not only by public law but everywhere propped up by cultural attitudes. Throughout her life, homemaking—the notion that women's mission was to provide a comfortable home for men who shared no similar responsibility—symbolized women's servility, women's bondage. To end that bondage, women as well as men needed to be educated and involved with their own life's work; and both women and men needed to function efficiently in the home.

On the other hand, Crystal Eastman insisted, women who wanted to work at home—or needed to work at home—should be paid for their labor. What is today referred to as "wages for housework" she called a "Motherhood Endowment." In "Now We Can Begin," she wrote that the only way for women "at least in a capitalist society" to achieve "real economic independence" was for the political government to recognize and subsidize housework as skilled labor.

From 1903 to 1911 Crystal Eastman lived among people who shared her views. A settlement house worker while studying for her M.A. in sociology at Columbia (1904) and for a law degree at New York University (1907), she lived in and became a leading member of the new feminist and radical community just then emerging in Greenwich Village. She lived with suffragists who were her close friends from Vassar or law school, notably Madeleine Doty, Inez Milholland, and Ida Rauh. Eventually Ida Rauh married Eastman's brother Max.

Comfortable in many worlds, Crystal Eastman moved with ease among artists, social workers, poets, anarchists, socialists, and progressive reformers. It was a time of experiment and change, and she was committed to both. Appalled by poverty and its senseless waste, she was a socialist by nature and conviction. Her concern for the poor, nurtured by her mother from childhood, and her anguish over brutal economic conditions intensified during this period.

In 1907 Crystal graduated from law school; she was second in her class and had a particular interest in labor law. When her good friend Paul U. Kellogg, then editor of the social-work magazine *Charities and the Commons*, organized the celebrated *Pittsburgh Survey* for the Russell Sage Foundation, an institution that supports social service research, he invited Crystal to join the staff. She remained in Pittsburgh for over a year to complete the first in-depth sociological investigation of industrial accidents ever made. This work catapulted her to prominence, and in June 1909 Governor Charles Evans Hughes appointed her New York's first woman commissioner, the only woman among fourteen members of the Employer's Liability Commission. As secretary of that prestigious commission, she drafted New York State's first workers' compensation law, which was soon used as a model by many other states.

She believed that industrial accidents happen almost inevitably because of organized neglect of workers' safety. Her goal was to shift the burden of guilt or blame from victim to industry and its management and to adopt, as almost every "civilized country except the United States" already had, the principle of workers' compensation. Industry's refusal to secure the safety and health of its workers remains today a primary labor issue. Unfortunately, corporations now often prefer to pay insurance fees rather than make the necessary capital investments to secure safe working conditions. But in 1910 when the loss of a leg or an eye or a life generally resulted in no compensation to the worker or the worker's family, Crystal Eastman's book *Work Accidents and the Law* resulted in a major progressive reform, although she herself considered the new legislation a minimal compromise.

The contribution Crystal Eastman made to labor law and industrial safety was internationally acclaimed. Moreover, her work in Pittsburgh and New York, and later Washington, confirmed her radical vision and clarified her understanding of economics. She began to identify herself as a socialist. In 1911 she wrote "Three Essentials for Accident Prevention," in which she referred to the Triangle Shirtwaist Company fire, in which 140 women locked into the room that was their "sweatshop" perished. When healthy women and men die because of preventable disasters, she wrote, we do not want to hear about "relief funds." "What we want is to start a revolution." Nothing short of revolution would finally end "this unnecessary killing and injuring of workers in the course of industry." Revolutionary change began, she wrote, by collecting the information necessary to prevent economic disaster and human suffering.

Suffrage was for Crystal Eastman a primary enthusiasm, and she expected the men in her life to be suffragists. She introduced her brother Max to political and social issues and, in 1909, encouraged him to organize the Men's League for Woman Suffrage. But the vote represented only a part of the power denied to women that Crystal Eastman believed women needed to reclaim.

Tall, almost six feet tall, athletic and robust herself, Crystal Eastman sought to extend the contours of women's strength and women's sphere far beyond suffrage. With Annette Kellerman, a champion swimmer and diver from Australia who was then in New York to entertain Broadway audiences with her aquatic skills, she attempted to work out a program for the physical "regeneration of the female sex."

To promote her vision of women's power, Crystal Eastman spoke before large audiences on "women's right to physical equality with men." Journalist Freda Kirchwey recalled that Eastman pictured a utopia of athletes, with women "unhampered by preconceived ideas of what was fit or proper or possible for their sex to achieve." Eastman believed that "when women were expected to be agile, they became agile; when they were expected to be brave, they developed courage; when they had to endure, their endurance broke all records." According to Kirchwey, who was at this time still a student at Barnard, as Crystal Eastman "stood there, herself an embodiment of tall, easy strength and valor, her words took on amazing life. . . ."

From adolescence onward Crystal Eastman was aware that fashion served to confine and limit women's ability to move freely. In matters of style, from short hair and short skirts to her insistence on wearing bathing suits without the customary stockings and skirt, her guiding principle was the achievement of greater and easier activity. Freedom involved discarding antique and unnecessary encumbrances. She never rode sidesaddle, and careened about her hometown "on a man's saddle in fluttering vast brown bloomers" that shocked polite Glenora society. When her neighbors complained to her father about her swimming clothes, she received her family's support. Although her father never said a word to her, she believed that he was "startled and embarrassed to see his only daughter in a man's bathing suit with bare brown legs for all the world to see. I think it shocked him to his dying day." But "he would not want to swim in a skirt and stockings. Why then should I?"

In 1911, shortly after her mother died, Crystal Eastman married a ruggedly handsome insurance salesman named Wallace Benedict ("Bennie"). Although she made it clear to her friends and family, including Max, that she was physically and romantically excited by Bennie, they remained puzzled by her decision actually to marry him. Nevertheless, Bennie believed in and supported her work, and according to Max, he was full of "admiring passion." But the marriage was burdened by the need to move to Bennie's home in Milwaukee, which for Eastman resulted in periods of deep melancholy. Within two years she returned to New York, and in 1916 married Walter Fuller. Crystal Eastman's time in Milwaukee was devoted largely to the suffrage campaign.

In 1911, Wisconsin was the only large industrial state east of the Mississippi where a suffrage referendum was pending. The entire suffrage movement focused on Wisconsin, and Crystal Eastman served as the campaign manager and chaired the Political Equality League, which directed all activities in and out of the state. When it was over, she attributed the suffrage defeat in Wisconsin to the dominating power of the brewery industry and its ability to pressure a variety of dependent industries: "There are whole cities of 20,000 . . . where not a single businessman dares to let his wife come out for suffrage . . . because practically every man's business is dependent . . . on the good will of the big breweries. . . ." The big corporations, she explained, generally "put their business . . . ahead of democracy, justice, simple human right."

In 1913, as a delegate to the Seventh Congress of the International Woman Suffrage Alliance at Budapest, Eastman met with the women who were soon to become the leaders of the movement for international peace: Hungary's Rosika Schwimmer, Holland's first woman physician, Dr. Aletta Jacobs, and English suffragist Emmeline Pethick-Lawrence. As soon as the European war was declared Crystal Eastman limited or suspended all other concerns to organize American sentiment against the war, against America's participation in the war, and against militarism generally. She feared that if the United States entered the European war all recently achieved reforms, such as her own efforts to improve and enforce industrial health and safety standards, would be ended. She regarded the European war as a war of colonial ambition and believed that because all wars were organized for efficient international murder, they inevitably threatened to destroy those interests that most concerned people: labor legislation, public health care, decent housing, the movement for new parks and playgrounds, and all democratic institutions or, as she wrote, "such beginnings of democracy as we have in America."

The international woman's movement, already organized on behalf of suffrage and allied with the major movements for economic and social change, seemed to Crystal Eastman to be ideally suited to become the major force behind a new, bold, and vigorous international peace movement.

In November 1914, Crystal Eastman called together the first meeting of the Woman's Peace Party (WPP) of New York City and invited

Emmeline Pethick-Lawrence to speak. A militant suffragist who had been imprisoned in Holloway gaol and brutally force-fed, Pethick-Lawrence maintained that there was "no life worth living, but a fighting life." It was time, she said, for the peace movement to learn from the women's movement. The established peace societies were "passive and negative," and it was time for women to be angry, "active and militant." Active and militant throughout the war, the Woman's Peace Party of New York, over which Crystal Eastman presided until 1919, differed dramatically in method and style from two other organizations she helped to create: the national Woman's Peace Party and the American Union Against Militarism.

To mobilize women for peace throughout the United States, Eastman persuaded Emmeline Pethick-Lawrence to go to Chicago and meet with Jane Addams. As a result, Jane Addams called a national conference of women's organizations in Chicago in January 1915 to found the national Woman's Peace Party, today called the Women's International League for Peace and Freedom. Also in 1914, Eastman met with Lillian Wald, the director of the Nurse's Settlement and the Visiting Home Nurse Service, Paul Kellogg, Rabbi Stephen Wise, Oswald Garrison Villard, the publisher of the *Nation,* Jane Addams, and others at Wald's Henry Street Settlement in New York to organize what was originally called the Anti-Preparedness Committee. Lillian Wald became the president of this organization, soon to be renamed the American Union Against Militarism (AUAM), and Crystal Eastman its executive director. The AUAM published antimilitarist analyses, lobbied in Washington against preparedness and conscription, and campaigned against U.S. imperialism in Latin America and the Caribbean.

The social reformers within the union believed that their testimony before congressional committees and their private meetings with President Wilson and his advisers (many of whom were personal friends or at least professional associates) were sufficient to make a difference in the forming of public policy. Their Washington lobbyist, Charles T. Hallinan, was well known and highly regarded. In the beginning their activities were analytic, educational, discreet, supportive of what they believed was the president's real desire: to keep the United States neutral. Crystal Eastman's ability as an administrator, the clarity of purpose she maintained during moments of high tension, enabled her not only to function effectively as the executive officer of the AUAM, but to persuade Lillian Wald and Paul Kellogg of the need to broaden the committee's vision and purpose, to expand and intensify its range of activities.

In November 1915 she launched a dramatic "Truth About Preparedness Campaign." Supported by both the AUAM and the Woman's

Peace Part of New York, the campaign emphasized that economic profiteering was behind the industrialists' propaganda for military increases. Crystal Eastman identified the economic interests of the members of such pro-war organizations as the Army League and the Navy League and called for a public investigation of America's defenses "to root out the graft and inefficiency" and to insist on the nationalization of the defense industries.

To counter Theodore Roosevelt's claim that the United States had "a puny little egg-shell of a navy," the AUAM's literature revealed the size and scope of the world's third largest fleet. When the AUAM's lobby failed and Wilson adopted a preparedness package that included a force of 400,000 trained "citizen soldiers," the antipreparedness activities intensified. The "Truth About Preparedness Campaign" held mass meetings in the largest halls of countless cities. AUAM speakers addressed thousands of people and "won hundreds of columns of publicity from an unwilling press." The AUAM grew from "a small emergency committee of fifteen members to an organization of 6,000 members with local committees in 22 cities. It conducted a national press bureau which served 1,601 papers—including labor and farm weeklies and regular dailies."

Under the auspices of the less restrained Woman's Peace Party of New York, Eastman organized public debates and forums between businessmen associated with the Navy League and antimilitarists. The leadership of New York's WPP was comprised largely of Eastman's closest friends—suffragists, socialists, militant feminists. Although there were many differences among them in age, affluence, and position, to the press and the general public they seemed all to wear bobbed hair, believe in "free love," and belong to New York's "Bohemia." The WPP of New York was dominated by women like Margaret Lane, Anne Herendeen, Freda Kirchwey, Katherine Anthony, Madeleine Doty, Marie Jennie Howe, Agnes Brown Leach. They were members of Heterodoxy, an extraordinary luncheon club that met on Saturday afternoons for over twenty years to discuss women, literature, and politics. They stood on street corners and handed out birth-control literature. They helped organize strike committees and were occasionally arrested. They were rude to authority and careless about adverse publicity. Booing and hissing the business advocates of preparedness became a regular feature of their public meetings. When their meetings were broken up by violent patriots, frequently in uniform, the WPP was criticized in the press despite the fact that the women were the victims of the violence. Such publicity created additional difficulties for Eastman in her work with the AUAM leadership.

But Crystal Eastman believed that the activities of both organizations were necessary for success. She was convinced that lobbying by respectable and influential progressive Americans such as Lillian Wald, Paul Kellogg, Amos Pinchot, and Jane Addams had not yet been rendered meaningless. She remained optimistic that democratic control of foreign policy might still play a role in presidential policies. Aware that the private lobbying of the AUAM without sustained public protest and as much publicity as possible would be futile, she supported entirely the more radical efforts of the WPP of New York. In addition, she believed that the international nature of the woman's peace movement was "unique and priceless" and urged women to "stand by it and strengthen it no matter what other peace organizations we may identify ourselves with."

Lillian Wald and Jane Addams shared Crystal Eastman's convictions and agreed with many of her political analyses. Their disagreements involved issues of emphasis, style. While Lillian Wald remained on the executive board of the New York party and Jane Addams maintained cordial relations with Crystal Eastman, the social reformers were unwilling to engage in certain kinds of public protest and opposed Eastman's more confrontational tactics.

Tensions over Crystal Eastman's flamboyant political methods and unconventional life persisted throughout the war. One example was a popular "War Against War" exhibit which drew crowds of five to ten thousand New Yorkers a day for several months. British pacifist Walter Fuller helped the WPP of New York erect this graphic exhibit, which featured a huge metallic dragon representing the war machine of Wall Street, vivid cartoons, colorful posters, and a series of militant speakers. The exhibit was costly and well publicized, and its spirited sense of protest became a major focus of contention.

Also at this, time Eastman divorced Bennie and married Walter Fuller, with whom she had been living. While such living arrangements would rarely be considered objectionable today, Eastman's private activities gave rise to additional criticism from her associates. Her good friends, however, delighted in her new happiness. Roger Baldwin recalled that Walter Fuller was "extremely witty and totally pacifist and worked hard to make Crystal laugh—and, you know, Crystal loved to laugh."

Others were not at all amused by his wit, especially as represented in the "War Against War" exhibit. Mabel Hyde Kittredge, a patron of causes associated with the Henry Street Settlement and later president of the national Woman's Peace Party, resigned in protest over the tone of the exhibit. She complained that the New York branch "made fun" of the munitions-makers and "ridiculed" certain American interests. Others complained that "the sentiments expressed" at the New York meetings were "very extreme and dangerous."

Crystal Eastman's conviction that public activity and private lobbying could have a real impact on presidential policy was bolstered by the union's success regarding Mexico in the summer of 1916. A massive publicity campaign to avert war in Mexico resulted in an "unofficial commission" of three Mexican and three U.S. antimilitarists that met through June and July at El Paso. Organized by Eastman, this effort at private mediation was supported by the American Federation of Labor, whose officials met with officials of sixty Mexican labor unions in "the most effective effort ever made by the workers of two countries to avoid war." On July 6, 1916, Crystal Eastman and her associates held a press conference in Washington with three Mexican delegates and issued a press release which compared the Mexican Revolution to the French Revolution and analyzed the issues which jeopardized Mexican-American relations, notably the fact that 75 percent of Mexico's national wealth was controlled by foreign capital, mostly North American. The AUAM feared that United States policy in Mexico would impose a "suzerainty from the Rio Grande to Panama," creating "a suspicious and embittered South America."

Crystal Eastman criticized the United States' entire Latin American policy, beginning with the Monroe Doctrine. Why not, she asked, substitute a truly "democratic union of American republics," so that the United States may "rid itself of the temptation to establish profitable protectorates" where anti-American attitudes were "growing and perhaps warranted."

Wilson's response to the union's activity was to appoint a Joint High Commission on Mexico to mediate differences, and war was averted. In "Suggestions to the AUAM for 1916–1917," Eastman wrote that "we must make the most of our Mexican experience. We must make it known to everybody that people acting directly—not through their governments or diplomats or armies—stopped that war, and can stop all wars if enough of them will act together and act quickly."

But 1916 was an election year, and the victory for peace in Mexico was the final victory for the antimilitarists. The AUAM campaigned for Wilson despite the fact that Justice Charles Evans Hughes, the Republican candidate, had been a progressive governor and had worked closely with Crystal Eastman, whom he had appointed to her post as commissioner, and with Lillian Wald—who had faith in his profound interest in protecting the "ordinary people." But Republican Hughes did not promise peace. He promised suffrage. Most of Crystal Eastman's closest friends in the radical suffrage movement supported Hughes, and campaigned vigorously against Wilson, who refused to endorse the suffrage amendment.

The year 1916 was a tense and bitter time for the suffragist women who led the United States peace forces. It foreshadowed the dilemma feminists faced over the Equal Rights Amendment during the 1920s. While there was no correct position, there were priorities. In 1916 suffragists against the war had to vote for one or the other: Hughes, who seemed to promise suffrage with war, or Wilson, who promised peace without suffrage.

Several months before the election, in June 1916, Crystal Eastman gave a rousing and enthusiastic speech at the "Suffrage First" luncheon of Alice Paul's National Woman's Party convention. Nevertheless, all the AUAM's election efforts endorsed Wilson. From the beginning one of the members of the executive committee of the Congressional Union (reorganized in 1916 as the National Woman's Party), Eastman now seemed to support the candidate some of her closest comrades—Doris Stevens, Alice Paul, Lavinia Dock, Inez Milholland—were picketing and jeering. It seemed incomprehensible.

One of Inez Milholland's last speeches before her sudden death during a lecture tour through the western states seemed specifically aimed at her friend Crystal Eastman: "Do not let anyone convince you that there is any more important issue in the country today than votes for women. . . . There are people who honestly believe—HONESTLY BELIEVE! . . . that there are more important issues before the country than suffrage. . . . Now I do not know what you feel about such a point of view . . . but it makes me mad. . . . We must say, 'Women First.' "

Personal divisions and anguish among the suffragists aroused by the election evaporated quickly, however. In December 1916 Crystal Eastman and Jane Addams testified on behalf of the national Woman's Peace Party before the House Judiciary Committee to endorse the federal amendment for women's suffrage. Moreover, Paul's National Woman's Party opposed the war with consistent vigor; and when it became clear that Wilson had betrayed the antimilitarists, the pages of the *Suffragist,* the official paper of the National Women's Party, rallied to their support.

Contradictions in political life are commonplace. In this case the intensity of profound friendships transcended them. And Inez Milholland's sudden death transcended the election of 1916. Eastman arranged the largest and last memorial service for the beloved Amazon who had given her life to the suffrage movement. The *Suffragist* reported that Crystal Eastman "expressed the feeling of all these personal friends when she said, 'Here we are today, the representatives of so many great movements—and we all claim Inez Milholland. This is very wonderful to me; it simply means that her whole aspiration was for fuller liberty.' "

On behalf of her own aspiration for liberty, Crystal Eastman worked sixteen to twenty hours a day in the months prior to the declaration of war in April 1917. With only a few weeks off following the birth of her first child, Jeffrey Fuller, Eastman campaigned tirelessly. In "War and Peace" she wrote that the radical peace movement had three major emphases: to stop the war in Europe, to organize the world for peace at the close of the war, and to defend democracy against the subtle dangers of militarism. Stimulated "by the self-interest of capitalists, imperialists, and war traders, but supported by . . . thousands who call themselves democrats," the people needed to be demystified about alleged benefits of military conscription and service. "We must make this great democracy know," she wrote, "that military training is bad for the bodies and minds and souls of boys; that free minds, and souls undrilled to obedience are vital to the life of democracy."

As the United States hurtled toward war, Crystal Eastman's continued commitment to civil liberties in wartime and her support for *Four Lights,* the newsletter of New York's WPP, created additional tensions within the AUAM leadership. First issued on January 27, 1917, *Four Lights* became the subject of the first serious antagonism between Eastman and Jane Addams (in her capacity as president of the national WPP) and Lillian Wald. Modeled on the *Masses* (a radical magazine edited by Max Eastman) in format and style, *Four Lights* was gay, impulsive, and entirely disrespectful of authority. Although each issue was independently edited, Crystal Eastman was directly responsible for its tone, and it was the official paper of the organization over which she presided. There was little doubt in the minds of WPP conservatives that Crystal Eastman was no longer a sound ally.

Four Lights gave them little choice. It devoted an entire issue, "The Sister Susie Number" to criticizing such women as Lucia Ames Mead, chair of the WPP's Boston branch, which abandoned its former position to assist in war relief work. Some WPP branches, complained the editors of *Four Lights,* spent the entire war knitting socks. Even Jane Addams and Lillian Wald, opposed to conscription in principle, administered registration programs in their settlement houses. In addition, Lillian Wald chaired the Council of National Defense's Committee on Public Health and Child Welfare, while Jane Addams volunteered to work for Herbert Hoover's Food Administration. As far as *Four Lights* was concerned Hoover had revealed "the cloven hoof of the military dictator," and without mentioning Addams by name, it editorialized that "Hoover Helpers" were those women "who accept their position beside the garbage cans as they have always accepted what God and man has put upon them to endure. . . ."

In its first editorial *Four Lights* promised to be "the voice of the young, uncompromising peace movement in America, whose aims are daring and immediate." Above all, *Four Lights* opposed the mounting tyranny and wartime violence that quickly followed the United States' declaration of war. Within three months after the United States entered the war *Four Lights* editorialized against one of the greatest wartime outrages, the race riot in East St. Louis in which scores of black people were beaten, lynched, burned, and drowned:

> Six weeks have passed since the East St. Louis riots and no public word of rebuke, no demand for the punishment of the offenders, has come from our Chief Executive. These American Negroes have died under more horrible conditions than any noncombatants who were sunk by German submarines. But to our President their death does not merit consideration.
>
> Our young men who don their khaki are thus taught that, as they go out to battle under the flag of the United States, they may outdo Belgian atrocities without rebuke if their enemy be of a darker race. And those who guard our land at home have learned that black men and women and little children may safely be mutilated and shot and burned while they stand idly by.

Moreover, *Four Lights* announced on March 24, 1917, in a dramatic banner headline that it hailed "the Russian Revolution with mad glad joy." It pledged itself to the cause of international democracy and claimed that all nations "must be democratized before a federated world can be achieved." It accused the United States of "busily forging weapons to menace the spirit of freedom struggling to life in an exhausted Europe."

Lillian Wald, Paul Kellogg, Oswald Garrison Villard, Jane Addams, and the other social reformers on the board of the AUAM did not disagree theoretically with Crystal Eastman's position. They endorsed her June 15, 1917, press release that announced that once the United States entered the war the AUAM sought victory "in harmony with the principles outlined by the Revolutionary government of Russia, namely, No forcible annexations, No punitive indemnities, Free development of Nationalities." They disapproved, however, of her forthright public style and the order of her priorities. They particularly disapproved of the AUAM's new committee, the Civil Liberties Bureau, founded by Crystal Eastman, Roger Baldwin, and Norman Thomas.

Wald and Kellogg, for example, did not want to be identified with an "anti-war agitation." They sought to influence the future peace negotiations in the interests of international democracy and federation after the war. Crystal Eastman insisted that the Civil Liberties Bureau represented a "democracy first" movement.

Lillan Wald wrote Crystal Eastman on August 28, 1917, that the AUAM had been accepted by the public as "a group of reflective liberals." It was dignified and respectable. Eastman's enthusiasm for organizations like the Civil Liberties Bureau and the newly organized People's Council represented "impulsive radicalism." Wald wrote that Crystal Eastman's new activities demanded either her resignation or Wald's. It "would be lacking in sincerity for us not to be perfectly frank with each other."

For Eastman, Baldwin, and Thomas the Civil Liberties Bureau was the inevitable development of all their convictions. On July 2, 1917, Crystal Eastman issued a press release to introduce the new bureau: "It is the tendency even of the most 'democratic' of governments embarked upon the most 'idealistic of wars' to sacrifice everything for complete military efficiency. To combat this tendency where it threatens free speech, free press, freedom of assembly, and freedom of conscience—the essentials of liberty and the heritage of all past wars worth fighting—that is the first function of the AUAM today. . . . To maintain something over here that will be worth coming back to when the weary war is over. . . ."

By November 1917 Crystal Eastman's activism and her associates in the Woman's Peace Party of New York, combined with the activities of the Civil Liberties Bureau, ended the once-powerful alliance the AUAM had represented. Of her own resignation and the AUAM's disintegration Lillian Wald wrote in her 1934 autobiography, *Windows on Henry Street:* "The fire and imagination of the Secretary, Crystal Eastman, were often impatient of more sober councils."

An extensive correspondence between Lucia Ames Mead, Jane Addams, and Emily Greene Balch reveals that despite Eastman's formidable efforts throughout the war, the national WPP hierarchy attempted to prevent her from attending the Second International Congress of Women in 1919. Supported only by Balch, others argued that Eastman's "extreme" radicalism and her "casual sex life" would confuse their mission and increase their difficulties.

To continue their public works on behalf of the poor, the social workers depended on the contributions of private financiers and government largesse. They placed a high value on cautious and respectable behavior, and feared to lose the kind of public approval Crystal Eastman never sought. Her openness threatened the closeted self-protectiveness of her critics.

During the postwar Red Scare when all social progress was suspended the attitude of the social reformers seemed justified. But it did not protect them. Their respectability was illusory. When Jane Addams, for example, denounced the food blockade and insisted that the "United States should not allow women and children of any nation to starve," she was vilified as a traitor. Like Crystal Eastman, she was followed by the FBI and assorted secret agents. During the 1920s both their names appeared on all the lists of "dangerous Reds," enemies of America. The states' rejection of the child labor amendment, portrayed as part of a massive communist plot, symbolizes the collapse of progressive reform. While the nominal respectability of social reformers availed them very little, the inability of progressives to work together during the postwar period strengthened the militarist and antidemocratic forces they had so vigorously opposed.

Crystal Eastman's last activity as president of New York's WPP was to organize the First Feminist Congress in the United States, held on March 1, 1919. In her opening statement, she examined the status of women in this self-congratulatory center of "freedom and democracy." Citing dismal statistics, including the fact that four-fifths of the women in America were "still denied the elementary political right of voting," she enumerated the essential changes required before women could be independent. She did not mean to catalog the restrictive laws and repressive social customs that burdened women in a spirit of "bitterness," and she fully recognized "the fact that women by their passivity have made these things possible." Her one goal for this First Feminist Congress was to "see the birth of a new spirit of humane and intelligent self-interest . . . which will lead women to declare: 'WE WILL NOT WAIT FOR THE SOCIAL REVOLUTION TO BRING US THE FREEDOM WE SHOULD HAVE WON IN THE 19TH CENTURY.' "

Throughout the postwar years, Eastman's entire effort involved feminism and the "social revolution," by which she meant socialism. As a feminist she had no illusions about the marginality of feminist principles among the male-dominated socialist parties in the United States and Europe. Her own position, expressed vigorously in "Now We Can Begin," was entirely clear.

> Many feminists are socialists, many are communists. . . . But the true feminist, no matter how far to the left she may be in the revolutionary movement, sees the woman's battle as distinct in its objects and different in its methods from the workers' battle for industrial freedom. She knows, of course, that the vast majority of women as well as men are without property, and are of necessity bread and

> butter slaves under a system of society which allows the very sources of life to be privately owned by a few, and she counts herself a loyal soldier in the working-class army that is marching to over-throw that system. But as a feminist she also knows that the whole of woman's slavery is not summed up in the profit system, not her complete emancipation assured by the downfall of capitalism. . . .
>
> If we should graduate into communism to-morrow . . . man's attitude to his wife would not be changed.

Her socialist position, as expressed in *The Liberator,* which she co-owned and coedited with Max from March 1918 until they both resigned in 1922, was equally clear. Crystal Eastman had been radicalized by her wartime experiences. Many of her closest friends had been imprisoned and abused because they sought the most rudimentary political power—the vote—by exercising the most basic rights of free speech and assembly. The abolition of civil liberties in wartime revealed the fragile nature of bourgeois rights even in a country that boasted fiercely of its democratic heritage. The Espionage Act of 1917 and the Sedition Act of May 1918 altered forever the nature of American freedom. Those laws rendered all Crystal Eastman's wartime activity illegal and resulted in the removal of all radical publications from the mails, including *Four Lights* and the *Masses,* as well as the imprisonment of countless dissenters, including her brother and Roger Baldwin. During the postwar Red Scare thousands of Americans were imprisoned or deported—anarchists, socialists, labor leaders, conscientious objectors.

War, the counterrevolutionary mobilization, and the secret Allied intervention in the Soviet Union (which was reported in the United States only in *The Liberator*) served to convince her that the only way to "restore liberty" was "to destroy the capitalist system." "The world's future," *The Liberator* editorialized in February 1919, "shall not be the League of Business Politicians at Versailles, but the New International, the League of the Working Classes of the World."

In March 1919 Crystal Eastman became the first American journalist to visit communist Hungary. Her report from Hungary is as valuable for its information as it is for her feelings regarding the inevitable conflicts and contradictions such situations present to "pacifist revolutionaries." There was, she concluded, nothing simple about the dilemma of force. On the other hand, the activities of the invading British, American, and Japanese armies and Admiral Kolchak's "monarchist forces" helped resolve the conflict. The military invasion, intent on destroying all revolutionary movements, suspended Crystal Eastman's pacifism.

The Liberator was the only monthly in the United States to publish information about socialist movements throughout the world, as well as news about the Allied intervention in Russia. In May 1919, for example, *The Liberator* published the startling news that "Japan has made an offer to England" to send troops to join the Allied intervention in Russia "and bear the expenses of the expedition alone—if she receives a mandate for Indo-China."

Filled with some of the most significant poetry and literature of the postwar period, this "journal of Revolutionary Progress" had an impact that reached far beyond the United States. Italian communist theorist Antonio Gramsci depended on it for international information, "so tight and bristling was the blockade around the Bolsheviks." *The Liberator* published John Reed and Louise Bryant from Russia, a regular column of international news by Alexander Trachtenberg (the founder of International publishers), Bertrand Russell's "Democracy and Freedom," the works of associate editor Floyd Dell, contributions by Helen Keller, Norman Thomas, Roger Baldwin, Lenin and Dorothy Day, and the poetry of Claude McKay.

McKay's poetry had never been accepted by the *Masses*, which had sent him "so sorry" rejections. But when Crystal Eastman read his work in *Pearson's*, a literary journal, she invited him to call at *The Liberator* office. One of the leading black poets of the Harlem Renaissance, McKay was still working on the railroads, writing poems on the trains whenever he had spare time. He wrote: "The moment I saw her and heard her voice I liked Crystal Eastman. I think she was the most beautiful white woman I ever knew. . . . Her beauty was not so much of her features . . . but in her magnificent presence. Her form was something after the pattern of a splendid draft horse and she had a way of holding her head like a large bird poised in a listening attitude." Their lifelong friendship began during that first meeting, and Claude McKay became associate editor of *The Liberator*.

After the war, Crystal Eastman with her husband and son lived communally with her brother Max, their childhood friend Ruth Pickering—who had also graduated from Vassar and was soon to marry Amos Pinchot—the actress Florence Deshon, and Eugen Boissevan—who commanded "a whole fleet of merchant ships" and had married first Inez Milholland and then Edna St. Vincent Millay. Crystal Eastman had engineered this "delightful half-way family" in 1918 to promote companionship and economy. With two houses and a collective courtyard and kitchen, they shared a comfortable communal space in Greenwich Village and also spent weekends and summers together in Croton-on-Hudson with, among others, Boardman Robinson, Margaret and Winthrop D. Lane, Floyd Dell, and—until they left for Russia—John Reed and Louise Bryant.

The communal harmony and pastoral happiness of those years were short-lived. From 1907 to 1921 Crystal Eastman's capacity for work was intense and varied. Before the war her paying jobs, whether as a social investigator or government appointee, occupied only part of her working day. Political activities and organizations occupied far more time. Like all "workaholics," Eastman thrived on work. It energized her and increased her strength. When she was not working she became morose and melancholic. Yet between 1911 and 1921 Crystal Eastman's physical constitution broke down several times. Her blood pressure was frequently and dangerously high, and she had a bad heart. Above all, there was nephritis. Diagnosed late and little understood then, it is now known to be a slowly consuming and painful kidney condition.

With complete disregard for her physical well-being, Crystal Eastman did not slow down until the birth of her second child, Annis, two months prematurely. At the insistence of doctors, she removed herself from the management of *The Liberator,* became a contributing editor, and agreed to rest while writing a book on feminism and taking more personal care of herself and her daughter.

Hospital and medical expenses and the loss of her full-time *Liberator* salary devastated the Eastman-Fuller household. In the spring of 1922, when Annis was three months old, Walter Fuller left for England to look for a better job. Evidently Fuller felt confined in their marriage, which was financially crushed by debts. On April 14, Crystal wrote that she was "so lonely it makes a sick feeling in my solar plexus . . . I hope you will come back." To encourage her husband's return she arranged with Kellogg to offer Fuller a job on the *Survey Graphic.* It entailed more money, and Crystal Eastman believed that he "could work with Paul—he is sensitive and whimsical and humorous. And they have money in sight to run the *Survey Graphic* for three years—just about as long as you like a job to last. . . ." But Fuller refused the offer.

In a subsequent letter dated June 27, Eastman discussed the possibilities of joining Walter in England as soon as she could raise sufficient funds and he could afford the company of his family. She wrote: "Don't worry about harsh words. Have I said any? If I have they certainly can be forgotten now. I knew you had to run away. That you couldn't even send me a line to say so and say you were sorry will forever be incomprehensible to me. But then four-fifths of you is a closed book to me and four-fifths of me is a closed book to you,—and yet we love each other a great deal. Don't we?"

"Marriage Under Two Roofs," written for *Cosmopolitan* magazine, largely for money, was not written largely as spoof. Crystal and her husband lived for years not only under two separate roofs, but in two separate countries. From 1922 to 1927 she and her children traveled back and forth between England and the United States with commuter regularity. Often she spent her summer vacations in the south of France with Jeannette Lowe and their children. Walter might visit occasionally. Very much like "Marriage Under Two Roofs."

Wherever Crystal Eastman spent her time during these years, her life consisted of a continual battle to find meaningful work, to help organize the Anglo-American women's movement on behalf of equal rights, and to ignore the physicians, and several medical quacks, who all agreed on one thing: Crystal Eastman needed rest. She hated to rest, she hated inactivity, and she hated to be without a steady job. Her inability to find work, the fact that she was actually barred from the kind of work she sought, was the hardest for her to comprehend. Today we are more familiar with the facts and effects of political blacklists. But Crystal Eastman, attorney, social investigator, noted orator and author, could not understand why a militant feminist, antimilitarist, and socialist could not between 1922 and 1928 find regular employment. She could not understand it even when old friends like Paul Kellogg told her specifically that there were "practical difficulties in making a fresh start which it does no good to minimize." The United States, wrote Kellogg in a letter, "is not as tolerant as England; we still have a lot of beating up of bugaboos, and you will get a touch of that in any public work . . . and your various espousals—such as the Woman's Party—would not help in some of the few quarters where industrial research is still carried on, etc." Throughout the last years of her life, Crystal's only income was derived from her two houses, in Croton and Greenwich Village, when she rented them, and from feminist articles contracted by the militant wing of the Anglo-American women's movement, notably Alice Paul's journal *Equal Rights*, and Lady Rhonnda's *Time and Tide.*

During the 1920s the contradictions between radicalism and reform, within the context of both socialism and feminism, were vividly apparent in the divisions of the women's movement. For twenty years social reformers like Jane Addams and Florence Kelley had championed protective legislation for women and children. To the extent that Crystal worked for protective legislation for workers, she too had been identified with that reform movement. She regarded protective laws as cruelly discriminatory when they regulated working conditions for women only.

In 1908 Jane Addams and Florence Kelley had rejoiced in a Supreme Court decision that established the principle of protective legislation for women. *Muller v. Oregon* introduced "sociological jurisprudence" into constitutional law. Florence Kelley and Josephine Goldmark had hired Louis D. Brandeis to defend a protective law that established a ten-hour day for women laundry workers. The first of the famous "Brandeis briefs," it demonstrated the physical inferiority of women, their need for protection—and the benefits for the human race should women's toil be specifically restricted by the state. Yes, declared the unanimous Court: "Woman's physical structure, and the performance of maternal functions . . . justify special legislation restricting or qualifying the conditions under which she should be permitted to toil." These restrictions were "not imposed solely for her benefit, but also largely for the benefit of all."

This was the principle that protectionist reformers sought to defend against erosion by the Equal Rights Amendment. When the National Woman's Party introduced this amendment in July 1923, at the seventy-fifth anniversary convention of the Seneca Falls equal rights meeting of 1848, the feminists and the women reformers became irreconcilably divided. *Muller v. Oregon* classed women with minors, and rested its decision on women's biological "inferiority," their potential maternity, and "natural dependence" on men. It represented everything Crystal Eastman had opposed since her first speech called "Woman."

Since she was fifteen Crystal had considered arguments of women's physical inferiority male myths created to keep women untutored, unpaid, and unhappy at home. Now, with all Europe moving toward socialism, working women were urged to return home. It was believed that without patriarchal order there would be anarchy. The working class required stability. Women needed protection. Protection would preserve the home, and the entire human race. All the men in unions seemed to agree.

During World War I women in large numbers had moved into numerous industries and professions from which they had previously been barred. With war's end a great effort to dismiss them emerged. In Cleveland, for example, 150 women streetcar conductors were dismissed after the men struck to eliminate women from the job because there was no longer a "manpower shortage." In Detroit white male conductors petitioned for the dismissal of women and black workers because their contract promised "women and Negroes could be employed only in an emergency, and the emergency was over." By 1919 protective laws forbidding night work were used as a pretext for dismissing women workers from lucrative, interesting, and sought-after jobs.

Nevertheless, Florence Kelley, Jane Addams, Dr. Alice Hamilton—all the friends of labor—opposed the equal rights movement because they did not want to lose hard-won protective laws. Organized labor women may have favored equality—but equality with protection; and they opted for protection first. Given the cruel hours and life-threatening conditions, most working women and their allies believed that it was absurd to abandon specific protective laws for the principle of equality that seemed both abstract and farfetched. Crystal Eastman's support for equal rights represented a socialist feminist tradition that has only recently begun to reemerge. As a socialist in the 1920s she was virtually alone among her allies in the National Woman's Party and its British counterpart, Lady Rhonnda's Six Point Group.

For Crystal Eastman protection was humanitarianism in the interests of "family welfare." It had nothing to do with the needs or rights or aspirations of women. It represented reformism at its worst. It served everywhere to bar women from well-paid jobs that men were eager to keep for themselves. Protective legislation protected male unionists who feared female competition and capitalist power, which used intra-class competition between women and men just as it used ethnic and racial differences: to block real workers' unity, the necessary sense of connectedness that might stimulate a real workers' movement.

Crystal Eastman's commitment to equal rights was not an abstract enthusiasm. With a rare empathy for all women, and an ability to imagine herself in each humiliating or repressive situation, her outrage was as specific as it was theoretical. In "Women, Rights and Privileges," she wrote that "this sudden concern for the health of women when they set out to earn their living in competition with men seems a little suspicious.... What working-class mother of small children ever had nine hours consecutive rest? ... What traditional union husband ever felt that it was his concern to see that she should have?"

By 1927, Crystal Eastman became desperate for challenging work. Besides, she never actually liked England very well. She loathed the climate and longed for the American seasons—the heat of the sun and the snow. She was neither well nor happy. In January she wrote to Paul Kellogg that she had decided, with finality, to return home. "I am rich in health and strength now.... Three lazy months at Antibes ... have given me back myself." And, she wrote, she "was simply crazy to work. England holds nothing for me.... I have tried for two years to get a job—research, organizing, editorial, speaking, anything." She returned to the United States with a temporary position organizing the *Nation's* tenth anniversary celebration. Walter was to join her when she secured more permanent work. But in September 1927 Walter Fuller died of a stroke, and within ten months Crystal Eastman too was dead.

The last months of Crystal Eastman's life were given over to hard work and her final battle, to heal "this good for nothing body of mine." Ravaged by nephritis which was never properly diagnosed or treated, she blamed herself for her headaches, her loss of energy. On October 11, 1927, she wrote to Cynthia Fuller, Walter's sister: "I am fighting so hard not to drown and to get my health and hold on to it, so that I'll be equal to supporting the children and making a happy home for them."

Crystal Eastman was forty-seven years old when she died. Her last thoughts were of her children and all the work she had left undone. Many friends offered to adopt the children; Agnes Brown Leach and Henry Goddard Leach did so. Agnes Brown Leach had been among the most consistent supporters of the American Union Against Militarism, treasurer of the New York branch of the Woman's Peace Party, and a member of the executive committee of the National Woman's Party.

Crystal Eastman was mourned by many. Claude McKay believed that Crystal Eastman joined "in her personality that daring freedom of thought and action—all that was fundamentally fine, noble and genuine in American democracy." She was, he wrote, "a great-hearted woman whose life was big with primitive and exceptional gestures. She never wrote that Book of Woman which was imprinted on her mind. She was poor, and fettered with a family. She had a grand idea for a group of us to go off to write in some quiet corner of the world, where living was cheap and easy. But it couldn't be realized. And so life was cheated of one contribution about women that no other woman could write."

Crystal Eastman's contemporaries considered her "a great leader." In Freda Kirchwey's memorial in the *Nation* she wrote that when Crystal Eastman "spoke to people—whether it was to a small committee or a swarming crowd—hearts beat faster and nerves tightened as she talked. She was simple, direct, dramatic. Force poured from her strong body and her rich voice, and people followed where she led. . . . In her personal as in her public life her enthusiasm and strength were spent without thought; she had no pride or sense of her own power. . . . Her strength . . . her rich and compelling personality—these she threw with reckless vigor into every cause that promised a finer life to the world. She spent herself wholly, and died—too young."

Alice Paul

(1885–1977)

Christine A. Lunardini

Born into a Quaker family in Moorestown, New Jersey, Alice Paul was reared in the intellectual tradition of her parents, William and Tacie Parry Paul. She attended Swarthmore College, and after graduation went to the New York School of Philanthropy (a school of social work) in 1905 on a fellowship from the College Settlement Association. For the next few years she was a social worker; during this time she cultivated her interest in women's rights. While active as a caseworker in the settlement house crusade in England from 1906 to 1909, she became involved in the suffrage movement. Paul was arrested for her suffrage agitation and endured force-feeding for almost a month during one hunger strike. Paul received a Ph.D. in sociology from the University of Pennsylvania in 1912 before launching into her full-time suffrage career. In 1914 she cofounded the Congressional Union for Women's Suffrage—a breakaway group from the National American Woman Suffrage Association. She led pickets at the White House and was sentenced to prison for suffrage protests. Paul founded the National Woman's Party in 1916 and was a pivotal factor in women securing passage of the Nineteenth Amendment in 1920. In 1923 she introduced the Equal Rights Amendment (ERA) and became a lifelong advocate for feminist reform, working in Europe as well as the United States. By 1944 the ERA was a plank within the American presidential campaigns of both major parties. Paul continued her fight for women's rights from National Woman's Party headquarters in Washington, but declining health forced her to relocate in 1972 to the Connecticut countryside. Paul promoted the cause for women from her wheelchair until she suffered a stroke in 1974. Paul died in her hometown of Moorestown, New Jersey, in 1977.

An article appearing in *Everybody's* magazine in July 1916 attempted to uncover the real Alice Paul amidst the myriad contradictory descriptions of her that made the rounds of both suffrage and political circles. With more than a touch of exasperated surrender, the author concluded that, "There is no Alice Paul. There is suffrage. She leads by being . . . her cause."[1] Most contemporary journalists assigned to cover Paul were baffled by her and often tried to make her more—or less—than human: "I tried to imagine Alice Paul married," one such writer confided to her readers, "and I almost succeeded when I heard she was taking dancing lessons last Spring."[2] To associate Paul with the ordinary events of middle-class life, however, was beyond the writer's ability. She went on to predict that Paul would follow the fiery road to revolution. To this journalist and many of her contemporaries, Paul's political activities and the ordinary events of life were clearly contradictory, if not mutually exclusive. That Paul should prove to be such an elusive subject was not surprising; she was not a mainstream suffragist. By the time Alice Paul arrived on the scene in 1912, the American suffrage movement had reached a virtual standstill—it had lost the urgency and excitement that Susan B. Anthony and Elizabeth Cady Stanton had generated in the decades following the Civil War. Since Stanton and Anthony's retirement from suffrage, the National American Woman Suffrage Association (NAWSA) had relinquished almost entirely any effort to secure a federal women's suffrage amendment, preferring instead to focus on the state level. NAWSA's new president, Anna Howard Shaw, was a fiery speaker but a lackluster leader. During her presidency of NAWSA, which was the only national suffrage organization in operation at this time, the suffrage movement became mired at the state and local level, settling into the low-keyed, plodding pace that characterized it until 1913. As late as 1912, there were only nine full-suffrage states in the entire country.[3] Alice Paul's arrival on the scene marked a sharp departure from this type of suffrage activity, and a return to a more radical approach.

From the time that she took over the reins of NAWSA's Congressional Committee in 1913, Paul made it clear that her objective would be to secure a federal amendment to the Constitution that would give women the vote with, in a manner of speaking, one stroke of pen. Paul borrowed liberally from the English suffrage movement, making publicity and high visibility the vehicles for educating an uninformed public. When NAWSA objected to her tactics, she broke away from that organization, forming first the Congressional Union in 1914, and then the National Woman's Party (NWP) in 1916. While NAWSA always sought to include on their membership roles women who would not necessarily play an active part in the suffrage battle, Paul wanted only those women who were prepared to lend not only their names, but their time and effort as well. Consequently, her organization never numbered more than fifty thousand members, compared to NAWSA's membership, which numbered in the hundreds of thousands.

The Woman's Party activists possessed many of the same characteristics as their counterparts in NAWSA. But they tended to be a bit younger, somewhat better educated, more career-oriented, less apt to be married, and more cosmopolitan than the NAWSA women. Most of them were from the ranks of the middle class, and in many ways they were typical of middle-class women of their generation. The critical factor that distinguished the women that joined NAWSA and the women that joined the Woman's Party was their brand of feminism. For both groups, suffrage was the issue around which they rallied. For the Woman's Party, however, militancy was the chief weapon. Picketing the White House and Congress both in time of peace and war, the Woman's Party members were fully prepared to risk social status, family approbation, and personal freedom in order to achieve their goal. NAWSA members, on the other hand, chose to adhere to the more traditional, socially acceptable, and much more conservative approach of using gentle persuasion.

Paul herself contrasted sharply with the entrenched suffrage leadership, being at once more aggressive and more willing to employ tactics considered radical in order to achieve her goal of a federal amendment. Paul was idolized and idealized by her suffrage followers, but she often appeared paradoxical. She was alternately described as "exceedingly charitable . . . and patient," and "cold, austere, and a little remote."[4] She elicited both profound and unquestioning loyalty from her coworkers and intense distrust and skepticism from her adversaries. More than one observer described her single-mindedness as "fanaticism." Outraged by Paul's campaign against the Democratic party in the summer of 1914 and its attendant publicity, Mrs. Medill McCormick, a NAWSA officer, described Paul as an "anaemic fanatic, well-intentioned and conscientious . . . but almost unbalanced because of her physical condition." McCormick was referring to Paul's frail appearance, which she attributed to Alice's alleged refusal to spend more than thirty cents a day on food. This, in McCormick's view, demonstrated Paul's instability and characterized her attitude towards suffrage: "She will be a *martyr* whether there is the slightest excuse for it in this country or not, and I am really convinced that she will die for the cause, but," McCormick added disparagingly, "it will be because of her 30 [cent] meals."[5]

Paul's followers were as lavish in their praise of her as her detractors were in their criticism. "I know of no modern leader with whom to compare her," said one admiring political observer. "I think she must possess many of the same qualities that Lenin does . . . cool, practical, rational. . . . And if she has demanded the ultimate of her followers, she has given it herself."[6] Maud Younger, the "millionaire waitress" from California, the founder and president of the waitresses' union in San Francisco and a skilled organizer, could not say enough about Paul's executive abilities: "She has in the first place, a devotion to the cause which is absolutely self-sacrificing. She has an indomitable will. . . . She has a clear, penetrating, analytic mind which cleaves straight to the heart of things. . . . She is a genius for organization, both in the mass and in detail."[7] In a similar vein, Lucy Burns, Paul's second-in-command, noted: "Her great assets, I should say, are her power, with a single leap of the imagination, to make plans on a national scale, and a supplementary power to see that it is done down to the last postage stamp."[8]

In substance, both views of Paul are accurate, although not necessarily in their particulars. The complexities of her personality revealed in such divergent views can be better understood in the context of her background and upbringing. Born on January 11, 1885, in the small Quaker community of Moorestown, New Jersey, nine miles east of Philadelphia, Alice was the oldest child of William M. and Tacie Parry Paul. Her family tree included, on her mother's side, William Penn, and on her father's side, the Winthrops of Massachusetts.[9] The first Paul to settle in New Jersey had fled England due to religious and political conflicts with the Crown.[10] Alice's father was a successful businessperson who served as president of the bank that he helped to found, the Burlington County Trust Company. He also held directorships on the boards of several local companies, invested in several profitable real estate ventures, and owned a working farm. Alice's mother was the daughter of one of the founders of Swarthmore College in Pennsylvania. Indeed, Tacie Parry would have been among the first women to graduate from Swarthmore had she not left in her senior year to marry William Paul. Alice eventually followed in her mother's footsteps, first attending a Quaker school in Moorestown, and then enrolling at Swarthmore, where she earned a degree. Both of the elder Pauls were active and devout Quakers and subscribed to traditional Quaker beliefs, including that of equality between the sexes.[11] Quakers have always been heavily represented in social justice movements. It is not surprising, then, that Quaker women were so heavily represented in the ranks of American suffragists. Their participation in public affairs at a time when most women did not engage in controversial activities stemmed in large part from the greater role that women had in the Quaker religion than women had in most other religions. Lucretia Mott, a prominent

Quaker, was one of the original organizers of the American suffrage movement at its founding in 1848, when she, along with Elizabeth Cady Stanton, called women to meet at Seneca Falls, New York, and issued the women's Declaration of Sentiments.

In addition to Alice, the Pauls had three other children: William, Jr., Helen, and Parry Haines Paul. Alice Paul's relationship with her parents was apparently good, although not very well documented. She was sixteen years old when her father died suddenly of pneumonia, but her recollections of his death were vague and she could say only that, "I just remember that life went on."[12] We do know, however, what William Paul thought of his oldest daughter, as revealed in a magazine article published in 1916. An interviewer, seeking hometown opinion regarding Paul's militant suffrage activity, asked Tacie Paul what she thought about her daughter. "Well," she sighed, "I remember that Mr. Paul used to say that whenever there was anything hard and disagreeable to do, 'I bank on Alice.' "[13] Although both William and Tacie Paul were suffrage advocates, the article implied that Tacie Paul did not quite understand her daughter's militant activities. Tacie Paul's attitude towards militancy may have been influenced by Alice Paul's uncle, Donald Paul. When William Paul died so suddenly, his wife and family, although well off financially, depended upon Donald for advice and guidance on money matters. Like many middle-class women, Tacie Paul had little knowledge of family finances and neither the experience nor the confidence necessary to take over when faced with the disaster of her husband's death. The circumstances of having the family finances taken over by an uncle did not affect Alice directly since she had already left home for college. But she was aware of her mother's new dependence and it influenced her own determination to be independent and self-sufficient.[14] In any case, her uncle did not approve of Alice's suffrage activity, and Tacie Paul may have withheld public approval in the magazine article in order to maintain harmony within the family.[15] Despite Tacie Paul's ambivalence regarding Alice's suffrage activities, and her reluctance to offend her brother-in-law, she nevertheless supported her daughter financially, which allowed Alice to devote full time to suffrage.[16]

The elder Pauls raised their children in an atmosphere of discipline, achievement, and service. In keeping with Quaker teaching, neither music nor dancing was encouraged as part of the younger Pauls' childhood experiences. The children knew that their Irish maids went off to dances but assumed that only "a sort of common people" engaged in such behavior.[17] Instead of music and dance, Paul's recreational activities centered on sports, especially tennis. Suffrage coworker Mabel Vernon, a year ahead of Paul at Swarthmore, remembered her as a shy, sports-minded young woman. In contrast to Paul's frail and sickly pallor that later caused much concern and comment, Vernon recalled Paul's healthy and vigorous appearance as a college student.[18]

Paul read voraciously, especially in the classics, and she haunted the local Friends library as a youth. She read every line written by Charles Dickens "over and over again."[19] Dickens's social commentary undoubtedly helped to shape her own sense of justice. Her suffrage coworker, Anne Martin, confided that one of the sacrifices that Paul made during the suffrage campaign was to stay away from Washington bookstores, to keep no books in her rooms, and not to read anything not specifically related to suffrage. She feared that any indulgence in reading for pleasure might tempt her to give less than 100 percent to the suffrage cause.[20]

At Swarthmore, Paul initially chose to major in biology. She did so not because she especially liked biology or the sciences, but because of a personal conviction that she would carry with her into adulthood. Opportunities for new adventure, to learn new things, had to be grasped immediately. To stick with the things she believed she already knew—English and Latin, for example—meant passing up an opportunity to engage in something about which she knew nothing. Biology was a new adventure, an unknown quantity, a challenge to be met.[21] Later on, this conviction would manifest itself in other ways as well. She was not a particularly introspective person. Paul always professed to believe that the past was past and ought not to be dwelt upon. As a result, she more often than not refused to talk about her past experiences, particularly when she believed that doing so would make her and not suffrage the focus of public attention.

Her commitment to biology was superficial at best, for she never really considered pursuing a career in the sciences. Paul's first introduction to political science and economics came only in her senior year when Swarthmore hired Professor Robert Brooks to teach those subjects. Paul was immediately attracted to both disciplines and did so well that Brooks recommended her for a College Settlement Association fellowship at the New York School of Philanthropy (later Columbia University School of Social Work).[22]

Paul spent several years after her graduation from Swarthmore in the study and practice of social work. After she completed her year at the New York School of Philanthropy, she earned a master's degree in sociology at the University of Pennsylvania in 1907, with minor fields in political science and economics. (Although she was no stranger to the problems women faced because of their legal status in an unequal society, she had not yet exhibited publicly a concern for the issue of equal suffrage. Paul had already begun research on the project that would become her doctoral dissertation, "Towards Equality," an examination of women's legal status in Pennsylvania.) Her familiarity with suffrage, however, reached back to her childhood. One of her earliest memories was accompanying her mother to suffrage meetings at the home of a neigboring Quaker family in Moorestown.[23]

Paul interrupted her graduate work at the University of Pennsylvania to accept a second fellowship to study social work in Woodbridge, England, the central training school for Quakers. As with biology, Paul's commitment to social work was not all-consuming. She arrived in England in the fall of 1907 with the belief that she was only marking time. "I knew in a very short time that I was never going to be a social worker, because I could see that social workers were not doing much good in the world. . . . You knew you couldn't *change* the situation by social work."[24]

It was while she was in England, however that Paul found the cause that integrated and brought into focus her family heritage, her service-oriented Quaker education, and her interest in economics, political science, and the status of women. Christabel Pankhurst, the English suffragist, was invited to speak at the University of Birmingham, where Paul was fulfilling the academic requirements of her fellowship. Suffrage at that time was even less popular than it was respectable. The Pankhursts, Christabel, her mother Emmeline, and her sister Sylvia, founders of the Women's Social and Political Union (WSPU), were avowed radicals who employed militant tactics to achieve their goals. Christabel Pankhurst's appearance at Birmingham incited the usually proper students to rowdy behavior. She was shouted down and the embarrassed Birmingham administration was forced summarily to cancel her talk. The reaction to Pankhurst's appearance both angered and surprised Paul. She had not encountered any opposition to suffrage at the meetings she had attended as a child. Now, as a young adult, it shocked her that people would react so violently to the idea. For Paul, such resistance was both foolish and ill-informed, and she left the auditorium thinking that even though her fellow students were so intolerant, the suffragettes "had anyway one heart and soul convert . . . that was myself."[25]

When Paul finished her year at Woodbridge, a representative of the Charity Organization Society of London invited her to become a caseworker in the working-class district of Dalston. By now she was determined to throw in her lot with the Pankhurst group; thus, she accepted the caseworker position because it placed her where she wanted to be. In the fall of 1908, she participated in her first suffrage parade and began an association with the WSPU that would last for two years. During that time she became thoroughly versed in the strategy and tactics of confrontational suffragism. Paul's participation in subsequent parades and demonstrations led to her arrest and imprisonment on several occasions over the next year on charges of disturbing the peace and disorderly conduct. Along with her English comrades, she took part in hunger strikes to protest against the British government's treatment of the suffrage prisoners.[26] It was a profoundly formative period in her political awakening for, prior to this time, Paul had evinced little interest in political activism. Indeed, aside from the meetings she had attended with her mother, and despite her academic interest in inequality, Paul had not been sufficiently inspired by the American suffrage movement to join any suffrage organizations at home.

While in Europe, Paul met only one other American active with the WSPU—Lucy Burns, a woman of Irish descent born in Brooklyn. Burns graduated from Vassar and then went on to Yale to do graduate work in languages at a time when women were not highly regarded by their male colleagues on that campus. She left Yale, returning to Brooklyn to teach English at Erasmus High School. In 1906, much to the dismay of her Erasmus students, she resigned her teaching position to study languages in Europe. Burns went first to the University of Berlin (1906–1908), and then to the University of Bonn (1908–1909). But Burns, much like Alice Paul, felt she was drifting along with no particular focus to her life. While she was vacationing in England, she met the Pankhursts and discovered her intense interest in the suffrage movement. By 1909, she had transferred to Oxford with the intention of pursuing her Ph.D., but by that time her only real concern was suffrage.[27] From 1909 to 1912, Burns worked with the WSPU as an organizer, primarily in Edinburgh. She, too, gained invaluable experience that would later serve the American suffrage cause well.

Alice Paul first met Lucy Burns at a London police station where both were waiting to be processed after having been arrested for demonstrating. Paul, noticing the tiny American flag pinned to Burns's lapel, maneuvered her way through the crowded station house and introduced herself. They found an empty tabletop and perched there, exchanging stories of their English experiences and talking about their hopes for the American women's movement.[28] The two became fast friends and worked closely together on their return to the United States.

In both style and appearance, Alice Paul and Lucy Burns provided a striking contrast to one another. Burns, much the better diplomat of the two, possessed a quicker wit and a readier sense of humor. She was spontaneous, outspoken, and laughed easily. Paul, on the other hand, was irrepressibly shy. Paul was reserved, soft-spoken, and appeared to be much more businesslike. Lucy Burns, with her red hair, sturdy build, and rugged Irish features, seemed equal to any task. Alice Paul was slight of build and almost timid-looking. She suffered periodic bouts of ill-health which, on several occasions, required hospitalization. Many of her later health problems stemmed from the hunger strikes in which she participated as a suffrage prisoner.[29] Mabel Vernon recalled how shocked she was the first time she saw Paul after the latter's return from England. Paul appeared on the verge of collapse. The painful and dangerous forced-feedings administered by British prison officials left her weak, pale, and underweight.[30] To even casual observers, the toll extracted for standing on principle was a harsh one. The experience also helped to shape the careless eating habits that later prompted Mrs. Medill McCormick to predict that Paul would become a self-made martyr. Nothing could have been further from the truth; Paul was much too pragmatic to choose martyrdom. She approached risky situations with a healthy degree of trepidation and never thought of herself as especially brave. When Emmeline Pankhurst asked her, in the spring of 1909, to take part in a demonstration against Herbert Asquith, the British prime minister, that would almost certainly lead to arrest and imprisonment, Paul recalled later: "I remember hesitating the longest time and writing the letter [accepting the invitation] and not being able to get up enough courage to post it, and going up and walking around the post office, wondering whether I dare put it in."[31]

But Lucy Burns was impressed with Paul's courage, as well as her "extraordinary mind . . . and remarkable executive ability." She thought the frail-looking Quaker had two serious disabilities that would hamper her effectiveness in a grueling political campaign: her apparent ill-health and a "lack of knowledge about human nature." Burns later acknowledged that "I was wrong in both."[32] Paul herself always believed that Burns possessed far greater courage than she, pointing out that Lucy Burns never hesitated to risk possible arrest on the picket lines, both in England and in the United States, despite Burns's phobic fear of rats and other animal life that inhabited the damp, dark prison cells.[33]

Paul and Burns worked so well together that observers often attributed to them one mind and spirit. One suffragist, when asked to describe the differences between the two, found more similarities than differences in their beliefs and attitudes. However, she was able to detect differences in temperament: "Both saw the situation exactly as it was, but they went at the problems with different methods. Alice Paul had a more acute sense of justice, Lucy Burns a more bitter sense of injustice. Lucy Burns would become angry because the President or the people did not do this or that. Alice Paul never expected anything of them."[34]

After her imprisonment in Hallowell Jail in 1910, Paul returned to the United States from England and resumed graduate study at the University of Pennsylvania. Burns, however, remained in Europe to organize for the WSPU, thus the two were not united again until 1912, when they joined forces to do suffrage work in America.

At NAWSA's annual convention in 1912, Alice Paul, along with Lucy Burns, petitioned for and was granted permission to take over NAWSA's Congressional Committee. The Congressional Committee was, theoretically, established to lobby for suffrage on the federal level, that is, to lobby for a women's suffrage amendment to the United States Constitution. In fact, NAWSA in this period focused its efforts almost exclusively on the states, with the goal of securing changes to each individual state constitution. Other than lip service, very little attention was paid to the idea of securing a federal amendment.

When Paul assumed leadership of NAWSA's Congressional Committee, most people who noticed such things would not have predicted the effect she was about to have, either on the suffrage movement or on the people who worked with her. Alice Paul possessed many of the same social and educational characteristics of other women suffragists. Her marital and professional status, while somewhat unusual, could not be viewed as extraordinary. She never married, but neither did many of her contemporaries. She collected a string of degrees that eventually included two law degrees and a Ph.D., but there were others as versatile. Yet Paul was an extraordinary personality, perhaps the single truly charismatic figure in the twentieth-century suffrage movement. Certainly she was the force that powered the militant suffrage movement. She successfully mobilized both impatient New Suffragists—the mostly younger generation of American women determined to secure their rights even if it required more militant tactics to do so—and the discontented Old Suffragists—women who had been engaged in the suffrage movement for years who were generally older and more conservative, but who were beginning to despair of ever realizing their goal by following the strategy employed by NAWSA. To the new suffragists, Paul represented the force that made them willing to take uncommon risks, including imprisonment and possible estrangement from families, friends, and peers.

When Max Weber wrote *The Sociology of Religion* in 1922, he might have used Alice Paul as his model in developing the concept of the charismatic leader. Such a person, Weber concluded, challenged the established order in ways both constructive and destructive, established boundaries by drawing on legitimacy from sources within herself or himself, and disregarded public opinion.[35] This certainly applied to Paul. When faced with a law or a convention that, if observed, would have nullified a particular plan of action, Paul usually just commented on the "absurdity" of the existing situation and proceeded to do exactly as she pleased.[36] When public opinion turned against her, as it did at various times, for example, during a suffrage parade in 1913 and again in 1917 when she picketed the White House while the country was at war, she either ignored the opposition or turned it to her own advantage. Publicity was one of the major tactics Paul employed. She did not desire nor incite the crowds to turn riotous during the suffrage parade of 1913, but when they did she exploited the resulting publicity to the benefit of both her organization and the suffrage movement in general.[37] In similar fashion, attacks on the White House picketers by hostile crowds during the First World War generated publicity that sometimes rivaled the war news for front-page coverage in the nations' newspapers.[38] For Paul, with her keen understanding of the media, publicity was the event.

In attempting to explain Paul, historians have often dismissed her as either well-meaning but harmlessly misguided, or as fanatical and dangerously misguided—in either case harmful to the suffrage movement. At best, she is given minimal credit for advancing suffrage.[39] Others have gone so far as to label her pathological—a personality who appealed only to persons on the fringes of the suffrage movement.[40] In a very limited sense, this explanation of Paul may be understandable. Contemporaries who responded to her were alienated from society to the extent that they willingly followed a leader who advocated what were considered extreme, radical tactics. Attempts by women to improve their status in society and to secure their rights more often than not have been criticized by those who held power and wished to maintain the status quo. Aggressive action, militancy, and perceived radicalism on the part of women have been even more severely criticized and condemned. Aggression, when attributed to women, has always been and remains to a large extent, a negative trait. But, as S. N. Eisenstadt, in his commentary on Weber's work, observed, "The search for meaning, consistency, order is not always something extraordinary, something which exists only . . . among pathological personalities, but also in all stable situations . . . focused within some specific parts of the social structure and of an individual's life space."[41]

American society in the early twentieth century often produced disorientation and alienation for women, particularly for middle-class women who had the desire, the means, the motivation, and the opportunity to be actively involved in pursuing equal rights. Their response to Alice Paul was a manifestation of their own search for balance and equality in a world they perceived to be disorderly. And Paul herself was motivated not by an unrealistic obsession that could justly be interpreted as pathological, but by a logically deduced expectation of equality for both sexes. Her charismatic appeal made her more effective in pursuing that goal, and a continually modernizing industrial society provided her with a constituency more receptive to her message.

Paul, although she professed to be unaware of her power or the source of it, nevertheless used her unfailing ability to motivate people to do things they did not necessarily want to do.[42] "I cannot say that I personally like to do the things that Alice Paul set us to do," wrote one less-than-enthusiastic worker, "But . . . I helped to picket the White House, to keep the fires burning near suffrage headquarters, and to pester congressmen and senators and did my little best to swell all sorts of parades and demonstrations."[43] More commonly, however, the women who worked in Paul's organization did so with great enthusiasm and were more than willing to follow Paul's instructions to the letter.

She may not have understood fully the source of her power, but Paul despite her protests to the contrary was aware of it and more important, she used it effectively. One suffrage volunteer vividly recalled how newcomers to the organization met Alice Paul for the first time. Those women who wanted to work for Paul were assigned tasks about the headquarters, but not specifically told which job they were being trained for or what precisely would be expected of them. Throughout their internship, Paul would receive reports on the volunteer's performance and potential from her coworkers. "And then Miss Paul sent for you," one such intern reported. "I will never forget that first interview. Miss Paul sat at a desk in a room seemingly completely dark except for a small desk lamp. . . . I felt she deliberately created an atmosphere of the tough executive. There was no subtlety about her. Direct, blunt, she asked why I wanted to do this. She wanted to probe sufficiently without wasting time, to discover if I had any weaknesses and to what extent she and the movement could depend on me."[44] This woman, like most others, left the meeting with a sense of deep commitment not only to suffrage but to Alice Paul as well. Not only was she determined not to let suffrage down, but she was even more determined not to let Alice Paul down.

Paul was more concerned about enthusiasm for the movement than she was with an individual's specific talents.[45] Ardent feminism and unwavering adherence to Paul's vision and goals were the criteria for acceptance in those whom she entrusted responsibility. Class, social standing, education, or experience did not particularly concern her. Thus, although her organization, like most suffrage groups, was largely white and middle-class, dedication to feminism and not an elite status was the common bond.[46] At the same time, Paul harbored many of the same biases and prejudices associated with her elite, white, upper-middle-class milieu. Clearly, she was much more comfortable with people of her own background and status. She could speak with no self-consciousness of her desire to find a quiet secluded home where there were still "some American people left."[47] While she claimed long-standing friendships with both African-Americans and Jews, at the same time she had a reputation for particularly noticeable prejudices against both groups.[48] She was, in short, neither better nor worse than the society in which she lived.

Whatever the degree of her racism, Paul's relationship with African-Americans often had less to do with an established racial policy—either articulated or unarticulated—than it did with her perception at the moment of how her organization might be affected. Thus her actions were not always predictable. In 1913, one of her coworkers, Elsie Hill, then in charge of the College Suffrage League's contingent in the Washington suffrage parade, informed Paul that several delegations of white marchers contested the inclusion of representatives from Howard University, one of the nation's most prestigious black universities at that time. These white marchers, Hill reported, were threatening to boycott the parade if the black women were allowed to participate. In 1913, Paul could easily have resolved the problem by refusing the black women a place in the line of march, without fear of creating a larger problem. Racism, both openly virulent and covert, prevailed throughout the country. Theodore Roosevelt, the Progressive party candidate in the election of 1912, conducted a "Lily White" campaign in order to secure southern votes. And the newly elected Wilson administration inaugurated a policy of racial segregation in federal government agencies within months of taking over the Oval Office.[49] Like professional politicians, most suffrage leaders perceived a danger in alienating white legislators, voters, and real or potential supporters of their cause. The social climate that encouraged and fostered discriminatory behavior also dictated that, with few exceptions, African-Americans were not asked to attend or to speak at suffrage meetings in most sections of the country.[50] For these reasons then, Paul could have appeased the white marchers by disallowing the Howard women to march. Instead, she refused to pull them from the parade. And, to protect them from possible harrassment or worse, Paul ordered that they march between two groups of male participants. This solution apparently mollified the white complainers and ensured the safety of the black women.[51]

Ironically, long after the Nineteenth Amendment was ratified, when the objections of white potential suffrage supporters towards the inclusion of blacks would have carried much less weight, Paul took a less charitable stand. The event was the post-ratification meeting of the National Woman's Party, the political party founded by Alice Paul in 1916. The convention was billed as an opportunity to discuss issues facing women in the post-ratification era, as well as an opportunity to set the agenda for the NWP. For Paul personally, her goal was to bid farewell to her party in an atmosphere free of dissension and discord—Paul had announced that she was retiring from the NWP after the convention. A number of minority groups requested time to speak at the convention, including a coalition of black women's clubs, one of which was the National Association of Colored Women. In this case, Paul decided almost petulantly that "these people" were "harassing" her and that they were "spoilers."[52] She allowed the African-American women to speak, but she did not give them a prominent place, nor did she give them more than a few minutes to address the convention.

These decisions were arbitrarily made. Paul certainly possessed her own prejudices, but she did not attempt actively to enforce a policy as such, regarding either race or class. Rather, she utilized a pragmatic approach that offered solutions dependent upon her perception of the moment. Her own racism, of course, had to influence her perceptions. Sometimes her decisions coincided with the prevailing social mores; often they did not. But they were always made, she believed, with an eye on the long-range goal.

Paul was not an easy person to know. Her public persona was that of a professional organizer, an astute politician, a forceful leader. Her private persona was enigmatic at best. At a time when most women were "other directed," Paul apparently had made the ego-identity shift to an individualistic ethic necessary for development as a strong individual.[53] Never introspective, Paul applied her abilities to the task at hand with a cool measuredness and without emotionalism. Her intellectualism and purposefulness made her seem aloof, coldly efficient, and abrupt to the point of rudeness and insensitivity. Frequently, however, what was interpreted as insensitivity was really absentmindedness. When it was pointed out to her that a volunteer worker had left in anger because Paul had not adequately appreciated the woman's efforts, Paul made a point to express gratitude to other workers and even went so far as to apologize for uncommitted transgressions.[54]

Despite her refusal to dwell on adversity or obstacles, Paul was not immune to attacks leveled against both her and her organization. She never forgot an incident in 1914, just after she had embarked on her first anti–Democratic party campaign. She went to Mississippi to attend a conference with NAWSA and other suffrage groups. But rather than enjoy the camaraderie of her fellow suffragists, Paul was shunned by the other delegates. The profound sense of isolation that she experienced was still with her sixty years later. "I remember going down in the morning for breakfast, and here were all these people from all the different states in the Union, and I remember not one human being spoke to me. I just felt *such* an outcast, and for a long time we were regarded in that way."[55]

Although she had many devoted admirers and loyal coworkers and friends, Paul had few intimate, long-term relationships. Most of her close friends were women who worked with her in the American and international women's movements. Although she never married, she certainly had no conflicts with the institution of marriage.[56] Her closest friend throughout her long career was Elsie Hill, a Connecticut congressperson's daughter who came to work for Paul in 1913. They were immediately drawn to one another and worked together almost constantly from then on. Much later, after the deaths of Elsie's husband and Alice's sister Helen, with whom Alice had made her home in the 1940s, the two friends moved in together and continued working on women's issues until Elsie's death in the late 1960s.[57]

Recent scholarship suggests that some relationships between women reformers and activists during this period were also sexual relationships. There is no evidence to date that suggests that this was true of Paul's relationship with Hill. The lack of such evidence is not, in and of itself, enough to conclude that Paul did not engage in sexual relationships with women friends (or men, for that matter).[58] But in her private life, Paul was as conservative as she was radical in her public life. She never hesitated to censor coworkers or to monitor their behavior about even the pettiest matters. She refused, for example, to allow her workers to smoke in the main floor offices of the suffrage headquarters. Moreover, she prohibited smoking in the upstairs secluded rooms on occasions when important visitors were scheduled to be in the building.[59] On more substantive issues, such as birth control, abortion, and divorce, party workers clearly understood that they were not to express their own personal opinions. Paul went so far as to chastise members for making statements that she had not personally authorized.[60] Other issues took a back seat to suffrage, for Paul adamantly insisted that the organization stick to its single-issue framework. In many instances, this strategic and tactical stance was reinforced by her personal conservatism and sense of morality which, for example, prompted her to express disdain for persons who advocated the right to sexual preference.[61] There is no evidence, therefore no reason, to suggest that her private conduct contradicted her public statements.

The contours of Paul's private life suggest that she monitored her own actions as relentlessly as she governed her coworkers—surely a strange practice for an advocate of women's freedom. Her followers, however much they may have chafed under her tight rein, did not view her as arrogant, presumptive, or unfaithful to their cause—at least not until after suffrage had been passed and new political lines had to be drawn in the women's movement. Regardless of how her public image changed over time, Paul always maintained a larger vision, one that transcended her own conservatism: "I think if we get freedom for women, then they are probably going to do a lot of things that I wish they wouldn't do; but it seems to me that isn't our business to say what they should do with it. It is our business to see that they are free."[62]

Freedom, for Paul, extended beyond suffrage. Her goal was to remove all legal inequalities from the statute books throughout the country through passage of a federal Equal Rights Amendment (ERA). Such a goal was, and is, profoundly revolutionary in nature. Equal suffrage was the most radical demand of the nineteenth-century women's rights movement because it propelled women into the public sphere.[63] Just so, the struggle for equal rights in the twentieth century demanded a radical redefinition of power relationships, one directed primarily at the public sphere, but that also had important and unavoidable consequences for the private sphere.

But securing support for an Equal Rights Amendment in the 1920s proved to be more difficult than its advocates anticipated. Battle lines very quickly were drawn between those who believed in equality for everyone, with special treatment or special legislation for no one, regardless of sex, and those who believed that protective legislation was necessary for women and children, especially in the workplace. And, since every major women's organization with the exception of the Woman's Party favored protective legislation, it was clear to all by 1925 that the ERA would be at least as difficult to secure as suffrage had been.

Many members of the Woman's Party retired from political activism after suffrage was won, for a variety of reasons. Some were simply exhausted and wanted to resume normal lives again. Others, like Lucy Burns, were both tired and a little bitter towards those who had sat out the suffrage movement. "I don't want to do anything more," Burns announced. "I think we have done all this for women, and we have sacrificed everything we possessed for them, and now let them . . . fight for it. I am not going to fight anymore."[64] For a while, there was some doubt regarding the role Alice Paul would play in activist politics. After the suffrage amendment was ratified, one of her goals was to get a law degree, which she did. But she could no more disassociate herself from seeking justice and equality for women than she could take up needlepoint as a full-time occupation. As one Washington reporter later observed, "Every other woman in Washington I can imagine without a cause. . . . Even over teacups I think of [Paul] as a political force, a will bound to express itself politically."[65]

Paul continued to express her will politically. After launching the National Woman's Party on the ERA road, she went to Europe and helped to found the World Woman's Party. She had always voiced discontent over the exclusion of women from participating in the League of Nations. For over a decade, until the start of World War II, Paul stayed in Europe, lobbying the League of Nations and working to involve women in international politics. When she returned from Europe, Paul threw herself back into the American ERA campaign. She was also instrumental in having a reference to sex equality included in the preamble to the United Nations Charter.[66]

After more than a decade in Europe, Paul found many changes in the National Woman's Party. It was still dedicated to promoting the ERA and had accomplished a great deal in the intervening years by persuading almost every major women's organization to support the ERA. But not everyone was happy to see Paul return to Washington and the national headquarters. Many believed she was trying to pick up where she had left off and that it was an unfair usurpation of power since she had chosen to spend so much of her time in Europe. In the late 1940s, a power struggle for control of the Woman's Party took placed amidst unfounded accusations that Paul had misused organization funds. Throughout the remainder of her life, however, Paul remained a leader of the National Woman's Party and active in the causes near and dear to her heart. In 1968 and 1969, already nearing her eighty-fifth birthday, Paul was on the front lines in the antiwar marches, and she continued to lobby for the ERA until a stroke in 1974 incapacited her. Alice Paul died on July 10, 1977, believing that the ERA, then three states short of ratification, would very soon be the law of the land. That was not to be, but Alice Paul will always be associated with equal rights. Late in her life, assessing her own career, Paul concluded, "The thing I think that was the most useful thing I ever did was having a part in getting the vote for all women."[67]

Notes

[1]Anne Herendeen, "What the Hometown Thinks of Alice Paul," *Everybody's* (July 1916), pp. 1127–1128.

[2]Ernestine Evans, "Women in the Washington Scene," *Century Magazine* (Sept. 1923), pp. 507–517.

[3]Full suffrage states as of November 1912 were Wyoming (1890; territory, 1869) Colorado (1893) Utah and Idaho (1896), Washington (1910), California (1911), and Oregon, Arizona and Kansas (1912).

[4]Inez Haynes Irwin, *The Story of the Woman's Party* (New York: Harcourt, Brace, 1921), pp. 14–16.

[5]Mrs. Medill McCormick to Harriet Vittam, 31 July 1914, Papers of the National American Woman Suffrage Association, the Library of Congress (hereafter cited as NAWSA Papers). The emphasis in the quotation is McCormick's.

[6]Doris Stevens, *Jailed For Freedom* (New York: Boni & Liveright, 1920), p. 17.

[7]Maud Younger, quoted in Inez Haynes Irwin, *Up Hill with Banners Flying* (Penobscot, ME: Traversity Press, 1964), pp. 15–16.

[8]Lucy Burns, quoted in Ibid., p. 16.

[9]Conversations with Alice Paul: Woman Suffrage and the Equal Rights Amendment, interview by Amelia Frye, 1971–73, Suffragists Oral History Project, Bancroft Library, University of California at Berkeley (1976), pp. 1–5, 279–284 (hereafter cited as Paul Interview).

[10]Ibid., p. 6.

[11]Robert Gallagher, "I Was Arrested Of Course . . . ," *American Heritage* 25 (February 1974), pp. 17–18.

[12]Paul Interview, pp. 7–8.

[13]Herendeen, "What the Hometown Thinks," p. 1128.

[14]Paul Interview, pp. 7–8.

[15]"LMWW" to Alice Paul, 26 October 1914, The Papers of the National Woman's Party, 1913–1920, The Suffrage Years, Library of Congress, Washington, D.C. (hereafter cited as NWP Papers). The letter, from a friend of Paul's who knew the family quite well, reports on a running argument between Paul's uncle and a cousin who supported Paul's activity.

[16]Paul Interview, pp. 67–70.

[17]Ibid., p. 16.

[18]Mabel Vernon to Amelia Frye, "Mabel Vernon, Speaker for Suffrage and Petitioner for Peace," Berkeley Oral History Project, Bancroft Library, University of California, pp. 33–34 (hereafter cited as Vernon Interview).

[19]Paul Interview, p. 16.

[20]Inez Haynes Irwin, *Up Hill with Banners Flying* (Penobscot, ME: Traversity Press, 1964), p. 24.

[21]Paul Interview, p. 17.

[22]Ibid., pp. 17–18.

[23]Ibid., p. 31.

[24]Ibid., p. 20.

[25]Ibid., pp. 31a, 34.

[26]Suffrage Scrapbooks, vol. 1, pp. 80, 95, Sophia Smith Collection, Smith College, Northampton, MA.

[27]"Lucy Burns," *Notable American Women: A Biographical Dictionary,* Edward L. James, et al., eds. (Cambridge, MA, and London: The Belknap Press of Harvard University, 1971–1980), vol. 4, pp. 124–125; also, Irwin, *Up Hill with Banners Flying,* pp. 14–18.

[28]Paul Interview, p. 48.

[29]Irwin, *The Story of the Woman's Party,* p. 16.

[30]Vernon Interview, pp. 35–36.

[31]Paul Interview, p. 47.

[32]Irwin, *The Story of the Woman's Party,* p. 16.

[33]Paul Interview, pp. 225–227; Irwin, *Up Hill with Banners Flying,* p. 18.

[34]Ibid., p. 18.

[35]Max Weber, *The Sociology of Religion* (London: Methuen, 1965), pp. 45–59.

[36]Irwin, *Up Hill with Banners Flying,* p. 26.

[37]See, for example, newspaper coverage in the *New York Times,* 4–6 March 1913.

[38]*New York Times,* 23 June and 7 and 8 July 1917; also *Washington Post,* 23, June 24, 7 July 1917.

[39]See, for example, Aileen Kraditor, *Ideas of the Woman Suffrage Movement, 1890–1920* (New York: Anchor Books, 1970); Eleanor Flexner, *Century of Struggle: The Woman's Rights Movement in the United States* (Cambridge, MA: The Belknap Press of Harvard University, 1975); and Anne Firor Scott and Andrew Scott, eds., *One Half the People: The Fight for Woman Suffrage* (Philadelphia: Lippincott, 1975).

[40]Foremost among historians who apply this interpretation to Paul is William O'Neill, *Everyone Was Brave: The Rise and Fall of Feminism in America* (Chicago: Quadrangle Books, 1969); and *The Woman Movement: Feminism in the United States and England* (Chicago: Quadrangle Books, 1969); and Robert Riegel, *American Feminism* (Lawrence, KS: University of Kansas Press, 1963).

[41]S. N. Eisenstadt, ed., *Max Weber on Charisma and Institution Building* (Chicago: University of Chicago Press, 1968), pp. xxiii–xxvi.

[42]In her interview with Amelia Frye, Paul, on several occasions, expressed wonderment over, for example, the reason why the Pankhursts singled her out of the hundreds of WSPU members and invested responsibility in her. She was inclined to attribute it more to the fact that she was an American

and therefore more noticeable than to the fact that people were drawn to her because of her charismatic personality.

[43]*Biographical Cyclopedia of American Women,* p. 125.

[44]Rebecca Hourwich Reyher to Amelia Frye, "Rebecca Hourwich Reyher: Search and Struggle for Equality and Independence," Suffragists Oral History Project, Bancroft Library, University of California at Berkeley (1977), pp. 45–50 (hereafter cited as Reyher Interview).

[45]Paul Interview, p. 189.

[46]Ibid., pp. 183–189.

[47]Ibid., p. 11.

[48]Vernon Interview, pp. 157–158; Frieda Kirchwey, "Alice Paul Pulls the Strings," *The Nation* (March 1921), p. 332.

[49]Arthur S. Link, "Theodore Roosevelt and the South in 1912," *North Carolina Historical Review* (July 1946), pp. 313–324, and "Correspondence Relating to the Progressive Party's 'Lily White' Policy in 1912," *Journal of Southern History* (November 1944), pp. 480–490; Nancy J. Weiss, "The Negro and the New Freedom: Fighting Wilsonian Segregation," *Political Science Quarterly* (March 1969), pp. 61–79; Christine A. Lunardini, "Standing Firm: William Monroe Trotter's Meetings with Woodrow Wilson, 1913–1914," *Journal of Negro History* (Summer 1979), pp. 244–264.

[50]Rebecca Hourwich Reyher: Search and Struggle for Equality and Independence. Interview conducted by Amelia R. Frye and Fenn Ingersoll, Suffragists Oral History Project, University of California at Berkeley (1971), pp. 61–62.

[51]Paul Interview pp. 132–133.

[52]Kirchwey, "Alice Paul Pulls the Strings," *Nation,* p. 332.

[53]Phyllis Chesler, *Women and Madness* (Garden City, NY: Doubleday, 1972), pp. 299–300.

[54]Irwin, *The Story of the Woman's Party,* pp. 14–15.

[55]Paul Interview, p. 110. The emphasis is Paul's.

[56]Ibid., pp. 267–272.

[56]Ibid., p. 250.

[58]Carroll Smith-Rosenberg, "The Female World of Love and Ritual: The Relations between Women in the Nineteenth-Century America," in Nancy Cott and Elizabeth Pleck, eds., *A Heritage of Her Own* (New York: Simon & Schuster, 1979), pp. 311–342; Blanche Weisen Cook, "Female Support Networks and Political Activism: Lillian Wald, Crystal Eastman, and Emma Goldman," Ibid., pp. 412–444.

[59]Reyher Interview, pp. 65–66.

[60]Dora Lewis to Alice Paul, 14 July 1916; Paul to Lewis, 25 July 1916, NWP Papers.

[61]Paul Interview, pp. 195–196.

[62]Ibid., p. 196.

[63]Ellen Carol DuBois, *Feminism and Suffrage: The Emergence of an Independent Women's Movement in America, 1848–1869* (Ithaca, NY: Cornell University Press, 1978), pp. 15–20.

[64]Paul Interview, p. 257; *Notable American Women*, Vol 4, pp. 124–125.

[65]Ernestine Evans, "Women in the Washington Scene," *Century Magazine*, CVL (September 1923), p. 514.

[66]Ibid., p. 514; *New York Times*, 10 July 1977, p. 42.

[67]Ibid., Paul Interview, p. 42.

PART VII

New Horizons

Following World War I, the business boom in America signaled an era of unprecendented economic speculation. The era was short-lived, however. The stockmarket crash in October 1929 initiated a traumatic shift for all Americans and ushered in the Great Depression. Popular perceptions of women's roles transformed dramatically within a period of a few years. As Americans were thrown into the business of survival and recovery, feminist demands took a backseat to larger economic concerns.

By 1933, over 25 percent of American workers were unemployed. But it was not only the unemployed who feared for their futures: hundreds of thousands of middle-class Americans found wages cut and job "security" threatened. Attitudes toward women's participation in the labor force were affected by these setbacks. Women out in the wage-earning economy—except female heads of household—were branded as barriers to full economic recovery. President Franklin D. Roosevelt's "New Deal," a myriad of platforms and agencies for economic recovery, instituted new government employment programs, many of which included women. Even a feminist leader such as Frances Perkins, who became the first woman to hold a cabinet post when she was appointed Secretary of Labor in 1933, was forced to denounce the "pin-money worker," the housewife who allegedly worked outside the home for petty cash to purchase luxury items.

The National Economy Act of 1933 forced many women out of the civil service by banning both spouses from working for the government. Three-fourths of the spouses who resigned, generally the lower paid of the couple, were women. Members of the League of Women Voters (the post-suffrage heir of the National American Woman Suffrage Association) supported this move: "We of the League are very much for the rights of women, but we are not feminists primarily; we are citizens." But many New Deal feminists, Eleanor Roosevelt among them, condemned this policy.

Public opinion and policy discriminated against women despite feminist opposition. Private businesses tried to keep women from competing with men for positions. The American Federation of Labor (AFL), the largest and most powerful union in its day, declared that married female workers with employed husbands should be banned from employment. Even women's colleges discouraged their graduates from taking paying jobs, trying to renew interest in the nineteenth-century ethic of domestic feminism. Married women were told they should volunteer their labor to do social housekeeping within their communities. Government policy and media campaigns worked well. By 1936, a Gallup poll found that 82 percent of all Americans believed that wives should not work if husbands were employed, and 75 percent of the women polled echoed this sentiment.

The depression affected nearly all aspects of American women's lives. The marriage rate dipped and the birth rate was in long-term decline, with 1933 as the nadir year. Birth control clinics grew during this period, not because of feminist demands, but because of the simple need to limit the number of mouths to be fed in a period of economic deprivation and instability. Feminists tried to push birth control into New Deal programs, but Congress resisted. Finally, reformers were able to win victories in the courts, with the result that doctors could distribute birth control information and devices unless prohibited by state law.

Women's roles in the marketplace changed as well as their family expectations. Rather than being conspicuous consumers of goods, women were expected to become thrifty and enterprising producers for the household. Wives hoped to save their husband's hard-earned cash for those essential goods that could not be provided by female domestic labor. Home industry replaced smart buying in advice columns in women's magazines. Eleanor Roosevelt provided special "White House menus" to spur homemakers into making more nutritious and thrifty meals. Some women transformed this new ideology into more activist roles by forming housewives' associations and women's groups committed to public housing.

Some scholars have found that the only women whose lives did not alter dramatically were the very rich or the very poor. Women in poverty in the South shared lives much like those of their mothers and grandmothers. They worked by their husbands' sides in the fields, tended large families, and were saddled with harsh household labor; they had only outdoor plumbing and primitive fuel supplies. Nevertheless, the depression could and did increase the number of hardships endured by rural families. Perhaps the decline of male status within society gave women the opportunity to demonstrate their enormous reserves of strength, while men crumpled under the weight of economic burdens. Women often held families together. Massive migrations wreaked havoc with family stability when thousands of farmers from the Dust Bowl ("Okies," as they were called) moved westward to California or other more prosperous states. Rural mothers resolutely tried to keep kinfolk fed and clothed and housed despite mighty challenges. Women did not welcome these opportunities, but met them with a courage that enhanced their family roles, a theme exemplified in John Steinbeck's classic novel, *The Grapes of Wrath*.

Another group of poor women who found its lot worsened was factory workers. While the closing of immigration in the 1920s should have created better conditions for industrial workers (by shutting the door on cheaper labor flowing into the marketplace), worse ones prevailed. Women found themselves working for reduced wages. Further, employers introduced the abusive "apprentice system" and hired apprentices (providing them with room and board but no pay) during a speedup, then fired them when orders were met. These and other hardships drove women into increasing labor militance. Women's roles in unionization drives were enhanced, given a boost by the National Industrial Recovery Act of 1933, which specifically guaranteed workers' rights to organize. Although women had been given the cold shoulder by the AFL (mainly craft and other skilled labor unions), they were warmly welcomed into the more accessible Congress of Industrial Organization (CIO) in 1938. The CIO was interested in organizing all workers, including the unskilled, and profited from mass-production industries such as textiles and auto manufacturing. Women were prominent in strike organization, "with babies and banners," walking on picket lines in the 1937 Chicago Republic Steel plant strike and organizing an Emergency Brigade in Flint, Michigan, during strikes at auto factories. By 1940, over 800,000 women were union members, tripling their participation since 1933.

Other groups, noting women's labor activism, began to draw women into their movements. Communist Party organizers were able to promise a greater equality for women within political organizations—something democratic and union leaders were unable to deliver. One woman who joined the Communist Party was Elizabeth Gurley Flynn, who began her activist career as a socialist and joined the International Workers of the World (IWW, known as "the Wobblies") in 1906. Helping organize the 1912 Lawrence, Massachusetts textile strike and the 1913 Paterson, New Jersey strike, she also spearheaded organizing in 1916 at the Mesabi Range in Minnesota. In 1917, Flynn and 168 fellow Wobblies were indicted for violation of the Espionage Act of 1917. Her legal defense activities led her to help found the American Civil Liberties Union in 1920, an organization from which, ironically, she was expelled when she joined the American Communist Party in 1937. She later headed the Party after serving time in jail for dissident activity. Although few women threw themselves so wholeheartedly into Communist activities, Flynn was one of thousands of young women who experimented with radical politics during the Depression decade.

Just as the Depression had given rise to a new ideological ethos for women, so the outbreak of World War II and America's entry into the war in December 1941 introduced yet another reshaping of concepts of ideal womanhood. The national emergency demanded women's mobilization as well as men's. The number of women in the wage-earning force increased by 57 percent during the war. Over 6 million women who had never worked for wages before took jobs, married women's labor force participation doubled, and unions gained 2.2 million women in a matter of four years. Not all of this was achieved without resistance, however. At the outset, most male managers were reluctant to employ women in all aspects of the defense industry, citing, for example, "the lack of adequate toilet facilities" as an excuse for not hiring women. But reservations were abandoned by necessity within the first year of war production. During the war, 60 percent of those polled in a Gallup canvass supported wives working in the war industry. The shift in perception from the Depression ethic was rapid and widespread.

American women, wooed with "Commando Mary" and "Rosie the Riveter" and other propaganda, responded positively to the call. Such campaigns were in no way linked to sexual egalitarianism nor feminism, but women were often exploited despite the fact that they were doing a "man's job." Employers hoped to maintain rigid gender roles despite women's massive participation in the war industries, and despite men and women's working side by side with little differentiation except pay. Although the National War Labor Board mandated equal pay for equal work, the government allowed job classifications which provided *de facto* separate pay scales for men and women. However, women complained little because the wages they received in the war industry were superior to any they might earn in the other sectors of the economy.

Further, the government response to the needs of mothers with federally funded daycare programs was feeble. In 1943 the Lanham Act provided for child care centers, but so few were built that only one in ten defense workers could take advantage of these facilities. Despite its limited effectiveness, this brief experiment served as an example for a future generation: with safe and inexpensive child care support, mothers might be vital contributors to the national economy. The unsolicited opportunities of wartime production offered women the means of balancing household responsibilities and wage-earning roles.

One group of women who had been balancing work and family for centuries, African-American women, improved their status as well. At the outbreak of war, almost three-fourths of African-American women wage-earners were employed as domestic servants. They were virtually excluded from clerical and retail positions outside the black community and they were discriminated against as factory operators. By 1944, this proportion was reduced by one-third as the number of African-American women working in factories grew to nearly 20 percent. This did not, however, represent status or wage equality. Indeed, black women testified that segregation of tasks was common in factories. White women were given jobs that were "cleaner" or "more skilled." Often, however, crunches on the assembly line inadvertently created the breakdown of barriers erected by prejudice. Although this did not signal a change in attitude, it gave African-American women opportunities for service and achievement—as well as disproving racist theories of inferiority.

The media worked to recreate women's images during both the Depression and the war. Government propaganda and advertising were central factors in dictating what roles women would have in the work force, and during the war, in shaping women's self-images: soap ads featured women with blow torches and coveralls and posters highlighted stenographers in uniform as "secretaries of war." A larger role in shaping women's self-images was played by an increasingly powerful medium: American movies. During the 1930s, film audiences included millions of young women seeking role models in the parade of stars. Film magazines and movies themselves refined and shaped star images and the models of womanhood to which many American women aspired.

During the early years of filmmaking, two separate screen images dominated—the virgin and the vamp. Mary Pickford, the most successful female film star of her day, typified the former. She was forced to play the role of a child onscreen until she was well past the age of thirty. Pickford's image was wedded to the American ideal of healthy, wholesome, and, above all, innocent beauty. The first Miss America, Margaret Gorman, chosen at a pageant dreamed up by Atlantic City promoters in the 1920s, bore a striking resemblance to Pickford.

A contrasting screen idol was embodied in the character of the vamp, an image that Theda Bara popularized during the silent film era. Eye makeup created for Bara by Helena Rubenstein was mass marketed, and the connection between movies and fashion flourished. Gloria Swanson, Marlene Dietrich, and Greta Garbo played variations of the vamp. It was no accident that many of these "exotic" roles were portrayed by foreign women imported for American audiences. The screen siren, although alluring, often met with tragic consequences to reinforce the values stamped on the American screen by Pickford and her celluloid descendants. The *femme fatale* character did not empower women in any real sense and nearly all these seductresses pursued a goal similar to that of their virginal sisters in film: a man.

During the 1930s, however, female film stars played a wider range of roles, and many more assertive and independent models emerged. The spunk and savvy demeanors of women played by Irene Dunne, Jean Arthur, and Myrna Loy paved the way for a stronger breed of screen women. Even the stars of comedies were able to create more daring roles: Carole Lombard transformed the "dizzy" blonde into her own intelligent brand of femininity and Claudette Colbert plunged zestfully into sexual banter, often besting her man. Although Jean Harlow may have been exploited as a "sex goddess" (and indeed led a tragic personal life before her premature death at twenty-nine), her screen characters projected more complexity than the one-dimensional women studio publicists tried to portray. Mae West, who by 1935 was earning over $480,000 per year, transformed the image of the sex symbol into much more than Hollywood bargained for when her tough-talking, wise-cracking characters projected power as well as appeal.

West was but one of a generation of women in Hollywood who began to command respect as well as shape ideals for an eager female audience. Others included Rosalind Russell, Bette Davis, Joan Crawford, and Katharine Hepburn. Hepburn was born into a socially prominent family in Connecticut, and her mother was a birth control crusader with Margaret Sanger, the most prominent twentieth century advocate of birth control. Hepburn attended Bryn Mawr before going on the stage in 1928 and began her film career in 1932. Hepburn has won four Academy Awards, but is perhaps best remembered for some of her dozen film collaborations with Spencer Tracy, classics such as *Woman of the Year,* in which she portrayed an outstanding woman journalist, *Pat and Mike,* in which she played a woman athlete, and *Adam's Rib,* where her portrait of a lawyer entangled in a "battle of the sexes" with her husband and courtroom adversary includes one of the most sophisticated treatments of feminism on the screen.

The rapid proliferation of opportunities for women on screen during the 1930s and 1940s reflected changes within society as a whole. Female journalists were gaining prominence and influence, as the careers of Dorothy Thompson, foreign correspondent-columnist, and Dorothy Day, founder of the *Catholic Worker,* demonstrate. Photographers Margaret Bourke-White and Dorothea Lange captured the American public's imagination, as well as bringing national and international events into dramatic visual focus. Mildred Ella (Babe) Didrickson became an Olympic gold medalist before becoming a professional golfer, and African-American Althea Gibson, a tennis star, was treated to a ticker-tape parade in New York City when she returned triumphant from Wimbledon in 1957, having won both the singles and the doubles titles. Female scholars such as anthropologist Margaret Mead and biologist Rachel Carson, whose *Silent Spring* stirred a generation into ecological awareness, began to have a wider impact on society. Artists such as Georgia O'Keeffe may not have garnered the critical attention and wide audience of their male counterparts, but their work would influence the art world and reshape perspectives on cultural aesthetics with the advent of the feminist renaissance in the 1960s.

The women of the generation between the World Wars found themselves caught within several snares. Many fought to fulfill the competing ideals ushered in by each new decade. Some struggled to hold the ground hard won by an earlier generation. Some women saw not a recycling of patterns but innovative and pioneering transformations—changes that might make a permanent difference in women's experiences. During this important era the majority of women looked to new horizons—new role models, images, and opportunities—to have greater control over their own lives and greater influence over the lives of others.

Eleanor Roosevelt

(1884–1962)

William H. Chafe

Eleanor Roosevelt was born October 11, 1884. Educated privately, in her youth she combined an upper-class social whirl with great interest in "social housekeeping," working for the National Consumers' League and at a New York settlement house. She married her cousin, Franklin Delano Roosevelt, in 1905; they had six children between 1906 and 1916. During World War I and the 1920s Eleanor Roosevelt emerged in the public world of reform politics. For the rest of her life she was an important leader in putting the concerns of working-class women, of African-Americans, of the poor, and of the politically oppressed worldwide, onto America's national political agenda. She did so only in part through her relationship with her husband, who was president from 1933 until 1945. While she always had an unprecedently equal working relationship with FDR, Eleanor Roosevelt established a separate living space for herself at Hyde Park, called Val-Kill, in 1926. After FDR's death in 1945, Roosevelt continued to campaign for social justice through her writings, speeches, and as the U.S. delegate to the United Nations. She maintained a deep involvement in the reform wing of the Democratic party until her death on November 7, 1962.

Anna Eleanor Roosevelt was born in New York City on October 11, 1884, the first child and only daughter of Elliott Roosevelt and Anna (Hall) Roosevelt. Descended on both sides from distinguished colonial families active in commerce, banking, and politics, she seemed destined to enjoy all the benefits of class and privilege. Yet by the time she was ten, both her parents had died, as had a younger brother Elliott, leaving her and her second brother Hall the only survivors.

As a youngster, Eleanor experienced emotional rejection almost from the time she could remember. "I was a solemn child," she recalled, "without beauty. I seemed like a little old woman entirely lacking in the spontaneous joy and mirth of youth." Her mother called her "Granny" and, at least in Eleanor's memory, treated her daughter differently than her son, warmly embracing the boy while being only "kindly and indifferent" to her little girl. From most of her family, young Eleanor received the message that she was "very plain," almost ugly, and certainly "old fashioned." When her parents died, she went to live with her grandmother, who was equally without warmth. As Eleanor's cousin Corinne later remarked, "it was the grimmest childhood I had ever known. Who did she have? Nobody."

In fact, Eleanor had one person—her father. "He was the one great love of my life as a child," she later wrote, "and . . . like many children, I have lived a dream life with him." Described by his friends as "charming, impetuous, high-spirited, big-hearted, generous, [and] friendly," Elliott exhibited ease and grace in his social interactions. With Eleanor, he developed an intimacy that seemed almost magical. "As soon as I could talk," she recalled, "I went into his dressing room every morning and chattered to him . . . I even danced with him, intoxicated by the pure joy of motion . . . until he would pick me up and throw me into the air." She dreamed of the time when they would go off together—"always he and I . . . and someday [we] would have a life of our own together."

But Elliott's capacity for ebullient play and love also contained the seeds of self-destruction—alcoholism, irresponsibility, cruelty. He never found an anchor, either in public life or business, to provide stability for himself and his family. Elliott's emotional imbalance quickly produced problems in his marriage and banishment from the household. The last four years of his life were like a roller coaster. Elliott nourished the emotional relationship with Eleanor through letters to "father's own little Nell," writing of "the wonderful long rides . . . through the grand snow-clad forests, over the white hills" that he wanted them to enjoy together. But when his long-awaited visits occurred, they often ended in disaster, as when Elliott left Eleanor with the doorman at New York's Knickerbocker Club, promising to return but going off on a drunken spree instead. The pain of betrayal was exceeded only by Eleanor's depth of love for the man she believed was "the only person who really cared." Looking back later in life for an explanation of her inability to express emotions spontaneously, she concluded that the trauma of her childhood was the main cause. "Something locked me up," she wrote.

After her father's death, an emotional void pervaded Eleanor's life until, at age fourteen, she enrolled in Allenswood, a girls' school outside London presided over by Marie Souvestre, daughter of a well-known French philosopher and radical. At Allenswood, the girl found a circle of warmth and support. "She was beloved by everybody," her cousin remarked. "Saturdays we were allowed a sortie in Putney which has stores where you could buy books, [and] flowers. Young girls had crushes and you left [gifts] in the room with the girl you were idolizing. Eleanor's room every Saturday would be full of flowers because she was so admired." Allenswood also provided educational inspiration. Souvestre passionately embraced unpopular causes, staunchly defending Dreyfus in France and the cause of the Boers in South Africa. "I consider the three years which I spent with her as the beginning of an entirely new outlook on life," Eleanor wrote. Marie Souvestre toured the continent with the girl, confiding in her and expressing the affection that made it possible for Eleanor to flower. Describing her stay at Allenswood as "the happiest years of my life," Eleanor noted that "whatever I have become since had its seeds in those three years of contact with a liberal mind and strong personality." The love and admiration were mutual. "I miss you every day of my life," Souvestre wrote her in 1902.

The imprint of Marie Souvestre was not lost when Eleanor returned to the United States at age seventeen to "come out" in New York society. Even in the rush of parties and dances, she kept her eye on the more serious world of ideas and social service. Souvestre had written her in 1901: "Even when success comes, as I'm sure it will, bear in mind that there are more quiet and enviable joys than to be among the most sought-after women at a ball." Heeding the injunction, Eleanor plunged into settlement-house work and social activism.

Much of Eleanor Roosevelt's subsequent political life can be traced to this early involvement with social reform. At age eighteen she joined the National Consumers' League, headed by Florence Kelley. The league was committed to securing health and safety for workers—especially women—in clothing factories and sweatshops. On visits to these workplaces, Eleanor learned firsthand the misery of the working poor and developed a lifelong commitment to their needs. At the same time, she joined the Junior League and commenced work at the Rivington Street Settlement House, where she taught calisthenics and dancing and witnessed both the deprivation of the poor and the courage of slum dwellers who sought to improve their lot. Eleanor discovered that she preferred social work to debutante parties. More and more, she came to be recognized as a key member of a network of social reformers in New York City.

At the same time, however, Eleanor was secretly planning to marry her cousin Franklin Roosevelt, an event that would be followed by a fifteen-year hiatus in her public activities. Like his godfather (Eleanor's father), Franklin was "a gay cavalier," spontaneous, warm, and gregarious. But unlike Elliott, Franklin also possessed good sense and singleness of purpose. Eleanor saw in him the spark of life that she remembered from her father. After their engagement, she even sent to Franklin a letter signed "little Nell," her father's favorite name for her. Franklin, in turn, saw in Eleanor the discipline that would curb his own instincts toward excess.

After their marriage on March 17, 1905, the young Roosevelts settled in New York City while Franklin finished his law studies at Columbia. Franklin's mother, Sara, had warned Eleanor that she should not continue her work at the settlement house because she might bring home the diseases of the slum, but soon Eleanor was preoccupied with other concerns. Within a year, Anna was born (1906), then the next year James (1907), and two years later Franklin. Although Eleanor cherished her children, it was not a happy time. Sara dominated the household and imposed her will on almost all issues, including the raising of the children. As Eleanor later recalled, her mother-in-law "wanted . . . to hold onto Franklin and his children; she wanted them to grow up as she wished. As it turned out, Franklin's children were more my mother-in-law's children than they were mine." Nor was Sara's possessiveness limited to the children. At the family estate at Hyde Park, she was in total control. At dinner, Franklin sat at one end of the table, his mother at the other, and Eleanor in the middle. Before the fireplace there were two wing chairs, one for the mother, the other for the son. Eleanor was like an uninvited guest.

Fearing that she would hurt Franklin and lose his affection, Eleanor did not rebel. But she did experience a profound sense of inadequacy about her abilities as a wife and mother. Daughter Anna described her mother as unpredictable and inconsistent with the children, sweet one moment, critical and demanding the next. "Mother was always stiff, never relaxed enough to romp . . . Mother loved all mankind, but she did not know how to let her children love her." Eleanor herself recognized the problem. "It did not come naturally to me to understand little children or to enjoy them," she later said. "Playing with children was difficult for me because play had not been an important part of my own childhood." Instead of comforting the children when they experienced pain, she urged upon them an attitude of stoicism and endurance, as if to say that expressing emotion was a sign of bad character. The death of her third child, Franklin, a few months after his birth only reinforced Eleanor's unhappiness and feeling of inadequacy. Three additional children were born in the next six years—Elliott in 1910, Franklin in 1914, and John in 1916. Eleanor was devoted to each, yet motherhood could not be fulfilling in a household ruled by a grandmother who referred to the children as "my children . . . your mother only bore you."

In the years between 1910 and the beginning of World War I, Eleanor Roosevelt's activities revolved more and more around Franklin's growing political career. Elected as the Democratic assemblyman from Dutchess County in 1910, he rapidly became a leader of insurgent anti-Tammany forces in Albany. In 1913 Franklin was appointed assistant secretary of the Navy, and Eleanor, in addition to managing a large household, became expert at hosting the multiple social events required of a subcabinet member, as well as moving the entire household at least twice each year—to Campobello in New Brunswick during the summer, then to Hyde Park and back to Washington. During these years, she fulfilled the many traditionally female social activities expected of her.

America's entry into World War I in 1917 provided the occasion for Eleanor to reassert the public side of her personality. As her biographer Joseph Lash has noted, "the war gave her a reason acceptable to her conscience to free herself of the social duties that she hated, to concentrate less on her household, and to plunge into work that fitted her aptitude." She rose at 5 a.m. to coordinate activities at the Union Station canteen for soldiers on their way to training camps, took charge of Red Cross activities, supervised the knitting rooms at the Navy department, and spoke at patriotic rallies. Her interest in social welfare led to her drive to improve conditions at St. Elizabeth's mental hospital, while her sensitivity to suffering came forth in the visits she paid to wounded soldiers. "[My son] always loved to see you come in," one mother wrote. "You always brought a ray of sunshine."

The war served as a transition for Eleanor's reemergence as a public personality during the 1920s. After Franklin's unsuccessful campaign for the vice-presidency on James Cox's ticket in 1920, the Roosevelts returned to New York where Eleanor became active in the League of Women Voters. At the time of her marriage, she had opposed suffrage, thinking it inconsistent with women's proper role; now, as coordinator of the league's legislative program, she kept track of bills that came before the Albany legislature, drafted laws providing for equal representation for men and women, and worked with Esther Lape and Elizabeth Read on the league's lobbying activities. In 1921 she also joined the Women's Trade Union League—then viewed as "left-leaning"—and found friends there as well as political allies. In addition to working for programs such as the regulation of maximum hours and minimum wages for women, Eleanor helped raise funds for the WTUL headquarters in New York City. Her warm ties to first- and second-generation immigrants like Rose Schneiderman and Maud Swartz highlighted how far Eleanor had moved from the upper-class provincialism of her early years.

When Franklin was paralyzed by polio in 1922, Eleanor's public life expanded still further: she now became her husband's personal representative in the political arena. With the aid of Louis Howe, Franklin's political mentor and her own close friend, Eleanor first mobilized Dutchess County women, then moved on to the state Democratic party, organizing all but five counties by 1924. "Organization," she noted, "is something to which [the men] are always ready to take off their hats." No one did the job better. Leading a delegation to the Democratic convention in 1924, she fought (unsuccessfully) for equal pay legislation, the child labor amendment, and other planks endorsed by women reformers.

By 1928, Eleanor Roosevelt had clearly become a political leader in her own right. Once just a "political wife," she gradually extended that role and used it as a vehicle for asserting her own personality and agenda. In 1928, as head of the national women's campaign for the Democratic party, she made sure that the party appealed to independent voters, to minorities, and to women. She was also instrumental in securing the appointment of Frances Perkins as commissioner of industrial relations in New York after Franklin had been elected governor there. Dictating as many as one hundred letters a day, speaking to countless groups, acting as an advocate of social reform and women's issues, she had become a political personality of the first rank.

Eleanor Roosevelt's talent for combining partisan political activity with devotion to social welfare causes made her the center of an ever-growing female reform network. Her associates included Marion Dickerman and Nancy Cook, former suffragists and Democratic party loyalists; Molly Dewson, a longtime research secretary of the National Consumers League; and Mary Dreier of the Women's Trade Union League. She walked on picket lines with Rose Schneiderman, edited the *Women's Democratic News,* and advised the League of Women Voters on political tactics. Her political sophistication grew. "To many women, and I am one of them," she noted, "it is difficult to care enough [about an issue] to cause disagreement or unpleasant feelings, but I have come to the conclusion that this must be done for a time so we can prove our strength and demand respect for our wishes." By standing up for women in politics, ER provided a model for others to follow. In the process, she also earned the admiring, if grudging, respect of men who recognized a superb organizer when they saw one.

During the 1932 campaign, which led to Franklin's election to the presidency, Eleanor coordinated the activities of the Women's Division of the Democratic National Committee. Working with Mary (Molly) W. Dewson, she mobilized thousands of women precinct workers to carry the party's program to local voters; for example, the women distributed hundreds of thousands of "rainbow fliers," colorful sheets containing facts on the party's approach to various issues. After the election, Molly Dewson took charge of the Women's Division, corresponding daily with Eleanor both about appointing women to office and securing action on issues that would appeal to minorities, women, and such professional groups as educators and social workers. The two friends were instrumental in bringing to Washington an unprecedented number of dynamic women activists. Ellen Woodward, Hilda Worthington Smith, and Florence Kerr all held executives offices in the Works Progress Administration, while Lorena Hickok acted as eyes and ears for WPA director Harry Hopkins as she traveled across the country to observe the impact of the New Deal's relief program. Mary Anderson, director of the Women's Bureau, recalled that women government officials had formerly dined together in a small university club. "Now," she said, "there are so many of them that we need a hall."

Eleanor Roosevelt not only provided the impetus for appointing these women but also offered a forum for transmitting their views and concerns across the country. Soon after she entered the White House, she began a series of regular press conferences to which *only* women reporters were admitted, and where the first lady insisted on making "hard" news as well as providing social tidbits for the "women's page." She introduced such women as Mary McLeod Bethune and Hilda Worthington Smith to talk about their work with the New Deal. These sessions provided new status and prestige for the female press corps and they also underlined the importance of women's issues to the first lady. Her efforts helped create a community of women reporters and government workers. When the all-male Gridiron Club held its annual dinner to spoof the president and his male colleagues, the first lady initiated a Gridiron Widows' Club where the women in Washington could engage in their own satire.

Largely as a result of ER's activities, women achieved a strong voice in the New Deal. The proportion of women appointed as postmasters shot up from 17.6 percent in 1930 to 26 percent between 1932 and 1938. More important, the social welfare policies of the administration reflected a reform perspective that women like Ellen Woodward and Florence Kerr shared with men like Harry Hopkins and Aubrey Williams. When a particularly difficult issue involving women came up, the first lady would invite Molly Dewson to the White House and seat her next to the president, where she could persuade him of her point of view. ER's own political role appears most clearly in her work on the reelection drive of 1936, when she coordinated the efforts of both men and women and used the "educational" approach developed by the Women's Division in 1932 as a major campaign weapon. More than sixty thousand women precinct workers canvassed the electorate, handing out "rainbow fliers" as the party's principal literature. For the first time women received equal representation on the Democratic Platform Committee, an event described by the *New York Times* as "the biggest coup for women in years."

Eleanor Roosevelt's fear that she would have no active role as a presidential wife had been unfounded. She toured the country repeatedly, surveying conditions in the coal mines, visiting relief projects, and speaking out for the human rights of the disadvantaged. Through her newspaper column "My Day," she entered the homes of millions. Her radio programs, her lectures, and her writings communicated to the country her deep compassion for those who suffered. At the White House, in turn, she acted as advocate of the poor and disenfranchised. "No one who ever saw Eleanor Roosevelt sit down facing her husband," Rexford Tugwell wrote, "and holding his eyes firmly, [and saying] to him 'Franklin, I think you should' . . . or, 'Franklin surely you will not' . . . will ever forget the experience. . . . It would be impossible to say how often and to what extent American governmental processes have been turned in a new direction because of her determination." She had become, in the words of columnist Raymond Clapper, a "Cabinet Minister without portfolio—the most influential woman of our times."

But if Eleanor had achieved an unparalleled measure of political influence, it was in place of, rather than because of, an intimate personal relationship with Franklin. In 1932 Eleanor described a perfect couple as one where two people did not even need to tell each other how they felt, but cared so much that a look and the sound of a voice would tell all. Probably at no time after their first few years together did Franklin and Eleanor achieve that degree of intimacy. Not only was Sara still a dominant presence, but Franklin had embarked on his own interests and enthusiasms, often different from Eleanor's. The differences in their temperaments became a permanent barrier that tormented their relationship. He loved to party; she held back and frowned on his willingness to "let go." In a letter to her daughter Anna from Warm Springs in 1934, Eleanor declared that she "always felt like a spoil-sport and policeman here. . . . I'm an idiotic puritan and I wish I had the right kind of sense of humor and could enjoy certain things. At least, thank God, none of you children have inherited that streak in me."

During the years he was assistant secretary of the Navy, Franklin acted more frequently on his fun-loving instincts. "He deserved a good time," Eleanor's cousin Alice Roosevelt acidly noted, "he was married to Eleanor." A frequent companion on Franklin's pleasurable excursions was Lucy Mercer, Eleanor's social secretary. Over time, the relationship between Lucy and Franklin became intimate, particularly during the summers when Eleanor was absent from Campobello. After Franklin was stricken with pneumonia in the fall of 1918, Eleanor discovered letters between Franklin and Lucy describing their affair. Although Franklin refused Eleanor's offer of divorce, and Sara engineered an agreement for them to stay together if Franklin stopped seeing Lucy, their marriage would never again achieve the magical possibility of being "for life, for death," one where a word or look would communicate everything. In the wake of the Mercer affair, James Roosevelt later wrote, his parents "agreed to go on for the sake of appearances, the children and the future, but as business partners, not as husband and wife. . . . After that, father and mother had an armed truce that endured until the day he died."

In the eyes of some, Eleanor Roosevelt's emergence as a public figure seemed a direct consequence of profound anger at her husband's betrayal. Yet Eleanor's activism predated her discovery of the Mercer affair. World War I provided the occasion for expressing long-suppressed talents and energies that could be traced back to her early involvement with the National Consumers' League and the settlement house and were rooted, ultimately, in her relationship with Marie Souvestre. The Lucy Mercer affair, like Franklin's polio, reinforced the move toward public self-assertion, but did not itself cause a transformation.

What the Mercer affair did cause was a gradual reallocation of emotional energy away from Franklin and toward others. Through the polio episode and afterward, Eleanor remained devoted to Franklin's care and career. During the 1920s a warmth of tone and feeling continued in her letters to and about him. Yet gradually their lives became separate. Franklin went off on his houseboat in Florida or to Warm Springs, Georgia, with his secretary Missy LeHand. Eleanor stayed away, as if intentionally ceding to others any emotional involvement with her husband. She might have been jealous of Missy (some have said Franklin had "an affair" with her) or even her daughter Anna for easily giving him the fun and enjoyment that was beyond her ability. But a part of her recognized that others must provide what she could not give.

Increasingly, Eleanor appeared to draw on her own family experience when offering advice to others. When a woman wrote her in 1930 about a marital problem, Eleanor replied: "All men who make successes of their work go through exactly the same kind of thing which you describe, and their wives, one way or another, have to adjust themselves. If it is possible to enter into his work in some way, that is the ideal solution. If not, they must develop something of their own and if possible make it such a success they will have something to interest their husbands." In a poignant piece entitled "On Being Forty-five," which she wrote for *Vogue* in 1930, Eleanor elaborated:

> Life is a school in which we live all our days, and by middle-age, we should know that happiness . . . is never ours by right, but we earn it through giving of ourselves. You must have learned self-control. No matter how much you care, how much you may feel that if you knew certain things you could help, you must not ask questions or offer help, you must wait until the confidence is freely given, and you must learn to love without criticism. . . . If you have learned these things by forty-five, if you have ceased to consider yourself as in any way important, but understand well the place that must be filled in the family, the role will be easy.

Above all, Eleanor concluded, the forty-five-year-old woman must

> keep an open and speculative mind . . . and [then] she will be ready to go out and try new adventures, create new work for others as well as herself, and strike deep roots in some community where her presence will make a difference in the lives of others. . . . One can no longer be interested in one's self, but one is thereby freed for greater interest in others and the lives of others become as engrossing as a fairy story of our childhood days.

Taking her own advice, Eleanor increasingly transferred the emotional focus of her life away from Franklin. The political network of women reformers of which she was the center provided intimate friendship as well as political camaraderie. During the 1920s she spent one night a week with Esther Lape and Elizabeth Read, reading books together and talking about common interests. She also became close friends with Women's Trade Union League women like

Rose Schneiderman, inviting them to Hyde Park for picnics. Molly Dewson became an especially close friend, and Eleanor wrote in 1932 that "the nicest thing about politics is lunching with you on Mondays." In a revealing comment made in 1927, Eleanor observed that "more than anything else, politics may serve to guard against the emptiness and loneliness that enter some women's lives after their children have grown."

Many of Eleanor's friendships during the 1920s and 1930s were with women who lived with other women. She had become particularly close to Nancy Cook and Marion Dickerman, who lived together in New York City. In 1926 she moved with them into Val-Kill, a newly constructed cottage at Hyde Park, an event that accurately symbolized her growing detachment from Franklin and his mother. Although she returned to the "Big House" at Hyde Park when Franklin was present, it was never without resentment and regret. She and Dickerman purchased Todhundter, a private school in New York, where Eleanor taught three days a week even after Franklin was elected governor of New York. The three women also jointly managed a furniture crafts factory at Val-Kill. The linen and towels at Val-Kill were monogrammed "EMN," and the three women together constituted as much a "family" for Eleanor during those years as Franklin and her children.

There were always "special" relationships, however, and during the 1930s these acquired an intensity and depth that were new to Eleanor's life. One of these was with her daughter Anna and Anna's new love, John Boettiger, a reporter whom Anna had met during the 1932 presidential campaign. Eleanor shared a special bond with her daughter, different from the one she had with her sons. Although the two women had had a difficult relationship during Anna's adolescence and early adulthood, caused partly by Anna's resentment of her mother's "distance" and preference for other, competing personalities like Louis Howe, the two women rekindled their affection during Anna's romance with John. Eleanor seemed to be re-living her early days with Franklin by investing enormous energy and love in Anna and wanting her daughter to find the kind of happiness she felt she had lost forever with her own husband. "I love Anna so dearly," Eleanor wrote John in 1935, "that I don't need to tell you that my willingness to let her go to you speaks much for my *trust and love* of you" (italics mine). Eleanor became a ready accomplice in the young couple's effort to find time alone together before their respective divorces and wrote constantly of her hopes for their happiness. One poignant letter to Anna on Christmas Eve 1935 speaks with particular power to the emotional ties that had developed between mother and daughter. "The dogs and I have felt sad every time we passed your door," she wrote. "It was hard to decorate the tree or get things distributed without you . . . and if anyone says much I shall weep for I have had a queer feeling in my throat when I thought of you. Anyway I am happy that you and John are together for I know you will be happy, so please give him a hug for me and tell him I am grateful for him and what he means to you for every day of my life."

Perhaps Eleanor's most carefree relationship during these years occurred with Earl Miller, a former state trooper who had been Governor Al Smith's bodyguard and who subsequently provided the same service to the Roosevelt family. He encouraged Eleanor to drive her own car, take up horseback riding again, and develop confidence in her own personality. He was strikingly different from her other friends—tall, handsome, a "man's man." Although they talked about ideas and politics, the relationship was more that of "boon companions." With Earl Miller, Eleanor found a way to escape the pressures of her political and social status. She went frequently to his home for visits, had him stay at Val-Kill or her New York apartment, and accompanied him whenever possible for long walks and late-evening suppers. Although some of her friends disliked his tendency to "manhandle" Eleanor, all understood the importance of the relationship, and Marion Dickerman even said that "Eleanor played with the idea of marriage with Earl." Miller himself denied that the subject had ever been raised. "You don't sleep with someone you call Mrs. Roosevelt," he said. But without question, the two had an extraordinarily close relationship, and James Roosevelt later observed that his mother's tie to Miller "may have been the one real romance in [her] life outside of marriage. . . . She seemed to draw strength from him when he was by her side, and she came to rely on him. . . . Above all, he made her feel like she was a woman."

It was Eleanor Roosevelt's relationship with Lorena Hickok, however, that proved most intense during the 1930s and that subsequently has caused the most controversy. The two women became close during the 1932 campaign, when Hickok was covering the prospective first lady in her role as a reporter for the Associated Press. "That woman is unhappy about something," Hickok noted. Eleanor had not wanted Franklin to become president and feared that life in the White House would destroy her independence and cast her in an empty role as hostess and figurehead. As the two women talked about their respective lives, they developed an intimacy and affection so close that Hickok felt compelled to resign her position as a reporter because she no longer could write "objectively" about the Roosevelts.

Within a short time, the two women were exchanging daily letters and phone calls, the contents of which suggested that each woman was deeply infatuated with the other. "Hick darling," Eleanor wrote on March 6, "how good it was to hear your voice. It was so inadequate to try to tell you what it meant. Jimmy was near and I could not say, *je t'aime et je t'adore* as I long to do but always remember I am saying it and I go to sleep thinking of you and repeating our little saying." The next night, Eleanor was writing again. "All day," she said, "I thought of you, and another birthday I *will* be with you and yet tonight you sounded so far away and formal. Oh! I want to put my arms around you. I ache to hold you close. Your ring is a great comfort. I look at it and think she does love me, or I wouldn't be wearing it!" The two women plotted ways to be together, to steal a few days in the country, to bridge the gap of physical separation that so often stood between them.

> Only eight more days [Hickok wrote]. Twenty-four hours from now it will be only seven more—just a week! I've been trying today to bring back your face—to remember just *how* you looked. . . . Most clearly I remember your eyes, with the kind of teasing smile in them, and the feeling of that soft spot just northeast of the corner of your mouth against my lips. I wonder what we will do when we meet—what we will say when we meet. Well—I'm rather proud of us, aren't you? I think we have done rather well.

Over time, the relationship cooled somewhat under the pressure of Hickok's demands on Eleanor's time and Eleanor's reluctance to give herself totally to her new friend. Hickok was jealous of Eleanor's other friends, even her children. "Darling," Eleanor wrote, "the love one has for one's children is different, and not even Anna could be to me what you are." From Eleanor's point of view, the two were like a married couple whose relationship had to "flower." "Dearest," she wrote, "strong relationships have to grow deep roots. We are growing them now, partly because we are separated. The foliage and the flowers will come somehow, I'm sure of it. . . ." But an impatient Hickok was jealous of Eleanor's other friends and unable to limit the ardor of her affection.

In time, the situation became too much for Eleanor. In an attempt to explain herself to Hickok, she wrote: "I know you often have a feeling for me which for one reason or another I may not return in kind, but I feel I love you just the same and so often we entirely satisfy each other that I feel there is a fundamental basis on which our relationship stands." "Hick" had to understand, Eleanor wrote, "that I love other people the same way or differently, but each one has their place and one cannot compare them." But in the end, Eleanor could not explain herself sufficiently to satisfy Hickok and concluded that she had failed her friend. "Of course dear," she wrote,

"I never meant to hurt you in any way but that is no excuse for having done it. It won't help you any but I'll never do to anyone else what I did to you." However much she might try, Eleanor could not let herself go emotionally. As a result, she said, "I am pulling myself back in all my contacts now. I have always done it with the children, and why I didn't know I couldn't give you (or anyone else who wanted or needed what you did) any real food, I can't now understand. Such cruelty and stupidity is unpardonable when you reach my age. Heaven knows I hope in some small and unimportant ways I have made life a little easier for you, but that doesn't compensate." Although the two women remained close during the 1930s and 1940s and continued to share the "special Christmases" that Eleanor reserved for her most intimate friends like Earl Miller, Nan Cook, and Hickok, the two women never resumed the intensity and ardor of their early relationship.

Many observers have speculated on the sexual significance of Roosevelt's relationship with Hickok. Hickok herself appears to have had numerous lesbian involvements, and the intimacy of her correspondence with Roosevelt has suggested to some that the love the two women shared must, inevitably, have had a sexual component as well. Many of Eleanor's other women friends lived together in what were called, at the time, "Boston marriages," and some of these associates undoubtedly found fulfillment through sexual relationships with other women. In all likelihood, Marie Souvestre was one of these. Nor has speculation about Eleanor's sexual life been limited to women. Her son James believed that she had an affair with Earl Miller, and later in her life some believed that she had sexual relationships with other men.

Although the accuracy of such speculation may ultimately be irrelevant, the preponderance of evidence suggests that Eleanor Roosevelt was unable to express her deep emotional needs in a sexual manner. Her friend Esther Lape has recalled the distaste and repugnance with which Eleanor responded to the issue of homosexuality when they discussed a French novel dealing with the topic in the 1920s. Eleanor herself told her daughter that sex was something to be "borne," not enjoyed. Eleanor's own reference to Hickok having "a feeling for me which for one reason or another I may not return in kind" may be an allusion to a sexual component of Hickok's desire that Roosevelt could not reciprocate. Earl Miller, and other men with whom Eleanor was rumored to have had a sexual relationship, have all denied—persuasively—the truth of such conjecture. Moreover, we must never forget that Eleanor was raised in a Victorian culture that attempted to repress the sexual drive. She tied her daughter's hands to the top bars of her crib in order to prevent her from masturbating. "The indication was clearly," Anna recalled, "that I had had a bad habit which had to be cured and about which one didn't talk!"

All of this conforms to Eleanor's own repeated declarations that she could never "let herself go" or express freely and spontaneously her full emotions. A person who had been raised to believe that self-control was all-important was unlikely to consider sexual expression of love—especially outside of marriage—a real option. She might sublimate her sexual drives and seek fulfillment of them through a series of deeply committed, even passionate, ties to a variety of people. But it is unlikely that she was ever able to fulfill these drives through actual sexual intimacy with those she cared most about. She was imprisoned in the cage of her culture, and her own bitter experiences through childhood and marriage reinforced her impulse toward self-control and repression. Within her world, she used verbal and emotional lovemaking to achieve whatever satisfaction she could. But ultimately, she could not liberate herself from that world. She would give to others as much as she could within the confines of her life, but she could not take from others—or give—in a manner that her culture defined as forbidden.

In this context, it is not surprising that Eleanor Roosevelt derived some of her emotional gratification from public life and by giving herself emotionally even to distant correspondents who somehow sensed her willingness to listen to their needs. Such expression of concern constituted the intersection of her public and private lives. Over and over again she answered pleas for help with either a sensitive letter, an admonition to a federal agency to take action, or even a personal check. When a policeman she knew suffered a paralyzing injury, she helped pay for his treatment, visited him repeatedly and, to encourage his rehabilitation, even asked him to help type a book she was composing about her father. The indigent wrote to her because they knew she cared, and in caring she found an outlet for her own powerful emotional needs.

The same compassion was manifested in Eleanor Roosevelt's advocacy of the oppressed. It was almost as though she could fully express her feelings only by externalizing them through political issues. Visiting the poverty-stricken countryside of West Virginia and hearing about the struggle of Appalachian farmers to reclaim land, she became a champion of the Arthurdale Resettlement Administration Project, devoting her lecture fees as well as influence to help the community regain autonomy. Poor textile workers in the South and garment union members in the North found her equally willing to embrace their cause. She invited their representatives to the White

House and seated them next to the president at dinner so that he might hear of their plight. She and Franklin had worked out a tacit understanding that permitted her to bring the cause of the oppressed to his attention and allowed him, in turn, to use her activism as a means of building alliances with groups to his left. The game had clear rules: Franklin was the politician, Eleanor the agitator, and frequently he refused to act as she wished. But at least the dispossessed had someone advocating their interests.

Largely because of Eleanor Roosevelt, the issue of civil rights for black Americans received a hearing at the White House. Although Roosevelt, like most white Americans, grew up in an environment suffused with racist and nativist attitudes, by the time she reached the White House she was one of the few voices in the administration insisting that racial discrimination had no place in American life. As always, she led by example. At a 1939 Birmingham meeting inaugurating the Southern Conference on Human Welfare, she insisted on placing her chair so that it straddled both the black and white sides of the aisle, thereby confounding local authorities who insisted that segregation must prevail. Her civil rights sympathies became most famous when in 1939 she resigned from the Daughters of the American Revolution after the organization denied Marian Anderson permission to perform at Constitution Hall. Instead, the great black artist sang to seventy-five thousand people from the Lincoln Memorial—an idea moved toward reality owing to support from the first lady.

Roosevelt also acted as behind-the-scenes lobbyist for civil rights legislation. She had an extensive correspondence with Walter White, executive secretary of the NAACP, who wished to secure her support for legislation defining lynching as a federal crime. She immediately accepted the role of intermediary and argued that the president should make such a bill an urgent national priority. She served as the primary advocate for the antilynching bill within the White House, and she and White became fast friends as they worked toward a common objective. When the NAACP sponsored a New York City exhibit of paintings and drawings dealing with lynching, Roosevelt agreed to be a patron and attended the showing along with her secretary. After White House Press Secretary Steve Early protested about White, she responded: "If I were colored, I think I should have about the same obsession [with lynching] that he has." To the president ER communicated her anger that "one could get nothing done." "I'm deeply troubled," she wrote, "by the whole situation, as it seems to me a terrible thing to stand by and let it continue and feel that one cannot speak out as to his feelings."

Although Eleanor lost out in her campaign for Franklin's strong endorsement of an antilynching bill, she continued to speak forthrightly for the cause of civil rights. In June 1939, in an address before the NAACP's annual meeting, she presented the organization's Spingarn Medal to Marian Anderson. A few weeks later, she formally joined the black protest organization.

As the threat of war increased, Roosevelt joined her black friends in arguing that America could not fight racism abroad yet tolerate it at home. Together with Walter White, Aubrey Williams, and others, she pressed the administration to act vigorously to eliminate discrimination in the Armed Forces and defense employment. Although civil rights forces were not satisfied with the administration's actions, especially the enforcement proceedings of the Fair Employment Practices Commission created to forestall A. Philip Randolph's 1941 march on Washington, the positive changes that did occur arose from the alliance of the first lady and civil rights forces. She would not give up the battle, nor would they, despite the national administration's evident reluctance to act.

Roosevelt brought the same fervor to her identification with young people. Fearing that democracy might lose a whole generation because of the depression, she reached out to make contact with the young. Despite warnings from White House aides that her young friends could not be trusted, between 1936 and 1940 she became deeply involved in the activities of the American Student Union and the American Youth Congress, groups committed to a democratic socialist program of massively expanded social-welfare programs. She advanced their point of view in White House circles and invited them to meet the president so that they might have the opportunity to persuade him of their point of view. To those who criticized her naiveté, she responded: "I wonder if it does us much harm. There is nothing as harmful as the knowledge in our hearts that we are afraid to face any group of young people." She was later betrayed by some of her young allies, who insisted on following the Communist party line and denouncing the European war as imperialistic after the Nazi-Soviet Non-Aggression Pact in 1940. Nonetheless, Eleanor Roosevelt continued to believe in the importance of remaining open to dissent. "I have never said anywhere that I would rather see young people sympathetic with communism," she wrote, "But I have said that I would rather see the young people actively at work, even if I considered they were doing things that were a mistake." It was through her contact with the American Student Union that she first met Joseph Lash, a vigorous leader of the anticommunist faction of the student movement, who would later become as close to her as anyone in her life.

With the onset of World War II, the first lady persisted in her efforts for the disadvantaged. When it appeared that women would be left out of the planning and staffing of wartime operations, she insisted that administration officials consult women activists and incorporate roles for women as a major part of their planning. Over and over again, she intervened with war-production agencies as well as the military to advocate fairer treatment for black Americans. After it seemed that many New Deal social-welfare programs would be threatened by war, she acted to protect and preserve measures directed at the young, tenant farmers, and blacks. Increasingly, she devoted herself to the dream of international cooperation, perceiving, more than most, the revolution rising in Africa and Asia, and the dangers posed by the threat of postwar conflict.

When Jewish refugees seeking a haven from Nazi persecution received less than an enthusiastic response from the State Department, it was Eleanor Roosevelt who intervened repeatedly, trying to improve the situation. Parents, wives, or children separated from loved ones always found an ally when they sought help from the first lady. Nowhere was Roosevelt's concern more poignantly expressed than in her visits to wounded veterans in army hospitals overseas. When the world of hot dogs and baseball seemed millions of miles away, suddenly Eleanor Roosevelt would appear, spending time at each bedside, taking names and addresses to write letters home, bringing the cherished message that someone cared.

Perhaps inevitably, given the stresses of the times, the worlds of Franklin and Eleanor became ever more separate in these years. As early as the 1936 reelection campaign, she confessed to feeling "indifferent" about Franklin's chances. "I realize more and more," she wrote Hickok, "that FDR's a great man, and he is nice, but as a person, I'm a stranger, and I don't want to be anything else!" As the war proceeded, Eleanor and Franklin more often became adversaries. He was less able to tolerate Eleanor's advocacy of unpopular causes, or her insistence on calling attention to areas of conflict within the administration. "She was invariably frank in her criticism of him," one of his speechwriters recalled, "[and] sometimes I thought she picked inappropriate times . . . perhaps a social and entertaining dinner." In search of release from the unbearable pressures of the war, Franklin came more and more to rely on the gaiety and laughter of his daughter Anna and other women companions. One of these was Lucy Mercer Rutherfurd, who began to come to White House dinners when Eleanor was away (with Anna's complicity) and who, unbeknownst to Eleanor, was with the president in Warm Springs when he was stricken by a cerebral hemorrhage and died in April 1945.

With great discipline and dignity, Eleanor bore both the pain of Franklin's death and the circumstances surrounding it. Her first concern was to carry forward the policies that she and Franklin had believed in and worked for despite their disagreements. Writing later about her relationship with Franklin, she said: "He might have been happier with a wife who had been completely uncritical. That I was never able to be and he had to find it in some other people. Nevertheless, I think that I sometimes acted as a spur, even though the spurring was not always wanted nor welcome. I was one of those who served his purposes." What she did not say was that Franklin had served her purposes as well. Though the two never retrieved the intimacy of their early relationship, they had created an unparalleled partnership to respond to the needs of a nation in crisis.

Not long after her husband's death, she told an inquiring reporter, "The story is over." But no one who cared so much for so many causes, and was so effective as a leader, could long remain on the sidelines. Twenty years earlier, ER had told her students at Todhunter: "Don't dry up by inaction, but go out and do new things. Learn new things and see new things with your own eyes." Her own instincts, as well as the demands of others, reaffirmed that advice. Over the next decade and a half, Roosevelt remained the most effective woman in American politics. She felt a responsibility not only to carry forward the politics of the New Deal, but also to further causes that frequently had gone beyond New Deal liberalism. In long letters to President Truman, she implored the administration to push forward with civil rights, maintain the Fair Employment Practices Committee, develop a foreign policy able to cope with the needs of other nations, and work toward a world system where atom bombs would cease to be negotiating chips in international relations.

Appropriately, President Truman nominated the former first lady to be one of America's delegates to the United Nations. At the UN, her name became synonymous with the effort to compose a declaration of human rights embodying standards that civilized humankind would accept as sacred and inalienable. For three years, she argued, debated, lobbied, and compromised until finally on December 10, 1948, the document she had fundamentally shaped passed the General Assembly. Delegates rose in a standing ovation to the woman who more than anyone else had come to symbolize the cause of human rights throughout the world. Even those in the United States who had most opposed her nomination to the delegation applauded her efforts. "I want to say that I take back everything I ever said about her," Senator Arthur Vandenberg of Michigan commented, "and believe me, it's been plenty." At times a figure of scorn and ridicule during the New Deal, Roosevelt was now fast becoming a national heroine, even to former enemies.

The cause of world peace quickly became as central to Eleanor

Roosevelt's efforts as anything in which she had engaged before. With the same emotional fervor that had earlier characterized her response to the dispossessed, Roosevelt reached out to the victims of war. "The weight of human misery here in Europe," she said after a visit to Germany and its concentration camps, "is something one can't get out of one's heart." In moving speeches that vividly portrayed the suffering wrought by war, she sought to educate America to its responsibilities in the postwar world. She had driven through England in 1928, she told her audience, noting the names of all the young men who had died during World War I. Now, she had completed the same kind of journey through Germany. "There is a feeling that spreads over the land," she said, "the feel of [a] civilization that of itself might have a hard time coming back." If America wished to avoid such a world, it must avoid isolationism and wake up to the necessity of helping those who had suffered.

Although Roosevelt disagreed profoundly with some of the military aspects of U.S. foreign policy, she supported the broad outlines of America's response to Russia in the developing Cold War. In debates at the UN, she learned quickly that Soviet delegates could be hypocritical, and on more than one occasion she responded to Russian charges of injustice in America by proposing that each country submit to investigation of its social conditions—a suggestion the Soviets refused. When Henry Wallace and other liberal Americans formed the Progressive party in 1947 with a platform of accommodation toward the Soviet Union, Roosevelt demurred. Instead, she spearheaded the drive by other liberals to build Americans for Democratic Action, a group that espoused social reform at home and support of Truman's stance toward Russia.

Through public speeches and her newspaper column, as well as her position at the UN, Roosevelt remained a singular public figure, able to galvanize the attention of millions by her statements. She became one of the staunchest advocates of a Jewish nation in Israel, argued vigorously for civil rights, and spoke forcefully against the witch-hunts of McCarthyism, attacking General Dwight Eisenhower when he failed to defend his friend George Marshall from Senator McCarthy's smears. Although Eisenhower did not reappoint her to the United Nations when he became president in 1953, she continued to work tirelessly through the American Association for the United Nations to mobilize public support for international cooperation. She also gave unstintingly of her time to the election campaigns in 1952 and 1956 of her dear friend Adlai Stevenson, a man who brought to politics a wit and sophistication Roosevelt always admired.

It was the private sphere, though, that remained most precious.

"The people I love," ER worte her friend and physician David Gurewitsch, "mean more to me than all the public things. . . . I only do the public things because there are a few close people whom I love dearly and who matter to me above everything else. There are not so many of them and you are now one of them." Gurewitsch was a constant companion after she met him in 1947. She traveled with him to Europe, mothered him, and depended upon him for devotion and nurturance. Some even thought he was her lover.

The same kind of relationship—perhaps even deeper—existed with Joe Lash, the young man from the American Student Union whom she had met in the late 1930s. Lash, too, became an intimate companion, spending evenings with her in her New York apartment and weeks at a time at Hyde Park. "I love to be with you dear boy," Eleanor wrote. "I never want to be alone when I'm with people I love." She brought him presents, corresponded with him almost daily, and looked forward eagerly to times when they could be together. "Do come up whenever you are free," she wrote Lash. "I'll be at the house soon after six waiting to both kiss and spank you and I would love it if you have nothing else that calls, to have you stay the night. It will be nice to tuck you in and say goodnight on your birthday!" With Lash too, she seemed to find a maternal role that had been absent in her relationship with most of her own children. "A little bit of my heart seems to be with you always Joe," she wrote during the war. Eleanor became deeply involved in Lash's love affair with Trude Pratt, doing all in her power to bring them together, to erase misunderstandings between them, and to make it possible for them to find the happiness in marriage that had eluded her and Franklin. Tragically, her involvement with Lash led to one of the most bizarre and disgraceful episodes of the war. Because of Lash's involvement with the American Student Union, he was suspected of being procommunist and was placed under counterintelligence surveillance during the war. Letters between the two were opened by government agents, and even the first lady's hotel room was bugged when she went to visit Lash. As a result of such surveillance, government spies made the unfounded allegation that she and Lash were having an affair, and Lash—a soldier at the time—was sent to the Far East.

During the last two decades of her life, Eleanor Roosevelt's children remained as much a trial as a comfort, with the possible exception of Anna. After Franklin's death, Eleanor lived at Val-Kill with Malvina Thompson, her secretary, and her son Elliott and his family. Anna and Elliott were both involved in radio and TV programs with their mother, while James and Franklin entered politics in California and New York. Among her children, only John carried out a life totally on his own. More often than not, family gatherings degenerated into bitter arguments. It was the grandchildren who brought joy—the grandchildren, old friends like Lash and Gurewitsch, and new friends like Allard Lowenstein and his young compatriots in the National Student Association, whom Eleanor befriended during the late 1940s and for the rest of her life. With Lowenstein, as with Lash and Gurewitsch, she adopted a maternal role, providing a constant inspiration to another young reformer who would try to transform America through political and social action.

As she entered her seventies, Eleanor Roosevelt was applauded as the first lady of the world. Traveling to India, Japan, and the Soviet Union, she spoke for the best that was in America. Although she did not initially approve of John Kennedy and would have much preferred to see Adlai Stevenson nominated again, she lived to see the spirit of impatience and reform return to Washington. As if to prove that the fire of protest was still alive in herself, in 1962 Roosevelt sponsored hearings in Washington, D.C., where young civil rights workers testified about the judicial and police harassment of black protestors in the South.

It was fitting that Eleanor Roosevelt's last major official office should be to chair President Kennedy's Commission on the Status of Women. More than anyone else of her generation, her life came to exemplify the political expertise and personal autonomy that were abiding themes of the first women's rights movement. Eleanor Roosevelt had not been a militant feminist. Like most social reformers, she publicly rejected the Equal Rights Amendment of the National Woman's Party until the early 1950s, believing that it would jeopardize protective labor legislation for women then on the statute books. Never an enthusiastic supporter of the ERA, neither she nor JFK's commission recommended the amendment. In addition, she accepted the popular argument during the Great Depression that, at least temporarily, some married women would have to leave the labor force in order to give the unemployed a better chance. At times, she also accepted male-oriented definitions of fulfillment. "You are successful," she wrote in a 1931 article, "when your husband feels that he has been a success and that life has been worthwhile."

But on the issue of women's equality, as in so many other areas, Eleanor Roosevelt most often affirmed the inalienable right of the human spirit to grow and seek fulfillment. Brought up amid anti-Semitic and antiblack attitudes, she had transcended her past to become one of the strongest champions of minority rights. Once opposed to suffrage, she grew to exemplify women's aspirations for a full life in politics. Throughout, she demonstrated a capacity for change grounded in a compassion for those who were victims.

There was, in fact, a direct line from Marie Souvestre's advocacy of intellectual independence to Eleanor Roosevelt's involvement in the settlement house, to her subsequent embrace of women's political activism in the 1920s and 1930s, and to her final role as leader of the Commission on the Status of Women. She had personified not only the right of women to act as equals with men in the political sphere, but the passion of social activists to ease pain, alleviate suffering, and affirm solidarity with the unequal and disenfranchised of the world.

On November 7, 1962, Eleanor Roosevelt died at home from a rare form of bone-marrow tuberculosis. Just twenty years earlier, she had written that all individuals must discover for themselves who they are and what they want from life. "You can never really live anyone else's life," she wrote, "not even your child's. The influence you exert is through your own life and what you've become yourself." Despite disappointment and tragedy, Eleanor Roosevelt had followed her own advice and because of it had affected the lives of millions. Although her daughter Anna concluded that Eleanor, throughout her life, suffered from depression, she had surely tried—and often succeeded—through her public advocacy of the oppressed and her private relationships with friends to find some measure of fulfillment and satisfaction.

"What other single human being," Adlai Stevenson asked at Eleanor Roosevelt's memorial service, "has touched and transformed the existence of so many? . . . She walked in the slums and ghettos of the world, not on a tour of inspection . . . but as one who could not feel contentment when others were hungry." Because of her life, millions of others experienced a new sense of possibility. It would be difficult to envision a more enduring or important legacy.

Sources

The Eleanor Roosevelt Papers at the Franklin Delano Roosevelt Library, Hyde Park, New York, represent the most comprehensive collection of material available. Of particular interest are her correspondence with Walter White of the NAACP, material about her family, especially her father, and drafts of articles and lectures. Other relevant collections at Hyde Park are the papers of Mary (Molly) Dewson, Hilda Worthington Smith, and Lorena Hickok; the papers of the Women's Division of the Democratic National Committee; and those of Anna Roosevelt Halstead. Several collections at the Schlesinger Library, Radcliffe College, bear directly on Eleanor Roosevelt's life: see especially the papers of Mary Anderson, Mary Dewson, Mary Dreier, and Ellen Woodward. Of Eleanor Roosevelt's own writings the most valuable are *This I Remember* (New York, 1949); *This Is My Story* (New York, 1937); *Autobiography* (New York, 1961); and *It's Up To the Women* (New York, 1933). She also wrote a monthly column, "If You Ask Me," for the *Ladies Home Journal* from June 1941 to spring 1949 and in *McCall's* after 1949. The best place to begin reading about her is Joseph Lash's excellent two-volume biography, *Eleanor and Franklin* (New York, 1971) and *Eleanor: The Years Alone* (New York, 1972). On Lash's personal relationship with Roosevelt, see *Love, Eleanor: Eleanor Roosevelt and Her Friends* (New York, 1982). Other books that cast light on the Roosevelt family include James Roosevelt, *My Parents: A Differing View* (Chicago, 1976) and Elliott Roosevelt with James Brough, *An Untold Story: The Roosevelts of Hyde Park* (New York, 1973), both of which offer personal views by the Roosevelt children. Even more revealing is Bernard Asbell, ed., *Mother and Daughter: The Letters of Eleanor and Anna Roosevelt* (New York, 1982).

Georgia O'Keeffe

(1887–1986)

Sarah Whitaker Peters

Georgia O'Keeffe, a major figure in the evolution of twentieth-century American art, was born November 15, 1887, on a farm near Sun Prairie, Wisconsin, the second child and first daughter of Francis Calixtus and Ida O'Keeffe. She attended parochial and private schools in Wisconsin, and graduated from the Chatham Episcopal Institute in Virginia (1905–1906). For the next two years, O'Keeffe studied at the Art Institute in Chicago and the Art Student's League in New York. In 1908 she returned to Chicago, where she worked as a freelance commercial artist until 1910. After this, she taught art in public schools and colleges in Texas and South Carolina, until 1914, when she began studying at Teachers College, Columbia University, in New York. In 1916, O'Keeffe met Alfred Stieglitz, the great photographer and advocate of modern art, who exhibited her first abstractions at his gallery, 291. He arranged shows for O'Keeffe nearly every year thereafter until his death in 1946. They began living together in 1918, and married in 1924. From 1916 on, her art was labeled erotic by many critics because of the different ways she unified the female body with the forms of nature. She, however, always denied this interpretation. By O'Keeffe's own account, the men of the inner "Stieglitz" circle did not want her around at first. But when her paintings of Manhattan (traditionally a male artist's preserve) sold well and received a good press, as indeed all her work did from the start, she won their respect as an artist—not a woman *artist. There were large retrospective exhibitions of O'Keeffe's work given at major museums around the country in 1943, 1946, 1960, 1970, and 1988. O'Keeffe published* Some Memories of Drawings *in 1974, consisting of a portfolio of drawings and her own text, and two years later,* Georgia O'Keeffe, *which featured 108 reproductions of her paintings, again with her own text. She died March 6, 1986, in Santa Fe, New Mexico.*

Georgia O'Keeffe has written that her first memory was of the brightness of light, and that she decided at age twelve (when she reached puberty) to become a painter.[1] Intentionally or not, these statements come across as profoundly mythic: metaphors of spiritual transformation and psychological change. O'Keeffe was like that—and so was her art.

Born on November 15, 1887, O'Keeffe grew up in a Wisconsin farm family of Irish, Hungarian, and Dutch descent, the second child of seven. Of her childhood O'Keeffe wrote: "I seem to be one of the few people I know of to have no complaints against my first twelve years."[2] Her mother, Ida Totto O'Keeffe, was a strong believer in education, and the young Georgia was sent to strict Catholic and Episcopal schools in Madison, Wisconsin, and Chatham, Virginia (near where the family moved in 1903). She would always like to learn new things, but she never quite mastered spelling—as her exceptionally intelligent and beautiful letters reveal.

At eighteen O'Keeffe went to study at the highly respected Art Institute of Chicago. There she received a rigorous academic training, drawing from casts and the human figure. In 1907, with the traditional (for women) idea of teaching in mind, she went to New York to work in oil, pastel, and watercolor at the Art Students League. Foremost among her instructors was the dedicated and flamboyant American impressionist William Merritt Chase, of whom she wrote: "There was something fresh and energetic and fierce and exacting about him that made him fun."[3] She learned much about the techniques of painting from Chase—and she was awarded first prize by him for a naturalistic still life.

During that same New York winter of 1908, O'Keeffe saw the historic first exhibitions in America of French artists Auguste Rodin and Henri Matisse at the avant-garde Little Galleries of the Photo-Secession, known as 291 from its location at 291 Fifth Avenue, which was directed by Alfred Stieglitz, the internationally famous photographer. For Stieglitz, the name "Photo-Secession" meant seceding from the accepted idea of what then constituted a photograph. Further, he was almost alone in believing that a photograph could have the significance of art. By 1912, he would be on the lookout for painting and sculpture that had also "seceded" from the accepted ways of making art. In a word, abstraction. But O'Keeffe was not yet ready to "see" radical European modernism. (Few in 1908 were.) Nor was she ready to listen to Stieglitz's enlightened, nonstop talk about it at 291. Although she had wanted to return to the League for another year of study, her parents had fallen upon hard times and she felt it necessary to find paid work instead.

For the next four years O'Keeffe gave up painting—the act, if not the dream. She returned to Chicago, where she could stay with relatives, and became a free-lance commercial artist. O'Keeffe has said very little about this humbling, hard-working artistic apprenticeship. We know only that she drew lace and embroidery advertisements, at two different fashion houses, for newspapers under deadline. Long an important center for arts and crafts in America, Chicago was still making outstanding contributions to the international art nouveau movement (the graphic designer Will H. Bradley and architect Louis Sullivan come to mind) during the years O'Keeffe studied and worked there. And it is quite certain that the infinite variety of art nouveau she saw in this city taught her first hand that line, color, and form have powers independent of subject matter—a crucial preparation, however unconscious, for her breakthrough abstractions of 1915.

Although O'Keeffe was not happy in her job, she kept at it resolutely for two years until a bad case of measles seriously affected her eyesight. Sent home to Virginia to recuperate, discouraged and at loose ends, she taught art for a time at her old school. In the summer of 1912, recovered at last, she registered rather indifferently for a drawing course at the University of Virginia. There, to her surprise, she became converted for life to the anti-academic composition theories of Arthur Wesley Dow. The timing seems to have been perfect, for Dow's unorthodox methods of art education—richly saturated with late nineteenth-century symbolist notions of correspondence (analogy), "visual music," and synesthesia (the overlap between the senses)—finally mustered her own latent creativity.

Dow had constructed his teaching system, or "synthesis," on the two-dimensional principles of Japanese picture making: harmoniously spaced linear design instead of descriptive analysis, and abstract arrangements of dark and light patterns (*notan*) instead of illusionistic effects of light and shadow (chiaroscuro). As O'Keeffe was later to describe it, "filling space in a beautiful way." For the next six years she taught the design exercises laid out in Dow's famous book *Composition* at schools and colleges in Virginia, South Carolina, and Texas. During this long, and sometimes frustrating, process she herself learned much about simplifying nature forms to their essence as shapes.

O'Keeffe was teaching in Amarillo, Texas, at the time of the scandalous 1913 Armory Show in New York, so she never saw it. Billed as "The International Exhibition of Modern Art," this large-scale presentation of the extremes of French fauvism and cubism was to reform—and transform—the direction of American art: how it was taught, how it was exhibited, and how it was collected.

As Barbara Novak has pointed out in her important study, *Ameri-*

can Painting of the Nineteenth Century, the qualities of form and modes of procedure most commonly denoted as "American," from the 1700s on, were nearly always a combination of indigenous (folk) styles, and transformations of European traditions. Novak also isolated several traits that can be called "national," since they reappeared in new contexts throughout the nineteenth century. These are: the preservation of literal fact, the unique relation of object to idea, a preoccupation with *things*, and a strong folk art tradition—which may actually have helped to restrain American artists from taking up the more decorative extremes of each successive European style.[4] Theodore Stebbins, in his recent survey of this early material, *A New World: Masterpieces of American Painting 1760–1910*, holds that the roots of a distinctly American culture were set right after the War of 1812, when writers such as Washington Irving, James Fenimore Cooper, and William Cullen Bryant identified American art with the American land—and thus set the stage for the rise of the Hudson River school of native landscape painters.[5]

As O'Keeffe's own formation demonstrates, would-be artists in America were trained along the unadventurous lines of the European academies. To exhibit and sell work, one had to paint in the academic mode. The first rebellion against this rigidly enforced rule was the so-called Ash Can school of painters, which included Robert Henri, John Sloan, William Glackens, and George Bellows. During the first decade of the twentieth century, these artists banded together in New York to paint the life they saw around them: young women drying their hair on a roof top, boxers in the ring, women shopping, and an election night in Herald Square. But if their subject matter was "modern," their styles were not—compared to what Stieglitz was showing at 291. Aware of this, the Association of American Painters and Sculptors, formed in 1911, began to make plans for an invitational exhibition of contemporary American art, one that would include some of the early native abstractionists already being extolled by Stieglitz. But the association had considerable difficulty in getting the show off the ground. Finally, Arthur B. Davies (who was well acquainted with the Paris avant-garde) stepped in as a fund-raiser. He also revamped the original plans—changing them to include some of the most extreme and celebrated European modernists. In the end, about 1,300 sculptures, paintings, and drawings were gathered together, mostly by Davies and the painter Walt Kuhn, for the opening on February 17, 1913. Although three-quarters of these works were by Americans, it was the contemporary Europeans who stole the show—*and* the headlines. Twenty-five-year-old Marcel Duchamps's cubist work *Nude Descending the Staircase No. 2* (1912) caused the most commotion: It was gleefully described as "the staircase descending a nude," and "explosion in a shingle factory." Former President Theodore Roosevelt attended, and warned against the European "lunatic fringe." (He thought the Duchamp looked like a Navajo blanket.) The *New York Times* called the exhibition "pathological." Other art critics labeled Kandinsky, Matisse, Picasso, and Brancusi as "lunatics" and "depravers." Nevertheless, the Armory Show, which traveled to Chicago and Boston, was seen by nearly 300,000 people.[6] Although it offered a flawed and incomplete picture of early modernist abstraction (the Italian futurists were completely ignored), collectors began almost immediately to collect it, and galleries other than Stieglitz's sprang up to show it. Encouraged and inspired, a small number of gifted American artists increasingly took up the advanced European challenge, inventing their own color abstractions, and their own variations on cubism. Although Georgia O'Keeffe did not know it in 1913, she too would ride this new wave of public and private interest in abstract art.

O'Keeffe returned to New York the fall of 1914 to study for six months with Dow himself at Columbia University's Teachers College. She was painting hard again (Dow rated her as exceptionally talented), and she went often to 291, where she saw important exhibitions of Picasso, Braque, Picabia, and the American abstract watercolorist John Marin. By now she was taking a direct personal notice of modern art—and of Stieglitz as well. Shortly after leaving the city to teach in South Carolina, she wrote her Columbia colleague Anita Pollitzer that "I believe I would rather have Stieglitz like something—anything I had done—than anyone else I know of."[7]

Actually, she had become increasingly dissatisfied with her own drawings and paintings—finding them stylistically derivative and, worse, reflective of other people's sensibilities. She was then twenty-eight, and she wanted to express *herself.* She resolved suddenly to start from scratch—jettisoning all the years of hard-won instruction. As she was to describe this turning point seven years later: "I have things in my head that are not like what anyone has taught me—shapes and ideas so near to me—so natural to my way of being and thinking that it hadn't occurred to me [before] to put them down. [And] I decided to . . . accept as true my own thinking."[8] Beginning with pastels and watercolors first and then stripping down from color to black and white, she spread large sheets of sketch paper on the floor, and with charcoal sticks, tried to put down in abstract shapes, as exactly as she could, the essence of her emotions. It was not easy. Her letters to Pollitzer tell of having too much inside herself for the "marks" she was transcribing, erasing, changing, throwing away and re-transcribing. She wrote, too, of disgust and elation, of cramps in her head, hands, and feet. Sometimes she called what she was doing a "fool's game." The worst was that she couldn't find words for the images that were beginning, mysteriously, to satisfy her. What was she saying with them anyway? She hoped and believed that what she had expressed was "a woman's feeling." In dire need of feedback, she sent several batches of these drawings to Pollitzer who wrote right back, saying, "They spoke to me, I swear they did . . . you ought to cry because you're so happy."[9] On January 1, 1916, Pollitzer, on her own initiative, took O'Keeffe's three-month-old venture into abstraction to Stieglitz at 291. To his experienced eye, these gender-based expressions of self looked like something that had never been done before. "Finally, a woman on paper," is what he would always remember himself as saying. A seeker of the "new," and determined to recognize and foster an indigenous American art, Stieglitz exhibited ten of O'Keeffe's drawings at 291 that May, to immediate public and critical interest. In 1917, he gave her a one-person show, which included the rhapsodic Texas landscape watercolors that are now considered to be among her finest achievements.

It has long been observed that behind her later flowers, stars, skyscrapers, trees, Penitente crosses, animal bones, hills, and clouds lurk the same organic geometries on which her first abstractions were based: specifically the ovoid, the vertical stalk, the spiral, the seed pod, the tendril, and the arabesque. O'Keeffe admitted as much: "I always say that my work was never as good as it was in the beginning. You may wander around a bit, but your work doesn't change much."[10] Yet, typically, she never said how or why she came to choose the basic language of her forms, and she would not acknowledge their often-remarked uterine, phallic, and esoteric overtones—*or* their thinly disguised art nouveau origins (all of the early drawings carry specific references to plant forms and wave motifs).

Promised financial support by Stieglitz, O'Keeffe moved to New York to paint full time in 1918. About him she has said in retrospect: "He gave a flight to the spirit and faith in their own way to more people—particularly young people—than anyone I have ever known."[11] Although Stieglitz was a generation older than she (he was exactly her mother's age), the two artists married in 1924, and he exhibited her work almost yearly until his death in 1946. From her first show at 291, O'Keeffe was presented to the art world as a native, naive American genius—one who had developed "without the help of the city of Paris," but this was far from the whole story. While true that O'Keeffe never studied in Europe (as had Stieglitz and all the other artists of his circle), she had, by the time of her 1915 abstractions, read (twice) Kandinsky's extremely influential 1912 essay *Concerning the Spiritual in Art*—the bible, so to speak, of early modernist abstraction. And she had obviously learned much from his theories about how to loosen color from line and make it "sing," as her Texas watercolors of 1917–1918 demonstrate. Apparently O'Keeffe was also familiar with Picabia's infamous—and incendiary—1913 statement: "I improvise my pictures as a musician improvises music. . . . Creating a picture without models is art."[12] (Her *Evening Star* and *Light Coming in on the Plains* series are cases in point.) Further, she had long kept up with the important art periodicals of her time, and was well read in contemporary politics, literature, and history. The letters to Pollitzer chart her keen reactions to books like Synge's *Riders to the Sea,* H. G. Wells' *Tono Bungay,* Chekhov's *Sea Gull,* Hardy's *Jude the Obscure,* Randolph Bourne's *Life and Youth,* and Floyd Dell's *Women as World Builders.* She was a subscriber to the doctrinaire journal *The Masses.* She also played the violin and tried her hand at poetry. But if O'Keeffe was never culturally naive, there is little question that Stieglitz changed her life. And he greatly influenced her art—even as she did his. A belief they both shared was that, in Stieglitz's words, "Woman feels the World differently than Man feels it. . . . The Woman receives the World through her Womb. That is the seat of her deepest feelings. Mind comes second."[13] This idea (so specious by present-day standards) may in fact be at the bottom of all her marvelous visual metaphors on the "womb," ranging from barns and shells to fruit and skyscrapers.

Between 1917 and 1937 O'Keeffe posed frequently for Stieglitz's camera. This wide-ranging, composite portrait of her many "Selves" (over 300 prints) remains one of his greatest contributions to the history of photography. Early on, by diverse means, he tried deliberately to link her with favorite artists who had already caused revolutionary change in painting—particularly Rodin, Whistler, and Matisse. The 1918 print of her shown on p. 517 was almost certainly based upon Whistler's famous *Symphony in White, No. 1: The White Girl* (1862). Stieglitz has altered and amended his nineteenth-century source, but he tells a similar visual truth. There is, to begin with, the resonance of the familiar name *The White Girl.* It was the highest form of approbation for Stieglitz to call someone, or some thing, "white," and of O'Keeffe, he said, "Georgia is a wonder . . . if ever there was a whiteness she is that."[14] Further, it must also have occurred to Stieglitz that Whistler's famous subject for this painting, Jo Hiffernan, was his model and mistress—even as O'Keeffe was then his. In a real sense this photograph is a triadic portrait, for it would seem quite certain that Stieglitz not only intended to link O'Keeffe with Whistler through his most famous painting, but with himself as well, in ways that are at once intimate, politic, and artistic.

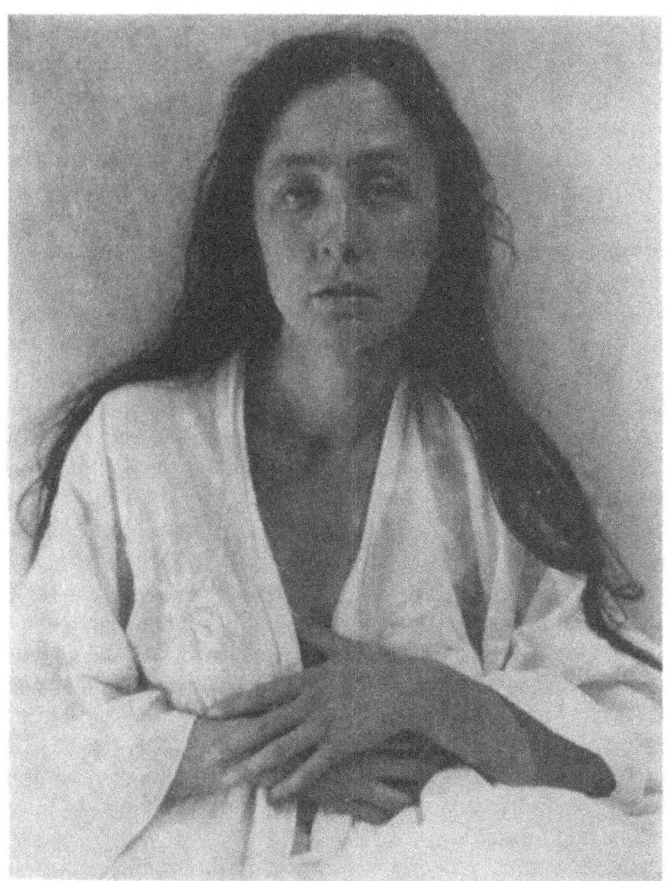

Courtesy, Museum of Fine Arts, Boston; Gift of Alfred Stieglitz, 1924

Stieglitz's exhibitions over the years of selections from this unique portrait helped to create the public personality of Georgia O'Keeffe that we know today: A preternaturally wise, sublimely self-confident, free-and-independent "priestess," who dared to paint "the very essence of womanhood"—as the writers of the first Freudian generation liked to put it. But she thought of herself very differently, and found the strictly sexual interpretations of her work (mostly by male critics) untrue, embarrassing, and extremely hard to live with. They made her feel "invaded," and (protesting, of course, too much) she fought ceaselessly against this reading of her images. (It is not without irony that several women artists in the 1970s—Miriam Schapiro and Judy Chicago among them—took up O'Keeffe's so-called vaginal iconography for specifically feminist intents and purposes.) One of the ways she tried to control matters was never to discuss her sources and intentions. For all her years of fame, O'Keeffe granted few interviews, and made relatively few public statements. Another was to change her style—to become more "objective." That is, to work from the motif instead of putting down what was already in her head.

It was with the intention of becoming more objective in her work that O'Keeffe began to cultivate an aesthetic interest of her own in photography. In a way, this was a logical progression, for she was inexorably drawn into the rich photographic culture of 291—which included such influential figures as Edward Steichen, Paul Strand, and Charles Sheeler—and she often helped Stieglitz with his various professional activities. Early in the 1920s she set about (covertly) isolating elements from the photographic process that could serve this new goal. Chief among them were the crop, the magnified close-up, the enlarged detail, the telephoto, and even such lens malfunctions as halation and flare (random internal reflections in the camera). But she would use them all for abstraction and expression rather than for verisimilitude. The most photo-optic (and perhaps the most metaphysical) of all her works may well be the thirty New York cityscapes she painted between 1925 and 1929. Her *East River from the Shelton* (1927–1928), for example, combines photographic data (halation and a telephoto view) with a spiritual vision of uncommon force and originality.

During their summers and autumns on the Stieglitz family property at Lake George, O'Keeffe and Stieglitz made frequent references to each other's work. Along with many other artists of their time, including Whistler, they were convinced, that all the arts should "aspire to the condition of music." If music, which is essentially non-mimetic could speak directly to the emotions, so also, they reasoned, could abstract painting and photography. Hence such titles as O'Keeffe's *Blue and Green Music* (1919) and Stieglitz's *Clouds in Ten Movements* (1922). As twentieth-century symbolists in the nineteenth-century tradition of poets Charles Baudelaire and Stéphane Mallarmé, they both believed that the artist should describe the effect an object produces rather than the object itself, should *suggest* rather than say. And whenever one looks at the images Stieglitz and O'Keeffe made, it is helpful to remember two things: First, that the symbolist artist regarded "true reality" as hidden; something that must be found. And second, that the viewer is meant to share with the artist the responsibility for finding it.

O'Keeffe had long been interested in the weather as an influence on and indicator of her emotions. Clouds, the most familiar and potent carriers of weather, are prevalent in her work. As for Stieglitz, he went so far as to describe his 1923 *Songs of the Sky* cloud photographs as "equivalents of my life experience." Many of these photographs hold shape-references to O'Keeffe's paintings, even as her pictures pay countless formal homages to his. In fact, it may be that these cross-references functioned as some sort of secret visual code between O'Keeffe and Stieglitz—especially during the years of their first lyrical happiness. In 1926, Stieglitz tipped his own hand somewhat with this recorded statement:

> Sometimes I've been talking with O'Keeffe. Some men express what they feel by holding a women's hand. But I have wanted to express the more, to express the thing that would bring us still closer. I would look at the sky, for the sky is the freest thing in the world, and I would make a photograph from the clouds and the sky and say to O'Keeffe, "Here is what we were talking about," she would say, "That's incredible, it's impossible."[15]

When their letters to each other are finally published, it may be possible to know more of the gist of these "conversations."

Stieglitz was never an easy, or even faithful, husband.[16] Long after he died, O'Keeffe wrote: "For me he was much more wonderful in his work than as a human being. I believe it was the work that kept me with him—though I loved him as a human being."[17] In addition to the stresses and strains of her marriage, O'Keeffe was becoming increasingly restless in the close and pretty greenness of upstate New York. In the 1926 painting *Lake George Barns,* her feelings of being hemmed in, stifled, imprisoned, are so clear as to be almost palpable. In plain fact, Lake George was not the psychic homeland for her that it was for Stieglitz, and her creative juices seemed to be drying up. She had never gotten over her Texan yen for open spaces, and in the spring of 1929, with Stieglitz's reluctant blessing, she went to Taos, New Mexico. The four months she spent there, with plenty of physical and mental solitude, reinvigorated her art. She was fascinated by the rich traditions of the Pueblo and Hispanic cultures—particularly the adobe buildings, ritualistic dances, and painted wood carvings. But more than anything she loved the light and the landscape. In the desert, "All is God," novelist D. H. Lawrence had written when he lived there, and among the nineteen paintings she did that first liberated summer is one called *The Lawrence Tree.* She described the southwestern light for herself as "the faraway nearby" and never tired of trying to capture it with paint. She thought that the Sangre de Cristo mountains looked like "miles of grey elephants."[18] And they are seen, just so, in the backgrounds of several of her Penitente Black Cross paintings.

When O'Keeffe left New Mexico that August to return to Stieglitz, she had already begun to recognize that she needed him *and* New Mexico. And that because he would never travel there she would have to get along with her "divided self" the best way she could.

After two more summers of separation and hard work (the New York public and critics loved her New Mexico paintings), O'Keeffe accepted a commission to paint a mural for the new Radio City Music Hall. Stieglitz had disapproved of the project from the start (he thought murals a second-rate art form, and that they were beneath what O'Keeffe should be doing), but O'Keeffe considered it to be a new and worthy challenge. A series of technical and contractual difficulties caused the plan to collapse—and after this so did she. Hospitalized for seven weeks with a mental and physical breakdown from an accumulation of stresses, it would be almost two years before she felt like painting again. After this, she (and Stieglitz—who always surrounded himself with people) understood better her intrinsic need for time alone.

In 1940, she bought a house (Ghost Ranch) in New Mexico, but continued to spend six months of the year in New York with Stieglitz. Things were now calmer and happier between them, although Stieglitz had stopped photographing in 1937 because of health problems. A touching glimpse into their lives at this time comes from a letter she wrote to the critic Henry McBride.

> I see Alfred as an old man that I am very fond of—growing older—so that it sometimes shocks and startles me when he looks particularly pale and tired—Aside from my fondness for him personally, I feel that he has been very important to something that has made my world for me—I like it that I can make him feel that I have hold of his hand to steady him as he goes on.[19]

Stieglitz died on July 13, 1946. She buried his ashes secretly at Lake George, writing later, "I put him where he would hear the Lake,"[20] and she never went there again. For the next three years she was completely occupied with settling his estate. He had acquired a vast collection of outstanding American and European art, and she undertook to divide it up so that it could be donated, in his name, to several American museums—among them the Metropolitan Museum of New York and the Art Institute of Chicago.

In 1949 O'Keeffe moved permanently to Abiquiu, New Mexico, where she could lead exactly the life of privacy and work in nature that suited her best. She did not forget Stieglitz, as is evident from a letter written in 1950: "He always seems oddly present here at the ranch—I was always so aware of him here for so many years [for] I wrote to him . . . so many many times."[21] She traveled resolutely to Europe and the Far East. Commenting on her travels, O'Keeffe wrote to a friend in 1953:

> Maybe I am queer that I am so singularly pleased with the life I have in New Mexico. I never even seem to see a dog that looks as fine as mine. . . . I keep wondering how this world would seem to me if I had seen it 40 years ago. . . . I will look at it—and I think I will be pleased to go home."[22]

In her later years, O'Keeffe was given retrospective exhibitions by the Worcester Art Museum (1960), the Amon Carter Museum of Western Art (1966), and the Whitney Museum (1970). In 1971 she lost her central vision and stopped painting, but she soon learned to be a hand potter and worked seriously at it. She also published two books about her art: *Some Memories of Drawings* (1974) and *Georgia O'Keeffe* (1976). In 1979 she wrote the introduction to a catalogue of Stieglitz's photographs of her exhibited at the Metropolitan Museum. She received many of the nation's highest honors and awards, including the Medal of Freedom (1977) and the National Medal of Arts (1985). On March 6, 1986, she died in Santa Fe at age ninety-eight. At her request there was no church service, and her ashes were scattered over the landscape she loved.

Way back in 1945, O'Keeffe may have unwittingly summed up her contribution to American art by what she wrote to James Johnson Sweeney, who was then organizing an exhibition of her work at the Museum of Modern Art in New York:

> I must say to you again that I am very pleased and flattered that you wish to do the show for me. It makes me feel inadequate and wish I were better. Stieglitz['s] efforts for me have often made me feel that way too— . . . For myself I feel no need of the showing. As I sit out here in my dry lonely country I feel even less need for all those things that go with the city. . . . When I say for myself I do not need that showing at the Museum . . . means—I should add that I think that I am one of the few who gives our country any voice of its own—I claim no credit—it is only that I have seen with my own eye and that I couldn't help seeing with my own eye.[23]

It should perhaps be borne in mind that this statement was made well before Jackson Pollock and the abstract expressionists of New York, directly inspired by surrealism's concern for the "unknown within," burst upon (and took over) the world art scene in the 1950s, with their abstraction based upon native American myth, the subconscious and personal gestural techniques.

Georgia O'Keeffe was one of the most autobiographical painters of the twentieth century. She herself admitted, "I find that I have painted my life—things happening in my life—without knowing."[24] But it may take generations before we are able to unlock the meaning of her pictorial forms—not least because critics, historians, and those who look closely always find new questions to ask of great visual images, and time may well put some of her paintings into this perennially radical category. For now, her depicted objects (however abstracted) should probably be read as ideas having to do with body and spirit. As with any major artist, however, no single perspective is possible. This is as true for the feminist viewpoint as for any other.[25] From her own words and actions, O'Keeffe comes across as one who sincerely believed that to separate painting, or music, or literature, into two sexes is to emphasize values in these forms that is *not* art. Hence her determination never to be billed as a "woman artist." She was, nonetheless, acutely aware of the role played by gender in the making of all art—and of her own in particular. She made her position on the issue of feminism very clear in a 1930 debate with Michael Gold, editor of *New Masses.* This remarkably forthcoming statement, elicited under pressure, is as revealing of her intelligence of vocation as anything she ever said publicly.

> I am interested in the oppression of women of all classes . . . though not nearly so definitely and so consistently as I am in the abstractions of painting. But one has affected the other. . . . I have had to go to men as sources in my painting because the past has left us so small an inheritance of woman's painting that has widened life. . . . Before I put a brush to canvas I question, "Is this mine? Is it all intrinsically of myself? Is it influenced by some idea or some photograph of an idea which I have acquired from some man?"
>
> That too implies a social consciousness, a social struggle. I am trying with all my skill to do painting that is all of a woman, as well as all of me. . . . I have no hesitancy in contending that my painting of a flower may be just as much a product of this age as a cartoon about the freedom of women—or the working class—or anything else.[26]

Sixty years later, we can see plainly that O'Keeffe did succeed in making an original art after herself. Her emotionally conceptual images were composed from many human and historical connections, but they gleam with her own rollicking wit, her maverick spirituality, and the doubts, fears, angers, and loves of a lifetime.

Notes

[1]Georgia O'Keeffe, *Georgia O'Keeffe,* (New York, 1976), unpaginated.

[2]O'Keeffe to Mitchell Kennerly, 20 January 1929, *Georgia O'Keeffe: Art and Letters,* Sarah Greenough, et al. (Boston, 1987), no. 41.

[3]O'Keeffe (1976).

[4]Barbara Novak, *American Painting of the Nineteenth Century* (New York, 1979), pp. 15, 55, 59.

[5]Theodore Stebbins, *A New World: Masterpieces of American Painting 1760–1910* (Boston, 1983), pp. 64–65.

[6]For a documented account of this historic exhibition see Milton W. Brown, *The Story of the Armory Show* (New York, 1963).

[7]O'Keeffe to Pollitzer, 11 October 1915, quoted in *A Woman on Paper,* Anita Pollitzer (New York, 1988), p. 24.

[8]Statement by Georgia O'Keeffe in *Alfred Stieglitz Presents One Hundred Pictures by Georgia O'Keeffe,* exhibition catalogue, the Anderson Galleries, 1923.

[9]Pollitzer to O'Keeffe, 1 January 1916, quoted in *The Art & Life of Georgia O'Keeffe,* Jan Garden Castro, (New York, 1985), p. 30.

[10]Quoted in Nessa Forman, "Georgia O'Keeffe and Her Art: Paint What's in Your Head," *Philadelphia Museum Art Bulletin,* 22 October 1971.

[11]*Georgia O'Keeffe: A Portrait by Alfred Stieglitz,* introduction by Georgia O'Keeffe (New York, 1978), unpaginated.

[12]As quoted in Arthur J. Eddy, *Cubists and Post Impressionism* (Chicago, 1914), pp. 96–97. In her correspondence with Pollitzer O'Keeffe cites reading this book.

[13]Quoted in Dorothy Norman, *Alfred Stieglitz : An American Seer* (New York, 1960), pp. 136–138.

[14]Stieglitz to Sherwood Anderson, 18 September 1923, Newberry Library, Chicago. White symbolism was an extremely popular theme in turn-of-the-century literature and painting, appearing often in the writings of Maurice Maeterlinck and Stéphane Mallarmé.

[15]Quoted in Herbert J. Seligmann, *Stieglitz Talking* (New Haven, 1966), p. 56.

[16]For a biography of this brilliant, charismatic man, see Sue Davidson Lowe, *Stieglitz* (New York, 1983). See also Laurie Lisle, *Portrait of an Artist: A Biography of Georgia O'Keeffe* (Albuquerque, New Mexico, 1986), and Roxana Robinson, *Georgia O'Keeffe: A Life* (New York: Harper and Row, 1989).

[17]*Georgia O'Keeffe: A Portrait by Alfred Stieglitz,* (New York, 1978), unpaginted.

[18]O'Keeffe (1976).

[19]O'Keeffe to Henry McBride, early 1940s, *Georgia O'Keeffe: Art and Letters,* no. 94.

[20]O'Keeffe to William Howard Schubart, 8 April 1950, in ibid., no. 103.

[21]O'Keeffe to Margaret Kiscadden, 9 March 1950, ibid, no. 104.

[22]O'Keeffe to William Howard Schubart, 4 January 1953, ibid, no. 112.

[23]O'Keeffe to James Johnson Sweeney, 11 June 1945, ibid, no. 90.

[24]O'Keeffe (1976).

[25]For an excellent summary of the important feminist perspective on art history during the last fifteen years, see Thalia Gouma-Peterson and Patricia Mathews, "The Feminist Critique of Art History," *Art Bulletin*, (September, 1987), pp. 326–357.

[26]O'Keeffe quoted in Gladys Oaks, "Radical Writer and Woman Artist Clash on Propaganda and its Uses," *New York World*, 16 March 1930, Woman's Sections, pp. 1,3.

Margaret Mead

(1901–1978)

Rosalind Rosenberg

Margaret Mead was born on December 16, 1901, in Philadelphia. Her mother, Emily Fogg Mead, was a feminist as well as an academic. After a year at DePauw University in Indiana, Margaret Mead transferred to Barnard College in New York City in 1920. There, her chief mentor was anthropologist Ruth Benedict. Mead earned two degrees at Columbia, an M.A. in psychology (1924) and a Ph.D. in anthropology (1929). She married sociologist Luther Cressman in 1923. Her fieldwork in Samoa in 1925 was the basis for Mead's Coming of Age in Samoa *(1928), a book "about the Samoa and the United States of 1926–1928." From this book and her other works emerge pictures both of Mead as an individual and of the changing facets of American feminism throughout the century. On her return from Samoa, Mead took up an appointment as assistant curator at the American Museum of Natural History of New York in 1926, and had a lifelong affiliation with Columbia. Mead published thirty-nine books and a vast number of articles, as well as making numerous records, tapes, and films. Mead divorced Cressman in 1928 to marry fellow anthropologist Reo Fortune, whom she divorced in 1935. Her third marriage to Gregory Bateson, lasted from 1936 to 1950. Bateson, too, was a famous anthropologist and psychologist. It was with Bateson that Mead had her only child, Mary Catherine Bateson, who published an account of her parents,* With a Daughter's Eye, *in 1984. Mead took a particular interest in world hunger and helped establish UNESCO, the United Nations agency committed to establishing world peace through cultural exchange. She was consulted as an expert on a wide range of issues, particularly in American culture. Her achievements have been widely honored. She died on November 15, 1978.*

Margaret Mead was born in 1901, the year Queen Victoria died, and throughout her life she radiated the confident optimism of the British monarch's final years. She achieved fame, however, not for her Victorian temperament, but for her anti-Victorian career. Working as an anthropologist among the primitive tribes of the South Pacific, Mead blasted the Victorians for their smug confidence in the superiority of Western culture, questioned their settled belief in the rightness of feminine subordination, and criticized their deep reticence about sexuality. For a century, Western governments had employed anthropology to influence and manipulate other cultures. Mead used it to challenge her own.

Mead came by her iconoclasm naturally. Her paternal grandmother had attended college, when fewer than 2 percent of Americans did so, and her parents were both social scientists. Her father, Professor Edward Mead, taught at the Wharton School of Business in Philadelphia, while her mother, Emily Fogg Mead, struggled to complete a Ph.D. in sociology while caring for five children. From the time Margaret was one year old until she was nine, the Meads spent each spring and fall in Hammonton, New Jersey. Margaret's mother selected Hammonton because of its large number of Italians, whom she could study for her dissertation on the acculturation of immigrants, but the small town proved educational for Margaret and her siblings as well. When they complained of the odd behavior of their playmates, Emily tried to make them understand that the neighborhood childred acted as they did, "not because of differences in the color of [their] skin or the shape of [their] heads," but because of "their life experience and the life experience of their ancestors."[1]

Margaret Mead absorbed her mother's critical spirit, but she struggled against her strict feminist principles. Emily Fogg Mead had reached maturity at the turn of the century, as the movement for women's rights was building to a crescendo. The social reform and suffrage movements of those years had captured her imagination and reinforced her sense of outrage at the special difficulties women faced in a male-dominated world. A fervent supporter of the American Association of University Women and the Women's Trade Union League, Emily sought to do her part to create broader opportunities for all women. Her eldest daughter, however, chafed under the private dimension of her mother's feminist commitment. "I wanted to wear a hat with ribbons and fluffy petticoats," Margaret Mead later remembered, "instead of the sensible bloomers that very advanced mothers put on their daughters so they could climb trees." In her moments of thwarted femininity Margaret turned to her paternal grandmother, who lived with the family and who seemed to Margaret less filled with "feminist aggrievement" than her mother.

Premature widowhood had limited Grandmother Mead to only one pregnancy, and Margaret later conceded that "had she borne five children and had little opportunity to use her special gifts and training," she might have taken as stern a view of feminist discipline as did her daughter-in-law. As it was, however, Grandmother Mead condoned the traditional trappings of femininity so long as they did not interfere with her granddaughter's intellectual development.[2]

Margaret could hardly have asked for greater encouragement than she received from her family, but she always regretted the unrelieved seriousness that accompanied it. Her mother had "no gift for play, and very little for pleasure or comfort," Mead later recalled. Her father had even less. He rarely reached toward his children, and when he did he lacked a tender touch. The only time he ever put Margaret's shoes on, the day her brother was born, he forced them onto the wrong feet. Only her grandmother provided the warmth she longed for, and even she could never satisfy Margaret's craving for affection. "I loved the feel of her soft skin," Margaret said years later, "but she never would let me give her an extra kiss."[3]

Not until Mead met Luther Cressman did she find the qualities she so missed in her family. Cressman was demonstrative, funny, and empathetic, all the things her relatives were not. Yet, unlike most of the boys she met as she was growing up, he took education seriously and respected ambition in girls. When he proposed to her in 1919, the year she completed high school and he graduated from Pennsylvania State College, she accepted. They agreed to defer marriage, however, so that he could study for the ministry, and she could go to college.[4]

But suddenly, the prospect of college looked doubtful for Mead. Serious losses in a business venture in the spring of 1919 undermined Edward Mead's commitment to his eldest child's education, and only the determination of Margaret's mother and grandmother stiffened his resolve. In the end, Margaret set off, not for Wellesley, Bryn Mawr, or Chicago, where her mother had studied, but for her father's college, DePauw. She left for Indiana with images of the great openness and freedom that her parents had always taught her the West represented. A year later she returned, bitterly denouncing the anti-intellectualism and antidemocratic atmosphere of an institution dominated by sororities and fraternities. Had her mother's conscientious schooling in the evils of prejudice not already penetrated her consciousness in childhood, the rejection she suffered from the sorority of her choice was enough to persuade her of bigotry's poison. For her sophomore year she transferred to Barnard College, the women's college of Columbia University.[5]

Barnard had always prided itself on its cosmopolitan character, but never more so than in the 1920s when New York City, from Greenwich Village to Harlem, was afire with cultural excitement. At Barnard, Mead had the further advantage of being near Cressman, who was studying at the General Theological Seminary on West Twenty-third Street. At a time when sexual appeal was becoming an increasingly important index of success for college women, having a fiancé relieved Mead from undue worry about her worth as a woman. As she later told a friend, being engaged was "very comfortable, and pleasant; it kept me from worrying about men or dates."[6]

Her popularity with men convincingly demonstrated, Mead spent most of her spare time with Barnard friends with whom she shared an apartment on the edge of campus. They called themselves the Ash Can Cats, which was what a Barnard professor said they looked like after staying up too late at night. Together they cooked, read Freud and Edna St. Vincent Millay, took the Fifth Avenue bus to Greenwich Village, and went constantly to the theater. Mead quickly took charge of the group, bossing them, nurturing them, worrying about their love affairs, and, in turn, being cared for by them. They became her extended family, filling in for the grandmother, parents, and siblings she had left behind and replacing the sorority that had rejected her.[7]

Pleased though she was to have won the approval of this sisterhood, her closest tie at Barnard was not to any other student, but rather to an anthropology instructor fifteen years her senior named Ruth Benedict. A 1909 graduate of Vassar, married, but childless, Benedict was a latecomer to anthropology. After unhappy stints as a charity worker, a high school teacher, and an amateur historian, she had returned to school in 1919, taking a series of lectures on anthropology at the New School for Social Research. Thrilled by the intellectual excitement generated in these classes, she enrolled at Columbia to study with Franz Boas, who at sixty-three was the unchallenged patriarch of American anthropology.[8]

A German Jew, Boas's commitment to egalitarian principles had been forged in his childhood by painful experiences with anti-Semitism, and confirmed in adulthood by American xenophobia.[9] When Benedict arrived at Columbia, Boas had just come through a particularly trying period. His unwillingness to speak out against Germany during World War I had put him in a unpopular position with University President Nicholas Murray Butler, who reduced the Columbia Anthropology Department to one member, Boas, and eliminated undergraduate instruction in anthropology at Columbia. By 1919 only Barnard students had permission to attend his courses.[10]

This clipping of his professional wings bothered Boas very little. He had long been dissatisfied with his Columbia undergraduates. "The quality of the Columbia students is on the whole not as good as I would like to see it," Boas had complained to President Butler. "I think it is largely due to the fact that a large percentage of the Columbia students prepare for professional work, and very few of the better class find time for an isolated subject such as anthropology." Boas much preferred teaching at Barnard, where preprofessionalism seemed less intense. In contrast to his Columbia undergraduates, Boas found that "the Barnard students are interested in the subject, intelligent, and take hold of it in a satisfactory way." With his undergraduate work now confined to Barnard, however, Boas decided that he should have a female assistant to lead discussions in his lecture course and to supervise field trips to the Museum of Natural History. He hired Ruth Benedict.[11]

Having found a purpose in life, Benedict lacked only "a companion in harness," someone who could explore anthropology with her and give her the love that her husband reserved for his medical research. She found that companion in Margaret Mead, who, entering her senior year as a psychology major, elected to take Boas's introductory course in general anthropology.[12]

Awed by Boas's demanding lectures, Mead looked for advice and support to his less intimidating assistant. Shy, beautiful, and dressed indifferently Ruth Benedict captivated the intense senior's attention. "Professor Boas and I have nothing to offer but an opportunity to do what matters," she told Mead in one of their many talks that year. Anthropology mattered, Benedict wrote in 1924, because it sought to resolve a fundamental issue of human life, "how far the forces at work in civilization are cultural, and how far organic or due to heredity." As a brilliant woman living in a society still deeply suspicious of female intelligence, Benedict was obsessed with the nature-nurture question. Primitive cultures seemed to offer a laboratory for exploring the question of how much of human behavior was universal, therefore presumably natural, and how much was socially induced, but year by year these cultures were passing away. "Anthropology had to be done *now*," Mead concluded, as she committed herself to Benedict and to anthropology. "Other things could wait."[13]

Having resolved to become an anthropologist, Mead also decided to marry. Her family did not understand why she was in such a rush. Cressman, who had begun graduate work in sociology at Columbia after completing his divinity studies, worried that they would not have enough to live on as students, but Mead was determined. Ruth Benedict had a husband, most women did. Mead seemed to feel that she ought to have one too. She did not intend, however, to cease being known as Margaret Mead. "I'm going to be famous some day," she declared at the end of a lively argument with her distraught father, "and I'm going to be known by my own name." Mead had her way. On September 2, 1923, she married Cressman in the little Episcopal church in Buckingham, Pennsylvania, where she had been baptized. As Cressman later recalled, she was twenty-one, he was twenty-six, and they were both virgins.[14]

Mead came to anthropology at a point when racism and xenophobia were reaching new heights in America. Still reeling from the most recent influx of immigrants from southern and eastern Europe, many white Americans were confronting African-Americans in large numbers for the first time. With the closing off of immigration during World War I, northern employers found that the only pool of unskilled labor they could still tap was that of blacks caught in southern poverty. Blacks began moving northward, only to be met by ugly race riots and an intensification of both anti-immigrant and anti-black feeling.[15]

Psychological tests conducted by the army during World War I reinforced the general hysteria. The tests purported to prove that recent immigrants and blacks were markedly less intelligent than other Americans. In doing so, they confirmed the biological determinism made popular by Eugenists, scientists who argued that America stood in danger of being swamped by mentally deficient and fecund lesser races. Boas denounced this belief in racial inferiority and sponsored numerous studies that sought to challenge it. One assignment went to Mead, who spent her first year after college earning an M.A. in psychology by studying her former Italian neighbors in Hammonton, New Jersey. Mead found that the longer her subjects had been in America and the more English they spoke at home, the better they did on tests that supposedly measured innate endowment. Her findings persuaded her that intelligence was no fixed quality, but a capacity that could either develop or be crippled, depending upon a person's surroundings.[16]

The year Mead completed her M.A. thesis, Congress virtually cut off immigration from southern and eastern Europe. In this hostile climate Boas believed that there was "a fundamental need for a scientific and detailed investigation of heredity and environmental conditions." The best way to challenge the hereditarians, he decided, would be through a study of adolescence in a culture markedly different from those of Western Europe and the United States, and the best person to do it would be his young student Margaret Mead.[17]

Scholars had been preoccupied with the topic of adolescence for many decades. Psychologist G. Stanley Hall had suggested in his massive study of adolescence in 1904 that the storm and stress of the teenage years stemmed from physiological forces. With the onset of puberty, Hall wrote, "the floodgates of heredity seem opened and . . .

passions and desires spring into vigorous life." Boys as well as girls suffered on the stormy seas of adolescence, but Hall, in common with many scholars of his day, believed that the special demands of girls' maturing reproductive organs made them particularly subject to the physiological dislocations of puberty, especially if they were unwisely subjected to the added strain of higher education. By the 1920s a few psychologists and sociologists were beginning to question Hall's "hereditary floodgates," but because they worked in the same culture, these researchers could only speculate about how much of the rebellion they observed among youths could be avoided. Only by looking at a culture free of Western influence could the issue of the inevitability of adolescent rebelliousness be examined in a fundamentally new way. This is what Boas wanted done.[18]

Mead entered graduate work in anthropology with the intention of working either with immigrant groups in the United States, as her mother had done, or of doing fieldwork among the Amerindians, as Ruth Benedict was doing. But a trip to the British Association for the Advancement of Science in Toronto in the summer of 1924 made the prospect of studying groups that others had already visited seem unexciting. In Toronto, she met professional anthropologists who were working among peoples in Africa and the South Pacific who had never seen an anthropologist before. Everyone talked about "my people," and she felt disadvantaged in having no people of her own.[19]

Mead asked Boas to let her go to the South Pacific; Boas said no. The topic he had in mind for her could be investigated just as well in America as in a region so far away. Besides, the South Pacific was too dangerous, especially for a small, twenty-three-year-old woman. Recounting "a sort of litany of young men who had died or been killed while they were working outside the United States," he insisted that she venture no farther than the American Southwest. Undaunted, Mead appealed to her mentor's egalitarian ideals. "I knew that there was one thing that mattered more to Boas than the direction taken by anthropological research. This was that he should behave like a liberal, democratic man, not a Prussian autocrat." Faced with the charge that he was dealing with a student in an arbitrary manner, and prodded by Ruth Benedict to relent, Boas compromised. If Mead would accept his project of a comparative study of female adolescence, he would support her. She agreed.[20]

For any other woman in the 1920s, the problems Mead faced in dealing with her adviser would have paled before the resistance she would have met from her family. But Mead, unique in so many ways, was especially blessed in her family relations. Trained as social scientists, her parents, as well as her new husband, understood the importance of fieldwork and supported her desire to do something original.

Mead and Cressman discussed the idea of his accompanying her, but Mead's attitude, as Cressman later ruefully recalled, "was that I didn't have the skills or the insights to go there." During the year she spent in the South Pacific, he studied in Europe.[21]

Mead wanted to visit as primitive and remote a people as she could so that the impact of Western influence would be minimized. Initially, she chose the remote Tuamotu Islands, part of French Polynesia, but Boas would not hear of her going there. He insisted that she choose an island to which a ship came regularly at least every three weeks. So she settled on American Samoa, a U.S. protectorate in the South Pacific, where the navy had a base and where her way could be eased by the surgeon general of the United States, a friend of her father-in-law.[22]

Samoa was far from untouched. Congregationalist missionaries from London had been there for over a hundred years, and now missionary schools dotted its islands and a pastor's house graced every village. Despite this Christian influence, however, Samoa remained primitive, and Mead was able to work on one of the most remote islands, the island of Tau, where she lived with the family of the naval officer who ran the dispensary in one of the villages. Each village on Tau was divided into between thirty and forty households whose composition varied from the biological family consisting of parents and children only, to households of fifteen and twenty people who were all related to the head of the household or to his wife by blood, marriage, or adoption. The villagers lived in beehive-shaped houses with floors of coral rubble and walls of perishable woven blinds that were kept rolled up except in bad weather. The villagers were Americanized to the point of attending church and wearing cotton cloth rather than the more traditional bark, but they spoke no English, and in much of their daily life they followed traditional customs, living a mostly self-sufficient existence of fishing and simple agriculture.[23]

Though Mead wanted to study adolescence, she realized that she could not understand the adolescent period without establishing its place within the entire female life cycle. Therefore in the nine months available to her for field work, she complimented her intensive study of fifty girls between the ages of ten and twenty with observations of the preadolescent girls and the grown women of the village.

The infant girl, Mead observed, entered the world without ceremony. Though she slept with her mother as long as she was nursing (two or three years), the principal responsibility for her care rested with an older girl of six or seven, who thereby freed the infant's mother for weaving, gardening, or fishing. Handed carelessly from one person to the next, the infant soon learned not to care "for one person greatly" nor to set "high hopes on any one relationship." At about six the little girl outgrew her guardian and became, in turn, the guardian of some new infant. Baby-tending remained her most important task until puberty, when she was relieved of it to work on the plantation, carry footstuffs down to the village, and learn the more elaborate household skills.[24]

Of girls at adolescence Mead observed, "It may be said with some justice that the worse period of their lives is over. Never again will they be so incessantly at the beck and call of their elders, never again so tyrannized by two-year-old tyrants. All the irritating, detailed routine of housekeeping, which in our civilization is accused of warping the souls and souring the tempers of grown women, is here performed by children under fourteen years of age." The adolescent girl was expected to become proficient in the work that would fall to her as an adult—weaving, planting, fishing. But she was in no hurry about this. "Proficiency would mean more work, and earlier marriage, and marriage is the inevitable to be deferred as long as possible."[25]

The greater freedom of adolescence and the casual attitude toward work and preparation for later responsibilities did much to diffuse any tension that might develop between a child and her parents, but perhaps even more important was the fact that every girl had multiple ties to adults in authority. "Few children live continuously in one household, but are always testing out other possibility residences . . . under the guise of visits. The minute that the mildest annoyance grows up at home, the possibility of flight moderates the discipline and alleviates the child's sense of dependency."[26]

With the onset of puberty came an awakening of interest in the opposite sex, but this new interest constituted no more than a variation of a long-standing sexual awareness. The girls had been masturbating since at least the age of six, had engaged in casual homosexuality, and had frequently witnessed intercourse. While "all expressions of affection are rigorously barred in public," Mead wrote, "the lack of privacy within the houses where mosquito netting marks off purely formal walls about the married couples, and the custom of young lovers using palm groves for their rendezvous makes it inevitable that children should see intercourse, often and between many different people." Sex was viewed as natural, and while there was a formal belief that girls should be virgins at marriage, many were not. With few exceptions, adolescence in Samoa "represented no period of crisis or stress, but was instead an orderly developing of a set of slowly maturing interests and activities."[27]

The United States, Mead concluded, had much to learn about adolescence from the Samoans. First, Americans could greatly minimize the conflicts of adolescence by finding ways of relieving the intense emotional pressure created by their small, tightly knit families. Samoan children could visit friends or relatives if parents became too overbearing; American children could not so easily do so. Remembering the mediating role her grandmother had played in her own childhood household, Margaret found among the Samoans confirmation for her belief that Americans would be much better off if parenting were more widely shared. Children should not be reared by mothers alone, but by a variety of other people as well—including, if necessary, social welfare agencies and psychiatrists.

Americans could further diffuse the emotional intensity of adolescence by adopting the Samoans' openness toward sex. Exposed to the sexual relations of others from early childhood, proficient in masturbation, and likely to have sexual experience before marriage, Samoan girls, Mead believed, did not suffer the intense sexual anxieties so prevalent among American teenagers.

Finally, Mead approved of the Samoan girls' early introduction to work. From earliest childhood, girls labored in a purposeful way, working their way into adult activities. American girls, by contrast, suffered from the sharp discontinuities of childhood play, followed by an education that was cut short by maternal drudgery. What children did as children in America, and especially what females did as children, had nothing to do with what they were to do as adults. The advances made by American women in higher education simply exacerbated the sense of discontinuity in their lives by giving women a sense of choice they later found difficult to exploit. The adolescent girl in America needed to know that her education was leading toward some purposeful end.[28]

Published in 1928 as *Coming of Age in Samoa*, Mead's study of adolescence won an immediate and enthusiastic audience in America. In a country increasingly concerned with the rebelliousness and sexual precocity of the young here was a book with some answers. Rebelliousness was not inevitable. Sex was not bad. Later anthropologists would take Mead to task for much that she said. Some charged that she had downplayed conflict in Samoan society, ignoring the passionate struggle for independence from American political control taking place all around her, exaggerating the degree of sexual freedom, and slighting the competition for rank in Samoan society. In 1969, responding to one particularly impassioned critic, Mead accepted some criticisms and attributed others to regional differences or to changes in Samoan society over time, but she concluded with an important point about perspective. "[T]o the young girl, . . . uninvolved in the rivalries that were related to rank and prestige, moving gently, unhurriedly toward adulthood, the preoccupations of the whole society may have seemed more remote than they would have appeared from any other vantage point. And this is the vantage point from which I saw it."[29]

Mead was a pioneer. In a profession dominated by men, who were interested in the concerns of their male subjects, she set off to study the experience of young women. The lesson that she taught in doing so has proved to be one of the most important of the twentieth century: each society is seen differently by those occupying different positions within it. Men had always looked at societies from the vantage point of chiefs and presidents. In a revolutionary turnabout, Mead advocated placing women at the center of any attempt to understand a culture's character.

On her way back from Samoa, Mead met Reo Fortune, a young New Zealand psychologist, whose work on Sigmund Freud's and W. H. R. River's theories of dreams had won him a fellowship to study in England. "We talked nonstop for six weeks," Mead later recalled, "fitting all that each of us had learned into a new approach to the study of primitive peoples." By the time Mead joined her husband, she found that she had fallen in love with the young New Zealander. Fortune gave her what Cressman could not, a brilliant understanding of the intellectual issues that consumed her and a passionate commitment to anthropological fieldwork. In the 1920s getting a divorce invited scandal, but when Mead reached Marseilles, she told Cressman that she saw no future in their marriage. Within two years she was married to Fortune.[30]

Back in New York Mead went to work as an assistant curator for ethnology at the American Museum of Natural History, taught a class at Columbia, and completed her Ph.D. with a thesis entitled, "An Inquiry into the Question of Cultural Stability in Polynesia" (1929). Though more than qualified for an assistant professorship, she settled for teaching on an adjunct basis at Columbia, while working at the Museum of Natural History. Boas had few academic jobs to distribute to his students, and he assigned those he had on the basis of financial need. Ruth Benedict did not have a full-time position at Columbia until she was divorced from her husband, and the jobs at Barnard always went to unmarried women with no other means of support. Because she was married, Mead could not expect Boas's assistance in finding an academic position, but the curatorship offered her by the Museum of Natural History while she was still in Samoa was more attractive in some ways than an academic appointment. Whereas in a university setting Mead would have had to pick her way through the hostile terrain of a male-dominated institution, in the southwest tower of the museum she was able to build her own fiefdom, one populated almost exclusively by young women chosen for their intelligence and the likelihood that they would move on to their own careers in a few years. These were the foot soldiers in Mead's anthropological army. They organized her field notes, picked up her laundry, and gave her backrubs. Mead achieved unprecedented success in a male world, but from the Ash Can Cats to her south-tower staff, she did so within the protective borders of a devoted female community.[31]

In writing *Coming of Age in Samoa,* Mead suggested that if the crisis of adolescence, with its discontinuities and conflict over goals, could be mitigated, women's lot would be far happier. But the more she talked with Ruth Benedict about the problem of women's nature and role, the more she came to believe that adolescence was simply a particularly dramatic episode in a larger pattern. The problem for American women was not so much the crisis of adolescence, but the absence of real choice in the matter of personal temperament at any stage of their lives. The West, Mead complained, was so accustomed to a thoroughgoing sexual polarity that no one seemed able to conceive of sexual relations without extreme sex differentiation. The pervasiveness of this assumption of sexual polarity found ample demonstration in a widely read feminist work of the 1920s written by Mathilde and Mathis Vaerting. The Vaertings argued that in early matriarchal societies women had dominated men and had shown all of the qualities of aggression that Western men later came to embody. To Mead this understanding of sex was incredibly narrow and culturally biased. So thoroughly did the Vaertings accept the polarization of the sexes that the only alternative to the Western pattern they could imagine was simple role reversal. Surely, Mead thought, there were other ways of patterning sexual behavior than either the one condoned by modern civilization or the flip side of that pattern championed by the Vaertings.[32]

In 1931 Mead traveled with her new husband Reo Fortune to New Guinea to study sexual differences in primitive cultures. They lived among three different peoples, starting with the Arapesh, a group they visited simply because their carriers did not want to transport their equipment all the way to their original destination and dumped it instead in the Arapesh's mountain village. The steep mountains made cultivation extremely difficult, and the possibility of starvation always threatened. Under these harsh conditions, this mountain people had fashioned a simple culture in which the personality and roles of men and women alike were "stylized as parental, cherishing and mildly sexed." For their second group Mead and Fortune journeyed to the cannibalistic region of the Yuat River and studied the Mundugumor, where both the men and the women were fiercely aggressive, highly sexed, and noncherishing toward their children. Finally, they studied the people living on the shore of Tchambuli Lake, where Mead found a surprising reversal of conventional Western roles, the women acting in a brisk, businesslike, and cooperative way and the men behaving in a catty, exhibitionist way, preoccupied with decorative and artistic activities. By the time they had finished with the Tchambuli, Mead had the theme she wanted. Sex was not necessarily as important a basis for behavioral differences as Americans, and indeed most Westerners, believed.[33]

"If those temperamental attitudes which we have traditionally regarded as feminine," wrote Mead, "such as passivity, responsiveness and willingness to cherish children—can so easily be set up as the masculine pattern in one tribe, and in another be outlawed for the majority of women as well as for the majority of men, we no longer have any basis for regarding such aspects of behavior as sex-linked." The sharply contrasting cultural styles of the Arapesh, Mundugumors, and Tchambuli persuaded Mead that "many, if not all of the personality traits which we have called masculine or feminine are as lightly linked to sex as are clothing, the manners and the form of head-dress that a society at a given period assigns to either sex." Human nature, she concluded, was "almost unbelieveably malleable."[34]

Published as *Sex and Temperament,* Mead's study of these three cultures further popularized the environmentalist beliefs of the Boasians. Not all critics accepted Mead's findings, however. Some found it incredible that she could have happened on three such neatly patterned societies. Her own husband and fieldwork partner, in an article entitled the "Arapesh Warrior," later questioned her characterization of the Arapesh as "passive" and "cherishing." Despite these criticisms, Mead believed that her fundamental insight remained unassailable. For anyone willing to look, the world displayed an extraordinary diversity of gender patterning. She found further support for her patterning idea from an English anthropologist who joined Mead and Fortune on the final stage of their research. This was Gregory Bateson, who worked nearby as they studied the Tchambuli. Seeing Gregory often, amid the exhilaration of fieldwork, Mead found herself falling in love once again.[35]

The Mead-Fortune marriage had proved rocky from the start. Mead was brilliant, but she was driven and uncompromising. Fortune was brilliant, but he was cranky and given to emotional outbursts. In the field these qualities did not mix well. The tall, gangly, charming Gregory Bateson seemed to combine Cressman's calm with Fortune's passion for anthropological fieldwork. He also looked like good father material. Mead relished the fame she had won as an anthropologist, but professional success did not make up for the fact that she was childless. Not that she had wanted children at first. Like most career women of her time she had believed that work precluded motherhood. But as she grew older, her views changed. She had her career, but she wanted to be a mother too. Not with Fortune, of course; Fortune would make a terrible father. But Bateson would be perfect.[36]

In 1935, Mead divorced for a second time, and, accompanying Bateson on a new field trip to Bali, began her third marriage. After suffering several miscarriages, she returned to New York in 1939 to have her daughter Mary Catherine Bateson. Gregory Bateson was in England at the time, trying to find a way to be useful to the English who were under attack from Hitler. But pediatrician Benjamin Spock, who would later write *Baby and Child Care,* was there, and Mead arranged for the event to be photographed just as she had photographed innumerable births in the field.[37]

Motherhood changed Mead's life. Drawing on the pattern of her childhood and of the primitive cultures she had studied, she set about creating an extended family to help her raise Cathy. At first she relied on Helen Burrows, an experienced English nanny with a fourteen-year-old child of her own to support. Then, when Cathy was two, the Mead-Batesons moved into the first floor of a Greenwich Village townhouse owned by Lawrence and Mary Frank. Lawrence Frank worked for the Rockefeller Foundation and spent his career holding conferences that brought together anthropologists, sociologists, psychologists, and psychoanalysts to work on various aspects of human development in the 1930s and 1940s. Cathy grew up with the Frank children, under the watchful eye of Mary Frank. Also drawn into the extended family network was Marie Eichelberger, one of Mead's friends from Barnard. "Aunt Marie," as Cathy called her, was a social worker, who served as Mead's general factotum. Throughout their lives together, Eichelberger served as Mead's banker and attorney; she helped her get ready for her field trips; and she helped raise Cathy. There were others, as well, who picked Cathy up after school, and cared for her when her mother was out of town. Mead's colleague Melville Herskovits once said, "You're certainly lucky, Margaret to have all these slaves." "They're not slaves, Mel," Mead replied, "they're people who like to help me." "They're slaves all the same," Herskovits replied.[38]

Mead doubled up on her teaching and cut back on her work at the museum to have more time for her daughter. She hired a maid to clean the apartment, but she made a ritual, when she was in New York, of breakfasting with Cathy each morning and returning home in the evening to prepare their dinner. Bateson contributed little to the complicated arrangements that surrounded Cathy's upbringing. To Mead's sorrow, he slowly drifted away. Unable to keep up with the frenetic pace that she set herself, he became involved with other women who could dote on him. In 1950, Mead and Bateson divorced.[39]

One of the ways in which motherhood changed Mead's life was in her approach to her work. Gradually, maternity came to take center stage in her depiction of gender roles in primitive cultures. The American celebration of family life that followed upon the sacrifices of fifteen years of depression and war reinforced this shift in Mead's thinking, and in 1949 she elaborated on her new sense of maternity's importance in her book *Male and Female.* In her earlier books motherhood had been but an incident in the life cycle, always positively depicted but never having a dominant impact on the culture at large. The power of the Eugenists in the 1920s and the rise of Hitler in the 1930s had made her especially sensitive to the evil uses to which biology could be put, and in her early writings she strove to minimize any suggestion of its importance in human life. By the time she wrote *Male and Female,* however, Mead had begun, tentatively, to discuss the ways in which biology might work dialectically with environmental forces to shape culture. Maternity became the central feature of this dialectic, the one great problem that Mead believed all cultures must confront in organizing gender roles. How, she tried to explain, do societies deal with regularities in the human condition, like pregnancy and childbirth? How do men around the world deal with the fact that they will never bear a child?[40]

While Mead emphasized the need to take maternity into account in explaining the differing ways that cultures pattern gender roles, she scorned the apotheosis of motherhood that was coming to pervade post World War II American society. She objected, in particular, to Ferdinand Lundberg and Marynia Farnham's Freudian inspired bestseller, *Modern Woman: The Lost Sex.* Lundberg and Farnham condemned what they saw as the the neurotic strivings of feminists and called for a return to passive, dependent femininity. Mead had long been interested in psychoanalysis, but she believed that Lundberg and Farnham erred badly in their uncritical acceptance of Freud's belief that "penis envy" lay at the root of the female personality structure. Women suffered not so much from "penis envy," Mead countered, as from envy of the special power and privilege that societies awarded to those who possessed penises. Moreover, any envy that girls might have of the male sex organs (and Mead believed that such envy sometimes did exist) was counterbalanced by the envy little boys often exhibited for the remarkable reproductive organs of the female sex. In contrast to Lundberg and Farnham's tales of penis envy, Mead reported primitive societies in which male ceremonials imitated gestation and childbearing in an obvious display of "womb-envy."[41]

Fourteen years later, Betty Friedan would include Mead in her list of the villainous creators of what she called the "Feminine Mystique," the postwar veneration of domesticated motherhood. Mead resented Friedan's characterization of her as someone caught in a "functional freeze." It was true that she talked in *Male and Female* about the ways in which societies used sexual characteristics to shape gender roles, that she emphasized the positive aspects of maternity, and that she warned of the difficulties society's interconnectedness placed in the way of reform. But her warnings about the difficulties of change stood alongside her warnings of the danger of stasis: "To the extent that either sex is disadvantaged, the whole culture is poorer, and the sex that, superficially, inherits the earth, inherits only a very partial legacy." Moreover, at a time when Friedan, having turned down a graduate fellowship in psychology, was newly married, pregnant, and headed for suburbia, Mead was regretting in *Male and Female* that so few cultures had found a way "to give women a divine discontent that will demand other satisfactions than those of child-bearing."[42]

Mead never called herself a feminist. Feminists were women like her mother whose "feminist aggrievement" made them unhappy about being women, or those like Alice Paul and other supporters of the Equal Rights Amendment who minimized differences in the experiences of men and women and therefore did not reckon with the difficulties those differences posed for comprehensive social reconstruction. "If the women's movement has done any harm," she once told newswoman Barbara Walters, "it's to make it seem as if it all were easy. It *isn't* easy!"[43]

Despite such criticisms as this, by the 1970s many had come to view her as a grandmother of modern feminism. She played that role in her own way, continuing to work until her death in 1978, returning again and again to the South Pacific, maintaining intimate friendships with both men and women, glorying in becoming a grandmother, writing books and articles, and lecturing on the themes that had informed her life's work. She tried to persuade her audiences that understanding the lives of other people could help them understand their own, that a greater ease with sexuality (homosexual as well as heterosexual) could enrich them, that building support networks for the overburdened nuclear family would bring greater well-being for all, and that motherhood and careers could and should go together. Through the 1920s when the Eugenists were railing against immigrants, the 1930s when Hitler was slaughtering the Jews of

Europe, the 1940s and 1950s when psychoanalysts and anticommunists were thundering about the dangers posed by homosexuals, feminists, and career women, Margaret Mead maintained a remarkably steady course. More than any other woman of her generation she forced those around her to think seriously about the ways in which the world could be a more open, more democratic place, a place where women could play a larger role.[44]

Notes

[1]Margaret Mead, *Blackberry Winter: My Earlier Years* (New York: Simon and Schuster, 1970), pp. 23–79; Rosalind Rosenberg, *Beyond Separate Spheres: Intellectual Roots of Modern Feminism* (New Haven: Yale University Press, 1982), pp. 207–213.

[2]Mead, *Blackberry Winter,* pp. 20, 45–54, 61.

[3]Ibid., pp. 26, 35, and 56.

[4]Jane Howard, *Margaret Mead: A Life* (New York: Simon and Schuster, 1984), p. 35.

[5]Mead, *Blackberry Winter,* pp. 93–109.

[6]Howard, *Margaret Mead,* p. 36.

[7]Ibid., pp. 43–50.

[8]Margaret Mead, ed., *An Anthropologist at Work: Writings of Ruth Benedict* (New York: Avon, 1959), pp. 3–11; Judith Schachter Modell, *Ruth Benedict: Patterns of a Life* (Philadelphia: University of Pennsylvania Press, 1983), pp. 1–143.

[9]Rosenberg, *Beyond Separate Spheres,* pp. 165–66.

[10]Ibid., pp. 213–18.

[11]Ibid.

[12]Howard, *Margaret Mead,* pp. 51–59.

[13]Mead, *Blackberry Winter,* pp. 114 and 111–15; Ruth Benedict, "Nature and Nurture," *The Nation* (1924): 118.

[14]Howard, *Margaret Mead,* pp. 60–62.

[15]James R. Green, *The World of the Worker: Labor in the Twentieth Century* (New York: Hill and Wang, 1980), pp. 98–99.

[16]Margaret Mead, "Intelligence Tests of Italian and American Children," Master's Thesis, Columbia University, 1924.

[17]Franz Boas, "The Question of Racial Purity," *American Mercury* 1 (1924): 153.

[18]G. Stanley Hall, *Adolescence: Its Psychology and Its Relations to Physiology, Anthropology, Sociology, Sex, Crime, Religion, and Education* (New York: Appleton, 1904), I:308.

[19]Mead, *Blackberry Winter*, pp. 100, 137, 124.

[20]Ibid., p. 139–40.

[21]Howard, *Margaret Mead*, p. 72.

[22]Mead, *Blackberry Winter*, p. 129.

[23]Margaret Mead, *Coming of Age in Samoa: A Psychological Study of Primitive Youth for Western Civilization* (New York: Morrow, 1928), pp. 266–77.

[24]Ibid., pp. 199, 20, 22, 28.

[24]Ibid., pp. 28, 38.

[26]Ibid., pp. 42, 209, 213.

[27]Ibid., pp. 134–35, 157, 136, 147–50. Mead does not discuss contraception, and it is not clear whether young women tend to be pregnant at marriage.

[28]Ibid., pp. 213–14, 216, 227.

[29]Margaret Mead, *The Social Organization of Manua* (1969 ed; Honolulu, Hawaii: Bishop Museum, 1930), addendum. Mead's best-known critic was Derek Freeman. See his *Margaret Mead and Samoa: The Making and Unmaking of an Anthropological Myth* (Cambridge: Harvard University Press, 1983), pp. 118, 131–140, 226–53.

[30]Mead, *Blackberry Winter*, pp. 167–80.

[31]Howard, *Margaret Mead*, p. 327; Rosenberg, *Beyond Separate Spheres*, pp. 232–33.

[32]For Mead's critique of Mathilde and Mathis Vaerting, *The Dominant Sex: A Study in the Sociology of Sex Differences* (London: Allen and Unwin, 1923), see Margaret Mead, *Sex and Temperament in Three Primitive Societies* (New York: Morrow, 1935), pp. x–xi.

[33]Margaret Mead, *Letters from the Field, 1925–1975* (New York: Harper and Row, 1977), pp. 201–02.

[34]Mead, *Sex and Temperament*, pp. 279–80.

[35]Reo Fortune, "Arapesh Warfare," *American Anthropologist* 41 (1939): 22–41; Mead, *Blackberry Winter*, pp. 227–43. For a more recent evaluation of the Tchambuli see Deborah B. Gewertz, *Sepik River Societies: A Historical Ethnography of the Chambia and Their Neighbors* (New Haven: Yale University, 1983).

[36]Mead, *Blackberry Winter*, pp. 225–26.

[37]Ibid., pp. 227–43, 265–82.

[38]Howard, *Margaret Mead*, pp. 73, 244; Mary Catherine Bateson, *With a Daughter's Eye: A Memoir of Margaret Mead and Gregory Bateson* (New York: William Morrow, 1984), pp. 37–48.

[39]Bateson, *With a Daughter's Eye*, pp. 49–57.

[40]Margaret Mead, *Male and Female: A Study of the Sexes in a Changing World* (New York: Morrow, 1949), p. 160; Virginia Yans-McLaughlin, "Science, Democracy, and Ethics: Mobilizing Culture and Personality for World War II," in George Stocking, ed., *Malinowski, Rivers, Benedict and Others: Essays on Culture and Personality* (Madison: University of Wisconsin Press, 1986), p. 204.

[41]Ferdinand Lundberg and Marynia Farnham, *Modern Woman: The Lost Sex* (New York: Harper and Brothers, 1947), passim; Mead, *Male and Female*, pp. 78–160.

[42]Mead, *Male and Female*, pp. 383, 160; Betty Friedan, "The Functional Freeze, the Feminine Protest, and Margaret Mead" in *The Feminine Mystique* (New York: Norton, 1963), ch. 6; Howard, *Margaret Mead*, p. 363; Marcia Cohen, *The Sisterhood: The True Story of the Women Who Changed the World* (New York: Simon and Schuster, 1988), pp. 62–71.

[43]Howard, *Margaret Mead*, pp. 364–65.

[44]Margaret Mead, "Bisexuality: A New Awareness," and "Women: A House Divided," in Margaret Mead and Rhoda Matraux, *Aspects of the Present* (New York: Morrow, 1980), pp. 57–76, 269–75.

PART VIII

Contemporary Lives

In the 1990s American women's lives are shaped by many transformations initiated immediately following World War II. Peacetime pressures on wives and mothers to return to domestic life and to quit working outside the home failed. Postwar inflation as well as the heightened material expectations of householders (for consumer goods and homeowning, for example) kept women in the wage-earning force. A postwar survey of women war workers indicated that 84 percent of the women who remained in the workforce or found new jobs after being mustered out of wartime industries claimed an economic rationale for their employment. Few were willing to claim personal satisfaction or economic autonomy as a reason for continued employment. Whatever the reason or claims, increasingly, married women without children and record numbers of young unmarried women entered the wage-earning force from the 1940s onward.

While only 20 percent of married women worked in 1950, this grew to 30 percent in 1960, over 40 percent by 1970 and since 1980 clearly the majority of American wives earn wages. This trend persisted through the postwar "baby boom" (1946–1964), when women produced on the average, 2.5 children each in 1960, compared with 1.9 in 1940. Concurrently, the divorce rate doubled from 1940 to 1945, and continued to climb thereafter, only leveling off in the late 1980s. Single mothers also form a sizeable chunk of the female labor force as we entered the 1990s.

While postwar American families shifted in size and composition, the American household underwent an even more dramatic change. Suburbs grew five times faster than cities, and with Veteran's Administration loans and the rise of the "subdivision," such as the Levittown prototype in suburban New York, row after row of homeowners with growing families became the norm within American society. These geographic and demographic factors transformed the lives of middle class women. Given physical isolation in the suburban community and the renewed preoccupation with mothering, chores for suburban mothers seemed to grow exponentially. In but one example, chauffeuring became a major time constraint for women within these "bedroom communities." Cars were turned over to women, but so were all the shopping, domestic and parenting responsibilities—after men were dropped off at the local train depot. Mothers were expected to serve as the primary work force within organizations such as the Parent Teacher Association (PTA), scouting societies (Campfire Girls, Girl Scouts of America, and others) as well as thousands of local voluntary organizations. Women were expected to embody self-sacrificing roles as wives and mothers. As it had in the previous decades, American advertising and media played a key role in trying to transform women's expectations and roles.

Cultural coercion was rampant during this era. Film stars projected roles of wholesome and harmonious domesticity—exemplified by the characters played by Doris Day and Debbie Reynolds. The new medium of television reinforced only maternal stereotypes for women, in programs such as *Father Knows Best* and *Ozzie and Harriet.* By the mid-fifties the majority of women who enrolled in colleges were dropping out before graduation to get married and start a family. Educational institutions increasingly became "husband-hunting grounds"—and even a venerable woman's college like Radcliffe had deans preaching the necessity of preparing students for their roles as wives and mothers. Despite the onslaught of propaganda, even while social scientists preached the positive effects of raising larger families, educated women increasingly manifested discontent with the status quo. These social tensions resulted in what came to be known as "women's dilemma," in reality a problem confronted by both sexes, but addressed in advice literature as a problem specifically for women.

Many psychologists and scholars, especially women in these fields, began to address the widespread disillusionment over traditional sex roles. Arguments and advice blossomed across a wide political spectrum. In 1947 the best-selling *Modern Woman: The Lost Sex* argued that the women's rights movement was a manifestation of women's "deep illness," that feminism "bade women commit suicide as women," that an "independent woman" was a contradiction in terms. Attacks upon women's independence and intellectual development were reinforced by other new "scientific sources." Intelligence Quotient (IQ) studies argued that males and females had measurable, verifiable mental differences, with women's greatest disadvantages showing up in tests of science and math skills—precisely those subjects considered most important to national progress in a politically tense, highly technological era.

Even those scholars skeptical of such scientific data conceded that socialization could produce "role conflict." As sociologist Mirra Komarovsky explained: women involved in culturally approved activities such as service clubs displayed the same traits of agressiveness and competence claimed as "masculine traits" in career women; socialization, not anatomy, determined behavior patterns. These theories gained prominence in the 1970s when psychologists cataloged what they called women's "fear of success." Despite fervent opposition, many women seem to have conquered their fears.

A new generation of women activists had tasted leadership opportunities and earned respect of men and women alike with roles in New Deal programs and wartime movements. Some of these women committed to leadership roles struggled against postwar propaganda and carved out significant careers in local, state and even national politics. Certainly the era marks the emergence of figures such as Clare Booth Luce, who began as an editor at *Vanity Fair,* became a successful playwright (*The Women*) and eventually the American ambassador to Italy, as well as Helen Gahagan Douglas, who started her career on the Broadway stage and went on to become a leading member of the California delegation to the House of Representatives and the Democratic candidate for the U.S. Senate, losing to Richard Nixon in 1946.

African-American women had always feared racism and other roadblocks rather than success; many saw their marginal wartime improvements slip away. Women joined their husbands and brothers in the campaign against segregation and racism. In 1955 Rosa Parks refused to give up her seat on a Montgomery, Alabama, bus. In her wake civil rights activists launched one of the most successful boycott campaigns in the modern era. The Montgomery bus boycott lasted over a year and gave birth to the Southern Christian Leadership Conference (SCLC) and the ascendancy of Martin Luther King, Jr.. Out of this renewed resistance thousands of blacks and whites joined in the crusade against discrimination that included the sit-in campaigns of the student-organized Student Nonviolent Coordinating Committee (SNCC). Hundreds of southern young people and scores of northern college students came South in summertime campaigns to try to register African-Americans to vote. The "Freedom Summer" of 1964 was one of the most dramatic grass-roots campaigns for civil rights ever staged. Ella Baker, Fannie Lou Hamer, and many other outspoken African-American women were in the forefront of this struggle. Hundreds upon thousands of younger women—black and white—participated in the civil rights campaigns in the South during this era. Many encountered sexism within the movement as well as racism outside their organizations.

Women found themselves "pushed off the agenda" within male-dominated political organizations. One such organization was Students for a Democratic Society (SDS), founded in 1962, which embodied the radical struggles of the "sixties" generation. Women were shouted off the stage at mass meetings; their claims on time and attention were subjected to ridicule, shouted down by obscenities. As a result, thousands of young women separated themselves into consciousness-raising (CR) groups and sought to reform society with or without the approval or cooperation of male comrades. This separate activism brought mixed results.

While younger women challenged political movements and formed separate groups, older women as well were re-evaluating their contributions and experiences. Betty Friedan's instantly famous *The Feminine Mystique* (1963) encouraged wives and mothers, and women generally, to examine their lives in light of contemporary developments. The aging of the American population meant that nearly all American women spend most of their mature years in an "empty nest," with children grown and out of the home. Thus, Friedan argued, the socialization of women to unpaid, unspecialized careers only as homemakers and maternal workers stunted women's development as well as rendering them unproductive and unfulfilled for most of their adult lives. Friedan was but one of a score of prominent women who counseled her contemporaries to seek vocations, to make lives outside of the confines of sex-role stereotypes.

President John F. Kennedy was the first Chief Executive to address explicitly questions of gender by establishing a Commission on the Status of Women. He appointed Eleanor Roosevelt to head the group in 1960. Roosevelt and other moderate activists wanted to work within legislative commissions. Betty Friedan, among others, was impatient with these channels. She and younger activists had no time to collect the paperwork demanded by government agencies. Further, many women saw these traditional tactics as stalling techniques developed by the establishment to defuse feminist anger. In an attempt to capture the energy of the moment and bring younger women into the movement, Friedan and her cohorts launched the National Organization for Women (NOW)—a direct-action campaign—in 1966.

These champions of social change witnessed a tidal wave of activist women breaking down barriers of prejudice and discrimination. Legal suits and media tactics loosened the constrictive bonds of gender stereotype. Women began to flood into law, business, and medical schools at an unprecedented rate. In 1972 *Ms.* magazine was launched by Gloria Steinem to give feminism a popular, monthly forum.

A virtual flood of feminist scholarship attracted an increasingly sympathetic readership, including Kate Millet's *Sexual Politics* (1970), Shulamith Firestone's *Dialectic of Sex* (1970), and Robin Morgan's *Sisterhood Is Powerful* (1970). Such writers illustrate the extraordinary vitality, variety, and sheer innovativeness of late twentieth-century feminist thought. In two related ways it was notably distinct from the feminism that culminated in the Nineteenth Amendment. These new feminists were prepared to take up issues of sexuality (both heterosexual and homosexual) in the most explicit and adventurous ways. And second, many women, especially those belonging to the poorest and most exploited cultures, were not persuaded by the white, middle-class tendency to view men's and women's campaigns for justice as fundamentally separate. To Cherrie Moraga, for example, the traditional "women's movement" was "devoid of race, class roots, what you ate at home, the smells in the air." Most lesbians and women of color refused to subsume their interests into a movement preoccupied with only the interests of white heterosexual females. The roots of feminist activism stem in large part from the civil rights struggle where large numbers of white women demonstrated their commitment to racial equality. Furthermore, in the earliest days of feminist organization and activism, lesbian women played a disproportionate role in organizing, staffing, and sustaining the movement. In the past quarter century some mainstream feminists have attempted to incorporate some of these challenges to broaden the base of their movement. Yet some critics have charged the opposite tactic, that American feminist organizations jettison issues which do not appeal to the white, heterosexual, middle-class majority to which the movement increasingly panders.

In contemporary society, women enjoy an unprecedented influence within certain discrete sectors. The majority of bookbuyers continue to be women, and the paperback book market is clearly dominated by the influence of female authors and readers. From the self-help literature (showing feminist influence by way of the pioneering work of the Boston Women's Health Collective which published *Our Bodies, Ourselves* in 1971), to the popularization of sexology (from Masters and Johnson's influential studies to the controversial volumes by Shere Hite), as well as the continuing boom in romance fiction (Harlequin novels hit the 100 million mark in annual sales in 1977 and continue to grow), the female audience is enormous and diverse.

Women increasingly are targeted by advertisers who recognize the growing earning power of women consumers. For example, auto manufacturers realize that the solo female buyer is on the increase and women are more likely to purchase a new car than their male counterpart. Not only are women expanding their range of consumption, but the growth of traditional women's consumer items is staggering. In America today, women contribute to a fiercely competitive billion dollar cosmetics industry, including millions of dollars worth of cosmetic surgery.

The power of this female audience is evident in other media. Women are expected to be the top consumers of "infotainment" news programs and daytime dramas (popularly known as soap operas). Women viewers in the 18–35-year-old range are sought by broadcasters for prime-time programming; this female audience can boost advertising revenues by millions. Today women are contributors to televangelical campaigns by a three-to-one margin. Ironically, many of these televangelists are fundamentalists who condemn "women's lib" as "the devil's work."

Not only women, but feminists have influenced media and the arts during the past quarter century. Female journalists increasingly work their way up the masthead, join "the boys on the bus" (the press corps assigned to political campaigns), and redefine the terms of "hard" and "soft" news. Women in broadcast journalism no longer only decorate weathermaps but also hold prestigious positions as anchors and investigative reporters on television programs. Female performers defy both stereotype and convention—on stage and screen both small and large, as dancers and singers, musicians and composers, stand-up comics, and orchestra conductors. Female novelists inventively refine women's roles within existing literary landscapes, such as Erica Jong, whose characters and language in *Fear of Flying* break down the traditional—and male imposed—boundaries for "women writers." African-American poet, novelist and essayist, Alice Walker writes what she calls "womanist" prose. Besides the celebration of the African-American spirit, both in Walker's *The Color Purple,* and in Toni Morrison's *Beloved,* readers witness the violent impact of racism on black lives.

Contemporary female artists rediscover neglected talents of the past century, such as painter Mary Cassatt and sculptor Harriet Hosmer, while pioneering their own distinctive styles. Contemporary historians have attempted to reclaim women's pasts, as this book illustrates. The training and experience of Judy Chicago (creator of explicitly feminist and collaborative work such as "The Dinner Party" and "The Birth Project") diverges radically from the climb to success taken by painter Helen Frankenthaler. Painters like Frankenthaler resist—like Georgia O'Keeffe before her—the notion that they should be identified as women painters or female artists, and especially object to critical interpretations which analyze art so rigidly in terms of gender.

In addition, during the past three decades, efforts to break down the barriers of gender discrimination have made great progress. Legislative inroads promise permanent change in women's status. First and foremost, Title VII of the Civil Rights Act of 1964 forbade discrimination in employment on the basis of sex. In 1967 the Equal Rights Amendment (ERA) was reintroduced in Congress and almost passed in 1972. That same year the 1972 Education Act forbade institutions of higher learning from discriminating on the basis of sex, threatening to curtail federal funding to those schools and programs that denied women equal access. Affirmative action campaigns were instituted and many employers were required to comply with quotas established to insure women's taking advantage of opportunities.

In 1973 the United States Supreme Court liberalized abortion policy with the *Roe v. Wade* decision that many women believed guaranteed them the right to control their own bodies. Nearly one quarter of a million women joined NOW in its campaign to secure passage of the Equal Rights Amendment; by 1982 thirty-five of the thirty-eight states required for ratification had passed.

Yet the ERA failed to be ratified by the necessary number of states, and the *Roe v. Wade* decision was assaulted by the *Webster v. Missouri* decision in 1989. Women have been prominent in the campaigns to defeat feminist interpretation of the law. Coalitions of fundamentalists and right-wing women have proven increasingly effective. Phyllis Schafly, whose Illinois-based "Eagle Forum" spearheaded the attack on the ERA, drew her strength from the South (in which no state ratified the amendment) and played on the fears of the American public that the ERA would create havoc within society by enforcing "unisex" public bathrooms and drafting women into combat. "Operation Rescue" and other "Pro-Life" activists ironically have borrowed the civil disobedience techniques of the 1960s, as have "Pro-Choice" workers on the barricades outside abortion clinics.

The backlash campaigns against feminism have been strong and, in some ways, successful. Authors such as Midge Decter, in *The New Chastity* (1972), and George Gilder, in *Sexual Suicide* (1973), decried the feminist agenda and identified its defenders as "man-hating, lesbian extremists." Many supporters of political feminism heeded this "lavender herring" and disassociated themselves from "the movement." For example, although many young women readers of *Ms.* embraced feminist principles (equal pay, breaking down sexual prejudice, and even increased toleration for all sexual preferences), the overwhelming majority did not belong to any women's liberation group in 1973. Increasingly, the *New York Times* and other major media labeled young women of the 1980s as the "post-feminist" generation with scarcely a ripple of response.

The real and potential political impact of women was exemplified by Democratic candidate, Walter Mondale's choice of a female running mate, Geraldine Ferraro, in the 1984 presidential campaign. While women were not nominees for the national office in the 1988 election, all candidates were forced to deal with the concerns of women one way or another—even if it meant conservative congressional candidates supporting federally-subsidized daycare and other "family issues."

Women from a variety of political camps have emerged. As yet we are unable to gauge the impact of the appointment of Sandra Day O'Connor to the U.S. Supreme Court by President Ronald Reagan in 1981. Although Sally Ride became the first American woman in space in 1983, her token accomplishment called attention to sexism as much as paved the way for future female astronauts. The same might be said for Barbara McClintock, whose work in genetics earned her the 1983 Nobel Prize in physiology.

Gains must be weighed in the balance of historical context. While the percentage of African-American women wage-earners working as domestics was cut from 30 percent in 1965 to less than 10 percent a decade later, we must remember that immigrant Hispanic women, along with female immigrants recently arrived from southeastern Asia have taken their place. Minority women in the United States face a range of staggering handicaps, including high rates of high school dropout, high rates of teenage pregnancy, high rates of alcoholism and drug use, and patterns of downward economic spirals that plague women of color especially. Although divorce is an unimpeded option for many women today, surveys demonstrate that following marital dissolution, female income drops by over 70 percent while male income increases by over 40 percent.

Today women can find equal representation on the floor of the Democratic National Convention and are approaching equity at the Republican party gatherings, yet less than a handful serve in the Senate, less than twenty in the House of Representatives, and women's showing in governor's mansions and state houses proves equally sparse. For all of the political strides and economic achievements of women during the last quarter century, the overwhelming majority of those underemployed and on welfare rolls (over 80 percent) remain women. Women in the U.S. earn on average less than $20,000 a year and need a college education to earn three-fourths the salary of a male high-school dropout. Further, the average woman continues to earn sixty cents for every dollar earned by a man, a statistic that has remained depressingly stable for nearly two hundred years. However, women's role in the nation's labor force is increasingly significant when predictions indicate that three out of every five new workers will be women.

Perhaps progress cannot merely be measured by weighing women's achievements in terms of men's: status, power, and money. Some women suggest that these measurements reinforce a "penarchy" (the domination of all other groups within society, including poor and minority males, by elite males who use political, economic and sexual control to maintain their status). To weigh women's achievements on these sexist scales perpetuates the stereotype of female inadequacy. Feminists argue that women must not merely measure up to the standards provided by males in power, but struggle to redefine the terms by which all individuals are measured to provide more space and value for alternative scales. Women have not merely entered the work force but are attempting to transform rules of employment as well as the workplace environment. Women have raised gender issues in the workplace, making headway on questions of sexual harassment, parental leave, childcare, care of elderly dependents and other "family issues."

One of the biggest problems facing American women today is the balancing of career and family. Over 60 percent of women with preschool children work outside the home, and the majority of women with infants seek daycare within the first year following birth. In addition to the demand for safe, affordable daycare and other means of lessening the burdens of motherhood, many feminists recognize that fathers should be added to the formula of caretaking. Some feminists like Friedan argue in favor of men participating more actively in parenting and shouldering more domestic responsibilities. This stems from an earlier "male liberation" movement, geared to allowing men to show more emotion and demonstrate nurturing qualities within the home and larger society. Feminists argue that women need not divest themselves completely of these important responsibilities nor shift all the burden onto men, but learn to redistribute more equitably the challenges and burdens of rearing children.

Over the past few decades feminist reformers increasingly have agitated to protect victims of rape and incest, to decrease homophobia and insure equal rights for gay citizens, to prevent child abuse and custody kidnapping, and to heighten awareness of pornographic exploitation and sex-trade violence. Comparable worth campaigns and demands for pay equity challenge women's second-class economic status. At the same time, female workers are in the forefront of many movements to improve productivity and dependability: on-site daycare, increased health benefits, flex-time (workers setting their own hours within a window of daily/weekly scheduling), and many other innovations.

While women struggle within women's movements they also

contribute enormously to peace campaigns throughout the globe, to toxic waste cleanups, to disarmament conferences, to animal rights campaigns, to nuclear power protests, and a range of radical issues. Women also appear in the forefront of anti-abortion violence and pro-Creationist struggles, protests against increased sex education and campaigns promoting quarantines for individuals carrying HIV, the AIDS virus. Sex roles have transformed and propelled women into both feminist and antifeminist camps. Women are free to enter any campaigns they choose, and, as in the past, women will participate on both sides of "women's issues," crusading *with* as well as *against* one another. The impact of these campaigns, the feminist agenda for the twenty-first century, and the meaning of gender for generations to come, remains uncharted.

Helen Gahagan Douglas

(1900–1980)

Ingrid Winther Scobie

Helen Gahagan Douglas was born November 15, 1900, to Lillian Rose Mussen Gahagan and Walter Hamer Gahagan II, a wealthy New York civil engineer. Douglas attended the Berkeley Institute in Brooklyn and the Capon School in Northhampton, Massachusetts, before entering Barnard College in 1920. In 1922 she made her debut on the Broadway stage and abandoned her formal education for a career in the theater as an actor and singer. She married actor Melvyn Douglas in 1931; the couple had two children, Peter (1933) and Mary Helen (1938), plus a son, Gregory, from Melvyn's first marriage. In addition to her film debut in She *(1935), Helen Gahagan Douglas continued her concert appearances and went on a European singing tour in 1937. She turned her energies to politics in 1939, when she was appointed to the State Advisory Committee of the National Youth Authority as well as the National Advisory Committee of the Works Progress Administration. The Douglases' friendship with Franklin and Eleanor Roosevelt drew them increasingly into Democratic party politics. In 1944 Helen Gahagan Douglas won the election in Los Angeles' fourteenth congressional district and was appointed to the House Foreign Affairs Committee. Reelected in 1946 and 1948 by wide margins, her reputation as a leading liberal grew. In 1946 President Harry S Truman appointed her as an alternate delegate to the UN General Assembly. She coauthored the Atomic Energy Act and won numerous plaudits and national attention. In 1950 she lost her race for the United States Senate against her congressional colleague, Richard M. Nixon. In 1951 she moved to New York and maintained her interest in politics, speaking out on disarmament and traveling in Latin America and the Middle East to broaden her political expertise. After Eleanor Roosevelt died in 1962, Douglas published a tribute to her,* The Eleanor Roosevelt We Remember *(1963). President Lyndon B. Johnson appointed her to represent him at the inauguration of the president of Liberia in 1964. That same year she was a delegate at the second Soviet-American Women's Conference sponsored by the Women's International League for Peace and Freedom. Douglas died on June 28, 1980. Her autobiography,* A Full Life, *was published posthumously in 1982.*

When Helen Gahagan Douglas died of cancer on June 28, 1980, at age seventy-nine, newspapers across the country reminded readers that in 1950 this actor-turned-politician lost her race against Richard M. Nixon for a United States Senate seat in California in perhaps the most celebrated red-smear campaign of the cold war years. The *Los Angeles Times,* which had virtually shut Douglas out of any significant news coverage during her six-year congressional career from 1944 to 1950, commented that Nixon's campaign "was a model of its kind—innuendo piled on innuendo." The paper cited Douglas's political courage as her most significant contribution to American politics. In a letter to the editor of the *Los Angeles Times,* a prominent San Francisco judge commented that to lose both the noted California writer Carey McWilliams and Douglas in the same week was "a tragic loss for American democracy" and called for "a requiem for the demise of an era." Former member of Congress Jerry Voorhis, himself a political loser to Nixon in 1946, predicted that this "noble" woman would live on as a "symbol of the Gallant American Lady." Tenant-farm worker organizer H. L. Mitchell called Douglas a "sainted person." United States Senators Alan Cranston and Howard Metzenbaum inserted lengthy newspaper obituaries in the *Congressional Record,* adding adulatory remarks of their own. While most obituaries and editorials concentrated on her political career, some also chronicled her accomplishments in theater and opera, noted her uncommon beauty and elegant demeanor, and mentioned her longtime association with Hollywood as the wife of the distinguished actor, Melvyn Douglas.[1]

In 1897, Walter Gahagan, a civil engineer born and raised in Ohio, and his bride Lillian, a teacher who had grown up in Wisconsin, moved to Brooklyn. In the summer of 1900, Lillian, Walter, and their two-year-old twins, Frederick and William, took up temporary residence in Boonton, New Jersey, where Walter had a contract to build a large reservoir. On November 20, Lillian gave birth to Helen, shortly before the family moved back into their Brooklyn home. Two years later, a second girl, Lillian, was born, and the Gahagans moved their growing, active family into an imposing, elegant brownstone house in the city's posh Park Slope area adjacent to Prospect Park and Grand Army Plaza. In 1910, a fifth child, Walter, Jr., added even more bustle to the busy household. Servants eased household work for mother Lillian.

Walter viewed hard work, constant reading, and education as the essentials for a successful life for men and women, but that did not mean to him that women should pursue careers. Lillian also believed in education, as well as exposure to the arts, and a good religious upbringing in the Presbyterian church. Unlike some of her contemporaries, Lillian disagreed with her husband over careers for women, a disagreement which intensified when Walter prohibited her from pursuing a promising singing career in opera. Yet when Helen developed an early interest in the theater, Lillian was as adamant as Walter in opposing it because it was not considered a "proper" profession for a "lady."

Aside from continual friction over her acting ambitions, Helen grew up feeling close to her family. Walter often took the children to his construction sites. Lillian invited musicians to the house to perform. She took the children down the street to the Brooklyn Museum and to the public library on Saturdays. Helen went with her mother to the Metropolitan Opera but did not enjoy it. Helen recalled, "I would be so unhappy sitting through long operas and I'd complain, 'They're all so *fat,* Mother.' " When Helen said she wanted to act, her mother responded, " 'Why do you want to be an actress? Why don't you want to be something really worthwhile—a singer?' "[2]

Summers were special times for the Gahagans. They visited family in the Midwest, and when the children became teenagers, the family traveled to Europe. In 1914, Walter bought Cliff Mull, a lovely Victorian house on a hill above Lake Morey near Fairlee, Vermont. After that, the family spent at least part of every summer in Vermont. Even in the last years of her life, Helen found Vermont an escape, a critical source of nourishment, beauty, and repose.

After a summer in the country, it was always a letdown for Helen to return to Brooklyn to begin school. She and her sister attended the Berkeley Institute, a private school in the neighborhood designed to prepare young women for college. Helen's perpetual dislike of school began in kindergarten, when Berkeley dropped her behind a grade because she could not spell, a problem that continued to plague her as an adult. Helen hated both her academic courses as well as the rules outlining proper behavior for "young ladies," and she consistently performed poorly. She much preferred to spend her time making up stories and acting them out. But theater had no place at Berkeley until Helen's freshman year in high school, when Elizabeth Grimball, a drama coach by training, joined the faculty. She quickly realized that this academically rebellious teenager had exceptional acting talent and considerable intelligence. Before long, Helen began starring in plays and participating on the debate team. Helen received excellent grades in Grimball's class, but her marks deteriorated in others. Much to Grimball's dismay, not to mention Helen's, the irate Gahagans pulled their daughter out of Berkeley and sent her to the elite Capon School in Northampton, Massachusetts, which primarily prepared students for admission into Smith College. Against her parents' instructions, Helen immediately involved herself in play productions and did little better academically. She did manage to graduate, but it took a summer of tutoring at Dartmouth for her to pass the entrance examinations for Barnard College in New York, the only school Helen would consider because it was near the theater scene.

Gahagan entered Barnard, the women's college of Columbia University, in the fall of 1920. The college had a strong tradition of dramatic activity, quite unusual for colleges and universities at that time. Wigs and Cues, a student theater organization, provided opportunities for acting and directing. Gahagan also appeared in several off-Broadway productions.

The noted actor Grace George, who had a reputation for finding young actors, saw Gahagan in a performance and insisted that Broadway producer William Brady, George's husband, see Gahagan perform. Brady asked the starry-eyed Gahagan to play the lead role in a Broadway production, *Dreams for Sale,* a new Owen Davis play about to go into rehearsal, and offered her a five-year contract for starring Broadway roles, a most unusual proposal which Helen accepted. Few actors, no matter how talented, stepped directly from any preparatory environment—stock company, drama school, or college theater—into a leading role contract with a New York producer.

The time could not have been more propitious, for the early 1920s marked the beginning of one of the most vibrant decades in the history of American drama. Gahagan's exciting propects, however, enraged her father. Although Brady eventually convinced Walter Gahagan that his daughter was not entering an "improper" profession for women from fine families, Walter deeply regretted his daughter's decision to quit school and found it difficult to accept her acting career.

Despite poor reviews for *Dreams for Sale,* Gahagan caught the critics' attention. In a comment typical of most of his colleagues, the eminent critic Alexander Woollcott called her an "indisputable talent." When the show closed, Gahagan moved on to other starring roles. From her debut, critics compared her style to that of Ethel Barrymore, and rarely failed to mention her uncommon beauty—tall at five feet seven inches, with a regal bearing. Unlike other fledgling stars, Gahagan had financial backing from her family and did not have to worry about supporting herself; she never hesitated, therefore, to turn down a role that did not interest her. In 1925, she left Brady for another veteran producer, George Tyler, whose gentle personality and innovative productions more suited Gahagan. But by 1927 Gahagan was restless with the stage, and under pressure from her mother to develop her singing, she decided to take voice lessons.

Gahagan began instruction with a noted voice coach, Sophia Cehanovska, and eventually immersed herself full time in her lessons. During a tour in Europe in 1929, her repertoire included the lead roles in *Tosca, Aida,* and *Cavalleria Rusticana.* Although she received mixed reviews, Gahagan had visions of auditioning for the Metropolitan Opera and a variety of American engagements. When none of this materialized, she sailed again to Europe in the summer of 1930 with the idea of staying two years.

This plan evaporated several months later when the aging theater legend David Belasco offered Helen the lead role in a new play, *Tonight or Never.* Belasco thought Gahagan ideal to play an opera singer whose agent is convinced she could sing better if she would only have an affair. The agent's predictions prove correct after the diva has a passionate evening with an "unknown gentleman" who turns out to be a Metropolitan Opera scout. With Gahagan's consent, Belasco selected an accomplished actor but a relative newcomer to Broadway, Melvyn Douglas, as the irresistable lover. During the rehearsal period, Gahagan and Douglas fell in love, and in April 1931, near the end of the play's long run, they married.

The couple's lives took an unexpected turn when in May 1931 Hollywood producer Samuel Goldwyn purchased the movie rights to *Tonight or Never* as a vehicle for Gloria Swanson to launch her singing career. The entire cast moved to Hollywood for the filming. The Douglases initially viewed this trip to California as a temporary one, but when movie offers continued to come Melvyn's way, and Helen had some singing and acting opportunities with theaters in San Francisco and Los Angeles, they began to consider California their home. Helen Gahagan Douglas, however, had little luck getting into film; she made only one movie, *She,* with RKO in 1935. The science-fiction fantasy failed at the box office. A radio contract also proved disappointing. The Douglases lives were further complicated by the births of the two children, Peter in 1933 and Mary Helen in 1938.

In the summer of 1937 Gahagan looked forward to a European singing tour culminating with a performance at the Salzburg Festival in Austria. Rather than operatic roles, she sang a solid repertoire of songs including German lieder. Gahagan enjoyed enthusiastic audiences. Despite the tense political situation resulting from the rapid spread of Nazism, no unpleasant incidents occurred until her stay in Salzburg, when a contact of a friend asked her to report on anti-Nazi activity in the United States. Horrified at the request, she canceled a fall engagement with the Vienna Opera and returned home, determined that she and Melvyn should become involved in antifascist activities in Hollywood. They first joined the 5000-member Hollywood Anti-Nazi League.

Helen initially considered her political activity of secondary interest, but after she returned from Europe she had lost much of the drive that had characterized her acting career. Part of the explanation lay in increasingly diminishing opportunities. Chances to sing in the United States had always been limited, and existing European doors were closing fast in 1938 and 1939. Professional theater opportunities on both coasts continued to decline as the depression decade wore on. But another part of the explanation involved Melvyn. By the end of the 1930s, he had become one of Hollywood's highest paid leading men, known for his fine comic timing, his handsome looks, and his ability to play well against Hollywood's female stars. While not all of his films offered him a chance to demonstrate his talent, *Ninotchka* (1939), eliminated any questions about his talent as a screen actor. Although Helen never resented Melvyn's success, she had always felt their careers should be equally successful. With his star rising, and hers on the decline, she was ready to be pulled off in another direction. Within a short time after Helen made her first step into the political foray, she had become a leading figure in the California Democratic party with considerable national visibility. Except for a few minor engagements, Helen neither acted nor sang again until the early 1950s. But she did not set aside her theatrical skills. Her rapid political climb was due in large part to her ability to shift her acting skills from the dramatic to the political stage.

The Douglases' heightened political awareness paralleled the dramatic change in Hollywood's political atmosphere. In the early 1930s, the movie colony had been a center of political indifference, but by 1937, the community had become a hotbed of radical and liberal organizing. Sensitivity to fascism increased throughout the country, although the most intense activity took place in Hollywood and New York City.

Helen Douglas's first serious move into politics began unexpectedly in the fall of 1938. Melvyn, who had become very active in the

Democratic party and other organizations during the previous year, offered the patio of the Douglases' spacious home to a Hollywood group, the John Steinbeck Committee to Aid Migratory Workers, for a meeting. Helen sat in on the meeting and found herself fascinated with the problems being discussed. Her initial curiosity evolved into a commitment to action: She organized a Christmas party for migrant children, attracting thousands. She read extensively, toured migrant camps, and attended government hearings and meetings of concerned citizens. In early 1939, she became the Steinbeck Committee's chair, working hard to publicize the problem, solicit money, and encourage the public to push for labor laws and social security programs that would include migrants. She also urged improvements in housing, health services, and food distribution centers. She listened attentively to experts. Groups sought her out as a speaker. She eventually drew the attention of Washington experts on migrants' problems, including Arthur Goldschmidt, who worked under Secretary of Interior Harold Ickes. Goldschmidt described his first encounter with Douglas: "I found myself subjected to an intense cross-examination—grilling might not be too strong a word. She accepted no vague generalities. . . . Her questions were not naive; . . . I came away . . . enchanted with a sense of wonder at Helen's display of energy—at the physical, emotional and mental drive of this beautiful and glamorous person."[3]

Aubrey Williams, head of the National Youth Authority, also learned about the activities of both Douglases. As he frequently suggested interesting people to Eleanor Roosevelt whom he thought she and FDR would like to meet, he wrote the Roosevelts about the Douglases. He mentioned that Melvyn could be a political asset to FDR for the 1940 campaign and that Helen's information about migrants would be useful to both Roosevelts. Eleanor Roosevelt was quick to respond; she invited the Douglases to dinner and to spend the night at the end of November 1939. The evening proved delightful; the two couples were drawn to each other, and a special friendship, from which both couples stood to benefit, took shape almost immediately.

During the next few days, the Douglases met a large group of high-ranking New Dealers, including Secretary of Labor Frances Perkins and Harold Ickes, who were as eager to rub shoulders with the bright, enthusiastic, and glamorous Hollywood couple as the Douglases were to meet Washington's political elite. The Douglases left Washington exhilarated. The Roosevelts offered them a standing invitation to stay at the White House when politics brought them to Washington, and Eleanor began a practice of visiting and often staying with her new friends on her trips to the West. Neither Douglas hesitated to contact the Roosevelts or the administration members they had met concerning their political activities. The President appointed both Douglases to various White House boards and remained in close touch with what each was doing. In turn, the Douglases devoted increasingly more time to supporting Roosevelt's policies.

When the Douglases returned to Los Angeles, Helen turned her attention to planning the Steinbeck Committee's second Christmas party, a massive gathering that attracted over eight thousand migrant workers. Shortly after the party Helen resigned from the committee because she learned of Communist infiltration into the organization. Before the Soviet-Nazi pact of September 1939, liberals of all persuasions were virtually indistinguishable from each other; they formed a United Front that supported the New Deal and opposed fascism. But after the pact, American Communists began to object to the anti-fascist stands of liberal organizations. The United Front fell apart quickly as non-Communist liberals dropped their membership. After Helen resigned, she wrote her friend Congressman Jerry Voorhis that she found herself in the "absurd position . . . of most liberals today. The Communists call us reactionaries and the reactionaries call us Communists!"[4]

At this juncture, Helen Douglas took her initial steps into the Women's Division of the Democratic party, steps that brought her closer to Eleanor Roosevelt and provided an entry into the power structure of Democratic politics. Douglas continued to lecture about migrants, and gained considerable attention with an article for the February 1940 issue of the *Democratic Digest*, the widely read monthly magazine of the national Women's Division office. She urged state and local governments to respond to migrants' needs, and communities to assimilate the migrant and "recognize him for his true worth—a vital and necessary element in the agriculture structure [and] a human being . . . whose welfare affects the country at large."[5] This article impelled Dorothy McAllister, a national director of the Women's Division, to invite Douglas to speak on migrant labor at the Division's first National Institute of Government in Washington, a conference to educate party women about campaign issues and party organization in preparation for the 1940 fall campaign. Also during the spring Helen and Melvyn arranged for Eleanor Roosevelt to come to California to visit migrant camps.

In July, the Douglases journeyed to Chicago for the party's nominating convention. Melvyn went as a delegate, Helen as an alternate. Two principal candidates surfaced among the delegates for the position of California's Democratic Party Committeewoman: Douglas and Nettie Jones, a longtime party worker, head of the Women's

Division in California, and a conservative. Douglas won, a victory that angered Jones, who legitimately felt resentful that Douglas had none of the traditional credentials required for this position. Douglas's appointment drew national attention.

After the convention, the Douglases plunged into a hectic campaign speaking schedule—Melvyn nationally and Helen throughout California. When Roosevelt took California by a landslide, party officials in Washington singled out the Douglases for their contributions to the victory. Helen's speaking abilities surpassed those of more seasoned politicians, and she had proved that she had the power to draw and hold a crowd no matter the size. Together the Douglases persuaded many Hollywood actors to speak publicly for Roosevelt and to make substantial campaign contributions. After the election, Helen decided to let political activities absorb all her energies. Through state party chair William Malone she gained two additional party positions: vice-chair of the state organization and head of the Women's Division.

During the first few months of 1941, Douglas strengthened the structure of the Women's Division and made new appointments down to the county level. She selected two women to head the counties in northern California while she and an assistant took responsibility for the south. She selected bright, capable, professional women, many of whom had never before been active in the Women's Division. Douglas then turned her attention to the major focus of the national Women's Division office—homefront defense plans and fundraising. She organized, for example, a regional conference held in September 1941 for party women's education. This conference, which included movie stars and national party figures, was a great success.

While the conference demonstrated Douglas's organizational ability, a more significant test of her political acumen lay ahead: the mobilization of California Democratic women for the 1942 election. The national and state picture looked gloomy. The congressional coalition between Republicans and conservative Democrats had continued to grow in strength since the 1936 election. Douglas directed the Women's Division to work outside of the regular party structure because she thought the women would be more effective this way. They wrote and distributed thousands of flyers, registered voters, raised money, and canvassed precincts. In the final election, despite Democratic Governor Culbert Olson's loss to Republican Earl Warren in the gubernatorial race, Democrats won three of six critical districts in Southern California and several other congressional seats. Washington Democrats were delighted with the Southern California victories, particularly since nationally the party had lost 70 of its 318 House seats. Although it is difficult to assess Douglas's role in these victories, many in both California and Washington gave her considerable credit.

Late in 1943, Representative Thomas Ford, a friend and an ardent New Dealer who represented the Fourteenth Congressional District in Los Angeles, suggested that Douglas run for his seat. He had planned to retire in 1944, and he regarded Douglas as an excellent replacement. Douglas found the idea of running somewhat overwhelming, and the dilemma raised questions of how to reorganize her personal life. Melvyn had joined the army and was in India. Peter and Mary Helen were eleven and seven, in need of parental attention. Politically she faced substantial odds. Not only was she a woman but her credentials did not resemble those of other congressional candidates, male or female. She did not live in the Fourteenth District, an ethnically and economically diverse area encompassing the downtown core of Los Angeles, but in the affluent residential hills of the adjacent Fifteenth District. Furthermore, state assemblyman Augustus Hawkins, a black from the district, was a logical successor. He had a distinguished record in his fight for labor and civil rights. During the war years, blacks in the fourteenth had grown to represent 25 percent of the population, and Hawkins had become a powerful voice in the community. But Ford and his political advisers felt Douglas would stand a better chance of winning. Despite Douglas's unfamiliarity with the district's problems, Ford believed the majority of the constituents would identify with her enthusiasm for the New Deal and Roosevelt. Furthermore, as he put it, the "people of the 14th are not going to vote for a Negro, however light-colored he may be."[6] Douglas finally agreed to run.

Hawkins decided not to file, but Loren Miller, a prominent black lawyer in the district, filed, as did several other candidates. Vicious literature began circulating immediately. One flyer reminded voters that Douglas was married to a Jew (Melvyn had a Jewish father) and that she was a Communist. Twelve years of the "communistic Tom Ford" was enough. The *Los Angeles Times* accused her of Communist ties because the Congress of Industrial Organizations (CIO) backed her. A poster from a Democratic opponent pictured Douglas, labeled "Lady Bountiful," coming down out of the hills of the fifteenth district asking a passerby, "Where's the Fourteenth District?" Douglas wrote Eleanor Roosevelt, "Well, I am really in the campaign and I never knew anything could be quite so repulsive."[7]

Douglas conducted an issue-oriented race, championing the New Deal record and emphasizing her confidence in FDR's leadership. Her campaign literature included a supportive statement from the president. In true Women's Division style, she went armed with facts, figures, and simple language, and refused to run down her opponents. While she only hinted that as a member of Congress she would see herself as representing a national constituency, she communicated that what was good for the country was good for the district. She held dozens of meetings in homes to help dissipate some of the hostility from housewives who could not envision a woman in Congress. She knew how to read an audience and could emotionally charge a group by using colorful language, vivid analogies, and large dramatic gestures.

Douglas won the primary despite the nasty opposition. She immediately turned her attention from the exhilaration of her primary victory to the July nominating convention, for which the Democratic National Committee had billed her as the principal woman among the convention speakers. The press played up the decision to include Douglas as a speaker, claiming that the Democrats were trying to compete with the Republicans who had placed the flashy celebrity Clare Booth Luce, a first-term Connecticut congresswoman, in a prominent spot in their June nominating convention. Much to the press's disappointment neither woman had any interest in a "catfight" or a glamour-girl competition.

Douglas began campaigning almost immediately, stressing once again her allegiance to the president who was running for a fourth term. Her Republican opponent, like her Democratic opposition in the primary, conducted a red-baiting campaign, emphasized the fact that she lived outside the district, and pointed out her connections with Hollywood to suggest a lack of qualifications. But Douglas pulled off a victory—barely—that was part of the tide that Roosevelt and California Democrats enjoyed. She won by less than 4,000 votes out of approximately 137,500 cast. Although she gained a majority of the black votes, few black leaders had rallied to her support. Not even the liberal black *California Eagle* which later became her strong advocate did much for her candidacy. Clearly she had a difficult challenge ahead of her to keep her district.

Douglas arrived in Washington early in January 1945. The Democrats controlled Congress, but the combination of conservative Democrats and Republicans formed a majority. Douglas discovered quickly that in order to have any impact as a new member, she would have to play a nontraditional role, and not just because liberal Democrats were in the minority. She was too impatient to wait the necessary length of time dictated by the behavior norms of the House for new members wishing to assume a position of power. She did not want to spend an inordinate amount of time learning the fine points of legislative procedure, realizing that even time did not guarantee power to women. Furthermore, she had a purist's theoretical notion of representative government. She saw political issues in terms of right and wrong. She had faith that government, run by and for the American people, would be improved simply by voters electing legislators who would work for the right programs. This philosophy set her apart from those who believed that legislative success came only with compromise.

Modeling herself after Eleanor Roosevelt, Douglas worked to develop policy for a national and often an international constituency of "ordinary people." She believed the economic interests of the national groups she deemed important, particularly labor and African-Americans, were identical to the key groups in her district. In foreign affairs, she saw herself speaking for every American who wanted peace. What was good for the world, therefore, was good for the country and for the district. She worked hard toward her goals on the floor of Congress, often lecturing her colleagues and inserting articles and speeches in the *Congressional Record.* She took her assignment to the Foreign Affairs Committee seriously. And she spoke before dozens of groups of concerned citizens all over the country, urging them to pressure members of Congress.

The outlines of Douglas's liberal philosophy took shape and matured during her first term, the Seventy-ninth Congress. Initially she had looked to FDR for policy guidelines. After his death in April 1945, her ideals came principally from Truman's Fair Deal program. She developed numerous statements including demands for the creation of a homeland for the Jews, support for the United Nations, a permanent Fair Employment Practices Commission (FEPC), the end of the poll tax, a full employment bill, extension of social security, the building of low-cost housing, the continuation of wartime rent and price controls, additional funds for day-care programs and school lunches, more farm loans, an increase in the minimum wage, support for labor's right to strike, and funding for cancer research. She called the economic need of veterans a national crisis, began a long-term investigation of the problems of water in California's Central Valley, and demanded more attention to the problems of migrant workers. Her principal legislative success was her cosponsorship of the Atomic Energy Act of 1946, a law that placed the development of atomic energy in civilian rather than military hands. Douglas struck out against those who red-baited her with a statement she entitled "My Democratic Credo" in which she explained that the way to keep communism out of the United States was by building a strong economy, controlling inflation, and providing jobs and affordable housing for all Americans.

Douglas's approach to the issue of civil rights illustrates her political style. She was a civil rights proponent in a style reflective of Eleanor Roosevelt. In the upper-class Brooklyn society of her childhood, her Republican family did not mix with blacks, thus Douglas became responsive to blacks only after she entered politics. Eleanor Roosevelt introduced Douglas to black leaders during the war, including Mary McLeod Bethune, head of the National Council of Negro Women (NCNW). In 1942, at the First Lady's request, Douglas called a meeting to discuss employment and housing discrimination problems for African-Americans in Los Angeles. She worked with FEPC investigations in defense industries. Once in Congress, Douglas aligned herself with a small handful of congressional representatives (including the two black representatives, Adam Clayton Powell and William Dawson) who persistently introduced FEPC, antilynching, and anti–poll tax bills despite continual failure to get these bills passed. Douglas not only tried to generate public pressure on Congress to pass civil rights legislation, but she also gave speeches for national and local branches of the National Association for the Advancement of Colored People (NAACP) and helped the NCNW raise funds. Blacks throughout the country recognized her contributions. The Scroll of Honor that she received in 1946 from the NCNW acclaimed her "superb statesmanship" for her first term in Congress.

Douglas's attitude towards civil rights was also politically astute. Her black consituency was an identifiable audience, and she needed to play to it as she looked ahead to the 1946 election. She publicized her civil rights efforts and worked to bring increased services for blacks into her district. She won the primary easily, but the fall campaign proved more challenging. Her Republican opponent, Frederick W. Roberts, a longtime state assemblyman, was black. Red-baiting issues surfaced again. Douglas could not campaign in person because Truman had appointed her to the 1946 General Assembly of the United Nations, an appointment that added to her prestige but kept her out of her district during the fall campaign season. But Douglas's liberal stance on issues in general, her work on behalf of blacks nationally, and her careful cultivation of the black community paid off as black Democratic leaders worked hard for her. While the Republicans enjoyed a landslide victory, gaining control of both the House and the Senate for the first time in sixteen years, Douglas almost doubled her margin from 1944. She was particularly delighted that she won by large majorities in the black precincts. She interpreted this to mean that she had won the confidence of blacks and that they felt their interests would be more effectively served by a white Democrat with a liberal record than by a black Republican.

When the Eightieth Congress opened in January 1947, the Democrats found the political scene in Washington dismal. While Douglas, like all liberals, found it impossible to do much for her supporters, she still played her part in the futile attempts to buck the Republicans. Liberal groups clamored for her attention; she stepped up her speaking schedule in an effort to reduce voter apathy. She considered the problem of inflation and federal funding for low-income housing the most pressing issues. She hired a black secretary from the district, becoming the first white member of Congress to have a black staff person, a move that created quite a stir in Washington.

Douglas also became more outspoken on women's issues, increasingly attacked the House Un-American Activities Committee (HUAC), and took strong positions on foreign policy issues. She urged the extension of social security to cover more women and supported legislation for equal pay for equal work. She opposed Equal Rights Amendment (ERA) efforts, as did all pro-labor legislators who feared that such an amendment would kill hard-earned special interest legislation favoring working women. Her opposition to the House Un-American Activities Committee focused on its mode of investigating, particularly its issuing of certain contempt citations during the committee's investigations into Hollywood in 1947. In foreign affairs, she deviated from Truman in opposing aid to Greece and Turkey in 1947 on the grounds that the aid should come from the United Nations, but she worked strongly for the Marshall Plan, a program for European economic recovery, both in committee, on the floor, and in public gatherings.

By early 1948, Douglas not only had blacks solidly behind her but labor as well. She had worked more closely with labor union leaders during the Eightieth Congress. She had campaigned against the anti-union Taft-Hartley Act of 1947, and her general stand on issues resulted in top ratings from labor unions and liberal magazines including *The Nation* and the *New Republic.* As expected, her Republican opponent in the 1948 election, William Braden, raised red-baiting issues once again, claiming Douglas was part of the left-wing influences in Congress. Braden's literature also played up her Fifteenth Congressional District residence—referring to her as the Hollywood representative who lived in the "hotsy-totsy area of Hollywood" as compared to the "modest home of our good neighbor and friend" Braden who lived in the district. Despite Braden's attacks, Douglas's total vote of approximately 88,000 to Braden's 43,000 surprised even Douglas. She clearly had established a safe congressional seat despite the dirty campaign tactics of her opponents.

In January 1949, at the opening of the Eighty-first Congress, Douglas enjoyed enormous popularity in the eyes of labor, blacks, Jews and other minority groups, and civil libertarians. Many of her supporters agreed with Douglas's somewhat egotistical self-evaluation that she was one of the few and possibly the most conscientious members of Congress. She saw herself as a "people's representative" fighting for America's working class. When Douglas announced late in 1949 that she intended to run for the United States Senate, she found many of her supporters dismayed and concerned. While they believed that she could continue to win her congressional seat, many did not think that she had the statewide political base or the experience to run for the Senate. Further, while her political views suited her district, they did not reflect the majority opinion in the state. But she remained undaunted.

Douglas explained her decision to run on her intense dislike for the aging incumbent, Sheridan Downey, a New Dealer who became progressively more conservative after the war. Douglas particularly opposed Downey's stand on a hotly-debated water rights issue in California. The federal government prohibited use of water from federal dams for any farm larger than 160 acres. Douglas favored this law that protected the small farmer; Downey sided with the corporate farmers who wanted to abolish the limitation. Downey also favored state control of California's offshore oil while Douglas felt that control by the federal government would best protect the average consumer. When Douglas entered the race, she presented herself as representing the lower-middle-income people of California—veterans, small farmers, women, blacks, ethnics and small businesspeople—and Downey as favoring the big farmer, private utilities, oil, and big business.

Although Downey had strong corporate support, Douglas made him nervous. His health was failing as well. At the end of March, he formally withdrew, throwing his support behind Manchester Boddy, the editor of the liberal *Los Angeles Daily News*, who had enthusiastically supported Douglas during her first two terms in the House. Boddy took Douglas and her supporters aback when he not only made clear that he agreed with Downey on the water and oil issues but he also turned to red-baiting as the key to his campaign strategy.

As always before, Douglas campaigned strictly on issues. She cited her support for Truman's Fair Deal program and made clear her role in the refining of foreign policy as a member of the House Foreign Affairs Committee. She stressed that while she opposed HUAC, she hated communism, as she had explained in her "Democratic Credo." Douglas's views cut her off from the major funding sources. The oil industry, big business, and corporate farmers all backed Boddy. Labor unions unanimously stood behind Douglas. She also got considerable help in communities throughout the state from ethnic groups, academics, Jews, farmers, blacks, and liberal women's groups. Eleanor Roosevelt conducted a major fundraising effort in her behalf, and many Hollywood friends offered time and money. Conservative

Democratic women found Douglas's views, particularly her stand against ERA, distasteful.

Douglas won the primary by a comfortable margin—gaining close to 890,000 votes to Boddy's 532,000. Despite Boddy's financial edge and his potentially devastating allegations that Douglas had Communist sympathies, his late entry in the campaign and sudden conservative turnaround after years of gaining a statewide reputation as the well-respected editor of a liberal paper cost him votes. He also did not have Douglas's charismatic appeal as a speaker, nor could he articulate issues clearly. But Douglas's primary victory did not foreshadow success in the fall campaign. She had a formidable Republican opponent in congressional representative Richard M. Nixon, who had won close to 1,060,000 votes in the primary. Nixon knew that if he could take most of Boddy's votes, he could easily beat Douglas.

A member of the House since 1946, a resident of Whittier, a Los Angeles suburb, Nixon had attained significant national visibility as a member of HUAC, particularly in his leadership of the committee's investigation of Alger Hiss and as the co-sponsor of the Mundt-Nixon Communist control bill. Nixon and Douglas, as members of the Southern California congressional delegation, had shared some concerns over nonpartisan issues. But Douglas was revolted by Nixon's HUAC activities and general political stand. Furthermore, in 1946 he had ousted New Dealer Jerry Voorhis, Douglas's close friend and colleague, in a ruthless red-baiting campaign.

Over the summer, Nixon decided that rather than conduct a broad-based issue campaign, he would follow Boddy's lead and concentrate on Douglas's vulnerability on the issue of "red-blooded Americanism." Both domestic and foreign events fed this decision. Americans were up in arms about the so-called fall of China to communism, blaming it on Truman's incompetence. In early 1950 United States Senator Joseph McCarthy embarked on his search for American Communists. McCarthy's "revelations" heightened irrational fears about internal security and resulted in a bipartisan Congress passing the Internal Security Act, even over Truman's veto (with Douglas one of the few voting against the bill). In June 1950 the Korean War began when Americans aided the South Koreans in their struggle against invading Communist troups from North Korea. All these events made Nixon's dubbing of Douglas as the "Pink Lady" an effective device.

Nixon won the election by a margin of 2,200,000 to 1,500,000. Most commentators credited the victory to what they called a vicious campaign. They placed her loss in the category of other leading liberals who also lost in red-baiting races, including Senator

Claude Pepper in the primary and Senators John Carroll, Elbert Thomas, Senate majority leader Scott Lucas, and several other House members in the fall. Setting aside the "dirty campaign" issue for a moment, however, it seems clear that Nixon still had an edge on Douglas. Nixon's position on issues such as taxation, government spending, labor, and farm policy reflected the general sentiment of Californians. Nixon matched Douglas's skill as a speaker; although their styles were different, Nixon could engage a crowd as effectively as his opponent. The Republicans also profited from a substantial financial edge, particularly in the Nixon campaign, and from poor Democratic party organization. Nixon also had the luxury of many "Democrats for Nixon" campaign workers, many of whom had initially backed Downey and Boddy. One of the most effective organizers of this group was George Creel, a prominent member of Woodrow Wilson's administration, who went beyond Nixon in his red-baiting. Finally, Californians had little precedent in electing a woman to statewide or national office.

Douglas remained optimistic even into election night, despite all evidence that her campaign had failed. The numbers of her enthusiastic workers had diminished during the fall. While many viewed her as a more attractive alternative to Nixon, they saw her as a losing candidate and turned away to work for others. Even the numerous Washington luminaries, including Vice-President Alben W. Barkley and cabinet members Charles P. Brannan, J. Howard McGrath, and Oscar Chapman who came to California to support Douglas could not change what seemed a foregone conclusion.

Douglas had mixed feelings about her Senate loss. Winning would have thrust her into a very unusual spot for a political woman, but she also felt relieved. Although her marriage was still intact, the previous eight years had placed a strain on Helen's relationship with Melvyn and their children. Melvyn had spent three years abroad during the war. When he returned, he based himself in Los Angeles, but his work frequently took him away from home for extended periods. The children, after several months with Helen in Washington at the beginning of her first term in Congress, attended boarding school in Los Angeles. In 1950 Helen knew it was critical to reassemble the family. She and Melvyn decided to make New York their home base as Melvyn wanted to leave movie production and return to the theater. Helen also hoped to spend more time in Vermont at the family home in Fairlee.

Once the family settled into a Manhattan apartment, Douglas spent the next thirty years lecturing on college campuses on various current topics, particularly disarmament, and serving on boards of numerous liberal civic and political organizations. She campaigned for presidential, state, and local candidates at the request of the Democratic National Committee and toured as a performer with programs combining singing and poetry reading. In 1973, as the Watergate scandal broke, she found herself once again in the national limelight. Bumper stickers abounded reading "Don't Blame Me, I Voted for Helen Gahagan Douglas." Women's groups suddenly saw her as a role model and asked for advice about how women "make it" in politics. *Ms.* featured her on its front cover. Colleges awarded her honorary degrees. In 1974, she underwent breast cancer surgery but continued to lead an active life. She had spent several years writing her autobiography; it was almost completed when she died in June 1980.

Douglas is remembered by only a handful as a leading Broadway star, and by almost no one as a singer. In Congress, she did not wield significant political power as traditionally defined; but she challenged the male power structure by her insistance on respect for her political style, and she gained that respect. Her passionate appeals for a better America for the average citizen and a peaceful world gave hope to the people she represented—not only those in her own district but around the country—that someone cared. Despite only three terms in Congress, she stood out among her colleagues as an idealist who was willing to take risks, who spoke persuasively and stood for goals that more pragmatic politicians hesitated to embrace, and it is that for which she is recognized. The outpouring of expression at the time of her death suggests that Helen Gahagan Douglas forged a durable legacy of political principle and action.

Notes

I wish to thank the National Endowment for the Humanities, the Eleanor Roosevelt Institute at the Franklin D. Roosevelt Library, and the American Philosophical Society for partial funding for the research and writing of my work on Douglas. A full-scale biographical study is forthcoming in 1991 from Oxford University Press.

[1]*Los Angeles Times*, 1 and 12 July 1980; Claremont *Courier*, 16 July 1980; and H. L. Mitchell, "In Memory of an Early Friend of the Farm Worker" [mimeographed, July 1980].

[2]Helen Gahagan Douglas, "Congresswoman, Actress, and Opera Singer," an oral history conducted in 1973, 1974, and 1976 by Amelia Fry, in Helen Gahagan Douglas Oral History Project, vol. 4, Regional Oral History Project, The Bancroft Library, University of California, Berkeley, 1982, p. 4.

[3]Goldschmidt, Douglas Memorial Service, 2 December 1980, New York City, author's collection of unpublished materials on Douglas.

[4]Douglas to Jerry Voorhis, 12 March 1940, University of Oklahoma, Carl Albert Congressional Research and Studies Center, Helen Gahagan Douglas Collection [HGD Papers], Box 212, Folder 9.

[5]Helen Gahagan, "FSA Aids Migratory Worker," *Democratic Digest* 17 (February 1940), p. 37.

[6]Thomas F. Ford to Douglas, 20 October 1943, HGD Papers, Box 163, Folder 1.

[7]Douglas to Eleanor Roosevelt, 16 March 1944, Franklin D. Roosevelt Library, Anna Eleanor Roosevelt Papers, Box 1756.

Ella Baker

(1903–1986)

Catherine Clinton

Born in Norfolk, Virginia, in 1903, Ella Baker never forgot her roots. Her father Blake was a waiter on the ferry to Washington, while her mother Georgianna was active in the church. When the family moved to Littleton, North Carolina in 1910, they settled on land once owned by Baker's grandparents' former master. Her parents prized education and Baker graduated from Shaw University, a black college in Raleigh, North Carolina, in 1927. She moved to New York City and became a journalist and reformer, participating in local New Deal politics. During the depression Baker became involved in the National Association for the Advancement of Colored People, and served as a field organizer into the 1940s. In the wake of the Montgomery, Alabama, bus boycott, Baker joined the Southern Christian Leadership Conference and became active in radical civil rights politics. She was the political and spiritual midwife for the Student Nonviolent Coordinating Committee and remained an activist until her death at the age of eighty-three.

When four young black men refused to vacate a lunch counter in Greensboro, North Carolina, in February 1960, turning the national spotlight onto segregation, sit-ins sprang up across the South in sympathy with the protest and in solidarity with the cause of racial equality. Some argue the modern civil rights protest movement was born in this heady rush to confrontation; if so, then we must acknowledge that the student movement was midwifed by Ella Baker.

By the spring of 1960 Baker was chafing within the Southern Christian Leadership Conference (SCLC), an organization founded in the wake of the Montogmery, Alabama, bus boycott, which she had joined "temporarily" in 1958. After nearly two years, she was unhappy as executive secretary and sought new directions. Baker enthusiastically embraced the alternative posed by students—youthful crusaders "interested not in being leaders as much as in developing leadership among other people."[1]

Black youth throughout the South were primed for protest in the spring of 1960. Chicago-born Diane Nash went to Howard University in Washington, D.C., before she transferred to Fisk University in Nashville, both black colleges. Segregation—the separation of white and black into two worlds—within American society made her feel "stifled and boxed in." Nash worked to break out by joining the student movement on campus where she met fellow activist Marion Barry. Barry was raised on a Mississippi farm and later moved to Memphis where he graduated from LeMoyne College. While attending graduate school at Fisk, he joined in the student crusade. (Barry would later become mayor of Washington, D.C.) Another politician in the making, John Lewis, was born in a tenant house in Alabama and began his career as a preacher while still in high school. He attended the American Baptist Theological Seminary in Nashville, and befriended other nonviolent activists. John Lawson was a northern-born college graduate who had refused to serve in the Korean War and spent time in prison. Paroled as a Methodist missionary in India for three years, he steeped himself in the philosophy of Mahatma Gandhi. Lawson was an active member of the Fellowship of Reconciliation (FOR), a group dedicated to nonviolent social action for instituting political reform, and became its first southern field secretary. He attended Oberlin College School of Theology before settling at the Vanderbilt School of Theology in 1958. Lawson organized workshops on nonviolence at Vanderbilt in 1959 and spearheaded the movement of 150 sit-in protestors in Nashville during the spring of 1960. These activities, ironically, earned him his expulsion from divinity school. These were but a few of the student activists primed for action in the winter of 1959–60.

Protests required tough self-discipline on the part of these young activists—courtesy and patience were demanded despite trying conditions. All participants were expected to turn the other cheek, never to retaliate despite verbal or physical abuse. The watchwords of this movement were *love* and *nonviolence.* When newspapers across the South erupted with reports of polite, persistent youths disrupting segregated facilities and filling local jails, the civil rights leadership, white segregationists, and lawmakers were all unprepared.

However, one person who responded with foresight and insight was Ella Baker. She knew that Rev. Martin Luther King, Jr., and other activists and ministers of the SCLC were interested in channeling the energy of youth into their own protest program, yet this fiercely energetic and independent woman fought to keep the students disentangled from "parent" organizations. Through Baker's efforts a network of student protestors led to the formation of the Student Nonviolent Coordinating Committee, Freedom Summer (the busing in of hundreds of college students and other civil rights workers in 1964 to register blacks to vote across the South), and one of the most dynamic chapters in the history of the modern civil rights movement.

Baker had recognized something new and exciting in the spontaneous protests in the first months of the new decade, at a time when she was increasingly disenchanted with her role in the SCLC. She had been on the brink of resigning her post when the youth revolution sparked new hope, and a new mission. Her long years of experience led her to believe this was not an opportunity to be missed and she moved rapidly to capitalize on the combustion of activity.

In the first months of 1960, Baker went to two leaders of the SCLC to request funding for a meeting, a Student Leadership Conference, where groups and leaders from across the South might gather. Baker was not concerned with bringing youth in line with the interests of the larger, ministerially dominated movement, yet the eight-hundred dollar donation by the SCLC was their investment in an attempt to maintain interest and, perhaps, exercise control. Apparently many within the leadership believed this financial pledge and Baker's involvement would guarantee SCLC dominance of the youth movement. But they underestimated both college activists' and Baker's commitment to an independent course.

Baker took responsibility for the meeting, using her contacts at her alma mater, Shaw University in Raleigh, North Carolina, to set up a conference on Easter weekend, April 16–18, 1960. Her call for the conference was co-signed by King, but the spirit and content of the message conveyed Baker's concerns. She took pains to insure that students would be featured on the podium, inviting John Lawson, a strong presence in the Nashville contingent, to offer the keynote address. She assured the invitees that the weekend goals were

"TO SHARE experience gained in recent protest demonstrations and TO HELP chart future goals for effective action," hoping to create "a more unified sense of direction for *training and action in Nonviolent Resistence.*" Further, Baker stipulated that the conference should be "youth centered" and those "Adult Freedom Fighters" present were only for "counsel and guidance."[2]

When the conferees gathered at Raleigh, the numbers and representation far exceeded Baker's estimates. Over 300 students attended, and the group was kaleidoscopic in its range and depth, including over 120 black student representatives from fifty-six colleges and high schools from twelve southern states and the District of Columbia. The conference attracted between fifty and sixty representatives from northern colleges and members of thirteen national or northern "observer organizations" (such as the National Student Association, the Students for a Democratic Society, and the National Student Christian Federation). Nearly a dozen southern white students attended. Members of the Congress of Racial Equality (CORE), FOR, and, of course, the SCLC leadership turned up. But the overwhelming majority of attendees were black youths eager to organize struggles, to join the wave of energy sweeping across southern campuses.

When the Southern Christian Leadership Conference funded the meeting, they had assumed that Baker would support their efforts to channel youthful energy into their larger organization. Martin Luther King, Jr. was a rising star within the movement who had begun to attract national attention. Indeed, he was forced to leave the conference early to appear on the nationally televised Sunday news program *Meet the Press.* So when King arrived in Raleigh he called a press conference and outlined his goals for the weekend: establish a permanent organization, pursue a policy of serving time in jail rather than paying fines, become more attuned to Gandhi's philosophy of nonviolent protest, and push the federal government to step in by spreading nonviolent confrontations throughout the South.[3]

King and his followers were distressed that this SCLC agenda was not the preoccupation of debating students; rather, the majority of the students struggled with the political and philosophical questions of building a movement. John Lawson's keynote address eschewed setting specific goals in favor of sharpening group appreciation of the spiritual and moral underpinnings of student protests. Students were not encouraged to become involved because of charismatic leadership or spontaneous whim, rather they were confronted with the serious business of commitment and continuing struggle—a strategy that provided important rewards in the months and years of conflict ahead. Lawson attacked the National Association for the Advancement of Colored People (NAACP) for "fund-raising and court action rather than developing our greatest resource, a people no longer the victims of racial evil who can act in a disciplined manner to implement the constitution."[4] Fellow delegates were concerned with defining the radical ideology with which the group wished to be associated. Almost all disdained the overtures made by established civil rights organizations.

Meanwhile, Ella Baker had reason to fear the plans of SCLC leaders. A reckoning was in the works because Baker had welcomed the student philosophy of "group centered leadership" as refreshing for those who "bore the scars of battle, the frustration and the disillusionment that come when the prophetic leader turns out to have heavy feet of clay."[5] This was a thinly veiled reference to King, among others.

Animosity between the two activists was growing and was apparently based on the simple fact that Ella Baker was unable to conform to the female stereotype envisioned by the conservative black male ministers leading the movement. Andrew Young suggests that this particular feud had to do with King's psychology.

> We had a hard job with domineering women in SCLC because Martin's mother, quiet as she was, was really a strong, domineering force in that family. She was never publicly saying anything, but she ran Daddy King and she ran the church and she ran Martin and so Martin's problems with Ella Baker, for instance, in the early days of the movement were directly related to his need to be free of that strong matriarchal influence.[6]

James Lawson concurred: "Martin had a real problem with having a woman in a high position."[7] King was neither the first, nor the last, of a long line of men with whom Baker would have to do battle. At Raleigh, in April 1960, Baker stood fast and, with the students, won independence.

On the second day of the conference, King, Rev. Ralph Abernathy (an important civil rights activist who would become King's lieutenant and successor), and Rev. Wyatt Walker (the incoming executive director of the SCLC) called a caucus with Baker to which no students were invited. At this meeting the three men, all Baptist ministers, argued that students should organize a "youth group" or a "student arm" of the SCLC. Walker even admitted to Baker that his motives were personal—in an attempt to strengthen the leadership role he was about to assume, he wanted the students "delivered" to his organization. King argued he could influence the Georgia delegation, and Abernathy assumed the Alabama students would follow dutifully Georgia's lead. Walker then argued that he could insure Virginia's cooperation and pull off his coup. Baker, however, resisted the ministers' efforts, and argued that the students should not settle on a structure at this meeting—especially one that suited the "Adult Freedom Fighters" rather than the youth on the front lines. When the ministers pressured her to make a motion to become a part of the SCLC, Baker walked out of the meeting. Her defiance defeated their purposes and the three left town later that night, before the end of the conference.

On April 17, 1960, with Baker's blessing, the students voted against any permanent affiliation with an established group. Ironically, the delegation from Petersburg, Virginia—which Walker thought was in his hip pocket—created the most strenuous opposition to affiliation with the SCLC, so intense that the meeting was forced to stop, sing, and pray.[8] Nevertheless, the students were willing to form a temporary Student Nonviolent Coordinating Committee (SNCC). This group planned to meet every month—"to continue the dialogue"—and Marion Barry was elected chair, a position he resigned in the fall to return to graduate school.

Baker found SNCC exhilarating, and reported in the *Southern Patriot* in May 1960 that "the Student Leadership Conference made it crystal clear that current sit-ins and other demonstrations are concerned with something much bigger than a hamburger or even a giant-sized Coke."[9] (She would later complain that the protests should not be about who got *served* a burger but about who could *afford* a burger in a segregated, racist America.) She applauded the perception that "it is important to keep the movement democratic and to avoid struggles for personal leadership"—especially as a refugee from the ministers' caucus. Finally, she concluded that "Many adults and youth characterized the Raleigh meeting as the greatest or most significant conference of our period."[10]

The group might have become mere footnote to the civil rights movement, if Baker had not continued to nurture it. Eleven SNCC members gathered in Atlanta on May 13 to coordinate efforts. Without money or mailing address, the students gratefully accepted Baker's offer to shelter the organization at the SCLC headquarters, a group with which Baker remained affiliated. Baker recruited Jane Stembridge, a white student from Virginia at the Union Theological Seminary in New York, to run the office. By June, Stembridge and other volunteers produced the *Student Voice*, the SNCC newsletter, full of statements of purpose, solicitation for funds and contributions from black campuses (the young Julian Bond penned a protest poem and sent it from Morehouse College where he was enrolled).

By the end of the summer, Baker officially broke ties with the SCLC and secured SNCC offices provided by a sympathetic donor on Auburn Avenue in Atlanta. She, Stembridge, and Bob Moses, a black

Harvard graduate student recruited by the SCLC for voter registration but who defected upon his arrival in Atlanta, were the unpaid staff that sustained the organization in its first months. The historian Clayborne Carson argues in his study of the organization: "SNCC would probably not have survived its first summer had it not been for the energy and skills of Baker and Stembridge. Whereas SNCC appeared to outsiders and even to many black student leaders to be merely a clearinghouse for the exchange of information about localized protest movements, to the two women it was potentially an organization for expanding the struggle beyond its campus base to include all classes of blacks."[11] And indeed it did accomplish some of these idealistic goals.

What drew the fifty-seven-year-old Baker into an organization staffed and sustained by students? Baker's personal style pulled her into this maelstrom of energy, and her youthful comrades responded enthusiastically. John Lewis, a SNCC veteran, later commented, "She was much older in terms of age, but I think in terms of ideas and philosophy and commitment she was one of the youngest persons in the movement."[12] Her willingness to meet the students on their own terms, without manipulation, taught them to trust her. Her patience through long hours—and in some cases days—of philosophical and political wrangles endeared her to the SNCC rank and file. One SNCC veteran fondly remembered her wearing a surgical mask to protect her against the cloud of smoke filling the room, sitting through endless strategy debates, which Baker had doubtless heard again, and again, and again.[13] But Baker's patience and endurance gave her the strength to impart decades of wisdom to the committed student activists.

Baker was born in Norfolk, Virginia, in 1903 to Georgianna and Blake Baker. Her father was a waiter on a ferry that ran from Norfolk to Washington, a job that kept him from home much of the time. In 1910 the family moved to Littleton, North Carolina, and settled near her maternal grandparents, who had been slaves. After emancipation, Baker's grandfather, a preacher, had settled on the land of his former owner in rural North Carolina, where he built a church. Baker used to be accorded a seat of privilege, placed in a chair next to the pulpit from which her grandfather delivered his sermon. He gathered his family around to form a tightly-knit clan. Baker recalled:

> There was a deep sense of community that prevailed in this little neck of the woods. It wasn't a town, it was just people. And each of them had their twenty-thirty-forty-fifty acre farms. . . . This community had been composed to a large extent by relatives. Over the hill

> was my grandfather's sister who was married to my Uncle Carter, and up the grove was another relative who had a place. . . .[14]

This sense of family was accomplished despite the circumstances of slavery over which Baker's maternal grandparents had triumphed. Baker recalled that her grandmother chose her grandfather instead of the partner the mistress had picked out. Under slavery, masters attempted to control every aspect of slaves' lives. It was not uncommon for a slave's owner to intervene in these matters, especially for a "favorite slave" and/or illegitimate offspring. Baker's grandmother's defiance created tension, both because she was the daughter of the master and because in rejecting the advice of her white owners she was banished to the fields instead of remaining a "house slave." The stories handed down strenghtened both Baker's resistance to white authority and her family ties.

Baker's family, especially her mother, played a large role in the community: "Mamma was always responding to the sick after we moved."[15] Baker's aunt was a midwife, and Baker learned about family responsibility by her example as well.

> My aunt who had thirteen children of her own raised three more. She had become a midwife, and a child was born who was covered with sores. Nobody was particularly wanting the child, so she took the child and raised him. He's one of the *best* of her brood. And another mother decided she didn't want to be bothered with two children. So my aunt took one and raised him. So they were part of the family.[16]

This sense of belonging to a "wider brotherhood" than just her immediate family nurtured Baker during her youth, and she had hopes of becoming a medical missionary.

She was educated at local schools and then graduated from Shaw University in Raleigh, North Carolina, in 1927. With her college degree in hand she struck out for Harlem, in New York City, to live with a cousin, but found her education no assistance against the great wall of prejudice. Because she was African-American she was limited to jobs waiting tables or working in a factory. When the stockmarket crashed in 1929 and the depression set in, Baker watched her own dreams fade. When she moved to Harlem she had hopes of saving her money so she could pursue a higher degree in sociology at the University of Chicago, a coeducational institution with a liberal race policy. The struggles within her own community due to the depression affected Baker deeply, "The tragedy of seeing long lines of people standing waiting, actually waiting on the bread line, for coffee or handouts, this had its impact."[17] Baker began to write for the *American West Indian News*, and by 1932 had joined the *Negro National News* as office manager and editorial assistant.

Also by this time Baker was fully committed to a career in activism. In 1932 she organized the Young Negroes Cooperative League and helped coordinate activities for the Works Progress Administration (WPA) consumer education program. Baker spearheaded the effort to offer classes in settlement houses, provide lecturers to women's clubs, and help sponsor cooperatives in housing projects; Baker believed in bringing collective strategies to the people. She saw the widespread collapse of the economy as something that created an opportunity for dramatic political change. The Manhattan circles within which she traveled honed her political perspective. Baker recalled: "New York was a hotbed of—let's call it radical thinking. You had every spectrum of radical thinking on WPA. We had a lovely time! Ignorant ones, like me, we had lots of opportunity to hear and to evaluate whether or not this was the kind of thing you wanted to get into. Boy it was good, *stimulating*."[18]

By the late 1930s, Baker's activism led her into the National Association for the Advancement of Colored People (NAACP). This group, founded in 1910, was an interracial organization dedicated to improving race relations and fighting white terrorism; in particular, the NAACP sought to push an antilynching bill through Congress. This and other legislative campaigns were aimed at insuring blacks their constitutionally guaranteed rights, rights that were abridged by segregation. By the early 1940s, Baker was an assistant field secretary for the NAACP, a position that kept her on the road. Despite her peripatetic life, Baker's roots kept her anchored: "I think these are the things [community and family] that helped to strengthen my concept about the need for people to have a sense of their own value, and *their* strengths, and it became accentuated when I began to travel in the forties for the National Association for the Advancement of Colored People."[19]

Baker faced challenges within and outside the black community when organizing in the field. As an organizer she would be dispatched to specific regions; she later remembered her first contacts in Florida: "You'd call up Reverend Brother so-and-so, and ask if you could appear before the congregation at such-and-such a time. Sometimes they'd give you three minutes, because, after all, many people weren't secure enough to run the risk, as they saw it, of being targeted as ready to challenge the powers that be." She regretted that a stalwart, Harry T. Moore, a black principal, was fired for speaking out in favor of equal pay for black and white teachers. Moore later died when his house was bombed on Christmas eve—a martyr to the cause of African-American resistance. Baker remembered, "You could go into that area of Florida and you could talk about the virtue of the NAACP, because they knew Harry T. Moore. They hadn't discussed a whole lot of theory." But there was a *man* who served *their* interests and who *identified* with them."[20]

Baker attempted to build a movement among a people, like all other peoples, divided by class prejudices. She confronted well-to-do blacks who were embarrassed by being reminded of the masses of uneducated, impoverished African-Americans. Baker reasoned: "The gal who has been able to buy her minks and whose husband is a professional, they live well. You can't insult her, you never go and tell her she's a so-and-so for taking, for *not* identifying. You try to point out where her interest lies in identifying with that other one across the tracks who doesn't have minks."[21] Even more common, she encountered "the little people" who resented the paternalism of NAACP organizers. When she first came to Florida, Baker recalled, "I got a contribution for a life membership in the NAACP, which was five-hundred dollars then, was from a longshoreman's union. They remembered somebody who had been there before from the NAACP, with a mink coat. When they gave this five-hundred dollar membership, somebody mentioned it. See, they had resented the mink coat. I don't think it was the mink coat they really resented. It was the *barrier* they could sense between them and the person in the coat."[22] But wardrobe was hardly the issue; rather, Baker used these examples to illustrate the visible ways in which invisible walls would have to be broken down to bring all the people into a movement for social justice.

Baker never married; however, in 1946 she took over the rearing of her seven-year-old niece and therefore resigned from the NAACP to devote time to raising the young girl in Baker's Harlem home. Although her retirement was ostensibly for personal reasons, in her letter of resignation, Baker voiced her disillusionment with the political dissent she increasingly faced. Baker admitted she was unwilling to defer to the male ministerial leadership she encountered; many men within the organization complained of her outspoken manner and her "disrespectful style."[23] And yet she was so loved by "the people" that several urged her to voice her concerns at the annual NAACP convention. Baker refused, not out of respect for male leaders, but because she did not want *her* role or personality to become the focus of a split within the movement. Increasingly Baker's grass-roots, collectivist party politics were replaced by hierarchy within African-American leadership. Baker saw alienation between these leaders and their poor, mainly rural black constituents.

Although the NAACP continued its organizational campaigns, the major thrust of the organization was focused on legal battles. In 1954 the *Brown v. Board of Education* Supreme Court decision signaled a new era for civil rights. Although lawmakers were unsure as to what "all deliberate speed" might mean, African-Americans believed their time had come. In 1955 Rosa Parks refused to give up her seat on a Montgomery city bus to a white passenger and the subsequent boycott of the bus system in the capital of Alabama lasted for over a year. Public transportation was shut down and a new civil rights militance was born. In 1957 the SCLC developed in the wake of this resistance and King, among others, hoped to export "nonviolent direct action" throughout the South. Three years later, SNCC renewed Baker's commitment and she in turn was able to train and nurture a cadre of youthful revolutionaries.

Resigning from the SCLC to work at her unpaid position with SNCC, Baker also signed up with the YWCA in Atlanta as a consultant in human relations. Her lifelong commitment to political organization gave her little economic security, as Baker confessed in 1979, "How did I make my living? I haven't. I have eked out existence."[24] When she began working for the NAACP, her salary was $2,000 a year. During the 1950s she supported herself by working for the New York Cancer Society. She thought of her political activities as a vocation, not a means of breadwinning. Her views differed dramatically from her youthful peers in SNCC: "I think today, people's concept of political organizing is like you're really out there night and day doing it all. See, young people today have had the luxury of a period in which they could give their all to this political organizing. They didn't have to be bothered by a whole lot of other things. But most of those who are older put it in with things that they had to do."[25]

Students gave their all in 1964 in the Freedom Summer when thousands of college students moved South in an effort to register blacks to vote. Baker was invaluable during this effort. She sent SNCC member Bob Moses to Amzie Moore, her coworker from her NAACP days: "I had gone down there and stayed with them and helped with meetings, so I knew the person. I knew he knew the state, and so Bob Moses was able to have an entrée. Here was a man who had never been to Mississippi, and he had somewhere to sleep, to eat, and he had somebody who knew something that could be useful."[26] When whites resisted the registration drive and it became apparent that blacks would continue to be denied their right to vote, SNCC organized a separate political entity, the Mississippi Freedom Democratic Party (MFDP). Baker was a keynote speaker at the party convention in Jackson, Mississippi. She also moved to the MFDP office in Washington and appeared on television to support the organization. When Fannie Lou Hamer became one of the visible leaders within the newly organized party, Baker felt no spirit of rivalry;

instead she confessed to intense pride in the movement: "Great fruit came of it in terms of arousing the people and getting them involved . . . like Mrs. Hamer. There's a woman that had been a timekeeper on a plantation for sixteen or more years, and when she attempted to register to vote she lost her job, her husband lost his, and then she was badly beaten."[27]

Hamer went on to be the keynote speaker for the MFDP in Atlantic City, New Jersey, at the Democratic National Convention. When President Lyndon Johnson, in an effort to compromise, engineered a separate and partial seating of MFDP delegates on the convention floor, Hamer and her comrades refused. They wanted the all-white segregated delegation thrown out and replaced by the representative MFDP people. Johnson's hammerlock on the convention prevented the issue from getting to the floor, but Hamer and her supporters rallied outside the hall and garnered media attention. In 1967 the MFDP campaign yielded electoral victory when Robert Clark became the first African-American to serve in the Mississippi state legislature since Reconstruction.

Baker's commitment to the cause of freedom continued past the Freedom Summer, and in 1967 she joined the Southern Conference Educational Fund, a group dedicated to interracial collective action in the South. Baker continued her travels and speeches on behalf of racial justice, arguing: "I keep going because I don't see the productive value of being bitter. What else *do* you do?"[28] In 1972 she became vice chairperson of the Mass Party Organizing Committee. She also served on the board of the Puerto Rican Solidarity Committee, and by the 1980s her role as an exemplary female leader brought her national recognition.

Not only did Baker midwife the student revolutionaries of the 1960s, but she served as a force for broadening the struggle for civil rights throughout her career. Although most midwives disappear from the life of the child after its birth, Baker was a stalwart exemplary force for social struggle and justice throughout the 1960s and into the 1980s. Her nonviolent stance was one she learned from early disappointment. Late in her life, Baker recalled the first incidence of race prejudice she encountered, when a young boy called her "nigger" on the streets of Norfolk, and she struck back by slapping him across the face. As a movement elder, she counseled that striking back was not enough, that retaliatory acts were feeble. Joining a collective movement, fighting side-by-side in nonviolent protest was a more effective means of permanent revenge. Baker believed that all people everywhere would have to unite in the struggle against prejudice and injustice.[29]

Baker's global concerns, like many of the young people she inspired, led her into movements against apartheid in South Africa, for liberation in Zimbabwe, and against American imperialism in Africa generally. But her commitments remained rooted in the family and community values she inherited from her kin and her people. She explained in 1979:

> To me, I'm part of the human family. What the human family will accomplish, I can't control. But it isn't impossible that what those who came along with me went through, might stimulate others to continue to fight for a society that does not have those kinds of problems. Somewhere down the line the numbers increase, the tribe increases. So how do you keep on? I can't help it. I don't claim to have any corner on an answer, but I believe that the struggle is eternal. Somebody else carries on.[30]

Her message of collective struggle struck a chord among "the people" throughout her life, but it especially uplifted a generation in turmoil during the 1960s.

Thus Ella Baker departed from a life filled with challenge and struggle in 1986. She provided a legacy that filmmaker Joanne Grant celebrated in her 1984 documentary *Fundi*. As Vincent Harding explains in the film, *fundi* is an African term of honor and respect for a person that signifies a fountain from which knowledge and power might flow. Baker, and many older African-American women like her, nurtured the grass-roots protest movement during the struggle for civil rights. The black church may have been headed by male ministers, but it was sustained by its female membership. Records of organizations, memoirs of participants, and films and other documentation demonstrate women's widespread, steadfast, and significant participation.

The hundreds of black women who opened their homes during boycotts and protests of the early 1960s, the steady parade of domestic servants who walked to work in Montgomery for over a year to make the bus boycott effective, the hundreds of thousands of women who canvassed and counseled and made voting rights a top priority for the civil rights agenda—all these women deserve their due. The ideology, the example of empowerment, and the tactical energizing of the civil rights movement would infuse the women's liberation movement that grew from it during the 1960s and into the 1970s.

Yet much of this legacy is missing from historical reconstructions of the period. Against all odds, women seem to be simultaneously celebrated while being erased. Some commentators, sensitive to gender issues, mention appreciatively those few women leaders who emerged from the male hierarchy dominating civil rights politics, a backhanded compliment at best. Yet perhaps this historical vision is a mirror of contemporary sexual politics; one civil rights leader recalled that the video or news teams would only turn on the lights and film men giving speeches during rallies, ignoring women who might also have featured roles.[31]

The current images of "the movement" illuminate this distortion. Scholarly attention that focuses almost exclusively on men remains the standard. Even the award-winning documentary *Eyes on the Prize* (Part I, 1987, Part II, 1990) reinforces this image problem by keeping women in the background, playing up the role of male leadership (with females following), and minimizing both women's significant organizational and political contributions as well as the tensions black feminism provoked—for example, the split produced by Shirley Chisholm's presidential candidacy in 1972. It is conventional wisdom that the feminist movement of the late 1960s and 1970s stemmed from, in large part, the civil rights movement, as activist Virginia Durr explains in her autobiography.

> I believe that the struggle of the blacks against segregation led to the women's movement. The women who took part in that struggle for black emanicipation began to realize that they weren't very well emancipated either. When your husband disassociates himself from you because you have been to a prayer meeting, you're not very free to go to those meetings. . . . These sweet church women, black and white, were scared to death of their husbands. . . . If you go to any of the Southern women's movement meetings, you would be surprised at the amount of passion that comes forth. They really feel held down and they are trying to break loose.[32]

Yet the power of memory and the current renaissance of black women's literature undercuts this convenient neglect of black women's crucial part in the empowerment of blacks in the South. The lack of scholarship on these issues will soon be met by a mighty wave of work, just as the noticeable absence of African-American women's literature has been supplanted by a virtual flood of literary work.[33] Ella Baker will not be remembered merely as a "midwife," but as a full and equal parent who participated in the conception, birth, and nurturing of not one but many movements for social justice. Baker fought equally for the rights of blacks and the status of women.

When an even younger generation looks back on this dynamic era of civil rights struggle, Ella Baker will take her rightful place, at the forefront of many movements, in the vanguard of political change—a comrade and an inspiration.

Notes

[1]James Forman, *The Making of Black Revolutionaries: A Personal Account* (New York: Macmillan, 1972), p. 217.

[2]Clayborne Carson, *In Struggle: SNCC and the Black Awakening of the 1960s* (Cambridge, MA: Harvard University Press, 1981), p. 20.

[3]Ibid., pp. 22–23.

[4]Ibid., p. 23.

[5]Ibid., p. 20.

[6]David Garrow, *Bearing the Cross: Martin Luther King and the SCLC* (New York: William Morrow, 1986), p. 654, n. 12.

[7]Ibid., p. 141.

[8]Forman, *Black Revolutionaries*, p. 217.

[9]Ibid.

[10]Ibid.

[11]Carson, *In Struggle*, pp. 25–26.

[12]Forman, *Black Revolutionaries*, p. 24.

[13]See *Fundi*, Joanne Grant (1984).

[14]Ellen Cantarow, *Moving the Mountain: Women Working for Social Change* (New York: Feminist Press, 1980), pp. 60–61.

[15]Ibid., p. 59.

[16]Ibid., p. 59.

[17]Ibid., p. 60.

[18]Ibid., p. 61.

[19]Ibid., p. 61.

[20]Ibid., pp. 69–20.

[21]Ibid., p. 70.

[22]Ibid., pp. 71–72.

[23]*Fundi* and Cantarow, *Moving the Mountain*, p. 156, n. 3.

[24]Cantarow, *Moving the Mountain*, p. 73.

[25]Ibid., p. 74.

[26]Ibid., p. 89.

[27]Ibid., p. 90.

[28]Ibid., p. 92.

[29]See *Fundi.*

[30]Cantarow, *Moving the Mountain*, p. 93.

[31]Dudley Clendinen, ed., *The Prevailing South* (Atlanta, GA: Longstreet Press, 1988), p. 192.

[32]Hollinger Barnard, ed., *Outside the Magic Circle: The Autobiography of Virginia Foster Durr* (New York: Simon and Schuster, 1987), p. 331.

[33]Two outstanding African-American novelists, Alice Walker and Toni Morrison, have won the Pulitzer Prize in the past five years. *The Color Purple* and *Beloved* received instant acclaim and "classic" status.

Betty Friedan

(b. 1921)

Donald Meyer

Betty Friedan was born Betty Naomi Goldstein on February 4, 1921, in Peoria, Illinois. From 1938 to 1942 she attended Smith College in Northampton, Massachusetts, graduating summa cum laude *in psychology. She then went to the University of California, Berkeley, for postgraduate study but left after a year to pursue a newspaper career in New York. She married Carl Friedan soon thereafter and had three children, Emily, Daniel, and Jonathan. She continued to write, publishing articles in women's magazines. In 1963, Friedan published* The Feminine Mystique. *The book gained Friedan immediate fame, and she began to lecture widely. In 1966 she was a founding member and first president of the National Organization for Women. Friedan was instrumental in establishing one of the nation's first women's studies programs, at Cornell in 1968. She attempted to move feminism into orthodox, national politics in 1968 along with other prominent women, supporting the antiwar candidacy of Eugene McCarthy, who had been the chief sponsor of the Equal Rights Amendment in Congress. In 1971 she joined feminists Bella Abzug, Gloria Steinem, and Shirley Chisholm in establishing the National Women's Political Caucus. In the early 1970s Friedan organized the First Women's Bank and Trust Company. Friedan published* It Changed My Life *in 1976 and* The Second Stage *in 1981.*

Betty Friedan, née Goldstein, was born in Peoria, Illinois, in 1921, and grew up there, living in the same house until she went off in 1938 to Smith College.[1] As she would recall it, this girlhood was by no means unclouded. School work came easy, but she was not one of the popular girls in high school. The chief trouble appeared at home, however. Like many other midwestern small-city families, the Goldsteins weathered the Great Depression without serious blight. The tension between Betty Goldstein's parents had deeper roots than that. Before marrying, her mother had written for a local newspaper. She gave up this potential career for husband and family. Soon she had found herself restless, discontent, resentful. She had more energy, more intelligence, more ambition than would be contained in the role of housewife, even in Community Chest work and other civic activities. In effect, the first person the future feminist knew, suffering from "the problem that had no name," was her own mother: "My own feminism somehow began in my mother's discontent. . . ."[2]

Yet it was the mother who prompted the daughter not to make the same mistake. She urged her daughter to try out for the school paper, get jobs, earn money, not out of family necessity but for independence. Her mother impelled her toward Smith. In college, perhaps as though compelled to understand her own upbringing, Betty Goldstein majored in psychology. Once again the work came easy: she graduated summa cum laude in 1942. She won a grant to work with the psychologist Erik Erikson in Berkeley. After a year there she got another grant, opening a highway to a Ph.D. and a professional career in psychology. Just exactly why she chose, instead, to go to New York City and work on newspapers, Friedan never said, but presently she married Carl Friedan and soon thereafter found herself a housewife, in the suburbs of Rockland County, with three children. In an autobiographical reminiscence forty years later, Friedan noted that she had not quit her newspaper job: she had been fired, during pregnancy, with no legal recourse. But she had not, she agreed, been victimized by this lack of legal equality. Instead, she had been "relieved" to be fired. Why? "I was determined to be 'fulfilled as a woman' as my mother was not."[3] Thus, Rockland County was not to be a repetition of Peoria: unlike her mother, Betty Friedan embraced motherhood and housewifery eagerly. In short, the exemplary victim of the feminine mystique would be herself.

Some of the persuasive power of Betty Friedan's famous bestseller, *The Feminine Mystique,* published in 1963, undoubtedly inhered in the utter conviction with which she presented women's need for a complete life, a conviction drawn from personal experience. Despite her wish to live by the standards of the feminine mystique, Friedan found that she could not. She was bored. Her need for greater activity, sterner challenge, true risk-taking would not be denied. She began free-lancing articles for women's magazines. In 1957 she composed a questionnaire which she sent to the members of the Smith College class of '42, inquiring of their lives since graduation. She undertook systematic research into popular women's magazine fiction, modern psychiatry and sociology, and modern educational theories—all respecting women. Literally, she had resumed the career she had forsaken. She then brought all this individual effort to stunning fruition in her book. The book in turn launched her on a new career, that of no longer just a writer but a leader.

W. W. Norton, the publishers of *The Feminine Mystique,* had reason to hope for good sales. Exposés of tedium in the picture-window suburbs, such as A. C. Spectorsky's *The Exurbanites* (1956) and Richard and Katherine Gordon's *The Split-Level Trap* (1960) had already been modest best-sellers. As far back as 1956, in a special issue devoted to "the American Woman," *Life* magazine in its otherwise conventionally upbeat portrait included several selections indicating all was not well for this paragon. By 1962 *Esquire*'s July issue on "the American Woman" more nearly approached lamentation than celebration. The most famous career woman of the epoch, Margaret Mead, had been deploring the "return of the cave woman." Even mass-circulation women's magazines which Friedan would criticize in her book as purveyors of the mystique at its worst had begun to carry articles diagnosing malaise. But, cautiously, the publisher printed a first run of only three thousand copies. By comparison with these other discussions, Friedan's manuscript was not journalistic in style. It had very little personal, autobiographical, confessional tang. True to Friedan's own academic training, it carried a heavy freightage of scholarly quotations and references. It treated psychology and sociology on levels of high scholarly theory. Even for its intended audience, college-educated women of her own generation, it could not have been thought easy reading. Yet the book took off immediately. Norton soon printed another sixty thousand copies. In ten years, sales swelled to 3 million. Obviously, a large audience had been waiting for such a book and was receptive to Friedan's message.

Paradoxically, then, the sway of the feminine mystique had already begun to decline before Friedan's book appeared. Still, that hardly explains why Friedan's book in particular won renown. One reason was her rhetorical strategy. While the mystique Friedan attacked—of women's fulfillment through domesticity—sometimes appeared to hover everywhere in the 1950s, in every sphere of American life, Friedan did not really think women had been seduced by the fiction in women's magazines or by advertising concocted by some Madison Avenue Institute for Motivational Research. This would have been to demean women's brains, and besides, "A mystique does not compel its own acceptance."[4] While Friedan then offered several guesses why so many women had in fact apparently accepted the beliefs making up the feminine mystique, she herself shrewdly—if "unconsciously"—illuminated the most powerful one by her own procedure. While pop fiction editors and ad men were not likely to mesmerize educated women, educated women were respectful of science. The most powerful underwriters of the feminine mystique were those—both men and women—who insisted that its tenets were not a "mystique" at all but scientific, validated by "research." By far, most of Friedan's book was devoted to identifying the contribution of scientists to the mystification of women: Sigmund Freud, the psychologist; Margaret Mead, the anthropologist; Talcott Parsons, Harvard's dean of modern "functional sociology"; and so on. If the feminine mystique was purveyed by such authorities, it enjoyed prestige indeed.

The prestige of social science could not be undermined simply by citing the feelings of boredom, frustration, and despair Friedan found among her classmates and the scores of other women she had interviewed. Feelings could not stand against science. Instead, by a kind of intellectual jujitsu, Friedan turned to still more social science as counter to the social science she had identified at the heart of the feminine mystique. Freud was not the only psychologist; there were Erik Erikson, A. H. Maslow, theorists of liberation. There was not just one Margaret Mead, author of the feminine mystique's *Male and Female*, but several Margaret Meads, including the critic of the return to the cave of domesticity. Functional sociology, it appeared, was not really a science at all, but a form of circular reasoning already under fire as a "myth." Not women's complaints alone—let alone "women's intuition"—demonstrated the falsity of the feminine mystique—but rather social science's self-criticism proved her point. In chapter after chapter, the heavy majority of Friedan's references were to scholarly articles, scholarly books, academic research. She thus had it both ways, assailing the feminine mystique in its central citadel, disguised as science, while still claiming the prestige of science for herself.

Friedan improved upon this basic strength with two rhetorical contributions of her own. Obviously, the subjective feelings of the victims of the feminine mystique might have been summed up in any number of plain words. *Boredom* comes first to mind perhaps. *Frustration* and *claustrophobia* offered a quasi-clinical ring. *Alienation* resonated back through fashionable radicalism to Karl Marx himself. Friedan's "the problem that has no name" escaped the limitations of all these. It meant something far deeper than boredom, far different from some pathology open to "treatment," and it did not carry the burden of a philosophy to be learned. It encouraged each victim of the "problem" to learn more about it, not by reading about it in more articles or books but by exploring it in her own heart and soul.

The other contribution was her title itself. What Friedan was examining was in truth a mystique "of"—or "about"—femininity. Transforming the noun *femininity* into the adjective *feminine* Friedan introduced an irreducible ambiguity, but one which strongly favored her polemical intent. Clearly, a "mystique of femininity" might be held by both men and women; in Friedan's book most of its exponents were indeed men. But Friedan's whole purpose was to induce women to abandon the mystique. With her choice of "the feminine mystique," she highlighted the myth in its appeal precisely to women, and the need, therefore, of women themselves to start thinking differently about themselves. How men might be induced to start thinking differently about women, while no doubt important, was quite another matter. *The Feminine Mystique* was a call upon women.

This central purpose meshed with certain other features of the book, conspicuous only to critical reflection. The book said nothing of politics. It offered no assessments of either major party. Among politicians, only Adlai Stevenson was mentioned, but only as just another standard exponent of the mystique, not as a liberal. Nor did religion appear significantly. With only a little historical scholarship to draw on, Friedan, evidently unaware of the considerable interdependence between nineteenth-century feminists and religion, wrote as though the two had been only at odds. Secular-minded herself, she simply ignored the issue in postwar America, and thus ignored the fact that women of Jewish and Catholic origins would loom far larger in modern feminism than they had in the nineteenth century,[5] when feminism had in some ways been part of Protestant evangelicalism. Finally, Friedan wrote very little of economics. In a chapter entitled, "The Sexual Sell," she did anticipate a theme that later socialist feminists would hammer hard: "The really important role that women serve as housewives is *to buy more things for the house.*" Once one realized that women are "the chief customers of American business," the feminine mystique made sense. But Friedan quickly backed away from any political implications in this. Apotheosis of the housewife-consumer had not followed from some deliberate conspiracy; "business" did not stand embattled against women's escape from the home. It was simply a "byproduct" of "our general confusion lately on ends with means; just something that happened to women. . . ."[6] In no way, then, did the feminine mystique derive from or rest on some basic structure of capitalism.

This indifference to religion, politics, and the economy both expressed and facilitated the central message of Friedan's book, the message that best explains its instant popularity: you can change yourself! In her last chapter, "A New Life Plan for Women," Friedan did not call for a new women's movement, a movement for women's liberation, a new "feminism." She did not call for a new economic system. She did not herald some new religious vision. Instead, she noted how, once a woman faced the pressure of the feminine mystique, "she begins to find her own answers."[7] True, the school system would have to purge itself of catering to the mystique of femininity. True, the collaboration of feminine mystique and the churches (and synagogues) would have to be broken. But these, as well as women's entry into politics, first at the local, then at higher levels, would follow as results even more than as causes of women's awakening. Women—a woman, any woman—need not wait for political wheels to turn, for economic revolutions, for religious transformations, before saving themselves from the deformations wrought by the mystique. The mystique was a scheme of ideas and feelings. It could be defeated by different ideas and feelings. The process of change took place in the mind and spirit. Mind and spirit were every woman's to fulfill. It was in this sense that *The Feminine Mystique* took its place among all those other perennial best-sellers in American culture, the "self-help" books according to which a *man* had only to get his mind straight and think right, think positively, in order to liberate himself from defeat. He did not need politics; he did not need—indeed, ought not want—a change in the economic rules. His religion need be simply an understanding of the powers of one's own mind. No such book had yet been written for women.

Finally, all this meshed perfectly with the historical dimension of the book. In 1963 Friedan still had only a sparse literature on which to draw for any understanding of nineteenth century feminism and of why feminism had faded away after 1920. But she did not really need it for her argument about the feminine mystique. Repeatedly, she contrasted the mystique of the fifties with previous decades when, she said, it had not flourished. Repeatedly, in her telling, the mystique was a creation of post–World War II advertisers, editors, and popular psychiatrists. (This included the somewhat paradoxical implication that Friedan herself had not grown up under its influence and indeed that her peers in the class of 1942 generally had not been its victims.[8]) In short, the feminine mystique did not have roots deep in history, deep in ancient religious myths, deep in the structures of millenial patriarchy. It followed that it would be easy to dispel. After all, why should the concoction of mere admen and popular magazine editors and pop-psychologists be hard to refute?

This foreshortening of modern women's history was a central feature of Friedan's appeal.

In 1966 Friedan helped found the National Organization for Women (NOW).[9] In 1964 congressional representative Martha Griffith (Michigan) and Senator Margaret Chase Smith (Maine) had made sure that the clause forbidding "sex discrimination"—introduced by a segregationist congressional representative in hopes of defeating the Civil Rights Act of 1964—was retained in Title VII of that act. Thousands of complaints from women were soon filed. It quickly became apparent, however, that meaningful enforcement of the act by the new Equal Economic Opportunity Commission (EEOC) depended on outside pressure. Old-line women's organizations, such as the League of Women Voters and the American Association of University women, although headquartered in Washington, did not see this as part of their purposes. The dozen or so women, several of them "closet" feminists in the federal government, who joined with Friedan to create NOW were thus primarily interested in opening to women the world of work outside the home. With Friedan as president, NOW set out to expose all forms of gender discrimination in the workplace, to insist upon a vigorous EEOC, to persuade unions and other organizations to recognize women's demands for equality, and to prompt the creation of local NOW groups for the same activities. With no money, no office, no staff, NOW in its early days relied wholly on what *The Feminine Mystique* had already revealed, a ground swell of demand among women for more opportunities. NOW's first significant success was its part in impelling President Johnson to sign an executive order forbidding sex discrimination in the federal government and by government contractors.

NOW had no particular interest in mass membership. It had no particular interest in evangelizing women themselves. Certainly it welcomed men as members; it did not proclaim "sisterhood." Friedan herself persistently linked equality for women with the equality long asserted in the Bill of Rights of the United States Constitution. Although NOW failed in seeking alliance with the black civil rights movement, its quest resembled that movement's, in striving to extend to still more persons what had remained, in effect, a right enjoyed by white men only. NOW called for no sweeping changes in political, economic, or cultural arrangements in the country. It wanted women to share equally in those arrangements. Quite consistently with this traditional liberalism, it got behind efforts to install an Equal Rights Amendment (ERA) in the Constitution. For fifty years ERA supporters had been opposed by those, including many women, who pointed out that an ERA would negate the many state laws protecting women from certain onerous conditions, laws passed often only after long struggle against crude exploitation. NOW insisted that the time had come to recognize that these protective laws had often been used to limit opportunity. Thus, the early NOW expressed women very like Friedan herself—middle class, middle aged, highly educated, ambitious, professional, white. It felt responsibility for "all" women, notably women in factories and black women, but it sought first of all the end to barriers for women most ready to seize the new opportunities awaiting.

By 1970 Friedan felt, on the one hand, that the potential for a great grass-roots women's movement had vastly increased and, on the other hand, that the women's movement was in serious danger of tearing itself to pieces. From her trips around the country, lecturing and organizing, she was convinced that eagerness for broader lives flourished among ordinary women—"Middle American" women—even more hotly than the response to her book had indicated. In addition, civil rights ferment among blacks had begun to invigorate black women ever more surely. Working-class women had begun to realize their stake in NOW's agenda. Young women on college campuses, often with links to the male-dominated Students for a Democratic Society (SDS), had begun insisting that the "New Left" purge itself of its own relegation of women to helper status. Women everywhere, it seemed, were becoming self-conscious about their marginality and determined in their readiness to do something about it.[10] But all this ferment held the potential also for division and conflict. Friedan urged young radical women to stop talking about "socialism" versus "capitalism."[11] She hoped black women would refrain from the temptations of racial confrontations. But above all, she warned against letting "sex" come to be the focus of women's liberation.

In 1970 the writer Kate Millett published *Sexual Politics*, a book instantly hailed by some women as the bible for a new feminism. In this book, relying heavily on her own reading of some American and English novelists, Millett celebrated a certain basic femininity as against various masculine propensities such as violence and power-oriented sexuality. Friedan felt sure this pointed the wrong way for women. Taking Millett to be arguing, in effect, that the explanation for women's condition consisted simply of "men," she feared that this opened the way to urging lesbianism as women's preferred escape from oppression. She was appalled when Millett allowed herself to be quoted, in a *Time* magazine cover story, as to her own personal sexual life. Any woman had a perfect right, Friedan said, to whatever sexual life suited her, but to make lesbianism into a political issue would amount to suicide for the women's movement. Middle American women were not interested in lesbian lives. Hard-pressed working women are not interested in undermining marriage and the family. Black women were not eager to attack black men. To attack men, marriage, and the family as the keys to women's oppression would lead only to defeat.

Friedan's personal history on this point was complicated. Her own marriage had long been in trouble. At the time of the publication of *The Feminine Mystique* she had been warned that a divorce would hurt her credibility. As her status in feminism grew, her status as wife suffered. She knew about the battered-wife syndrome before the feminists of the seventies made it a part of their agenda.[12] When she finally did get a divorce, in 1969, she kept it secret, flying in and out of Mexico on a single day during a lecture tour.[13] Thus Friedan had reason to sympathize with the militancy rising around her, but she never ceased deploring what she felt to be an "anti-man" feeling being vented in certain sectors of the movement.

Hoping to head off division, Friedan promoted the idea of a women's national strike for August 16, 1970, the fiftieth anniversary of the ratification of the Nineteenth Amendment to the Constitution.[14] Soon refocused as a parade in which women of every sort could share, the action would be symbolic of women's solidarity. On the appointed day, several tens of thousands of women—plus many men—marched down Fifth Avenue in New York City, in a demonstration reminiscent of the suffrage parades that had preceded the triumph of 1920. Friedan meant to follow up on this moment through an overtly political organization, the National Women's Political Caucus (NWPC), started in July 1971.[15] Any hopes she might have had for personal leadership in the NWPC were quickly dispelled. Feminist outreach to politics immediately interested women already in politics, notably a recently elected congressperson, Bella Abzug of New York. At the Democrats' National Convention in Miami in 1972, Friedan found herself effectively bypassed.

Friedan's leadership dimmed also within the increasingly heterogeneous world of feminism itself. While Millett's notoriety of 1970 soon faded, another, far more compelling figure had emerged, far more adapted than Friedan to represent feminism in the mass media. For Friedan, Gloria Steinem embodied an especially painful issue: "Gloria is assuredly blonder, younger, prettier than I am. . . ."[16] But Steinem was far more than just a pretty face. She understood the logic of modern mass media. She had a clear sense of the new constituency for feminism, women younger than those to whom Friedan had addressed her book, often better educated, not yet married, often vehement in their impatience with both the sexual as well as the economic roles still the norm for women. Steinem founded a Women's Action Alliance, obviously competitive with NOW. In June 1971 Steinem, not Friedan, was invited to address the graduating class at

Smith (Steinem's alma mater too) on feminism. The feminism she hailed resembled Friedan's hardly at all. In August 1971 Steinem made the cover of *Newsweek*: "A Liberated Woman Despite Beauty, Chic and Success." In January 1972 the first issue of *Ms.* magazine appeared, with Steinem as editor. It was an immediate hit. In the years ahead, *Ms.* proved to be feminism's one popular media success. While many radical feminists would score *Ms.* as bland, sentimental, and edited by the same yardsticks used by mass circulation organs, it gave first space to some of the best rising young feminist novelists, including Alice Walker. Friedan never appeared in *Ms.*, and was rarely mentioned. At the First National Women's Conference held in Houston in 1977, a kind of exercise to celebrate the triumphs of feminism with no fewer than three First Ladies in attendance, Betty Friedan had no official, scheduled place.

Although it had become resonably clear as early as 1969 that for feminism as a movement much was at stake in its appearance in the mass media, Friedan experienced much ambivalence about her own role. She stepped down as president of NOW in 1970, as the organization, still only three thousand members strong, in an obvious bid to widen its appeal, elected a woman of both black and Hispanic roots, Aileen Hernandez, as its new head. "I've often been asked," Friedan wrote, "if I voluntarily bowed out. . . ." Six years later she could only say: "That's a hard question to answer."[17] Retrospectively, she attributed her failures in the National Women's Political Caucus to personal deficiencies: "I was scared enough by . . . tactics used against me to stay away . . . from any confrontation whatsoever. . . . I now see that my own cowardice, my faint-heartedness, my unwillingness to compete in a really rough fight" had induced her retreat.[18] Yet there were those who had regarded Friedan as often imperious, demanding, and tactless in dealing with others.[19] On balance, Friedan did seem to have lacked those intuitions guiding an effective leader. In appearances at such high-visibility international conferences as one in Teheran in 1974, on the initiative of the sister of the Shah of Iran, and another in Mexico City in 1975, under United Nations auspices, Friedan did not seem aware, nor was she to become fully aware upon reflection, that these affairs had been completely stage-managed for ulterior purposes, her own feminist purposes not being among them.[20]

Instead, Friedan's route seemed more surely that of further thought and writing. This too did not prove easy, however. Prompted by the success of *The Feminine Mystique*, Random House had offered her a contract for a second book. Working with the title "The Unfinished Revolution," then "The New Woman," finally "Humansex," Friedan could not bring her manuscript to completion. As books that were more direct and radical about sex appeared—Millett's *Sexual Politics*, Shulamith Firestone's *The Dialectic of Sex*, Ti-Grace Atkinson's *Amazon Odyssey*, Germaine Greer's *The Female Eunuch*, among others—Friedan grew more sure of where the women's movement was going wrong than she was of some new dispensation. She was drawn to writing a column, "Betty Friedan's Notebook," for *McCall's*, a magazine she had stigmatized as one of the more blatant purveyors of the feminine mystique. Why not *Ms.*? "I always saw the women's movement as a movement of the mainstream. . . . I was interested in writing for those 8,000,000 woman's magazine readers, the suburban housewives," not for the "already convinced," "especially within the framework of a new kind of feminist conformity."[21] In 1976 Friedan cobbled together a selection from her speeches, notebooks, and other writing, together with updating comments, into a volume entitled *It Changed My Life*. Concluding that book with "An Open Letter to the Women's Movement," she noted the convulsions that had racked NOW in 1975 over a "Majority Caucus" pledged to take NOW "out of the mainstream, into the revolution." She noted the failure of state ERAs in New York and New Jersey and the stalling of the national ERA four states short of ratification. Public opinion polls still showed overwhelming endorsement, among men as well as among women, for greater opportunities for women, but this tremendous reservoir of goodwill was being wasted, she argued, by leadership preoccupied with "racism, poverty, rape and lesbian rights."[22] Antifeminist women, Friedan argued, in such groups as "Total Womanhood," "The League of Housewives," and the "Pussycat League,"—"fearful sisters," "truly vicious," filled with "icy, burning rage"[23]—were themselves symptoms rather than the cause of feminism's failure. The fears driving the antifeminist women had a taproot in reality. Almost in proportion as women were moving out into the public marketplace, women were finding themselves economically hard-pressed. Indeed, what impelled far more women out of housewifery into jobs was hard necessity rather than eager ambition. Attacks upon marriage and family, upon "patriarchy," upon "compulsory heterosexuality," meant less than nothing to most women. Feminism, Friedan argued, needed a new bearing.

In 1981 Freidan published *The Second Stage*. In this book she took for granted the death of the feminine mystique. That old ideology had had but to be exposed to the light of criticism for it to shrivel away. But the collapse of the feminine mystique had not automatically been followed by equality and liberation. The ERA had been stalled. By 1981 it faced the likelihood of defeat. Millions more women were at work in the marketplace than ever before, but most of them still crowded into poorly paid "pink collar" ghettos. Millions more women with young children were at work, without help. While more kinds of careers for professional women had opened than ever before, all sorts of signs of stress and disillusion among even such privileged women had begun to appear. Supposedly egalitarian new divorce laws had backfired badly for tens of thousands of women. While the false idyll of "fifties" domesticity had long dissipated, life in 1981 fulfilled no one's fantasy.

Friedan did not doubt that forces quite independent of the women's movement had much to do with some of these problems: inflation, continuing racism, the peculiar forms of the new "post-industrial" service economy, the apparent turn to the political Right, the rise of the religious Right. But *The Second Stage* returned to what Friedan regarded as self-inflicted wounds. Citing Kate Millett, Susan Brownmiller, Mary Daly, and Shulamith Firestone among others, Friedan repeated her insistence that preoccupation with sexual issues had got feminism out of touch with the mainstream of American women who had indeed been eager to liberate themselves from the feminine mystique but had never wanted destruction of the family, repudiation of marriage, or sexual war against men. But the second-generation feminists, the daughters, as it were, younger, impatient with restraint, stimulated by media success, had generated a new mystique, a "feminist" mystique, far more dangerous to feminist success than the old, discredited feminine mystique. Still sensitive to rhetorical tactics, Friedan criticized the language both NOW and feminist radicals were using in the defense of the Supreme Court's 1973 decision, *Roe v. Wade*, invalidating states' prohibitions on abortion. Feminists had let their opponents steal the banner of "pro-life."[24] Certainly no woman should be denied an abortion, but claiming a "right" to abortion was comparable to claiming a "right" to a mastectomy or any other medical operation. Abortions ought to be defended as functions of need, failure, and despair, not of equality and sexual freedom.

Friedan was convinced that mainstream political success awaited a feminism that concentrated on family issues. Reaching out to churches, neighborhood groups, local unions, to all varieties of private associations with a stake in social health and vitality, such a feminism would far more closely approach mainstream politics than NOW, let alone the smaller feminist groups, had ever been able to do. Ultimately, the basic reason for this was that the most important collaborators with this feminism would be men. Friedan had always deplored the "anti-man" note she heard in certain radical feminists. She had felt it to be pragmatically foolish, as well as misguided sexually. Without men's goodwill, even the final collapse of the feminine mystique would not mean women's liberation. Allowed, even encouraged and urged, to move out into jobs and careers, women were already finding themselves trying to juggle two roles, two full-time responsibilities: home and work, children and office. Many women had adjusted by trying to postpone home, limit children, even abandon marriage altogether. This was the old pattern urged on college women by Bryn Mawr college's M. Carey Thomas back before World War I: do not waste your training in domesticity. Friedan felt sure the vast majority of modern American women refused to make any such choice. They would not forsake marriage, home, children. But they wanted to work, or had to work. What then was the only way to avoid exhaustion? Men had to share the homework, share "parenting," share in the private sphere.

Back in 1971, NOW itself had already set up a "Task Force on the Masculine Mystique," postulated on the idea that myths of normative "masculinity" oppressed men just as the feminine mystique had oppressed women.[25] Her own father, Friedan felt, had been such a victim. Like women, men too had only to wake up to their oppression to begin quickly to free themselves from it. The task force got nowhere. While its premise was rickety enough, its basic weakness was political. Norms of "masculinity" may or may not have weighed hurtfully on some men, but the masculine mystique had not done to men what the feminine mystique had done to women: held them out of the marketplace, inhibited them from money-making, discouraged them from competing for power. Why should men sacrifice any of these privileges? If most men had come to accept money-earning women in the marketplace, did that mean they must themselves retreat a little from the marketplace in order to spend more time at home?

In *The Second Stage* Friedan still wanted to believe that it was in men's self-interest to become a little less competitive while women became more competitive, to be a little less aggressive while women were becoming more. She did not exalt some vision of androgyny as had many feminists on the Left, but she clearly evoked a picture of the sexes sharing domesticity that, she felt, would allow women to fulfill basic needs for home and motherhood while still at work in the world. Instead of trying to construct a parallel scheme of fulfillment for men, however, she followed a quite different line, one that left her hopes—and feminism's—still adrift. The reason there was a "quiet movement" away from coercive masculinity among men was not so much that men were beginning to understand the attractions of a new sharing as that the old rewards of masculinity were being undermined. "[Many] of the old bases for men's identity have become shaky."[26] The work world was changing. Good jobs, jobs that made men "feel like men," were becoming scarce. "Only one out of every five men now says that work means more to him than leisure."[27] The war in Vietnam too had undermined a certain machismo in national life. And so on. But this approach contained its own paradoxes. If the work world was becoming less rewarding, why should women insist upon being included in it? No doubt no more Vietnam Wars were wanted, but women were not likely to find reform of politics simply a matter of androgynous psychology. Still as much a realistic observer as a hopeful reformer, Friedan could not deny another kind of evidence also. Something like a male backlash against the sex equalities was already in progress, as attested by the macho heroes in the novels of John Updike, Philip Roth, Saul Bellow, and Thomas Pynchon; the proliferation of pornography; and a clinically attested increase in impotence. Certainly these were as telling as the feelings she cited among men whom she interviewed on the waning influence of the masculine mystique. In the end, Friedan appealed once again to the old idea that, however probable the gender revolution might or might not be, it was not only desirable but necessary: the world could no longer afford leadership of the "stereotypical male."[28]

Whether or not men were yet collaborating on the necessary "convergence" of the sexes, a feminist could take hope, finally, in the fact that the "changing sex roles of both men and women are a massive, evolutionary development."[29] Friedan was almost surely unaware that the same claim had been made by one of the greatest of the earlier feminists, Charlotte Perkins Gilman, in 1898. Whatever men and women might want, the change to sexual equality, Gilman wrote, "is not a thing to prophesy and plead for. It is a change already instituted. . . , the same great force of social evolution which brought us into the old relation [of inequality] is bringing us out. . . ."[30] By the end of her life Gilman was complaining bitterly that the young women of the 1920s had forsaken the cause. However flaming their youth, they had wrought no "social improvement that I have heard of."[31] Equality had not been quite so inevitable after all.

The Second Stage won no such popularity as had *The Feminine Mystique* eighteen years before. It could not have. For the individual woman reader, it evoked no personal awakening as had the earlier book. For any man who might have read it, it only promoted ambivalence. The book did register the end of what might be called the utopian phase of modern American feminism. By 1981 college women were assuming work and careers as a matter of course, often with little sense of the efforts that had had to be made to guarantee them their opportunities. At the same time, a revolution had occurred in both the American marketplace and American home life: the single wage-earner family was increasingly rare. The stresses and pains this single fact implied for marriage, child-rearing, and home life specifically, as well as for sexual culture at large, outran even the most radical feminist alarm. Condensed to a nub, Friedan's message constituted both a warning and a hope. If feminists followed an agenda forged only in their own fantasies of revolution, they would be reduced to the isolated sect they sometimes seemed to have become by the mid-eighties. On the other hand, so long as feminists drew their agenda from issues close to the experiences of mainstream, middle-class American women, they could not fail to prosper. If there were "massive, evolutionary" developments that would carry mainstream America on into the nineties, it seemed quite clear feminists would have plenty of problems to care about. As she herself arrived at late middle age, Friedan continued to make herself available, at conferences, workshops, conventions, encouraging activity, confident of the energies she had helped unlock.

Notes

[1]Autobiographical fragments are to be found scattered through all three of Friedan's books, but especially in *It Changed My Life* (New York, 1976). See also Paul Wilkes, "Mother Superior to Women's Lib," *New York Times Magazine,* 29 Nov., 1970.

[2]*The Second Stage* (New York, 1981), p. 93.

[3]Ibid.

[4]*The Feminine Mystique* (New York, 1963), p. 182.

[5]She did note how Catholic and Jewish women faced a "housewife image" enshrined in their churches' dogmas, ibid., p. 351.

[6]Important role, ibid., p. 206; customers, ibid., p. 207; byproduct, ibid.

[7]Ibid., p. 338.

[8]"[These Smith] graduates of 1942 were among the last American women educated before the feminine mystique," ibid., p. 360.

[9]In addition to Friedan, in *It Changed My Life,* Part 2, Jo Freeman, *The Politics of Women's Liberation* (New York, 1975), examines NOW: Rolande Ballorain, *Le nouveau feminisme americain* (Paris, 1972), is particularly interesting for its interviews with the new feminist leaders, including Friedan. Donald Meyer, *Sex and Power: The Rise of Women in America, Russia, Sweden and Italy* (Middletown, 1987), ch. 10, discusses NOW.

[10]A more or less instant history is in Judith Hole and Edith Levine, *Rebirth of Feminism* (New York, 1971); Mary Lou Thompson, ed., *Voices of the New Feminism* (Boston, 1970), offers readings including Friedan. Recent histories include Meyer, *Sex and Power,* ch. 10, and Marcia Cohen, *The Sisterhood:*

The True Story of the Women Who Changed the World (New York, 1988) is a paean in the breathless style of Tom Wolfe.

[11]Friedan, *It Changed My Life*, p. 389.

[12]Cohen, *The Sisterhood*, pp. 17–18.

[13]Friedan, *It Changed My Life*, p. 137.

[14]Ibid., pp. 137ff.

[15]Ibid., pp. 165ff.

[16]Ibid., p. 179; Cohen, *The Sisterhood*, offers many pages on Steinem.

[17]Friedan, *It Changed My Life*, p. 140.

[18]Ibid., pp. 181, 183.

[19]For example, see Germaine Greer, "Women's Glib," *Vanity Fair*, June 1988.

[20]Friedan, "Scary Doings in Mexico City," *It Changed My Life*, pp. 342ff.

[21]Ibid., p. 188.

[22]Ibid., p. 379.

[23]Ibid., p. 382.

[24]*The Second Stage*, pp. 107–108.

[25]See the discussion in Meyer, *Sex and Power*, pp. 416–420.

[26]*The Second Stage*, p. 130.

[27]Ibid., p. 134.

[28]Ibid., p. 156.

[29]Ibid., p. 142.

[30]C. P. Gilman, *Women and Economics* (New York, 1966), p. 316, quoted in Meyer, *Sex and Power*, p. 341.

[31]C. P. Gilman, *The Living of Charlotte Perkins Gilman* (New York, 1935), pp. 318–319, quoted in Meyer, *Sex and Power*, p. 347.

Credits

"Pocahontas" by Philip Young. Originally published as "The Mother of Us All: Pocahontas Reconsidered," *Kenyon Review*, Vol. 24, Summer, 1962, rights owned by Young.

"Anne Hutchinson" courtesy of M. J. Lewis.

"Phillis Wheatley" by Charles Scruggs. Parts of this essay were published previously in "Phillis Wheatley and the Poetical Legacy of Eighteenth-Century England," *Studies in Eighteenth-Century Culture*, Vol. 10. Courtesy of University of Wisconsin Press.

"Catharine Beecher" by Kathryn Kish Sklar. Previously published as "Catharine Beecher's *A Treatise on Domestic Economy:* A Document in Domestic Feminism," ed. by Earl A. French and Diana Royce, *Portraits of a Nineteenth-Century Family* (Hartford, Conn.: Stowe-Day Foundation, 1976), Courtesy of Stowe-Day Foundation.

"Margaret Fuller" by Bell Gale Chevigny. Reprinted with permission of Charles Scribner's Sons, an imprint of Macmillan Publishing Company, from *American Writers*, Supplement II, edited by Leonard Unger and A. Walton Litz. Copyright © 1960, 1961, 1963, 1964, 1965, 1968, 1969, 1970, 1971 by the University of Minnesota.

"Charlotte Forten" by Brenda Stevenson. From *The Journals of Charlotte Forten Grimk(*, edited by Brenda Stevenson. Copyright © 1988 by Oxford University Press, Inc. Reprinted by permission.

"Charlotte Perkins Gilman" by Carol Berkin. Berkin, Carol Ruth, Mary Beth Norton. *Women of America: A History*. Copyright © 1979 by Houghton Mifflin Company. Used with permission.

"Crystal Eastman" by Blanche Wiesen Cook. Courtesy of Blanche Wiesen Cook.

"Eleanor Roosevelt" by William Chafe. Courtesy of William Chafe.

"Georgia O'Keeffe" by Sarah Whitaker Peters. Sarah Whitaker Peters © 1989.

"Helen Gahagan Douglas" by Ingrid Winther Scobie. Parts of this essay were previously published as "Helen Gahagan Douglas: Broadway Star as California Politician" *California History*, Vol. LXVI, No. 4 December 1987.

Photo Credits

Page 12, "Pocahontas." Pocahontas, c. 1595-1617. Daughter of Powhatan chief. Unidentified artist, English school, after the 1616 engraving by Simon van de Passe. Oil on canvas, 76.8 X 64.1 cm. (30¼ X 25¼ in.) after 1616. NPG.65.61. National Portrait Gallery, Smithsonian Institution; Transfer from the National Gallery of Art; gift of Andrew W. Mellon, 1942.

Page 34, Statue of Anne Hutchinson at Boston State House." Photo by Daniel L. Colbert.

Page 64, "Mansion House of Charles and Eliza Lucas Pinckney." From an engraving by Samuel Smith from Thomas Leitch's 1774 *Painting of Charles Towne*, Courtesy of the Museum of Early Southern Decorative Arts, Winston-Salem.

Page 82, "Stone Mortuary Figure at Etowah Indian Mounds, Georgia." Courtesy of Georgia Department of Natural Resources.

Page 102, "Phillis Wheatley." From copy in Rare Book Collection, UNC Library, Chapel Hill.

Page 120, "Mercy Otis Warren." Bequest of Winslow Warren. Courtesy of the Museum of Fine Arts, Boston.

Page 146, "Maria Weston Chapman," courtesy of Stephen Alcorn.

Page 168, "Catharine Beecher." The Schlesinger Library, Radcliffe College. Stowe-Day Foundation.

Page 188, "Margaret Fuller." Picture Collection, The Branch Libraries, The New York Public Library.

Page 220, "Elizabeth Cady Stanton." Courtesy of Rhoda Barney Jenkins.

Page 240, "Mary Todd Lincoln." Courtesy of Lloyd Ostendorf Collection, Dayton, Ohio.

Page 258, "Varina Davis." Davis,Varina Howell, 1826-1906. Wife of Jefferson Davis. John Wood Dodge, 1807-1893. Watercolor on ivory, 6.5 X 5.3 cm. (2½ X 2 in.), © 1849. NPG.80.113. National Portrait Gallery, Smithsonian Institution. Gift of Varina Webb Stewart.

Page 278, "Charlotte Forten." Moorland-Spingarn Research

Center, Howard University.

Page 310, "Charlotte Perkins Gilman." Courtesy of Bryn Mawr College Archives.

Page 338, "Jane Addams." Jane Addams Memorial Collection. Special Collections. The University Library, The University of Illinois at Chicago.

Page 378, "Rose Schneiderman." Rose Schneiderman Photo Collection, Tamiment Institute Library, New York University.

Page 402, "Crystal Eastman." Courtesy of Annis Young.

Page 428, "Alice Paul." Courtesy of National Woman's Party Papers, Library of Congress. Photo by Edmunston.

Page 462, "Eleanor Roosevelt," National Archives.

Page 488, "Georgia O'Keeffe," National Archives.

Page 497, "Georgia O'Keeffe." Gift of Alfred Stieglitz, 1924. Courtesy, Museum of Fine Arts, Boston.

Page 506, "Margaret Mead." Courtesy of Barnard College Library.

Page 540, "Helen Gahagan Douglas." Carl Albert Center Congressional Archives, University of Oklahoma.

Page 560, "Ella Baker." *Southern Patriot Photo.* Courtesy of Anne Braden.

Page 578, "Betty Friedan. Susan Wood © 1984.

About the Authors

Jean H. Baker is Professor of History at Goucher College. Among her most recent books are *Affairs of Party, Mary Lincoln: A Biography,* and *The Stevensons: Biography of an American Family.*

G.J. Barker-Benfield teaches history at the State University of New York, Albany. He has written *The Horrors of the Half-Known Life: Male Attitudes Towards Sexuality in Nineteenth-Century America* (1976) and *The Culture of Sensibility: Sex and Society in Eighteenth Century Britain* (1992). He is now writing a book on sensibility and gender in America.

Carol Ruth Berkin is Professor of History at Baruch College and the City University Graduate Center. She is author of *Jonathan Sewall: Odyssey of an American Loyalist* (1972) and, most recently, *First Generations: Women in Colonial America* (1996). She is co-editor, with Mary Beth Norton, of *Women of America: A History* (1980) and, with Clara Lovett, of *Women, War and Revolution* (1980). She is currently working on a study of four prominent loyalists in the American Revolution.

Joan E. Cashin is Associate Professor of History at Ohio State University and is the author of *A Family Venture: Men and Women on the Southern Frontier* (1991) and *Our Common Affairs: Texts from Women in the Old South* (1996). She is currently working on a biography of Varina Howell Davis.

William H. Chafe is Alice Mary Baldwin Professor of American History and Dean of the Faculty of Arts and Sciences at Duke University. His books include *The Unfinished Journey* (1986), *Civilities and Civil Rights* (1980), and *Never Stop Running* (1993), a biography of Allard Lowenstein.

Bell Gale Chevigny is professor emerita of literature at Purchase College, State University of New York. A revised and greatly expanded edition of *The Woman and the Myth: Margaret Fuller's Life and Writing* was published in 1994, which includes a bibliographical essay of recent work on Fuller and a supplement of newly-uncovered work by and about Fuller. She is co-editor of *Reinventing the Americas: Comparative Studies of Literature of the United States and Spanish America* (1986) and

Chloe and Olivia (1990), a novel. In journals including *Feminist Studies, The Nation, Double Take, Harpers,* and *Michigan Quarterly Review,* she continues to publish fiction, memoir, literary criticism and essays on social and cultural matters.

Catherine Clinton is the Douglas Southall Freeman Visiting Chair of History at the University of Richmond (1997-98) and author of several books, including *The Plantation Mistress* (1982), *Tara Revisited* (1995), and *Civil War Stories* (1998). She is the editor of a forthcoming series from Oxford University Press, Viewpoints on American Culture.

Blanche Wiesen Cook is University Distinguished Professor at John Jay College and at the Graduate Center at the City University of New York. The author of *Crystal Eastman* (1978) and *The Declassified Eisenhower* (1981), she is currently working on her biography of Eleanor Roosevelt: *Eleanor Roosevelt,* Vol. 1 (1992); Vols. 2 & 3, forthcoming.

Marianne B. Geiger teaches history at Fordham University.

M.J. Lewis is completing a study of which the Anne Hutchinson narrative is an abridgment, a shortened version of an historical conflict that has been inadvertently—and unrecognizably—transmuted into a political myth. Her larger study is more than alternative or supplementary interpretation of the event; it offers a new perspective and encourages a healthier approach to historiography.

Christine A. Lunardini is a writer living in Manhattan. She is the author of *From Equal Suffrage to Equal Rights: Alice Paul and the National Women's Party* (1986), *What Every American Should Know about Women's History* (1994) and, most recently, *Women's Rights* (1996).

Donald Meyer is emeritus Professor of History at Wesleyan University, Middletown, Connecticut. He is the author of *The Protestant Search for Political Realism, The Positive Thinkers* and *Sex and Power: The Rise of Women in America, Russia, Sweden and Italy.* He is presently at work on a cultural history of the United States.

Bruce Miroff is professor and chair of political science at the State

University of New York, Albany. He is the author of *Icons of Democracy: American Leaders as Heroes, Aristocrats, Dissenters and Democrats* (1993) and co-author of *The Democratic Debate: An Introduction to American Politics* (Second Edition, 1998).

Annelise Orleck is Associate Professor of History and Co-Chair of Women's Studies at Dartmouth College. She is the author of *Common Sense and a Little Fire: Women and Working-Class Politics in the United States* and co-editor of *The Politics of Motherhood: Activist Voices from Left to Right*. She is currently at work on a history of race, gender and welfare rights activism in Las Vegas, Nevada entitled *Gambling With Human Lives: Women, Children and Welfare.*

Theda Perdue is Professor of History at the University of Kentucky. She is the author of *Slavery and the Evolution of Cherokee Society* (1979), *Native Carolinians* (1985), *The Cherokee* (1988) and *Cherokee Women: A Study in Changing Gender Roles* (1998); and is the editor of *Nations Remembered: An Oral History of the Five Civilized Tribes* (1980) and *Cherokee Editor* (1983).

Sarah Whitaker Peters was formerly Adjunct Assistant Professor of Art History at the University of Long Island, C.W. Post campus, and a free lance critic for *Art in America*. She is the author of *Becoming O'Keeffe* (1991) and wrote the entry on O'Keeffe for *The Dictionary of Art* (1996). She is currently preparing a catalogue essay on O'Keeffe for the Staatiliche Kunsthalle, Baden-Baden, Germany.

Rosalind Rosenberg is Professor of History at Barnard College. She is the author of *Beyond Separate Spheres: Intellectual Roots of Modern Feminism* and *Divided Lives: American Women in the Twentieth Century.*

Constance B. Schulz is the Director of the Applied History Program at the University of South Carolina. She is creator of *The American History Videodisc*, and its companion CD-Rom version, and of *The History of South Carolina Slide Collection*, and author of *Bust to Boom: Documentary Photographs of Kansas, 1936-49* and *A South Carolina Album, 1936-1948*. She has written articles on the history of childhood for the colonial and early national period. She is currently completing work on books documenting photography for Michigan during the Great Depression, and of the Pittsburgh Photographic Project's record of the Pittsburgh Renaissance, 1950-51.

Ingrid Winther Scobie is Professor of History at Texas Woman's University. She is the author of *Center Stage: Helen Gahagan Douglas, a Life* (OUP, 1992) and co-editor of *The Challenge of Feminist Biography: Writing the Lives of Modern American Women* (1992). She has published numerous articles on 20th century political history, women's history and oral history. In 1994-95 she held the Mary Ball Washington Chair in American History at University College, Dublin. She is currently working on a forthcoming manuscript: *The Women of '74: Women in Congress in Postwar America.*

Charles Scruggs is a professor of American Literature at the University of Arizona. He is the author of *The Sage in Harlem: H. L. Mencken and the Black Writers of the 1920s* (1984) and *Sweet Home: Invisible Cities in the Afro-American Novel* (1993). He is also the author of articles on Jonathan Swift, Alexander Pope and Jean Toomer.

Kathryn Kish Sklar is Distinguished Professor of History at the State University of New York, Binghampton. She is author of *Catharine Beecher: A Study in American Domesticity* and, most recently, *Florence Kelley and the Nation's Work: the Rise of Women's Political Culture, 1830-1900.*

Brenda E. Stevenson is Associate Professor of History at the University of California at Los Angeles. She is the author of *Life in Black and White: Family and Community in the Slave South* (OUP, 1996) and the editor of *The Journals of Charlotte Forten Grimke* (OUP, 1988).

Philip Young was Evan Pugh Professor Emeritus of English at Pennsylvania State University. He published *Ernest Hemingway* (1952), *Ernest Hemingway: A Reconsideration* (1966), *Three Bags Full: Essays in American Fiction* (1971), *Revolutionary Ladies* (1977), *Hawthorne's Secret: An Untold Tale* (1984), and, posthumously, *The Private Melville,* ed. by Katherine Young (1992).